P9-DVT-356

Nova Scotia,
New Brunswick &
Prince Edward Island

Newfoundland
& Labrador
p169

Prince Edward
Island
p143

New
Brunswick
p101

Nova Scotia
p40

THIS EDITION WRITTEN AND RESEARCHED BY
Korina Miller, Benedict Walker
Kate Armstrong, Carolyn McCarthy

PLAN YOUR TRIP

ON THE ROAD

NATALIA BRATSLAVSKY / SHUTTERSTOCK ©

COLORFUL BUOYS, PEGGY'S COVE (P58), NOVA SCOTIA

GREG AND JAN RITCHIE / SHUTTERSTOCK ©

PUFFINS, P193

Contents

Welcome to Nova Scotia, New Brunswick & Prince Edward Island

Fashioned by the mighty Atlantic, these open-armed Canadian provinces beckon you for chats, chowder and the chance to see whales breach in the distance.

Watery Wonderland

Scanning the horizon from the blustery clifftop, you discern a fine spray shooting up from what appears to be an upturned boat, before it suddenly vanishes. Seconds later, whooshing up, the enormous whale-body arcs and rolls into the air, slapping its broad tail flukes against the icy surface. Such moments of aquatic wonder aren't uncommon in Atlantic Canada: perhaps as you bike past a lupine-fringed red-sand beach on Prince Edward Island, fly-fish the abundant rivers of New Brunswick, mount a tidal bore wave aboard a dinghy in Nova Scotia, or contemplate the passing of icebergs in Newfoundland and Labrador.

Light the Way

Welcome to what's perhaps the lighthouse capital of the world. Reached by winding sealed and unsealed roads, countless windswept craggy coves provide the photogenic backdrops for these picture-perfect beacons, many still in service. More house volunteer-operated museums, where you can climb to the top to marvel at the ocean and wonder about how many lives have been saved over the years by these Maritime sentinels. Not all lighthouses are open or in great shape, but they're universally in wild and wonderful locations, poignant reminders of a lost age.

A Foot-Tapping Good Time

Here's a culture defined by fiddle playing and wearing out the dancing shoes. Maritimers are well-practiced in the art of partying and like nothing more than to share the good times with all who visit. If these come-one-come-all get-togethers don't make you tap your feet, check your pulse. Outdoor festivals fill the summer calendar as locals make the most of long daylight hours. Folks of Acadian and Gaelic roots each celebrate their heritage through their own distinct music and all are invited: be there by six!

Shellfish Bliss

Gear-up with your bib, pick and lobster fork and forget about getting butter in your hair: crustaceans (lobster, crab, shrimp) and bivalves (scallops, mussels, oysters) form the mainstay of Atlantic Canada's marine bounty. Confused about how to get the meat out of that lobster leg? This thoughtful bunch often supplies you with instructions on the placemat of how to master the beast with your chosen utensils. Part surgeon, part warrior, part gourmand, the experience of eating these briny critters is almost as good as they taste.

Why I Love Nova Scotia, New Brunswick & Prince Edward Island

By Benedict Walker, Writer

My arrival in Halifax began as one of those rainy, weary, almost-missing-your-flight kind of mornings, after weeks of long days on the road. Always the penny-pincher, I opted, despite my lethargy, for the airport shuttle over a taxi. As the only passenger I sat up front with the driver, who regaled me with his latest tales as if I were an old friend. His warm demeanor soon thawed my frosty mood – these were people who'd already welcomed me many times and captured my heart. I was home, safe. Visit and you'll see what I mean.

For more about our writers, see p280

Above: West Point Lighthouse, Cedar Dunes Provincial Park (p166), Prince Edward Island

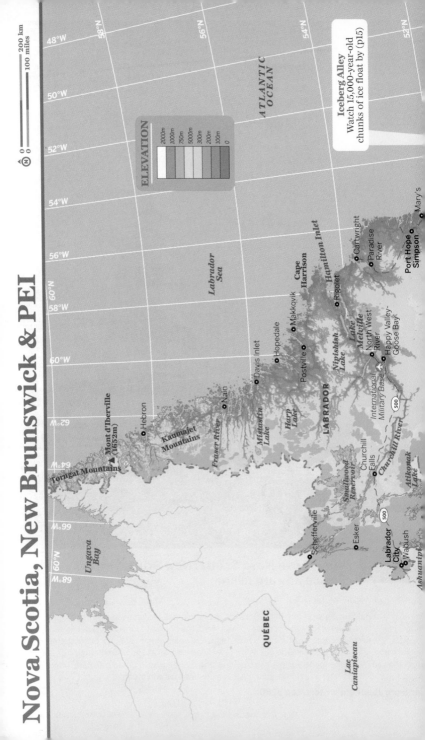

Nova Scotia, New Brunswick & PEI

ELEVATION

2000m
1000m
750m
5000m
300m
200m
100m
0

Iceberg Alley
Watch 15,000-year-old chunks of ice float by (p15)

ATLANTIC OCEAN

Labrador Sea

Cape Harrison

Hamilton Inlet

Mary's

Cartwright

Paradise River

Port Hope Simpson

Rigolet

Makkovik

Hopedale

Postville

Davis Inlet

Lake Melville

North West River

Happy Valley-Goose Bay

Nain

Mistastin Lake

Harp Lake

Nipishish Lake

LABRADOR

International Military Base

500

Churchill Falls

Churchill River

Fraser River

Hebron

▲ Mont d'Iberville (1652m)

Kaumajet Mountains

Torngat Mountains

Ungava Bay

Schefferville

Esker

Smallwood Reservoir

Attikonak Lake

500

Labrador City

Wabush

Ashuanipi

QUÉBEC

Lac Caniapiscau

200 km
100 miles

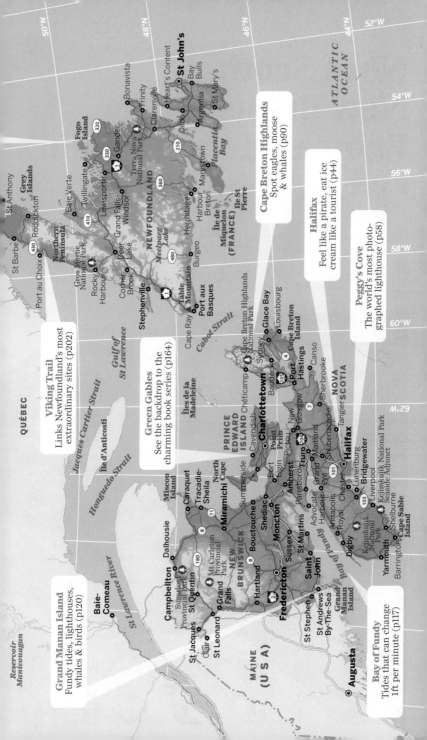

Grand Manan Island
Fundy tides, lighthouses, whales & birds (p120)

Viking Trail
Links Newfoundland's most extraordinary sites (p202)

Green Gables
See the backdrop to the charming book series (p164)

Cape Breton Highlands
Spot eagles, moose & whales (p90)

Halifax
Feel like a pirate, eat ice cream like a tourist (p44)

Peggy's Cove
The world's most photographed lighthouse (p58)

Bay of Fundy
Tides that can change 1ft per minute (p117)

ATLANTIC OCEAN

QUÉBEC

MAINE (USA)

NEW BRUNSWICK

NOVA SCOTIA

PRINCE EDWARD ISLAND

NEWFOUNDLAND

Nova Scotia, New Brunswick & Prince Edward Island's
Top 10

Cape Breton Highlands

1 Circuitous roads traverse forested ridgelines and dramatic coastal cliffs where eagles soar, whales spout in the distance and moose amble by the roadside. Tackle this national park (p90) as a one- to three-day trip, but make sure you buckle your boots at least once to explore trails that pass by pristine streams, waterfalls and abundant wildflowers to ever more stunning vistas. On the coast, paddle a kayak or take a whale-watching tour to look for minke whales, seabirds and seals. Half the fun is getting there. Cabot Trail (p89), Halifax

Bay of Fundy

2 The Bay of Fundy (p117) in New Brunswick is home to the highest tides in the world. Boats look hopelessly beached on mud flats and piers look ridiculously lofty at low tide. Then, when one billion tonnes of water flow back into the bay, boats bob up to 15m above where they were six hours earlier – it's surreal. Get right into the tidal action by rafting the tidal bore, or relax with a whale-watching cruise, on which you might see blue whales, minke or the rare fin whale.

Charlottetown and Green Gables

3 Base yourself in postcard-perfect Charlottetown (p146), a gourmand's haven that lends new credence to the farm-to-table movement. From here it takes less than an hour to reach the real-life sites that provided the backdrop to the *Anne of Green Gables* books, loved by children around the world. You'll find Anne all over Prince Edward Island: in gift shops, as countless pretty redheads dressed as our heroine, among antiques and old-time memorabilia, and in places that understandably inspired names such as the 'Lake of Shining Waters' and 'White Way of Delight.' Green Gables Heritage Place (p164), Cavendish

Halifax

4 When the fog is in, the tall ships and piers of the Halifax Waterfront (pictured top right; p44) take on the air of an eerie pirate-movie set. You can almost imagine the cold, dingy scene of yesteryear as the foghorns blow. Then the fog lifts, the sun comes out and everything turns festive: street buskers sing, laughter peels from beery pub patios and kids giggle with dribbling ice-cream cones as the container ships, frigates and sailboats chug across the sparkling bay. Hop on the Dartmouth ferry to enjoy the view back to Halifax's boxy downtown.

The Viking Trail

5 The Viking Trail (p202), aka Rte 430, connects Newfoundland two World Heritage sites on the northern peninsu Gros Morne National Pa with its fjordlike lakes and geological oddities rests at its base, while th sublime, 1000-year-old Viking settlement at L'Ar aux Meadows (pictured bottom right; p206) – Le Eriksson's pad – stares from the peninsula's tip. The road is an attraction in its own right, holding close to the sea as it hea resolutely north past the ancient burial grounds of Port au Choix and the fer jump-off to Labrador.

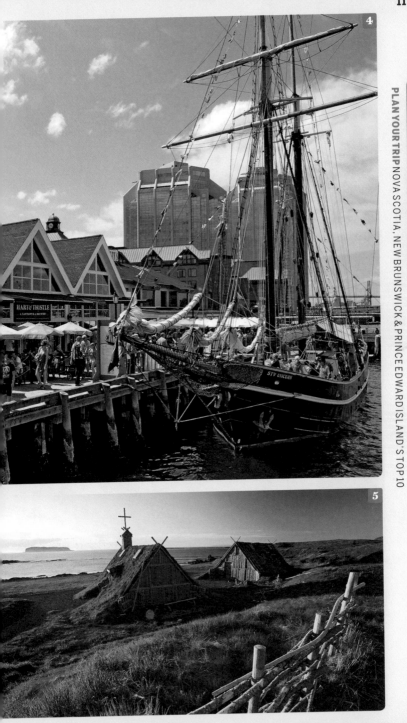

Peggy's Cove

6 Despite being clogged with tour buses all summer long, Peggy's Cove (p58) in Nova Scotia makes all the postcards and enchants all who visit. The lighthouse, the blue-grey sea and the tiny sheltered bay scattered with crab traps and Popeye-esque boat docks are all straight out of a sailor's yarn. To get beyond the snapshot take time to meander and experience a glimpse of life in a very, very small Maritime village. It's surprising Disney hasn't made a film here yet.

Scottish & Acadian Music

7 Long cold winters have been endured for centuries with the help of lively fiddle playing and dancing. Call it a ceilidh, kitchen party or concert, but don't miss the chance to experience something that brings joy to much of this part of the world (p232). Listen to bagpipes or watch young fiddle virtuosos play while the oldies get up and step dance. Music is practiced indoors all winter to be let loose to party in summer at community halls, pubs, parks and festivals. Bagpipe player at Citadel Hill National Historic Site (p45), Halifax

6

Lobster Suppers

8 Slapping on a bib was never so much fun. Join the crowds of hungry revelers attacking their plate-sized, orangered crustacean with forks, pickers and nutcrackers. Get covered in lobster juice; dunk each mouthful in butter and enjoy. Don't forget to leave room for the feast's common accompaniments: mussels, chowder, fresh biscuits, salad and strawberry shortcake for dessert. You can get the lobster supper experience (p240) at restaurants but the best, cheapest and most fun meals are at local churches and town halls.

Grand Manan Island

9 From windy, jagged cliffs and marshland to spruce forests and sloping points with storybook lighthouses, Grand Manan (p120) in New Brunswick has incredible natural diversity along its 30km length. There are dozens of trails to wande and coves to explore but no fast-food restaurants or traffic. The silence is broken or by the rhythmic ocean surf. You feel about a million nautical miles away from anything not windswept, rugged or overwhelmingly natural. To get out of a peaceful stupor, go kayaking, cycling, whale-watching or birding. Swallowtail Lighthouse (p120)

10

Floating Iceberg Alley

10 They shimmer from white to electric blue as they float down the grey-black Atlantic (p208). It's a wonder that these icebergs have broken away from their Greenland home to create such a show, but even more amazing is that some of the ice is more than 15,000 years old. While icebergs have been floating around here for centuries, they are doing so at an ever-increasing rate. For an unusual treat cool down a summer drink with the world's most ancient ice cubes. Iceberg-watching near Twillingate Island (p198), Newfoundland

Need to Know

For more information, see Survival Guide (p251)

Currency
Canadian dollar ($)

Language
English, French

Visas
With the exception of US nationals, all visitors to Canada require either an electronic travel authorization (eTA; visa-waiver) or a formal visa.

Money
ATMs are widely available and credit and debit cards are accepted almost everywhere.

Cell Phones
Local SIM cards can be used in unlocked GSM 850/1900 compatible phones.

Time
Atlantic (GMT minus four hours)

When to Go

Mild summers, cold winters
Cold climate

L'Anse aux Meadows
National Historic Site
GO Jun–Sep

St John's
GO Dec–Apr

Charlottetown
GO May–Sep

Cape Breton Island
GO May–Oct

Grand Manan Island
GO May–Sep

Annapolis Valley
GO May–Sep

High Season
(Jul & Aug)

➡ Warm weather and long sunny days mean busy highways and slower travel times.

➡ The whole region plunges into festival mode, with theater, music and food extravaganzas.

➡ Attractions and visitor centers keep longer summer hours.

Shoulder
(May–Jun & Sep–Oct)

➡ Wildflowers in spring and crimson leaves in the fall.

➡ Cool but comfortable. You may have things all to yourself.

➡ Some lodgings close and restaurants may open under reduced hours.

Low Season
(Nov–Apr)

➡ Few lodgings and attractions outside the big cities and ski resorts remain open.

➡ Darkness and cold take over. Driving can be fraught with challenges.

➡ Christmas festivals liven up December and January.

Websites

The official websites of each province's tourism boards are:

Nova Scotia Tourism (www.novascotia.com)

Tourism New Brunswick (www.tourismnewbrunswick.ca)

Tourism Prince Edward Island (www.tourismpei.com)

Newfoundland & Labrador Tourism (www.newfoundlandlabrador.com)

Parks Canada (www.pc.gc.ca) Official website of the National Parks Service.

Lonely Planet (www.lonelyplanet.com/canada) Destination information, hotel bookings, traveller forum and more.

Important Numbers

Nova Scotia and Prince Edward Island's area code is 🕿902, New Brunswick is 🕿506, and Newfoundland and Labrador is 🕿709. Many accommodations have toll-free numbers that are free to dial from Canada and the USA. For local calls, you need to use the area code but not the country code.

Country Code	🕿1
International Access Code	🕿011
Emergency	🕿911
Directory Assistance	🕿411

Exchange Rates

Australia	A$1	C$0.98
Europe	€1	C$1.40
Japan	¥100	C$1.25
New Zealand	NZ$1	C$0.92
UK	UK£1	C$1.70
US	US$1	C$1.30

For current exchange rates, see www.xe.com.

Daily Costs

**Budget:
Less than $100**

➡ Dorm bed: $25–40

➡ Campsite: $20–35

➡ Plenty of markets and supermarkets for self-catering

Midrange: $100–250

➡ B&B or room in a midrange hotel: $90–180

➡ Restaurant meal: from $15 plus drinks

➡ Rental car: $25–70 per day

➡ Attractions: $5–25

**Top End:
More than $250**

➡ Four-star hotel room or luxury B&B: from $180

➡ Three-course meal in a top restaurant: from $45 plus drinks

➡ Sea kayaking or canoe day tour: $65–175

Opening Hours

The following list provides standard opening hours for high-season operating times.

Banks 10am to 5pm Monday to Friday, some open 9am to noon Saturday

Museums 10am to 5pm, may close on Monday

Restaurants 8am to 11am & 11:30am to 2:30pm Monday to Friday, 5pm to 9:30pm daily, some open 8am to 1pm weekends

Bars 5pm to 2am

Clubs 9pm to 2am Wednesday to Saturday

Shops 10am to 6pm Monday to Saturday, noon to 5pm Sunday

Supermarkets 9am to 8pm, some open 24 hours

Arriving

Halifax Stanfield International Airport (p56) MetroX bus 320 runs every 30 to 60 minutes (5:45am to 12:15am). Taxis cost $60 to downtown (30 minutes).

St John's International Airport (p183) Taxis cost $30 plus $3 for each additional passenger to downtown (10 minutes).

Land Border Crossings The Canadian Border Services Agency (p262) posts updated wait times hourly; it's usually less than 30 minutes.

Getting Around

Public transportation is available in cities and between larger towns, but most visitors rent a car.

Car Good-value rentals are available in Nova Scotia and New Brunswick. Prince Edward Island and Newfoundland have fewer vehicles and higher prices.

Train Clean, economical and reliable VIA Rail connects Halifax to Montréal via New Brunswick.

Bus Cover more ground than trains; places not serviced by buses usually have private shuttle services for similar fares, more cramped seating and door-to-door service.

Keep in Mind

Remember the large scale of Canada's Atlantic provinces: distances can be long and travel times slow. Consider exploring just one or two regions in depth.

Blackflies and mosquitoes can be a major annoyance in the summer. Bring insect repellent and clothing to cover up, especially in northern, woodsy regions.

Transportation (rental car, ferry) and sleeping reservations are important in July and August.

For much more on **getting around**, see p261

If You Like...

Seafood

Sweet Atlantic lobsters are ubiquitous and other underwater delicacies such as Digby scallops and Malpeque oysters are world-famous for their quality.

Lobster Suppers A Maritime seafood feast best taken in churches and town halls. (p240)

Lobster Pound & Moore Takes lobster suppers into gourmet territory, plus serves the best lobster ravioli on the planet. (p96)

Water Prince Corner Shop Scarf a scallop burger or get a lobster to eat there or to go. (p152)

Norseman Restaurant & Art Gallery Put on rubber boots to handpick your crustacean right on the shore. (p207)

Wine & Spirit Tasting

Drive the wineries of Nova Scotia's Annapolis Valley and Bear River, which have the same latitude as Bordeaux, France. Other areas produce harder stuff: whisky, vodka and good old-fashioned moonshine.

Glenora Inn & Distillery Canada's only single-malt whisky is produced here; tour the distillery and take a swig. (p87)

Rossignol Estate Winery Specializes in fruit wines including an award-winning (and delicious) blackberry mead. (p154)

Prince Edward Distillery Famed for its fine potato vodka and other spirits. (p159)

Auk Island Winery Try fruit wines made with iceberg water and local fruit. (p199)

Ironworks Distillery A bottle of smooth Bluenose Rum makes the perfect souvenir. (p61)

Myriad View Makes legal moonshine so potent it evaporates on the tongue. (p159)

Historic Sites

Leif Erikson was the first European to set foot in the Americas in Newfoundland, marking the beginning of this region's rich European history. Folks get into it too, dressing up in period garb and acting the part, bringing the sites to life.

Louisbourg The size and authenticity of this recreated site is like a time machine back to the 18th century. (p98)

L'Anse aux Meadows National Historical Site It's easy to imagine what life was like when the Vikings first landed here. (p206)

King's Landing Historical Settlement Family fun at this recreated 19th-century Loyalist village includes pub grub and children's programs. (p104)

Canadian Museum of Immigration at Pier 21 Marvel at the stories of the more than one million immigrants who have landed here. (p45)

Rendez-Vous de la Baie Learn about the troubled history of the Acadian people at this interpretative center and museum. (p67)

Lighthouses

When most people envision the Atlantic and Maritime provinces, there's a lighthouse in the image somewhere. A drive to any coastal spit will usually turn up a red-and-white beacon just waiting to be photographed.

Peggy's Cove Quintessential Maritime: a red-and-white storybook lighthouse on rolling granite backed by the cold Atlantic. (p58)

Cape Enrage Watch the rise and fall of the Fundy tides from this windswept, 150-year-old beacon. (p130)

Long Point Spot icebergs in May and June from the 360-degree view in this 1876 lighthouse. (p199)

Swallowtail Lighthouse White-washed perfection on a grassy bluff where you can watch seals raiding ancient fish traps. (p120)

Point Amour Lighthouse Provincial Historic Site The tallest lighthouse in Atlantic Canada also has a small maritime history museum. (p218)

Point Prim PEI's prettiest beacon with views over the island; try the hand-pump fog horn. (p151)

Cap D'Or Stay overnight in the guesthouse at this remote outpost. (p82)

Hiking & Walking

This is a forested region with so many fantastic hiking possibilities that we can hardly list them all. From coastal jaunts to deep woods, mountains, lakes and valleys, you'll be on the lookout for birds, moose and whales from majestic clifftops.

Cape Breton Highlands National Park Winding roads to ocean vistas perfect for spotting whales, moose or eagles. (p90)

Fundy National Park See the highest rise and fall of the tides from forested bliss. (p128)

Mt Carleton Start out in French cowboy country to discover rugged hiking and quiet lakes. (p109)

East Coast Trail Part easy walking, part tough wilderness trail, often with free guided hikes. (p184)

Cape Split There's no better place to hike along the Fundy tidal shore. (p76)

p: Louisbourg National Historic Site (p98), Nova Scotia

ttom: Hopewell Rocks (p132), New Brunswick

PLAN YOUR TRIP IF YOU LIKE...

Kayaking & Canoeing

Perhaps the most Canadian of sports and a spectacular way to experience this region from a watery perspective. From mellow lake paddles to high action in the waves past spouting whales, the water is a huge part of what makes these provinces tick.

Eastern Shore Nova Scotia's forgotten coast is studded with islands and calm bays, perfect for paddling. (p99)

Mt Carleton Gorgeous canoeing through a string of wilderness lakes surrounded by tree-clad mountains. (p109)

North Rustico Scoot off from the red-sand beach and burn the calories you'll replenish later that night. (p161)

Whale-Watching

Thar she blows! Humpbacks and minke are the most common whales you'll spot in this region, but lucky souls will see elusive blue whales and the endangered fin whale, two of the largest creatures on Earth.

Long Island Get way out into the Bay of Fundy for your best chance for a sighting. (p70)

Pleasant Bay Plenty of folks lead tours up here, and eagles soar close to shore too. (p92)

Fundy Isles The whales are here, but you'll also see plenty of seals and bird life. (p117)

Witless Bay Ecological Reserve Just when you thought all your dreams had been realized, an iceberg floats by. (p185)

Music

Whether it's Scottish, folk or rock, music rings everywhere in this corner of Canada. Ceilidhs, kitchen parties and some awesome festivals liven up the summer and extend into the fall.

Ceilidh Trail Nonstop kitchen parties and ceilidhs await; finish up in Chéticamp for Acadian rhythms. (p87)

Halifax There are tons of bars, and nearly every one of them swells with live music. (p44)

Stan Rogers Folk Festival Intimate vibe and awesome music, from bluegrass to Celtic. (p100)

Cavendish Beach Music Festival Camp near the beach and enjoy A-list country music headliners and rock and folk kick-starters. (p164)

Acadian Culture

The fascinating history of these French speakers has given rise to a unique culture with its own tricolor flag, a soulful brand of fiddle music and a delicious cuisine specializing in delicately spiced meat pies.

Northeastern New Brunswick Staunchly Acadian and sporting one of the region's best historical sites, the Acadian Historic Village. (p139)

Chéticamp, Nova Scotia Get into the culture via summer music, theater performances and Acadian restaurants. (p89)

West Pubnico, Nova Scotia Out of the way but friendly; has its own historical re-creation, Le Village Historique Acadien. (p69)

Acadian Shores, Nova Scotia Less touristed than Chéticamp but equally authentic, it's a great place to try rappie pie. (p67)

Month by Month

February

This is not a popular month to visit this part of Canada unless you're looking for deep snow and hard ice, but you'll be sure of a warm welcome during one of the year's coldest months.

🏃 Skiing

Atlantic Canada's best skiing is at Marble Mountain in Corner Brook, Newfoundland, open from December to April. It's challenging terrain, lift lines are short and the snow is plentiful.

🏃 World Pond Hockey Tournament, New Brunswick

Hockey purists, don't miss this event. All proceeds go toward building an arena for the folks of Tobique Valley, but until then the ponds are cleared and more than 120 teams come to shoot pucks around the ice.

April

The land is usually thawing by April and trees are sprouting new leaves, but if you visit you'll be enjoying it all with very few other people around.

💥 Mi-Carême

Mid-Lent, usually in March or April, is marked in the Acadian town of Chéticamp by going in disguise and visiting neighborhood homes to see if anyone can guess who you are. Meanwhile music, feasts and entertainment are found around town.

🍴 PEI Burger Love

Carnivores go crazy at this month-long celebration of the humble burger. Restaurants around the province devise mouthwatering creations that compete for the title of Most Loved Burger: all are crafted with love and imagination using homegrown ingredients.

June

June weather can be sunny but brisk. In some areas, many tourist-oriented attractions may still be shut or keep low-season hours, but in general you'll find the Maritime provinces ramping up for the summer season.

🏃 Whale-Watching

Whales begin to be seen in the Bay of Fundy and off the coast of Newfoundland this month, then hang around to feed until around October or November. Meanwhile, on Nova Scotia's South Shore, the season runs from July to October.

🏃 Drifting Icebergs

Spring and early summer are the best times to see some of the tens of thousands of icebergs that break off in Greenland to sail down the coast of Newfoundland's 'Iceberg Alley.' The iceberg-tracking site www.icebergfinder.com can help you plan where to go and what times of year are best to visit.

☆ Acadian Concerts

In late June you'll start to find summer Acadian concerts and kitchen parties along the Nova Scotia coast between Yarmouth and Digby. More are scheduled through July, and by August you can find a performance most nights of the week.

July

Summer starts to heat up, days are long and festivals bring music and food to the streets. All outdoor activities are go! If you're lucky, things can still be relatively uncrowded early in the month.

Lobster Suppers

During the summer lobster season (depends on the region), tasty crustaceans get boiled up en masse and served to hungry crowds with all-you-can-eat fixings and pie for dessert.

Ceilidhs

Cape Breton is the capital of these foot-tapping Scottish music performances where most people in the small communities participate, show up as audience and get up and dance. While found year-round, they occur almost every night in July and August.

Canada Day

Canada's national holiday is celebrated throughout the region with parades, fireworks, music and picnics. Many businesses close their doors in observance of the holidays so be sure to have plans and a picnic packed before the big day, July 1.

Cavendish Beach Music Festival

Some of the biggest names in country music head to Cavendish, Prince Edward Island, to perform at one of the largest outdoor music festivals held in North America.

Indian River Festival

As an antidote to Cavendish partying, this festival from the June to October showcases classical, jazz and world music in an acoustically sublime St Mary's Church. The French Gothic architecture beautiful music in a wonderful summer experience.

Peak of Lupine Season

Lupine usually begin blooming in June but by July they cover hillsides, colorfully border the highways and decorate home fronts. Purple is the dominant color but you'll also see scatterings of pink lupine, especially in PEI.

Halifax Pride

Halifax booms with events for Pride Week, the largest this side of Montréal. Don't miss the annual, highly entertaining Dykes vs Divas softball game, the Queer Acts Theater Festival, nightly parties and one hell of a parade.

Bastille Day

Celebrate the July 14 French national holiday with bona-fide French nationals in St-Pierre. The town comes alive with music, food stalls and family-oriented games for nonstop fun. Stop in for a few éclairs while you're there as well.

August

High season is in full swing by August. The weather is at its sunniest, everything is open extended hours and festivals are going on everywhere.

Stan Rogers Folk Festival

The tiny remote seaside town of Canso swells with visitors once a year for what many claim is one of the best music festivals in the Maritimes. It's a mellow scene with camping, easy-going people and amazing live performances.

Halifax International Busker Festival

Comics, daredevils and more from Canada and around the world perform on several outdoor stages over 11 days. This is the oldest festival of its kind in Canada and the audience usually exceeds 500,000 people.

Bakeapple Season

Called 'cloudberries' throughout much of the rest of the world, this rare and delectable berry is in full season by mid-August – then it's tossed liberally into pies and jam.

Digby Scallop Days

Celebrating Digby's massive scallop fleet, this five-day festival in early August lets you try out different styles of preparation. Alongside it are parades, dances, car shows and even a kids' pie-eating contest.

Miramichi Folksong Festival

Another superlative event, this is North America's oldest folk-fest set along its winding, namesake river in New Brunswick. Expect a low-key family vibe set to the tune of fiddlers and singers with all the old folks getting up to boogie.

🏃 Royal St John's Regatta

Newfoundland keeps up the action with this rowing regatta, claimed to be the oldest sporting event in North America, on Quidi Vidi Lake. St John's becomes a ghost town as thousands head to watch and enjoy the sunshine.

September

Summer gets extended for a slew of music festivals, while the harvest of food and wine is enjoyed to the fullest. Temperatures become more brisk but the sun still makes regular appearances.

✖ PEI Fall Flavours

Called 'the biggest kitchen party in Canada,' here you get your hands juicy with interactive culinary demos, gorge on the best seafood in the world and enjoy two chowder championships. Meanwhile there's live music, a widely regarded oyster-shucking contest and chef challenges.

☆ Atlantic Film Festival

Atlantic Canada and Canada's best films plus some gems from around the world get screened at this intimate yet internationally recognized festival in Halifax. Of course, this is Nova Scotia so there are plenty of music performances scheduled alongside.

☆ Deep Roots Music Festival

Enjoy folk music and move to the beats of Mi'kmaw, Acadian and other unique musical genres, all with Canadian roots, in the fun university town of Wolfville. Workshops are available with some of the artists.

🍷 Nova Scotia Fall Wine Festival

There's no better moment to enjoy Nova Scotia's wines than at this event where you can meet winemakers and enjoy their vintages paired with meals prepared by renowned chefs.

October

Ah, the colors of fall. As the world turns from green to red and the temperatures start to drop, there's still plenty to enjoy in the Maritimes. Canadian Thanksgiving is the perfect time to experience the hospitality of the locals.

◉ Fall Foliage

One of nature's most spectacular shows of color begins late September and peaks in October. Panoramas are filled with brick reds, rust, gold and copper that eventually turn brown before dropping to the ground.

🎊 Thanksgiving

Unlike the US, Canadian Thanksgiving is celebrated on the first Monday in October in thanks for the harvest. Families enjoy their turkey feasts over the weekend, while a few fall festivals surround the big day.

☆ Celtic Colours

The who's who of the Maritimes' music world make it to this Cape Breton music festival, which is highly regarded among lovers of Celtic music.

December

🎊 Christmas

The festivities begin in November with Christmas parades and festivals of light that then move into Father Christmas greetings and Christmas markets. The big day is of course on 25 December when most families get together for holiday supper.

Itineraries

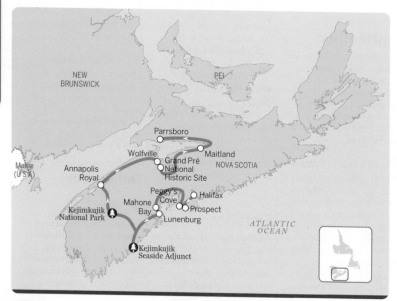

Nova Scotia Sampler

This compact itinerary showcases the historic and natural diversity within easy reach of Halifax. Soak up some music and culture in **Halifax** then travel to nearby **Peggy's Cove** and jostle for position to snap the most photographed lighthouse in the world. Don't forget your sunscreen in **Mahone Bay**, where the sun shines on great craft shopping and sea kayaking. Move on slightly south to **Lunenburg**, a World Heritage site known for its colorful boxy buildings and *Bluenose* schooner. The **Kejimkujik National Park** offers a range of terrain from its coastal beaches (in the section of park known as the **Kejim-kujik Seaside Adjunct**) to inland rivers, which are the perfect spot to float a canoe and drift through the woods. Cross the province to **Annapolis Royal** to stay at a heritage bed and breakfast; explore its fort by day and graveyard by night. The next day visit the wineries around the fabulous college town of **Wolfville** and the **Grand Pré National Historic site**, before stopping to down a meal at a fine vineyard restaurant. Lastly, explore the Fundy coast around **Parrsboro** and Advocate Harbour, or go to **Maitland** to get right in and raft the tidal bore.

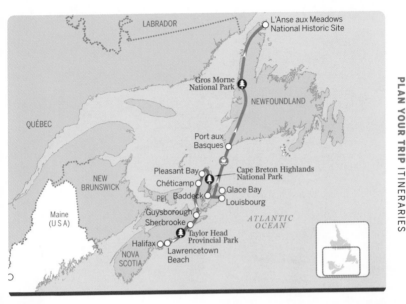

Cabot & Viking Trails

2 WEEKS

Experience the living world at its most magnificent and explore the juxtaposing cultures that have shaped eastern Canada in this grand northerly tour, best suited to those who love hiking, wildlife and photography. Spend a couple days in **Halifax** enjoying lively bars and a nonstop music scene, then hit the road up the Atlantic Coast. Stop for a chilly surf at Lawrencetown Beach or a hike through pine forest to a spectacular white-sand beach at **Taylor Head Provincial Park**. Visit the historical village at **Sherbrooke** then either cut up Hwy 7 for a shortcut to Cape Breton Island or, with an extra day or two, continue on the coast to the sheltered hamlet of **Guysborough**. Just after arriving on Cape Breton from the causeway, veer left toward Hwy 30 and stop in at one of the many ceilidh music gatherings along this route. Hook up with the **Cabot Trail** at **Chéticamp**, a deeply Acadian town. Next you can watch whales or chant with monks at the Tibetan monastery in **Pleasant Bay** and look for moose and nesting bald eagles in **Cape Breton Highlands National Park**. Get your art fix at the studios dotted along the last section of the trail before heading over to **Baddeck** to learn everything you ever wanted to know about Alexander Graham Bell at the town's fabulous museum. From here take a jaunt east to **Louisbourg** to visit the massive, windy restored French Fort complete with costumed thespians and activities to take you back to the 18th century. Stop at the **Miners' Museum** in Glace Bay before arriving in industrial North Sydney for the ferry to Newfoundland.

It's a six-hour sail over the sometimes rough swell of the Cabot Strait to Port aux Basques. Alight and drive north to **Gros Morne National Park**, rich with mountain hikes, sea-kayak tours, fjords and weird rock formations. Take the Viking Trail from here to its awe-inspiring endpoint: **L'Anse aux Meadows National Historic Site**, North America's first settlement. Leif Erikson and his Viking pals homesteaded the place 1000 years ago, and it probably looked much the same then as it does now. After coming all this way, you too will feel like an Atlantic explorer.

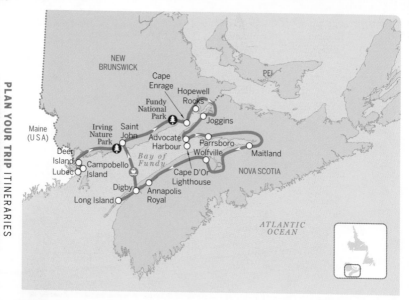

10 DAYS Bay of Fundy Tidal Tour

Experience the dramatic Fundy tides and its wildlife on this loop that can be tackled from Maine, USA. Cross the bridge to **Campobello Island**, the childhood home of 32nd US president Franklin D Roosevelt, from **Lubec**, Maine, then visit the Roosevelt's home that's now a fascinating museum. The next day take the car ferry to fisher-funky **Deer Island** to check out Old Sow, the world's second-largest natural tidal whirlpool, before boarding another ferry that shuttles you to the mainland. Drive north to gritty yet cosmopolitan **Saint John** to fill up on fine dining, and warm up your hiking boots at **Irving Nature Park** the following day to see hundreds of birds and possibly seals. Spend the next few days really breaking your boots in throughout **Fundy National Park** and its extensive coastal trails. Continue north to **Cape Enrage** to take a tour of the lighthouse, and sea kayak or rappel down the rock cliffs that meet the rise and fall of the powerful tides. Move on to a day trip to the bizarre **Hopewell Rocks** formations, a must-see, but expect hundreds of visitors.

Now it's time to change provinces. Drive across the border to Nova Scotia and down to **Joggins** to see the Unesco Heritage fossil cliffs. Continue along driftwood-strewn Chignecto Bay to stop for lunch in **Advocate Harbour**, then move onto **Parrsboro** via the **Cape D'Or Lighthouse**, to look for semiprecious stones on the beach and stay the night. Enjoy the views of the Cobequid Bay tides, which can change up to a foot per minute, until you reach **Maitland** where you can get into inflatable dinghies for an exhilarating rafting adventure on the tidal bore. Scoot southwest to fabulous **Wolfville** for a night or two to explore the surrounding countryside, before heading deeper into the Annapolis Valley to delightful **Annapolis Royal**, and onwards to **Digby** where you can dine on succulent scallops before resting your weary head. In the morning, head over to **Long Island**, home to the region's most spectacular whale-watching, before turning back to Digby for the car ferry to Saint John, New Brunswick, where the adventure began.

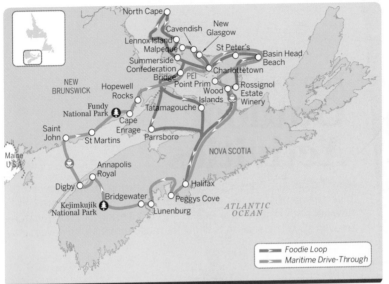

Foodie Loop / 1 WEEK

Maritime Drive-Through legend:
- Foodie Loop
- Maritime Drive-Through

Foodie Loop
1 WEEK

This tour explores the Maritimes' locavore dining scene. Start by eating and drinking your way through **Halifax**, then take the car ferry to **Wood Islands**, Prince Edward Island (PEI). Spend your first day in Canada's cutest province exploring the east; stop at **Rossignol Estate Winery** and quirky distilleries, and stroll on **Basin Head Beach**. Dine in **St Peter's** before moving on to **Charlottetown** where you can base yourself for the next few days to explore the central part of the province. The capital is a hotbed of farm-to-table restaurants and B&Bs. Head to **Malpeque** for oysters, say hello to Anne of Green Gables in **Cavendish**, then gorge on lobster in **New Glasgow**, if you can stomach all that seafood.

Spend a night or two in **Summerside** to explore western PEI with a drive up the scenic west coast through Acadian villages to lighthouse vistas. Gape at the windmills of **North Cape** before looping back on the east coast, stopping to learn about Mi'kmaq culture on **Lennox Island**.

Take the **Confederation Bridge** to drive back to Halifax via the wine region around **Tatamagouche**, or head down the Fundy Coast to **Parrsboro**.

Maritime Drive-Through
8 DAYS

Short on time but want to see as much as possible? Enjoy **Halifax** for a day before swinging down to snap a few photos at **Peggy's Cove**, then stop for the night in World Heritage–listed **Lunenburg** with your camera at the ready at every turn. The next day cross via Bridgewater up Hwy 8, stopping for a day hike or a paddle in **Kejimkujik National Park**, then stay in **Annapolis Royal** and take the town's famous nighttime graveyard tour, if you're not easily spooked! Take a short drive to **Digby** for a lunch of fried scallops, then take the ferry to **Saint John**, New Brunswick. If you're a nature lover, press on to camp in **Fundy National Park**, otherwise, stay in adorable **St Martins**. Spend the next day hiking and continuing up the Fundy Coast to view the tides at **Cape Enrage** and **Hopewell Rocks**. The next day, drive across the **Confederation Bridge** into Prince Edward Island (PEI) and **Charlottetown**. Meet Anne of Green Gables in **Cavendish**, have a lobster supper then tour PEI's east coast the following day, with a stop at **Point Prim**, before taking the car ferry back to Nova Scotia and Halifax.

Outdoor Activities

Atlantic Canada does a good job of harnessing its abundance of diverse and pristine terrain for outdoor adventures. Visitors can now get out in the sun (or rain or fog) to hike, kayak, whale-watch or even surf. The season is short for most activities, however (May to October).

On the Water

Best Places to Whale-Watch

Twillingate Island, Newfoundland

Digby Neck, Nova Scotia

Grand Manan Island, New Brunswick

Pleasant Bay, Nova Scotia

Witless Bay Ecological Reserve, Newfoundland

Best Paddling Locations

Eastern and south shores, Nova Scotia

Cape Breton, Nova Scotia

Fundy Isles, New Brunswick

Eastern Fundy shore, New Brunswick

Cartwright, Labrador

Witless Bay, Newfoundland

North Rustico, Prince Edward Island

Kayaking & Canoeing

Atlantic Canada is chock-full of possibilities to get out on the water, be it a lazy canoe trip or a battle with rolling rapids. Sea kayaking has exploded here, with myriad places to paddle. A unique activity in the region is tidal-bore rafting, where you harness the blasting force of the famous Fundy tides.

National and provincial parks are excellent places to start if you've never dipped an oar. Maps and equipment rentals are usually available from the park information centers, where the staff can also give route recommendations.

Canoeing doesn't have the cachet of sea kayaking in the region, but there are still some lovely opportunities. The sport is best suited to inland lakes and rivers, so it's no shocker that Kejimkujik National Park ranks high on the list. It's a good place to paddle into the backcountry and camp. In New Brunswick, the place for canoeing is pristine though moose- and bear-trodden Mt Carleton Provincial Park, while those who wish to remain closer to city life can push off from Fredericton and paddle through the Saint John River. Canoeing in Newfoundland centers on the region's Terra Nova National Park.

Whale-Watching

One of Atlantic Canada's most precious gifts to visitors is the sheer thrill of whale-watching.

More than 22 species of whale and porpoise lurk offshore throughout Atlantic Canada, drawn to the rich fishy feeding waters. The standout species include the leaping and diving humpback whale, the highly endangered North Atlantic right whale and the largest leviathan of all, the mighty blue whale.

Whale-watching boat operators are ubiquitous and will bring you close to the creatures. Popular tour areas include Cape Breton and Nova Scotia's Cabot Trail coastline, especially around Pleasant Bay. The most common sightings here are humpback, minke and pilot whales. In New Brunswick, right whales and blue whales are frequently observed along the eastern Fundy Shore and around the Fundy Isles. Newfoundland is generally surrounded by whales, with humpback and minke commonly seen; tour operators cluster around Witless Bay Ecological Reserve and Twillingate.

Some tours get you closer to the action in Zodiacs while others are on big, relatively comfortable ferry-like motorboats. Look for smaller tours such as Ocean Explorations Whale Cruises (p70) on Digby Neck, which are led by marine biologists. Many tours take in more than just whales and will take you to see seals, puffins or other seabirds as well.

Standard trips last about two hours and cost around $60 to $90 per adult. The sighting success rate is often posted and you should ask if there's any sort of money-back guarantee if you do not see whales. Remember, you're heading out on open sea for most of these tours, so be prepared for a wavy ride. If you're at all prone to seasickness, medicate beforehand. It's also cold out there, so take a jacket or sweater. The season varies by location but usually is in July and August.

And while whale-watching tours are great, never underestimate what you can see from shore, especially from places such as Cape Breton's Cabot Trail and throughout Newfoundland's Avalon Peninsula. Seeing the far away spout of a whale from a clifftop while a bald eagle soars overhead is a true Maritime experience.

TYING KNOTS

Unleash your inner sailor (or fisher or rock climber) by learning to tie a half hitch, bowline and others with *Knots and Splices* (2006) by Cyrus Day and Colin Jarman. Also helpful for budding escape artists.

SEA KAYAKING

If there's any one activity that is Atlantic Canada's specialty, it's sea kayaking. It's everywhere and is absolutely the best way to see the remarkable coastlines. You'll often be kayaking alongside whales, seals and a huge amount of bird life.

Most companies cater to beginners, so no need to feel unworthy if you've never kayaked before. Conversely, advanced paddlers can rent crafts and head out on their own. It can be very rough out there due to volatile weather, high winds and strong currents, so know your limits. The Canadian government publishes an excellent resource titled *Sea Kayaking Safety Guide* available via download from **Transport Canada** (www.tc.gc.ca). The guide details each province's weather and kayaking terrain, and also provides trip-planning tips.

Trips range from paddling around icebergs in Newfoundland to navigating protected inlets ringed by forest on uninhabited isles along the Eastern Shore of Nova Scotia. If you're a beginner, the best place to start are calm waters where your boat won't get jostled around by waves or currents. Some companies make multiday trips, including camping in places you couldn't get to otherwise.

Hiking

Trails – from gentle jaunts around an interpretive path to breath-sapping slogs up a mountain – crisscross the area's national and provincial parks. Hiking them can be the most enjoyable and inexpensive way to absorb the region.

The hiking season runs from May to October, with optimal conditions from June onwards, when the trails are fully thawed. Early in the season, you'll frequently find yourself blissfully (depending on your incli-nation) alone. During the height of the season (July and August), especially on popular sections of the Cabot Trail and other well-publicized walks, you'll be sharing your isolated paradise with scores of other hikers. Having realistic expectations will help you choose when to set out. Maps are available at park centers, although for extended hikes you may need topographic maps.

Canada is notably home to one of the most ambitious paths ever conceived, the **Trans Canada Trail** (www.thegreattrail.ca), which, by its completion, will span approximately 24,000km from Cape Spear

STRAP ON YOUR HIKING BOOTS

Nova Scotia

Nova Scotia holds such a variety of terrain and well-tended backcountry that you'll be spoiled with options.

➡ **Cape Breton Highlands National Park** (p90) offers exquisite hiking over dramatic coastline. The Skyline Trail is the most popular path, but it's hard to go wrong with any of them.

➡ **Cape Split** (p76) is one of the best hikes to view the Fundy tides plus wilderness scenery.

➡ **Taylor Head Provincial Park** (p100) occupies a slender sprig of land on the eastern shore and has trails traversing forest and beach.

New Brunswick

Rugged, forested New Brunswick holds an unlistable number of hiking options ranging from mountains and river valleys to the dramatic Fundy coastline.

➡ **Fundy National Park** (p128) and Fundy Trail Parkway (p125) have a variety of paths along the wooded coastline.

➡ **Mt Carleton Provincial Park** (p109) offers adventurous hikes over mountain peaks to river valleys and lakes. Expect to see wildlife but few humans.

➡ **Grand Manan Island** (p120) shines as the provincial jewel for seaside-themed mellow hikes. Cliffs, marshes and lighthouses are all on the paths.

Newfoundland

Remnants of old walking paths that used to connect local communities and provided escape routes inland from pirates now make for fantastic hiking. Most clutch the shoreline and often provide whale views.

➡ **East Coast Trail** (p184) runs along the Avalon Peninsula.

➡ **Skerwink Trail** (p191) on the Bonavista Peninsula, a fabulous 5km loop reveals picture-perfect coastal vistas.

➡ **Gros Morne National Park** (p202) is renowned for its spectacular landscapes.

Prince Edward Island

PEI is very flat, so there are far fewer hiking opportunities than the other provinces. That said, there are plenty of beaches to stroll.

➡ **Prince Edward Island National Park** (p158) is the best choice if you feel the need to use your feet.

in Newfoundland to Victoria, British Columbia. At time of writing, more than 86% of the trail was open to hikers and many provincial trails already link up to it.

> **MARINE CONDITIONS**
> ....
> Kayakers, fisherfolk and anyone else sailing out to sea can check www.buoyweather.com for marine conditions all around Atlantic Canada.

Birdwatching

No need to be a binocular-toting ornithologist to get into the scene here. Birds swarm the region, and whether you're a birder or not, you'll find it tough to resist the charm of a funny-looking puffin or common murre.

Seabirds are the top draw. Many whale-watching tours also take visitors to seabird colonies as whales and birds share a taste for the same fish. You'll be able to feast your eyes upon razorbills, kittiwakes, arctic terns, and yes, puffins and murres. The colonies can be up to one million strong, their shrieks deafening and their smell, well, not so fresh. Still, it's an amazing sight to behold.

Also impressive to watch are the Arctic-nesting shorebirds that migrate south through the Bay of Fundy. Each year millions of tiny sandpipers refuel in the rich mudflats exposed by the world's highest tides. The prime time is mid-August, and the prime places are around Windsor and Grand Pré in Nova Scotia's Annapolis Valley.

The *Sibley Field Guide to Birds of Eastern North America* (2003) by David Sibley makes an excellent, illustrated and portable companion for bird-watchers.

Cycling & Mountain Biking

After PEI's main rail line ceased operations in 1989, the province cleverly converted its defunct railway bed into a 435km cycling route they named the **Confederation Trail** (www.tourismpei.com/pei-confederation-trail). The move landed PEI on the map as an international cycling destination, and cycling the trail remains one of the most popular ways to experience the province today. Traversing the length of the island, with feeder paths connecting most towns, the trail is lined with top-notch services

and facilities, many provided in quaint, reconditioned train stations. This access to services, combined with manageable distances between sections and predominantly flat, scenic terrain, make cycling here an attractive prospect even for those with limited experience. The seaside stretch from St Peters to Mt Stewart is particularly inspiring.

Although not yet a cohesive entity, the **New Brunswick Trail** (www.nbtrail.com) is in similar vain and offers unconnected sections of trail around the province. Rewarding rides include the Fundy Trail Parkway (p125) along coastal wilderness, and paths through the backcountry in Kouchibouguac National Park (p136).

In Nova Scotia, the area around Lunenburg and Mahone Bay is a cyclist's dream with few hills, gorgeous ocean views and little vehicular traffic. Cape Breton Highlands National Park (p90) is hard to match for scenery, but peak-season traffic and its sections of sheer elevation make it tough going for inexperienced cyclists.

Rugged terrain, high winds, poor road conditions and long stretches of road between towns make Newfoundland a difficult cycling destination. If you want to give it a try, Gros Morne National Park (p202) and CA Pippy Park (p175) in St John's are options.

For a more urban experience, you can rent bikes and explore Halifax's waterfront with even more wind in your hair.

Fishing

Fly-fishing in this region is downright mythical. Avid anglers get all slack-jawed and weak-kneed when names such as 'Miramichi' and 'Margaree' are invoked. No, these aren't beautiful women, but rather places to cast a line for Atlantic salmon and trout (speckled and brown, among the many).

FISHING RULES & LICENSES

Staff at any tourist office will have the most current information about fishing regulations and outfitters. Each province also produces its own 'angler's guide' booklet that includes licensing rules. License prices vary by province and by species fished; a seven-day license costs anywhere from $35 to $95. Check with each province's environmental or natural resources department for further information.

Newfoundland & Labrador (www.env.gov.nl.ca/env/wildlife/angling)

New Brunswick (www2.gnb.ca/content/gnb/en/departments/erd.html)

Nova Scotia (www.gov.ns.ca/fish)

Prince Edward Island (www.gov.pe.ca/forestry/licence)

On the tranquil Miramichi River in New Brunswick, everyone from Prince Charles to Dick Cheney to Marilyn Monroe has reeled one in. The Humber River in Newfoundland and Pinware River in Labrador Straits are known for salmon fishing. If the latter isn't remote enough, Labrador offers several fly-in lodges that have hosted the likes of George Bush Sr.

Deep-sea fishing is huge around North Rustico in PEI where you can sign on with any of a fleet of fishing boats, often captained by bearded seamen who come from long generations of plying the waters. There are plenty of other opportunities to cast a line for the big one – try boats around Lunenberg and along the Cabot Trail in Nova Scotia.

And finally, lobster fishing provides a unique experience, one that kids will love. Haul up crustacean-filled pots in Lunenburg in Nova Scotia. Then grab a bucket and a shovel to go clamming in PEI.

especially plentiful in the colder months. So bundle up in your 7mm wetsuit, try not to freeze your ass off in the almost freezing water and join the lineup. People do surf at warmer times of the year, too. Board rentals cost about $40 per day, lessons about $90.

Kejimkujik National Park (Seaside Adjunct) provides additional waves and the prices are similar.

Perhaps even more radical than surfing is kitesurfing, in which you cruise in, over and out of waves using some cool equipment. Shippagan in northeastern New Brunswick is a good place to try it. Lawrencetown Beach in Nova Scotia is a great place to watch a spectacular show of kitesurfers flying along and over waves.

A stand-up paddleboard (SUP) option is now available in calm Malpeque Bay in PEI, a perfect spot for beginners. Work up an appetite thinking of all those yummy oysters growing beneath you.

Board Sports

Surfing seems an unusual sport for Atlantic Canada – too damn cold, right? Think again. People do surf here and not only is it cold, it's bloody freezing, since the best waves break in winter. Luckily, the best time for beginners is summer when the waves are smaller and the water is at least a little bit warmer.

The place to partake of the madness is Lawrencetown Beach on Nova Scotia's eastern shore. L-town, as it's called, faces due south and picks up stormy weather from hundreds of kilometers away; this results in exceptional wrapping waves,

Skiing & Snowboarding

Atlantic Canada's best skiing and snowboarding take place at Newfoundland's Marble Mountain (p209) outside Corner Brook. It may not have the height of Whistler or other top resorts, but it's lower cost with shorter lift lines, so you get more time on the slopes.

Marble has 39 trails, four lifts, a 519m vertical drop and annual snowfall of 5m. There are snowboarding and tubing parks, as well as night skiing on Friday. The region caters to cross-country skiers at Blow-Me-Down Cross Country Ski Park (p210), about 10 minutes from the mountain.

Serious cross-country skiers will want to head far north to where the Canadian national team trains in Labrador West. The Wapusakatto Mountains let loose with good, cold, dry snow from late October to late April, a much longer season than elsewhere in the region – or anywhere in Canada.

Wentworth (www.skiwentworth.ca) is the favorite spot in Nova Scotia, although it's small with 815 vertical feet and 20 runs. The park also offers cross-country skiing and snowshoeing.

New Brunswick has three ski parks, the biggest being **Poley Mountain** (www.poleymountain.com) near Sussex, with more than 40 hectares of skiable terrain and 10 night skiing trails.

For further information contact the Canadian Ski Council.

Other Winter Sports

Windsor, Nova Scotia, claims to be the birthplace of hockey so as you'd expect, there are plenty of ice-skating areas around the region, although not many cater to visitors. Your best bet for gliding across the ice is the world-class Emera Oval in downtown Halifax where you can even borrow skates for free.

Fundy National Park (p128), New Bruns

Travel with Children

These Canadian provinces were made for kids. As if seeing moose, eagles and whales or running around in the snow or on the beach all day wasn't fun enough, everywhere you turn those crafty Canadians have cooked up some hands-on learning experience, living history lesson or child-oriented theater.

Best Regions for Kids

Halifax, Nova Scotia

Cartoonlike tug-boat rides, cycling, kayaking, a free year-round skating area, parks and family-friendly festivals galore through summer.

Prince Edward Island's Beaches

Sandy stretches of white or pink sand with lightly lapping, bearably cool waves.

Fundy National Park, New Brunswick

Low-tide flats to putter around, trails to waterfalls, lakes to swim in.

St John's, Newfoundland

Nearby whale-watching tours.

Nova Scotia, New Brunswick & PEI for Kids

Between learning about pirate history on antique sailing vessels, playing on low-key beaches and climbing to the top of lighthouses, it's impossible to make a bad decision about where to take your kids in these provinces. Canada caters to families better than nearly anywhere else in the world and the mix of coast and forest, easy-to-manage cities and lakes galore make this region a top choice in the country. The food isn't daunting, people are friendly and there's a prevalent sense of peace and welcome.

Museums, Monuments & Lighthouses

Halifax, Saint John and St John's all have science museums that specialize in hands-on activities to get all ages involved, while at historic sites strewn across the region costumed thespians get you right into the period and often have demonstrations of everything from blacksmithing to cooking. At some of these places there are also puppet or theatrical performances for children and other events such as hayrides. Teens often enjoy these sites as well, since they are large, diverse and great for exploration.

Lighthouses seem to be perched on every headland and you can climb up to the top of many of them, usually for a small fee. If you're lucky there will be a hand pump horn to set off.

Outdoor Activities

Endless coastlines, fresh air, wildlife, snow, sand, rivers, lakes and mountains make almost any outdoor activity you may be yearning for entirely possible. Prince Edward Island's mostly flat Confederation Trail traverses the island and can be picked up from almost any point; the coastline of the Prince Edward Island National Park has dedicated cycling lanes that run scenically along the beaches. The Halifax waterfront is also a great place for family bike rentals. Canoeing is a Canadian activity par excellence, available in lakes in Nova Scotia and New Brunswick and most sea-kayaking outfits throughout the region cater to families. Skiing and snowboarding are available at small family-friendly slopes in winter.

But perhaps the most exciting thing to do with all the surrounding seas is to set sail, either to explore and feel the wind in your hair or to look for the many species of whale thriving in the Bay of Fundy, Cabot Straight and the mighty Atlantic Ocean.

Eating Out

Fast food is ubiquitous in Canada so healthy eaters may find that the biggest hurdle is finding food that's not processed or fried. Cabins and family suites often have kitchens so you can self-cater; in cities you'll find options fit for any type of diet.

Most budget to midrange restaurants offer booster seats. As an alternative to kids' menus, you can often ask for half-portions of mains on the adult menu.

Children's Highlights

A History Lesson

➡ **European Colonization** L'Anse aux Meadows (Newfoundland), Louisbourg (Nova Scotia), King's Landing Historic Settlement (New Brunswick)

➡ **Fossils** Joggins Fossil Centre (Nova Scotia)

➡ **First Nations** Lennox Island (PEI), Port au Choix National Historic Site (Newfoundland)

➡ **Pirates & the Titanic** Halifax Waterfront, Maritime Museum of the Atlantic (Halifax), Titanic Burial Grounds (Halifax)

Out in Nature

➡ **Whale- and Sealife-Watching** Brier Island (Nova Scotia), Witless Bay Ecological Reserve (Newfoundland), Grand Manan Island (New Brunswick)

➡ **Wild Waters** Rafting the Fundy tidal bore (Nova Scotia), sea kayaking (Nova Scotia), clamming at Point Prim (PEI)

➡ **Beaches** Prince Edward Island National Park (PEI), Kejimkujik National Park Seaside Adjunct (Nova Scotia), Parlee Beach Provincial Park (New Brunswick)

➡ **Forests & Lakes** Anchors Above Zipline Adventure (Nova Scotia), Kejimkujik National Park (Nova Scotia), Mt Carleton (New Brunswick)

Theme Park Delight

➡ **Upper Clements Park** (www.upperclements parks.com) Wild rides, zip lines and a wildlife park near Annapolis Royal, Nova Scotia.

➡ **Magic Mountain Water Park** (www. magicmountain.ca) Steep and fast slides to lazy floats make this great for all ages in Moncton, New Brunswick.

➡ **Avonlea** (www.avonlea.ca) Brings the *Anne of Green Gables* books to life in PEI.

➡ **Ross Farm Museum** (www.museum.gov. ns.ca/rfm/) Recreates 1800s Nova Scotian farm life, including hands-on animal experiences and sleigh rides in winter.

Cape Breton Island (p87), Nova Sc

Once in Canada, kids receive a wide range of discounts on attraction admissions and transportation fares. Usually kids aged six to 17 are half-price; younger children are free. Ask about family admissions if your posse consists of two adults and two or more kids.

Kids often stay for free in hotels and motels. B&Bs are not so gracious, and may even refuse to accept kids. Ask when booking. Most restaurants other than fine-dining establishments will usually offer you booster seats and anything else you might need. Children's menus are widely available as well.

Baby food, infant formula, milk, disposable diapers (nappies) and the like are widely available in drugstores and supermarkets. Breastfeeding in public is legal. In all vehicles, children under 18kg must be restrained in safety seats.

Most tourist offices can lead you to resources for children's programs, childcare facilities and pediatricians.

Planning

Children who are traveling to Canada without both parents need authorization from the nonaccompanying parent.

Regions at a Glance

Yaar! This is the Canada for enjoying steel-colored seascapes and salt air with a big bowl of chowder and a pint of ale to wash it down. Everything here revolves around the cold Atlantic Ocean, from today's whale-watching adventures and lobster feasts to the history of Vikings and pirates. While tied together by geography and history, each province has its own personality, from the iceberg-clad desolation of Newfoundland to the forested inland rivers and lakes of New Brunswick, the storybook farmlands of Prince Edward Island (PEI) and the never-ending coastal and cultural variations of Nova Scotia. Wherever you choose to go, you'll never be far from the sound of waves crashing on a beach or a simple supper of fresh fish.

Nova Scotia

Culture
Activities
History

Cultural Mishmash

Tartan shops, French-speaking villages and aboriginal communities are all within kilometers of each other. Throw in some African Nova Scotians and Pier 21, Canada's entry point for more than a million immigrants, and you have the definition of a cultural melting pot.

Coves, Cliffs & Tides

Coastal coves between evergreen islets are bird and marine-mammal habitats that beg you to go paddling. On the Fundy Coast the highest tides in the world constantly change the landscape. Cape Breton Island's coastal cliffs are home to moose and nesting bald eagles.

Time Warp

Nova Scotians don't just preserve their historical vestiges, they get in period costume and do old-time activities from sewing to blacksmithing, recreating the scene as it might have been hundreds of years ago.

p40

New Brunswick

Activities
Fishing
Wildlife

You in a Canoe

From the tranquil Chiput-neticook Lakes to the quicksilver Tobique River, New Brunswick is tops for canoeing, the most Canadian of activities. You can even meet artisans who still make canoes the old-fashioned way – a dying art.

Tie your Flies

Baseball stars and captains of industry used to come to New Brunswick to cast their fly rods into the province's salmon- and trout-choked rivers. Why not do the same?

Puffin Lovin'

Whether you're a hard-core birdwatcher or just want to be able to tell your friends you saw a moose, New Brunswick's got plenty of animal action to go around. Your best bet: observing rare Atlantic puffins on desolate Machias Seal Island.

p101

Prince Edward Island

Cuisine
Culture
Beaches

Lobster Suppers, Oysters & Potatoes

Although the area vies with Idaho as potato capital of the Americas, you'll pass vine-covered hills to reach town halls serving fisher-sized suppers of fresh lobster before hitting coves of sunlit fishing boats pulling up succulent Malpeque oysters. PEI is a must for the serious foodie.

It's All About Anne

Personified by Anne Shirley, LM Montgomery's red-headed star of the *Anne of Green Gables* series, Prince Edward Island (PEI) is as pretty as it's portrayed in the books. Red dirt and sands mimic Anne's hair, while white-picket fences and fields of wildflowers paint the real-life backdrop.

White & Pink Beaches

PEI has sienna beach flats topped by red-and-white lighthouses, cream-colored road-eating dunes, stretches of white sands that 'sing' when you walk on them and some of the warmest waters in the Gulf of St Lawrence.

p143

Newfoundland & Labrador

Seascapes
Culture
History

Great Big Sea

'There's one,' someone shouts, and sure enough a barnacled humpback steams through the water. Or maybe they're referring to the icebergs. Whether you're along-shore, out in a boat or by your window, Newfoundland's sea delivers.

Strange Brew

The peculiar brogue is vaguely Irish, the slang indecipherable enough to merit its own dictionary, plates arrive with cod tongues, bakeapple jam and figgy duff (sweet pudding made with raisins and molasses), while towns have names such as Dildo and Jerry's Nose. This region is so offbeat it even has its own time zone: a *half*-hour ahead of the mainland.

Viking Vestiges

They've taken a low-key approach at L'Anse aux Meadows, Leif Erikson's 1000-year-old settlement, but the forlorn sweep of land is more powerful that way. You can feel the Vikings' isolation.

p169

On the Road

Newfoundland & Labrador
p169

Prince Edward Island
p143

New Brunswick
p101

Nova Scotia
p40

Nova Scotia

Includes ➜

Best Places to Eat

➜ Wild Caraway (p83)

➜ Le Caveau (p77)

➜ Black Spoon (p96)

➜ Lincoln Street Food (p63)

➜ 2 Doors Down (p52)

➜ Shanty Cafe (p69)

Best Places to Sleep

➜ Keltic Lodge at the Highlands (p92)

➜ Cabot Links (p88)

➜ Queen Anne Inn (p74)

➜ Roselawn Lodging (p77)

➜ Maple Inn (p81)

➜ Jumping Mouse Campground (p93)

Why Go?

If Nova Scotia were a film, its protagonists would be rugged yet kind-hearted, burnt by the wind and at one with the sea. It would be shot against a backdrop of rolling green fields and high sea-cliffs; its soundtrack would feature fiddles, drums and evocative piano scores; and its plot would be a spirited romp around themes of history, community and family.

Nova Scotia is the real deal. Its wild and wonderfully varied landscape is home to a diverse population of resourceful, hospitable folk, who love to sing and dance but who'd happily break you at dodgeball in a second.

Short-lived summers are a sheer delight, as the locals emerge from the cold to celebrate life: accommodations fill fast and prices hike. As difficult as the late spring and peak fall conditions are becoming to predict, these times afford spectacular scenery and a milder climate, while long, white winters are harsh but beautiful affairs.

When to Go

Halifax

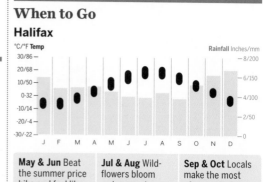

May & Jun Beat the summer price hike and feel like you have the province to yourself.

Jul & Aug Wildflowers bloom as temperatures and prices rise, while days go on forever.

Sep & Oct Locals make the most of stunning fall foliage before the long winter comes.

History

From time immemorial, the Mi'kmaq First Nation lived throughout present-day Nova Scotia. When the French established the first European settlement at Port Royal (today's Annapolis Royal) in 1605, Grand Chief Membertou offered them hospitality and became a frequent guest of Samuel de Champlain.

That close relationship with the French led to suspicions by the British after they gained control of Nova Scotia, and rewards were offered for Mi'kmaw scalps. Starting in 1755 most French-speaking Acadians were deported to Louisiana (where they became known as Cajuns) and elsewhere for refusing to swear allegiance to the British Crown.

Nova Scotia was repopulated by some 35,000 United Empire Loyalists retreating from the American Revolution, including a small number of African slaves owned by Loyalists and freed Black Loyalists. New England planters settled other communities and from 1773 waves of Highland Scots arrived.

Most Nova Scotians trace their ancestry to the British Isles, as a look at the lengthy 'Mac' and 'Mc' sections of the phone book easily confirms. Acadians who managed to return from Louisiana after 1764 found their lands in the Annapolis Valley occupied. They settled instead along the French Shore between Yarmouth and Digby, on Cape Breton Island around Chéticamp, and on Isle Madame. Today Acadians make up some 12% of the population, although not as many still identify French as their first language. African Nova Scotians make up about 5% of the population. Nova Scotia has close to 34,000 people of Aboriginal identity, of which around 22,000 are First Nations people, predominantly from 18 different Mi'kmaq communities.

Local Culture

With nearly 8000km of coastline, Nova Scotia has a culture that revolves around the sea. Historically, it has been a hard-working region of coal mines and fisheries. The current culture is still very blue-collar but, with the decline of the primary industries, many young Nova Scotians are forced to leave their province in search of work.

Perhaps because of the long winters and hard-working days, an enormous number of Nova Scotians play music. Family get-togethers, particularly Acadian and Scottish, consist of strumming, fiddling, foot-tapping and dancing.

FAST FACTS

➡ Population: 942,930
➡ Area: 55,284 sq km
➡ Capital: Halifax
➡ Quirky fact: Has the only tidal power plant in the western hemisphere

NOVA SCOTIA

ⓘ Getting There & Away

AIR

There are multiple flights daily between **Halifax Stanfield International Airport** (p56) and Toronto, Montréal, Ottawa, Saint John and Moncton, and less frequent flights to Boston and New York. In summer and fall there are direct flights to London and Iceland. Airlines covering these routes include Air Canada, Condor, Delta, Iceland Air, United and Westjet.

PAL Airlines (PB; ☎ 800-563-2800; www.palairlines.ca) can be useful for getting to Nova Scotia from regional locations in Quebec, New Brunswick and Newfoundland.

Air St-Pierre (PJ; ☎ 877-277-7765; www.airsaintpierre.com) also flies to the French territories of St Pierre and Miquelon from **Sydney JA Douglas McCurdy Airport** (YQY; ☎ 902-564-7720; www.sydneyairport.ca; 280 Silver Dart Way), which otherwise only services domestic routes.

BOAT
New Brunswick

Bay Ferries (☎ 877-762-7245; www.ferries.ca) operates boats from Digby to Saint John, NB (adult/child one-way from $36/20, from 2½ hours). Rates for vehicles start at $107 (including a fuel surcharge).

Newfoundland

Marine Atlantic (☎ 800-341-7981; www.marine-atlantic.ca) ferries ply the route between North Sydney and Port aux Basques, Newfoundland (adult/child one-way from $44/21, six to eight hours), year round. In summer, ferries also travel to Argentia (adult/child one-way from $116/65, 16 hours) on Newfoundland's east coast. Reservations are required for either trip.

Factor in an extra $114 to bring a standard-sized vehicle to Port aux Basques, and an extra $203 to Argentia.

Prince Edward Island

Bay Ferries cruises between Caribou, near Pictou, and Wood Islands on Prince Edward Island (PEI) up to nine times daily (adult/child from $19/free, 1¼ hours). A standard vehicle costs $81. No reservations are required, but it's wise to show up half an hour before departure.

Nova Scotia Highlights

① **Cabot Trail** (p89) Driving Cape Breton Island's breathtaking twists and turns.

② **Louisbourg National Historic Site** (p98)

Marveling at the province's long colonial history.

③ **Canadian Museum of Immigration at Pier 21** (p45) Contemplating Canada's multicultural roots.

④ **Memory Lane Heritage Village** (p98) Celebrating how a community has preserved its history at this re-created village in Lake Charlotte.

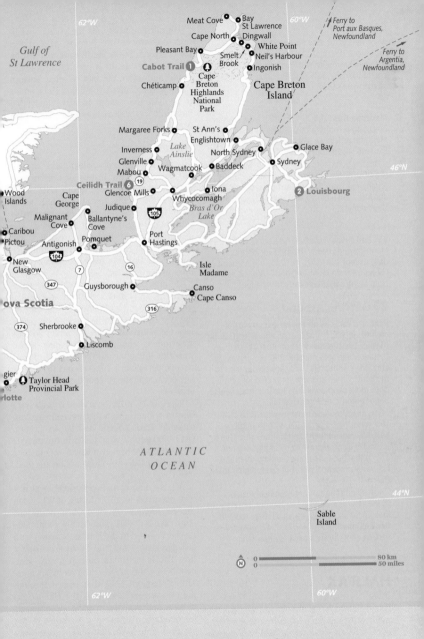

5 **Ironworks Distillery**
(p61) Sampling a Bluenose Rum in World Heritage–listed Lunenburg.

6 **Glenora Inn & Distillery**
(p87) Observing how a single malt is made at this distillery on the Ceilidh Trail.

7 **Joggins Fossil Centre**
(p80) Contemplating evolution at these wondrous, well-preserved cliff faces.

8 **Grand Pré National Historic Site** (p75)
Remembering the plight of the Acadians.

9 **Cape d'Or Lighthouse**
(p82) Gawking at the view.

USA

As of June 2016, **Bay Ferries** (p41) commenced services of a high-speed car catamaran between Yarmouth and Portland, Maine (adult/child $107/65, 5½ hours). Bringing a vehicle will cost an extra $199.

BUS

Maritime Bus (☑ 800-575-1807; www.maritime bus.com) provides a bus service through the Maritime provinces and connects with Orleans Express buses from Québec.

Destinations from Halifax include Sydney ($63.50, five hours, two daily), Charlottetown (change at Truro; $103, nine hours, two daily) and Moncton (change at Truro; $83, eight hours, three daily).

TRAIN

VIA Rail (www.viarail.ca) runs services between Montréal and Halifax (from $134, 22 hours, daily except Tuesday), with stops in Amherst (17 hours from Montréal) and Truro (18 hours from Montréal). Book early for cheaper fares.

ⓘ Getting Around

Renting a car is by far the easiest way to get around and can be more economical than taking the bus. Shuttle buses are another alternative. Distances are very manageable; you can easily stay in the Annapolis Valley and do day trips to the South Shore and vice versa. The longest drive most people will do is the four-hour haul to Cape Breton Island from Halifax.

The direct route to most places will be on a 100-series highway (eg 101, 102, 103); these have high speed-limits and limited exits. There is usually a corresponding older highway (eg 1, 2, 3) that passes through communities and has varying speed limits, but rarely higher than 80km/h.

The ubiquitous car rental agencies can be found at airports and in larger cities, but if you're looking for something with a bit more room, try **Cruise Canada** (☑ 800-671-8042; www.cruise-canada.com) for RV and camper rentals.

HALIFAX

☑ 902 / POP 390,100

Proud Halifax locals (known as Haligonians), many of whom have come from other parts of Nova Scotia, have a great quality of life: sea breezes keep the air clean; leafy, manicured parks and gardens nestle between heritage buildings; there's a thriving arts, theater and culinary scene; and the numerous pubs, with their craft-brew culture and love for bands, quite simply, go off.

It's not just a city for the young – Halifax's longevity ensures something of appeal for everyone. Stroll the historic waterfront, check out a museum or two, catch some live music and enjoy the best of what Eastern Canada has to offer – you'll find Haligonians to be more than happy to share their fabulous little city with visitors from around the world.

History

Pirates, warring colonialists and exploding ships make the history of Halifax read like an adventure story. From 1749, when Edward Cornwallis founded Halifax along what is today Barrington St, the British settlement expanded and flourished. The destruction of the French fortress at Louisbourg in 1760 increased British dominance and sealed Halifax's place as Nova Scotia's most important city.

Despite being home to two universities from the early 1800s, Halifax was still a rough-and-ready sailors' nest that, during the War of 1812, became a center for privateer black-market trade. As piracy lost its government endorsement, Halifax sailed smoothly into a mercantile era, and the city streets, particularly Market and Brunswick Sts, became home to countless taverns and brothels.

On April 14, 1912, three Halifax ships were sent in response to a distress call: the 'unsinkable' RMS *Titanic* had hit an iceberg. Over 1500 people were killed in the tragedy and many were buried at Fairview Cemetery, next to the Fairview Overpass on the Bedford Hwy.

A lesser-known piece of tragic local history occurred in 1917, during WWI, when the SS *Mont-Blanc*, a French munitions ship carrying TNT and highly flammable benzol, collided in the Halifax Narrows with a Norwegian vessel, the *SS Imo*, causing a fire. The French ship burned for 20 minutes before the fire reached its toxic cargo. The subsequent blast that ripped through the city became known as the Halifax Explosion and was the world's most powerful detonation prior to the testing of the atomic bomb. More than 1900 people were killed, and 9000 injured. The entire suburb of Richmond was leveled by the blast and First Nations Mi'kmaq communities along the shoreline were inundated by a resultant tsunami. The event remains the most significant disaster in Haligonian history.

⊙ Sights

⊙ Downtown

★**Canadian Museum
of Immigration at Pier 21**   MUSEUM
(☑902-425-7770; www.pier21.ca; 1055 Marginal Rd; adult/child $11/7; ⊙9:30am-5:30pm May-Nov, reduced hours Dec-Apr) Pier 21 was to Canada what Ellis Island was to the USA. Between 1928 and 1971 over a million immigrants entered Canada here. Their stories and the historical context that led them to abandon their homelands form the basis of this brilliant museum, the compelling permanent exhibits of which include the recently renovated 'Pier 21 Story' and the new 'Canadian Immigration Story.' The collection, featuring firsthand testimonies and artifacts, is complemented by visiting exhibitions along related themes.

★**Citadel Hill
National Historic Site**   HISTORIC SITE
(☑902-426-5080; www.pc.gc.ca; 5425 Sackville St; adult/child $12/6; ⊙9am-5pm) Canada's most visited national historic site, the huge and arguably spooky Citadel is a star-shaped fort atop Halifax's central hill. Construction began in 1749 with the founding of Halifax; this version of the Citadel is the fourth, built from 1818 to 1861. Guided tours explain the fort's shape and history. The grounds inside the fort are open year-round, with free admission when the exhibits are closed.

From November to May, while the grounds remain open, visitor experience services are limited.

Art Gallery of Nova Scotia   GALLERY
(☑902-424-5280; www.artgalleryofnovascotia.ca; 1723 Hollis St; adult/child $12/5, 5-9pm Thu free; ⊙10am-5pm Wed, Fri & Sat, to 9pm Thu, noon-5pm Sun) Don't miss the permanent, tear-jerking 'Maud Lewis Painted House' exhibit, which includes the tiny house (3m by 4m) that Lewis lived in most of her adult life. The main exhibit in the lower hall changes regularly, featuring anything from ancient art to the avant-garde. Free tours are given at 2pm Sunday year-round and daily during July and August.

Museum of Natural History   MUSEUM
(☑902-424-7353; http://naturalhistory.novascotia.ca; 1747 Summer St; adult/child $6.30/5.25; ⊙9am-8pm Wed, to 5pm Thu-Tue mid-May–Oct, closed Mon Nov–mid-May; ⊕) Daily summer programs introduce children to Gus the go-pher tortoise and demonstrate the cooking of bugs. Exhibits on history and the natural world will keep parents engaged, too.

Halifax Public Gardens   GARDENS
(www.halifaxpublicgardens.ca; 5665 Spring Garden Rd; ⊙sunrise-sunset) **FREE** Formally established in 1867 in celebration of Canada's Confederation, Halifax's delightful central public gardens are considered by many to be the finest Victorian city gardens in North America. Oldies bands perform off-key concerts in the gazebo on Sunday afternoons in summer, tai chi practitioners go through their paces, and anyone who brings checkers can play on outside tables.

St Paul's Church   CHURCH
(☑902-429-2240; www.stpaulshalifax.org; 1749 Argyle St; ⊙9am-4pm Mon-Sat, Mass 10am Sun) The oldest surviving building in Halifax is also the oldest Protestant place of worship in Canada. Established in 1749 with the founding of Halifax, St Paul's Anglican Church once served parishioners from as far and wide as Newfoundland to Ontario. Drop in any time for a guided or self-directed tour of this fascinating building.

**Alexander Keith's
Nova Scotia Brewery**   BREWERY
(☑902-455-1474; www.keiths.ca; 1496 Lower Water St, Brewery Market; adult/child $26/12; ⊙11:30am-8pm Mon-Sat, to 6pm Sun) A tour of this brewery takes you to 19th-century Halifax via costumed thespians, quality brews and dark corridors. Finish your hour-long tour with a party in the basement pub, with beer on tap and ale-inspired yarns. Note that you'll need your ID. Kids are kept happy with lemonade. Multiple tours run daily from June to October, and from Friday to Sunday from November to May; check the website for tour times.

Maritime Museum of the Atlantic MUSEUM
(☑902-424-7490; http://maritimemuseum.nova scotia.ca; 1675 Lower Water St; adult/child May-Oct $9.50/5, Nov-Apr $5/3; ⊙9:30am-5pm May-Oct, reduced hours Nov-Apr) Part of this popular waterfront museum used to be a chandlery, where all the gear needed to outfit a vessel was sold. You can smell the charred ropes, cured to protect them from saltwater. There's a range of permanent exhibits including displays on the RMS *Titanic* and the Halifax Explosion. Outside at the dock you can explore the CSS *Acadia,* a retired hydrographic vessel from England.

Halifax

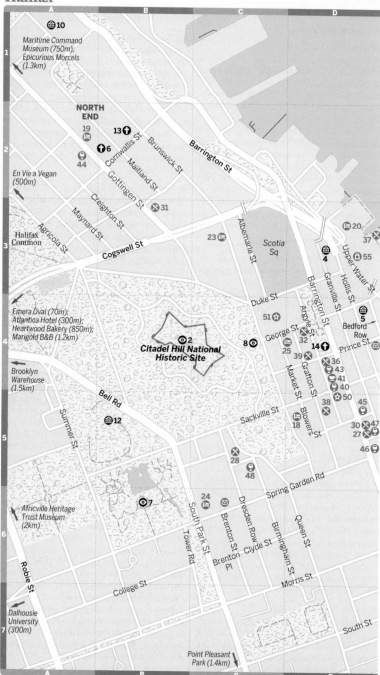

Maritime Command Museum (750m); Epicurious Morcels (1.3km)

NORTH END

En Vie a Vegan (500m)

Halifax Common

Scotia Sq

Emera Oval (70m); Atlantica Hotel (300m); Heartwood Bakery (850m); Marigold B&B (1.2km)

Brooklyn Warehouse (1.5km)

Citadel Hill National Historic Site

Bedford Row

Africville Heritage Trust Museum (2km)

Dalhousie University (300m)

Point Pleasant Park (1.4km)

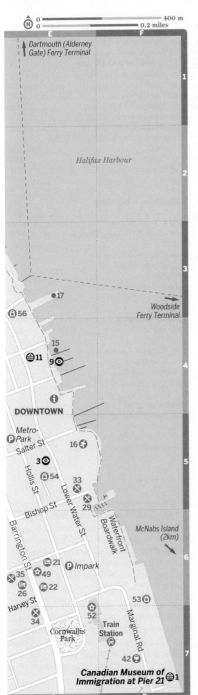

Canada's official Naval Memorial, the last WWII corvette, **HMCS Sackville** (☑902-429-2132; www.hmcssackville.ca; adult/child $3/2; ☉10am-5pm Jun-Oct), is docked outside and staffed by the Canadian Navy.

Anna Leonowens Gallery   GALLERY

(☑902-494-8223; http://alg.nscad.ca; 1891 Granville St; ☉11am-5pm Tue-Fri, noon-4pm Sat) **FREE**
Off the pedestrian area on Granville St, this gallery shows work by students and faculty of the Nova Scotia College of Art & Design. The gallery is named for the founder of the college, who was immortalized in *The King and I* for her relationship with the king of Siam.

Halifax Town Clock   NOTABLE BUILDING

(Old Town Clock; Brunswick St) Atop Citadel Hill, Halifax's Palladian-styled town clock looks like it would be more at home in a Venetian lane, but has been faithfully keeping time here for over 200 years. The inner workings arrived in Halifax from London in 1803, after being ordered by Prince Edward, the Duke of Kent.

Fairview Lawn Cemetery   HISTORIC SITE

(☑902-490-4883; 3720 Windsor St) When the RMS *Titanic* sank, the bodies not lost at sea were brought to Halifax. Among other sites, there are 19 graves at **Mt Olivet Catholic Cemetery** (7076 Mumford Rd) and 121 here at the Fairview Lawn Cemetery, including that of J Dawson, whose name was the basis for Leonardo DiCaprio's character in the film *Titanic*. Those with a keen eye will be able to locate the touching Celtic Cross and Unknown Child monuments.

◉ North End

The North End has been a distinct neighborhood for almost as long as Halifax has existed. In the early 1750s the 'North Suburbs' area became popular and subsequently grew thanks to its larger building lots.

Africville Heritage Trust Museum   MUSEUM

(www.africvillemuseum.org; 5795 Africville Rd; adult/child $4/2.30; ☉10am-4pm Tue-Sun Jun-Aug, 10am-4pm Tue-Fri Sep-May) Learn the story of Africville, Halifax's predominantly African suburb, the residents of which were evicted and their homes razed in what became the local scandal of the 1960s. In 2010 Halifax's mayor issued a formal apology to the community. Poignantly, the museum is housed in a replica of the Seaview United

Halifax

Baptist Church that was once the center of the community.

Maritime Command Museum　　MUSEUM
(☏902-721-8250;　　www.psphalifax.ca/marcom museum; 2725 Gottingen St; ☉9am-3:30pm Mon-Fri) FREE The admiral of the British navy for all of North America was based in Halifax until 1819 and threw grand parties at Admiralty House, now the Maritime Command Museum. Apart from the beautiful Georgian architecture, the museum is worth a visit for its eclectic collections, including cigarette lighters, silverware and ship's bells, to name but a few.

St George's Round Church　　CHURCH
(☏902-423-1059; www.roundchurch.ca; 2222 Brunswick St) Built in 1800, this church is a rare example of a circular church built in the Palladian style, with a main rotunda 18m in diameter. Tours here, and of the affiliated **Little Dutch Church** (2393 Brunswick St; ☉by appointment Jul-Sep) FREE, are by arrangement.

Cornwallis Street Baptist Church　　CHURCH
(☏902-429-5573; www.cornwallisstreetbaptist.ca; 5457 Cornwallis St) The Cornwallis Street Baptist Church has been serving African Nova Scotians since the 1830s. Walk by on Sunday morning and hear the gospel music flow through its walls.

Outside the Centre

**Crystal Crescent Beach
Provincial Park** STATE PARK

(http://parks.novascotia.ca/content/crystal-crescent-beach; 223 Sambro Creek Rd) Eighteen kilometers south of Halifax, near the village of Sambro, this gorgeous provincial park boasts three distinct beaches in separate coves; the third one out, toward the southwest, is clothing-optional and gay-friendly. An 8.5km hiking trail begins just inland and heads through barrens, bogs and boulders to Pennant Point.

🏃 Activities

Cycling is a great way to see sites on the outskirts of Halifax. You can take bikes on the ferries to Dartmouth or cycle over the MacDonald Bridge. In summer, there's usually a few outfitters renting out bikes along the waterfront around Bishop's Landing (at the end of Bishop St).

There are short and long hikes surprisingly close to downtown. Hemlock Ravine is an 80-hectare wooded area that has five trails, suitable for all levels. To get there, take the Bedford Hwy from central Halifax then turn left at Kent Ave; there's parking and a map of the trail at the end of this road. See www.novatrails.com for more detailed trail descriptions and directions to other trailheads.

McNabs Island HIKING

(www.mcnabsisland.ca) Fine sand and cobblestone shorelines, salt marshes, forests and abandoned military fortifications paint the landscape of this 400-hectare island in Halifax Harbour, where with a little imagination you could transport yourself back in time. Refer to the website for information on the various ways to get here, what to do (and what not to do) when here, and for a downloadable map.

Point Pleasant Park HIKING

(☑ 902-490-4700; 5718 Point Pleasant Dr; ☉ sunrise-sunset; ☐ 9) Some 39km of nature trails, picnic spots and a beautiful 18th-century Martello Tower are all found within this 75-hectare sanctuary, just 1.5km south of the city center. Trails around the perimeter of the park offer views of McNabs Island, the open ocean and the North West Arm.

I Heart Bikes CYCLING

(☑ 902-406-7774; www.iheartbikeshfx.com; 1507 Lower Water St; rentals per hour from $12) If you

prefer two wheels to two legs, you'll heart these folks, too. Centrally located near the Halifax Waterfront, it's a great spot to pick up a chariot and start pedaling. Both rentals and cycling tours are available.

👉 Tours

Halifax Free Tours WALKING

(www.halifaxfreetours.wixsite.com/halifaxfreetours; ☉10am & 3pm Jun-Sep) FREE You can't beat the price of these free 1½-hour walking tours of downtown Halifax, led by friendly local guides. Send an email to reserve a spot and please remember to tip!

Adventure Canada ECOTOUR

(☑ 905-271-4000; www.adventurecanada.com) This provider of group eco- and adventure tours is one of the few companies permitted to operate on Sable Island (p50), with its population of wild horses and the world's largest breeding colony of grey seals.

Murphy's the Cable Wharf CRUISE

(☑ 902-420-1015; www.mtcw.ca; 1751 Lower Water St) This tourism giant runs a range of tours on Halifax Harbour, from deep-sea fishing and two-hour scenic cruises to the crowd-pleasing 55-minute Harbour Hopper Tours (adult/child $35/20) on an amphibious bus, and Theodore the Tugboat's Big Harbour Adventure tours ($20/10), wildly popular with youngsters.

Pedal & Sea Adventures CYCLING

(☑ 877-777-5699; www.pedalandseaadventures.com; bicycle rental per day/week from $35/149) Offers unique, all-inclusive cycling tours in Nova Scotia, as well as quality bike rentals, where they'll deliver the bike to you (for two-day rentals or longer), complete with helmet, lock and repair kit.

OFF THE BEATEN TRACK

SABLE ISLAND

This ever-shifting, 44km-long spit of sand lies some 300km southeast of Halifax and has caused more than 350 documented shipwrecks. But what makes Sable Island most famous is that it's home to one of the world's only truly wild horse populations, as well as the planet's largest breeding colony of grey seals.

The first 60 ancestors of today's Sable Island horses were shipped to the island in 1760 when Acadians were being deported from Nova Scotia by the British. The Acadians were forced to abandon their livestock and it appears that Boston merchant ship owner Thomas Hancock helped himself to their horses – then put them to pasture on Sable Island to keep it low-profile. The horses that survived became wild.

Today the island works as a research center: scientists come every year to study the horses and other wildlife, and to keep an eye on any impact from their neighbor, the ExxonMobil Sable Offshore Energy Project. Just 10km away, this site has been harvesting natural gas since 1999, although decommissioning plans are currently underway.

It's complicated and expensive – but not impossible – to visit Sable Island as a layperson; about 50 to 100 adventurous souls make it to the island each year. Contact **Sable Island Station** (☏ 902-426-1993; www.pc.gc.ca), in conjunction with Environment Canada, for information about how to get the necessary permissions and to independently arrange transport. Otherwise, Adventure Canada (p49) operates group tours.

Tall Ship Silva BOATING
(☏ 902-420-1015; www.tallshipsilva.com; 1751 Lower Water St; cruises adult/child $30/19) Lend a hand or sit back and relax while taking a 1½-hour daytime cruise or a two-hour evening party cruise on Halifax's square-masted tall ship. Check the website for sailing times.

Bluenose Sidecar Tours DRIVING
(☏ 902-579-7433; www.bluenosesidecartours.com; tours from $89) Enjoy free and breezy views from fun, old-school motorcycle sidecars on tours around Halifax or to Peggy's Cove, Lunenburg and the South Shore.

Bluenose II BOATING
(☏ 800-763-1963; www.bluenose.novascotia.ca; Lower Water St; 2hr cruises adult/child $20/10) This classic replica of the *Bluenose* racing schooner is sometimes in Halifax and sometimes in Lunenburg. Check the website for details.

Great Earth Expeditions ECOTOUR
(☏ 902-223-2409; www.greatearthexpeditions.com; tours from $90) Half- and full-day ecotours led from Halifax can include hiking, kayaking or historical themes, including a tour to McNabs Island in Halifax Harbour. Also offers longer four-day tours up the Cabot Trail (p89) and through Kejimkujik National Park (p64).

Local Tasting Tours FOOD & DRINK
(☏ 902-818-9055; www.localtastingtours.com; tours from $40) Eat your way around Halifax's burgeoning restaurant scene on these fun, foodie-themed tours, featuring up to six local restaurants per tour.

Tattle Tours WALKING
(☏ 902-494-0525; www.tattletours.ca; ☉ 7:30pm Wed-Sun) Lively two-hour tours depart from the Old Town Clock and are filled with local gossip, pirate tales and ghost stories. Walking tours are also available on demand. Rates vary depending on the number in your party.

East Coast Balloon Adventures BALLOONING
(☏ 902-306-0095; www.eastcoastballoonadventures.com; 45min flights $275) Float from Halifax over the patchwork fields of Annapolis Valley at sunrise or sunset for the ultimate, peaceful views of this stunning province. Minimum age for children is eight.

🎆 Festivals & Events

Halifax Pride Week LGBT
(www.halifaxpride.com; ☉ Jul) The largest LGBTI Pride festival east of Montreal paints the town pink and every other shade of the rainbow, with its massive grab-bag of fun, inclusive events and performances.

Nova Scotia Tattoo CULTURAL
(www.nstattoo.ca; tickets from $32; ☉ Jul) The world's 'largest annual indoor show' is a military-style event with lots of marching bands.

TD Halifax Jazz Festival MUSIC
(www.halifaxjazzfestival.ca; tickets from $28; ☉ Jul) Now in its fourth decade, Halifax's well-loved jazz festival boasts free outdoor jazz

concerts and evening performances ranging from world music to classic jazz trios.

Halifax International Busker Festival
PERFORMING ARTS
(www.buskers.ca; ☺ Aug) The oldest and largest festival of its kind in Canada draws comics, mimes, daredevils and musicians from around the world to the Halifax waterfront.

Atlantic Film Festival
FILM
(www.atlanticfilm.com; tickets $10-16; ☺ Sep) A week of great flicks from the Atlantic region and around the world.

Atlantic Fringe Festival
THEATER
(www.atlanticfringe.ca; ☺ Sep) The theater comes to town for ten days in September, showcasing offbeat and experimental works by emerging and established artists.

Halifax Pop Explosion
MUSIC
(www.halifaxpopexplosion.com; day passes from $59; ☺ Oct) Around 150 artists from genres as diverse as hip-hop, punk, indie rock and folk perform in 15 venues over a four-day period.

🛏 Sleeping

Marigold B&B
B&B $
(☎ 902-423-4798; www.marigoldbedandbreakfast.com; 6318 Norwood St; s/d $75/85; P ☺ 🏠) Feel at home in this welcoming artist's nest full of bright floral paintings and fluffy cats, if that's your kind of vibe. Marigold is located in a tree-lined residential area in the North End, with easy public transport access.

Dalhousie University
HOSTEL $
(☎ 902-494-8840; www.dal.ca/dept/summer-accommodations.html; 6230 Coburg Rd; s/d $49/69; ☺ May-Aug; P 🏠 🏊) Single and twin dorm rooms with shared bathrooms are clean but bland. Most are adjacent to all the included university amenities, a short walk from the Spring Garden Rd area.

HI Nova Scotia
HOSTEL $
(☎ 902-422-3863; www.hihostels.ca; 1253 Barrington St; dm/r $30/68; 🏠) Expect a dark and dormy night and a bright and cheery do-it-yourself breakfast at this exceptionally central 75-bed hostel. The staff are friendly, the shared kitchen is lively and the house is Victorian. Reserve ahead in summer. Slight rate reduction for HI members.

Halifax Backpackers Hostel
HOSTEL $
(☎ 888-431-3170; www.halifaxbackpackers.com; 2193 Gottingen St; dm/d/tr $23/55/65; 🏠) Coed dorms at this hip, 36-bed North End hostel

hold no more than six beds. It draws a funky young crowd and everyone congregates at the downstairs cafe to swill strong coffee, eat cheap breakfasts and mingle with the eclectic local regulars. City buses stop right in front, but it's a slightly rough-edged neighborhood. Best suited for high-energy travelers who like to party and socialize.

★ Cambridge Suites Halifax
HOTEL $$
(☎ 902-420-0555; www.cambridgesuiteshalifax.com; 1583 Brunswick St; d $149-209, ste $169-299; P ☺ ❄ 🏠) For those who value the comforts of home, this recently updated hotel features a wide range of studio rooms and suites featuring tasteful furnishings with dark woods and colorful, stylish accents. One-bedroom suites and above are oversized and have a fabulous, clever layout with windows that open. On top of all that, the location can't be beat. Free continental breakfast, wi-fi and local telephone calls are included in the rate.

★ Prince George Hotel
HOTEL $$
(☎ 902-425-1986; www.princegeorgehotel.com; 1725 Market St; d $179-269; P ❄ @ 🏊 🏠) A suave and debonair gem, central Prince George has all the details covered. Garden patios are a great place to take a drink or a meal, or even work, as an alternative to indoor meeting areas. Guestrooms and suites are as classy as you'll find in Halifax and the hotel's common areas ooze urban-chic.

Homewood Suites by Hilton Halifax-Downtown
HOTEL $$
(☎ 855-605-0320; www.hilton.com; 1960 Brunswick St; r/ste from $119/$159; P ☺ ❄ 🏠 🏊) As the brand name implies, this centrally located property is better suited for long-stay guests or traveling families who value the comforts of home; all suites, from studios to two-bedroom hospitality suites, feature full kitchens. Daily breakfast and an 'evening social' (Monday to Thursday) are included in the rates, which vary dramatically by season.

Pebble Bed & Breakfast
B&B $$
(☎ 902-423-3369; www.thepebble.ca; 1839 Armview Tce; r $195-265; ☺ 🏠 🏊) The two suites of this luxurious B&B feature plush, high beds, gorgeous bathrooms and a modern-meets-antique decor. Irish owner Elizabeth grew up with a pub-owning family and brings lively, joyous energy from the Emerald Isle to her delightful home in a posh, waterfront residential area, a stone's throw from downtown. There's a two-night minimum stay from June to October.

Atlantica Hotel
HOTEL $$

(☎902-423-1161; www.atlanticahotelhalifax.com; 1980 Robie St; d $139-199; P⊖❄🛜🏊) Older hotels have solid bones and the Atlantica is no exception. Freshly updated in 2016, this well-located, privately owned hotel has everything in place to ensure a pleasant stay, from well-trained staff to a range of guestroom types, all generously proportioned and neutrally decorated. The on-site restaurant with room service and light-filled indoor pool add to the value proposition.

Waverley Inn
INN $$

(☎902-423-9346; www.waverleyinn.com; 1266 Barrington St; d $135-235; P❄@🛜) Every room in this historic inn is unique, furnished dramatically with bold antiques and luxurious linens. Both Oscar Wilde and PT Barnum once stayed here and probably would again today if they were still alive. On the downside, guestroom and bathroom dimensions aren't huge, but the location makes up for such shortfalls. One for those who value originality and flair.

Lord Nelson Hotel & Suites
HOTEL $$

(☎902-423-5130; www.lordnelsonhotel.com; 1515 S Park St; d $159-239, ste $229-349; P⊖❄@🛜) The Lord Nelson has long had a reputation for being where the stars, like the Rolling Stones, stay when they come to town, but that doesn't mean it's Halifax's top hotel. Rooms vary in size from compact guest rooms to oversized suites dressed in an elegant (but not stuffy) style. It's a great choice for those who value history and individuality.

Halliburton
INN $$

(☎902-420-0658; www.thehalliburton.com; 5184 Morris St; d $125-195, ste $235-305; P❄@🛜) Class without fuss can be found at this comfortable and well-serviced historic hotel right in downtown. Colorful rooms with Keurig coffee machines and iPod docking stations range in size from compact 'petit rooms' to small suites with patios or four-poster beds.

Halifax Marriott Harbourfront
HOTEL $$$

(☎902-421-1700; www.marriott.com; 1919 Upper Water St; d $229-369) The sprawling Marriott Harbourfront hotel occupies a prime location on, you guessed it, the Halifax waterfront. Plush rooms could do with a little more zing for the price, but the main draws are the property's impressive common areas, from the marble lobby to the bar and the fitness center.

✕ Eating

Heartwood Bakery
VEGETARIAN $

(☎902-425-2808; www.iloveheartwood.ca; 6250 Quinpool Rd; mains $11-16; ⊙11am-8pm; 🍴) Try the local organic salad bar or amazing baked goods, along with a cup of fair-trade coffee. Otherwise there's soup, sandwiches, pizza and veggie burgers.

Annie's Place Cafe
BREAKFAST $

(www.anniesplacecafe.ca; 1592b Queen St; breakfasts $4-10; ⊙7am-3pm Mon-Fri, 8am-2pm Sat) A slice of small town in the heart of Halifax, Annie welcomes you in and cooks up a hearty breakfast, including freshly baked bread and homemade chai. You'll have a whole new set of friends by the time you leave.

★ En Vie a Vegan
VEGETARIAN $$

(☎902-492-4077; www.enviehalifax.com; 5775 Charles St; mains $11-18; ⊙11am-9pm Tue-Fri, 10am-9pm Sat & Sun; 🍴) Finally, a restaurant focused on sustainable, organic, locally sourced plant-based eating that has universal appeal. There's nothing bland or boring about what's on offer here. Most menu items, from the coconut shrimp to the double-bacon cheeseburger, feature the original name of their non-vegan counterpart; there's no animal products in any of the dishes, but the ruse is highly convincing.

★ 2 Doors Down
MODERN CANADIAN $$

(☎902-422-4224; www.go2doorsdown.com; 1533 Barrington St; mains $10-20; ⊙11am-10pm) Reservations aren't accepted at this food-lovers haunt that tempts with a welcome array of staples such as burgers, curries, and fish-and-chips, as well as more elevated offerings such as shrimp-and-snow-crab-stuffed shitake caps and plenty of gluten-free goodness. The word is out about this cozy haunt, so be prepared for a short wait at busy times.

★ Henry House
PUB FOOD $$

(☎902-423-5660; www.henryhouse.ca; 1222 Barrington St; mains $11-24; ⊙11:30am-midnight) Jazz and classical music lilt above the din of respectably dressed diners chatting by the open fire in this handsome 1834 ironstone, serving upscale pub fare. When the gorgeous yet unpretentious Drawing Room upstairs is open (6pm to midnight, Friday and Saturday) you'll be able to dazzle your date with your extensive knowledge of the fine house whiskeys and smoked cocktails.

Brooklyn Warehouse   CANADIAN $$

(☑ 902-446-8181; www.brooklynwarehouse.ca; 2795 Windsor St; mains lunch $10-18, dinner $16-30; ⊙11:30am-10pm Mon-Sat; 🖋) This North End hot spot is loaded with vegetarian and vegan options – the eggplant moussaka stack is excellent. It has a huge beer and cocktail menu, and an atmosphere that feels like a hip, modern version of *Cheers* – but with way better food.

Wooden Monkey   CANADIAN $$

(☑ 902-444-3844; www.thewoodenmonkey.ca; 1707 Grafton St; mains $15-30; ⊙11am-10pm; 🖋) 🖋 This dark, cozy nook with outdoor sidewalk seating on sunny days adamantly supports local organic farms and is a fab place to get superb gluten-free and vegan meals, as well as a selection of seafood and meat dishes prepared with conscience.

Salty's   SEAFOOD $$

(☑ 902-423-6818; www.saltys.ca; 1869 Upper Water St; mains bar & grill $12-22, restaurant $25-30) Choose between the casual bar and grill downstairs or the upstairs dining room of this tourist-friendly waterfront seafood restaurant. Fortunately, hyped-up Salty's delivers tasty, well-presented seafood in a busy and thoroughly Halifax setting. Nightly specials are good value.

Stubborn Goat   PUB FOOD $$

(☑ 902-405-4554; www.stubborngoat.ca; 1579 Grafton St; small plates $9-19, mains $16-29; ⊙11:30am-2am) Self-billed as a gastropub, the Goat goes beyond pub grub to serve fancy top-nosh small plates such as mouthwatering salmon-belly tartare and the always-popular 'balls' (meatballs stuffed with cheese). Mains such as lobster and smoked meatloaf are bound to tempt. You can also keep it simple with beer and a burger. Check the website for the location and hours of the Goat's seasonal waterfront beer garden.

Edna   MODERN CANADIAN $$

(www.ednarestaurant.com; 2053 Gottingen St; brunch $12-20, mains $18-35; ⊙5-10pm Tue-Fri, 10am-2:30pm & 5-10pm Sat & Sun) From the Southern-fried rock hen to the filled-with-everything-good-from-the-sea Atlantic bouillabaisse, you'll find something to love here. You can dine at a big wooden table where guests from everywhere chat and mingle, at the bar for a little less socializing, or at a regular old table for two. It's a unique, vivacious, food-and-drink-loving atmosphere.

Hamachi Steakhouse   JAPANESE $$

(☑ 902-425-1600; www.hamachirestaurants.com; 1477 Lower Water St; mains $12-28, teppanyaki $28-39; ⊙11:30am-10pm Mon-Sat, 4-10pm Sun) Watch the show grill-side while your chef slices, dices and sets the stove aflame to cook up the meats, seafood and veggies that make a crowd-pleasing Japanese teppanyaki. For a less theatrical experience, grab a table and enjoy the teppanyaki, sushi or Alberta steaks quietly, with a beautiful view of the harbor.

Morris East   ITALIAN $$

(☑ 902-444-7663; www.morriseast.com; 5212 Morris St; pizzas $15-20; ⊙11:30am-9pm) At this cosmopolitan cafe, you'll find creative, wood-fired pizzas on your choice of white, whole-wheat or gluten-free ($3.50 extra) dough; try the peach, rosemary aioli and prosciutto pizza. There's also snazzy cocktails, such as a basil, lime and vodka punch.

Epicurious Morcels   FUSION $$

(☑ 902-455-0955; www.epicuriousmorsels.com; 5529 Young St; mains $10-29; ⊙11:30am-2:30pm & 5-8:30pm Tue-Sun) The specialties on this diverse menu include smoked salmon, gravlax (dill-cured salmon) and a range of tasty, creative soups. There's something here for everyone.

★ Bicycle Thief   ITALIAN $$$

(☑ 902-425-7993; www.bicyclethief.ca; 1475 Lower Water St; mains lunch $10-26, dinner $20-39; ⊙11.30am-late Mon-Fri, 5:30pm-late Sat) Named for the classic 1948 Italian film, this shabby-chic waterfront restaurant has won similar critical acclaim by local foodies – and with good reason. Start with regional oysters or polenta with wild mushroom ragout, then continue with dishes such as pistachio-honey-roasted salmon or pancetta-wrapped pork tenderloin. The wine and cocktail list is several pages longer than the food menu.

Press Gang Restaurant
& Oyster Bar   SEAFOOD $$$

(☑ 902-423-8816; www.thepressgang.ca; 5218 Prince St; single oysters $3.25, mains $36-40; ⊙5-10pm Sun-Wed, to midnight Thu-Sat) Order any number and combination of Nova Scotia and PEI oysters raw or baked – if you're a fan of the briny bivalves, you've found nirvana. Otherwise, choose from a short but impressive menu of delicious appetizers and mains and soak up the atmosphere of this slick and stylish outfit. Dress to impress.

Five Fishermen
SEAFOOD $$$

(☎ 902-422-4421; www.fivefishermen.com; 1740 Argyle St; mains $29-39; ☺ noon-10pm Mon-Fri, 5-10pm Sat & Sun) This fabulous restaurant housed in what was once the John Snow funeral home that interred many of Halifax's 150 *Titanic* victims doesn't have to rely on this macabre and quirky fact to put bums on seats: thankfully, the seafood sells itself. Expect elevated oceanic delicacies, with lamb and steak thrown in for good measure.

Chives Canadian Bistro
CANADIAN $$$

(☎ 902-420-9626; www.chives.ca; 1537 Barrington St; mains $24-35; ☺ 5-9:30pm) The menu changes with what's seasonally available and uses mostly local ingredients. The food is fine dining, while the low-lit cozy ambience is upscale casual.

Da Maurizio
ITALIAN $$$

(☎ 902-423-0859; www.damaurizio.ca; 1496 Lower Water St; mains $28-39; ☺ 5-10pm Mon-Sat) Many locals cite this as their favorite Halifax restaurant, with exposed brick and clean lines bringing out all the flavors of the heritage brewery building. The cuisine is as fine as the ambience. Reservations are strongly recommended.

🍷 Drinking & Nightlife

★ Lot Six
COCKTAIL BAR

(☎ 902-428-7428; www.lotsix.ca; 1685 Argyle St; ☺ 4pm-2am) This slick bar and restaurant has a fabulous glass atrium that delivers extra atmosphere points, whatever the season. Score a cushy seat at the counter if you're flying solo or an extra-cute two-person booth if you're angling for *amour*.

Tom's Little Havana
BAR

(☎ 902-423-8667; www.tomslittlehavana.wix.com/cafe; 1540 Birmingham St; 11:30am-2am) Craft beers, game nights, Scotch nights and a daily happy hour (5pm to 8pm) make Tom's feel like an extension of the living room at your best mate's place. There's a warm and friendly vibe here, which gets even warmer as the night wears on.

Durty Nelly's
IRISH PUB

(☎ 902-406-7640; www.durtynellys.ca; cnr Argyle & Sackville Sts; ☺ 11:30am-1am) There are lots of reasons to come to Halifax's uberpopular Irish Pub, from open-mic and rib nights to regular live music, cold ales, great food and a fun and friendly atmosphere.

Middle Spoon
COCKTAIL BAR

(☎ 902-407-4002; www.themiddlespoon.ca; 1559 Barrington St; ☺ 4-11pm Mon-Sat) What could be better than a place that serves only beer, wine, creative cocktails and decadent desserts? How about one with a super secret? (Should we even be writing this?) It has a speakeasy-inspired lounge downstairs that serves even better cocktails. Get the password by clicking on the >: symbol on the website and don't tell anyone we told you...

Economy Shoe Shop Cafe Bar
CAFE

(☎ 902-423-8845; www.economyshoeshop.ca; 1663 Argyle St; ☺ 11:30am-midnight Mon-Thu, to 2am Fri-Sun) This has been the 'it' place to drink and people-watch in Halifax for well over a decade. On weekend nights, actors and journalists figure heavily in the crush. It's a pleasant place for afternoon drinks and the kitchen dishes out tapas until last call at 1:45am.

Pacifico
CLUB

(☎ 902-422-3633; www.pacifico.ca; 1505 Barrington St; ☺ 9pm-2am Fri & Sat) Halifax's hottest hangout sprawls beneath Barrington and Salter Sts, with high-energy DJs, bottle service and party people.

Garrison Brewing Company
BREWERY

(☎ 902-453-5343; www.garrisonbrewing.com; 1149 Marginal Rd; ☺ 10am-8pm Sun-Thu, to 10pm Fri & Sat) Not much beats a $2 taster glass of craft beer on a sunny patio, except maybe *five* varieties of tasters, which is how many the brewery serves on tap each day. Other bottled beers are sold in the shop but because they're not legally a bar (and Canada has complicated liquor laws), you can't drink them on the premises.

Gay & Lesbian

Reflections Cabaret
GAY & LESBIAN

(☎ 902-422-2957; www.reflectionscabaret.com; 5187 Salter St; ☺ 10pm-3am Thu-Mon) If you're looking to get your glam on, this mainly gay disco attracts a mixed crowd. Nightly entertainment ranges from wrestling to drag shows to sensory stage shows. Check the website for events listings.

Menz and Mollyz Bar
GAY & LESBIAN

(☎ 902-446-6969; www.facebook.com/menznmollyz; 2182 Gottingen St; ☺ 4pm-2:30am) Self-billed as Atlantic Canada's premier LGBTQI destination, Menz and Mollyz can be hit or miss, but that can be said for many community bars since the advent of phone-dating apps. Keep it friendly and rock up when there's an event on and you're bound to have a good time.

☆ Entertainment

Check out the *Coast* (www.thecoast.ca) to see what's on. This free weekly publication, available around town, is the essential guide for music, theater, film and events.

Live Music

Halifax loves its music, with folk, hip-hop, alternative, country and rock gigs around town every weekend. Cover charges depend on the band.

Seahorse Tavern   LIVE MUSIC
(☑902-423-7200; www.theseahorsetavern.ca; 1665 Argyle St) This joint hosts events that attract the crowds who are actually cool (not just faux-cool). Punk, indie, metal, funk, Motown, soul...and monthly themed dance parties. Check the website for what's on and when.

Bearly's House of Blues & Ribs LIVE MUSIC
(☑902-423-2526; www.bearlys.ca; 1269 Barrington St; ☺5pm-midnight) The best blues musicians in Atlantic Canada play here at incredibly low cover charges. Wednesday karaoke nights draw a crowd and some fine singers.

Carleton   LIVE MUSIC
(☑902-422-6335; www.thecarleton.ca; 1685 Argyle St; ☺noon-2am) Catch acoustic sets, then enjoy the meals, including a late-night menu.

Theatre

Shakespeare by the Sea   THEATER
(☑902-422-0295; www.shakespearebythesea.ca; Point Pleasant Park; ☺Jun-Sep) Fine performances of the Bard's works at the Cambridge Battery, an old fortification in the middle of Point Pleasant Park. Another reason to love Halifax! Check the website for a map and details.

Neptune Theatre   THEATER
(☑902-429-7070; www.neptunetheatre.com; 1593 Argyle St) This downtown theater presents musicals and well-known plays on its main stage (from $35) and edgier stuff in the studio (from $15).

Yuk Yuks   COMEDY
(☑902-429-9857; www.yukyuks.com/halifax; 1181 Hollis St) This is the place to go for local and international stand-up and improv gigs: check the website for what's on when.

Sports

Scotiabank Centre   STADIUM
(☑902-451-1221; www.scotiabank-centre.com; 1800 Argyle St; ☺box office 9am-5pm) Halifax's premier multipurpose indoor arena is smack-bang in the heart of downtown. The biggest matches, games and concerts to come to town are held here.

🛍 Shopping

★**Halifax Seaport
Farmers Market**   MARKET
(☑902-492-4043; www.halifaxfarmersmarket.com; 1209 Marginal Rd; ☺10am-5pm Mon-Fri, 7am-3pm Sat, 9am-3pm Sun) Although it has operated in several locations since its inception in 1750, what's now known as the Halifax Seaport Farmers Market (in its present location since 2010) is North America's longest continuously operating market. With over 250 vendors from a province that prides itself on strong farm-to-table and maritime traditions, it's well worth a visit.

Historic Properties   SHOPPING CENTRE
(www.historicproperties.ca; 1869 Upper Water St; ☺store hours vary) The Historic Properties are a group of restored warehouse buildings on Upper Water St, built between 1800 and 1905, that have been converted into boutiques, restaurants and bars connected by waterfront boardwalks. The 1814 **Privateers Warehouse** was the former storehouse of government-sanctioned pirates and is the area's oldest stone building. Among the other vintage buildings are the wooden **Old Red Store**, and **Simon's Warehouse**, built in 1854.

Nova Scotian Crystal   ARTS & CRAFTS
(☑888-977-2797; www.novascotiancrystal.com; 5080 George St; ☺9am-6pm Mon-Fri, 10am-5pm Sat & Sun) As much of a show as a place to shop – watch glass blowers form beautiful crystal glasses and vases, then pick the ones you want in the classy adjacent boutique.

Historic Farmers Market   MARKET
(☑902-329-3276; www.historicfarmersmarket.ca; 1496 Lower Water St; ☺7am-1pm Sat) If you're in Halifax on a Saturday morning, pop by this grassroots, member-run, non-profit cooperative market, housed in a beautiful 1820s stone building.

ℹ Orientation

The downtown area, three universities and older residential neighborhoods are contained on a compact peninsula cut off from mainland Halifax by an inlet called the North West Arm. Almost all sights of interest to visitors are concentrated in this area, making walking the best way to get around. Point Pleasant Park is at the extreme southern end of the peninsula, and the lively and multicultural North End neighborhood – home to African Nova Scotians, art-school students and most of Halifax's gay bars – stretches from the midpoint to the northern extreme.

Two bridges span the harbor, connecting Halifax to Dartmouth and leading to highways north (for the airport) and east. The MacDonald Bridge at the eastern end of North St is closest to downtown.

ℹ Information

INTERNET ACCESS

Halifax Central Library (☑ 902-490-5700; www.halifaxcentrallibrary.ca; 5440 Spring Garden Rd; ☺9am-9pm Mon-Thu, to 6pm Fri & Sat, noon-6pm Sun; ☏)

MEDICAL SERVICES

Family Focus (☑ 902-420-2038; www.thefamily focus.ca; 5991 Spring Garden Rd; ☺8:30am-9pm Mon-Fri, 11am-5pm Sat & Sun) Walk-in or same-day appointments.

Halifax Infirmary (Charles V Keating Emergency and Trauma Centre; ☑ 902-473-3383, 902-473-7605; www.cdha.nshealth.ca; 1796 Summer St; ☺24hr) For emergencies.

POST

Lawton's Drugs (☑ 902-429-0088; 5675 Spring Garden Rd; ☺8am-10pm Mon-Fri, 9am-9pm Sat, noon-8pm Sun) There's a post office in the rear of this pharmacy.

Main Post Office (☑ 902-494-4670; www.canadapost.ca; 1660 Bedford Row; ☺9am-5pm Mon-Fri)

TOURIST INFORMATION

Tourism Nova Scotia (☑ 800-565-0000, 902-425-5781; www.novascotia.com) Operates visitors information centers in Halifax and other locations within Nova Scotia province, plus a free booking service for accommodations, which is useful when rooms are scarce in midsummer. It publishes the *Doers & Dreamers Guide*, which lists places to stay, attractions and tour operators.

Visitor Information Centre (VIC; ☑ 902-424-4248; www.novascotia.com; 1655 Lower Water St; ☺9am-5pm) On the Halifax Waterfront, this official province-run plaza is a great place to start your wanderings of downtown Halifax; they'll load you up with maps and friendly advice. There is also an official VIC welcome center at the **airport** (☑ 902-873-1223; Halifax International Airport; ☺9am-9pm).

USEFUL WEBSITES

Destination Halifax (www.halifaxinfo.com)

Halifax Regional Municipality (www.halifax.ca)

ℹ Getting There & Away

AIR

Most air services in Nova Scotia go to/from Halifax and there are multiple daily flights to Toronto, Calgary and Vancouver.

International destinations serviced include Boston, New York and London.

Halifax Stanfield International Airport (YHZ; ☑ 902-873-4422; www.hiaa.ca; 1 Bell Blvd) is 32km northeast of town on Hwy 102, toward Truro.

BUS

The only province-wide (and beyond) bus company is **Maritime Bus** (p44), which services the main highways from Kentville to Halifax and up to Truro. From Truro the routes fork: toward North Sydney in one direction and toward Amherst and on to New Brunswick in the other.

Advance Shuttle (☑ 877-886-3322; www.advanceshuttle.ca) offers slow-going shuttle services from Halifax airport and downtown hotels to Prince Edward Island (from $69).

Cloud Nine Shuttle (☑ 902-742-3992; www.thecloudnineshuttle.com) can drop you at points along the South Shore as far as Yarmouth. Fares start at $75 and the journey takes about 3½ hours.

TRAIN

One of the few examples of monumental Canadian train station architecture left in the Maritimes is found at 1161 Hollis St. **VIA Rail** (www.viarail.ca) operates an overnight service to Montréal (from $134, 21 hours, daily except Tuesdays).

ℹ Getting Around

TO/FROM THE AIRPORT

The cheapest way to get to the airport is by Metro Transit public bus 320, which runs half-hourly to hourly between 5am and midnight from the Metro X bus stop on Albemarle St between Duke and Cogswell Sts.

If you arrive in the middle of the night, as many flights do, your only choice is a taxi, which costs $56 to downtown Halifax. There are often not enough taxis, so it's prudent to reserve one in advance. Try **Halifax Airport Taxi** (☑ 902-999-2434; www.halifaxairportlimotaxi.com), which has 24-hour airport service. The journey shouldn't take much longer than 30 minutes.

Maritime Bus (www.maritimebus.com) operates an airport shuttle ($22, 30 to 45 minutes) between May and October.

CAR & MOTORCYCLE

Pedestrians almost always have right of way in Halifax, so watch out for cars stopping suddenly.

Outside the downtown core, you can usually find free on-street parking for up to two hours. Halifax's parking meters are enforced from 8am to 6pm Monday to Friday.

All the major national car-rental chains are represented at the airport and in downtown Halifax. Some will let you pick up in town and drop off at the airport free of charge.

PUBLIC TRANSPORTATION

Halifax Transit (☑ 902-480-8000; www. halifax.ca/transit; single ride $2.50-3.50) runs the city bus system and the ferries to Dartmouth. Maps and schedules are available at the ferry terminals and at the information booth in Scotia Sq mall.

Bus 7 cuts through downtown and North End Halifax via Robie St and Gottingen St, passing both of Halifax's hostels. Bus 1 travels along Spring Garden Rd, Barrington St and the south part of Gottingen St before crossing the bridge to Dartmouth.

AROUND HALIFAX

Dartmouth

Founded in 1750, just one year after its counterpart across the harbor, working-class Dartmouth had long been regarded as Halifax's grubby little brother. In recent years, its proximity to Eastern Shore beaches, ease of access to downtown Halifax and a spate of waterfront redevelopment projects have rejuvenated Dartmouth's demographic and contributed to its growing popularity.

◎ Sights

Dartmouth's compact, historic downtown is a pleasant place for a stroll and a pint: getting here on the ferry from Halifax – the oldest saltwater ferry system in North America – is half the fun, especially at sunset. Before you return, head west on Alderney Dr to climb the bluffs of **Dartmouth Commons** for excellent views across the harbor. Exercise the usual caution in the park after dark.

Quaker House   HISTORIC BUILDING
(☑ 902-464-2300; www.dartmouthheritagemuseum. ns.ca; 59 Ochterloney St; $5; ⊙10am-5pm Tue-Sun Jun-Aug) Built in 1786 by Quaker whalers from Nantucket who fled the American Revolution, Quaker house is the oldest surviving house in the Halifax area. Admission includes entry into the Dartmouth Heritage Museum housed in nearby Evergreen House.

Dartmouth Heritage Museum   MUSEUM
(☑ 902-464-2300; www.dartmouthheritagemuseum. ns.ca; 26 Newcastle St; $5; ⊙10am-5pm Tue-Sat) An eclectic collection of local historic artifacts is displayed here in **Evergreen House**, the former home of folklorist Helen Creighton, who traversed the province in the early 20th century, recording stories and songs. Tickets include same-day admission to the 1786 Quaker House.

✖ Eating

Portland Street Creperie   CREPERIE $
(☑ 902-466-7686;   www.portlandstreetcreperie. com; 55 Portland St; crepes $4-9; ⊙8:30am-5pm Mon-Thu & Sat, to 7pm Fri, 10am-1pm Sun) There's a crepe for everyone at this local favorite. From the savory 'mushroom melt' to the sweet, sweet 'honeycomb,' drizzled with Nova Scotian honey and butter, these tempting treats are priced such that you mightn't be able to stop at just one.

Nena's All Day Breakfast   DINER $
(☑ 902-406-0006; www.nenasbreakfast.com; 273 Wyse Rd; meals $6-16; ⊙7am-3pm) On a drab street corner surrounded by used-car lots and mechanic workshops you'll find this hopping, spotlessly clean breakfast joint, serving diner-style greasy faves. Breakfast is served all day, but there's a lunch menu also. If you're a fan of french fries (or home fries) and Canadian gravy, you're advised to stop by.

Two If By Sea   BAKERY $
(☑ 902-469-0721; www.twoifbyseacafe.ca; 66 Ochterloney St; pastries $3-5; ⊙7am-6pm Mon-Fri, 8am-5pm Sat & Sun) Be warned...if you're wanting to gorge on the massive buttery chocolate croissants that TIBS are famous for, get in quick: they're often sold out by 1pm. Even sans pastries, it's a hip place to stop for coffee and people-watching on a sunny day, with a home-proud Dartmouth atmosphere.

▽ Drinking & Nightlife

★**Battery Park Beer**
Bar & Eatery   MICROBREWERY
(☑ 902-446-2337; www.batterypark.ca; 62 Ochterloney St; ⊙2pm-midnight Wed-Mon) This local collaboration is the talk of the town for its small-batch specialty beers and out-of-this-world tasting menus, best shared. The aesthetic is wooden-industrial, the crowd is hip and the bacon fudge is addictive.

NOVA SCOTIA DARTMOUTH

Celtic Corner PUB

(☑902-464-0764; www.celticcorner.ca; 69 Alderney Dr; ☺11am-midnight) Dartmouth's most popular and centrally located pub, with live music most nights and a wide variety of beers on tap and hearty pub food (mains $10 to $17).

Just Us! Coffee Roaster's Co-Op CAFE

(www.justuscoffee.com; 15 King's Wharf; ☺7am-5:30pm Mon-Thu, to 9pm Fri & Sat; ☎) This bright yet cozy cafe serves up fair-trade, house-roasted coffee and baked goods made from locally sourced ingredients. What originally started in 1995 as Canada's first fair-trade coffee roaster now has a handful of outlets around the province, all with free wi-fi thrown in. Check the website for other locations.

🛍 Shopping

Alderney Landing MARKET

(☑902-461-4698; www.alderneylanding.com; 2 Ochterloney St; ☺9:30am-5pm Mon-Fri) This multipurpose venue houses a theater, market and a variety of cafes, restaurants and shops.

❶ Getting There & Away

Halifax Transit (www.halifax.ca/transit) operates an extensive, easy-to-use network of buses and ferries. In Dartmouth, catch the ferry to Halifax ($2.50, 20 minutes) from the **Dartmouth Ferry Terminal** (replete with public-use piano) at Alderney Gate.

Peggy's Cove

Peggy's Cove is one of the most visited fishing villages in Canada, and for good reason: the rolling granite cove, highlighted by a perfect red-and-white lighthouse, exudes a dreamy seaside calm, even through the parading tour buses. Visit before 10am, after 6pm, or in the off-season to avoid the jam and to appreciate the true beauty and tranquility of the place.

If you're looking for the same kind of vibe without the mass of visitors, cute-as-a-button **Lower Prospect** is 30km to the east via Terrence Bay.

⊙ Sights

★William E deGarthe

Gallery & Monument GALLERY

(☑902-823-2256; 109 Peggy's Point Rd; $2; ☺gallery 9am-5pm May-Oct) Finnish-born local artist William deGarthe (1907–83) sculpted the magnificent *Lasting Monument to Nova Scotian Fishermen* into a 30m granite outcropping behind his home. The sculpture

depicts 32 fishermen, their wives and children, St Elmo with wings spread, and the legendary Peggy of her eponymous Cove. The homestead is now a gallery showcasing 65 of deGarthe's other works.

Swissair 111 Memorial MEMORIAL

(8250 Hwy 333) This moving memorial commemorates the 229 people who lost their lives on September 2, 1998, when Swissair Flight 111, bound for Geneva, Switzerland, plunged into the ocean 8km off the coast of Peggy's Cove.

Peggy's Point Lighthouse LIGHTHOUSE

(185 Peggys Point Rd; ☺9:30am-5:30pm May-Oct) The highlight of the cove is this picture-perfect lighthouse, which for many years was a working post office. Meander around the granite landscape that undulates much like the icy sea beyond.

🛏 Sleeping & Eating

Wayside Camping Park CAMPGROUND $

(☑902-823-2271; www.waysidecampground.com; 10295 Hwy 333, Glen Margaret; tent/RV sites $25/35; ☺May-Oct; ☎🐕) About 10km north of Peggy's Cove and 36km from Halifax, this camping park has lots of shady sites on a hill. It gets crowded in midsummer.

Oceanstone Seaside Resort RESORT $$

(☑902-823-2160; www.oceanstoneresort.com; 8650 Peggy's Cove Rd, Indian Harbour; r $105-195, cottages $195-335; P✦❄@☎🐕) Whimsically decorated cottages are a stone's throw from the beach and just a short drive from Peggy's Cove. Guests can use paddleboats to venture to small islands. **Rhubarb**, the inn's dining room, is considered one of the best seafood restaurants in the region.

Peggy's Cove Bed & Breakfast B&B $$

(☑902-823-2265; www.peggyscovebb.com; 17 Church Rd; d $155; ☺Apr-Oct; ☎) The only place to stay in the cove itself, this B&B has an enviable position with one of the best views in Nova Scotia, overlooking the fishing docks and the lighthouse; it was once owned by artist William deGarthe. You'll definitely need advance reservations.

Dee Dee's ICE CREAM $

(www.deedees.ca; 110 Peggy's Cove Rd; cones from $3.50; ☺noon-6pm May-Sep) On hot days, explore the area while licking a delicious homemade-with-local-ingredients ice-cream cone from Dee Dee's. It's near the tourist information center.

☆ Entertainment

Old Red Schoolhouse   THEATER
(☑902-823-2099; www.beales.ns.ca; 126 Peggy's Point Rd; suggested donation $10) This performance venue puts on comedies and music performances through the high season. A few shows per season are serviced by shuttle vans that offer round-trips to Halifax hotels. Check the website for details.

❶ Information

Visitor Information Centre (VIC; ☑902-823-2253; 109 Peggy's Cove Rd; ⊙9am-7pm May-Oct) There's a free parking area with washrooms and a tourist information office as you enter the village. Free 45-minute **walking tours** are led from the tourist office daily from mid-June through August.

SOUTH SHORE

This is Nova Scotia's most visited coastline and it's here you'll find those quintessential lighthouses, forested coves with white beaches, and fishing villages turned tourist towns. The area from Halifax to Lunenburg is cottage country for the city's elite and ever-popular with day-trippers.

Chester

Established in 1759, the town of Chester has become a choice spot for well-to-do Americans and Haligonians to have a summer home. It's had a colorful history as the haunt of pirates and Prohibition-era bathtub-gin smugglers and it keeps its color today via the many artists' studios about town. It holds a large regatta in mid-August.

◉ Sights

Tancook Island   ISLAND
(www.tancookislandtourism.ca) This island (population 190) is a 45-minute ferry ride from Chester's government wharf (round-trip $5.50, four services daily Monday to Friday, two daily on weekends). Settled by Germans and French Huguenots in the early 19th century, the island is famous for its sauerkraut, and is crisscrossed with **walking trails**. The last ferry from Chester each day overnights in Tancook Island.

Lordly House Museum   MUSEUM
(☑902-275-3842; 133 Central St; ⊙10am-4pm Tue-Sat Jun-Sep) FREE A fine example of Georgian architecture from 1806, the Lordly House Museum has three period rooms illustrating 19th-century upper-class life and Chester history. The museum is also an artists' studio.

🛏 Sleeping & Eating

Graves Island Provincial Park CAMPGROUND $
(☑902-275-4425; www.parks.gov.ns.ca; campsites $24) An island in Mahone Bay connected by a causeway to the mainland has 64 wooded and open campsites. RVs usually park in the middle of the area, but some shady, isolated tent sites are tucked away on the flanks of the central plateau.

Mecklenburgh Inn B&B   B&B $$
(☑902-275-4638; www.mecklenburghinn.ca; 78 Queen St; r $135-155; ⊙May-Dec; 🛜) This casual four-room inn, built in 1890, has a breezy 2nd-floor veranda. Some rooms have private adjacent balconies; most have private bathrooms. The owner is a Cordon Bleu chef, so expect an excellent breakfast.

Kiwi Café   CAFE $
(☑902-275-1492; www.kiwicafechester.com; 19 Pleasant St; mains $9-16; ⊙8am-4pm Sun-Wed, to 8pm Thu-Sat; 🛜🅿) A New Zealand chef prepares excellent soups, salads, sandwiches and baked goods that you can eat in or take away. The walls are painted kiwi green and there's beer, wine and a relaxed atmosphere.

Rope Loft   PUB
(☑902-275-3430; www.ropeloft.com; 36 Water St; ⊙11:30am-11pm) You couldn't find a better setting for an ale than this bayside pub. Hearty pub food is served indoors or out.

☆ Entertainment

Chester Playhouse   THEATER
(☑902-275-3933; www.chesterplayhouse.ca; 22 Pleasant St; tickets around $25) This older theater space has great acoustics for live performances. Plays or dinner theater are presented most nights in July and August, with occasional concerts during spring and fall.

❶ Information

Chester Visitor Information Centre (☑902-275-4616; www.vic.chesterchamber.ca; 20 Smith Rd; ⊙9:30am-5:30pm) In the old train depot near the Chester turnoff, proud local staff are a font of knowledge.

Mahone Bay

The sun shines more often in Mahone Bay than anywhere else along the coast. With more than 100 islands in the bay, and less than 100km from Halifax, it's a great base for exploring this section of the South Shore. Take out a kayak or a bike or simply stroll down Main St, which skirts the harbor and is scattered with shops selling antiques, quilts, pottery and works by local painters.

◉ Sights & Activities

Mahone Bay's seafront skyline is punctuated by three magnificent old **churches** that draw in many keen photographers and also host live classical music in the summer.

Mahone Bay Settlers' Museum　　MUSEUM
(☑ 902-624-6263; www.mahonebaymuseum.com; 578 Main St; ⊙10am-4pm Jun–mid-Oct) `FREE`
Exhibits on the area's architecture and its settlement by 'Foreign Protestants' in 1754.

Sweet Ride Cycling　　CYCLING
(☑ 902-531-3026; sweetridecycling.com; 523 Main St; half-/full-day rentals $20/30; ⊙10am-5pm Mon-Sat, noon-5pm Sun) Pick up a sweet ride here and check in with the friendly staff for the best routes in the area.

⌘ Tours

South Shore Boat Tours　　CRUISE
(☑ 902-543-5107; www.southshoreboattours.com; tours from $45; ⊙Jun-Oct) Join Captain Chris for fascinating cruises around Mahone Bay, offering insight into the local wildlife and traditional fishing and boatbuilding industries.

✲ Festivals & Events

Great Scarecrow Festival &
Antiques Fair　　CULTURAL
(www.mahonebayscarecrowfestival.com; ⊙Oct) Locals make outlandish scarecrows and carve pumpkins to display outside their homes on the first weekend in October. Meanwhile, a popular antique fair rages on.

⊨ Sleeping & Eating

Kip & Kaboodle
Backpackers Hostel　　HOSTEL $
(☑ 902-531-5494; www.kiwikaboodle.com; 9466 Hwy 3; dm/d/tr $30/69/105; ⊙Apr-Oct; P🎐) This friendly nine-bed hostel is superbly located, 3km from the attractions of Mahone Bay and 7km from Lunenburg. Owners offer town pick-up, as well as economical tours, a shuttle service, barbecues and bonfires, and excellent area tips. There are also bike rentals and one private room.

Fisherman's Daughter　　B&B $$
(☑ 902-624-0483; www.fishermans-daughter. com; 97 Edgewater St; r $135-145; 🎐🎐) Set on the bay by the three beautiful churches, this very old house (1840) has been meticulously remodeled for comfort, while retaining all the charm. Two rooms have views through sharply pitched Gothic-style windows, and all four rooms have good-sized attached bathrooms. It has all the friendly service you'd want from a top B&B.

Three Thistles B&B　　B&B $$
(☑ 902-624-0517; www.three-thistles.com; 389 W Main St; r $115-150; P🎐🎐) 🍴 Owner Ama Phyllis uses environmentally conscious cleaning agents and cooks with organic foods. Rooms are sparkling-clean and there's a back garden that stretches to a wooded area. Yoga classes are available and the loft apartment is a real delight.

Biscuit Eater　　CAFE $
(☑ 902-624-2665; www.biscuiteater.ca; 16 Orchard St; mains $8-20; ⊙9am-5pm Wed-Mon; 🎐) Dine on fabulous organic meals from soups to salads and sandwiches while surrounded by books. Or just stop for a fair-trade coffee and to Skype the folks back home.

LaHave Bakery　　DELI $
(☑ 902-624-1420; www.lahavebakery.com; 3 Edgewater; sandwiches $5-9.50; ⊙8:30am-6:30pm; 🍴) This bakery is famous for its hearty bread. Sandwiches are made on thick slabs of it.

★ Mateus Bistro　　MODERN CANADIAN $$$
(☑ 902-531-3711; www.mateusbistro.com; 533 Main St; mains $22-35; ⊙5-9pm Tue & Wed, 11:30am-9pm Thu-Mon) Tucked into a little gallery with an outdoor patio, this place may not have the sea views, but once you hit the cocktails, wine and food, you'll likely not care. The European-inspired menu changes with what's fresh locally, from oysters and Fundy scallops to duck and a rainbow of veggies.

⛉ Shopping

Amos Pewter　　ARTS & CRAFTS
(☑ 800-565-3369; www.amospewter.com; 589 Main St; ⊙9am-7pm Mon-Sat, 10am-7pm Sun) Watch demonstrations in the art of pewter making, then buy wares in the attached store.

A PIRATE'S TREASURE

Oak Island, near Mahone Bay, is home to a so-called 'money pit' that has cost over $2 million in excavation expenses – and six lives. Few facts are known about what the pit is or what might be buried there, but if you're keen to find out more, *The Curse of Oak Island*, an ongoing reality TV series, seeks to expound all the theories – and maybe find some treasure!

The mystery began in 1795 when three inhabitants of the island came across a depression in the ground. Knowing that pirates had once frequented the area, they decided to dig and see what they could find. Just over half a meter down, they hit a layer of neatly placed flagstone; another 2.5m turned up one oak platform, then another. After digging to 9m, the men temporarily gave up, but returned eight years later with the Onslow Company, a professional crew.

The Onslow excavation made it down 27.5m; when the crew returned the next morning, the shaft had flooded and they were forced to halt the digging. A year later, the company returned to dig 33.5m down in a parallel shaft, which also flooded. It was confirmed in 1850 that the pit was booby-trapped via five box drains at Smith Cove, 150m from the pit. The beach was found to be artificial.

Ever since, people have come to seek their fortune from far and wide at the 'money pit.' Only a few links of gold chain, some parchment, a cement vault and an inscribed stone have been found.

ℹ Information

Mahone Bay (www.mahonebay.com) Links to restaurants and accommodations.

Mahone Bay Visitor Information Centre (☑ 902-624-6151; 165 Edgewater St; ☺ 9am-6pm May-Oct) Has do-it-yourself walking tour brochures.

Lunenburg

The largest of the South Shore fishing villages is historic Lunenburg, the region's only Unesco World Heritage site and the first British settlement outside Halifax. The town is at its most picturesque viewed from the sea around sunset, when the boxy, brightly painted old buildings literally glow behind the ship-filled port.

Lunenburg was settled largely by Germans, Swiss and Protestant French, who were first recruited by the British as a workforce for Halifax, then later became fishermen. Today Nova Scotia has been hard hit by dwindling fish stocks, but Lunenburg's burgeoning tourism trade has helped shore up the local economy.

◉ Sights & Activities

Look out around town for the distinctive 'Lunenburg Bump,' a distinctive architectural feature of older buildings whereby a five-sided dormer window on the 2nd floor overhangs the 1st floor.

Ironworks Distillery　　　DISTILLERY

(☑ 902-640-2424; www.ironworksdistillery.com; 2 Kempt St; ☺ noon-5pm Wed-Mon) Tastings are free but good luck getting out of this old ironworks building without buying a bottle of something. Local ingredients craft a changing selection of liqueurs, a strong apple brandy and a very quaffable black spiced rum.

Knaut-Rhuland House　　　MUSEUM

(☑ 902-634-3498; 125 Pelham St; $3; ☺ 11am-5pm Tue-Sat, 1-5pm Sun Jun-Sep) Knaut-Rhuland House is considered the finest example of Georgian architecture in the province. This 1793 house has costumed guides who point out its features.

Fisheries Museum of the Atlantic　　MUSEUM

(☑ 902-634-4794; http://fisheriesmuseum.nova scotia.ca; 68 Bluenose Dr; adult/child $10/3; ☺ 9:30am-5pm) The knowledgeable staff at the Fisheries Museum of the Atlantic includes a number of retired fisherfolk who can give firsthand explanations of the fishing industry. A cute aquarium on the 1st floor lets you get eye-to-eye with halibut, a 6kg lobster and other sea creatures. Film screenings and talks take place throughout the day.

Pleasant Paddling　　　KAYAKING

(☑ 902-541-9233; www.pleasantpaddling.com; 221 The Point Rd; kayak rentals from $35, tours from $50; ☺ May-Oct) The knowledgeable folks at this beautiful place to paddle offer rentals and tours in single or double kayaks.

Lunenburg

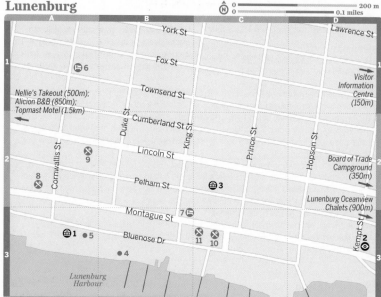

Lunenburg

⊙ Sights

1	Fisheries Museum of the Atlantic.......A3
2	Ironworks Distillery.................................D3
3	Knaut-Rhuland House.........................C2

⊕ Activities, Courses & Tours

4	Bluenose II B3
5	Trot in Time A3

🛏 Sleeping

6	1775 Solomon House B&B..................A1
7	Sail Inn B&B..B3

⊗ Eating

8	Fleur de Sel A2
9	Lincoln Street Food A2
10	Magnolia's Grill....................................C3
11	Salt Shaker Deli...................................C3

☞ Tours

Lunenburg Walking Tours   WALKING
(☏ 902-521-6867;   www.lunenburgwalkingtours.
com; tours adult/child from $20/10) Enthusiastic
and very experienced Sheila Allen and her
team lead leisurely tours during the day or
spooky lantern-lit ones at night.

Trot in Time   TOURS
(☏ 902-634-8917; www.trotintime.ca; adult/child
$20/10; ⊙ Jun–mid-Oct) Take a half-hour tour
of town in a horse-drawn cart. Leaves from
outside the Fisheries Museum of the Atlantic.

Bluenose II   BOATING
(☏ 902-634-1963;   www.bluenose.novascotia.
ca; 2hr cruises adult/child $20/10) This classic
replica of the *Bluenose* racing schooner is
sometimes in Halifax and sometimes in
Lunenburg. Check the website for details.

✺ Festivals & Events

Boxwood Festival   MUSIC
(www.boxwood.org; festival pass $50; ⊙ Jul) Flau-
tists and pipers from around the world put
on stellar public concerts.

Lunenburg Folk Harbour Festival   MUSIC
(☏ 902-634-3180; www.folkharbour.com; ⊙ Aug)
Singer-songwriters from Canada and beyond, plus traditional music and gospel.

Nova Scotia Folk Art Festival   ART
(www.nsfolkartfestival.com; ⊙ Aug) Buffet dinner, artist talks and then a big art show and
sale on the first Sunday in August.

🛏 Sleeping

Board of Trade Campground   CAMPGROUND $
(☏ 902-634-8100;   www.lunenburgns.com/camp
ground; 11 Blockhouse Hill Rd; tent/RV sites
$28/40; 🕾) This campground perched on

the hill above Lunenburg has great views and a lot of gravel RV sites. Grassy tent sites are closely packed together and lack shade.

Sail Inn B&B
B&B $$

(☎902-634-3537; www.sailinn.ca; 99 Montague St; r $110-180; P❧☎) Rooms have a view over the waterfront and are bright, airy and modern, with an antique twist. You get a free sail on the owner's 15m ketch with your stay. Don't miss the old well on the ground floor that has been turned into a lighted fish pond.

Alicion B&B
B&B $$

(☎902-634-9358; www.alicionbb.com; 66 McDonald St; r $139-169; P❧❄☎) ♨ This classic 1911 B&B with its wraparound porch set on a leafy hill a healthy walk from downtown oozes Canadiana. Classic but not stuffy, the four airy, light-filled bedrooms make you want to kick back and read, if there just wasn't so much to see and do in town. Breakfasts are beautifully prepared and the owners are enviro-aware.

Lunenburg Oceanview Chalets
COTTAGE $$

(☎902-640-3344; www.lunenburgoceanview.com; 78 Old Blue Rocks Rd; cottages $139-179; P❧☎) For something a little different, these rustic log cabins with private decks atop a hill on the outskirts of Lunenburg might be just what the doctor ordered. They're fully self-contained, have wi-fi, log fires, ocean views (at a distance), and the refreshing sound of horses neighing in the meadows. Relaxing, romantic and reasonably priced. Two-night minimum stay June to September.

Topmast Motel
MOTEL $$

(☎902-634-4661; www.topmastmotel.ca; 76 Masons Beach Rd; d $105-155) No other accommodation in town has the incredible view of Lunenburg across the harbor that rooms at this simple, bright and spotlessly clean motel enjoy. Its manager is one of the friendliest hosts you could hope to find. An excellent alternative if you're looking for the privacy and isolation that B&Bs sometimes lack.

1775 Solomon House B&B
B&B $$

(☎902-634-3477; solomonhouse@ns.sympatico.ca; 69 Townsend St; d $135; ☎) A wonderful place with undulating floors and low door frames, this B&B has an extraordinarily cordial and helpful owner. Rooms are cozy amid the aging walls and you'll be talking about the breakfasts for the rest of your trip. The only drawbacks are the minuscule bathrooms.

🍴 Eating

Salt Shaker Deli
DELI $

(☎902-640-3434; www.saltshakerdeli.com; 124 Montague St; mains $9-17; ⊙11am-9pm) With a clean-cut modern atmosphere, a waterfront deck and amazing food, it's no wonder this deli-restaurant is always packed. Try the thin-crust pizzas or a pound of mussels cooked in the style of your choosing.

Nellie's Takeout
FAST FOOD $

(☎902-634-4574; www.facebook.com/nelliestakeout; 53 Falkland St; items $4-9; ⊙11am-6pm Mon-Sat, noon-6pm Sun) Near the frequently overlooked chunk of the Berlin Wall (yes, it's legit), Nellie's food truck is a local favorite that not too many tourists have yet discovered. That could all be about to change. We're talking fish-and-chips, fried scallops, burgers and all sorts of greasy goodness at down-to-earth prices.

Magnolia's Grill
DINER $

(☎902-634-3287; www.magnolias-grill.com; 128 Montague St; mains $9-17; ⊙11am-9pm Mon-Sat) Try one of the many soups of the day at this diner-style locals' favorite. Seafood, including Solomon Gundy, and an extensive wine list are also available.

★ Lincoln Street Food
CANADIAN $$$

(☎902-640-3002; www.lincolnstreetfood.ca; mains $24-29, 3-course prix fixe $45; ⊙5-9pm Wed-Sat, 11am-2pm & 5-9pm Sun; ⫶) This spot is turning heads with its market-inspired fresh food that includes vegan, vegetarian and sustainable fish and meat options. The meals are complemented by a preservative-free wine list and an uber-chic interior that looks like it's straight out of NYC's Lower East Side.

Fleur de Sel
FRENCH $$$

(☎902-640-2121; www.fleurdesel.net; 53 Montague St; mains $22-38; ⊙11am-2pm & 5-10pm; ⫶) On sabbatical in 2016 after 12 years knocking the socks off diners from far and wide, owners Martin and Sylvie promise to return to the helm of their elegant establishment serving French-inspired dishes made from organic produce for the 2017 season. Check the website to hold them to their promise.

ℹ Information

Explore Lunenburg (www.explorelunenburg.ca) Local history and tourism information.

Visitor Information Centre (VIC; ☎902-634-8100; 11 Blockhouse Hill Rd; ⊙9am-8pm May-Oct) Perched high above town, this helpful center has maps and will help with finding beds when accommodations are in short supply.

Lunenburg Public Library (☑902-634-8008; 19 Pelham St; ☺10am-6pm Tue, Wed & Fri, to 8pm Thu, to 5pm Sat; ☎) Free internet access.

ⓘ Getting There & Away

Lunenburg is just shy of 100km from Halifax on Hwy 103. There is currently no scheduled public bus service between Halifax and Lunenburg.

Liverpool

There is plenty to see and do in historic Liverpool, one of the South Shore's larger centers. It's a pretty town with some fine heritage architecture, and is well situated for exploring several gorgeous beaches, as well as Kejimkujik National Park (69km to the north) and its Seaside Adjunct (32km southwest), but lacks a little of the seaside charm found in villages to its north.

⊙ Sights

Rossignol Cultural Centre MUSEUM
(☑902-354-3067; www.rossignolculturalcentre. com; 205 Church St; adult/child $5/3; ☺10am-5:30pm Mon-Sat) Local character Sherman Hines' most fabulous endeavor is a must-see for anyone who enjoys the offbeat. There are halls of taxidermy animals, cases of gorgeous aboriginal beadwork, walls of Hines' beautiful photography (including from his Mongolian adventures), and a room dedicated to outhouses around the world.

Hank Snow Home Town Museum MUSEUM
(☑902-354-4675; www.hanksnow.com; 148 Bristol Ave; $4; ☺9am-5pm Mon-Sat, noon-5pm Sun) This museum sheds light on Nova Scotia's status as a northern Nashville. In the old train station, it captures the history of Snow, Wilf Carter and other crooners and yodelers.

Fort Point Lighthouse LIGHTHOUSE
(☑902-354-5260; 21 Fort Lane; ☺10am-6pm May-Oct) FREE At Fort Point a cairn marks the site where Frenchman Samuel de Champlain landed in 1604. You can blow the hand-pumped foghorn in the lighthouse at the end of Main St.

Queen's County Museum MUSEUM
(☑902-354-4058; www.queenscountymuseum. com; 109 Main St; $4; ☺9:30am-5:30pm Mon-Sat, 1-5:30pm Sun) This museum has First Nations artifacts and materials relating to town history, as well as some writings by early citizens.

Perkins House Museum MUSEUM
(☑902-354-4058; http://perkinshouse.novascotia. ca; 105 Main St; adult/child $4/2; ☺9:30am-5:30pm Mon-Sat, 1-5:30pm Sun Jun-Oct) Perkins House Museum displays articles and furniture from the colonial period. Built in 1766, it's the oldest house belonging to the Nova Scotia Museum.

★ Festivals & Events

Privateer Days CULTURAL
(www.privateerdays.ca; ☺Jun) This three-day summer festival is a celebration of piracy and the town's history.

🛏 Sleeping & Eating

Geranium House B&B $
(☑902-354-4484; 87 Milton Rd; r $60; ☺May-Sep) This B&B on a large wooded property next to the Mersey River has three rooms with shared bathroom – ideal for cyclists and families – and a fascinating host.

Lane's Privateer Inn INN $$
(☑902-354-3456; www.lanesprivateerinn.com; 27 Bristol Ave; d $135-190; ☎) Originally the home of a swashbuckling privateer, this 200-year-old inn has all the modern updates and is a clean and pleasant place to stay. It's the center of action in summer, with live music on weekends and special events such as wine tastings. There's also an excellent dining room (mains $10 to $25, open 7am to 10pm).

☆ Entertainment

Astor Theatre THEATER
(☑902-354-5250; www.astortheatre.ns.ca; 59 Gorham St) The Astor is the oldest continuously operating performance venue in the province. Built in 1902 as the Liverpool Opera House, it presents films, plays and live music.

Kejimkujik National Park

Some of Nova Scotia's most unique, magnificent and unspoiled terrain is found in the Kejimkujik National Park (shortened to 'Keji' by locals). The main park occupies 381 sq km in the center of the mainland, while its smaller Seaside Adjunct is located 107km to the south.

Less than 20% of Keji's wilderness is accessible by car; the rest is reached on foot or by canoe. Bird-watchers will be in their element, while wildlife ranges from porcupines to black bear. On a less joyful note, biting insects are rampant; watch out for eel-like leeches in the lakes and some seriously large mosquitoes.

The 'Keji Adjunct' protects landscapes of rolling low brush, wildflowers, white sandy coves and the granite outcrops spreading between Port Joli and Port Mouton Bay.

The Port Joli Basin contains the **Point Joli Migratory Bird Sanctuary**, with waterfowl and shorebirds in great numbers. It's only easily accessible by kayak.

🏃 Activities

September to early October is prime hiking time; the bugs in the spring would drive you mad. More than a dozen lakes are connected by a system of portages, allowing canoe trips of up to seven days. A topographical map ($10) should be acquired for ambitious multiday trips.

The main hiking loop in the main park, the **George Lake Trail** is a 60km trek that begins at the east end of George Lake and ends at the Big Dam Lake trailhead. A shorter loop, ideal for an overnight trek, is the 26km **Channel Lake Trail**, which begins and ends at Big Dam Lake.

In the adjunct section of the park, two mostly flat trails lead to the coast from the parking lot. **Harbour Rocks Trail** (5.2km return) follows an old cart road through mixed forest to a beach where seals are often seen. The **Port Joli Head Trail** is an 8.7km loop.

Rossignol Surf Shop　　　　SURFING
(☑ 902-354-7100; www.surfnovascotia.com; White Point Beach Resort, White Point; ⊙ 10am-5pm Jul-Aug) The Rossignol Surf Shop, 32km from Keji Adjunct, rents surfboards (half-/full-day rental $20/35) and offers two-hour surfing lessons ($85). The schedule is limited; check the website for details.

Keji Outfitters　　　　CANOEING
(☑ 902-682-2282;　　www.whynotadventure.ca; ⊙ 8am-9pm Jun-Sep) Rent canoes and other equipment in the park at Jakes Landing. One-/24-hour hire of a double kayak, canoe or bike is $15/40. One-week hire for any of these is $165. It's open during the off-season by appointment.

🛏 Sleeping

Jeremy's Bay Campground　　CAMPGROUND $
(☑ 877-737-3783;　www.pc.gc.ca; tent/RV sites $26/30; ⊙ May-Oct) Of the 360 campsites within the park, 30% are assigned on a first-come, first-served basis. It costs from $10 to reserve a site.

Caledonia Country Hostel　　HOSTEL $
(☑ 902-682-3266;　www.caledoniacountryhostel.com; 9960 Hwy 8, Caledonia; dm/d $30/70; ☎) In the heart of Caledonia – the only town near the park that has an internet cafe, a gas station and a grocery store – this spotless hostel has beds on the 2nd floor of an adorable Victorian-style home. Cozy nooks with TV, books and old-style upholstered chairs abound. Tours and shuttle services available.

Raven Haven Hostel & Family Park　HOSTEL $
(☑ 902-532-7320; www.hihostels.ca; 2239 Virginia Rd, South Milford; dm/cabins $24/72, tent/RV sites $20/24; ⊙ Jun-Aug; ℗ ☕ ☎) This HI hostel and campground is 25km south of Annapolis Royal and 27km north of Kejimkujik National Park. The four-bed hostel is in a cabin near the beach, and rustic two-bedroom cabins have equipped kitchens but no linens. There are 15 campsites, but the camping in the park is better. Canoes and paddleboats can be rented.

Mersey River Chalets　　CABIN $$
(☑ 902-682-2447;　www.merseyriverchalets.ns.ca; 315 Mersey River Chalets Road E, Caledonia; tipis $90-115, cabins $175-195; ☕ ☎) Comfy cabins have pine floors, wood-burning stoves and very private porches complete with barbecue; rooms in the lodge have private decks with lake views; and cozy tipis have fully equipped kitchens. Free canoes and kayaks are available for guests.

Thomas Raddall Provincial Park　CAMPGROUND
(☑ 902-683-2664; http://parks.novascotia.ca/content/thomas-raddall; campsites $24; ⊙ May-Oct) Thomas Raddall Provincial Park, across Port Joli Harbour from Keji Adjunct, has large, private campsites, eight of which are walk-in. The forested campground extends out onto awesome beaches.

ℹ Information

Kejimkujik National Park Visitor Centre
(☑ 902-682-2772; www.parkscanada.gc.ca/keji; 3005 Main Pkwy, Maitland Bridge; park entrance adult/child $6/3; ⊙ 8:30am-8pm Jul-Sep, to 4:30pm May, Jun & Oct) Get an entry permit and park maps and reserve backcountry sites here. If you're into birding, see if they have a copy of *Nova Scotia Birding on the Lighthouse Route*.

ℹ Getting There & Away

Entrance to the Kejimkujik National Park is through the visitor center on Hwy 8, which can be approached from Annapolis Royal, 49km to the northwest. From the east, the park is 69km from Liverpool, or 68km from Bridgewater, from where it's another 19km to Lunenburg.

The only access into Kejimkujik National Park Seaside Adjunct is via Hwy 103 and then along a 6.5km gravel road. The park is 47km east of Shelburne and 32km west of Liverpool. For GPS navigation systems, search for 1188 Saint Catherine's River Road, Port Joli.

Shelburne

Shelburne's historic waterfront bobs with sailboats and has 17 homes that were built pre-1800 – it feels like a historical re-creation. The wonderfully maintained, low-in-the-earth buildings once housed Loyalists who retreated here from the American Revolution. In 1783 Shelburne was the largest community in British North America, with 16,000 residents, many from the New York aristocracy, who exploited the labor of Black Loyalists living in nearby Birchtown. Shelburne's history is celebrated with **Founders' Days** over the last weekend of July.

◉ Sights

From mid-June to mid-August Shelburne boasts a slew of daily demonstrations around town by folks in period costume, including old-style cooking, sewing, music, military exercises, carving and more; schedules change daily but start around 1pm. Check with the visitor information center for details.

Black Loyalist Heritage Centre　MUSEUM
(📞902-875-1310; http://blackloyalist.novascotia.ca; 119 Old Birchtown Rd; adult/child $8/5; ⊙10am-5pm) Birchtown's Black Loyalist Heritage Centre and museum was moved to its shiny new facility in 2015, 7km outside town, on the site of what was Canada's largest free African settlement in the 1780s. The museum offers a fascinating insight into this largely untold Canadian story. There's a **trail** for hiking or cycling the 6km to Birchtown across from Spencer's Garden Centre at the far south end of Main St.

Dory Shop Museum　MUSEUM
(📞902-875-3219; http://doryshop.novascotia.ca; 11 Dock St; adult/child $4/free; ⊙9:30am-5:30pm Jun–mid-Oct) Shelburne dories (small open boats once used for fishing from a mother schooner) are still made to order at the Dory Shop Museum for use as lifeboats.

BLACK LOYALIST BIRCHTOWN

Just as Shelburne was once the largest settlement in British North America, so Birchtown was once the largest settlement of freed African slaves in North America. After the American Revolution, about 3500 Black Loyalists were rewarded by the British with land for settlements near Shelburne, Halifax, Digby and Guysborough. Nine years later, in 1792, after barely surviving harsh winters and unequal treatment, 1200 of them boarded 15 ships bound for Sierra Leone, in West Africa, where they founded Freetown. An additional 2000 from the USA settled in the Maritimes after the War of 1812, and others came from the Caribbean in the 1890s to work in the Cape Breton Island coal mines.

Ross-Thomson House　MUSEUM
(📞902-875-3141; http://rossthomson.novascotia.ca; 9 Charlotte Lane; adult/child $4/free; ⊙9:30am-5:30pm Jun–mid-Oct) Built in 1784, Ross-Thomson House belonged to well-to-do Loyalist merchants who arrived in Shelburne from Cape Cod. Furniture, paintings and original goods from the store are on display. The house is surrounded by authentic period gardens. Admission is free on Sunday mornings.

Shelburne County Museum　MUSEUM
(📞902-875-3219; www.shelburnemuseums.com; 20 Dock St; ⊙by appointment) **FREE** A c 1787 Loyalist house is now the Shelburne County Museum. It has a collection of Loyalist furnishings, displays on the history of the local fishery, and a small collection of Mi'kmaw artifacts.

🛏 Sleeping & Eating

Islands Provincial Park　CAMPGROUND **$**
(📞902-875-4304; http://parks.novascotia.ca/content/islands; 183 Barracks Rd; campsites $24; ⊙Jun-Oct) Across the harbor from Shelburne are 65 campsites in mature forest and a beach for swimming.

★ Cooper's Inn B&B　B&B **$$**
(📞902-875-4656; www.thecoopersinn.com; 36 Dock St; r $130-220; 🖥) Part of this waterfront building dates to 1784 and was brought here from Boston. Now it's a relatively modern but still charmingly heritage-style inn with six rooms. There's also a flower-filled garden, where you can drink your complimentary bottle of Jost wine at sunset.

Bean Dock
CAFE **$**

(☑ 902-875-1302; sandwiches $3.50-7; ☺ 10am-4pm Mon, Tue & Thu-Sat, to 8pm Wed) Grab a wooden table overlooking the bay for coffee, grilled sandwiches and light mains, from fish cakes to sun-dried tomato pasta salad. The giant Adirondack chair out front is worth chatting about.

★ Charlotte Lane
MODERN CANADIAN **$$$**

(☑ 902-875-3314; www.charlottelane.ca; 13 Charlotte Lane; mains $18-33; ☺ 11:30am-2:30pm & 5-8pm Tue-Sat) People drive from Halifax to eat here, and rave about it; evening reservations are highly recommended. Swiss chef Roland Glauser is constantly revising an extensive, annotated wine list to accompany his ever-changing menu of local seafood, meat and pasta dishes.

ⓘ Information

Visitor Information Centre (VIC; ☑ 902-875-4547; 43 Dock St; ☺ 9am-4pm May-Sep) Has copies of an excellent self-guided historic district walking tour.

ACADIAN SHORES

Along the Acadian Shores (which include a smaller area known as the French Shore) you'll be regularly waved to by the Stella Maris, the single-starred, tricolored Acadian flag. With the exception of British-feeling Yarmouth – the largest town in the area, first settled by the Acadians but later a stronghold for the New Empire Loyalists – this region comprises small communities who proudly uphold their French-Acadian language and traditions. This is the place to admire elaborate Catholic churches, learn about the historical struggles of the resilient Acadian people and take a stroll along a fine sandy beach. If you stay longer, don't miss the chance to sample the region's foot-tapping music performances that take place in summer.

The Acadian Shores are located along an approximately 120km-long stretch of mostly coastal land between Digby to the north and the city of Yarmouth and the communities of the Pubnicos to the south. There's no public transport outside Yarmouth and, unless you're a spirited cyclist, the distances between communities make self-driving the only practical way of exploring the region.

French Shore

The villages of Church Point, Grosses-Coques, Belliveau Cove and St Bernard, on the mainland directly across St Mary's Bay from Digby Neck, make up the heart of the French Shore. This is where Acadians settled when, after trekking back to Nova Scotia following deportation, they found their homesteads in the Annapolis Valley already occupied. Now linked by Hwy 1 – pretty much the only road in each town – these are small fishing communities.

The best way to explore this fading but unique part of the province is to follow Hwy 1 as it hugs the shoreline, from Belliveau Cove to as far south as Mavilette Beach. It can be approached equally in the reverse direction.

⊙ Sights & Activities

Rendez-Vous de la Baie CULTURAL CENTER
(www.rendezvousdelabaie.com; 23 Lighthouse Road, Church Point; ☺ 7am-7pm Mon-Fri, 9am-5pm Sat & Sun) **FREE** If there's one essential stop along this coast, this is it. Learn about Acadian history and culture at the museum; check out local art at the gallery; watch musical performances and more at the theater; and get tourist tips at the information center. The center also runs Acadian-themed tours.

Smuggler's Cove Provincial Park STATE PARK
(http://parks.novascotia.ca; 7651 Hwy 1, Meteghan; ☺ mid-May–mid-Oct) Named for its popularity with 19th-century pirates, this park is today frequented by picnickers. A hundred wooden stairs take you down to a rocky beach. There are picnic sites with barbecue pits at the top of the stairs, and a view across St Mary's Bay to Brier Island.

Gilbert's Cove Lighthouse LIGHTHOUSE
(☑ 902-837-5584; www.gilbertscovelighthouse.com; 244 Lighthouse Rd, Gilbert's Cove; ☺ 10am-4pm Mon-Sat, noon-4pm Sun May-Sep) **FREE** Built in 1904, this gorgeous little lighthouse had only two light-keepers throughout its years of service. It was rescued in 1982 from vandalism and decay by the local historical society, who have turned it into a charming museum. There's a scenic picnic area and a great spot for beachcombing and swimming.

Église St Bernard CHURCH
(St Bernard's Church; ☑ 902-837-5687; 3623 Hwy 1, St Bernard; ☺ 9am-5pm May-Nov) St Bernard is known for its church, a huge granite

structure built by locals who added one row of blocks each year between 1910 and 1942. It has incredible acoustics, showcased each summer in regular musical performances.

Belliveau Beach   BEACH

Belliveau Beach, near the southern end of Belliveau Cove, is made up of masses of sea-polished stones broken up by small clumps of incredibly hardy fir trees. Just behind the beach, a **cemetery** and **monument** recall the struggles of the early Acadian settlers of the French Shore.

Hinterland Adventures & Gear   KAYAKING

(✉ 902-837-4092; www.kayakingnovascotia.com; 54 Gates Lane, Weymouth; kayak rentals per 1hr/day $8/42, tours from $48) Running tours for over 15 years, this respected kayaking and canoeing outfit specializes in paddling tours of St Mary's Bay and the Sissiboo River.

⭐ Festivals & Events

Festival Acadien de Clare   CULTURAL

(www.festivalacadiendeclare.ca; ⊙ Aug) The largest and oldest of the annual Acadian cultural festivals is held over seven days in and around the village of Church Point.

🛏 Sleeping & Eating

À la Maison d'Amitié B&B   B&B $$

(✉ 902-645-2601; www.houseoffriendship.ca; 169 Baseline Rd, Mavilette; r $185; ⊙ Jun-Oct; 🐾) À la Maison d'Amitié B&B is perched dramatically on a cliff close to the beach on six private hectares. The huge, American-style home has cathedral ceilings and sky-high windows with views on all sides.

Roadside Grill   ACADIAN $

(✉ 902-837-5047; 3334 Hwy 1, Belliveau Cove; mains $9-18; ⊙ 8am-9pm) Try the steamed clams or the *rappie* pie at this pleasantly old-fashioned and long-running local restaurant. It also rents out three small cabins (singles/doubles $60/80) with cable TV and microwaves. There's live Acadian music Tuesday nights from 5:30pm to 7:30pm June through August.

La Cuisine Robicheau   ACADIAN $$

(www.lacuisinerobicheau.ca; 9651 Hwy 1, Saulnierville; mains $10-25; ⊙ 8am-9pm Tue-Sun) This is the most elevated of Acadian cuisine found on this coast. The *rappie* pie, seafood lasagna and chocolate pie are so good and affordable they may make you exclaim *'sacre bleu!'*. It's family-run, always busy, and there's often live music at suppertime during summer.

Yarmouth

Founded in 1761 by New Englanders from Massachusetts, Yarmouth reached the peak of its prosperity in the 1870s. It's still the biggest town in southern Nova Scotia due to the ferry that once linked the province to Bar Harbor (Maine, USA). When that service was terminated in 2010, Yarmouth had it tough, with locals lobbying unsuccessfully to get it back. What they did get, however, is in many people's eyes even better: a high-speed passenger and vehicle catamaran linking Yarmouth with Portland, Maine's largest city.

The **Collins Heritage Conservation District**, centered on Collins St, boasts some beautiful Victorian buildings to complement Yarmouth's handful of interesting attractions, but there's no compelling reason to stick around. That said, with its recent re-positioning as the gateway to exploring the quiet, gentle pleasures of the Acadian Shores and Annapolis Valley, the locals hope you will – stick around, that is.

◉ Sights

★ Cape Forchu Lightstation   LIGHTHOUSE

(Yarmouth Light; ✉ 902-742-4522; www.cape forchulight.com; Hwy 304; ⊙ 9am-5pm Jun-Sep) **FREE** Resembling a giant red-and-white-striped candlestick, this local icon celebrated its 175th birthday in 2015. The lighthouse affords spectacular views and there's a tearoom below. The drive in and out is also a little bit magical.

Art Gallery of Nova Scotia   GALLERY

(✉ 902-749-2248; www.artgalleryofnovascotia.ca; 341 Main St; adult/child $6/free, Thu after 5pm free; ⊙ 10am-5pm Tue, Wed, Fri & Sat, to 9pm Thu, noon-5pm Sun) Practical Yarmouth is the unexpected home to this refreshingly cosmopolitan branch of the Art Gallery of Nova Scotia. The ultra-modern building houses well-selected works from mostly Maritime artists.

Yarmouth County Museum   MUSEUM

(✉ 902-742-5539; www.yarmouthcountymuseum. ca; 22 Collins St; adult/student $5/2; ⊙ 9am-5pm Mon-Sat Jun-Sep, 2-5pm Tue-Sat Oct-May) This museum in a former church contains five period rooms related to the sea. The ticket includes Pelton-Fuller House next door.

Pelton-Fuller House   HISTORIC BUILDING

(✉ 902-742-5539; www.yarmouthcountymuseum. ca; 20 Collins St; adult/student $5/2; ⊙ hours vary Jun-Sep) Step back in time in this 1892 wooden home built in the Victorian Italianate style, filled with antiques and memorabilia, and with a meticulously cared-for rose garden out back. Admission includes entry to the neighboring Yarmouth County Museum.

🛏 Sleeping & Eating

★ MacKinnon-Cann House Historic Inn
INN $$

(📞 866-698-3142; www.mackinnoncanninn.com; 27 Willow St; r $169-239; 🛜) Each of the six rooms represents a decade, ranging from the Victorian 1900s to the groovy 1960s, depicting the era at its most stylish while managing to stay calming and comfortable. Two rooms can be joined to create a family suite.

Best Western Mermaid
MOTEL $$

(📞 902-742-7821; www.bwmermaid.com; 545 Main St; d $115-165; 🅿 ♻ ❄ 🛜 ✤) Close to the ferry terminal, this chain motel is in good shape and has the important bits covered: clean rooms, good water pressure and comfy beds. There's also a pool the kids will love in the warmer months, plus free breakfast and wi-fi.

Lakelawn B&B Motel
MOTEL $$

(📞 902-742-3588; www.lakelawnmotel.com; 641 Main St; r $109-159; 🛜 ✤) This place is as cute and service-oriented as motels come. Rooms are clean and basic, and some of the better meals in town are available in the country-style dining area. Go even classier in the four B&B-style rooms in the central Victorian house.

★ Shanty Cafe
CAFE $

(📞 902-742-5918; www.shantycafe.ca; 6b Central St; items $4-9; ⊙ 7am-7pm Mon-Sat; ✐) It's almost worth coming to Yarmouth just to start your day with something delicious and healthy from this proudly sparkling cafe, where you can tell it's a labor of love for all concerned. For lunch, Indian and Mexican flavors spice up Western favorites on a menu that's as inexpensive as it is diverse.

Rudder's Brew Pub
PUB FOOD $

(📞 902-742-7311; www.ruddersbrewpub.com; 96 Water St; pub menu $8-14, dinner mains $14-32; ⊙ 11am-late) The 300 seats at this waterfront pub and restaurant fill fast. A mean ale is brewed on-site and there's a wide-ranging menu. Drinks are poured until the wee hours on busy summer nights.

WORTH A TRIP

ACADIAN VILLAGE

The 17-acre **Le Village historique acadien de la Nouvelle-Écosse** (Historical Acadian Village of Nova Scotia; 📞 902-762-2530; http://levillage.novascotia.ca; 91 Old Church Rd, Lower West Pubnico; adult/child $7/3; ⊙ 9am-5pm Jun-Oct) overlooking Pubnico Harbour re-creates an Acadian village, with vintage Acadian buildings and a cemetery. The village is located in West Pubnico, one of Nova Scotia's original Acadian communities (and not to be confused with all the other nearby Pubnicos), about a 40-minute drive southeast of Yarmouth.

Marco's Grill and Pasta House
ITALIAN $$

(📞 902-742-7716; www.marcosgrill.com; 624 Main St; mains $10-24; ⊙ 11am-9pm) If you've been traveling around the province for a while, there'll come a day when the thought of eating another lobster or bucket of mussels will tip you over the edge. That's when Marco's fabulous, very Italian pastas will be the most comforting thing since mom's lasagna. Don't pass up the breaded mushrooms.

Stanley Lobster Pound
SEAFOOD $$

(📞 902-742-8291; www.stanleylobster.com; 1066 Overton Rd; market price varies; ⊙ 3-8pm Wed-Sat) You can't get more authentic than choosing your own lobster and walking it home. Well, not really, but you can have your lobster two ways – live or cooked. It's a lot easier to have the little critter boiled up, so you can dine by campfire overlooking the Bay of Fundy. Down-home Nova Scotia atmosphere aplenty.

ℹ Information

Visitors Information Centre (VIC; 📞 902-742-5033; 228 Main St; ⊙ 7:30am-9pm May-Oct) Ask for a local walking tour map.

Izaak Walton Killam Memorial Library (📞 902-742-2486; 405 Main St; ⊙ 10am-4pm Mon-Sat; 🛜) Has free internet access.

ℹ Getting There & Away

Yarmouth is 300km southwest of Halifax on Hwy 103, and 104km south of Digby on Hwy 101.

There are no scheduled bus services from Yarmouth to Halifax and beyond, but Cloud Nine Shuttle (p56) can get you to the capital or to Halifax International Airport.

As of June 2016, Yarmouth is once again connected to the USA by sea. The trip, operated by **Bay Ferries** (www.ferries.ca) travels to Portland, Maine (adult/child $107/65, 5½ hours). Bringing a vehicle will cost an extra $199.

ⓘ Getting Around

You can rent bikes and surreys (four-wheeled covered bicycles) from **Wheelhouse** (☑ 902-307-7433; www.thewheelhouse.ca; 5 Collins Street; bikes per hour from $12; ☺ 9am-5pm) for a fun way to explore Yarmouth.

ANNAPOLIS VALLEY

Historically, the fertile and sparsely populated Annapolis Valley was known as the breadbasket of colonial Canada. Today, the region still produces much of Nova Scotia's fresh produce, especially apples, but the real excitement surrounds the growth of the valley's viticulture industry. The wineries boast a similar latitude to Bordeaux, France, and have taken advantage of the sandy soil and reconnected with the area's French roots.

Regional highlights include the **Annapolis Valley Apple Blossom Festival** (www.appleblossom.com), visits to the Fundy coast at Annapolis Royal for tidal vistas over patchwork farmland, the vibrant and spirited town of Wolfville, and taking a moment to contemplate the past while gazing upon the World Heritage landscape of Grand Pré.

ⓘ Getting There & Away

Hwy 101, which begins on the outskirts of Halifax, continues for 74km to Wolfville at the northern extent of the Annapolis Valley, then runs straight down to Digby in the south. Because of the distances between towns and the many and varied side-trips to discover, self-driving is the most practical and enjoyable way to explore the region.

At Digby, **Bay Ferries** (www.ferries.ca) links Nova Scotia to Saint John, NB, via car ferry. The journey takes approximately 2¼ hours in peak season and 2¾ hours during off season. Check the website for schedules.

ⓘ Getting Around

The **Kings Transit** (www.kingstransit.ns.ca) bus line runs every other hour from 6am to around 7pm from Weymouth (just north of Church Point) to Bridgetown (just north of Annapolis Royal) and then as far as Wolfville, stopping in every little town along the way.

Long Island

The long and narrow strip of land that resembles a giraffe's neck craning out to take a peek into the Bay of Fundy is known as **Digby Neck**. At the far western end of this appendage, Long Island, and then Brier Island, are connected by ferry with the rest of the peninsula. The entire area is a haven for whale and seabird watchers.

Many people head straight to Brier Island, but Long Island is easier to get to and has a few more residents. At the northeastern edge of Long Island, **Tiverton** (population 300) is a tiny fishing community. Continuing along the main road for 15km, you'll reach the southwestern end of the island and the village of **Freeport** (population 250), central for exploring both Brier and Long Islands.

In the center of the island, **Central Grove Provincial Park** has a muddy, 2km-long hiking trail to the Bay of Fundy.

◉ Sights & Activities

Island Museum   MUSEUM
(☑ 902-839-2034; www.islandshistoricalsociety. com; 243 Hwy 217, Freeport; by donation; ☺ 9:30am-4:30pm Jun-Sep) This local history museum has exhibits on island life and a tourist information desk.

★**Ocean Explorations
Whale Cruises**   WHALE WATCHING
(☑ 902-839-2417; www.oceanexplorations.ca; tours from $75; ☺ Jun-Oct) One of the best whale-watching tours in the province is led by biologist Tom Goodwin and has the adventurous approach of getting you down low to whale level in a Zodiac. Shimmy into an orange coastguard-approved flotation suit and hold on tight! Goodwin has been leading whale-watching tours since 1980 and regularly donates to wildlife conservation and environmental education organizations.

✗ Eating

Lavena's Catch Café   CAFE $
(☑ 902-839-2517; 15 Hwy 217, Freeport; mains $7-18; ☺ 11:30am-8pm; ☏) Lavena's Catch Café is a country-style cafe directly above the wharf at Freeport; it's the perfect spot to enjoy a sunset and you might even see a whale from the balcony. There's occasional live music in the evenings.

ℹ Getting There & Away

Long island is connected to Digby Neck by a ferry (foot passenger/car free/$5), which runs from the aptly named East Ferry to Tiverton, every hour on the half-hour from 9:30am to 4:30pm, and returns on the hour.

Brier Island

Brier Island bills itself as a top ecotourism destination. The island was home to Joshua Slocum who, in 1895, became the first man to sail solo around the world. Westport, Brier Island's only permanent settlement, is a quaint fishing village and a good base for exploring the numerous excellent, if rugged and windy, hiking trails around the island. Columnar basalt rocks are seen all along the coast and agates can be found on the beaches.

Plankton stirred up by the strong Fundy tides attracts finback, minke and humpback whales, and this is the best place in the world to see the endangered North Atlantic right whale. Blue whales, the world's largest animal, are also sighted on occasion, plus you're almost certain to see plenty of seals.

Bring plenty of warm clothing (regardless of how hot it seems), sunblock and binoculars; motion-sickness pills are recommended.

◉ Sights & Activities

Brier Island Lighthouse   LIGHTHOUSE
(Western Light; 720 Lighthouse Rd) Originally built in 1809, this rugged outpost has seen many incarnations over the years. Its present form, a striking red-and-white-striped concrete tower standing 18.3m tall, was built in 1944 and has been automated since 1987.

Brier Island Whale &
Seabird Cruises   WHALE WATCHING
(☑902-839-2995;   www.brierislandwhalewatch.com; adult/child from $50/28; ☺ Jun-Oct) You can book excellent whale-watching tours (2½ to five hours, depending on where the whales are) with this eco-conscious company.

⌆ Sleeping

Brier Island Lodge   LODGE $$
(☑902-839-2300; www.brierisland.com; 557 Water Street, Westport; r $109-169; ☺ May-Oct; ☻ ☎ ☺) Atop cliffs 1km east of Westport, Brier Island Lodge has 37 rooms, many with ocean views. Its restaurant (mains $8 to $29) has views on two sides, friendly service and fabulously fresh seafood. Boxed lunches are available.

ℹ Getting There & Away

Brier Island is fairly remote, even by Canadian standards. It's just over 70km from Digby (itself a little removed from the rest of Nova Scotia) via Long Island and two car-ferry crossings. The best way to understand ferry timings is to check out www.brierisland.org/info.html. Needless to say, you'll need your own wheels.

Digby

Nestled in a protected inlet off the Bay of Fundy, Digby is known for its scallops, mild climate and daily ferry to Saint John, NB. Settled by United Empire Loyalists in 1783, it's now home to the largest fleet of scallop boats in the world.

Emigration in recent years has been hard on Digby, parts of which are looking a little rough around the edges. The town lacks the architectural charm of starlets such as Lunenburg, Wolfville and Annapolis Royal, but it remains a logical base for explorations of Digby Neck, Long and Brier Islands, and the French Shore.

If you're here in passing, the best things to do are to stroll the waterfront, watch the scallop draggers come and go, eat as much of their catch as you can, then squeeze in a sunset at Point Prim.

◉ Sights

Admiral Digby Museum   MUSEUM
(☑902-245-6322;   www.admiraldigbymuseum.ca; 95 Montague Row; by donation; ☺9am-5pm Mon-Sat) The only real sight in town is the Admiral Digby Museum, a mid-19th-century Georgian home that contains exhibits of the town's marine history and early settlement.

✦ Festivals & Events

Digby Scallop Days   FOOD & DRINK
(www.digbyscallopdays.com; ☺Aug) If you're around in summer, reserve even more space in your belly and itinerary for this delicious seafood festival.

Wharf Rat Rally   MOTORCYCLE
(www.wharfratrally.com; ☺late Aug–early Sep) Rev your engines for the Wharf Rat Rally at the end of August, where tens of thousands of bikers roar into town for motorcycle-oriented contests, tours and general mingling. Book your accommodations well in advance.

🛏 Sleeping & Eating

Digby Backpackers Inn HOSTEL $
(📞902-245-4573; www.digbyhostel.com; 168 Queen St; dm/r $30/65; 🛜) Saskia and Claude keep the solid four-bed dorm rooms spotless and often spontaneously host barbecues or take the whole hostel out to see the sunset. The heritage house has plenty of communal areas, including a deck, and there's a welcoming vibe. Internet access, a light breakfast and towels are included in the price. Cash only.

Digby Pines Golf Resort & Spa RESORT $$
(📞902-245-2511; www.digbypines.ca; 103 Shore Rd; d/ste/cottage from $140/195/265; ⊙May-Oct; 🅿🍴@🛜🏊🐾) Although standard rooms are elegantly furnished with dark woods and comfy bedding, they're small for the price, and the resort could do with some general TLC. That said, Digby Pines still offers the town's highest standard of accommodation, with attentive staff, an excellent restaurant and fabulous, family-friendly facilities, which include a world-class golf course, outdoor pool and day-spa.

Josie's Place DINER $
(📞902-245-2952; 88 Warwick St; mains $7-18; ⊙7am-8pm) There's nothing fancy about Josie's – just good, old-fashioned, no-frills diner-style cooking, from fry-up breakfasts to meatloaf like your mom used to make, along with sandwiches, salads, and fish-and-chips. Cheap and cheery. There's a line out the door when the bikers are in town.

Shoreline Restaurant SEAFOOD $$
(📞902-245-6667; 88 Water St; mains $12-28; ⊙11am-9pm) Walk through the gift store to the restaurant out back, where you can choose a table by the window or a booth on the deck overlooking a grassy lawn and the harbor beyond. Daily specials and all your seafood faves are on the menu (including bacon-wrapped scallops!), as well as steaks, burgers and salads.

ℹ Information

Western Counties Regional Library (📞902-245-2163; www.westerncounties.ca; 84 Warwick St; ⊙12:30-5pm & 6-8pm Tue-Thu, 10am-5pm Fri, 10am-2pm Sat; 🛜) Free internet access.

ℹ Transport

Digby is 32km southwest of Annapolis Royal, just off Hwy 1. From Yarmouth, it's 104km along Hwy 101, heading northeast.

Kings Transit (📞902-628-7310; www.kingstransit.ns.ca; one-way fare adult/child $3.50/1.75) operates a local bus service that runs as far north as to Wolfville, via Annapolis Royal.

Bay Ferries (www.ferries.ca) operates a daily car-ferry service to Saint John, NB, on the *Fundy Rose* (adult/child from $36/20, 2¼ to 2¾ hours). Rates for vehicles start at $107, including fuel surcharge.

Bear River

Bear River is a delightful riverside enclave popular with artists and those who moved here from larger centers for a 'tree change'. There's a strong Mi'kmaq presence mixed in with Scottish roots, giving Bear River a unique vibe. Some buildings near the river are on stilts, while other historic homes nestle on the steep hills of the valley. A few wineries are starting to pop up just out of town.

◉ Sights

Bear River First Nation Heritage & Cultural Centre CULTURAL CENTER
(📞902-467-0301; 194 Reservation Rd; $3) Bear River First Nation is a five-minute drive from Bear River town: turn left after crossing the bridge, then take a left where the road forks. A 1km trail starts behind the center and highlights plants with traditional medicinal uses. The Heritage & Cultural Centre offers demonstrations of traditional crafts and hands-on workshops, but unfortunately it's open infrequently.

Annapolis Highland Vineyards WINERY
(📞902-467-0363; www.annapolishighlandvineyards.com; 2635 Clementsvale Rd; ⊙10am-5pm Mon-Sat, noon-5pm Sun) Don't miss the gold-medal White Wedding dessert wine if you come in for a free tasting at this rather commercial winery. Delicious fruit wines are also available.

Bear River Winery WINERY
(📞902-467-4156; www.wine.travel; 133 Chute Rd; ⊙by appointment) 🚳 All estate-produced, award-winning wines made at this adorable little winery are created using solar energy, biodiesel, wind power and the natural slope of the property. Stop by to take a free tour and tasting (July to September) or stay longer at friendly hosts Chris and Peggy's one-room **B&B** ($140 per night) to enjoy wine-making workshops and retreats.

X Eating

Myrtle and Rosie's Cafe CAFE $
(☑ 902-467-0176; 1880 Clementsvale Rd; mains $7-14; ☺10am-5pm Tue-Sun) Stop in to chat with locals, have coffee over a slice of pie, or chow down on a delicious BLT or a juicy burger, and enjoy the view of Bear River.

🔒 Shopping

Flight of Fancy GIFTS & SOUVENIRS
(☑ 902-467-4171; www.theflight.ca; 1869 Clementsvale Rd; ☺10am-6pm) This exquisitely curated craft store and gallery has work by close to 200 artists and craftspeople. If you want to buy just one treasure to take away from Nova Scotia, this is a good place to find it.

Annapolis Royal

The community's efforts to restore and promote their village as a tourist destination have made Annapolis Royal one of the most delightful places to visit in the region. At the time of writing, it remained one of the only well-trodden towns in the province without a ubiquitous Tim Horton's coffee and donut franchise.

As teeny-tiny as it feels, Annapolis Royal is dripping with historical significance: the area was the location of Canada's first permanent European settlement and was capital of Nova Scotia until the founding of Halifax in 1749. Formerly called Port Royal, it was founded by French explorer Samuel de Champlain in 1605. As the British and French battled, the settlement often changed hands. In 1710 the British had a decisive victory and changed the town's name to Annapolis Royal in honor of Queen Anne.

⊙ Sights

★Fort Anne
National Historic Site HISTORIC SITE
(☑ 902-532-2397; www.parkscanada.gc.ca/fortanne; Upper St George St; adult/child $4/2; ☺9am-5:30pm) This historic site in the town center preserves the memory of the early Acadian settlement, plus the remains of the 1635 French fort. Entry to the extensive grounds is free, but you'll also want to visit the museum, where artifacts are contained in various period rooms. An extraordinary four-panel tapestry, crafted in needlepoint by more than 100 volunteers, depicts 400 years of history.

Port Royal
National Historic Site HISTORIC SITE
(☑ 902-532-2898; www.pc.gc.ca; 53 Historic Lane; adult/child $4/2; ☺9am-6pm) Some 14km northwest of Annapolis Royal, Port Royal National Historic Site is the actual location of the first permanent European settlement north of Florida. The site is a replica of de Champlain's 1605 fur-trading habitation, where costumed workers help tell the story of this early settlement.

Annapolis Royal
Historic Gardens GARDENS
(☑ 902-532-7018; www.historicgardens.com; 441 St George St; adult/child $14.50/6; ☺9am-8pm Jul & Aug, to 5pm May, Jun, Sep & Oct) These gorgeous gardens cover a rambling 6.5 hectares with various themed areas such as an Acadian kitchen garden one might have seen in the late 1600s, and an innovative modern one. Munch on blueberries, ogle the vegetables and look for frogs. The **Secret Garden Café** offers lunches and German-style baked goods.

🏃 Activities

★Tour Annapolis Royal WALKING
(www.tourannapolisroyal.com; tours adult/child $9/5; ☺Jul-Oct) This outfit runs several history-oriented tours. The best is a creepy tour of the Fort Anne graveyard led by an undertaker-garbed guide. Everyone carries a lantern and winds through the headstones to discover this town's history. Proceeds go to the local historical society. Hour-long tours begin at 9:30pm; check the website for dates.

Delap's Cove Wilderness Trail HIKING
Over the North Mountain from Annapolis Royal, Delap's Cove Wilderness Trail lets you get out on the Fundy shore. It consists of two loop trails connected by an old inland road that used to serve a Black Loyalist community. Today, only relics of old foundations and apple trees remain in the woods. Both the loop trails are a 9km round-trip.

🛏 Sleeping & Eating

Dunromin Campground CAMPGROUND $
(☑ 902-532-2808; www.dunromincampground.ca; 4618 Hwy 1, Granville Ferry; tent/RV sites from $30/45, cabins/caravans from $70/145; ☺May-Oct; P 🛜 🐕) This popular, offbeat campground has some secluded riverside sites, as well as nifty options such as a tipi for up to six people and a gypsy caravan. Canoes are available to rent ($10 per hour).

Croft House B&B
B&B $

(☎ 902-532-0584; www.crofthouse.ca; 51 Riverview Lane; d from $85; P ⬡ ❀) This farmhouse stands on approximately 40 hectares of land, about a five-minute drive from Annapolis Royal across the river. One of the enthusiastic owners is a chef and he whips up a fine breakfast with organic ingredients.

★ Queen Anne Inn
INN $$

(☎ 902-532-7850; www.queenanneinn.ns.ca; 494 Upper St George St; r $129-179, carriage house from $189; ☻ May-Oct; P ✳ ❀) Arguably the most elegant property in Annapolis Royal, this B&B is the perfect balance of period decor and subtle grace. It's so beautiful, with the Tiffany lamp replicas, manicured grounds and sweeping staircases, that it might seem stuffy were it not for the friendly owners, who make you feel like you could (almost) kick your feet up on the antique coffee table.

Bailey House B&B
B&B $$

(☎ 902-532-1285; www.baileyhouse.ca; 150 Lower St George St; r $145; P ❀) The only B&B on the waterfront, Bailey House is also the oldest inn and one of the best in the area. The friendly owners have managed to keep the vintage charm (anyone over 6ft might hit their head on the doorways!), while adding all the modern comforts and conveniences.

★ Cafe Restaurant Compose
EUROPEAN $$

(☎ 902-532-1251; www.restaurantcompose.com; 235 St George St; mains lunch $11-18, dinner $18-34; ☻ 5-8:30pm Wed, 11:30am-2:30pm & 5-8:30pm Thu-Tue; ❀) This cafe offers fine dining in a relaxed setting, with wonderful views of the Bay of Fundy. Dine alfresco (in season) to get even closer to the shore. With an emphasis on fresh seafood and local produce, the menu reads well and is executed beautifully, with something for everyone.

Bistro East
BISTRO $$

(☎ 902-532-7992; www.bistroeast.com; 274 St George St; mains $12-28; ☻ 11am-10pm) Great for lunch and dinner, Bistro East has been serving juicy steaks, fresh seafood and handmade pasta for almost a decade. Friday and Saturday nights feature live, good-for-the-ambience music from 8pm. This is one of those jovial little establishments where it's genuinely difficult to be disappointed.

German Bakery & Sachsen Cafe
GERMAN $$

(☎ 902-532-1990; www.germanbakery.ca; 358 St George St; mains $9-20; ☻ 9am-7pm) In an area where seafood is king, it's nice to find hearty German breads, schnitzels and desserts in this casual, although slightly over-priced, cafe.

🍷 Drinking & Entertainment

Ye Olde Pub
PUB

(☎ 902-532-2244; 9 Church St; ☻ 11am-11pm Mon-Sat, noon-8pm Sun) Rumored to be Nova Scotia's smallest pub, it's by no means the dullest. On sunny days drink beer and eat pub grub (mains $5 to $15) on the outdoor terrace; when it's cooler, slip into the dark and cozy old bar, which was once a bank.

King's Theatre
THEATER

(☎ 902-532-7704; www.kingstheatre.ca; 209 St George St; movies $10, live shows from $15) Right on the waterfront, this nonprofit theater presents musicals, dramas and concerts most evenings in July and August, and occasionally during the rest of the year. Hollywood films are screened on most weekends and independent films most Tuesdays year-round.

🛍 Shopping

Farmers & Traders Market
MARKET

(www.annapolisroyalfarmersmarket.com; cnr St George & Church Sts; ☻ 8am-noon Sat May-Oct, also 10am-2pm Wed Jul & Aug) Annapolis Royal's thriving community of artists and artisans offer their wares alongside local farm produce at this popular market. There's live entertainment most Saturday mornings.

ℹ Information

Tourist Information Centre (☎ 902-532-5769; www.annapolisroyal.com; 236 Prince Albert Rd; ☻ 10am-6pm May-Oct) At the Tidal Power Project; pick up a historic walking tour pamphlet.

Wolfville & Grand Pré

Visually arresting, Wolfville has a perfect blend of old-college-town culture, small-town homeyness and a culinary scene that has developed in concert with the surrounding wine industry. Combined with the town's permanent residents, the students and faculty of local Acadia University bump the town's residential population to over 7000, injecting a youthful vigor to this otherwise quiet district and making Wolfville one of the province's most livable and ethnically diverse towns.

Essentially just down the road, Grand Pré, Wolfville's bucolic neighbor, is a small bilingual community. In the 1750s, however, it was

WOLFVILLE & GRAND PRÉ WINERIES

Most of Nova Scotia's best wineries and vineyards are found in the rolling hills and valleys around Wolfville and Grand Pré. Our pick of the bunch (so to speak):

Luckett Vineyards (☑ 902-542-2600; www.luckettvineyards.com; 1293 Grand Pré Rd, Wolfville; tastings from $5; ☉ 10am-5pm May-Oct) Palatial views over the vines and hillsides down to the Bay of Fundy cliffs. Sample the red, white, fruit and dessert wines, and the particularly good ice wine, then stay for lunch on the patio.

Gaspereau Vineyards (☑ 902-542-1455; www.gaspereauwine.com; 2239 White Rock Rd, Gaspereau; ☉ 10am-5pm May-Oct, tours noon, 2pm & 4pm) One of the province's best-known wineries, with award-winning ice wine, an elegant Estate Riesling, and super-friendly staff.

Domaine de Grand Pré (☑ 902-542-1753; www.grandprewines.ns.ca; 11611 Hwy 1, Grand Pré; tours $9; ☉ 10am-6pm, tours 11am, 3pm & 5pm) A great destination winery and one of the best known in the province. It features a delicious spicy muscat and a nice sparkling Champlain Brut.

L'Acadie Vineyards (☑ 902-542-8463; www.lacadievineyards.ca; 310 Slayter Rd, Wolfville; ☉ 10am-5pm May-Oct) 🖉 Overlooking Gaspereau Valley, this geothermally powered winery grows certified-organic grapes to make traditional-method sparkling and dried-grape wines.

Blomidon Estate Winery (☑ 902-582-7565; www.blomidonwine.ca; 10318 Hwy 221, Canning; tastings from $5; ☉ 10am-6pm Jun-Sep) The friendly and laid-back winemaker comes out to chat with those tasting wines. The sparkling wines and Tidal Bay are probably the best, but the oaky red merits a try.

If you don't want to drive, hop on the **Wolfville Magic Winery Bus**, which runs from June through mid-October.

the site of one of the most tragic but compelling stories in eastern Canada's history, the Acadian deportation. In 2012, the marshland and polder farmland of Grand Pré were given Unesco World Heritage status.

Beyond the two towns, you'll find Acadian dikes, scenic drives and some of the best hiking along the Fundy Coast.

👁 Sights

★ Grand Pré

National Historic Site   HISTORIC SITE
(☑ 902-542-3631; www.pc.gc.ca; 2205 Grand Pré Rd, Grand Pré; adult/child $8/4; ☉ 9am-6pm May-Oct) This interpretive center explains the historical context for the deportation of the French-Acadian people from Acadian, Mi'kmaw and British perspectives and traces the many routes Acadians took from, and back to, the Maritimes. Beside the center, a serene park contains gardens, an Acadian-style stone church, and a bust of American poet Henry Wadsworth Longfellow, who chronicled the Acadian saga in *Evangeline: A Tale of Acadie,* and a statue of his fictional Evangeline, now a romantic symbol of her people.

★ Tangled Garden   GARDENS
(☑ 902-542-9811; www.tangledgardenherbs.ca; 11827 Hwy 1, Grand Pré; garden $5; ☉ 10am-6pm) These unique, sumptuous terraced gardens afford wonderful views of the surrounding countryside. A labor of love, the meticulous grounds are the perfect spot to wander, picnic or contemplate, especially when walking the meditative labyrinth. The gift shop is probably the best-smelling shopping experience in Nova Scotia. Be sure to pick up a jar of the phenomenal rosemary quince jelly.

Randall House Museum   MUSEUM
(☑ 902-542-9775; 171 Main St, Wolfville; by donation; ☉ 10am-5pm Mon-Sat, 2-5pm Sun Jun-Sep) Randall House Museum relates the history of the New England planters and colonists who replaced the expelled Acadians.

Waterfront Park   PARK
(cnr Gaspereau Ave & Front St, Wolfville) Waterfront Park offers a stunning view of the tidal mudflats, Minas Basin and the red cliffs of Cape Blomidon. Displays explain the tides, dikes, flora and fauna, and the history of the area. This is an easy spot to start a walk or cycle on top of the dikes.

CAPE BLOMIDON & THE UPPER ANNAPOLIS VALLEY

The North Mountain, which ends at the dramatic Cape Blomidon, defines one edge of the Annapolis Valley. On the other side of the mountain are fishing communities on the Bay of Fundy. The valley floor is crisscrossed with small highways lined with farms and orchards. It's a great place to get out your road map – or throw it away – and explore.

Around 3km from the village of Port Williams, the 1814 **Prescott House Museum** (☑ 902-542-3984; http://prescotthouse.novascotia.ca; 1633 Starr's Point Rd; adult/student $4/3; ☺ 10am-5pm Mon-Sat, 1-5pm Sun Jun-Sep) – considered to be one of the finest examples of Georgian architecture in Nova Scotia – was the former home of the horticulturalist who introduced many of the apple varieties grown in the Annapolis Valley.

In the quaint, historic town of Canning, stop for a fair-trade coffee (or an art class) at **Art Can Gallery & Café** (☑ 902-582-7071; www.artcan.com; 9850 Main St; mains $10-14; ☺ 9am-5pm; 🛜) or head just out of town to sample wines at Blomidon Estate Winery (p75).

North out of Canning, along Hwy 358, stop at the well-signposted Look-Off. About 200m above the Annapolis Valley, it's the perfect spot to view the farmlands below and, if you're lucky, bald eagles above: from November to March they number in the hundreds, attracted by local chicken farms.

Hwy 358 ends in Scots Bay, where the dramatic 14km **Cape Split hiking trail** (www.scottsbay.com/cape-split) leads to views of the Minas Basin and the Bay of Fundy. If you're not up for the hike, nearby **Blomidon Provincial Park** (☑ 902-582-7319; www.parks.gov.ns.ca; 3138 Pereau Rd, Canning) has a picnic area and plenty of easier walks.

For some lunch after all that fresh air, head to Centreville's **Hall's Harbour Lobster Pound** (☑ 902-679-5299; www.hallsharbourlobster.com; 1157 W Halls Harbour Rd; mains $13-24; ☺ noon-7pm May-Oct) and gorge yourself on ocean delicacies, straight from the source.

Round out your afternoon with a visit to Kentville, the county seat for the area, where you can rent a bike at **Valley Stove & Cycle** (☑ 902-542-7280; www.valleystoveandcycle.com; 353 Main St; bike rental half/full day $25/35) to admire the town's stately old homes, or check out the region's apple farming history at **Blair House Museum** (Kentville Agricultural Centre; ☑ 902-678-1093; 32 Main St; ☺ 8:30am-4:30pm Mon-Fri Jun-Sep) **FREE** or other local history and art at **Old King's County Museum** (☑ 902-678-6237; www.kingscountymuseum.ca; 37 Cornwallis Ave; ☺ 9am-4pm Mon-Sat Jun-Aug, closed Sat Apr, May & Sep–mid-Dec) **FREE**.

🕝 Tours

Wolfville Magic Winery Bus BUS
(☑ 902-542-4093; www.wolfvillemagicwinerybus.ca; hop-on/hop-off bus passes $30; ☺ Thu-Sun Jun-Oct) If you think you'd like to sample more than a few wines in the area's four amazing vineyards, best have a local drive you around – on a classic British double-decker, no less!

✯✯ Festivals & Events

Canadian Deep Roots Festival MUSIC
(www.deeprootsmusic.ca; ☺ late Sep) If you're in Wolfville in early fall, rock out to modern roots music at this annual festival.

🛏 Sleeping

Garden House B&B B&B $
(☑ 902-542-1703; www.gardenhouse.ca; 220 Main St, Wolfville; r $85-120; 🛜) This antique house retains its old-time feel in the most comfortable way. Creaky floors, a rustic breakfast table decorated with wildflowers, and a lived-in vibe you instantly feel a part of (everyone is encouraged to take off their shoes). Bathrooms are shared.

★ **Olde Lantern Inn & Vineyard** INN $$
(☑ 902-542-1389; www.oldlanterninn.com; 11575 Hwy 1, Grand Pré; r $129-150; 🛜) Clean lines, a friendly welcome and attention to every comfort makes this a great place to stay. The vineyard grounds overlook Minas Basin, where you can watch the rise and fall of the Fundy tides and gaze over the World Heritage Grand Pré landscape.

★ **Blomidon Inn** INN $$
(☑ 800-565-2291; www.blomidon.ns.ca; 195 Main St, Wolfville; d $139-159, ste $179-269; ❈ @ 🛜) Grand Victorian architecture and old-world extravagance make this a very upper-crust-feeling inn. Set in 2.5 hectares of perfectly maintained gardens, with rooms just as well groomed. Check online for package deals.

★ Roselawn Lodging
MOTEL $$

(☑ 902-542-3420; www.roselawnlodging.ca; 32 Main St, Wolfville; d $95-185; P ⊜ @ ⋑) This wonderful little 1960s-style complex features a variety of motel-style rooms and freshly updated cute-as-a-button cottages with full kitchens, and makes a welcome alternative to Wolfville's lofty B&Bs. With a pool, tennis court and spacious grounds, it's easy to make this place your little home away from home.

Victoria's Historic Inn
INN $$

(☑ 902-542-5744; www.victoriashistoricinn.com; 600 Main St, Wolfville; r $149-229) This elegant inn is directly opposite Acadia University. Each of its luxuriously appointed rooms vary in style, but all are decorated with excellent taste and attention to detail. Expect indulgences such as four-poster beds, period furnishings, fine linens, and memorable full breakfasts. Check the website to pick your favorite room; the Chase suite is hard to beat.

Gingerbread House Inn
INN $$

(☑ 902-542-1458; www.gingerbreadhouse.ca; 8 Robie Tufts Dr, Wolfville; d $125, ste $185-210; ⋑ ⋑) Although not in bad taste, the exterior of this unique, floral and frilly, B&B is like a big pink birthday cake with lacy white edging.

✖ Eating

Wolfville's proximity to local vineyards and growing reputation as *the* culinary hot spot outside Halifax means there's no shortage of great food to enjoy, from tasty student-priced eateries to fabulous fine dining.

Dining in Grand Pré is limited to the region's selection of higher-end winery cafes and restaurants.

Naked Crepe
CREPERIE $

(☑ 902-542-0653; www.thenakedcrepebistro.ca; 402 Main St, Wolfville; crepes $3-12; ⊙ 9am-11pm) Who doesn't enjoy a wafer-thin, flaky crepe filled with delicious sweet or savory goodness? Catering to both the breakfast crowd *and* the late-nighters, Naked Crepe boasts a huge range of inventive fillings. Excellent value.

Tin Pan
CAFE $

(☑ 902-691-0020; 978 Main St, Port Williams; mains $6-14; ⊙ 8am-8pm Mon-Sat) Only a blink away from Wolfville on Hwy 358 is the Tin Pan, a favorite for motorcyclists who head here on Saturday mornings for hearty breakfasts.

Troy
MEDITERRANEAN $$

(☑ 902-542-4425; www.troyrestaurant.ca; 12 Elm Ave, Wolfville; mains $16-26; ⊙ noon-8pm) It's refreshing to taste the spectacular flavors of healthy Mediterranean cuisine, presented in a modern and incredibly colorful restaurant, in otherwise mostly unadventurous, rural Nova Scotia. A range of light appetizers, which work equally well in a tapas-style presentation, is complemented by predominantly meat-based kebabs and mains, with some vegetarian and gluten-free options.

★ Le Caveau
EUROPEAN $$$

(☑ 902-542-1753; www.grandprewines.ns.ca/restaurant; 11611 Hwy 1, Grand Pré; mains lunch $12-18, dinner $20-34; ⊙ 11:30am-2pm & 5-9pm May-Oct) Considered to be the finest Northern European–style restaurant in the province, this Swiss restaurant is on the grounds of Domaine de Grand Pré (p75). The beautiful outdoor patio is paved with fieldstones and shaded with grapevines.

Privet House
FUSION $$$

(☑ 902-542-7525; www.facebook.com/PrivetHouse Restaurant; 268 Main St, Wolfville; mains lunch $12-20, dinner $19-38; ⊙ 11:30am-3pm & 5-9pm Tue-Sun) The finest dining in town serves up aged Atlantic beef, local seafood and game (all ingredients are Canadian) prepared with everything from European to Indian and Thai influences. Tablecloths are white, the wine list is long and the service is top-notch.

➌ Drinking & Entertainment

Library Pub & Wine Tavern
PUB

(☑ 902-542-4315; www.thelibrarypub.ca; 472 Main St, Wolfville; ⊙ 11am-midnight) Wolfville's Main St drinking establishment is a jolly place in a quaint historic building. If you're flying solo and of an agreeable temperament, you're bound to make some new friends here.

Acadia Cinema's Al Whittle Theatre
THEATER

(☑ 902-542-3344; www.alwhittletheatre.ca; 450 Main St, Wolfville) Operated by the volunteer-run Acadia Cinema Co-op, this fabulous historic building, a Wolfville cultural icon, functions as a multipurpose cinema, theater and performance space. Check the website for regular events listings and screening times and to learn about the theater's history.

❶ Information

Wolfville Memorial Library (☑ 902-542-5760; 21 Elm Ave, Wolfville; ⊙ 10am-5pm Tue-Sat, 1-5pm Sun; ⋑) Free internet access.

Tourist Information Centre (☑ 902-542-7000; www.wolfville.ca; 11 Willow Ave, Wolfville; ⊙ 9am-9pm May-Oct)

Getting There & Away

Wolfville is linked to Halifax by Hwy 101; the journey takes an hour in good traffic.

Maritime Bus (www.maritimebus.com) services from Halifax stop at Acadia University in front of Wheelock Hall off Highland Ave. **Kings Transit** (www.kingstransit.ns.ca) buses run between Cornwallis (southwest of Annapolis Royal) and Wolfville, stopping at 209 Main St.

Windsor

Windsor was once the only British stronghold in this region, but today it's just a graying little town eking out an existence between the highway and the Avon River. Windsor is a place to enjoy bluegrass music – think lots of fast banjo picking.

While in town, check out **Haliburton House** ([☑]902-798-2915; http://haliburtonhouse. novascotia.ca; 414 Clifton Ave; adult/student $4/3; [☉]10am-5pm Mon-Sat, 1-5pm Sun Jun-Oct), once home to Judge Thomas Chandler Haliburton (1796–1865), writer of the Sam Slick stories. Many of Haliburton's expressions, such as 'quick as a wink' and 'city slicker', are still used. There's also a **blues festival** (www. smokinbluesfest.ca), Windsor's hottest ticket.

Stay the night at the **Clockmaker's Inn** ([☑]902-792-2573; www.theclockmakersinn.com; 1399 King St; d incl breakfast $99-179; [P][☎]), a French-château–style mansion with curved bay windows, lots of stained glass and sweeping hardwood staircases. It's gay-friendly and afternoon tea is served daily.

CENTRAL NOVA SCOTIA

Hiking, rafting and rockhounding are the activities of choice around this pleasant and often overlooked region. For those traveling overland from the rest of Canada, the town of **Amherst**, geographic center of the Maritimes and a crossroads between New Brunswick, Prince Edward Island and Nova Scotia, will be your first taste of the province, if you swing off the Trans-Canada Hwy (Hwy 104 at this point).

From Amherst you can follow the 'Glooscap Trail' – named for the figure in Mi'kmaw legend who created the unique geography of the Bay of Fundy – as far as Wolfville in the Annapolis Valley, or take the road less travelled and hug the shoreline, visiting the World Heritage–listed Joggins Fossil Cliffs, the delightful hamlet of Advocate Harbour and the village of Parrsboro. This is the part of Nova Scotia famed for the legendary Fundy Tides and tidal bore rafting.

Information

Amherst Visitor Information Centre (VIC; [☑]902-667-8429; Amherst; [☉]8:30am-8pm) This massive visitor information center is at exit 1 off Hwy 104, just as you cross the border from New Brunswick.

Getting There & Away

Amherst is the gateway to Nova Scotia for visitors arriving by land, although the town itself is largely bypassed by the Trans-Canada Hwy (Hwy 104).

Maritime Bus (www.maritimebus.com) connects Amherst with Moncton, NB ($14, one hour, three daily), and Truro with Halifax ($25.50, 1½ hours, five daily).

Shubenacadie

Shubenacadie, or simply 'Shube,' 35km south of Truro off Hwy 2, is best known for the **Shubenacadie Provincial Wildlife Park** ([☑]902-758-2040; www.wildlifepark. novascotia.ca; 149 Creighton Rd; adult/child $5/3; [☉]9am-6:30pm daily mid-May–mid-Oct, 9am-3pm Sat & Sun mid-Oct–mid-May). It's the place to commune with Nova Scotia's fauna. You can hand-feed the deer and, if you're lucky, pet a moose. The animals were either born in captivity or once kept as 'pets' and thus cannot be released into the wild – they live in large enclosures. Turn off Hwy 102 at exit 11 and follow Hwy 2 to the park entrance.

Maitland

Tiny Maitland is the place to go rafting on the white water that is created by the outflow of the Shubenacadie River meeting the blasting force of the incoming Fundy tides. It's also one of the oldest towns in Canada.

Wave heights are dependent on the phases of the moon; get information from your rafting company about the tides for your chosen day as your experience (either mild or exhilarating) will be dictated by them. Outboard-powered Zodiacs plunge right through the white water for the two to three hours that the rapids exist. Prepare to get very, very wet – no experience is needed.

✹ Activities

★ Shubenacadie River Runners   RAFTING

(☑ 902-261-2770; www.tidalborerafting.com; 8681 Hwy 215; half-day rafting $60-70) The region's largest rafting company is organized and professional in every way. Prices depend on how big the tide and waves are; refer to the website for the lowdown on how it all works.

Shubenacadie River Adventures   RAFTING

(☑ 902-261-2222; www.shubie.com; 10061 Hwy 15; tours from $60) Besides the exciting tidal-bore-rafting day trips, mellow half-day river tours are also on offer. Check the website for tide times and the full details of what's available.

🛏 Sleeping

Cresthaven by the Sea   B&B $$

(☑ 902-261-2001; www.cresthavenbythesea.com; r $139-149; ⊘ May-Oct; 🛜) Stay here for what is possibly the best view over the Fundy tides. The immaculate white Victorian house sits on a bluff right over the point where the Shubenacadie River meets the bay. All the rooms have river views and the lower ones are wheelchair-accessible.

Tidal Life Guesthouse   B&B $$

(☑ 902-261-2583; www.thetidallife.ca; 9568 Cedar St; dm/r $55/110; ⊘ May-Oct; 🅿 🛜 🐾) This old beauty of a house has grand, airy rooms and large windows overlooking grassy fields. Artistically designed communal spaces are everywhere, including the back porch with requisite hammock. All accommodations include a big, healthy, locally sourced breakfast. Bathrooms are shared.

Truro

Several major highways converge here, along with a VIA Rail line, so it's no wonder Truro is known as the hub of Nova Scotia. While the town does look somewhat like an aging shopping mall, it's exceptionally well serviced and can make a good stop to pick up that nagging item you need or just to stock up on food.

Escape Truro's busy streets at **Victoria Park** (Park St, off Brunswick St) 400 hectares of green space in the very center of town that includes a deep gorge and two waterfalls. The park attracts dozens of bird species.

The best time to visit Truro is when Millbrook First Nation hosts its **annual pow-wow** (☑ 902-897-9199; www.millbrookfirstnation.

THE POWER OF THE BORE

The tidal bore phenomenon occurs when the first surge of the extreme Bay of Fundy tides flows upriver at high tide. Sometimes the advancing wave is only a ripple but, with the right phase of the moon, it can be a meter or so in height, giving the impression that the river is flowing backwards. You'll have to sit awhile to see the changes in the tide; a good place to watch is from the lookout on Tidal Bore Rd, off Hwy 236 just west of exit 14 from Hwy 102 on the northwest side of Truro.

Visit the **Environment Canada** website (www.tides.gc.ca/eng/find/zone/30) for the arrival time of the tidal bore at a variety of locations.

---

net; ⊘ Aug). Campsites and showers are available; drugs and alcohol are prohibited.

If you're looking for a place to stay in Truro, **Baker's Chest B&B** (☑ 902-893-4824; www.bakerschest.ca; 53 Farnham Rd; r $110-130; 🛜 🏊) is a newly restored classic older home with a fitness room, a pool and a hot tub. The famous **tearoom** is open from noon to 2pm on weekdays and is an adorable stop for soups, snacks and, of course, a nice cup of tea.

ℹ Information

Truro Welcome Centre (☑ 902-893-2922; 695 Prince St; ⊘ 9am-5pm May-Oct; 🛜) Offers internet access and a guide to the tree sculptures around town, which were carved after the region was affected by Dutch elm disease more than 30 years ago.

ℹ Getting There & Away

Hwy 102 from Halifax (95km) and the Trans-Canada Hwy (Hwy 104) intersect in Truro, along with a number of other highways and secondary roads.

Maritime Bus (www.maritimebus.com) services from Halifax ($25.50, 1½ hours) stop in Truro en route to Amherst ($25.50, 1¼ hours).

Economy & Five Islands

Hwy 2 hugs the shore of the Minas Basin, the northeast arm of the Bay of Fundy. Economy is the first sizable community that you'll arrive at west of Truro, followed by the aptly named Five Islands. There's some great hiking and views in the area, as well as several interesting sights.

WORTH A TRIP

JOGGINS FOSSIL CLIFFS

The wealth of fossils in this 15km stretch of seaside cliffs, including rare land species, are preserved in their original setting. The site is said to be the penultimate location to see what life on earth was like in the late Carboniferous period – 300 million years ago!

The state-of-the-art **Joggins Fossil Centre** (www.jogginsfossilcliffs.net; 100 Main St, Joggins; tours from $10.50; ⊗10am-4pm mid-Apr–Oct, by appointment Nov–mid-Apr) is the place to start your visit, and explains through displays and film what you can see in the Unesco World Heritage–listed cliffs below. The best time to visit the cliffs is at low tide when all of the beaches can be accessed – otherwise you'll be cut off from some of the more interesting sites by high water. Check the website to understand the various tours available and the level of difficulty for each. Note that tours leave on an irregular schedule, depending on the tides, and can be reserved in advance.

◉ Sights & Activities

Cobequid Interpretive Centre MUSEUM
(☑902-647-2600; www.cobequidinterpretive centre.com; 2 River Philip Rd, Economy; by donation; ⊗9am-4:30pm Jun-Sep) Stop here for good exhibits on the region's ecology and history. Climb a WWII observation tower for a bird's-eye view of the surrounding area and pick up hiking information from the staff. The nearby **Thomas Cove Coastal Trail** is actually two 3.5km loops with great views across the Minas Basin and the Cobequid Mountains. The trails begin down Economy Point Rd, 500m east of the interpretive centre. Follow the signs to a parking area.

Five Islands Provincial Park STATE PARK
(☑902-254-2980; http://parks.novascotia.ca/ content/five-islands) Just 7km west of Economy, are several hikes in this park. The 4.5km **Red Head Trail** is well developed, with look-outs, benches and great views.

Economy Falls HIKING
The most challenging hikes in the area are around Economy Falls. The **Devil's Bend Trail** begins 7km up River Phillip Rd toward the Cobequid Mountains. The 6.5km (one-way) trail follows the river to the falls. The 20km-loop **Kenomee Canyon Trail** begins at the top of the falls and twists up the river to a protected wilderness area.

Note that on the latter option, several streams have to be forded; there are designated campsites, making this a good two-day adventurous trek.

⌂ Sleeping & Eating

High Tide B&B B&B $
(☑902-647-2788; www.hightidebb.com; 2240 Hwy 2, Lower Economy; d $85-95; ☜) This friendly, modern bungalow has great views. Janet, one of the owners, will have you down on the beach for a clam boil in no time.

Four Seasons Retreat RESORT $$
(☑902-647-2628; www.fourseasonsretreat.ns.ca; 320 Cove Rd, Upper Economy; cottages $120-255; 🅿☺☏☒☸) Fully equipped cottages are surrounded by trees and face the Minas Basin. In summer, there's a hot tub near the pool; on a chilly night there are woodstoves.

That Dutchman's Cheese Farm CAFE $
(☑902-647-2751; www.facebook.com/ThatDutch mansCheeseFarm; 112 Brown Rd, Upper Economy; mains $8-13; ⊗11am-5pm Jul & Aug) The yummy cafe here offers sandwiches, soups and plates of the eccentric farmer's own Gouda. You can tour the farm for a small fee.

Parrsboro

Rock hounds come from far and wide to forage the shores of Parrsboro, the largest of the towns along the Minas Basin. The Fundy Geological Museum has wonderful exhibits and good programs that take you to the beach areas known as Nova Scotia's 'Jurassic Park.'

◉ Sights

FORCE RESEARCH STATION
(Fundy Ocean Research Center for Energy; ☑902-254-2510; www.fundyforce.ca; 1156 West Bay Road, Black Rock; ⊗10am-5pm Thu-Mon Jun-Oct) FREE Science and environment buffs will get a kick from this fascinating leading research center for in-stream tidal energy, which welcomes visitors. It's best to phone ahead to express your interest.

Ottawa House Museum MUSEUM
(☑902-254-2376; 1155 Whitehall Rd; $2; ⊗10am-6pm) This 21-room mansion was once

the summer home of Sir Charles Tupper (1821–1915), who served as both premier of Nova Scotia and prime minister of Canada. The museum has exhibits on shipbuilding, rum-running and the former settlement on Partridge Island.

Fundy Geological Museum MUSEUM
(☑902-254-3814; http://fundygeological.nova scotia.ca; 162 Two Islands Rd; adult/child $9/5; ☉10am-5pm) This award-winning museum got a million-dollar makeover in 2010 and uses interactive exhibits to help its visitors 'time travel' to when the fossils littering Parrsboro's beaches were living creatures. You can see a lab where dinosaur bones are being cleaned and assembled. **Beach tours** are included in the admission price and focus on minerals or fossils; times, length and frequency are dependent on the tides.

⭐ Festivals & Events

Nova Scotia Gem & Mineral Show GEM SHOW
(http://fundygeological.novascotia.ca/gemshow; ☉mid-Aug) This annual three-day event is the biggest in Parrsboro's calendar, when rock hounds from far and wide descend on the Fundy Shore in search of treasure.

🛏 Sleeping & Eating

Riverview Cottages COTTAGE $
(☑902-254-2388; www.riverviewcottages.ca; 3575 Eastern Ave; cottages $60-105; ☉May-Nov; P🐾🛜🐶) These rustic, country-cute, completely equipped cottages are a steal. You can canoe and fish on the bordering river and there's a big lawn perfect for a barbecue. It really is like going back in time to a 1960s holiday camp, but in an exceptionally well-maintained kind of way.

Mad Hatter Hostel HOSTEL $
(☑902-254-3167; www.madhatterhostel.webs. com; 16 Prince St; dm/s/d $20/35/50; 🛜) More like a few rooms and beds upstairs in an inviting home, this 'hostel' offers a ton of hospitality, kitchen use and a great location right in town.

⭐Sunshine Inn MOTEL $$
(☑877-706-6835; www.thesunshineinn.net; 4487 Hwy 2; r $110, cottages $139-149; ☉May-Nov; P🐾🛜) Let the Sunshine In! It certainly does on this bright, windswept address 3km north of Parrsboro. Choose between immaculately kept and beautifully updated 1970s-style motel rooms or a range of inviting self-contained cottages, equally well maintained and scattered about the beautiful property, which also boasts its own lake. Excellent-value good vibes all round.

⭐Maple Inn B&B $$
(☑902-254-3735; www.mapleinn.ca; 2358 Western Ave; d $99-169; ☉May-Oct; P🐾❄🛜) This elegant B&B in what was once the town's hospital is a true credit to its friendly owners. The wonderfully appointed rooms are filled with gorgeous antiques from Canada and Austria and updated unobtrusively with modern conveniences such as Jacuzzis, jet showers, wi-fi and flat-screen TVs. Delicious breakfasts kick-start the day.

Evangeline's Tower B&B B&B $$
(☑902-254-3383; www.evangelinestower.ca; 322 Main St; d $95-110; P🛜🐶) This elegantly decorated 1890s Victorian home has three rooms; two can be combined into a two-room suite for families. The generous, home-cooked breakfasts are delicious and cyclists are welcome.

⭐Black Rock Bistro BISTRO $$
(☑902-728-3006; www.blackrockbistro.ca; 151 Main St; mains $14-24; ☉noon-9pm May-Oct; P) Friendly, attentive service and beautifully executed meals – from delicate homemade pastas to fresh seafood (seared scallops, lobster lollipops!) and tender juicy steaks – are complemented by an excellent wine list and infrequent visiting musicians in the adjacent wine room. Be sure to leave room for the decadent desserts.

Harbour View Restaurant CANADIAN $$
(☑902-254-3507; 476 Pier Rd; mains $12-24; ☉7am-8pm) Hang out with the local fishers devouring Parrsboro's best fish-and-chips, along with chowder, homemade pies and more at this casual, family-friendly restaurant, right on the water.

WORTH A TRIP

AGE OF SAIL

Stop for tea, baked goods and a tour at the **Age of Sail Heritage Centre** (☑902-348-2030; www.ageofsailmuseum. ca; 8334 Highway 209, Port Greville; $4; ☉10am-6pm May-Oct) in Port Greville, about 20km to the west of Parrsboro on Rte 209. Capturing the area's shipbuilding heritage, the site also includes a restored 1857 Methodist church and a working blacksmith shop.

☆ Entertainment

Ship's Company Theatre   THEATER
(☑ 902-254-3000; www.shipscompanytheatre.com; 18 Lower Main St; tickets from $15; ⊙ Jul-Sep) This innovative theater company performs new Canadian and Maritime works 'on board' the MV *Kipawo,* the last of the Minas Basin ferries, now integrated into a new theater. There's high-quality theater for kids, improv comedy, readings and concerts.

🛍 Shopping

Tysons' Fine Minerals   ROCKS & MINERALS
(☑ 902-254-2376; www.tysonsfineminerals.com; 249 Whitehall Rd; ⊙ 10am-4pm) This place is more like a museum than a shop, with some of the most sparkling, massive and colorful minerals on display you're likely to see anywhere. Sometimes Helen takes visitors in to see the Tysons' own private collection, which is even more breathtaking.

Advocate Harbour

Advocate Harbour is a breathtaking little place with a 5km-long beach piled high with driftwood that changes dramatically with the tides. Behind the beach, salt marshes – reclaimed with dikes by the Acadians – are now replete with birds.

Most visitors pass through here on the scenic route to Amherst or en route to the famous Unesco World Heritage fossil cliffs (p80) in Joggins, 32km south of Amherst.

⊙ Sights & Activities

★ **Cape d'Or Lighthouse**   LIGHTHOUSE
(☑ 902-670-0534; www.capedor.ca; 1 Cape d'Or Rd, Diligent River) This spectacular cape of sheer cliffs was misnamed Cape d'Or (Cape of Gold) by Samuel de Champlain in 1604 – the glittering veins he saw in the cliffs were actually made of copper. Mining took place between 1897 and 1905 and removed the sparkle. The present lighthouse was added in 1922. Access is by the partially unsealed side road off Hwy 209 to Cape d'Or, then hike down the dirt trail. If you can't bring yourself to leave, there's a guesthouse.

Cape Chignecto Provincial Park   STATE PARK
(☑ 902-392-2085; http://parks.novascotia.ca/content/cape-chignecto; W Advocate Rd; hiking permits per day/year $5/25; ⊙ May-Oct) This isolated wilderness park in the Bay of Fundy features vast sea cliffs, pristine coastline, sheltered bays, and rare flora and fauna. It's best known for the **Cape Chignecto Coastal Trail**, a rugged 60km, four-day hiking loop that showcases the park's natural beauty. All park visitors must register and leave an itinerary at the visitors center; camping in the backcountry requires reservations.

Easier overnight hikes include the **Mill Brook Canyon Trail** (15km), the hike to **Refugee Cove** (20km), and the **Eatonville Trail** (28km), sections of which can be tackled as a day trip. All trails require a good level of fitness.

Some hikers have tried to avoid the ups and downs of the trails by taking shortcuts along the beach at low tide and have been cut off by Bay of Fundy tides. Get a tide table and ask park staff about current conditions before setting out.

Nova Shores Adventures   KAYAKING
(☑ 866-638-4118; www.novashores.com; 3838 Hwy 209; day tours from $100) Kayak through Cape Chignecto Provincial Park with Nova Shores Adventures. You'll often see seals and bears. Overnight tours include accommodations and food.

🛏 Sleeping & Eating

Cape d'Or Kitchen & Guest House   INN $$
(☑ 902-670-0534; www.capedor.ca; 1 Cape d'Or Rd, Diligent River; r $80-110, whole house $340; ⊙ May-Oct; 🛜🐾) The original lighthouse keeper's residence is now a laid-back four-room guesthouse at what is perhaps one of the most perfect spots in Nova Scotia (even more so when the sun's out). Its cosmopolitan **restaurant** has views to die for and serves lunch (mains $7 to $15) and dinner (mains $12 to $30), including seafood, meat and vegetarian dishes. To get here, take the partly unsealed road off Hwy 209 signposted to Cape d'Or. From the car park, you need to walk about 150m down a steep dirt trail.

Cape Chignecto Provincial Park Campgrounds   CAMPGROUND
(☑ 902-392-2085; http://parks.novascotia.ca/content/cape-chignecto; campsites $24; ⊙ May-Oct) In addition to 51 wilderness campsites at six points along the coastal trail and 27 walk-in sites near the visitor center, there is also a bunkhouse and a wilderness cabin (both $55 for up to four people). There are no drive-up sites in the park. All campsite reservations can be made online.

★ Wild Caraway Restaurant & Cafe
CANADIAN $$

(✆902-392-2889; www.wildcaraway.com; 3721 Hwy 209; mains lunch $7-16, dinner $18-28; ⊙11am-8pm Thu-Mon; 🐾) This gorgeous cafe-restaurant has some of the best locavore dining you'll find along this coast; it's also pretty as a postcard. Try the ploughman's lunch with house-smoked pork and cheese from That Dutchman's Cheese Farm (p80), or dine on applewood-smoked mackerel or a selection of seasonal specials.

SUNRISE TRAIL

It's claimed that the Northumberland Strait between Nova Scotia's north shore and PEI has some of the warmest waters north of the US Carolinas, with water temperatures averaging slightly over 20°C during summer. The Sunrise Trail is a prime area for beach-hopping, cycling and exploring friendly countryside towns.

Tatamagouche

The Malagash Peninsula, which juts out into protected Tatamagouche Bay, is a low-key, bucolic loop for a drive or bike ride. Taste local wines, go beachcombing or take a peek in some interesting museums found just inland. Tatamagouche is the largest town on the Northumberland Shore coast west of Pictou and makes a great base for exploring the region.

⦿ Sights

Balmoral Grist Mill HISTORIC SITE
(✆902-657-3016; http://balmoralgristmill.novascotia.ca; 544 Peter MacDonald Rd, Balmoral Mills; adult/child $4/3; ⊙9:30am-5:30pm Mon-Sat, 1-5:30pm Sun) In a gorgeous setting on the stream that once provided it with power, the Balmoral Grist Mill still grinds wheat in summer. From Tatamagouche, turn south on Hwy 311 (at the east edge of town) and then east on Hwy 256.

Jost Winery WINERY
(✆902-257-2636; www.devoniancoast.ca; 48 Vintage Ln, Malagash; tours $5; ⊙wine store 10am-5pm Mar-Dec, tours noon & 3pm Jun-Sep) Take a tour of the scenically located Jost Winery. While regular wine is free to taste, the ice wine costs $5. If you want to try all three ice wine varieties, ask to have three small glasses for the price of one large one. Winery signs direct you about 5km off Hwy 6.

Wallace Bay National Wildlife Area BIRD SANCTUARY
(✆800-668-6767; www.ec.gc.ca) About 30km northwest of town, this vast sanctuary protects 585 hectares, including tidal and freshwater wetlands. In the spring, keep your eyes peeled for bald eagles nesting near the parking lot, which is on the left just before the causeway.

Blue Sea Beach BEACH
(651 Blue Sea Rd, Malagash Point) Blue Sea Beach on the Malagash Peninsula has warm water and fine sand, and a marsh area just inland that's ideal for **bird-watching**. There are picnic tables and shelters to change in.

Rushton's Beach Provincial Park STATE PARK
(http://parks.novascotia.ca/content/rushtons-beach; 723 Hwy 6, Brule) Small cottages crowd around Rushton's Beach, just east of Tatamagouche in Brule. It's worth a visit to look for seals (turn left at the end of the boardwalk and walk toward the end of the beach) and birdlife in the adjoining salt marsh.

Sutherland Steam Mill HISTORIC SITE
(✆902-657-3365; http://sutherlandsteammill.novascotia.ca; 3169 Denmark Station Rd, Denmark; adult/child $4/3; ⊙9:30am-5:30pm Mon-Sat, 1-5:30pm Sun Jun-Oct) Built in 1894, the Sutherland Steam Mill produced lumber, carriages, wagons and windows until 1958. To get here from Tatamagouche, follow Hwy 6 for about 10km until the junction with Hwy 326, then drive south for 4km.

Wallace Museum MUSEUM
(✆902-257-2191; www.wallaceandareamuseum.com; 13440 Hwy 6; by donation; ⊙9am-5pm Mon-Fri Mar-Nov) The tourist information center is at the Wallace Museum. Collections of baskets woven by the Mi'kmaq, period dresses and shipbuilding memorabilia are displayed.

✷✷ Festivals & Events

Oktoberfest BEER
(✆902-657-2380; www.nsoktoberfest.ca; tickets $10-20; ⊙Sep) The wildly popular Oktoberfest is held the last weekend in September – yes, September.

🛏 Sleeping & Eating

Wentworth Hostel HOSTEL $
(✆902-548-2379; www.hihostels.ca; 249 Wentworth Station Rd, Cumberland; dm/r $30/50; 🐾) From Tatamagouche, follow Hwy 246 south for 26km until you reach Hwy 4. The 24-bed Wentworth Hostel is 1.3km west of Hwy 4

on Valley Rd, up steep, unsealed Wentworth Station Rd. The rambling farmhouse, built in 1866, has been used as a hostel for decades. It's a central base for both the Sunrise Trail and much of the Minas Basin shore.

Trails for hiking and mountain biking start just outside the door; the hostel gets particularly booked up in winter for the cross-country and downhill skiing nearby.

★ Train Station Inn   INN $$

(☑ 902-657-3222; www.tatatrainstation.com; 21 Station Rd; carriages $109-199; ⊙ May-Nov; 🛜 🐾) It's a museum, it's a kooky gift shop, it's a restaurant, it's a hotel and…it's a stationary train. Each unique carriage suite is a train-spotter's dream, decorated with period train posters, toy trains and locomotive books.

The dreamer behind the inn, James Le-Fresne, grew up across the tracks and saved the train station from demolition. Dine on delicious seafood, meat and salads in the c 1928 dining car or have a blueberry pancake breakfast in the station house. Free self-guided tours are available from the gift shop.

Sugar Moon Farm   CANADIAN $$

(☑ 902-657-3348; www.sugarmoon.ca; 221 Alex MacDonald Rd, Earltown; mains $12-30; ⊙ 9am-4pm Jul & Aug, reduced hours Sep-Jun) The food – simple, delicious pancakes and locally made sausages served with maple syrup – is the highlight of this working maple farm and woodlot. Check online for special happenings. To reach the farm from Tatamagouche, simply follow Hwy 311 south for 25km, then follow the signs on Alex MacDonald Rd.

🛍 Shopping

Lismore Sheep Farm   GIFTS & SOUVENIRS

(☑ 902-351-2889; www.lismoresheepfarmwoolshop. com; 1389 Louisville Rd, River John; ⊙ 9am-5pm) A working farm with more than 300 sheep, this is a fun destination even if you don't buy a rug, a blanket or socks. From May to October, the barn is open for visitors to pat the lambs and learn all about producing wool. The farm is 19km east of Tatamagouche off Hwy 6.

ℹ Information

Fraser Cultural Centre (☑ 902-657-3285; www.fraserculturalcentre.org; 362 Main St; ⊙ 10am-5pm Mon-Fri, to 4pm Sat, 11am-3pm Sun Jun-Sep; 🛜) Tourist information, internet access and local history displays.

Pictou

Many people stop in Pictou for a side trip or as a stopover via the ferry from Prince Edward Island, but it's also an enjoyable base for exploring Northumberland Strait. Water St, the main street, is lined with interesting shops and beautiful old stone buildings (but unfortunately the sea views are blighted by a giant smoking mill in the distance). The town is known as the 'Birthplace of New Scotland' because the first Scottish immigrants to Nova Scotia landed here in 1773.

◎ Sights & Activities

Picnic and swim at **Caribou-Munroes Island Provincial Park**, a 10-minute drive from town.

Hector   SHIP

(☑ 902-485-4371; www.shiphector.com; 33 Caladh Ave; adult/child $8/6; ⊙ 10am-4pm Jun-Oct) A replica of the ship *Hector*, which carried the first 200 Highland Scots to Nova Scotia, is tied up for viewing. Descend into the large hull crammed with bunks to get a feel of how challenging the crossing would have been. The ticket includes admission to Hector Heritage Quay.

Hector Heritage Quay   MUSEUM

(☑ 902-485-4371; 33 Caladh Ave; adult/child $8/6; ⊙ 10am-4pm Jun-Oct) Ticket price also includes admission to the good ship *Hector*. The Quay has an interpretive center, a re-created blacksmith shop, a collection of shipbuilding artifacts, and displays about the *Hector* and its passengers.

Northumberland Fisheries Museum   MUSEUM

(☑ 902-485-8925; 21 Caladh Ave; $5; ⊙ 10am-6pm Mon-Sat) Located in the old train station, this museum explores the area's fishing heritage. Exhibits include strange sea creatures and the spiffy *Silver Bullet,* an early 1930s lobster boat.

★☆ Festivals & Events

Pictou Landing First Nation Powwow   CULTURAL

(☑ 902-752-4912; www.plfn.ca/cultural-history/yearly-events/powwow; ⊙ Jun) Across the Pictou Harbour (a 25-minute drive through New Glasgow), this annual powwow on the first weekend in June features sunrise ceremonies, drumming and craft demonstrations.

THE ROAD TO CAPE GEORGE POINT

The eastern arm of the Sunrise Trail, from New Glasgow to Antigonish has some gorgeous diversions – perfect for a half-day excursion when the weather is fine. Be sure to pack some snacks and remember your beach towel.

Perhaps start your day with a hands-on visit to the Museum of Industry (p86), especially if you have kids in tow, then head along the coast to pretty **Arisaig Provincial Park** (☑ 902-863-4513; 5704 Hwy 245), where you can take a dip or search for fossils. Continue on to **Malignant Cove**. From here, the 55km coastal stretch of Hwy 245 has been compared in beauty to parts of the Cabot Trail, although less mountainous and more accessible.

After a short drive east you'll reach **Cape George Point Lighthouse** (www.parl. ns.ca/lighthouse), the handsome jewel in the day's crown, where you can look out over the calm waters of St Georges Bay. If it's nearing lunch time, head just around the cape to the fish-and-chip truck near the **Ballantyne's Cove Tuna Interpretive Centre** (57 Ballantyne's Cove Wharf Rd), then work off the fried goodness with a dip or a stroll at Crystal Cliffs Beach (p87).

Just 15 minutes south, there's plenty to see and do in Antigonish (p86), or keep up the outdoorsy theme and round out the day with a roar, high above the trees at **Anchors Above Zipline Adventure** (☑ 902-922-3265; www.anchorsabovezipline.ca; 464 McGrath Mountain Rd, French River; 1 ride $30; ☺ 10am-5pm), about 40km from Antigonish – watch for the signs on the Trans-Canada Hwy (Hwy 104).

Camping and food are available on-site; it's strictly alcohol- and drug-free.

Lobster Carnival   FOOD & DRINK
(☑ 902-485-5150; www.pictoulobstercarnival.ca; ☺ Jul) Started in 1934 as the Carnival of the Fisherfolk, this four-day event now offers free entertainment, boat races and lots of chances to feast on lobster.

🛏 Sleeping

Caribou-Munroes Island Provincial Park   CAMPGROUND $
(☑ 902-485-6134; www.parks.gov.ns.ca; 2119 Three Brooks Rd; campsites $24) Less than 10km from Pictou, this park is set on a gorgeous beach. Sites 1 to 22 abut the day-use area and are less private; sites 78 to 95 are gravel and suited for RVs. The rest are wooded and private.

★ **Pictou Lodge**   RESORT $$
(☑ 902-485-4322; www.pictoulodge.com; 172 Lodge Rd; r $129-239, cottages $189-429; ☎ ≋ ☻) This atmospheric 1920s resort is on more than 60 hectares of wooded land between Caribou-Munroes Island Provincial Park and Pictou. Beautifully renovated oceanside log cabins have original stone fireplaces. Motel rooms are also available. There's a life-sized checkerboard, paddleboats, a private beach and the best **restaurant** in town.

Willow House Inn   B&B $$
(☑ 902-485-5740; www.willowhouseinn.com; 11 Willow St; r $90-130; ☎ ☻) This historic c 1840 home is a labyrinth of staircases and cozy, antique rooms. The owners whip up great breakfasts, as well as conversation and tips for what to do around town.

Customs House Inn   INN $$
(☑ 902-485-4546; www.customshouseinn.ca; 38 Depot St; d $90-125; ☎) The tall stone walls here are at once imposingly chic and reassuringly solid. The chunky antique decor is as sturdy and elegant as the architecture, and many rooms have waterfront views. You'll be left pretty much to your own devices, including at the continental breakfast in the basement, which can be a nice break after days of B&B chitchat.

☆ Entertainment

deCoste Centre   LIVE PERFORMANCE
(☑ 902-485-8848; https://decostecentre.ca; 91 Water St; tickets from $20; ☺ box office 11:30am-5pm Mon-Fri, 1-5pm Sat & Sun) Opposite the waterfront, this impressive performing arts center stages a range of live shows. Experience some top-notch Scottish music during a summer series of ceilidhs (*kay*-lees; adult/child $15/7). Check the website for performance dates and times.

ⓘ Information

Eastern and Northumberland Shores Visitor Information Centre (☑ 902-485-8540; Pictou Rotary; ⊗ 9am-5pm) Large info center situated northwest of town to meet travelers arriving from the PEI ferry.

Town of Pictou (www.townofpictou.ca) Links to sights and festivals.

Pictou Public Library (☑ 902-485-5021; 40 Water St; ⊗ noon-9pm Tue & Thu, to 5pm Wed, 10am-5pm Fri & Sat; 🕲) Free internet access.

ⓘ Getting There & Away

Bay Ferries (p41) services to PEI leave from a terminal a few kilometers from Pictou. New Glasgow, 17km south, is the nearest town of any size.

New Glasgow

The largest town on the Northumberland Shore, New Glasgow has always been an industrial hub; the first mine opened in neighboring Stellarton in 1807. Still, it's a pleasant town with plenty of aging architecture and a pretty river running through the center. The few major local attractions are in **Stellarton**, a 5km drive south.

◉ Sights

Crombie House   GALLERY
(☑ 902-755-4440; www.sobeyartfoundation.com; 1780 Granton Abercrombie Rd, Pictou; ⊗ tours hourly 9-11am & 1-4pm Wed Jul & Aug) 𝗙𝗥𝗘𝗘 A 10-minute drive north of town, in the personal residence of the founder of the Sobeys supermarket chain, this private gallery has an excellent collection of 19th- and early 20th-century Canadian art, including works by Cornelius Krieghoff and the Group of Seven.

Museum of Industry   MUSEUM
(☑ 902-755-5425; http://museumofindustry.nova scotia.ca; 147 N Foord St, Stellarton; adult/child $9/4; ⊗ 9am-5pm Mon-Sat, 10am-5pm Sun Jul-Oct; 👶) This is a wonderful place for kids. There's a hands-on water-power exhibit and an assembly line to try to keep up with.

🛏 Sleeping & Eating

Comfort Inn   MOTEL $
(☑ 902-755-6450; www.newglasgowcomfortinn. com; 740 Westville Rd; d $79-139; 🅿 🕲) Our pick of the New Glasgow motels, the recently updated Comfort Inn has drive-up rooms and is well maintained. It's in a good location for cheap and easy eats.

The Bistro   MODERN CANADIAN $$
(☑ 902-752-4988; www.thebistronewglasgow.com; 216 Archimedes St; mains $19-32; ⊗ from 5pm Tue-Sat) The only constant on the Bistro menu is creativity in spicing and sauces. The menu changes daily according to what's available and in summer everything is organic. The local art on display is also for sale.

Hebel's   INTERNATIONAL $$$
(☑ 902-695-5955; www.hebelsrestaurant.ca; 71 Stellarton Rd; mains lunch $10-14, dinner $18-36; ⊗ 11:30am-2pm Tue-Fri, 5-9pm Tue-Sat) Flavors from all over the world are mingled with fresh Nova Scotian ingredients at this bright and homey, fire-warmed spot in an elegant Victorian. Choices may include anything from seafood creole or beef Stroganoff to miso-glazed salmon on Japanese noodles.

Antigonish

Beautiful beaches and hiking possibilities north of town could easily keep you busy for a couple of days, but Antigonish town itself is lively enough and has some great places to eat. Catholic Scots settled and established St Francis Xavier University and today the university still dominates the ambience of the town. Antigonish is known for the Highland Games held here each July since 1861.

◉ Sights

St Francis Xavier University   UNIVERSITY
(www.stfx.ca) The attractive campus of this 125-year-old university makes for an interesting stroll. The **Hall of the Clans** is on the 3rd floor of the old wing of the Angus L MacDonald Library, just beyond the St Ninian's Cathedral parking lot. In the hall, crests of all the Scottish clans that settled this area are displayed. Those clans gather each July for the Antigonish Highland Games.

St Ninian's Cathedral   CHURCH
(120 St Ninian St; ⊗ 7:30am-8pm) The area's Catholic cathedral, completed in 1874, is a fine example of Canadian Romanesque architecture.

Antigonish Heritage Museum   MUSEUM
(☑ 902-863-6160; www.heritageantigonish.ca; 20 East Main St; ⊗ 10am-5pm Mon-Sat Jul & Aug, 10am-noon & 1-5pm Mon-Fri Sep-Jun; 🅿) 𝗙𝗥𝗘𝗘 In the town's former railway station, this compact museum features displays devoted to remembering the history of Antigonish and its residents.

⚡ Activities

Crystal Cliffs Beach
SWIMMING

(Crystal Cliffs Farm Rd) About 15km northeast of Antigonish, turn off Hwy 337 and head down Crystal Cliffs Farm Rd to this popular beach for swimming and beach walks.

Antigonish Landing
HIKING

A 4km hiking and cycling trail to the nature reserve at Antigonish Landing begins just across the train tracks from the Antigonish Heritage Museum, then 400m down Adam St. The landing's estuary is a good **bird-watching** area where you might see eagles, ducks and ospreys.

🎭 Festivals & Events

Antigonish Highland Games
CULTURAL

(www.antigonishhighlandgames.ca; ⊘ Jul) An extravaganza of dancing, pipe-playing, and heavy-lifting events involving hewn logs and iron balls.

🍴 Eating

Gabrieau's Bistro
MODERN CANADIAN $$

(☑ 902-863-1925; www.gabrieaus.com; 350 Main St; mains lunch $10-16, dinner $18-30; ⊘ 10am-9pm Mon-Fri, 4-9:30pm Sat; ☑) Dine on any of a number of imaginative vegetarian dishes, salads, meats and seafood for lunch or dinner. Locals credit chef Mark Gabrieau for setting the culinary high-water mark in Antigonish. Dishes such as Thai shrimp and lobster risotto make frequent appearances on the exotic menu.

ℹ️ Information

Antigonish Visitor Information Centre
(☑ 902-863-4921; 145 Church St; ⊘ 10am-8pm Jun-Sep; 🛜) Brochures, free local calls and free internet access. Located in the Antigonish Mall parking lot at the junction of Hwys 104 and 7.

Antigonish Public Library (☑ 902-863-4276; 274 Main St; ⊘ 10am-9pm Tue & Thu, to 5pm Wed, Fri & Sat; 🛜) Free internet access. Enter off College St.

ℹ️ Getting There & Away

Antigonish is at the northern end of Hwy 7, 62km from Sherbrooke. New Glasgow is 57km to the west on the Trans-Canada Hwy (Hwy 104).

Maritime Bus (www.maritimebus.com) services to Halifax ($42, 3½ hours) and Sydney ($46, 3¼ hours) stop at Bloomfield Centre at St Francis Xavier University.

CAPE BRETON ISLAND

Floating over the rest of Nova Scotia like an island halo, Cape Breton Island is a heavenly, forested realm of bald eagles, migrating whales, palpable history and foot-tapping music. Starting up the Ceilidh Trail along the western coastline, Celtic music vibrates through the pubs and community centers, eventually morphing into more eclectic Acadian-style tunes around Chéticamp.

Linked to the rest of mainland Nova Scotia by a steel swing bridge, the island proudly claims the jewel in Nova Scotia's tourism crown: the 297km-long **Cabot Trail**, which twists and climbs its way through and around Cape Breton Highlands National Park. The trail traverses coastal mountains with glorious ocean views, passes plenty of loose moose on the roads (watch out!) and boasts dozens of challenging trails to bring you back to nature.

Most tourists visit in July and August, and many restaurants, accommodations and attractions are only open from June through October. **Celtic Colours** (www.celtic-colours. com; ⊘ Oct), a popular roving music festival that attracts top musicians from countries with Celtic connections, helps extend the tourist season on Cape Breton Island into the fall, a superb time to visit.

Ceilidh Trail

From Port Hastings, the Ceilidh Trail (Hwy 19) snakes along the western coast of Cape Breton Island. This area was settled by Scots and is renowned for its ceilidh music performances, square dances and parties.

Mabou is the hot spot of Cape Breton's Celtic music scene, where you can hike away your days and dance away your nights with a little help from that single-malt whiskey from the distillery down the road.

The trail continues to the former coal mining town of **Inverness**, with its sandy beach and 1km-long boardwalk, and then twists north to **Margaree Forks**, where you can pick up the Cabot Trail.

👁 Sights

⭐ Glenora Inn & Distillery
DISTILLERY

(☑ 902-258-2662; www.glenoradistillery.com; 13727 Route 19, Glenville; guided tours incl tasting $7; ⊘ tours hourly 9am-5pm Jun-Oct) Take a tour and taste the rocket fuel at the only distillery making single-malt whisky in Canada. Stay for an excellent meal at the gourmet pub (there are daily lunchtime and dinner ceilidhs) or even for the night. Cave-like rooms ($125 to $150) are perfect for sleeping it off if you've been drinking the local beverage; the chalets ($175 to $240) are a better choice if you want brighter surroundings.

Inverness County Centre
for the Arts
CULTURAL CENTER

(☑902-258-2533; www.invernessarts.ca; 16080 Hwy 19, Inverness; ⊙10am-5pm) Inverness County Centre for the Arts is a beautiful establishment with several galleries and an upmarket gift shop featuring works by local and regional artists. It's also a music venue, with a floor built for dancing, of course.

Celtic Music Interpretive Centre
MUSEUM

(☑902-787-2708; www.celticmusiccentre.com; 5473 Hwy 19, Judique; exhibit room $8; ⊙10am-5pm Mon-Fri Jun-Aug) Offers a great introduction to local culture. Half-hour **tours** (which can be self-guided if you arrive when no guides are available) may include a fiddle lesson and a dance step or two. The location and times of local square dances are advertised around the admissions desk and ceilidhs are also held at the center; inquire for details.

Inverness Miners' Museum
MUSEUM

(☑902-258-3822; 62 Lower Railway St, Inverness; by donation; ⊙9am-5pm Mon-Fri, noon-5pm Sat & Sun Jun-Oct) In the old train station just back from the beach, the Inverness Miners' Museum presents local history.

🏃 Activities

Cape Mabou Highlands
HIKING

Within the Cape Mabou Highlands, an extensive network of hiking trails extends between Mabou and Inverness toward the coast west of Hwy 19. The trails are sometimes closed when the fire danger is high; otherwise, hikes ranging from 4km to 12km start from three different trailheads. An excellent trail guide ($5) is available at the grocery store across the road from Mabou's Mull Café & Deli when the trails are open. Maps are also posted at the trailheads.

🛏 Sleeping & Eating

MacLeods Inn
INN $$

(☑902-253-3360; www.macleods.com; 30 Broad Cove Marsh Rd, Inverness; r $160-180; ⊙Jun-Oct; P⊜🐾) MacLeods Inn is a high-end B&B about 5km north of Inverness. The house

is big and modern, but the decoration is in keeping with Cape Breton heritage.

Duncreigan Country Inn
INN $$

(☑902-945-2207; www.duncreigan.ca; 11411 Hwy 19, Mabou; r $145-220; 🐾) Nestled in oak trees on the banks of the river, this inn has private, spacious rooms, some with terraces and water views. Bikes are available to guests and there's a licensed **dining room** that serves breakfast to guests or dinner by reservation (mains $10 to $23).

Clayton Farm B&B
B&B $$

(☑902-945-2719; 11247 Hwy 19, Mabou; s/d $80/105; ⊙May-Nov; @🐾) This 1835 farmhouse sits on a working Red Angus ranch and is run by hardworking Isaac Smith. Paraphernalia of old Cape Breton life and of Isaac's family are casually scattered throughout the common areas and comfortable guest rooms. It's rustically perfect.

★Cabot Links
RESORT $$$

(☑855-652-2268; www.cabotlinks.com; 15933 Central Ave, Inverness; r $295-435, villas from $975; ⊙May-Oct; P⊜❋🐾) Even if you don't play golf, you might want to consider this slick resort for a night or two of guaranteed luxury. Accommodations range from stylish hotel rooms in the main lodge to private villas overlooking the greens to truly indulgent (and expensive) multi-room residences. Expect to rub shoulders with a gentrified crowd.

★Red Shoe Pub
PUB FOOD $$

(☑902-945-2996; www.redshoepub.com; 11533 Hwy 19, Mabou; mains $13-25; ⊙noon-11pm Sun-Wed, to 2am Thu-Sat) Straddling the spine of the Ceilidh Trail, this pub is the beating heart of Mabou. Listen to a local fiddle player (often from the Rankin family) while enjoying a pint and a superb meal. The desserts, including the gingerbread with rum-butterscotch sauce and fruit compote, are divine.

🛍 Shopping

Bear Paw
BOOKS

(☑902-258-2528; 15788 Central Ave, Inverness; ⊙9am-5pm Mon-Fri) This little book shop sells the works of local Canadian novelist Alistair MacLeod (1936–2014).

ℹ Information

Visitor Information Centre (VIC; ☑902-625-4201; 96 Hwy 4, Port Hastings; ⊙9am-8pm) This big and busy visitor info center is on your right as you drive onto Cape Breton Island.

It's definitely worth a stop; there are few other information centers on the island, especially outside of July and August, and the staff are very well informed.

Cabot Trail

Driving the Cabot Trail is Nova Scotia's most famous recreational activity, taking you along winding roads, by serene lakes, beneath soaring eagles and on to cliff-top vistas that are sure to make your jaw drop.

Along the way, artists' workshops dot the southeastern flank of the trail like Easter eggs, from Englishtown to St Ann's Bay. Seize this treasure: drop in to a studio or two to meet an interesting mishmash of characters. You'll find pottery, leather, glass and pewter workers, painters and sculptors, and discover living remnants of Mi'kmaw and Acadian culture.

The most breathtaking scenery is found on the island's northwestern shore as the trail slopes down to Pleasant Bay and Chéticamp. Keep your eyes on the circuitous road, as tempting as the views become: there are plenty of places to stop, look and hike through a tapestry of terrain for boundless vistas over the endless, icy ocean.

Accommodations around the 298km trail are limited. If you intend to drive the trail in one or two days, plan to base yourself at Baddeck or Ingonish on its eastern flank, or Chéticamp or Pleasant Bay on its west. In the peak times of July and August, be sure to make bookings well in advance.

If you're looking for an ecofriendly stay, consider spending a night at **Chanterelle Country Inn & Cottages** (☑ 902-929-2263; www.chanterelleinn.com; 48678 Cabot Trail, North River; r from $145; ⊘ May-Nov; 🐾) 🍴 overlooking 60 hectares of rolling pastures and bucolic bliss, about 35km north of Baddeck. Meals (a separate cost) are served on the screened-in porch of the main inn.

Predictably, dining options on the trail are limited and seafood is king. If you have dietary restrictions or an aversion to crustaceans, it's pertinent to research your options in advance. Settle on some accommodations and then inquire with your innkeeper about what will be best for you. Locals are generally super-friendly and more than happy to help.

At **Dancing Goat** (☑ 902-248-2727; www.facebook.com/DancingGoatCafe; 6289 Cabot Trail, Margaree Valley; items $5-13; ⊘ 8am-5pm Sat-Thu, to 8pm Fri; 🐾) everything is homemade, most ingredients are local, and hearty breakfasts are as good as you'll get on Cape Breton. Big sandwiches and salads can be eaten in or taken away for hiking. It's also one of the few establishments open year-round.

Chéticamp

Chéticamp is not only the western gateway to Cape Breton Highlands National Park, it's more importantly Nova Scotia's most vibrant and thriving Acadian community, owing much of its cultural preservation to its geographical isolation – the road didn't make it this far until 1949. Upon entering the town from either direction you'll immediately feel like you've arrived in a little French village, although the landscape is decidedly reminiscent of the rugged Scottish highlands.

In the warmer months, there's always something going on, with plenty of opportunities to observe and experience Acadian culture, from interesting museums to sampling folk crafts (Chéticamp is famed for its hooked rugs) and toe-tapping live-music performances.

⊙ Sights

Le Centre de la Mi-Carême   MUSEUM
(☑ 902-224-1016; www.micareme.ca; 51 Old Cabot Trail Rd, Grand Étang; adult/child $5/4; ⊘ 10am-4pm Jun-Oct) Mi-Carême, celebrated in the middle of Lent, is Chéticamp's answer to Mardi Gras. Locals wear masks and disguises and visit houses, trying to get people to guess who they are. This museum covers the history of the celebration and displays traditional masks.

Les Trois Pignons   MUSEUM
(☑ 902-224-2642; www.lestroispignons.com; 15584 Cabot Trail; adult/child $5/4; ⊘ 9am-4pm May-Oct) This excellent museum explains how rug hooking went from being a home-based activity to an international business. Artifacts, including hooked rugs, illustrate early life and artisanship in Chéticamp. Almost everything here – from bottles to rugs – was collected by one eccentric local resident.

Église St Pierre   CHURCH
(St Peter's Church; ☑ 902-224-2064; 5 Aucoin Rd) The unique and photogenic 1893 Église St Pierre dominates the town with its silver spire and colorful frescoes.

☞ Tours

Love Boat Whale Cruises   WHALE WATCHING
(☑902-224-2899; www.loveboatwhalecruises.ca;
Quai Mathieu; tours from $40; ☺Jun-Oct) Friendly captains and regular sailings make this operator of whale-watching tours one of the better choices in Chéticamp. A minimum of six passengers is required for a sailing. Tours last from 2½ to three hours, and though there are no guarantees that whales will be sighted, guest reports are good.

🛏 Sleeping

Albert's Motel   MOTEL $
(☑902-224-2077; 15086 Cabot Trail; d $79-129;
☺May-Oct; P☺☺) This quaint motel has four cozy rooms with delightful patchwork quilts, mini-fridges, microwaves and large TVs, plus a communal deck overlooking the harbor. The place is spotlessly clean and the hosts are as friendly as they come.

★Maison Fiset House   B&B $$
(☑902-224-1794; www.maisonfisethouse.com;
15050 Cabot Trail; d/ste $169/219; P☺☺) A little luxury in Chéticamp is found in this grand old 1895 home. If you're in a suite, lounge in your Jacuzzi tub and enjoy the ocean views. Most importantly, experience the fully fledged Acadian hospitality from your host. Inquire about the rental units at the rear of the property. Open year-round.

Cornerstone Motel   MOTEL $$
(☑902-224-3232; www.cornerstonemotel.com;
16537 Cabot Trail; d $99-169; ☺May-Oct; P☺☺) The local 1950s motels always look fabulous with a coat of paint and a few updates. This one, at the very edge of Cape Breton Highlands National Park, 7km from town, fits that bill. All the standard features are here, with comfy bedding and hot showers, a fire pit, and a lovely outlook, perfect for that real road-trip vibe. Bikers welcome.

🍴 Eating

La Boulangerie Aucoin   BAKERY $
(☑902-224-3220; www.aucoinbakery.com; 14 La-pointe Rd; items $3.50-9; ☺7am-5pm Mon-Sat;
☺☺) This is the place to go for fresh-baked French- and American-style loaves, pastries, cakes, pies and ready-made sandwiches perfect for that picnic on the Cabot Trail. Family-owned and operated since 1959.

Harbour Restaurant   CANADIAN $$
(☑902-224-1144; www.baywindsuites.com; 15299 Cabot Trail; mains $14-30) At the Harbour Restaurant, local harbor-front dining at its best includes a range of Canadian and Acadian meals, not limited to oceanic treats. That said, the mushroom-topped scallops and Acadian *morue en cabane* (slow-cooked cod with pork and chives) are a great combination to share if you're dining with a companion.

All Aboard   CANADIAN $$
(☑902-224-2288; www.facebook.com/AllAboard
Restaurant; 14925 Cabot Trail; mains $10-24; ☺noon-9pm Wed-Mon; 🚼) This family-friendly restaurant serving seafood (including lobster, haddock and local salmon), steaks, burgers, pasta and salad is fast becoming an area favorite. Delicious and great value.

🍷 Drinking & Nightlife

Doryman Pub & Grill   PUB
(☑902-224-9909; www.doryman.ca; 15528 Cabot Trail) This is the joint to swing by for live fiddler and piano sessions every Saturday (2pm to 6pm). Live entertainment most weeknights.

ℹ Information

Tourist Information Centre (☑902-224-2642;
www.lestroispignons.com/visitor-information;
15584 Cabot Trail; ☺8:30am-5pm May-Oct)
Housed in the same building as Le Trois Pignons cultural center.

Cape Breton Highlands National Park

The **Cape Breton Highlands National Park**
(☑902-224-2306; www.pc.gc.ca; adult/child/
vehicle & passengers $8/4/20) offers visitors some of Eastern Canada's most dramatic scenery. It's accessible via the famous Cabot Trail, one-third of which runs through the park. Here you'll find expanses of woodland, tundra and bog, and startling sea views. Established in 1936 and encompassing 20% of Cape Breton's landmass, it's the fancy feather in Nova Scotia's island cap.

There are two park entrances, one at Chéticamp and one at Ingonish Beach; purchase an entry permit at either. A one-day pass is good until noon the next day. Wheelchair-accessible trails are indicated on the free map available at either entrance.

THE ACADIANS

When the French first settled the area around the Minas Basin, they called the region Arcadia, a Greek and Roman term for 'pastoral paradise.' This became Acadia and, by the 18th century, the Acadians felt more connection with the land here than with the distant Loire Valley they'd come from.

To the English, however, they would always be French, with whom rivalry and suspicion was constant. Considering it an affront to their Catholic faith, the Acadians refused to take an oath of allegiance to the English king after the Treaty of Utrecht granted Nova Scotia to the British. When hard-line lieutenant governor Charles Lawrence was appointed in 1754, he became fed up with the Acadians and ordered their deportation. The English burned many villages and forced some 14,000 Acadians onto ships.

Many Acadians headed for Louisiana and New Orleans; others went to various Maritime points, New England, Martinique in the Caribbean, Santo Domingo in the Dominican Republic, or back to Europe. Some hid out and remained in Acadia. In later years many of the deported people returned but found their lands occupied. In Nova Scotia, Acadians resettled the Chéticamp area on Cape Breton Island and the French Shore north of Yarmouth.

🏃 Activities

Hiking

Two trails on the west coast of the park have spectacular ocean views. **Fishing Cove Trail** gently descends 330m over 8km to the mouth of rugged Fishing Cove River. You can opt for a steeper and shorter hike of 2.8km from a second trailhead about 5km north of the first. Double the distances if you plan to return the same day. Otherwise, you must preregister for one of eight backcountry sites ($10) at the Chéticamp Information Centre. Reviews of trails in and near the park are available at www.cabottrail.com.

Most other trails are shorter and close to the road, many leading to ridge tops for impressive views of the coast. The best of these is the **Skyline Trail**, a 7km loop that puts you on the edge of a headland cliff right above the water. The trailhead is about 5.5km north of Corney Brook Campground.

Just south of Neil's Harbour, on the eastern coast of the park, the **Coastal Trail** runs 11km round-trip and traverses more gentle coastline.

Cycling

Don't make this your inaugural trip: the riding is tough, there are no shoulders in many sections and you must be comfortable sharing the incredible scenery with RVs. Alternatively, you can mountain bike on four inland trails in the park; only Branch Pond Lookoff Trail offers ocean views.

Sea Spray Outdoor Adventures CYCLING (☑ 902-383-2552; www.cabot-trail-outdoors.com; 299 Shore Rd, Dingwall; bicycle rental per day/week from $45/160; ☺ 9am-5pm Jun-Oct) In Smelt Brook near Dingwall, this outfitter rents bikes and does emergency repairs. It also offers help planning trips and leads organized cycling, kayaking and hiking tours.

🛏 Sleeping

Cape Breton Highlands National Park Campgrounds CAMPGROUND (tent sites/RV sites/oTENTiks from $18/30/100) Cape Breton Highlands National Park has six drive-in campgrounds. Most sites are first-come, first-served, but wheelchair-accessible sites, group campsites and backcountry sites can be reserved for $9.80. In the smaller campgrounds further from the park entrances, just pick a site and self-register. To camp at any of the three larger ones near the park entrances, register at an information center.

Chéticamp and Broad Cove campgrounds now have ready-made tent sites (oTENTiks), which are wildly popular.

From late October to early May, you can camp at the Chéticamp and Ingonish Campgrounds for $22, including firewood. In truly inclement weather, tenters can take refuge in cooking shelters with wood stoves.

ℹ Information

Chéticamp Information Centre (☑ 902-224-2306; www.parkscanada.gc.ca; 16646 Cabot Trail; ☺ 8:30am-7pm) Has displays and a relief map of the park, plus a bookstore. Ask the staff for advice on hiking or camping.

Ingonish Beach Information Centre (☑ 902-285-2535; 37677 Cabot Trail; ☺ 8am-8pm May-Oct) On the eastern edge of the park, with displays, maps and friendly bilingual staff.

Pleasant Bay

A perfect base for exploring the Cape Breton Highlands National Park, Pleasant Bay is a carved-out bit of civilization hemmed in on all sides by wilderness. It's also an active fishing harbor known for its whale-watching tours and for its Tibetan monastery.

⊙ Sights & Activities

Gampo Abbey   MONASTERY
(☎ 902-224-2752; www.gampoabbey.org; 1533 Pleasant Bay Rd; ⊙ tours 1:30-3:30pm Mon-Fri Jun-Sep) This abbey, 8km north of Pleasant Bay past the village of Red River, is a monastery for followers of Tibetan Buddhism. Ane Pema Chödrön is the founding director of the abbey and a noted Buddhist author, but you aren't likely to see her here as she is often on the road. You can visit the grounds any time during the day, but you'll get a more authentic experience with an escorted tour.

Whale Interpretive Centre   MUSEUM
(☎ 902-224-1411; 104 Harbour Rd; adult/child $5/4; ⊙ 9am-5pm Jun-Oct) Stop here before taking a whale-watching tour from the adjacent wharf. Park entrance permits are for sale, and internet access is available downstairs.

**Captain Mark's Whale &
Seal Cruise**   WHALE WATCHING
(☎ 902-224-1316; www.whaleandsealcruise.com; adult/child $55/35; ⊙ May-Sep) Depending on the season, two to five tours depart, either in the lower-priced *Double Hookup* motorboat (adult/child $45/20) or closer to the action in a Zodiac. Captain Mark promises not only guaranteed whale sightings, but also time to see seabirds and seals, as well as Gampo Abbey. Tours leave from the wharf next to the Whale Interpretive Centre.

Pollett's Cove   HIKING
The popular, challenging, 20km round-trip hiking trail to Pollett's Cove begins at the end of the road to Gampo Abbey. There are great views along the way and perfect spots to camp when you arrive at the abandoned fishing community. This is not a Parks Canada trail, so it can be rough underfoot.

🛏 Sleeping

HI-Cabot Trail Hostel   HOSTEL $
(☎ 902-224-1976; www.cabottrailhostel.com; 23349 Cabot Trail; dm/r $28/68; @ 🖥) Bright and basic, this very friendly 18-bed hostel has a common kitchen and barbecue area.

Ingonish

At the eastern entrance to Cape Breton Highlands National Park are Ingonish and Ingonish Beach (along with Ingonish Ferry, Ingonish Harbour and Ingonish Centre), small towns lost in the background of motels and cottages. This is a long-standing and popular tourist destination, but there are few real attractions. There are several hiking trails and an information center nearby in the national park.

⊙ Sights & Activities

Ingonish Beach   BEACH
This long, wide strip of sand is tucked in a bay surrounded by green hills.

Highlands Links Golf Course   GOLF
(☎ 902-285-2600; 275 Keltic Inn Rd; green fees from $60; ⊙ 6am-6pm May-Oct) Avid golfers in the know report that this 18-hole, par-72 course, designed by world-renowned Stanley Thompson, is one of the most beautiful and challenging in Canada.

🛏 Sleeping & Eating

Driftwood Lodge   INN $
(☎ 902-285-2558; www.driftwoodlodge.ca; 36125 Cabot Trail, North Ingonish; d/ste from $55/80; ⊙ May-Nov; 🅿 🖥 🐾) Located 8km north of the Ingonish park entrance, this funky cabin-meets-hotel establishment is a steal. The owner works at the national park and is a mine of info about hiking and activities. There's a fine-sand beach just below the lodge.

Maven Gypsy B&B & Cottages   B&B $$
(☎ 902-929-2246; www.themavengypsy.com; 41682 Cabot Trail, Wreck Cove; r $105-135; ⊙ Jun-Nov; 🖥 🐾) With fresh-baked goods for breakfast and friendly hosts, this adorable butter-yellow cottage is only three minutes' walk to the beach.

★**Keltic Lodge at the Highlands** LODGE $$$
(☎ 902-285-2880; www.kelticlodge.ca; Ingonish Beach; r $155-285, cottages $329-589; ⊙ May-Oct; 🖥 🏊 🐾) Extensively renovated in 2016, the finest digs in the area are scattered around this clifftop Tudor-style resort erected in 1940, sharing Middle Head Peninsula with its eponymous golf course. A range of room types, from guestrooms to apartments to gorgeous rustic cottages, are available; check the website for details. The day-spa and pool are like no other in Nova Scotia.

Clucking Hen Deli & Bakery CAFE **$**
(✆902-929-2501; 45073 Cabot Trail; mains $7-18; ☷7am-7pm May-Oct) Listen to the locals cluck away while you eat a delicious meal of home-made breads, soup and salad.

★**Main Street Restaurant & Bakery** CANADIAN **$$**
(✆902-285-2225; www.mainstreetrestaurantandbakery.ca; 37764 Cabot Trail, Ingonish Beach; mains $10-24; ☷7am-9pm Tue-Sat) By far the best breakfast stop near Cape Breton Highlands National Park and also a great stop for lunch and dinner. Sandwiches and French toast are made with thick, fresh bread, and the seafood plates are immense. Try the lobster angel-hair pasta with crab and mussels in a brandy cream sauce: you won't be disappointed.

The Far North

North of Ingonish, the first village outside Cape Breton Highlands National Park is **Neil's Harbour**, the nicest of the area's remote outposts. Continue on via New Haven Road to come to **White Point**. Both are simple, hard-working communities where fishing boats outnumber houses. If neither village floats your boat, follow twisty, wind-swept White Point Rd to get back onto the Cabot Trail.

If you're determined to get to the top of Nova Scotia, follow Bay St Lawrence Rd to take a look at the pretty, eponymous settlement. From here on, the road gets rougher and the scenery gets wilder. The last 7km of the 13km stretch of hectic, slow-going road between **Bay St Lawrence** and the unfortunately named **Meat Cove** is gravel. If you're not an avid camper/hiker, Meat Cove might not be your cup of tea.

◉ Sights & Activities

Cabots Landing Provincial Park STATE PARK
(✆902-662-3030; http://parks.novascotia.ca) Stop in this wonderful provincial park, 10km north of the Cabot Trail en route to Bay St Lawrence, to enjoy Aspy Bay and its spectacular beach.

Grassy Point HIKING
You can't beat the views over the coast from Grassy Point, accessible via a small foot trail (about 40 minutes round-trip) that starts just past the Meat Cove Campground. Sit for a while at the point to look for whales and nesting bald eagles.

Cape St Lawrence Lighthouse HIKING
From Meat Cove, a 16km hiking trail heads west to Cape St Lawrence lighthouse and **Lowland Cove**. Spend an hour gazing over the ocean and you're guaranteed to see pods of pilot whales. They frolic here all spring and summer and into the fall. Carry a compass and refrain from exploring side paths; locals have gotten lost in this area.

Captain Cox's Whale Watch WHALE WATCHING
(✆902-383-2981; www.whalewatching-novascotia.com; 578 Meat Cove Rd, St Margaret Village; adult/child $45/25) Captain Cox has been taking people to see whales aboard the 35ft *Northern Gannet* since 1986. He offers trips at 10:30am, 1:30pm and 4:30pm in July and August. Call for spring and fall schedules.

🛏 Sleeping & Eating

★**Jumping Mouse Campground** CAMPGROUND **$**
(✆902-383-2914; www.ecocamping.ca; 3360 Bay St Lawrence Rd, Bay St Lawrence; tent sites/cabin $30/60; ☷Jun-Sep) This ecofriendly campground is the best reason to get off the Cabot Trail, with 10 magical oceanfront sites and a beautifully built four-bunk cabin. There are hot showers, pit toilets, a cooking shelter and frequent whale sightings, and the whole place is nearly bug-free.

Two Tittle B&B **$**
(✆902-383-2817; www.twotittle.com; 2119 White Point Rd, White Point; r $60-100; 🅿🛜) Stay the night at homey Two Tittle, which smells like supper. Don't miss the short but gorgeous walk out back to the Two Tittle Islands the B&B is named for – and look out for whales and eagles.

Hine's Ocean View Lodge LODGE **$**
(✆902-383-2512; www.hinesoceanviewlodge.ca; Meat Cove; r $60, whole house $200; 🛜🍽) This isolated spot, high up its own road (signposted off Meat Cove Rd), has plain, almost-dormitory style rooms and a shared kitchen. The views are truly breathtaking, but it's not for those who don't like the feeling of being isolated. Cash only.

Meat Cove Campground CAMPGROUND **$**
(✆902-383-2379; www.meatcovecampground.ca; 2475 Meat Cove Rd, Capstick; tent sites/cabins from $30/60; ☷Jun-Nov; 🛜) This remote campground is in an undoubtedly spectacular spot, perched on a grassy bluff high above the ocean in the middle of nowhere. Four cabins with no electricity or plumbing share

the view; bring your own bedding. Note: there are no protective railings and campers have fallen to their death here. Not great for kids. Be prepared for high winds.

Chowder House SEAFOOD $$
(☑902-336-2463; 90 Lighthouse Rd, Neil's Harbour; chowder $7-12, mains $14-24; ☺11am-8pm May-Oct) This establishment, out beyond the lighthouse at Neil's Harbour, is the perfect stop for lunch or dinner. It's famous for its chowder, but also serves great-value suppers of snow crab, lobster, mussels and more. There are plenty of dining locals, who like to chat with folks from far away while they splatter themselves with seafood juice.

ℹ️ Information

Meat Cove Welcome Center (☑902-383-2284; 2296 Meat Cove Rd, Meat Cove; ☺8am-8:30pm Jul-Sep; 🛜) Stop by to get excellent info on hiking trails, check email, and grab a bite to eat (from sandwiches to lobster suppers). Leave your car here if there's no room at the trailhead.

Baddeck

The highlands meet the lowlands in Baddeck, an aging resort town in a pastoral setting on the northern shore of Bras d'Or Lake – a veritable inland saltwater sea, where eagles nest and puffins play. At 1099 sq km, the lake is the biggest in Nova Scotia and all but cleaves Cape Breton Island in two. Just south of Baddeck, **Wagmatcook First Nation** (www.wagmatcook.com) is composed of two Mi'kmaq communities.

◉ Sights

★ Alexander Graham Bell National Historic Site MUSEUM
(☑902-295-2069; www.pc.gc.ca; 559 Chebucto St; adult/child $8/4; ☺9am-6pm May-Oct) The inventor of the telephone is buried near his summer home, **Beinn Bhreagh**, which is visible across the bay from Baddeck. The excellent museum of the Alexander Graham Bell National Historic Site, at the eastern edge of town, covers all aspects of his inventions and innovations. Although nothing looks spectacular at first glance, it's the story of the man that will hook you. See medical and electrical devices, telegraphs, telephones, kites and seaplanes, and then learn how they all work.

Great Hall of the Clans Museum MUSEUM
(☑902-295-3411; www.gaeliccollege.edu/great-hall-of-the-clans; 51779 Cabot Trail, Englishtown; adult/child $8/6; ☺9am-5pm Mon-Fri Jun-Oct) This museum at the Gaelic College of Celtic Arts & Crafts, about 20km north of Baddeck, traces Celtic history from ancient times to the Highland clearances.

Wagmatcook Culture & Heritage Centre MUSEUM
(☑902-295-2999; www.wagmatcookcentre.com; Hwy 105, Wagmatcook; ☺9am-8pm May-Oct, reduced hours Nov-Apr) Stop in the Mi'kmaw community of Wagmatcook just west of Baddeck to visit the Wagmatcook Culture & Heritage Centre. This somewhat empty cultural attraction offers an entryway into Mi'kmaw culture and history.

☞ Tours

Amoeba CRUISE
(☑902-295-7780; www.amoebasailingtours.com; 2hr tours adult/child $25/10; ☺Jun-Oct) Classic schooner sailing tours on the Bras d'Or Lake bring you past Alexander Graham Bell's grand Beinn Bhreagh mansion and under soaring bald eagles.

🛏️ Sleeping

Bear on the Lake Guesthouse HOSTEL $
(☑866-718-5253; www.bearonthelake.com; 10705 Hwy 105, Aberdeen; dm/r $32/78; P😊🛜) Bear on the Lake Guesthouse, between Wagmatcook and the next town of Whycocomagh, is a fun place overlooking the lake. Dorm and private rooms are available, plus there's inviting communal areas and a large sunny deck. Backpackers should note that, without a vehicle, the location is quite isolated, with no facilities or transport nearby.

★ Silver Dart Lodge LODGE $$
(☑902-295-2340; www.maritimeinns.com; 257 Shore Road; r/chalet from $150/180; P😊❄️🛜🏊) The Silver Dart boasts recently and thoroughly renovated rooms, ranging from quaint chalets with kitchenettes at the rear of the property to motel-style units. McCurdy's Dining Room, the on-site bar-restaurant, has good food and lovely views. There's even a decent-sized pool for those hot summer days.

Dunlop Inn B&B $$
(☑902-295-1100; www.dunlopinn.com; 552 Chebucto St; d $120-170; P❄️🛜) This quaint, historic B&B offers an unrivaled position

with immediate water-frontage on Bras d'Or Lake. Subsequently, water views abound. Its five self-contained rooms are tastefully decorated, and the self-service breakfast kitchen is fresh from renovation.

Lynwood Inn INN $$
(902-295-1995; www.lynwoodinn.com; 441 Shore Rd; d from $100;) Rooms in this enormous inn go far beyond the hotel standard, with Victorian wooden beds, muted color schemes and airy living spaces. There's a family-style restaurant downstairs that serves breakfast, lunch and dinner; breakfast is not included in room rates.

Broadwater Inn & Cottages INN $$
(902-295-1101; www.broadwaterinn.com; 975 Bay Rd; r $129-159, cottages $149-289; May-Nov;) In a tranquil spot 2km northeast of Baddeck, this c 1830 home once belonged to JAD McCurdy, who worked with Alexander Graham Bell on early aircraft designs. The rooms in the inn are full of character, have bay views and are decorated with subtle prints and lots of flair. Modern cottages are set in the woods and are great for families.

Eating & Drinking

Herring Choker Deli DELI $
(902-295-2275; www.herringchokerdeli.com; 1958 Hwy 105; items $6-15; 9am-6pm May-Oct;) On Hwy 105, 12km southwest of Baddeck, this deli is one of the region's best pit stops for gourmet sandwiches, soups and salads.

High Wheeler Cafe CAFE $
(902-295-3006; 486 Chebucto St; sandwiches $9; 6am-8pm May-Oct;) This place bakes great bread and goodies (some gluten-free) and makes big, tasty sandwiches, quesadillas, soups and more. Finish off on the sunny deck licking an ice-cream cone. Box lunches for hikers also available.

★Baddeck Lobster Suppers SEAFOOD $$$
(902-925-3307; www.baddecklobstersuppers.ca; 17 Ross St; mains $22-28; 4-9pm Jun-Oct) In the former legion hall, this institution offers your choice of lobster, salmon, snow crab or strip-loin with all-you-can-eat mussels, chowder and dessert for $38. Feast on delicacies without the fuss of fancy fine-dining.

Big Spruce Brewing MICROBREWERY
(902-295-2537; www.bigspruce.ca; 64 Yankee Line Rd, Nyanza; noon-7pm) Pop into this farmyard brewery, about 14km southwest of Baddeck, to grab yourself a growler of unfiltered, unpasteurized, 'unbelievably good,' locally brewed beer.

☆ Entertainment

Baddeck Gathering Ceilidhs LIVE MUSIC
(902-295-0971; www.baddeckgathering.com; 8 Old Margaree Rd, St Michael's Parish Hall; adult/child from $10/5; 7:30pm Jul & Aug) Nightly fiddling and dancing. The parish hall is just opposite the tourist information center in the middle of town.

ⓘ Information

Visit Baddeck (www.visitbaddeck.com) Has maps, plus info on tour operators, golf courses and more.

Tourist Information Centre (902-295-1911; 454 Chebucto St; 10am-4pm Jun-Oct)

ⓘ Getting There & Away

Baddeck is located on the Trans-Canada Hwy (Hwy 105), 78km southwest of Sydney.

Maritime Bus (www.maritimebus.com) has one or two services daily to Sydney ($21, 1½ hours) and Halifax ($64, 5½ hours).

North Sydney

North Sydney is a small and friendly industrial town, although there's not much to see or do here. The main reason you'll be passing through is if you're heading to the Cabot Trail from Sydney, or heading to or from Newfoundland on the ferry.

🛏 Sleeping & Eating

A Boat to Sea B&B $$
(902-794-8326; www.aboattosea.com; 61 Queen St; r $100-110;) Right on the waterfront and surrounded by beautiful gardens (look for bald eagles), this grand home is decorated with stained glass and a quirky antiques collection. Relax on the waterfront patio and enjoy hearty breakfasts. There are only three rooms, so book ahead in high season, when there's a two-night minimum stay.

Heritage Home B&B B&B $$
(902-794-4815; www.bedandbreakfastnorthsydney.com; 110 Queen St; r $110-120;) This exceptionally well decorated and maintained Victorian home is an extremely elegant place to stay for the price. Breakfasts are home-cooked and most rooms have private bathrooms.

Bette's Kitchen
SEAFOOD **$**

(📞902-794-4452; 138 Queen St; mains $9-18; ⊙noon-8pm) This is *the* place on Cape Breton Island for a good ole-fashioned fry-up. Fried scallops, tender battered fish and golden, crunchy fries... It's *all* good, but perhaps not so good for you. Run with the adage: you only live once.

★ Black Spoon
MODERN CANADIAN **$$**

(📞902-241-3300; www.blackspoonbistro.com; 320 Commercial St; mains $12-19; ⊙11am-8pm Mon-Thu, to 9pm Fri & Sat) At this hip black-and-beige restaurant, dine on local faves with a delectable twist such as breaded haddock with mango salsa or the colorful grilled vegetable salad with goat's cheese. There's also espresso drinks, cocktails and a reasonable wine list.

Lobster Pound & Moore
SEAFOOD **$$$**

(📞902-794-2992; 161 Queen St; mains $24-38; ⊙noon-8pm Tue-Sun) With the standard lobster here weighing in at almost a kilo (2lb), show up hungry because portions are massive. But big quantity doesn't affect the freshness, high quality and all around deliciousness of the food. Try Korean grilled steaks, seafood stew, or the ravioli stuffed with fresh lobster and topped with even more. Decor is chic bistro meets seafood shack.

ⓘ Getting There & Away

North Sydney is 21km from Sydney, and 48km from the Cabot Trail at Indian Brook via the 24-hour vehicular Englishtown ferry ($7, five minutes).

The town is the boarding point for **Marine Atlantic ferry** (📞800-341-7981; www.marineatlantic.ca) services to Port-aux-Basques, NL (one-way adult/child $44/21, six to eight hours), and Argentia, NL (one-way adult/child $116/65, 16 hours). It costs an extra $114 to bring a standard-sized vehicle to Port-aux-Basques and an extra $203 to Argentia.

Sydney

📞902 / POP 31,600

The second-biggest city in Nova Scotia and the only real city on Cape Breton Island, Sydney is the embattled core of the island's collapsed industrial belt. The now-closed steel mill and coal mines were the region's largest employers and now the city feels a bit empty, but there are some lovely older houses, especially in the North End residential areas where most of the B&Bs are found. Overall, the city is well serviced and you get more bang for your buck staying here as a base to explore Louisbourg and the Cabot Trail than you would in more scenic areas.

◉ Sights

Downtown, Charlotte St is lined with stores and restaurants and there's a pleasant **boardwalk** along Esplanade.

The North End historic district has a gritty charm. There are eight buildings older than 1802 in a two-block radius in North End. Three are open to the public.

★ Cape Breton Miners' Museum
MUSEUM

(📞902-849-4522; www.minersmuseum.com; 42 Birkley St, Glace Bay; tour & mine visit adult/child $15/13; ⊙10am-6pm) Glace Bay, 6km northeast of Sydney, would be just another fading coal town were it not for this exceptional museum, the highlight of which is the 'Men of the Deeps' adventure under the seafloor to visit decommissioned mines with a retired miner as a guide – not for the claustrophobic. The museum's restaurant (11am to 8pm) is highly recommended, and offers seafood, sandwiches and burgers (mains $13 to $28); there's a daily lunch buffet from noon to 2pm.

Jost Heritage House
HISTORIC BUILDING

(📞902-539-0366; 54 Charlotte St; $3; ⊙9am-5pm Mon-Sat, 1-5:30pm Sun) Jost Heritage House features a collection of model ships and an assortment of medicines used by an early 20th-century apothecary.

Cape Breton Centre for Heritage & Science
MUSEUM

(📞902-539-1572; 225 George St; $2; ⊙9am-4pm Mon-Sat) This humble local history center explores the social and natural history of Cape Breton Island.

St Patrick's Church Museum
HISTORIC BUILDING

(📞902-562-8237; 87 Esplanade; $2; ⊙9am-5pm Mon-Sat Jun-Oct) Built in 1828 in the Pioneer Gothic style, St Patrick's Church is the oldest Catholic church on Cape Breton Island and now houses a museum recounting Sydney's religious past.

Cossit House
HISTORIC BUILDING

(📞902-539-7973; http://cossithouse.novascotia.ca; 75 Charlotte St; adult/concession $2/1; ⊙9am-5pm Mon-Sat, 1-5pm Sun Jun-Oct) Built in 1787, this is the oldest house in Sydney and one of the oldest surviving buildings in Nova Scotia.

🤚 Tours

Ghosts & Legends of
Historic Sydney   WALKING

(☑ 902-539-1572; www.oldsydney.com; tours $13;
⊙ 6:30pm Thu Jul & Aug) This walking tour, designed to scare the pants off you, leaves from
St Patrick's Church Museum, does a loop of
historic buildings and finishes with tea and
scones.

🛏 Sleeping & Eating

Sydney has some solid chain-hotel choices
and, unlike much of the rest of the island,
most properties here are open year-round.

⭐ Colby House   B&B $$

(☑ 902-539-4095; www.colbyhousebb.com; 10 Park
St; r $100-125; 🛜) It's worth staying in Sydney
for the affordable luxury of this exceptional
B&B. The owner used to travel around Canada for work and decided to offer everything
she wished she'd had on the road. The result
is a mix of heritage and modern design, the
softest sheets you can imagine, guest bath-
robes, and too many other comfort-giving
details to list.

Hampton Inn by Hilton   HOTEL $$

(☑ 855-605-0317; www.hilton.com; 60 Maillard St;
d $149-269; P ➛ ❄ 🛜 ☰) A little way from the
action of Sydney's waterfront area, this impressive tourist hotel is particularly popular
with families. Oversized, stylish and comfortable rooms exceed brand standards, and
the hotel staff are excellent.

Cambridge Suites Sydney   HOTEL $$

(☑ 902-562-6500;   www.cambridgesuitessydney.
com; 380 Esplanade; d $139-239; P ❄ 🛜) This
smart hotel in a hard-to-beat, downtown location has comfortable, nicely renovated rooms
in a variety of configurations, many with
water views. Rates include a decent serve-
yourself breakfast spread and free wi-fi.

Gathering House B&B   B&B $$

(☑ 902-539-7172; kmp38@msn.com; 148 Crescent
St; r $85-125; P ➛ ❄ 🛜 ☰) This welcoming,
ramshackle Victorian home is close to the
heart of town. Staying here makes you feel
like you're part of a big, lively family.

Governors Pub & Eatery   PUB FOOD $$

(☑ 902-562-7646; www.governorseatery.com; 233
Esplanade; mains $9-22; ⊙ 11am-11pm) Easily
the most popular place in Sydney. Stop in to
mingle with the after-work crowd for drinks,
dine on gourmet pub grub made with local
ingredients, and stay for live-music events

such as the Wednesday-night Irish jam sessions. Check the website for what's on.

Flavor on the Water   MODERN CANADIAN $$

(☑ 902-567-1043;   www.cbflavor.com/flavor;   60
Esplanade; mains $11-28; ⊙ 11am-8pm; 🖊) Syd-
ney's swankiest restaurant on the Esplanade
offers artfully presented dishes made from
local ingredients, from salads, sandwiches
and burgers for lunch to fish, chicken and
steak for dinner. The restaurant itself, with
its high ceilings and waterfront location, is
both stylish and impressive. Check the website to learn about its humble origins and
other local branches.

☆ Entertainment

Fiddlers and other traditional musicians
from the west coast of the island and a lot of
touring bands perform in the area.

Savoy Theatre   THEATER

(☑ 902-842-1577;   www.savoytheatre.com;   116
Commercial St, Glace Bay) Six kilometres from
Sydney, Glace Bay's grand 1920 Savoy Theatre is the region's premier entertainment
venue.

Casino Nova Scotia   CASINO

(☑ 902-563-7777;   www.sydney.casinonovascotia.
com; 525 George St; ⊙ 11am-3am) This popular
casino (there's not a great deal else to do in
town) has hundreds of slot machines, black-
jack and poker tables and live entertainment.

ⓘ Information

Sydney Port Tourist Information (☑ 902-539-
9876; 74 Esplanade; ⊙ 8:30am-6pm) Offers
maps and brochures on Sydney and Cape Breton.

ⓘ Getting There & Away

Sydney is 403km by road from Halifax. **Maritime
Bus** (www.maritimebus.com) travels from Sydney to Halifax ($72.50, seven hours) and Truro
($63.50, five hours) from where you can connect
to services bound for New Brunswick and Prince
Edward Island.

   If you're able to book in advance and they have
a driver available, **Bay Luxury Shuttle** (☑ 855-
673-8083; www.capebretonshuttle.ca) runs
from Glace Bay to Halifax (one-way from $65)
via North Sydney, Sydney and Hwy 105.

   Both Air Canada and Westjet offer direct services to Halifax and Toronto from Sydney's compact **JA Douglas McCurdy Airport** (p41),
which is 13km from downtown.

   Air St-Pierre (☑ 877-277-7765; www.airsaint-
pierre.com) offers less frequent, seasonal flights
to the French territory of St-Pierre and Miquelon.

Louisbourg

Louisbourg, 35km southeast of Sydney, is famous for its historic fortress. The town itself, with its working fishing docks, old-timers and friendly vibe, has plenty of soul.

◉ Sights

★ Louisbourg National Historic Site
HISTORIC SITE

(☑ 902-733-3552; www.fortressoflouisbourg.ca; 58 Wolfe St; adult/child $18/9; ⊙ 9:30am-5pm) You'll need at least a few hours to fully explore this extraordinary historic site that faithfully re-creates the Louisbourg Fortress as it was in 1744, right down to the people – costumed thespians take their characters and run with them. Free guided tours around the site are offered throughout the day. Travelers with mobility problems can ask for a pass to drive their car up to the site.

Built to protect French interests in the region, the fortress was also a base for cod fishing and an administrative capital. Louisbourg was worked on continually from 1719 to about 1745. The British took it in a 46-day siege in 1745, but it would change hands twice more. In 1760, after British troops under the command of General James Wolfe took Québec City, the walls of Louisbourg were destroyed and the city burned to the ground.

In 1961, with the closing of many Cape Breton Island coal mines, the federal government funded the largest historical reconstruction in Canadian history as a way to generate employment.

WORTH A TRIP

MEMORY LANE HERITAGE VILLAGE

A 20-minute drive from Tangier, this outstanding example of how a community can work together to preserve its history re-creates a 1940s Eastern Shore village (☑ 877-287-0697; www.heritagevillage.ca; 5435 Clam Harbour Rd, Lake Charlotte; ⊙ 11am-4pm Jun-Sep) in a series of lovingly relocated and restored buildings, chock full of hands-on antiques, as if frozen in time. You'll find vintage cars, a farmstead with animals (great for kids), a schoolhouse, a church, a miner's hut, a blacksmith, shipbuilding shops and so much more. A must for history buffs of any kind.

Though the scale of the reconstruction is massive, three-quarters of Louisbourg is still in ruins. The 2.5km **Ruins Walk** guides you through the untouched terrain. A short interpretive walk discusses the relationship between the French and the Mi'kmaq.

Louisbourg Lighthouse
LIGHTHOUSE

(555 Havenside Rd) Canada's first lighthouse was built on this wild, rugged and extremely scenic site in 1734. The present lighthouse was opened in 1923. You can't go in, but it's worth a visit to explore the site and the rugged 6km **trail** that follows the coast over bogs and Precambrian polished granite.

🛏 Sleeping & Eating

★ Cranberry Cove Inn
INN $$

(☑ 902-733-2171; www.cranberrycoveinn.com; 12 Wolfe St; r $105-160; ⊙ May-Nov; 🛜) From the dark-pink facade to the period-perfect interior, you'll be transported back in time through rose-colored glasses at this stunning B&B. Each room is different, and several have Jacuzzis and fireplaces.

Point of View Suites
INN $$

(☑ 888-374-8439; www.louisbourgpointofview.com; 15 Commercial St Extension; r $125-265; P 🐾 ❄ 🛜) If B&Bs aren't your thing, your best bet in town is this inn comprising a range of accommodation types, from motel-style rooms to self-contained apartments with full kitchens. Most have wonderful views over the harbor.

Grubstake
CANADIAN $$

(☑ 902-733-2308; www.grubstake.ca; 7499 Main St; mains lunch $8-18, dinner $16-35; ⊙ 11am-8pm) This informal restaurant is the best place to eat in town. The menu features burger platters at lunch and pastas and fresh seafood for dinner.

Beggar's Banquet
SEAFOOD $$$

(☑ 888-374-8439; www.louisbourgpointofview.com; 15 Commercial St Extension; meals $38; ⊙ 6-8pm Jul-Sep) Finally, here's a chance for you to get into period costume and gorge on a feast of local seafood in a replicated 18th-century tavern. There's a choice of four delicious and copious mains, including crab and lobster.

☆ Entertainment

Louisbourg Playhouse
THEATER

(☑ 902-733-2996; www.louisbourgplayhouse.ca; 11 Lower Warren St; tickets from $15; ⊙ 8pm-late Jun-Aug) A cast of young local musicians entertain in this 17th-century-style theater.

Information

Tourist Information Office (☑ 902-733-2720; 7495 Main St; ☺ 9am-7pm) Operated by the Destination Cape Breton Association; located in the center of town.

EASTERN SHORE

If you want to escape into the fog, away from summer crowds, this pristine region is the place to explore. Running from the outskirts of Dartmouth, across the harbor from Halifax, to Cape Canso at the extreme eastern tip of the mainland, the Eastern Shore has no large towns and the main road is almost as convoluted as the rugged shoreline it follows. For those seeking wildlife and barely touched wilderness, and opportunities to enjoy hiking, kayaking or fishing, this is your heaven.

Historically, villages in the region were linked only by boat, then by rail, which was later taken away. Spirited and resilient, these close-knit communities have maintained their traditions for decade upon decade.

◉ Sights & Activities

There are beautiful, long, white-sand beaches all along the Eastern Shore, although the water never gets very warm. The closest and busiest of the Eastern Shore beaches, 1km-long **Rainbow Haven** has washrooms, showers, a canteen and a boardwalk with wheelchair access to the beach. Lifeguards supervise a swimming area.

The most popular surf destination, cobblestone **Lawrencetown Beach** faces directly south and often gets big waves, compliments of hurricanes or tropical storms hundreds of kilometers away. It boasts a supervised swimming area, washrooms and a canteen. If you want to try surfing, but don't have a board or don't know what to do, **East Coast Surf School** (☑ 902-449-9488; www.ecsurfschool.com; 4348 Lawrencetown Rd, East Lawrencetown; lessons from $75) will get you vertical on the water.

The longest swimming beach in Nova Scotia and the prettiest in the area, with more than 3km of grass-backed white sand, is **Martinique Beach**. Even if you find the water too cold for a swim, it's a beautiful place to walk, watch birds or play Frisbee.

⊨ Sleeping & Eating

Liscombe Lodge Resort   RESORT $$
(☑ 902-779-2307; www.liscombelodge.ca; 2884 Nova Scotia Trunk 7, Marie Joseph; r $149-199, chalet

$175-285; ☺ May-Oct) A nature lover's dream, this rambling country lodge comprises 30 spacious, nicely decorated riverside rooms in the main lodge, a rustic three-bedroom Canadian-style cottage and 17 sweeter-than-sweet chalets with fireplaces and decks overlooking the woodsy grounds and river.

Dobbit Bakehouse   BAKERY $
(☑ 902-889-2919; 7896 Hwy 7, Musquodoboit Harbour; baked goods $2-6; ☺ 8am-5pm; ☎) Come chat with the friendly baker, a font of local knowledge, at this wonderful country bakery, which boasts rustic fresh breads and baked goods free from preservatives and using only seasonal local ingredients wherever possible. The selection changes daily. Free wi-fi.

Guysborough

Sleepy Guysborough was settled by United Empire Loyalists after the American Revolution. Despite such a long history, the town has become another particularly scenic yet economically challenged Eastern Shore community. Some degree of investment over recent years, however, has seen a flicker of renewed tourist appeal.

◉ Sights & Activities

The 26km **Guysborough Trail**, part of the Trans Canada Trail (TCT), is great for biking and hiking, and the region's sheltered coves and bays beg to be kayaked.

Old Court House Museum   MUSEUM
(☑ 902-533-4008; 106 Church St; ☺ 9am-5pm Mon-Fri, 10am-4pm Sat & Sun) **FREE** The Old Court House Museum displays artifacts related to early farming and housekeeping. It also offers tourist information and guides to hiking trails.

⊨ Sleeping & Eating

Boylston Provincial Park   CAMPGROUND $
(☑ 902-533-3326; www.parks.gov.ns.ca; off Hwy 16; campsites $18) The 36 shaded sites are never all taken. From the picnic area on the highway below the campground, a footbridge leads to a small island off the coast about 12km north of Guysborough.

Desbarres Manor   INN $$
(☑ 902-533-2099; www.desbarresmanor.com; 90 Church St; r $189-259; ☎) This tastefully renovated 1830 grand mansion with opulent rooms, some with water glimpses, is a good choice if you're spending a night in town.

DON'T MISS

TAYLOR HEAD PROVINCIAL PARK

A little-known scenic highlight of Nova Scotia, this spectacular **park** (☑ 902-772-2218; http://parks.novascotia.ca/content/taylor-head; 20140 Hwy 7, Spry Bay) encompasses a peninsula jutting 6.5km into the Atlantic. On one side is a long, very fine, sandy beach fronting a protected bay. Some 17km of hiking trails cut through the spruce and fir forests. The **Headland Trail** is the longest at 8km round-trip and follows the rugged coastline to scenic views at **Taylor Head**. The shorter **Bob Bluff Trail** is a 3km round-trip hike to a bluff with good views.

Rare Bird Pub PUB FOOD $$
(☑ 902-533-2128; www.rarebirdpub.com; 80 Main St; mains $12-18; ⊙ 11:30am-8pm May-Oct) The Bird is a logical stop for a swig of local ale, a pot of mussels, some East Coast music on the weekend, and occasional fiddlers on the wharf. Check the website for schedules.

Canso

One of North America's oldest seaports, Canso today stands as a lonely cluster of boxy fishers' homes on a treeless bank of Chedabucto Bay. Long dependent on the fishery, Canso has been decimated by emigration and unemployment since the northern cod stocks collapsed around 1990.

◉ Sights & Activities

Grassy Island National Historic Site HISTORIC SITE
(☑ 902-366-3136; www.pc.gc.ca; 1465 Union Street; suggested donation $3.50; ⊙ 10am-6pm Jun-Sep) An interpretive center on the waterfront tells the story of Grassy Island National Historic Site, which lies just offshore and can be visited by boat until 4pm. In 1720 the British built a small fort to offset the French, who had their headquarters in Louisbourg, but it was totally destroyed in 1744. Among the ruins today, there's a self-guided **hiking trail** with eight interpretive stops explaining the history of the area. The boat to Grassy Island departs from the center upon demand, weather permitting.

Whitman House Museum MUSEUM
(☑ 902-366-2170; 1297 Union St; ⊙ 9am-5pm Jun-Sep) **FREE** The 1885 Whitman House Museum holds reminders of the town's history and offers a wonderful view from the widow's walk on the roof. The museum also serves as Canso's unoffical tourist information office.

Chapel Gully Trail HIKING
This 10km boardwalk and hiking trail along an estuary and out to the coast begins near the lighthouse on the hill behind the hospital at the eastern end of Canso.

★ Festivals & Events

★ Stan Rogers Folk Festival MUSIC
(www.stanfest.com; ⊙ Jul) Most people who come to Canso come for the Stan Rogers Folk Festival, the biggest festival in Nova Scotia. It quadruples the town's population, with six stages showcasing folk, blues and traditional musicians from around the world.

⌂ Sleeping

Last Port Motel MOTEL $$
(☑ 902-366-2400; www.lastportmotel.ca; 10 Hwy 16; r $80-100; P ⚡) The only place to stay in Canso is this basic though spotlessly clean and super-friendly motel, just outside town.

Tangier

About 10km southwest of Taylor Head Provincial Park, Tangier is one of the best settings for **kayaking** in the Maritimes.

Highly recommended **Coastal Adventures Sea Kayaking** (☑ 902-772-2774; www.coastaladventures.com; off Hwy 7; tours from $75, single/double kayak rental from $50/70; ⊙ Jun-Sep) offers introductory sea-kayaking trips, extended guided tours and kayak rentals, and has cosy rooms if you choose to stick around.

Unless you're camping or hanging with your kayaking crew, the nearest accommodations are in Dartmouth. Be sure to bring your own food if you plan on spending any time paddling around the area's coves and bays. Services in the area are limited. **Murphy's Camping on the Ocean** (☑ 902-772-2700; www.murphyscamping.ca; 291 Murphy's Rd; tent/RV sites $27/39; ⊙ May-Oct; ⚡ ☀) gets you out of your tent and into the water to collect mussels; you eat your labors at a beach barbecue to the music of yarns told by Brian, the owner. There are RV sites, RV rentals, secluded tent sites and a very rudimentary room above the dock that can sleep four people.

New Brunswick

Best Places to Eat

➡ Rossmount Inn Restaurant (p115)

➡ Port City Royal (p125)

➡ Naru (p107)

➡ Inn at Whale Cove (p121)

➡ Manuka (p133)

Best Places to Sleep

➡ Quartermain House B&B (p106)

➡ Algonquin Resort (p115)

➡ Mahogany Manor (p124)

➡ Hotel Paulin (p140)

➡ Treadwell Inn (p115)

Why Go?

In the early 20th century, New Brunswick was a very big deal. Millionaire businesspeople, major-league baseball players and US presidents journeyed here to fish salmon from its silver rivers and camp at rustic lodges in its deep primeval forests. But over the decades, New Brunswick slipped back into relative obscurity. Today some joke that it's the 'drive-through province,' as vacationers tend to hotfoot it to its better-known neighbors Prince Edward Island (PEI) and Nova Scotia.

But the unspoiled wilderness is still here. There are rivers and coastal islands for kayaking, snowy mountains for skiing and quaint Acadian villages for exploring. So do yourself a favor, and don't just drive through. PEI will still be there when you're done, we promise.

When to Go
Fredericton

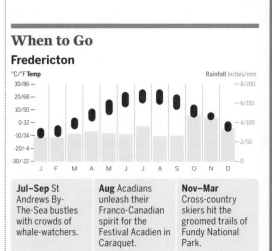

Jul–Sep St Andrews By-The-Sea bustles with crowds of whale-watchers.

Aug Acadians unleash their Franco-Canadian spirit for the Festival Acadien in Caraquet.

Nov–Mar Cross-country skiers hit the groomed trails of Fundy National Park.

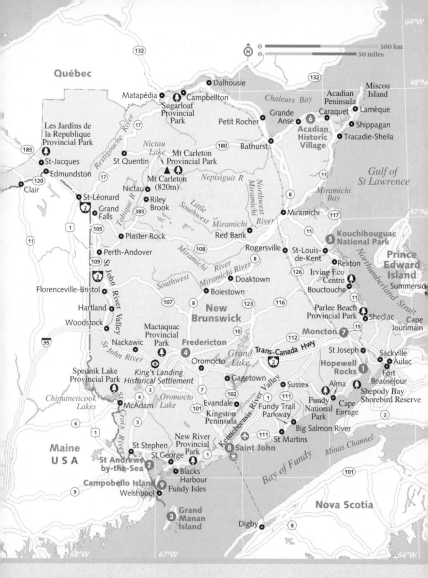

New Brunswick Highlights

1 **Hopewell Rocks** (p132) Feeling the power of the highest tides in the world.

2 **St Andrews By-The-Sea** (p114) Discovering this picturesque seaside town.

3 **Grand Manan Island** (p120) Breathing in the fresh sea air and unwinding on the peaceful, isolated island.

4 **Fredericton** (p103) Soaking up the past of a historic capital.

5 **Kouchibouguac National Park** (p136) Stretching out on the sandy beach or splashing in the lagoon.

6 **Acadian Historic Village** (p139) Living Acadian history at this reconstructed scene.

7 **Moncton** (p132) Tasting delicacies at the city's local markets.

8 **Saint John** (p122) Sipping on a local brew before hitting the hipster foodie scene.

9 **Campobello Island** (p119) Filling the shoes of Franklin D Roosevelt at his favorite holiday retreat.

History

What is now New Brunswick was originally the land of the Mi'kmaq and, in the western and southern areas, the Maliseet Aboriginals. Many places still bear their aboriginal names, although the Aboriginal people (who today number around 17,000) are now concentrated on small pockets of land.

Following in the wake of explorer Samuel de Champlain, French colonists arrived in the 1600s. The Acadians, as they came to be known, farmed the area around the Bay of Fundy. In 1755 they were expelled by the English, many returning to settle along the Bay of Chaleur. In the years following, the outbreak of the American Revolution brought an influx of British Loyalists from Boston and New York seeking refuge in the wilds of New Brunswick. These refugees settled the valleys of the Saint John and St Croix Rivers, established the city of Saint John and bolstered the garrison town at Fredericton.

Through the 1800s, lumbering and shipbuilding boomed, and by the start of the 20th century, other industries, including fishing, had developed. That era of prosperity ended with the Great Depression. Today, pulp and paper, oil refining and potato farming are the major industries.

Land & Climate

The province encompasses a varied geography of moist, rocky coastal areas, temperate inland river valleys and a heavily forested and mountainous interior. Summers are generally mild with occasional hot days. The Fundy shore is prone to fog, particularly in the spring and early summer. The primary tourist season lasts from late June to early September. Many tourist facilities (beaches, organized tours and some accommodations in resort areas) shut down for the remainder of the year.

Language

New Brunswick is Canada's only officially bilingual province; one-third speak French as their first language. You'll rarely have a problem being understood in English or French.

❶ Getting There & Away

AIR

Air Canada has several daily flights from Halifax, Montréal, Ottawa and Toronto into Moncton, Saint John, Fredericton and Bathurst. Moncton has WestJet services from Toronto. WestJet also flies into Fredericton.

> ## NEW BUNSWICK FAST FACTS
> ➡ Population: 756,800
> ➡ Area: 73,400 sq km
> ➡ Capital: Fredericton
> ➡ Quirky fact: Home to the world's biggest fake lobster (Shediac), axe (Nackawic) and fiddlehead (Plaster Rock).

BOAT

The **Bay Ferries** (☑ 877-762-7245; www.bayferries.com; adult/child/senior $46/31/36, car/bicycle $92/10) sails between Saint John and Digby, Nova Scotia, year-round. The three-hour crossing can save a lot of driving.

Free government ferries service Deer Island and White Head Island; **East Coast Ferries** (☑ 506-747-2159; www.eastcoastferries.nb.ca; car & driver $16, additional passenger $3; ☉ 9am-7pm) runs between Campobello Island and Deer Island. Another private ferry company also serves Grand Manan Island. Reserve ahead.

BUS

Maritime Bus (☑ 800-575-1807; www.maritimebus.com) services the major transportation routes in New Brunswick, with service to Nova Scotia, PEI and into Québec as far as Rivière-du-Loup, where buses connect with **Orléans Express** (☑ 888-999-3977; www.orleansexpress.com) services to points west.

CAR & MOTORCYCLE

For drivers, the main access points into New Brunswick are the cities of Edmundston and Houlton, and can be accessed from Nova Scotia and PEI, as well as Maine (USA). If you're going to PEI, there's no charge to use the Confederation Bridge eastbound from Cape Jourmain – you pay on the way back. Traffic is generally light, although crossing the Maine border usually means a delay at customs.

TRAIN

VIA Rail (☑ 888-842-7245; www.viarail.ca) operates passenger services between Montréal and Halifax, with stops in Campbellton, Bathurst, Miramichi and Moncton.

FREDERICTON

POP 56,000

This gorgeous provincial capital does quaint very well. The Saint John River curves lazily through Fredericton, past the stately government buildings on the waterfront and the university on the hill. Its neatly mowed, tree-lined banks are dotted with fountains, walking paths and playing fields. On warm weekends, 'The Green,' as it's known, looks like something out of a watercolor painting – families strolling, kids kicking soccer balls, couples picnicking.

On a flat, broad curve in the riverbank, the small downtown commercial district is a neat grid of redbrick storefronts. Surrounding it are residential streets lined with tall, graceful elms shading beautifully maintained Georgian and Victorian houses and abundant flower beds. A canopy of trees spreads over the downtown, pierced here and there by church spires.

⊙ Sights

The two-block strip along Queen St between York and Regent Sts is known as the Historic Garrison District. It comprises Barracks Square and Officers' Square. In 1875 Fredericton became the capital of the newly formed province of New Brunswick, and the garrison housed British soldiers for much of the late 18th and early 19th centuries. It's now a lively multiuse area with impressive stone architecture.

★ **Beaverbrook Art Gallery** MUSEUM
(www.beaverbrookartgallery.org; 703 Queen St; adult/child $10/free; ⊙10am-5pm Mon-Wed, Fri & Sat, to 9pm Thu, noon-5pm Sun) This excellent gallery was a gift to the town from Lord Beaverbrook (see Beaverbrook House, p427). The exceptional collection includes works by international heavyweights and is well worth an hour or so. Among others you will see Dalí, Freud, Gainsborough and Turner, Canadian artists Tom Thompson, Emily Carr and Cornelius Kreighoff, as well as changing contemporary exhibits of Atlantic art.

At the time of writing it was undergoing a multi-million-dollar expansion to be completed in 2017.

Barracks Square SQUARE
(497 Queen St) Part of the Garrison District (two city blocks and an important national historic site), Barracks Square is framed by the Soldiers' Barracks and the Guard House. You can see how the common soldier lived in the 1820s (lousy food, too much drink). When a guard was not on his beat, he could rest at the Guard House, built in 1828, on a bed made of hard planks. Conditions (especially for those in the cells) were nasty at best.

Loyalist Village HISTORIC SITE
(☎506-363-4999; www.kingslanding.nb.ca; 5804 Rte 102, Prince William; adult/child/family $18/12.50/42; ⊙10am-5pm mid-Jun–Oct) One of the province's best sites is this re-creation of an early-19th-century Loyalist village, 36km west of Fredericton. A community of costumed staff create a living museum by role-playing in houses, a school, church, store and sawmill typical of those used a century ago, providing a glimpse and taste of pioneer life in the Maritime provinces. Demonstrations and events are staged throughout the day and horse-drawn carts shunt visitors around. It offers excellent children's programs and special events occur regularly.

The King's Head Inn, a mid-1800s pub, serves traditional food and beverages by candlelight. It's not hard to while away a good half-day or more. The prosperous Loyalist life reflected here can be tellingly compared to that at the Acadian Historic Village (p139) in Caraquet.

Old Loyalist Burial Ground CEMETERY
(Brunswick St; ⊙8am-9pm) This Loyalist cemetery, dating back to 1784, is an atmospheric, thought-provoking history lesson of its own, revealing large families and kids dying tragically young. The Loyalists arrived from the 13 colonies after the American Revolution of 1776.

Christ Church Cathedral CHURCH
(http://cccath.ca/wp; 168 Church St) Built in 1853, this cathedral is a fine early example of 19th-century Gothic Revival style and has exquisite stained glass. It was modeled after St Mary's in Snettisham, Norfolk.

Government House HISTORIC BUILDING
(www.gnb.ca/lg/ogh; 51 Woodstock Rd; ⊙10am-4pm Mon-Sat, noon-4pm Sun) FREE This magnificent sandstone palace was erected for the British governor in 1826. The representative of the queen moved out in 1893 after the province refused to continue paying his expenses, and during most of the 20th century the complex was a Royal Canadian Mounted Police (RCMP) headquarters. It now evocatively captures a moment in time with tours led by staff in period costume.

Officers' Square HISTORIC SITE
(www.historicgarrisondistrict.ca; btwn Carleton & Regent Sts; ⊙ceremonies 11am & 4pm daily, plus 7pm Tue & Thu Jul & Aug) Once the military parade ground, the Garrison District's

Fredericton

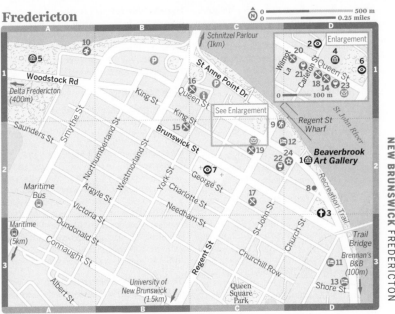

Fredericton

Officers' Sq now hosts a full-uniform changing-of-the-guard ceremony in summertime. Also in summer the Calithumpians Outdoor Summer Theatre performs daily at 12:15pm weekdays and 2pm weekends; the free historical skits are laced with humor. Summer evenings bring jazz, Celtic and rock concerts, see the website for schedules.

Fredericton Region Museum   MUSEUM
(📞506-455-6041; www.frederictonregionmuseum. com; Officers' Sq; adult/student $5/2; ⏱10am-5pm Jul & Aug, to 4pm Apr-Jun & Sep-Nov, by appointment Dec-Mar) Housed in the 19th-century officers' quarters on the western side of Officers' Sq, this museum's collection preserves the city's past. Displays feature military pieces used by local regiments and by British and German

armies from the Boer War and both world wars; furniture from a Loyalist sitting room and a Victorian bedroom; and aboriginal and Acadian artifacts. Don't miss the Coleman Frog, a 42lb creature of Fredericton legend. Real or plaster? Decide for yourself.

🏃 Activities

Lighthouse on the Green
HIKING, BIKING

(cnr Regent St & St Anne Point Dr; ⊙ 9am-6pm) There are 87km of recreational trails around town and along the river that either begin or intersect at this riverfront lighthouse (one part of the Trans Canada Trail), which doubles as a licensed patio-restaurant.

Second Nature Outdoors
BOATING

(www.secondnatureoutdoors.com; off Woodstock Rd; kayak per hour $15, half-day bike rental $15; ⊙ May-Sep) Operating out of the Small Craft Aquatic Centre, on the St John River beside Government House, Second Nature Outdoors rents out canoes, kayaks, paddleboards and bikes. They will drop you at Heart Island Resort and you can paddle downstream to your heart's and muscle's content...

Haunted Hikes
WALKING

(📞 506-457-1975; www.calithumpians.com; 796a Queen St; adult/child $14/9; ⊙ 9pm Mon-Sat Jul & Aug) Actors from the university masquerading as ghoulish thespians run entertaining Fredericton ghost tours.

Heritage Walking Tours
WALKING

(📞 506 457 1975; 796 Queen St; ⊙ 10am, 2:30pm & 5pm daily Jul & Aug, 4pm Jun, Sep & Oct) FREE Enthusiastic young people wearing historic costumes lead good, free hour-long tours of the river, the government district or the Historic Garrison District, departing from City Hall.

🎉 Festivals & Events

New Brunswick Highland Games Festival
CULTURAL

(⊙ late Jul) Kilts, clans and all things positively Celtic are exposed at this fun highlands games extravaganza held annually on the grounds of Government House. Competitors and visitors are drawn to its celebration of all things Scottish culture: dancing, caber toss competitions, whisky tastings, piped music and more.

Silver Wave Film Festival
FILM

(www.swfilmfest.com; ⊙ early Nov) Three days of New Brunswick, Canadian and international films and lectures organized by the NB Filmmakers' Cooperative.

Harvest Jazz & Blues Festival
MUSIC

(www.harvestjazzandblues.com; ⊙ Sep) This weeklong event transforms the downtown area into the 'New Orleans of the North.' Jazz, blues and Dixieland performers arrive from across North America.

🛏 Sleeping

There are a number of budget and midrange motels along Bishop Drive and Prospect St (southwest of town).

Mactaquac Provincial Park Campground
CAMPGROUND $

(📞 506-444-5205; https://parcsnbparks.ca/ Mactaquac; 1256 Hwy 105; campsites & RV sites $32; ⊙ Jun-Oct) Twenty-six kilometers west of Fredericton (and 10km north of Kings Landing Settlement), the resort-like and child-friendly Mactaquac Provincial Park has swimming beaches, fishing, hiking, picnic sites, boat rentals and a huge campground.

★ Quartermain House B&B
B&B $$

(📞 506-206-5255; www.quartermainhouse.com; 92 Waterloo Row; r $110-145) By far the most superior accommodations of its kind in New Brunswick, Quartermain ticks all the right boxes: delightful period home on Fredericton's exclusive Waterloo Row; warm, professional host; and incredible breakfasts. The price is ridiculous in comparison to other places in the region, but if you're going to splurge anywhere, this is the place.

Delta Fredericton
BUSINESS HOTEL $$

(📞 506-457-7000; www.marriott.com; 225 Woodstock Rd; r from $159; P 🛜 🏊) For a 'predictable' chain-hotel experience, this one surprises. Its location on the banks of Saint John River and a river trail is ideal. And recent renovations have brought a sleek, sharp focus: large and very pleasant rooms, plus trimmings (pools, restaurants and gym). Breakfast is not included in the price. The hotel is within walking distance of the center.

University of New Brunswick
UNIVERSITY ACCOMMODATIONS $$

(📞 506-447-3227; http://stay.unb.ca; 20 Bairley Dr; s/d/tr with private bath $54/84/115; s/d with shared bath $40/62.50; ⊙ 7am-11pm May–mid-Aug; P 🛜) Fredericton's only budget accommodations is located at the university. It's a great deal, but the catch is, rooms are available in summer only. Traditional rooms have shared bathrooms but a light continental breakfast is offered. The 'suites' have private bathrooms and kitchenettes. Rooms may be a bit sparse, but it's a lovely campus with views over Fredericton and the Saint John River.

Brennan's B&B
B&B $$

(☑ 506-455-7346; www.bbcanada.com/3892. html; 146 Waterloo Row; s $115-195, d $125-210, incl breakfast; P ⊖ ❀ @) Built for a wealthy wood-merchant family in 1885, this turreted white riverfront mansion is now a handsome six-room B&B; three of the rooms boast water views and two have kitchenettes. There's stunning original fretwork throughout.

Carriage House Inn
B&B $$

(☑ 506-452-9924; www.carriagehouse-inn.net; 230 University Ave; r incl breakfast $129-149; P ⊖ ❀ 🛜) In a shady Victorian neighborhood near the Green, this 1875 Queen Anne was built for a lumber baron and former Fredericton mayor. The grand common room has polished hardwood floors, antiques, comfy sofas, fireplaces and a grand piano. Upstairs, things deteriorate. Although charming, rooms are faded, their high ceilings, floral wallpapers and vintage artwork showing age (and little upkeep). There is a deep verandah for lounging.

Crowne Plaza Lord Beaverbrook
HOTEL $$$

(☑ 506-455-3371; www.cpfredericton.com; 659 Queen St; r $120-270; P ❀ 🛜 ⛱) Always bustling with weddings, conventions and business travelers, this 1948 downtown hotel is another one of Lord Beaverbrook's legacies to the city. The beaver mosaics on the facade are wonderful and the lobby has a touch of vintage glamour, but the 168 rooms, if comfortable, are showing signs of wear. Check online for specials.

✕ Eating

Chess Piece Patisserie & Cafe
CAFE $

(www.chesspiece.ca; 361 Queen St; snacks $3-8; ⊙ 7am-9pm Mon-Fri, 8am-9pm Sat, 10am-4pm Sun) A wonderful new addition to the local scene, this little laid-back cafe has an in-house patisserie bakery. Although it's one of Fredericton's best places for coffee and soup, the things to devour are the generously proportioned cakes and pastries, made on the premises using quality ingredients. And oh so sweet to both the eye and the taste buds.

Fredericton Boyce Farmers Market
MARKET $

(www.frederictonfarmersmarket.ca; 665 George St; ⊙ 6am-1pm Sat) This Fredericton institution is great for picking up fresh fruit, vegetables, meat, cheese, handicrafts, dessert and flowers. Many of the 150 or so stalls recall the city's European heritage, with everything from German-style sausages to French duck pâtés to British marmalade. There is also an eatery where Frederictonians queue to chat and people-watch.

★ Ten Resto
INTERNATIONAL $$

(☑ 506-206-3951; www.facebook.com/tenresto; 87 Regent St; mains $19-30; ⊙ 5-9pm Tue-Sat; 🍴) Coming here is a bit of an unorthodox numbers game. This pleasant locale has 10 tables and a choice of 10 dishes per sitting (and 10 menu changes a year). This means that you can be in an empty or very full restaurant, depending on the reservation timings. The reasons? Owners Keith and Shelley like you to feel at home.

★ Naru
JAPANESE $$

(536 Queen St; mains $12-15; ⊙ 11am-9pm Mon-Thu & Sat, to 10pm Fri; 🍴) A word of warning for purists of Japanese cuisine: this top-quality Japanese restaurant incorporates local Canadian produce and ideas into its recipes. But, given the high-quality Canadian seafood and produce, and the delicate presentation, the results are sublime. The sashimi, *maki* and tempura selections are fabulous; but look no further than the grilled scallop roll, topped with Parmesan cheese and *tobiko*. Good range of vegetarian options too.

The Palate
INTERNATIONAL $$

(www.thepalate.com; 462 Queen St; mains $19-22; ⊙ 11am-3pm & 5-9pm Mon-Fri, 10am-3pm & 5-9pm Sat) This modest, family-friendly place has an Italian-bistro feel and stands out because it doesn't blow its own trumpet. It has stood the test of time among Fredericton's thriving gastropub scene, doing what it does best for 16 years: preparing unpretentious but enjoyable seafood, chicken and pasta dishes with fresh produce, including some from its own gardens.

540 Kitchen & Bar
INTERNATIONAL $$

(540 Queen St; mains $14-32; ⊙ 11:30am-9pm Mon & Tue, to 10pm Wed & Thu, to 11pm Fri & Sat; 🍴) A fabulous gastropub that sticks to its mantra: locally sourced produce, everything made from scratch, seasonal menu. Wash down the likes of pork belly or rack of Spring lamb with a choice of beer. There are 10 taps that represent local micro-breweries. Good veggie options too. Get here early or reserve; it's popular.

Caribbean Flavas CARIBBEAN $$
(www.caribbeanflavas.ca; 123 York St; mains $15-30; ⊘11:30am-2:30pm Tue-Fri, plus 4:30-8pm Tue-Sat) A bright nook dishing up the tastes and colors of the Caribbean. Great for a casual, flavorful meal and a fruit-based drink (read: this place is alcohol-free).

Schnitzel Parlour GERMAN $$
(⊉506-450-2520; www.theschnitzelparlour.com; 304 Union St; mains $15-21; ⊘5:30-8pm Tue-Sat) Specializing in hearty, old-fashioned German fare, this cozy countryside restaurant on the northern side of the river has richly spiced goulash (the secret ingredient is chocolate), wild-boar stew and nine kinds of schnitzel on homemade spätzle (soft egg noodles). BYOB. The on-site Chocolaterie Fackleman (with the same hours as the restaurant) sells truffles and traditional Central European tortes.

🍷 Drinking & Nightlife

In the evenings the bars, pubs and rooftop patios of King and Queen Sts come alive. Craft beer (and a great ciderhouse) are the rage here. Younger things hit the one-stop (drinking) shop quadrant known as The Tannery.

Red Rover Ciderhouse BAR
(www.facebook.com/redroverbrew; 546 Queen St; ⊘5-9pm Mon, noon-9pm Tue-Thu, noon-10pm Fri & Sat) If you're up to your esophagus with craft beer, or you prefer wine or cocktails, you're in a win:win situation at this convivial, industrial chic ciderhouse. It serves craft cider made by New Brunswick's first (and very passionate) cider producers. They're constantly perfecting their brews and flavors (14 to date) using Canadian apples. And they're receiving awards for their efforts.

Lunar Rogue Pub PUB
(www.lunarrogue.com; 625 King St; ⊘11am-late Mon-Sat, to 10pm Sun) Named a 'great whisky bar of the world' for good reason: this jolly locals' joint has a fine assortment of single malts, part of the 500-plus whiskey collection. Work your way through the drams on the outdoor patio; it's wildly popular during the warmer weather.

Soak up the intake with a mighty fine breakfast or a selection from the bar menu (mains $8 to $14).

Boom! Nightclub CLUB
(www.boomnightclub.ca; 474 Queen St; cover charge $5-8; ⊘8pm-late Wed-Sun) A hip gay bar and dance club welcoming folks of all stripes.

☆ Entertainment

In summer downtown venues from Officers' Sq to the Lighthouse on the Green feature **outdoor summer concerts** (www.tourismfredericton.ca) with ranging from highland bagpipes and drums to country and blues. Check the website for schedules.

Playhouse THEATER
(⊉866-884-5800; www.theplayhouse.nb.ca; 686 Queen St) Stages concerts, theater, ballet and shows throughout the year.

❶ Information

The entire CBD is wired for free internet access. Otherwise, **Fredericton Public Library** (12 Carleton St; ⊘10am-5pm Mon, Tue & Thu, to 9pm Wed & Fri) has free internet access on a first-come, first-served basis.

Dr Everett Chalmers Hospital (⊉506-452-5400; 700 Priestman St) Located 2km south of the city center.

Main post office (⊉506-444-8602; 570 Queen St; ⊘8am-5pm Mon-Fri)

Visitor Information Centre (⊉506-460-2129; www.tourismfredericton.ca; City Hall, 397 Queen St; ⊘10am-8pm Jul & Aug, to 5pm Jun & Sep, to 4.30pm May & Oct) Provides free city parking passes. A secondary office opens in summer at Kings Landing (42 Prince William Rd, Prince William; ⊘10:30am-5:30pm Jun-Oct).

❶ Getting There & Away

AIR

Fredericton International Airport (YFC; ⊉506-460-0920; www.frederictonairport.ca) is on Hwy 102, 14km southeast of town. AirCanada has flights between Fredericton and the US, including New York City and Orlando (via other Canadian cities), as well flights to London, UK. Fredericton is also part of a good network of domestic flights.

BUS

The **Maritime Bus** (⊉506-455-2049; www.maritimebus.com; 105 Dundonald St; ⊘8am-8pm Mon-Fri, 10am-8pm Sat & Sun) terminal is a few kilometers southwest of downtown. Some useful destinations include Moncton ($44, 2¼ hours, two daily); Charlottetown, PEI ($69, 5½ hours, two daily); Bangor, ME ($58, 7½ hours, one daily); and Saint John ($31, 1½ hours, two daily).

CAR & MOTORCYCLE

Cars with out-of-province license plates are eligible for a free three-day parking pass for downtown Fredericton May to October, available at the **visitor center** (p108) at City Hall. In-province visitors can get a one-day pass. The major car-rental agencies all have desks at the airport.

❶ Getting Around

A taxi to the airport costs $18 to $22.

The city has a decent bus system; tickets cost $3 and include free transfers. Service runs Monday through Saturday from 6:15am to 11pm. Most city bus routes begin at King's Place Mall, on King St between York and Carleton.

Bicycle rentals are available at **Radical Edge** (☑506-459-3478; www.radicaledge.ca; 386 Queen St; rental per day $25).

UPPER ST JOHN RIVER VALLEY

The St John River winds along the western border of the province past forests and lush farmland. It drifts through Fredericton between tree-lined banks and around flat islands between rolling hills before emptying into the Bay of Fundy 700km later. The river is the province's dominant feature and for centuries has been its major thoroughfare. The valley's eye-pleasing landscape makes for scenic touring by car, or by bicycle on the Trans Canada Trail (TCT), which follows the river for most of its length.

Two automobile routes carve through the valley: the quicker Trans-Canada Hwy (Hwy 2), mostly on the western side of the river, and the more scenic old Hwy 105 on the eastern side, which meanders through many villages. Branching off from the valley are Hwy 17 (at St-Léonard) and Rte 385 (at Perth-Andover), which cut northeast through the Appalachian highlands and lead to rugged Mt Carleton Provincial Park.

Mt Carleton Provincial Park & the Tobique Valley

The 17,427-hectare provincial park is one of the region's best-kept secrets. It offers visitors a wilderness of mountains, valleys, rivers and wildlife including moose, deer and bear. The park's main feature is a series of rounded glaciated peaks and ridges, including Mt Carleton (820m). This range is an extension of the Appalachian Mountains, which begin in Georgia, USA, and end in Québec. Mt Carleton is little known and relatively unvisited, even in midsummer.

The park is open from mid-May to October. All roads are gravel-surfaced. The nearest towns are Riley Brook, 40km to the south, and St Quentin, 42km to the north, so bring all food and a full tank of gas.

🏃 Activities

Canoeing

The Mt Carleton area boasts superb wilderness canoeing. In the park itself, the Nictau and Nepisiguit chains of lakes offer easy day-tripping through a landscape of tree-clad mountains. For experienced canoeists, the shallow and swift Little Tobique River rises at Big Nictau Lake, winding in tight curls through dense woods until it joins the Tobique itself at Nictau. The more remote Nepisiguit River flows out of the Nepisiguit Lakes through the wilderness until it empties into the Bay of Chaleur at Bathurst, over 100km away.

The lower reaches of the Tobique, from Nictau, through minute Riley Brook and down to Plaster Rock is a straight, easy paddle through forest and meadow that gives way to farmland as the valley broadens, with a couple of waterfront campgrounds along the way. The easy 10km between Nictau and the Bear's Lair landing in Riley Brook makes for a relaxing afternoon paddle.

Bill Miller CANOEING
(☑506-356-2409; www.millercanoes.com; 4160 Rte 385, Nictau) Bill Miller welcomes visitors to his cluttered canoe-making workshop in Nictau (population roughly 8), on the forested banks of the Tobique River at the foot of Mt Carleton, where he and his father and grandfather before him have handcrafted wooden canoes since 1922.

Guildo Martel WATER SPORTS
(☑506-235-0286; kayak & canoe per day $40; ☉Jun-Sep) Guildo Martel rents canoes and kayaks for the day and will deliver them where required. He's located 4km from the park toward St Quentin. He will guide for a total of $100 on top of rental prices (for up to six people).

Bear's Lair KAYAKING
(☑506-356-8351; www.bearslairhunting.com; 3349 Rte 385, Riley Brook; kayak/canoe rental per day $35/50) Owners will drop you off upriver so you can paddle and float your way downstream and back to home base, Bear's Lair, the cozy lodge.

Hiking

The best way to explore Mt Carleton is on foot. The park has nearly 70km network of trails: most of them are loops winding to the handful of rocky knobs that are the peaks. The **International Appalachian Trail** (IAT) passes through here.

DON'T MISS

FLORENCEVILLE-BRISTOL

The tidy and green riverside village of Florenceville-Bristol is ground zero of the global french-fry industry. It's home to the McCain Foods frozen-foods empire, which is sustained by the thousands of hectares of potato farms that surround it in every direction. Started by the McCain brothers in 1957, the company produces one-third of the world's french-fry supply at its Florenceville factory. That adds up to 453,600kg of chips churned out every hour and $5.8 billion in annual net sales. To get your head around the spud industry, head to **Potato World** (www.potatoworld.ca; Rte 110; tours adult/family $5/16, experiential tours $10/32; ⏱ 9am-6pm Mon-Fri, to 5pm Sat & Sun Jun-Aug, 9am-5pm Mon-Fri Sep–mid-Oct), a tasteful, top-class interactive exposition of the history of the humble potato in these parts.

The easiest peak to climb is **Mt Bailey**; a 7.5km loop trail to the 564m hillock begins near the day-use area. Most hikers can walk this route in three hours. The highest peak is reached via the **Mt Carleton Trail**, a 10km route that skirts over the 820m knob, where there's a fire tower. Plan on five hours for the trek and pack your parka; the wind above the tree line can be brutal.

The most challenging hike (and the most rewarding for the views) is the **Sagamook Trail**, a 6km loop to a 777m peak with superlative vistas of Nictau Lake and the highlands area to the north of it; allow four hours for this trek. The **Mountain Head Trail** connects the Mt Carleton and Sagamook Trails (the latter being part of the Appalachian Trail), making a long transit of the range possible.

All hikers intending to follow any long trails must register at the visitors center (p111) before hitting the trail. Outside the camping season (mid-May to mid-September), you should call ahead to make sure the main gate will be open, as the Mt Carleton trailhead is 13.5km from the park entrance. Otherwise, park your car at the entrance and walk in – the Mt Bailey trailhead is only 2.5km from the gate.

🎊 Festivals & Events

World Pond Hockey Tournament SPORTS
(www.worldpondhockey.com; Rte 109, Plaster Rock; admission free; ⏱ Feb) The forest town of Plaster Rock (population 1200), 84km from Mt Carleton, hosts the World Pond Hockey Tournament. Over 20 rinks are plowed on Roulston Lake, which is ringed by tall evergreens, hot-chocolate stands and straw-bale seating for the thousands of spectators drawn to the four-day event. Over 120 amateur four-person teams come from around the world.

If you want to play, register early. If you want to watch, pack your long johns and a *toque* (wool hat) and book your accommodations early. The organizers keep a list of local folks willing to billet out-of-towners in their homes.

Fiddles on the Tobique MUSIC
(📞 506-356-2409; ⏱ late Jun) This weekend festival is held annually in Nictau and Riley Brook. It is a magical idea: a round of community-hall suppers, jam sessions and concerts culminating in a Sunday-afternoon floating concert down the Tobique River from Nictau to Riley Brook. Upward of 800 canoes and kayaks join the flotilla each year – some stocked with musicians, some just with paddlers – and 8000 spectators line the riverbanks to watch. By some accounts, the event has been damaged by its own popularity, devolving into a boisterous booze cruise. Others call it a grand party and good fun.

🛏 Sleeping

Heritage Cottages COTTAGE $
(📞 506-235-0793; www.nbparks.ca; Mt Carleton Provincial Park; d $60-90) Eleven delightful, restored cottages (the originals date from the late 1800s) sit on Bathurst Lakes and at Little Nictau. You must bring everything, including bedding, pots and pans. Some share facilities; others have their own kitchens and bathrooms.

Armstrong Brook Campground CAMPGROUND $
(📞 506-235-0793; www.nbparks.ca; campsites/RV sites $28/28; ⏱ May-Oct) The park's largest campground has 88 sites nestled among the spruce on the northern side of Nictau Lake, 3km from the entrance. It has toilets, showers and a kitchen shelter, but no sites with hookups. Recreational vehicle (RV) drivers often have their noisy generators running, so tenters should check out the eight tent-only sites on the northern side of the campground.

Bear's Lair INN $
(☑ 506-356-8351; www.bearslairhunting.com; 3349 Rte 385, Riley Brook; r from $65; ☺ May-Sep; P ☺) If any place in the province captures the essence of life in the north woods, this is it. A cozy log hunting lodge set on the banks of the Tobique River, it is busiest during fall hunting season – the high-ceilinged main lodge is adorned with numerous taxidermied specimens – but is also a relaxing base for outdoor enthusiasts year-round.

🛈 Information

Visitors center (☑ 506-235-0793; www. nbparks.ca; off Rte 385; per vehicle $10; ☺ 8am-8pm May-Sep, to 6pm Oct) At the entrance to the park. Has maps and information. Park entry is paid here.

Grand Falls

With a drop of around 25m and a 1.6km-long gorge with walls as high as 80m, these falls merit a stop in this otherwise-unscenic town. The Grand Falls are best when the dam gates are open (often after rain) – in summer much of the water is diverted for generating hydroelectricity – yet the gorge is appealing any time.

🏃 Activities

Open Sky Adventures ADVENTURE SPORTS
(☑ 506-477-9799; 16087 Rte 105, Drummond; ☺ Jun-Oct) Gorge yourself silly on Open Sky Adventures' activities. A one-hour boat trip costs $25 ($15 per child), plus there's deepelling (apparently that's face-forward rappelling; $100), zip-lining ($35) and kayaking (from $30 per day).

La Rochelle OUTDOORS
(1 Chapel St; tours adult/child $5/2; ☺ Jul & Aug) A 401-step stairway down into the gorge begins at La Rochelle, across the bridge from the Malabeam Reception & Interpretation Centre and left on Victoria St.

🛏 Sleeping & Eating

Falls & Gorge Campground CAMPGROUND $
(☑ 506-475-7769; 120 Manse St; campsites/RV sites $25/35; ☺ Jun-Sep) If you do decide to spend the night in Grand Falls, there are dramatically situated tent and RV sites here.

Le Grand Saut AMERICAN $$
(www.legrandsautristorante.com; 155 Broadway Blvd; mains $11-20; ☺ 10:30am-10pm) For a half

reasonable feed, Le Grand Saut, a popular, two-tiered spot with an inviting deck out front, serves up generous portions of salads, pastas, pizzas and steaks.

🛈 Information

Malabeam Tourist & Interpretation Centre
(☑ 506-475-7788; www.grandfalls.com; 25 Madawaska Rd; admission free; ☺ 10am-6pm May & Jun, 9:30am-6pm Jul & Aug, 10am-5pm Sep & Oct) In the middle of town, overlooking the falls, the Malabeam Reception & Interpretation Centre doubles as a tourist office. Among the displays is a scale model of the gorge showing its extensive trail system. The newer interpretation wing affords fabulous views of the falls.

🛈 Getting There & Away

Maritime Bus (☑ 506-473-4862; www. maritimebus.com; 555 Madawaska Rd; ☺ noon-midnight) services stop at the Esso station, just west of downtown.

Hwy 108 (known locally as the Renous Hwy) cuts across the province through Plaster Rock to the East Coast, slicing through forest for nearly its entirety. It is tedious, but fast. Watch out for deer and moose.

Edmundston & Around

Working-class Edmundston has a large paper mill, a utilitarian town center and a mainly bilingual French citizenry. There's few sights, but it makes a convenient stopover for those traveling east from Québec.

◉ Sights

Petis Témis Interprovincial Linear Park PARK
(Edmundston) Edmundston is the eastern terminus of the Petis Témis Interprovincial Linear Park, a 134km cycling and hiking trail between Edmundston and Rivière-du-Loup, Québec. It follows an old railbed along the Madawaska River and the shores of Lake Témiscouata, passing by several small villages and campgrounds along the way. Mountain bikers can hit the 45km of single mountain-bike trails in the surrounding Appalachian mountain range.

New Brunswick Botanical Garden GARDENS
(www.jardinnbgarden.com; off Rte 2, St-Jacques; adult/child $14/7; ☺ 9am-5pm May, Jun & Sep, to 8pm Jul & Aug) Halfway between the Québec border and Edmundston in the small community of St-Jacques is the New Brunswick

Botanical Garden. Here there are 80,000 plants, a herb pavilion and 3D flower sculptures to brighten your day, all accompanied by classical music. Kids might prefer the neat temporary exhibitions, such as a butterfly garden.

🛏 Sleeping & Eating

Look out for the *ploye*, a kind of buckwheat pancake and an important part of history and tradition for the Madawaska Valley. It's often eaten with butter, sugar or maple syrup.

Local restaurants that use and promote local products are listed at www.acadiegourmet.ca; for a complete list of eateries, see the tourist office website.

Auberge Les Jardins   INN $$
(📞 506-739-5514; www.lesjardinsinn.com; 60 Rue Principale, St-Jacques; r $119-175; 🅿 🛜 🕱) Get out of gritty Edmundston and sleep next to the botanical gardens at Auberge Les Jardins, a gracious inn with 17 rooms that are each decorated with a different Canadian flower or tree theme. There's also a modern motel in back, and a wood-and-stained-glass dining room that's considered one of the best restaurants in the province (check out the fabulous wine list).

Restaurant le Patrimoine   PIZZA $$
(http://pizzalepatrimoine.com; 115 Chemin Rivière-à-la-Truite, St-Jacques; pizzas $12-20; ⏰ 4-9pm Wed & Sun, to 10pm Thu, to 11pm Fri & Sat) Housed in a former golf clubhouse, this is way above par with its quality pizzas. It strikes the sweet spot every time with white- and whole-crust pizzas with gourmet toppings served up direct from its wood-fired oven. *Squisito* (delicious)!

ℹ Information

Edmunston Visitor Information Centre (www.tourismedmundston.com; 121 Victoria St; ⏰ 9am-7pm Jun-Aug, to 5pm Mon-Fri Sep-May) Has information on Edmunston and the locale.

Saint Jacques Provincial Visitor Information Centre (www.tourismnewbrunswick.ca; 17412 Rte 2, Saint Jacques; ⏰ 9:30am-6:30pm May, Jun & Sep, to 7:30pm Jul & Aug) This regional tourist office, about 20km north at the Québec border, has information on New Brunswick.

ℹ Getting There & Away

The **Maritime Bus** (📞 506-739-8309; www.maritimebus.com; 191 Victoria St, Edmundston; ⏰ 5am-midnight) network stops in Edmunston and heads south to Fredericton ($53.25, 3½

hours, one or two daily) and beyond, or westward into Rivière-du-Loup ($29.50, 30 minutes, one or two daily), from where you can catch connections into Québec.

WESTERN FUNDY SHORE

Almost the entire southern edge of New Brunswick is presided over by the constantly rising and falling waters of the Bay of Fundy.

The resort town of St Andrews By-The-Sea, the serene Fundy Isles, fine seaside scenery and rich history make this easily one of the most appealing regions of the province. Whale-watching is a thrilling area activity. Most commonly seen are the fin, humpback and minke; less so, the increasingly rare right whale. Porpoises and dolphins are plentiful. And let's not overlook the seafood – it's bountiful and delicious.

St Stephen

Right on the US border across the river from Calais, ME, St Stephen is a busy entry point with small-town charm and one tasty attraction. It is home to Ganong, a family-run chocolate business operating since 1873; its products are known around eastern Canada. The 5¢ chocolate nut bar was invented by the Ganong brothers in 1910, and they can also be credited with developing the heart-shaped box of chocolates seen everywhere on Valentine's Day.

◉ Sights & Tours

Chocolate Museum   MUSEUM
(📞 506-466-7848; www.chocolatemuseum.ca; 73 Milltown Blvd; adult/student/family $10/8.50/30; ⏰ 10am-4pm Mon-Fri, 11am-3pm Sat & Sun Apr-Nov) The Chocolate Museum has tasteful (and tasty) interactive displays of everything from antique chocolate boxes to manufacturing equipment.

Chocolate Museum Guided Heritage Walking Tour   WALKING
(adult/child $15/13.50; ⏰ Jul & Aug) In summer the museum (p112) arranges guided heritage walking tours of St Stephen, led by local students.

✰ Festivals & Events

Chocolate Fest   FOOD & DRINK
(www.chocolate-fest.ca; ⏰ early Aug) It's all things cocoa and sugar at St Stephen's Chocolate

WORTH A TRIP

SCENIC DRIVE: LOWER SAINT JOHN RIVER VALLEY

The main highway (Rte 7) between the capital and the port city of Saint John barrels south through a vast expanse of trees, trees and more trees. A far more scenic route (albeit about twice as long) follows the gentle, meandering Saint John River through rolling farmland and a couple of historic villages down to the Fundy coast.

Start on the north side of the river in Fredericton, and follow Rte 105 south through Maugerville to Jemseg. Follow the new bridge across Hwy 2 West. (This is in place of the Gagetown ferry which stopped operating in 2015; locals are protesting against its closure. Check to see if it's open.)

Head to the pretty 18th-century village of **Gagetown** – well worth a look-see. Front St is lined with craft studios and shops and a couple of inviting cafes. Stop into the excellent **Queen's County Museum** (16 Court House Rd, Gagetown; adult/child $3/free; ⏱10am-5pm mid-Jun–mid-Sep), the town's first court as well as the **Tilley House** (69 Front St, Gagetown; adult/child $3/free; ⏱10am-5pm mid-Jun–mid-Sep), Sir Leonard Tilley's childhood home. The top-notch staff will show you through the exhibits spanning pre-Colonial aboriginal history in the area, 18th-century settler life, and up to WWII.

From Gagetown, head south on Rte 102, known locally as 'the **Old River Road**,' denoting its status as the major thoroughfare up the valley in the kinder, simpler era between the decline of the river steamboats and the construction of the modern, divided highway. The grand old farmhouses and weathered hay barns dotted at intervals along the valley belong to that earlier age. The hilly 42km piece of road between Gagetown and the **Evandale ferry landing** (⏱24hr year-round) is especially picturesque, with glorious panoramic views of fields full of wildflowers, white farmhouses and clots of green and gold islands set in the intensely blue water of the river.

A hundred years ago, tiny Evandale was a bustling little place, where a dance band would entertain riverboat passengers. Across the water, Rte 124 takes you the short distance to the **Belleisle ferry** (⏱24hr year-round) which deposits you on the rural Kingston Peninsula, where you can cross the peninsula to catch the **Gondola Point Ferry** (p129) and head directly into Saint John.

Fest, when the town celebrates all things chocolate with a parade, tours of the local Ganong factory and unlimited sampling of the goods (yes, really!), and games for the kids.

🛏 Sleeping & Eating

Blair House INN $$
(☎506-466-2233; www.blairhouseheritageinn.com; 38 Prince William St; r incl breakfast from $100; P❄✳🖢) The five eclectic but comfortable rooms are complemented by a quiet garden at this fabulous Victorian home. Affable David serves up a generous cooked breakfast. You can walk to the main street easily from here.

Something's Brewing CAFE $
(www.somethingsbrewingcafe.ca; 140 Milltown Blvd; snacks $4-10; ⏱7am-8pm, to 10pm Fri) A lovely little local cafe and just the spot for a coffee – a range of fair-trade and organic coffees, in fact (if you count soy chai latte, which a purist definitely wouldn't). In any case, there are also great teas and wonderful home-baked cakes and pastries.

Carman's Diner DINER $
(☎506-466-3528; 164 King St; mains $4-16; ⏱7am-10pm) Home cooking is served up at this 1960s throwback with counter stools and your own mini (and working) jukeboxes at the tables. There's everything from burgers to sandwiches, but the homemade pies are the things to go for. It's only convenient if you have a car, as it's not in the center of town.

🔒 Shopping

Chocolate Museum Shop FOOD
(www.chocolatemuseum.ca; 73 Milltown Blvd; ⏱9am-5pm) The Chocolate Museum shop sells boxes of Ganong hand-dipped chocolates and is free to visit. Try the iconic chicken bone (chocolate-filled cinnamon sticks) or the old-fashioned Pal-O-Mine candy bar.

ℹ Information

Tourist office (www.tourismnewbrunswick.ca; Rte 170, Unit 4; ⏱9am-6pm May & Jun, Sep & Oct, to 7pm Jul & Aug) This new office in the Circle K Irving Complex at the junction as you enter town has information on the province.

① Getting There & Away

Across the border in Calais, ME, **West's Coastal Connection** (② 800-596-2823; www.westbus-service.com) buses head to Bangor (one-way ticket $27, four hours, one daily). In Bangor, buses use the Greyhound terminal and connect to Bangor airport.

St Andrews By-The-Sea

St Andrews is a genteel summer resort town. Blessed with a fine climate and picturesque beauty, it also has a colorful history. Founded by Loyalists in 1783, it's one of the oldest towns in the province. It's busy with holiday-makers and summer residents in July and August, but the rest of the year there are more seagulls than people.

The town sits on a peninsula pointing southward into the Bay of Fundy. Its main drag, Water St, is lined with restaurants and several craft shops.

⊙ Sights

Minister's Island   ISLAND
(② 506-529-5081; www.ministersisland.ca; adult/child under 8yr $10/free; ⊙ May-Oct) This pictur-esque tidal island was once used as a retreat by William Cornelius Van Horne, builder of the Canadian Pacific Railway and one of Canada's wealthiest men. As well as touring the island on foot along four marked trails of varying lengths, you can visit **Covenhoven**, his splendid 50-room Edwardian cottage, plus the towerlike stone bathhouse, tidal swimming pool and château-like barn (the largest freestanding wooden structure in Canada).

Important: the island can be visited at low tide, when you can drive (or walk, or bike) on the hard-packed sea floor. A few hours later it's 3m under water, so be careful. During high tide, a ferry departs from Bar Rd. To get to Minister's Island from downtown St Andrews, follow Rte 127 northeast for about 1km and then turn right on Bar Rd.

Wild Salmon Nature Centre   MUSEUM, AQUARIUM
(② 506-529-1384; http://wildsalmonnaturecentre. ca; Chamcook Lake No 1 Rd, off Rte 127; adult/student/child $6/4/3; ⊙ 9am-5pm Mon-Sat, noon-5pm Sun May-Aug) This handsome lodge has an in-stream aquarium, guided tours and displays devoted to the life and trials of the endangered wild Atlantic salmon.

Sheriff Andrew House   HISTORIC BUILDING
(② 506-529-5080; cnr King & Queen Sts; admission by donation; ⊙ 9:30am-4:30pm Tue-Sun mid-Jun–Sep) This 1820 neoclassical house has been restored to look like a middle-class home in the 1800s, and it's attended by lively and informative costumed guides.

St Andrews Blockhouse   HISTORIC BUILDING
(Joe's Point Rd; ⊙ 10am-6pm Jun-Aug) `FREE` The restored wooden Blockhouse Historic Site is the only one left of several that were built here for protection in the War of 1812. If the tide is out, there's a path that extends from the blockhouse out across the tidal flats.

Kingsbrae Garden   GARDENS
(② 506-529-3335; www.kingsbraegarden.com; 220 King St; adult/student/family $16/12/38, tours per person $3; ⊙ 9am-6pm May-Oct, to 8pm Jul & Aug) Extensive, multihued Kingsbrae Garden is considered one of the best horticultural displays in Canada. Check out the wollemi pine, one of the world's oldest and rarest trees.

Fundy Discovery Aquarium   AQUARIUM
(www.huntsmanmarine.com/aquarium; 1 Lower Campus Rd; adult/child $14.25/10; ⊙ 10am-5pm) This aquatic center focuses on the local marine ecology; a 20,000-sq-ft aquarium has most specimens that are found in Bay of Fundy waters, including seals (feedings at 11am and 4pm), seahorses (feedings at 10.15am and 3.30pm), salmon (feedings at 10.35am and 3pm), lobsters and sturgeon. Kids (and parents) love the touch pool reserved just for slippery skates.

🏃 Activities

Numerous companies offering boat trips and whale-watching cruises have offices by the wharf at the foot of King St. They're open from mid-June to early September. The cruises (around $60) take in the lovely coast. Seabirds are commonplace and seeing whales is the norm. The ideal waters for watching these beasts are further out in the bay, however, so if you're heading for the Fundy Isles, do your trip there.

Two Meadows Walking Trail   WALKING
The 800m Two Meadows Walking Trail, a boardwalk and footpath through fields and woodlands, begins opposite 165 Joe's Point Rd beyond the blockhouse.

Eastern Outdoors   CYCLING, KAYAKING
(② 506-529-4662; www.easternoutdoors.com; 165 Water St; mountain bikes per hour/day $20/30, kayaks per day $60; ⊙ May-Oct) This St Andrews–based outfitter offers a variety of trips, including a three-hour trip around nearby

Navy Island ($60), and full-day trips to Passamaquoddy Bay ($125) and Deer Island ($125).

Quoddy Link Marine
BOATING

(☑ 506-529-2600; http://quoddylinkmarine.com/; adult/child $58/28; ☺ mid-Jun–Oct) Serious whale-watchers should hop aboard this catamaran, staffed by trained marine biologists. There are one to three tours daily.

Jolly Breeze
BOATING

(☑ 506-529-8116; www.jollybreeze.com; adult/child $60/40; ☺ tours 9am, 12:45pm & 4:30pm Jun-Oct) This antique-style tall ship sails around Passamaquoddy Bay looking for seals and whales as well as porpoises and eagles.

🛏 Sleeping

Kiwanis Oceanfront Camping
CAMPGROUND $

(☑ 877-393-7070; www.kiwanisoceanfrontcamping. com; 550 Water St; campsites/RV sites $31/39; ☺ Apr-Oct) After the green and quaintness of St Andrews, this unattractive place – mostly a gravel parking area for trailers – comes as a shock. There's a few spaces for tents if you can squeeze in. It's situated at the far eastern end of town on Indian Point.

Picket Fence Motel
MOTEL $

(☑ 506-529-8985; www.picketfencenb.com; 102 Reed Ave; r $85-110; P ❄ 🛜) They're neat-as-a-pin, if dated motel-style rooms on approach into town but within walking distance of the main drag. It's among the cheapest you'll find in St Andrews, and while management is ultrafriendly, we're not convinced by its price-to-quality ratio.

⭐Treadwell Inn
B&B $$

(☑ 506-529-1011, 888-529-1011; www.treadwellinn. com; 129 Water St; r incl breakfast $179-229; ☺ May-Sep; ❄ ❄ 🛜) Big, light, airy handsome rooms in an 1820 ship chandler's house. Each of the four rooms has private decks and ocean views. Delightful Tom keeps things ship-shape. Breakfast is buffet continental.

Garden Gate
B&B $$

(☑ 506-529-4453; www.bbgardengate.com; 364 Montague St; r $150; P 🛜) Sunlight pours through the three spotless rooms in this handsome home several blocks behind the ocean. Excellent cooked breakfasts and small touches such as tea and cookies make for a pleasant experience.

Rossmount Inn
INN $$

(☑ 506-529-3351; www.rossmountinn.com; 4599 Rte 127; r $129-138; ☺ Apr-Dec; P ❄ 🛜 ☀) Flags flap in the breeze in front of this stately yellow summer cottage, perched atop a manicured slope overlooking Passamaquoddy Bay. Inside, the 18 rooms have a stylish mix of antiques and modern decor, with hand-carved wooden furniture and snowy white linens. It's about 4.5km north of downtown St Andrews on Rte 127.

Breakfast costs $6 (continental style) or $9 (full). The hotel restaurant is not only the town's best – we'd extend that to New Brunswick.

⭐Algonquin Resort
HOTEL $$$

(☑ 855-529-8693, 506-529-8823; www.algonquin resort.com; 184 Adolphus St; r from $229; P ❄ 🛜 ☀) The doyenne of New Brunswick hotels, this Tudor-style 'Castle-by-the-Sea' has sat on a hill overlooking town since 1889 and was given a makeover in 2015. With its elegant verandah, gardens, rooftop terrace, golf course, tennis courts and indoor pool with water slides, it's worth a look even if you're not spending the night. Prices vary according to seasons and demand.

🍴 Eating

Clam Digger
SEAFOOD $

(4468 Hwy 127, Chamcook; mains $6-15; ☺ 11:30am-3pm & 5-9pm Apr-Sep) Cars park three-deep outside this teeny red-and-white seafood shack that's a summertime tradition in these parts. In short: locals go nuts for it. Order your clam platter or dripping (yes, that would be the grease) cheeseburger, and claim one of the red-painted picnic tables. It's 3.5km north of the visitor center.

Honeybeans
CAFE $

(157a Water St; snacks $3-6; ☺ 7.30am-5pm Wed-Mon, 10am-5pm Sun) Listen to the gossip (it's a magnet for the locals) over a cup of good espresso-based coffee and a freshly baked treat.

⭐Rossmount Inn Restaurant
MODERN CANADIAN $$

(☑ 506-529-3351; www.rossmountinn.com; 4599 Rte 127; mains $18-30; ☺ 5-9:30pm) The Swiss chef-owner makes wonderful use of local bounty in this warm, art-filled dining room. The ever-changing menu might include foraged goose-tongue greens and wild mushrooms, periwinkles or New Brunswick lobster. They each play a part in complex, exquisite dishes – say, lobster with nasturtium-flower dumplings and vanilla bisque, or foie gras with cacao nibs and bee balm–poached peach.

St Andrews by-the-Sea

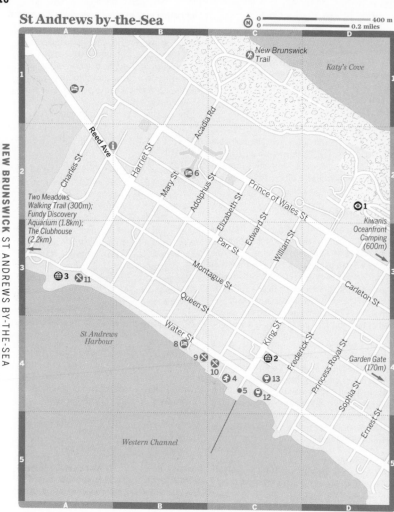

New Brunswick Trail

Katy's Cove

Reed Ave

Charles St

Harriet St

Mary St

Adolphus St

Acadia Rd

Elizabeth St

Edward St

Prince of Wales St

William St

Parr St

Montague St

Queen St

Water St

King St

Frederick St

Carleton St

Princess Royal St

Sophia St

Ernest St

Two Meadows Walking Trail (300m); Fundy Discovery Aquarium (1.8km); The Clubhouse (2.2km);

Kiwanis Oceanfront Camping (600m)

St Andrews Harbour

Garden Gate (170m)

Western Channel

Gables SEAFOOD $$

(506-529-3440; 143 Water St; mains $10-20; 11am-10pm) Seafood and views of Navy Island through a row of tall windows dominate this comfortable place. To enter, head down the alley onto a gardenlike patio on the water's edge.

Kingsbrae Garden Cafe CAFE $$

(www.kingsbraegarden.com; 220 King St; mains $10-18; 10am-5pm May-Oct, to 7pm Jul & Aug) At the beautiful Kingsbrae Garden, the terrace cafe serves sandwiches and salads for lunch with a glass of wine or local ale. Excellent brunches include salmon and scrambled eggs ($15).

Niger Reef Tea House CANADIAN

(www.nigerreefteahouse.com; 1 Joes Point Rd; mains $12-29; 11am-9pm May-Oct) Located in a historic building near the blockhouse overlooking the water, its interior murals date from the 1920s. Owner-chef David blends fresh, local ingredients (whatever is going that day) to create some beautiful salads, and the likes of curry lamb ragout and fiddlehead soup.

St Andrews by-the-Sea

🍸 Drinking & Nightlife

The Clubhouse   BAR
(http://algonquinresort.com; 465 Brandy Cove Rd;
⊙ 7am-9pm May-Oct) Kick back with a beer,
wine or cocktail at the '19th tee' and watch
as the punters come up the 18th hole of this
stunning golf course. The Clubhouse's inviting terrace has one of the region's best vistas.

Red Herring Pub   PUB
(211 Water St; ⊙ noon-2am Mar-Jan) A fun, slightly divey downtown watering hole with pool
tables, live music and frosty Canadian beers.

Shiretown Pub   PUB
(www.kennedyinn.ca; 218 Water St; ⊙ 11am-2am)
On the ground floor of the delightfully
creaky Kennedy Inn, this extremely old-
school English pub draws a mixed-age
crowd of partiers. Early afternoons mean
sipping New Brunswick–brewed Picaroons
bitter on the porch, while late nights bring
live music and raucous karaoke.

ⓘ Information

Tourist office (www.townofstandrews.ca; 46
Reed Ave; ⊙ 9am-7pm Jul & Aug, to 5pm May,
Jun, Sep & Oct; 🛜) This well organized office has
free walking-tour brochures that include a map
and brief description of some of the most note-
worthy places. It also has free internet access.

New River Provincial Park

Just off Hwy 1, about 35km west of Saint
John on the way to St Stephen, this large
park (☎ 506-755-4046; https://parcsnbparks.ca)
has one of the best beaches along the Fundy shore, a wide stretch of sand bordered
on one side by the rugged coastline of Barnaby Head. During camping season the park
charges a $10 fee per vehicle for day use,
which includes parking at the beach and
Barnaby Head trailhead.

You can spend an enjoyable few hours
hiking Barnaby Head along a 5km network
of nature trails. The **Chittick's Beach Trail**
leads through coastal forest and past four
coves, where you can check the catch in
a herring weir or examine tidal pools for
marine life. Extending from this loop is the
2.5km **Barnaby Head Trail**, which hugs the
shoreline most of the way and rises to the
edge of a cliff 15m above the Bay of Fundy.

The park's **campground** (☎ 506-755-4046;
https://parcsnbparks.ca; 78 New River Beach Rd;
campsites/RV sites $28/31; ⊙ May-Sep) is across
the road from the beach and features 100 secluded sites, both rustic and with hookups,
in a wooded setting. Drawbacks are the
gravel emplacements and traffic noise.

FUNDY ISLES

The thinly populated, unspoiled Fundy Isles
are ideal for a tranquil, nature-based escape.
With grand scenery, colorful fishing wharves
tucked into coves, supreme whale-watching,
uncluttered walking trails and steaming
dishes of seafood, the islands will make your
everyday stresses fade away and your blood
pressure ease. The three main islands each
have a distinct personality and offer a memorable, gradually absorbed peace. Outside of
the summer season, all are nearly devoid of
visitors and most services are shut.

Deer Island

Deer Island, the closest of the three main
Fundy Isles, is a modest fishing settlement
with a lived-in look. The 16km-by-5km island has been inhabited since 1770, and
1000 people live here year-round. It's well
forested, and deer are still plentiful. Lobster
is the main catch and there are half a dozen
wharves around the island.

Fundy Isles

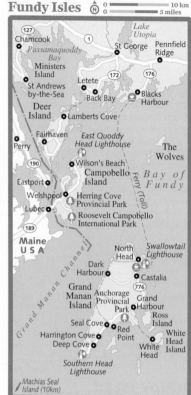

Deer Island can be easily explored on a day trip. Narrow, winding roads run south down each side toward Campobello Island and the ferry.

⊙ Sights

At the end of Cranberry Head Rd is a deserted beach. Most land on the island is privately owned, so there are no hiking trails.

Lobster Pound   VIEWPOINT

(Lambers Cove) At Lamberts Cove is a huge lobster pound used to hold live lobster (it could well be the world's largest). Another massive pound squirms at Northern Harbor.

Old Sow Whirlpool   WATERFRONT

(Deer Island Point Park) From the shores of the pretty, community-run 16-hectare Deer Island Point Park, Old Sow, the world's second-largest natural tidal whirlpool, is seen offshore a few hours before high tide. Whales pass occasionally too.

⟁ Tours

Whales usually arrive in mid-June and stay until October. You can be lucky enough to spot these offshore; for a closer look, head out on a kayak tour with **Seascape Kayak Tours** (☑506-747-1884; www.seascapekayaktours.com; 40 NW Harbour Branch Rd, Richardson, Deer Island; half-/full-day trips $85/150; ☉mid-May–mid-Sep).

🛏 Sleeping & Eating

Deer Island Inn   GUESTHOUSE $

(☑506-747-1998; www.deerislandinn.com; 272 Route 772, Lord's Cove; r incl breakfast $85-105; ☉May–mid-Oct) If island-stays are your thing, this excellent-value, conveniently located home brings a touch of Deer Island heritage and has five pleasantly appointed rooms. Excellent full breakfasts set you up for taking on the local sights.

Deer Island Point Park   CAMPGROUND $

(☑506-747-2423; www.deerislandpointpark.com; 195 Deer Island Point Rd; campsites $25-30; ☉Jun-Sep) Set up your tent on the high bluff and spend an evening watching the Old Sow whirlpool. The campground is directly above the Campobello ferry landing.

The Pilgrim's Rest   FAST FOOD $

(18 Cooks Lane, Lord's Cove; snacks $4-12, lobster rolls $11.50; ☉noon-8pm Sat & Sun May–mid-Jun, noon-8pm Tue-Sun mid-Jun–late Sep) An apt name for an apt spot. The Pilgrim's Rest is a simple, hole-in-the-wall eatery and is the place to get your fill of seafood (much of it fried) plus great lobster rolls to enjoy on the small patio or to take out for a picnic.

ⓘ Information

Tourist information (☑506-747-0119; www.deerisland.nb.ca; 193 Rte 772, Lords Cove; ☉10am-5pm Jul-Sep) This helpful place run by local volunteers out of the community centre.

ⓘ Getting There & Away

A free government-run ferry (25 minutes) runs to Deer Island from Letete, which is 14.5km south of St George on Hwy 172 via Back Bay. The ferries run year-round every half-hour from 6am to 7pm, and hourly from 7pm to 10pm. Get in line early on a busy day.

In summer **East Coast Ferries** (☑506-747-2159; www.eastcoastferries.nb.ca; car & driver $20, additional passenger $4; ☉8:30am-6:30pm late Jun–mid-Sep) services Campobello Island.

Campobello Island

The wealthy have long been enjoying Campobello, a gentle and prosperous island, as a summer retreat. Due to the island's accessibility to New England, it feels as much a part of the USA as of Canada, and most of the tourists here are Americans.

Like many moneyed families, the Roosevelts bought property in this peaceful coastal area at the end of the 1800s. The southern half of Campobello is almost all park, and a golf course occupies still more.

Come to the island prepared. The island's biggest community, Wilson's Beach, 10km north of Roosevelt Park, has just a grocery store and post office. An ATM is at Welshpool. The island has no gas station – the 1000 residents of the 16km-long Campobello must cross the bridge to Lubec, ME, to fill their tanks.

◉ Sights

★**Roosevelt Campobello International Park**   PARK

(☏506-752-2922; www.fdr.net; Hwy 774) **FREE** The southernmost green area of Campobello Island is this 1100-hectare park. Its biggest visitor attraction is the **Roosevelt Cottage**, the 34-room lodge where Franklin D Roosevelt grew up (between 1905 and 1921) and visited periodically throughout his time as US president (1933–45). The arts-and-crafts-style structure is furnished with original Roosevelt furniture and artifacts. Adjacent **Hubbard House**, built in 1891, is also open to visitors.

The park is just 2.5km from the Lubec bridge, and from the Roosevelt mansion's front porch you can look directly across to Eastport, ME. You'd hardly know you were in Canada.

Unlike the manicured museum area, most of the international park has been left in its natural state to preserve the flora and fauna that Roosevelt appreciated so much. A couple of gravel roads meander through it, leading to beaches and 7.5km of nature trails. It's a surprisingly wild, little-visited part of Campobello Island. Deer, moose and coyotes call it home, and seals can sometimes be seen offshore on the ledges near Lower Duck Pond, 6km from the visitor center. Look for eagles, ospreys and loons.

Herring Cove Provincial Park   PARK

FREE Along the northern boundary of Roosevelt Campobello International Park is Herring Cove Provincial Park. This park has 10km of walking trails as well as a campground and a picnic area on an arching 1.5km beach. It makes a fine, picturesque place for lunch.

East Quoddy Head Lighthouse   LIGHTHOUSE

Four kilometers north of Wilson's Beach is East Quoddy Head Lighthouse. Whales browse offshore and many people sit along the rocky shoreline with binoculars enjoying the sea breezes.

☞ Tours

Island Cruises   CRUISE

(☏506-752-1107; www.bayoffundywhales.com; 62 Harbour Head Rd, Wilson's Beach; adult/child $50/40; ☉Jul-Oct) Offers 2½-hour whale-watching cruises.

🛏 Sleeping & Eating

Herring Cove Provincial Park   CAMPGROUND $

(☏506-752-7010; www.campobello.com/cmpgrd-fe.html; 136 Herring Cove Rd; campsites/RV sites $22/24; ☉Jun-Sep) This 76-site park on the eastern side of the island, 3km from the Deer Island ferry, has some nice secluded sites in a forest setting, plus there's a sandy beach and ample hiking.

Owen House B&B   B&B $$

(☏506-752-2977; www.owenhouse.ca; 11 Welshpool St, Welshpool; d incl breakfast private/shared bath from $115/104; P) A classic seaside vacation home of yesteryear, complete with antique spool beds made up with quilts, cozy reading nooks and lots of windows on the ocean.

Pollock Cove Cottages   COTTAGE $$

(☏506-328-7932; pollockcove@gmail.com; 2455 Rte 774, Wilson's Beach; cottages $75-175; P@) Simple, clean one- and two-bedroom cottages with million-dollar views. All have kitchens.

Fireside Restaurant   MODERN AMERICAN $$

(☏506-752-6055; www.fdr.net; Roosevelt Park; luncheon special $12-18, mains $12-28; ☉noon-5pm Sun-Wed, to 9pm Thu-Sat late May–mid-Oct) Housed in a former summer residence of the Adams family (Mrs Adams was a cousin of President Roosevelt), this lovely spot has a daily luncheon special, salads, pastas and, of course, lobster rolls (price varies according to the lobster market).

Family Fisheries Restaurant   SEAFOOD $$

(www.familyfisheries.com; 1977 Rte 774, Wilson's Beach; mains $9-25; ☉11:30am-9pm Apr-Sep) Part of a fresh-fish market, this ultracasual seafood shack specializes in fish-and-chips (all the seafood is caught by family members), plus lip-smacking chowders and lobster rolls.

❶ Information

Visitors Center (☑ 506-752-2922; www.fdr. net; Hwy 774; ☉10am-5pm) Principally an information center for the Roosevelt Campobello International Park, but can point you in the right direction to elsewhere on the island.

❶ Getting There & Away

East Coast Ferries (p103) Connects Deer Island to Welshpool (25 minutes, half-hourly) on Campobello Island.

Grand Manan Island

Grand Manan is a peaceful, unspoiled place. There are no fast-food restaurants, no trendy coffeehouses or nightclubs, no traffic lights and no traffic. Just a ruggedly beautiful coastline of high cliffs and sandy coves interspersed with spruce forest and fields of long grass. Wonderful lighthouses, including the famous Swallowtail Lighthouse, stand guard above cliffs. Along the eastern shore and joined by a meandering coastal road sit a string of pretty and prosperous fishing villages. There is plenty of fresh sea air and that rare and precious commodity in the modern world: silence, broken only by the rhythmic ocean surf. Some people make it a day trip, but lingering is recommended.

❍ Sights

Grand Manan Art Gallery   GALLERY
(☑506-662-3662;   www.grandmananartgallery. com; 21 Cedar St, Castalia; $2; ☉noon-6pm Mon-Sat, 1pm-5pm Sun mid-Jun–late Sep) This lovely, not-for-profit local gallery showcases local, seasonal and regional artists, as well as well-known historic and emerging figures. Definitely worth checking out.

Fishing Weirs   LANDMARK
Those round contraptions comprising wooden posts that you see dotting the waters around Grand Manan are based on the design of ancient fishing traps; some of those you see date back to the 19th century, though, sadly, only a few remain these days. They were formerly labelled with names such as 'Ruin,' 'Winner,' 'Outside Chance' and 'Spite,' evoking the heartbreak of relying on an indifferent sea for a living.

Seal Cove   HISTORIC SITE
Seal Cove is the island's prettiest village. Much of its charm comes from the fishing boats, wharves and herring-smoking sheds clustered around the tidal creek mouth. For a century, smoked herring was king on Grand Manan. A thousand men and women worked splitting, stringing and drying fish in 300 smokehouses up and down the island. The last smokehouse shut down in 1996. Although herrings are still big business around here, they're now processed at a modern cannery.

Grand Manan Historical Museum   MUSEUM
(☑506-662-3524;   www.grandmananmuseum.ca; 1141 Rte 776, Grand Harbour; adult/student & senior $5/3; ☉9am-5pm Mon-Fri Jun-Sep, plus Sat Jul & Aug) This museum makes a good destination on a foggy day. Its diverse collection of local artifacts provides a quick primer on island history. You can see a display on shipwreck lore and the original kerosene lamp from nearby Gannet Rock lighthouse (1904). There is also a room stuffed with 200-plus taxidermied birds (including the now-extinct passenger pigeon).

Swallowtail Lighthouse   LIGHTHOUSE
(www.tourismnewbrunswick.ca; adult/under 12yr $5/free; ☉Jul & Aug) Whitewashed Swallowtail Lighthouse (1860) is the island's signature vista, cleaving to a rocky promontory about 1km north of the ferry wharf. Access is via steep stairs and a wooden footbridge. Since the light was automated in 1986, the site has been left to the elements. Nevertheless, the grassy bluff is a stupendous setting for a picnic. You can explore the lighthouse on your own (for a fee); even when it's closed it's illuminating, set where it is and all.

⏃ Activities

Around 70km of hiking trails crisscross and circle the island. Grab the comprehensive guide *Heritage Trails and Footpaths on Grand Manan* ($5), available at most island shops. Stay well away from the cliff edges as unstable, undercut ground can give way beneath your feet.

For an easy hike, try the 1.6km shoreline (boardwalk) path from Long Pond to Red Point (about one hour round-trip; suitable for children). In Whale Cove, the Hole-in-the-Wall is an often photographed natural arch jutting into the sea. It's a short hike from the parking area.

Sea Watch Tours BIRDWATCHING

(📞877-662-8552, 506-662-8552; www.seawatch-tours.com; Seal Cove Fisherman's Wharf; adult/child $115/56; ⊙Mon-Sat Jul & Aug) Make the pilgrimage out to isolated **Machias Seal Island** to see the Atlantic puffins waddle and play on their home turf. Access is limited to 15 visitors a day, so reserve well in advance. Getting onto the island can be tricky, as the waves are high and the rocks slippery. Wear sturdy shoes.

Whales-n-Sails Adventures BOATING

(📞888-994-4044, 506-662-1999; www.whales-n-sails.com; North Head Fisherman's Wharf; adult/child $66/46; ⊙Jul-Sep) A marine biologist narrates these exhilarating whale-watching tours aboard the sailboat *Elsie Menota*. You'll often see puffins, razorbills, murre and other seabirds.

Adventure High KAYAKING, CYCLING

(📞506-662-3563; www.adventurehigh.com; 83 Rte 776, North Head; day tours $45-110, bicycles per half-day/day/week $18/25/125; ⊙May-Oct) This outfitter offers tours of the Grand Manan coastline ranging from lovely two-hour sunset paddles to multiday Bay of Fundy adventures. Excellent educational information along the way.

🛌 Sleeping

You'll need to reserve ahead in summer to stay on Grand Manan.

Hole-in-the-Wall Campground CAMPGROUND $

(📞506-662-3152; www.grandmanancamping.com; 42 Old Airport Rd, North Head; campsites/cabins $28/42; ⊙May-Oct) These spectacular cliff-top campsites are secluded among the rocks and trees, with fire pits, picnic tables and breathtaking views. Choose an inland site if you sleepwalk or suffer from vertigo. Showers and laundry facilities are available, as well as a couple of spotless, simple cabins (linen provided).

Anchorage Camping CAMPGROUND $

(📞506-662-7022; Rte 776, Anchorage; campsites/RV sites $24/26; ⊙May-Sep) Family-friendly camping in a large field surrounded by tall evergreens, a former provincial park, located at Anchorage, between Grand Harbour and Seal Cove. There's a kitchen shelter for rainy days, a playground, laundry and a long pebbly beach. Get down by the trees to block the wind. The areas adjoins marshes, which comprise a migratory bird sanctuary, and there are several short hiking trails.

Inn at Whale Cove INN $$

(📞506-662-3181; www.whalecovecottages.ca; Whistle Rd, North Head; s/d incl breakfast $145/155; ⊙May-Oct; P❄) 'Serving rusticators since 1910', including writer Willa Cather, who wrote several of her novels here in the 1920s and '30s. The main lodge (built in 1816) and six shingled cottages (two with fully equipped kitchens) retain the charm of that earlier era. They are fitted with polished pine floors and stone fireplaces, antiques, chintz curtains and well-stocked bookshelves.

They're pricey for singles, but head here for the holistic experience. Trails lead to Whale Cove and the area is full of wildflowers.

McLaughlin's GUESTHOUSE $$

(📞506-662-3672; www.mclaughlinswharfinn.ca; 1863 Rte 776, Seal Cove; r $109) If it were any closer to the historic smoke shacks you'd be smoked yourselves. Perched on a wharf in Seal Cove is this atmospheric and very homely B&B with quilted beds and unique outlooks.

Compass Rose B&B $$

(📞506-662-3563; www.compassroseinn.com; 65 Rte 776, North Head; r incl breakfast $99-165; P❄🛜) It's hard to go wrong at this neat little spot, which has had a recent makeover and features airy and comfortable guest rooms, all with harbor views. It's within walking distance of the ferry dock, and has one of the island's most atmospheric restaurants attached. Handily, the owner, Kevin, runs the local kayaking company.

🍴 Eating

The island's scant options are nearly nonexistent in the off-season. For the few decent places that are open for dinner, reservations are essential. Be sure to try dulse, a dark purple seaweed harvested locally and eaten like crisps (chips) by locals. Chefs use it as a seasoning. You might even see a 'DLT sandwich' (yep, that's dulse instead of bacon).

⭐**Inn at Whale Cove** MODERN CANADIAN $$$

(📞506-662-3181; www.whalecovecottages.ca; Whistle Rd, North Head; mains $22-28; ⊙5-7pm) Wonderful food in a relaxed country setting on Whale Cove. The menu changes daily, but includes mouth-watering meals such as pulled pork and tagliatelle, seafood bouillabaise and a to-die-for hazelnut crème caramel for dessert. Come early and have a cocktail by the fire in the cozy, old-fashioned parlor.

Be on time (or risk the owner's wrath – all in the name of protecting the tranquillity of her inn guests, however).

Food for Thought CAFE
(922 Rte 776; snacks $4.25-7; ⊘ 6:30am-5pm Mon & Tue, to 6pm Wed & Thu, to 8pm Fri, 7am-3pm Sat Apr-Dec) This welcome relative newcomer to Grand Manan may not look like much from the outside, but step over the threshold and you'll find a cozy spot that churns out fresh and fabulous made-on-the-premises items, from excellent rolls and salads for picnics to hearty soups. The cookies and pastries are worth coming for alone (don't miss the cinnamon buns!) The owner is a caterer, and it's easy to see why.

🔒 Shopping

Roland's Sea Vegetables MARKET
(174 Hill Rd; ⊘ 9am-5pm) This is the spot in the world to learn about dulse. Grand Manan is one of the few remaining producers of dulse, a type of seaweed that is used as a snack food or seasoning in Atlantic Canada and around the world. Dulse gatherers wade among the rocks at low tide to pick the seaweed, then lay it out on beds of rocks to dry, just as they've been doing for hundreds of years.

ℹ️ Information

Tourist Information Office (☑ 506-662-3442; www.grandmanannb.com; 130 Rte 776, North Head; ⊘ mid-Jun–late Aug) Locally run tourist organization that has maps, brochures and ferry schedules.

ℹ️ Getting There & Away

The only way to get from Blacks Harbour on the mainland to North Head on Grand Manan is by a private ferry company, **Coastal Transport** (☑ 506-662-3724; http://grandmanan. coastaltransport.ca; adult/child/car/bicycle $12/6/36/4.10). The crossing takes 1½ hours, and there are around three to four daily departures from each port in summer. Reserve and pay in advance as it gets busy. It's best to pay for a return trip, rather than one way, so you don't get stuck on the island. Watch for harbor porpoises and whales en route.

The ferry dock is within walking distance of several hotels, restaurants, shops and tour operators. To explore the whole of the island, bring your own car, as there is no rental company on Grand Manan.

ℹ️ Getting Around

The ferry disembarks at the village of North Head at the northern end of the island. The main road, Rte 776, runs 28.5km down the length of the island along the eastern shore. It connects all of Grand Manan's settlements en route to the lighthouse, which is perched atop a bluff at South Head. You can drive from end to end in about 45 minutes. The western side of Grand Manan is uninhabited and more or less impenetrable: a sheer rock wall rising out the sea, backed by dense forest and bog, broken only at Dark Harbour where a steep road drops down to the water's edge. Hiking trails provides access to this wilderness.

Adventure High (p121) rents out bicycles. Be aware, though, that the roads are winding and high season is busy. At other times, keen cyclists can enjoy the undulating routes.

SAINT JOHN

POP 70,100

Saint John is the economic engine room of the province, a gritty port city with a dynamism that's missing from the demure capital. The setting is impressive – a ring of rocky bluffs, sheer cliffs, coves and peninsulas surrounding a deep natural harbor where the mighty Saint John and Kennebecasis Rivers empty into the Bay of Fundy. It can take a bit of imagination to appreciate this natural beauty, obscured as it is by the smokestacks of a pulp mill, oil refinery and garden-variety urban blight. But those who push their way through all this to the historic core are rewarded with beautifully preserved redbrick and sandstone 19th-century architecture and glimpses of the sea down steep, narrow side streets.

Originally a French colony, the city was incorporated by British Loyalists in 1785 to become Canada's first legal city. Thousands of Irish immigrants arrived during the potato famine of the mid-1800s and helped build the city into a prosperous industrial town, important particularly for its wooden shipbuilding. Today, a large percentage of the population works in heavy industry, including pulp mills, refineries and the Moosehead Brewery. There is also a large IT knowledge cluster.

⦿ Sights

The Bay of Fundy tides and their effects are a predominant regional characteristic. The rapids here on the Saint John River are part

Saint John

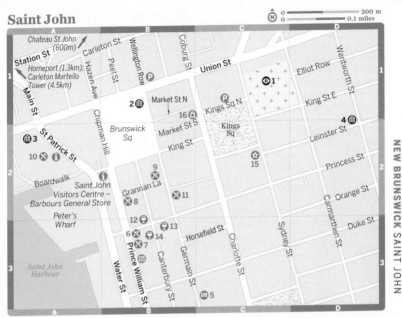

Saint John

⊙ Sights
1 Loyalist Burial Ground	C1
2 Loyalist House	B1
3 New Brunswick Museum	A2
4 Saint John Jewish Historical Museum	D2

⊜ Sleeping
5 Mahogany Manor	C3

⊗ Eating
Billy's Seafood Company	(see 16)
6 Britt's Pub & Eatery	B3
7 East Coast Bistro	B3
8 Java Moose	B2
9 Port City Royal	B2
10 Saint John Ale House	A2
11 Taco Pica	B2

⊜ Drinking & Nightlife
12 Big Tide Brewing Company	B3
13 Happinez Wine Bar	B3
14 O'Leary's	B3

⊛ Entertainment
15 Imperial Theatre	C2

⊜ Shopping
16 Old City Market	B1

of that and are one of the best-known sites in the province. Known as 'reversing rapids', the name is a bit of a misnomer. When the high tides at Bay of Fundy rise, the current in the river reverses, causing the water to flow upstream. When the tides go down (up to 8.5m), the water flows in the normal way. Generally, it looks like rapids.

Saint John Visitors Centre – Reversing Rapids (p127), next to the bridge over the river, can supply a tides table that explains where in the cycle you are.

Loyalist Burial Ground　　　　CEMETERY
This solemn cemetery, with tombstones from as early as 1784, is just off Kings Sq in a park-style setting in the center of town.

Saint John Jewish Historical Museum　　　　MUSEUM
(91 Leinster St; admission by donation; ⊙10am-4pm Mon-Fri Jun-Oct, plus 1-4pm Sun Jul & Aug) This modest museum traces the history of Saint John's once-thriving Jewish community, whose members included Louis B Mayer of Metro-Goldwyn-Mayer (MGM) Hollywood fame.

Irving Nature Park
PARK

(☉ 8am-dusk May-Oct) For those who have vehicles and like nature, Irving Nature Park, 9km southwest of Saint John, is a must for its rugged, unspoiled coastal topography. It's also a remarkable place for bird-watching, with hundreds of species regularly spotted. Seals sometimes gather on the rocks offshore. Seven trails lead around beaches, cliffs, woods, mudflats, marsh and rocks. Wear sturdy footwear. Take Hwy 1 west from town and turn south at Exit 107, Bleury St. Then take a right on Sand Cove Rd and continue for 2km to the entrance.

New Brunswick Museum
MUSEUM

(www.nbm-mnb.ca; 1 Market Sq; adult/student/family $10/6/22; ☉ 9am-5pm Mon-Wed & Fri, to 9pm Thu, 10am-5pm Sat, noon-5pm Sun) One of Canada's oldest (and New Brunswick's finest) museums, the New Brunswick Museum has a varied and interesting collection. There's a captivating section on marine wildlife with an outstanding section on whales, including a life-size specimen. There are also hands-on exhibits, models of old sailing ships and a stunning collection of Canadian and international artwork on the top floor. Well worth a visit.

Carleton Martello Tower
HISTORIC BUILDING

(454 Whipple St; adult/child $3.90/1.90; ☉ 10am-5:30pm late Jun-Sep) Built during the War of 1812 for defence purposes, this round stone fort features a restored barracks and other historical displays, but the real reason to go is the panoramic view over Saint John and the Bay of Fundy from the hilltop locale.

Loyalist House
HISTORIC BUILDING

(☎ 506-652-3590; www.loyalisthouse.com; 120 Union St; adult/child/family $5/2/7; ☉ 10am-5pm late May-Sep) Dating from 1810, the Georgian-style Loyalist House is one of the city's oldest unchanged buildings. It's now a museum, depicting the Loyalist period, and contains some fine carpentry.

🏃 Activities & Tours

As a popular stop for cruise-ship travelers, Saint John has a large range of tour options. Whale-watching, unfortunately, is not an attraction in Saint John, save for the very occasional, very wayward minke.

Harbour Passage
WALKING

Beginning on a boardwalk at Market Sq (behind the Hilton Hotel), Harbour Passage is a red-paved walk and cycle trail that leads around the harbor, up Bennett St and down Douglas Ave to the Reversing Falls bridge and lookout. Informative plaques line the route and it's about a one-hour walk one way.

Roy's Tour
DRIVING

(www.roystours.webs.com; tours per group per hour $60) Knowledgeable local Roy Flowers narrates personalized five- to six-hour taxi tours of the city and surrounds.

Walks 'n Talks with David Goss
WALKING

(☎ 506-672-8601; walks free-$5; ☉ 7pm Tue Jun-Sep) For nearly 30 years David Goss has led themed walks throughout the city and natural environments. The walks have so much flair that locals as well as visitors frequent the fun. Departure locations and hours vary; check with the visitor center.

🛏 Sleeping

Saint John motels sit primarily along Manawagonish Rd, 7km west of uptown. There are also a couple of upscale chain hotels uptown.

University of New Brunswick Summer Residences
RESIDENCE HALL $

(☎ 506-648-5755; www.unbsj.ca; off Sandy Point Rd, near Rockwood Park; s/d/ste $40/50/80; 🛜) From May to August, the University of New Brunswick's Saint John campus offers simple rooms and rather spartan kitchenette suites in two residence halls. The university is 6km north of the city center. Take a bus from Kings Sq; for the correct number, look for 'University' on the schedules.

Rockwood Park
CAMPGROUND $

(☎ 506-652-4050; www.rockwoodparkcampground. com; Lake Dr S; campsites/RV sites $29/39; ☉ May-Sep; 🛜) A couple of kilometers north of the downtown area is huge Rockwood Park, with small lakes, a woodland crisscrossed by walking paths, and a campground in a small open field.

★ Mahogany Manor
B&B $$

(☎ 506-636-8000; www.sjnow.com/mm; 220 Germain St; d incl breakfast from $110; 🅿️😊🛜) On the loveliest street in Saint John, this gay-friendly, antique-filled Victorian is a wonderful place to temporarily call home. Five light and airy rooms are a comfy mix of antiques and plush, modern bedding. The upbeat owners know more about the city than you'll be able to absorb – even which meal to order at which restaurant!

DON'T MISS

SCENIC DRIVE: FUNDY TRAIL

This magnificent **trail** (www.fundytrailparkway.com; adult/child/family $7.50/5/23; ⊙ 6am-8pm May-Oct) is not one track, per se, but comprises a network of roads, trails and footpaths along the Bay of Fundy coast. The main auto-parkway traverses a rugged section of what has been called the only remaining coastal wilderness between Florida and Newfoundland. The 19km-long parkway to Long Beach (opened in 2016) via Salmon River put an end to the unspoiled wilderness part, but it's still beautiful; off here are numerous viewpoints (lookouts), picnic areas and parking places. In 2018, the parkway will extend to Fundy National Park (30.5km total).

Running parallel to the parkway is a separate 11km-long multiuse trail for walkers and cyclists. In the off-season, the main gate is closed, but you can park at the entrance and hike or pedal in.

At Big Salmon River visit the **Big Salmon River Interpretative Center** (⊙ 8:30am-8pm mid-May–mid-Oct), which has exhibits from when a logging community lived here. Near there, a suspension bridge leads to a vast wilderness hiking area beyond the end of the road. This is known as the **Fundy Footpath**, but this is for hard-core hikers only – it's a solid five-day trek from Big Salmon River to Goose River in Fundy National Park. Think wilderness, rocky scree, tidal crossings and a rope ladder or two. You must register at either end.

Chateau Saint John BUSINESS HOTEL $$
(✆ 506-644-4444; www.chateausaintjohn.ca; 369 Rockland Rd; r from $155; P ✳ 🛜) Despite its behemoth appearance, situated on a main road on the edge of the CBD, Chateau Saint John surprises with large, spacious rooms and city views. Professional service and the price to quality ratio make this a good choice. It's a 15-minute walk into town and there's ample parking on-site. It's popular with groups and business people.

Homeport B&B $$
(✆ 888-678-7678, 506-672-7255; www.homeport.nb.ca; 60 Douglas Ave; r incl breakfast $109-175; P ➠ ✳ 🛜) Perched above once-grand Douglas Ave, this imposing Italianate-style B&B was once two separate mansions belonging to shipbuilder brothers. It has a boutique-hotel vibe, with a stately parlor, a full bar and 10 elegant old-world guest rooms (try to snag one with a claw-foot bathtub). It's about 1km west of the uptown peninsula.

🍴 Eating

Java Moose CAFE $
(www.javamoose.com; 84 Prince William St; snacks $3-6; ⊙ 8am-6pm; 🛜) Get your caffeine fix (fab or otherwise depending on your local or international taste buds) at this homegrown coffeehouse.

Taco Pica MEXICAN, GUATEMALAN $
(www.tacopica.ca; 96 Germain St; mains $14-24; ⊙ 10am-10pm Mon-Sat) A fusion of authentic Guatemalan and Mexican fare is served in this colorful cantina and is a welcome alternative to standard fare. An economical introduction to the cuisine is Taco Pica's *pepian* – a simple but spicy beef stew that is as good as you'll find in any Guatemalan household. The hardworking Guatemalan owner has been here for years. Live music is also often on the menu.

★ Port City Royal INTERNATIONAL $$
(✆ 506-631-3714; www.portcityroyal.com; 45 Grannan St; share plates $12-14; ⊙ 11:30am-late Tue-Fri, 2pm-late Sat) Owner-chef Jacob heads up this revered spot, housed in a renovated historic building. He declares that 'the menu is constantly in a state of evolution and never quite finished'. He loves experimenting with local produce, using whole animals (and their every last scrap for pâtés, soups and sausages) and his dishes (mainly share plates) are ever changing.

★ East Coast Bistro INTERNATIONAL $$
(✆ 506-696-3278; www.eastcoastbistro.com; 60 Prince William St; mains $20-31; ⊙ 11am-4pm Mon, to 9pm Tue-Thu, to 11pm Fri, to 10pm Sat) East Coast Bistro is one of the standout restaurants in Saint John, offering top-notch cuisine at digestible prices. Sustainable, local cuisine is the real deal here – it even makes its own bread. The menu changes seasonally, but braised Atlantic beef-cheek agnolotti and seafood sauté are just two of the luscious dishes whipped up in this casual space.

Britt's Pub & Eatery
MODERN AMERICAN **$$**

(www.brittspub.ca; 42 Princess St; mains $14-24; ⊙7:30am-1am Mon-Wed, to 2am Thu & Fri, 9am-2am Sat, 9am-midnight Sun) This cheery spot is one of the more affordable eating places around so it attracts a crowd. It's meant to emulate a British pub (though we're not so sure it does that), but it has good, modern fare and drinks. Good for single travelers who can enjoy the experience without standing out like a Union Jack–waving Brit in a Canadian pub.

Saint John Ale House
MODERN AMERICAN **$$$**

(www.sjah.ca; 1 Market Sq; mains $18-40; ⊙11am-late Mon-Fri, 10:30am-late Sat & Sun) On the lips of most locals who suggest the ale house for a great selection of beers, both craft and on tap (served in a pub downstairs) as well as its sleek, sprawling bistro and hearty meals based on the 'eat local and forage' mantra (menu changes daily). It offers a great brunch menu too, from the likes of pulled pork and eggs to frittata.

Billy's Seafood Company
SEAFOOD **$$$**

(www.billysseafood.com; 49 Charlotte St; mains $25-32; ⊙11am-10pm Mon-Sat, 4-10pm Sun) Since we are on the East Coast after all... This popular casual restaurant at the top of the City Market does reasonable seafood dishes. It's one of the few eateries open on Sunday evening.

Kingston Farmers Market
MARKET

(Rte 845, Kingston; ⊙8am-1pm Sat) A favorite (and fun) Saturday-morning activity for Saint Johners, head here for your fix of fresh fruits and vegetables and various ethnic foods.

THE TIDES OF FUNDY

The tides of the Bay of Fundy are the highest in the world. A Mi'kmaq legend explains the tide as the effect of a whale's thrashing tail sending the water forever sloshing back and forth. A more prosaic explanation is in the length, depth and gradual funnel shape of the bay itself.

The contrasts between the high and ebb tide are most pronounced at the eastern end of the bay and around the Minas Basin, with tides of 10m to 15m twice daily 12½ hours apart. The highest tide ever recorded anywhere was 16.6m, the height of a four-story building, at Burncoat Head near Noel, Nova Scotia.

🍷 Drinking & Entertainment

O'Leary's
PUB

(www.olearyspub.com; 46 Princess St; ⊙11:30am-11pm Mon & Tue, to 2am Wed-Fri, 3pm-2am Sat) Shoot the breeze with local barflies at this divey but friendly downtown institution.

Happinez Wine Bar
BAR

(www.happinezwinebar.com; 42 Princess St; ⊙4pm-midnight Wed & Thu, to 1am Fri, 5pm-1am Sat) For a quiet tipple in a sleek urban environment, duck into this intimate little wine bar. Cellar wines by the bottle come with a hefty price tag, but wines by the glass are available too.

Big Tide Brewing Company
BREWERY

(www.bigtidebrew.com; 47 Princess St; ⊙11am-midnight Mon-Sat, 3-9pm Sun) This subterranean brewpub is a cozy spot for a pint (try the Confederation Cream Ale or the Whistlepig Stout), a selection from the pub menu or a friendly game of trivia. All tap beer is brewed on the premises.

Imperial Theatre
THEATER

(☑506-674-4100; www.imperialtheatre.nb.ca; 24 Kings Sq S) Now restored to its original 1913 splendor, this is the city's premier venue for performances ranging from classical music to live theater.

🛍 Shopping

Old City Market
MARKET

(☑658 2820; 47 Charlotte St; ⊙7:30-6pm Mon-Fri, to 5pm Sat) Wedged between North and South Market Sts, this sense-stunning food hall has been home to wheeling and dealing since 1876. The interior of the impressive brick building is packed with produce stalls, bakeries, fishmongers and butcher shops, as well as numerous counters selling a range of delectable prepared meals. Locals head to the lunch counter at Slocum and Ferris.

ℹ Information

Main post office (126 Prince William St)

Saint John Library (1 Market Sq; ⊙9am-5pm Mon & Tue, 10am-9pm Wed & Thu, 10am-5pm Fri-Sun) Free internet access.

Saint John Regional Hospital (☑506-648-6000; 400 University Ave; ⊙24hr) Northwest of the town center.

Saint John Visitors Centre – Barbours General Store (St Andrew's Bicentennial Green; ⊙10am-6pm mid-May–Sep) Conveniently located in the old-fashioned Barbours General Store, at the central St Andrew's Bicentennial Green.

Saint John Visitors Centre – Reversing Rapids (450 Bridge Rd; ⊘ 9am-6pm mid-May–Sep, to 7pm Jul & Aug)

Visitor & Convention Bureau (☑ 506-658-2990; www.discoversaintjohn.com; City Hall, 15 Market Sq; ⊘ 9am-6pm mid-May–mid-Oct, to 7pm Jul & Aug) Knowledgeable, friendly staff. Ask for the self-guided walking-tour pamphlets.

ⓘ Getting There & Away

AIR

The airport is 5km east of town on Loch Lomond Rd toward St Martins. Air Canada runs daily flights to Toronto, Montréal and Halifax.

BOAT

The **Bay Ferries** (p103) sails daily between Saint John and Digby, Nova Scotia, year-round. The three-hour crossing can save a lot of driving.

Arrive early or call ahead for vehicle reservations, as the ferry is very busy in July and August. Even with a reservation, arrive an hour before departure. Walk-ons and cyclists should be OK any time. There's a restaurant and a bar.

BUS

Long-haul bus services are operated by **Maritime Bus** (☑ 506-672-2055; www.maritimebus.com; 125 Station St; ⊘ 8am-8pm Mon-Fri, 9am-8pm Sat & Sun). Routes include Fredericton ($25.50, 1½ hours) and Moncton ($34, two to four hours).

ⓘ Getting Around

Downtown (known as Uptown) Saint John sits on a square, hilly peninsula between the mouth of the Saint John River and Courtenay Bay. Kings Sq marks the nucleus of town, and its pathways duplicate the pattern of the Union Jack.

West over the Harbour Bridge is Saint John West. Many of the street names in this section of the city are identical to those of Saint John proper, and to avoid confusion, they end in a west designation, such as Charlotte St W. Saint John West has the ferries to Digby, Nova Scotia.

EASTERN FUNDY SHORE

Much of the rugged, unspoiled Eastern Fundy Shore from Saint John to Hopewell Cape has been incorporated into the Fundy Trail Parkway, both a 19km-long road and parallel 10km trail that will soon link up with the Fundy National Park. Indeed, hikers, cyclists, kayakers and all nature-lovers will be enchanted by this marvelous coast, edged by dramatic cliffs and tides. Since it's not yet possible to drive directly along the coastline from St Martins to Fundy National Park, a detour inland by Sussex is necessary.

St Martins

A 40km drive east of Saint John, St Martins is a winsome seaside hamlet surrounded by steep cliffs and flower-studded pastureland. Once a major wooden shipbuilding center, this (now sedate) spot springs to life in the summer. Hikers, bikers and scenic-drivers flock to the 19km Fundy Trail Parkway (p125), which starts east of the village and winds along a jaw-dropping stretch of coastline. In town, check out the impressive red sandstone sea caves of Mac's Beach, accessible by foot when the tide is low. The village's twin covered bridges are a popular photo op, so bring your camera.

☞ Tours

Red Rock Adventure   KAYAKING, WALKING
(☑ 506-833-2231; www.redrockadventure.ca; 415 Main St; per person walking tours $30-50, kayaking trips $125) Located opposite the St Martins Wharf and its pretty covered bridge, Red Rock Adventures offers walking tours, including one of historic St Martins, and kayaking adventures.

River Bay Adventures   KAYAKING
(☑ 506-663-9530; www.riverbayadventures.com; tours from $65) Runs two- to three-hour guided sea-kayaking trips to the caves and islands along the coast.

🛏 Sleeping & Eating

Salmon River B&B   B&B $$
(☑ 506-833-1110; www.salmonriverbandb.com; 4 Snows Lane; r $105-125; ⊘ mid-May–mid-Oct) Eight plain but pleasant rooms above Fiori's restaurant, run by the same folk. It's in a handy location bang in the middle of town.

The Caves   RESTAURANT $
(82 Bayview Rd; mains $10-27; ⊘ 11am-7pm May-Oct, to 8:30pm Jul & Aug) One of two seaside spots known for their creamy chowder sitting side by side on Mac's Beach. Also serves salads, burgers and sandwiches.

Seaside Restaurant & Take Out   SEAFOOD $$
(80 Big Salmon River Rd; mains $10-20; ⊘ 11am-8pm Mar-Nov) Right on Mac's Beach, the spacious but simple Seaside Restaurant serves fish-and-chips, scallops, chowder and more. Now you know you are on holiday.

Fundy National Park

Fundy National Park (www.pc.gc.ca/eng/pn-np/nb/fundy; daily permit adult/child/family $7.80/3.90/19.60; ☺May-Oct) is the region's most popular. Highlights include the world's highest tides, the irregularly eroded sandstone cliffs and the wide beach at low tide that makes exploring the shore for small marine life and debris such a treat. The park is delightfully wooded and lush and features an extensive network of impressive hiking trails.

🏃 Activities

Cycling
Mountain biking is permitted on six trails: Goose River, Marven Lake, Black Hole, East Branch, Bennett Brook (partially open) and Maple Grove. Surprisingly, at last report there were no bicycle rentals in Fundy National Park or in nearby Alma. Contact the visitor centers to find current information on this.

Hiking
Fundy features 120km of walking trails, where it's possible to enjoy anything from a short stroll to a three-day trek. Several trails require hikers to ford rivers, so be prepared.

The most popular backpacking route is the **Fundy Circuit**, a three-day trek of 45km through the heart of the park. Hikers generally spend their first night at Tracy Lake and their second at Bruin Lake, returning via the Upper Salmon River. You must reserve your wilderness campsites online ($10 per night).

Enjoyable day hikes in Fundy National Park include the **Matthews Head Loop**, a 4.5km stretch with the nicest coastal views of the park (ranked moderate to difficult); and the **Third Vault Falls Trail**, a challenging one-way hike of 3.7km to the park's tallest falls. Alternatively, a short and pleasant stroll along a boardwalk takes you to **Dickson Falls**.

For serious, experienced hikers, the most popular one-night backcountry trek is the **Goose River Trail**. It joins the **Fundy Footpath** (not to be confused with Fundy Circuit). The Fundy Footpath is an undeveloped five-day wilderness trek and one of the most difficult in the province. While you can cycle to Goose River, the trail beyond can only be done on foot.

In summer, rangers lead a variety of family-friendly educational programs, including night hikes.

Swimming
The ocean is pretty bracing here. A heated saltwater **swimming pool** (☺11am-6:30pm Jul & Aug), located near the park's southern entrance, is currently being renovated. It, along with a splash pad, is due to reopen in 2017.

🛌 Sleeping

Point Wolfe Campground   CAMPGROUND $
(✆877-737-3783; http://reservation.pc.gc.ca; campsites $26) This lovely campground (with 146 sites and 10 Otentiks), 8km southwest of the visitor center, is a little more secluded than the park's other mainstream campgrounds; it's the closest of all the campgrounds to the water. Twelve sites have water and electricity; this means that you may encounter RVs.

Chignecto North   CAMPGROUND $
(✆877-737-3783; http://reservation.pc.gc.ca; campsites/RV sites $26/36) This beautifully wooded campground (with 251 sites in total) is popular with families as it has playgrounds and good facilities. Sites are secluded and private, despite its generous size, and it's a 4km drive from the beach. Also has yurts and Otentiks (both $100).

Headquarters Campground   CAMPGROUND $
(✆877-737-3783; http://reservation.pc.gc.ca; campsites/RV sites $26/37, Otentiks/yurts $100/115) Of all the campsites in Fundy National Park, this is the most mainstream, and the only one close to both the beach and Alma village. It has 101 sites and offers yurts and Otentiks for those who don't have their own camping gear. It's not entirely wooded but the tent sites are grassy.

★ **Fundy Highlands Motel & Chalets**   CABIN, MOTEL $$
(✆888-883-8639, 506-887-2930; www.fundyhighlands.com; 8714 Hwy 114; r $99, cabins from $125; ☺May-Oct) The only private accommodations in Fundy National Park, this spot has charming little cabins, all with decks, kitchenettes and superlative views. On the same premises is a small, well-kept motel that offers rooms with kitchenettes. While not luxurious, it's got an appealing touch of retro and the delightful owners and staff ensure happy guests.

SCENIC DRIVE: KENNEBECASIS RIVER VALLEY

On a Saturday in summer, do what loads of Saint Johners do and take the **Gondola Point Ferry** (signposted off Hwy 1 at Exit 141) to the bucolic Kingston Peninsula, then follow Rte 845 east to the Kingston Farmers Market (p126). Sample the fresh fruits and vegetables and various ethnic foods on offer, or stop for lunch at the restored **1810 Carter House Tea Room** (www.facebook.com/1810CarterHouse; 874 Rte 845, Kingston; cakes & teas $5-9; ⊗9am-4pm Tue-Sat Jun-Aug), which is, of course, haunted – by a ghost who likes to tidy up and rearrange the books.

Leave the city folk behind, continuing on Rte 845 into the bustling community of Hampton, where you pick up Rte 121, which follows the northern side of the Kennebecasis River through farm country and the villages of Norton and Apohaqui into **Sussex** (population 4200).

Sussex is a working farming community nestled in a green valley dotted with dairy farms. The old-fashioned main street could be a movie set for a heartwarming 1950s coming-of-age story (but please, enough with the outdoor murals!). The well-preserved railway station houses the tourist information center, a small museum devoted to the area's military regiment, and an ice-cream parlour.

Gasthof Old Bavarian (☑506-433-4735; www.oldbavarian.ca; 1130 Knightville Rd, Studholm; mains $10-24; ⊗noon-10pm Fri-Sun) is the place for a truly memorable meal in the countryside. On a country road in a quiet valley settled by German and Dutch farmers, this place could have been transported – beer steins and all – from the Black Forest. Despite being more or less in the middle of nowhere, this place is always packed for dinner, so reservations are recommended. It's cash only.

Hang a left out of Gasthof's back onto the Knightville Rd, then left again onto Country View Rd at Anagance Ridge, then right onto Rte 890 into Petitcodiac. This stretch of road affords breathtaking vistas of rolling green countryside that will make you want to sell up, move here and raise chickens. If you can work up an appetite, stroll through the greenhouses and have a healthy organic lunch or tea and cake at **Cornhill Nursery & Cedar Cafe** (www.cornhillnursery.com; 2700 Rte 890, Cornhill; mains $9-15; ⊗10am-4pm Sun-Thu, to 9pm Fri & Sat May-Oct). From Petitcodiac you can rejoin Hwy 1, heading east to Moncton or west back to Fundy Park and Saint John. The views of the valley from Hwy 1 between Hampton and Sussex are also lovely.

❶ Information

Headquarters Visitors Centre (☑506-887-6000; ⊗10am-6pm May-Oct, to 8pm Jun & Jul) At the park's southern entrance.

❶ Getting There & Away

If heading east, it's yet not possible to drive directly along the coastline from St Martins to Fundy National Park; instead, a detour inland by Sussex is necessary. There's no public transport in the area.

Alma

The tiny, fully fledged fishing village of Alma is a useful supply center for Fundy National Park. It has accommodations, restaurants, a small gas station, grocery store, liquor outlet and laundry. Most facilities close in winter, when it becomes a ghost town, all except for the presence of Molly Kool (okay, statue of), the first female sea captain on the continent.

Fresh Air Adventure (☑800-545-0020, 506-887-2249; www.freshairadventure.com; 16 Fundy View Dr; tours from $69; ⊗Jun-Sep) offers myriad kayaking tours, from two-hour trips to multiday excursions, in and around Fundy.

🛏 Sleeping & Eating

Parkland Village Inn　　　　　INN $$
(☑506-887-2313; www.parklandvillageinn.com; 8601 Hwy 114; r $125-165) Parkland Village Inn is a busy 60-year-old inn with comfy, renovated rooms, some with killer Bay of Fundy views. Breakfast is only included out of high season.

The Beach House B&B　　　　　B&B
(☑506-887-9880; http://thebeachhousebedandbreakfastalma.com; 24 Foster Rd; r $100; ⊗May-Oct; 🅿🤶) Run by friendly British expats,

Lynn and Jeff, this modest, comfortable spot offers two spacious and neat rooms, conveniently located yet off the busy main drag. Lynn supplies a generous breakfast and there's satellite TV.

Octopus's Garden Café   CAFE $
(8561 Main St; snacks $4-12, mains $18; ⊙7am-10pm June-Oct; ?) A welcome addition to Alma's seafood-oriented food scene, the Octopus's tentacles extend as far as Italy. It serves up fabulous homemade pasta and sauces, good panini and, joy of joy, dishes such as muesli and yogurt. And, wait for it, there's an espresso machine. And yes, staff seem to know how to use it (a rarity in these parts).

Kelly's Bake Shop   BAKERY $
(www.facebook.com/homeofthestickybun; 8587 Main St; snacks from $2.50; ⊙7am-6pm) Sweet-lovers from far and wide flock here for one thing: the cinnamon sticky buns. Follow their lead.

Cape Enrage & Mary's Point

The 150-year-old lightstation at windblown and suitably named Cape Enrage (www.cape enrage.ca; off Rte 905; adult/child $6/5; ⊙10am-5pm mid-May–Oct, to 8pm Jul & Aug) is, these days, a not-for-profit organisation that earns its keep through the admission entry and adventure activities: rappelling off the steep rock faces and a zip line. Or you can simply wander the beach looking for fossils (low tide only!). Its lighthouse was one of the first 12 built in New Brunswick and still operates, albeit with an automated light.

At Mary's Point, 22km east of Cape Enrage, is the Shepody Bay Shorebird Reserve (Mary's Point Rd, off Hwy 915) FREE. From mid-July to mid-August hundreds of thousands of shorebirds, primarily sandpipers, gather here, at Mary's Point. Nature trails and boardwalks lead through the dikes and marsh. The interpretive center is open from late June to early September, but you can use the 6.5km of trails any time.

When all that activity gets you hungry, head to the Cape House Restaurant (www. facebook.com/CapeHouseRestaurant; mains $14-33; ⊙11:30am-11pm) in the original light-house-keeper's house, where you can enjoy the dramatic view while dining on pan-seared local scallops, hearty steaks and lobster chowder.

SOUTHEASTERN NEW BRUNSWICK

The southeastern corner of New Brunswick province is a flat coastal plain sliced by tidal rivers and salt marshes. Moncton, known as 'Hub City,' is a major crossroads with two well-known attractions where nature appears to defy gravity. Southeast, toward Nova Scotia, are significant historical and birdlife attractions.

Moncton

Once a major wooden shipbuilding port, Moncton is now the fastest-growing city in the Maritime provinces, with an economy built on transportation and call centers drawn here by the bilingual workforce. It's a pleasant, suburban city, with a small red-brick downtown along the muddy banks of the Petitcodiac River. There are some decent restaurants and bars, a bustling Acadian farmers market and an interesting museum at the Resurgo Place complex. Apart from that, there is little to detain the visitor.

⊙ Sights

Moncton Museum & Transport Discovery Centre   MUSEUM
(☑506-856-4383;   http://resurgo.ca/moncton museum; 20 Mountain Rd; adult/child/youth $10/5/7; ⊙10am-5pm Mon-Sat, noon-5pm Sun, closed Mon Sep-May) A visit to these interesting exhibitions will teach you about Moncton and its growth through artefacts and photographs that cover information on the Mi'kmaqs to the present day, plus Acadian history and agriculture and shipbuilding industries. The neighbouring Transport Discovery Centre, with its interactive displays relating to anything that moves, will appeal to kids especially. Check out the traveling exhibitions as well.

Magnetic Hill   AMUSEMENT PARK
(cnr Mountain Rd & Hwy 2; admission per car $5; ⊙8am-8pm May-Sep) At Magnetic Hill, one of Canada's best-known (though not best-loved) attractions, gravity appears to work in reverse. Start at the bottom of the hill in a car, and you'll drift upward. You figure it out. After hours and out of season, admission is free. It's a goofy novelty, worth the head-scratching laugh, but all the money-generating, spin-off

Moncton

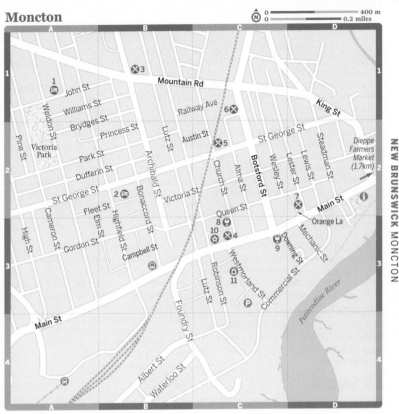

Moncton

🛌 Sleeping
1	Auberge au Bois Dormant Inn	A1
2	C'mon Inn	B2
	L'Hotel St James	(see 8)

🍴 Eating
3	Cafe Archibald	B1
4	Cafe C'est la Vie	C3
5	Calactus	C2
6	Manuka	C1
7	Pump House	D2

🍷 Drinking & Nightlife
8	Saint James' Gate	C3
9	Tide & Boar	C3

⭐ Entertainment
10	Capitol Theatre	C3

🛍 Shopping
11	Moncton Market	C3

hoopla now surrounding the hill is a bit much. The family-oriented attractions include a zoo, a faux village hawking ice cream and souvenirs, and a water park. Magnetic Hill is located about 10km northwest of downtown off Mountain Rd.

👉 Tours

Roads to Sea BUS
(☑506-850-7623; www.roadstosea.com; per person $173; ☉May-Oct) Roads to Sea offers nine-hour bus tours to Hopewell Rocks (p132) and the Bay of Fundy (including the

HOPEWELL ROCKS

At Hopewell Cape, where the Petitcodiac River empties into Shepody Bay, are the **Hopewell Rocks** (www.thehopewellrocks.ca; off Hwy 114; adult/child/family $10/7.25/25.50, shuttle per person $2; ☺ 9am-5pm May-Oct, longer hours summer; ♿). The 'rocks' are bizarre sandstone erosion formations known as 'flowerpots,' which rise from the ocean floor. They resemble giant arches, stone mushrooms and ice-cream cones. Visitors marvel at their Dr Seussian look, making the rocks New Brunswick's top attraction (and certainly one of its most crowded). You can only walk amid the rocks at low tide – check the tide tables at any tourist office or area hotel. At high tide, the rock towers are still visible from the well-trafficked trails that wind through the woods above. For a different perspective, **Baymount Outdoor Adventures** (p132) offers two-hour kayaking tours around the rocks.

The park features a large interpretive center with educational displays, two cafes and picnic areas (stock up and take your own). In high season there are traffic jams and a lot of people (on the staircases). Despite tourist buses being available, Hopewell Rocks is easiest visited with your own wheels. There is a massive car park, though this gets packed in summer.

Fundy National Park and Cape Enrage, plus lighthouses and covered bridges). The company's unique marketing pitch is that you get to see extreme high and low tides in the same day. The bus seats 12 people.

Baymount Outdoor Adventures KAYAKING
(☎ 877-601-2660; www.baymountadventures.com; tours adult/child $69/59; ☺ Jun-Sep) Offers two-hour paddling tours in kayaks around the Hopewell Rocks.

🛏 Sleeping

Reservations are a good idea as the city is a major conference destination and often gets packed solid. Most chain hotels are clustered around Magnetic Hill and on Main St.

C'mon Inn HOSTEL $
(☎ 506-530-0905, 506-854-8155; www.moncton hostel.ca; 47 Fleet St; dm $37, r $78-83; P @ ☎) One of Moncton's two hostels is housed in a rambling Victorian two blocks from the bus station. Two small dorms (one female only) and private doubles with shared bathroom are nothing fancy, but they are clean and comfortable. There is a kitchen for guest use and lots of space for lounging on the verandahs. The owner, Monique, is very helpful.

Auberge au Bois Dormant Inn B&B $$
(☎ 506-855-6767; www.auberge-auboisdormant. com; 67 John St; s $85-140, d $95-150; ☺ ✻ ☎) A gracious Victorian renovated with crisp modern flair. This gay-friendly establishment is on a quiet, tree-lined residential street and an excellent breakfast is served. Some of the rooms have access to balconies and the attic room is lovely.

L'Hotel St James BOUTIQUE HOTEL $$$
(☎ 888-782-1414; www.stjamesgatecanada.com; 14 Church St; r $169-289; P ✻ ☎) On the 2nd floor of a 19th-century brick shop building, this downtown boutique hotel has 10 stylish urban-chic guest rooms that wouldn't look a bit out of place in Montréal or New York. Swank design touches include mod tile walls, crisp white linens, huge flat-screen TVs and iPod docks. Downstairs there's a popular pub (p133) and restaurant.

🍴 Eating

Two excellent markets, the **Dieppe Farmers Market** (www.marchedieppemarket.com; cnr Acadie Ave & Gauvin Rd, Dieppe; ☺ 7am-1:30pm Sat) and **Moncton Market** (www.marchemoncton-market.ca; 120 Westmoreland St; ☺ 7am-2pm), are the places to buy fresh produce, baked goods and all kinds of ethnic dishes.

Calactus VEGETARIAN $
(☎ 506-388-4833; www.calactus.ca; 125 Church St; mains $11-17; ☺ 11am-10pm; ✎) Shangri-la for vegetarians! Enjoy the freedom to order anything off the globally inspired menu, which includes falafel plates, tofu cheese pizza and fried Indian *pakoras*. The natural wood, warm earth colors and burbling fountain create a soothing atmosphere. Wonderful service further heightens the experience.

Cafe C'est la Vie CAFE $
(www.cafecestlavie.ca; 75 Main St; snacks $6.50-7.50, bibimbap $10; ☺ 7:30am-6pm Mon-Wed, to 8pm Thu & Fri, 9am-6pm Sat & Sun) A useful spot for a quick and easy filling lunch, such as good sandwiches, panini and salads. The

Korean owners serve up great *bibimbap* (Korean mixed rice dish) options.

Cafe Archibald
FRENCH, CANADIAN $
(221 Mountain Rd; mains $8-13; ⊙9am-11pm Mon-Thu, to midnight Fri, 8:30am-midnight Sat & Sun) The bistro looks a bit tired but the cuisine is good. Crêpes are the house specialty, whipped up in the open kitchen and served at redwood banquettes or on the screened-in porch. Alternatively, feast on the smoked salmon and mozzarella pizza with a leafy salad.

★ Manuka
INTERNATIONAL $$
(☑506-851-5540; www.facebook.com/restomanuka; 184 Alma St; lunch mains $12-14, 3-course dinner menu $25; ⊙11am-2pm Tue-Fri, 5-9pm Wed-Sat) Housed incongruously in a yellow clapboard home, Belgian-owned Manuka is a bit like going to a friend's house for dinner...only the friend happens to be a very good cook. It's a fine-dining experience and one of the town's best gourmet options, where the chefs make everything from scratch.

Pump House
BREWERY $$
(www.pumphousebrewery.ca; 5 Orange Lane; mains $12-15; ⊙11am-late Mon-Sat, noon-midnight Sun) The Pump is where the locals unwind and you can get a good burger, steak-based meal or wood-fired pizza. Of the brews made on the premises, the blueberry ale is popular and the Muddy River stout is tasty – or better still, try the beer sampling tray.

Little Louis'
MODERN CANADIAN $$$
(☑506-855-5022; www.littlelouis.ca; 245 Collishaw St; mains $24-36; ⊙5-10pm) The odd location of this nouvelle cuisine bistro – upstairs in a faceless industrial strip mall – only adds to its speakeasy vibe. The atmosphere is cozy, with low lights, white tablecloths and jazzy live music. Local foodies rave about dishes like pan-seared scallop, fried beef, roasted cauliflower and beluga lentils.

🍷 Drinking & Entertainment

Saint James' Gate
BAR
(www.stjamesgate.ca; 14 Church St; ⊙11am-2am Mon-Fri, 10am-2am Sat & Sun) An upmarket tavern with a hum that reverberates off its interior Moorish-style arches. The bar, with its faux-leather-and-studded seats, is a pleasant place to prop yourself up, while a small outdoor patio brings in the summer cocktail crowd. Also serves up fancy food (mains $18 to $33). Upstairs is the boutique hotel L'Hotel St James (p132).

Tide & Boar
PUB
(☑506-857-9118; www.tideandboar.com; 700 Main St; ⊙11am-midnight Mon-Wed, to 2am Thu-Sat, noon-midnight Sun) A classy gastro pub that serves an interesting selection of beer (types you wouldn't find elsewhere), plus wines and quirky cocktails. Serves up a positive vibe and has music on weekends.

Capitol Theatre
THEATER
(www.capitol.nb.ca; 811 Main St) You can sip a glass of wine during the interval at the grand Capitol Theatre, a 1922 vaudeville house that has been restored to its original glory. It's the venue for concerts and live theater throughout the year.

ℹ Information

Moncton Hospital (☑506-857-5111; 135 MacBeath Ave) Emergency room.

Moncton Public Library (https://monctonpubliclibrary.ca; 644 Main St; ⊙10am-5pm Thu-Mon, to 9pm Tue & Wed; 🛜) Free internet access.

Visitors Information Centre (20 Mountain Rd, Resurgo Pl; ⊙10am-5pm Mon-Sat, noon-5pm Sun) This new center is in the recently opened Moncton Museum.

ℹ Getting There & Away

AIR

Greater Moncton International Airport (YQM; ☑506-856-5444; www.gmia.ca) is about 6km east of Champlain Place Shopping Centre via Champlain St. Air Canada runs daily flights to Toronto and Montréal.

BUS

Maritime Bus (☑506-854-2023; www.maritimebus.com; 1240 Main St) services Fredericton ($41.75, 2½ hours); Saint John ($33.75, two hours); Charlottetown, PEI ($41.75, three hours); and Halifax ($53.25, four hours).

CAR & MOTORCYCLE

There are six municipal parking lots around town, plus several private lots. Public parking meters cost $1 to $2.50 per hour. The municipal parking lot at Moncton Market on Westmorland St is free on Saturday, Sunday and evenings after 6pm. The city uses HotSpot Parking, a mobile payment service where you can pay for parking (and top up your metered space parking time) with your cell phone. Rates and maps can be found at www.moncton.ca.

TRAIN

With **VIA Rail** (☑506-857-9830; www.viarail.ca; 1240 Main St), the Ocean line (Montreal–Halifax) goes through northern New Brunswick, including Miramichi and Campbellton, and into Québec, on its way to Montréal. The train to Halifax (from $39) departs three days a week.

ℹ Getting Around

The airport is served by bus 20 from Champlain Pl nine times a day on weekdays. A taxi to the center of town costs about $15 to $20.

Codiac Transit (www.codiactranspo.ca) is the local bus system, with 40 wi-fi-equipped buses going all over town.

If you need wheels, there are car-rental desks at the airport, or try **Discount Car Rentals** (☑ 506-857-2309; www.discountcar.com; 470 Mountain Rd, cnr High St; ⊙ 7:30am-5.30pm Mon-Fri, 8am-midday Sat) in town.

Sackville

Sackville is a small, very quaint university town that's in the right place for a pit stop – for birds and people (when in town, students double the population). The Sackville Water-fowl Park is on a major bird migration route.

Sackville Waterfowl Park   BIRD SANCTUARY
(⊙ 24hr) FREE The Sackville Waterfowl Park, across the road from the university off East Main St, is on a major bird migration route. It's worth taking a quick stroll around the boardwalk trail. Interpretive signs explain a little about the area.

The Black Duck   CAFE $
(www.theblackduck.ca; 19 Bridge St; meals $6.50-8; ⊙ 7am-9pm) Popular among university students for its contemporary vibe and offerings, this bakery and cafe whips up wonderful baked goods on the premises. Excellent grilled sandwiches, bagels and reasonable coffee are on the menu here; perfect for the full gamut of meals.

Mel's Tea Room   DINER $
(17 Bridge St; mains $5-11; ⊙ 8:30am-8:30pm) Take a fun trip down memory lane at Mel's Tea Room. It's been operating in the center of town since 1919, now with the charm of a 1950s diner – with a jukebox and prices to match. Serves up good breakfast egg dishes, plus milkshakes and ice cream.

Coy Wolf Bistro   INTERNATIONAL $$
(☑ 506-536-8084; www.coywolfbistro.ca; 19 Bridge St; mains $20-30; ⊙ 5-9pm Wed-Sun) This cutting-edge eatery should howl its menu from the rooftops, so to speak. It follows the 'eat sustainable and local' philosophy and whips up creative dishes and a constantly

evolving menu. Think the likes of Northumberland clam chowder or the wolf burger, a local beef with gourmet filling. Funky decor without being try-hard cool is a bonus too.

ℹ Information

Sackville Visitor Information Centre (https://sackville.com/explore-sackville/visitor-information; 34 Mallard Drive; ⊙ 9am-5pm May-Oct, to 8pm Jul & Aug)

ℹ Getting There & Away

Buses run between Sackville and Moncton ($14.25, 45 minutes, three daily).

NORTHUMBERLAND SHORE

New Brunswick's Northumberland Shore stretches from the Confederation Bridge to Kouchibouguac National Park and is dotted with fishing villages and summer cottages. Shediac, on all lobster-lovers' itineraries, is a popular resort town in a strip of summer seaside and beach playgrounds. A good part of the population here is French-speaking, and Bouctouche is an Acadian stronghold. Further north, Kouchibouguac National Park protects a swath of scenic coastal ecosystems.

Cape Jourimain

Set on the Northumberland Strait, the 675-hectare **Cape Jourimain Nature Centre** (☑ 506-538-2220; www.capejourimain.ca; Rte 16; admission free; ⊙ 8am-7pm May-Oct) has 13km of walking trails, a museum with information on the area and a restaurant. A four-storey tower affords great views of the Confederation Bridge (that crosses to PEI) and the Cape Jourimain Lighthouse that was built in 1869. It's a twitcher's favorite for the migratory birds.

Shediac

Shediac, a self-proclaimed lobster capital, is a busy summer beach town and home of the annual July lobster fest. Have your picture taken with the 'World's Largest Lobster' sculpture – you can't miss it! (If the big claw doesn't grab your attention, it's handily located near the helpful tourist office.)

It seems on any hot weekend that half the province is flaked out on the sand at **Parlee**

Beach. South at Cap-Pelé are vast stretches of more sandy shorelines. Terrific Aboiteau Beach comprises over 5km of unsupervised sand, while others have all amenities and lifeguards.

Popular Shediac Bay Cruises (☏888-894-2002, 506-532-2175; www.lobstertales.ca; Pointe-du-Chene wharf; adult/child/family $70/48/204) takes passengers out on the water, pulls up lobster traps, then shows you how to cook and eat (that is, crack!) 'em.

After dinner, catch a flick at wonderfully retro Neptune Drive-In (www.neptunedrivein.ca; 691 Main St; per person/carload $10/20; ⊗Jun-Sep).

🍴 Sleeping & Eating

Auberge Gabriele Inn INN $$
(☏506-532-8007; www.aubergegabrieleinn.com; 296 Main St; r $125-170; P😊❋☏) One of the better options in Shediac, this attractive yellow building gets an extra tick for its good on-site restaurant. Rooms above are pleasant, if slightly dated, and offer a homey mix of antiques and modern.

Maison Tait INN $$
(☏506-532-4233; www.maisontaithouse.com; 293 Main St; r incl breakfast from $149; ☏) Lodgings at Maison Tait, a luxurious 1911 mansion, consist of nine sun-drenched rooms. Despite the fact they are outdated, they are upscale enough to enjoy.

Captain Dan's SEAFOOD $$
(www.captaindans.ca; Pointe-du-Chêne wharf; mains $11-28; ⊗11am-10pm Jun-Sep) Grab fresh seafood and strawberry daiquiris at always-packed Captain Dan's at the busy Pointe-du-Chêne wharf.

Paturel's Shore House SEAFOOD $$
(☏506-532-4774; www.paturelrestaurant.ca; 2 Cap Bimet Rd, Grand-Barachois; mains $17-33; ⊗4-10pm Tue-Sun late May–mid-Sep) Tops for dining out on fresh seafood at this simple place that resembles a large white house, located near to the shore. It's 7km east of Shediac; turn off Main St, direction north on Cap Bimet Road.

ⓘ Information

Visitors Information Centre (☏506-533-7925; www.shediac.ca; 229 Main St; ⊗9am-5pm May-Sep, to 9pm Jul & Aug) Provides excellent information on New Brunswick and maps of Shediac and surrounds.

ⓘ Getting There & Away

Maritime Bus (www.maritimebus.com) Runs from Shediac to Moncton ($12.25, 30 minutes, one daily) and Fredericton ($46, three hours, one daily); you must reserve 24 hours in advance. Buses also run from Shediac to Halifax, Nova Scotia.

Bouctouche

This small, surprisingly busy waterside town is an Acadian cultural focal point with several unique attractions. The visitors information center at the town's south entrance features an impressive boardwalk that extends over the salt marsh.

⊙ Sights & Activities

Irving Eco Centre PARK
(www.irvingecocentre.com; 1932 Rte 475, St-Édouard-de-Kent; ⊗interpretive center 10am-6pm late May-late Sep) On the coast 9km northeast of Bouctouche, this nature center protects and makes accessible 'La Dune de Bouctouche,' a beautiful, long sandspit jutting into the strait. The interpretive center has displays on the flora and fauna, but the highlight is the boardwalk that snakes above the sea grass along the dunes for 1km. The peninsula itself is 12km long, taking four to six hours to hike over the loose sand and back. There's a 12km hiking/cycling trail through mixed forest to Bouctouche town, which begins at the Eco Centre parking lot.

Le Pays de la Sagouine PARK
(☏506-743-1400; www.sagouine.com; 57 Acadie St; adult/student/family $20/15/45; ⊗10am-5:30pm Jul & Aug) Sitting on a small island in the Bouctouche River, this reconstructed Acadian village has daily programs in English and French. There are interactive cooking and craft demos, historical-house tours and live music, as well as several cafes in which to sample old-fashioned Acadian cuisine. In July and August there are regular supper theater performances (tickets from $20).

Olivier Soapery MUSEUM
(www.oliviersoaps.com; 831 Rte 505, Ste-Anne-de-Kent; ⊗9am-7pm Jun-Aug, 8:30am-4.30pm Mon-Fri Sep-May) An old-fashioned soap factory that promotes its 'museum'. It's really more of a store, with tons of luscious-smelling hand-molded soaps, but it does have regular scheduled talks on the soap-making process and a few interesting historical displays.

NEW BRUNSWICK BOUCTOUCHE

MR BIG

Kenneth Colin (KC) Irving was born in Bouctouche in 1899. From a modest beginning selling cars, he built up a business Goliath spanning oil refining, shipyards, mass media, transportation, pulp and paper, gas stations, convenience stores and more. The Irving name is everywhere. At least 8% of the province's workforce is employed by an Irving endeavor. KC died in 1992, leaving his three sons to carry on the vast Irving Group empire.

🛏 Sleeping & Eating

Chez les Maury   CAMPGROUND **$**
(☑506-743-5347; www.fermemaury.com; 2021 Rte 475, St-Édouard-de-Kent; campsites $25-30; ☺May-early Oct) On the grounds of a family-run vineyard, 200m from the Irving Eco Centre, this small, basic campground has toilets, showers and a tiny private beach across the way. A bell rings at 6.30pm for the 7pm free sampling of its wares – we're talking the likes of elderberry and strawberry wines (and they're good).

Le Vieux Presbytère   INN **$$**
(☑506-743-5568; www.vieuxpresbytere.nb.ca; 157 Chemin du Couvent; apt $160; ☎) This former priest's residence was once a popular religious retreat for Acadians from across the province. Several unpretentious but lovely apartments with high molded ceilings and delightfully sunny decor are up for grabs. All have kitchen and garden and water outlooks. There is a three-night minimum stay.

SCKS Société culturelle Kent-Sud   CAFE **$**
(www.sckentsud.com; 5 Blvd Irving; snacks $9-11; ☺8am-3pm Tue-Sat Sep-May, to 5pm daily Jun-Aug) A little not-for-profit cafe and a pleasant place to stop for coffee (read: espresso machine) and simple French-style snack lunches using, where possible, local produce.

Restaurant La Sagouine   ACADIAN **$**
(www.sagouine.nb.ca; 43 Blvd Irving; mains $8-18; ☺6am-10pm) Fried clams or a traditional Acadian dinner are on offer at this simple, old-fashioned spot that has (understandably) a slightly fuggy aroma of cooked seafood. In summer there are seats on the outdoor patio.

ℹ Information

Visitors Information Center (☑506-743-8811; www.tourismnewbrunswick.ca; 14 Acadie St; ☺10am-3pm late May-late Sep, longer hours summer)

Kouchibouguac National Park

Beaches, lagoons and offshore sand dunes extend for 25km here, inviting strolling, bird-watching and clam-digging. The **park** (www.pc.gc.ca; adult/child $7.80/3.90; ☺8am-dusk year-round) encompasses hectares of forest and salt marshes, crisscrossed or skirted by bike paths, hiking trails and groomed cross-country ski tracks. Kouchibouguac (*koosh*-e-boo-gwack), a Mi'kmaq word meaning 'River of Long Tides,' also has moose, deer and sometimes black bear.

🏃 Activities

Kouchibouguac has 60km of bikeways, crushed gravel paths that wind through the park's backcountry.

The calm, shallow water between the shore and the dunes, which run for 25km north and south, makes for a serene morning paddle. **Voyageur Canoe** (☑506-876-2443; per person $29.40) offers a must-do activity, especially for nonhikers. You paddle a four- or eight-person Canadian canoe to the sandy barrier islands, learning about the Mi'kmaq way of life plus viewing birds. The highlight is observing the grey seals; between 300 to 600 return to these feeding grounds each summer.

The park has 10 trails, mostly short and flat. The excellent **Bog Trail** (1.9km) is a boardwalk beyond the observation tower, and only the first few hundred meters are crushed gravel. The **Cedars Trail** (1.3km) is a lovely boardwalk trail with interpretation boards. The **Osprey Trail** (5.1km) is a loop trail through the forest. **Kelly's Beach Boardwalk** (600m one way) floats above the grass-covered dunes. When you reach the beach, turn right and hike around 6km to the end of the dune (the limits vary according to the location of the piping plover's nesting grounds). Take drinking water.

For swimmers, the lagoon area is shallow, warm and safe for children, while adults will find the deep water on the ocean side invigorating.

🛏 Sleeping

Kouchibouguac has two drive-in campgrounds and three primitive camping areas totaling 360 sites. The camping season is from mid-May to mid-October, and the park is very busy throughout July and August, especially on weekends. Camping reservations are necessary for the majority of the sites. The park entry fee is extra.

The three primitive campgrounds cost $10 per person per night; they have only vault (pump) toilets. You should take your own water to both Sipu and Petit-Large. Pointe-a-Maxime is the most difficult to get to (access by water only), but this does not translate into remote seclusion. There is a constant stream of passing motorized boat traffic from the fishing wharf nearby.

Cote-a-Fabien   CAMPGROUND $
(☑877-737-3783; www.pccamping.ca; campsites drivein/walk-in $21/11) On the northern side of Kouchibouguac River, this is the best choice for those seeking a bit of peace and privacy. There is water and vault toilets, but no showers. Some sites are on the shore, others nestled among the trees, with a dozen walk-in sites (100m; wheelbarrows provided for luggage) for those who want a car-free environment. The Osprey hiking trail starts here.

South Kouchibouguac   CAMPGROUND $
(☑877-737-3783; www.pccamping.ca; campsites/ Otentiks $28/15) South Kouchibouguac is the largest campground. It's 13km inside the park near the beaches in a large open field ringed by trees, with Otentiks (a type of yurt), plus sites for tents and RVs, showers and a kitchen shelter.

ℹ Information

Visitors Center (☑506-876-2443; www. pc.gc.ca/kouchibouguac; 186 Rte 117; ⊗8am-4:30pm Oct-May, to 8pm Jul-Sep) Has maps and helpful staff with good information and maps. If the center is closed, visit the administration office opposite, which is open all year.

ℹ Getting There & Around

It's difficult to get to and around the park without a car or bicycle. From the park gate it's at least 10km to the campgrounds and beaches.

The nearest bus stop is in Rexton, 16km south of the park, where **Maritime** (☑800-575-1807; www.maritimebus.com; 126 Main St) buses stop at the Irving Circle K gas station. Daily buses head south to Moncton ($20.25) and head north to Miramichi ($14.25).

MIRAMICHI RIVER VALLEY AREA

In New Brunswick, the word Miramichi refers to both the city and the river, but it connotes even more: an intangible, captivating mystique. The spell the region casts emanates partially from the Acadian and Irish mix of folklore, legends, superstitions and tales of ghosts. It also seeps from the dense forests and wilderness of the area and from the character of the residents, who wrestle a livelihood from these natural resources. The fabled river adds its serpentine cross-country course, crystal tributaries and salmon fishing. The region produces some wonderful rootsy music and inspires artists, including noted writer David Adams Richards, whose work skillfully mines the temper of the region.

Miramichi

The working-class mill town of Miramichi (formerly Newcastle) is an amalgam of the towns of Chatham, Newcastle, Douglastown, Loggieville, Nelson and several others for a 12km stretch on both sides of the Miramichi River. Miramichi – with its First Nations plus Irish, Scottish and French background – is an English-speaking enclave in the middle of a predominantly French-speaking region.

Traditional folk-music enthusiasts might want to visit here for the **Irish Festival** (www.canadasirishfest.com; ⊗mid-Jul) and the **Miramichi Folksong Festival** (www.mira michifolksongfestival.com; ⊗early Aug), the oldest of its kind in North America.

◉ Sights

Beaverbrook House   MUSEUM
(www.beaverbrookhouse.com; 518 King George Hwy; ⊗9am-5pm Mon-Sat, 1-5pm Sun Jun-Sep) FREE In the central square of Miramichi is a statue to Lord Beaverbrook (1879–1964), one of the most powerful press barons in British history and a major benefactor of his home province. His ashes lie under the statue presented as a memorial to him by the town. The 1877 Beaverbrook House, Beaverbrook's boyhood home, is now a museum.

🛏 Sleeping & Eating

Enclosure Campground   CAMPGROUND $
(☑506-622-0680; http://enclosurecampground. com; 8 Enclosure Rd, Derby Junction; campsites/

HISTORICAL MUSEUM OF TRACADIE

Unmasking a little-known but gripping story, the Historical Museum of Tracadie (Rue du Couvent; adult/child $5/free; ⊙ 9am-5pm Mon-Fri, noon-5pm Sat & Sun mid-Jun–early Sep) focuses on the leprosy colony based here from 1849 to as late as 1965. It's the only place in Canada providing details on a leprosarium. The nearby cemetery has the graves of 59 victims of Hansen's Disease (leprosy). Tracadie-Sheila is 77km northeast of Miramichi.

RV sites $31/36; ⊙ May-Oct) Southwest of Newcastle off Hwy 8, this former provincial park has a beautiful wooded area with spacious quasi-wilderness sites for tenters. Despite the website promoting a restaurant, this no longer operates.

Rodd Miramichi River   HOTEL $$
(☑ 506-773-3111; www.roddmiramichi.com; 1809 Water St; r from $200; P ❋ 🛜 ☀) One of Miramichi's more upmarket hotels, the massive Rodd sprawls along the waterfront on the southern side of the river. It has all the mod cons of a business hotel, but with a resort-like feel. Check online for specials.

Governor's Mansion   B&B $$
(☑ 506-622-3036; www.governorsmansion.ca; 62 St Patrick's Dr; r incl breakfast $89-159; P ❋ 🛜) On the southern side of the river overlooking Beaubears Island is the creaky, but elegant, antique-filled Victorian Governor's Mansion (1860), onetime home of the first Irish lieutenant governor of the province. Rooms are lovely, if ever so tired, but it provides a cozy place to rest your head.

Bistro 140   INTERNATIONAL $$
(www.facebook.com/Bistro140; 295 Pleasant St; mains $15-25; ⊙ 11:30am-9pm Mon-Thu, 4-10pm Fri & Sat) It's referred to by locals as Miramichi's 'fine-dining option', and while that might be taking it a bit far, it's a friendly bistro and serves up decent food with surprising quirks and an emphasis on local (seasonal fiddleheads as a vegetable side). The entrance is through an office-style building.

❶ Getting There & Away

Maritime Bus (☑ 506-773-5515; www.maritimebus.com; 186 King St) services depart from the Best Value Inn. Daily buses leave for Fredericton ($63.50, five hours), Saint John ($65.05, five hours) and Campbellton ($38.75, three hours).

The **VIA Rail station** (www.viarail.ca; 251 Station St, cnr George St) is in Newcastle. Trains from Montréal and Halifax stop here.

Miramichi River Valley

The Miramichi is actually a complex web of rivers and tributaries draining much of central New Brunswick. The main branch, the 217km-long Southwest Miramichi River, flows from near Hartland through forest to Miramichi where it meets the other main fork, the Northwest Miramichi.

For over a hundred years, the entire system has inspired reverent awe for its tranquil beauty and incredible Atlantic salmon fly-fishing. Famous business tycoons, international politicians, sports and entertainment stars and Prince Charles have all wet lines here. Even Marilyn Monroe is said to have dipped her toes in the water.

The legendary fishery has had some ups and downs with overfishing, poaching and unknown causes (perhaps global warming) affecting stocks, and there is ongoing debate as to the best way of sustaining levels: to introduce stocks or let nature take its course. While sportfishing is on the wane, the area is beautiful all the same.

❍ Sights

Metepenagiag Heritage Park   HISTORIC SITE
(☑ 506-836-6118; www.metpark.ca; 2156 Micmac Rd, Red Bank; adult/child $8/6; ⊙ 10am-5pm May-Oct) Forty kilometers northwest of Miramichi, on the Esk River, the Metepenagiag Heritage Park has interpretive tours of Mi'kmaq culture and history on a 3000-year-old archaeological site.

Atlantic Salmon Museum   MUSEUM
(www.atlanticsalmonmuseum.com; 263 Main St, Doaktown; adult/child $5/3; ⊙ 9am-5pm Mon-Sat, noon-5pm Sun Jun-Oct) Learn about historic Doaktown's storied fishing history, plus wonderful artworks and anthropological gems at this lodgelike museum. Doaktown is 90km southwest of Miramichi.

✖ Activities

The **Miramichi Trail**, a walking and cycling path along an abandoned rail line, is now partially complete, with 75km of the projected 200km usable.

At McNamee, 15km southwest of Doaktown, the pedestrian Priceville Suspension Bridge spans the river. It's a popular put-in spot for **canoeists and kayakers** spending half a day paddling downriver to Doaktown. Ask around about equipment rentals, shuttle services and guided trips for leisurely canoe, kayak or even tubing trips along the river.

Sportfishing is not something you come and do in a day. It's a multiday activity and, as such, few travellers take it up spontaneously. For those who do fish, it's tightly controlled for conservation. Licenses are required and all anglers must employ a registered guide. A three-day license for nonresidents is $60. All fish must be released. (Most of the salmon served up in the province is, in fact, salmon farmed in the Bay of Fundy.)

🛏 Sleeping

Beautiful rustic lodges and camps abound, many replicating the halcyon days of the 1930s and '40s. Check out www.miramichirivertourism.com for more accommodations and fishing outfitters.

Storeytown Cottages　　COTTAGE $$
(☎506-365-7636; www.facebook.com/storeytowncottages; 439 Storeytown Rd, Doaktown; cottages from $129) Run by a dynamic young couple, this place has simple but cozy log cabins on the riverbank. Outdoor activities include tubing ($10), kayaking ($35), canoeing ($40) and stand-up paddleboarding ($35). For $5, they'll shuttle you upriver so you can float or paddle back down. Bring mosquito repellent.

🛍 Shopping

WW Doak & Sons　　SPORTS & OUTDOORS
(www.doak.com; 331 Main St, Doaktown; ⊙8am-5pm Mon-Sat) WW Doak & Sons is one of Canada's best fly-fishing shops.

ℹ Information

Visitor Information Centre (www.doaktown.com; 263 Main St, Doaktown; ⊙9am-5pm Mon-Sat, noon-5pm Sun Jun-Oct) The tourist office is in the Salmon Museum in Doaktown, the center of most valley activity.

NORTHEASTERN NEW BRUNSWICK

The North Shore, as it is known to New Brunswickers, is the heartland of Acadian culture in the province. The region was settled 250 years ago by French farmers and fishers, starting from scratch again after the upheaval of the Expulsion (when the British deported some 14,000 Acadians from the region), frequently intermarrying with the original Mi'kmaq inhabitants. The coastal road north from Miramichi, around the Acadian Peninsula and along Chaleurs Bay to Campbellton passes through small fishing settlements and peaceful ocean vistas. At Sugarloaf Provincial Park, the Appalachian Mountain Range comes down to the edge of the sea. Behind it, stretching hundreds of kilometers into the interior of the province, is a vast, trackless wilderness of rivers and dense forest, rarely explored.

Caraquet

The oldest of the Acadian villages, Caraquet was founded in 1757 by refugees from forcibly abandoned homesteads further south. It's now the quiet, working-class center of the peninsula's French community. Caraquet's colorful, bustling fishing port, off Blvd St-Pierre Est, has an assortment of moored vessels splashing at the dock. East and West Blvd St-Pierre are divided at Rue le Portage.

It's a self-proclaimed 'cultural capital of Acadia'; each August the town is the proud host of the massive **Festival Acadien** (www.festivalacadien.ca; ⊙Aug), a historic occasion that celebrates their survival. It draws 100,000 visitors, and more than 200 performers including singers, musicians, actors, and dancers from Acadia and other French regions (some from overseas).

⊙ Sights

Acadian Historic Village　　PARK
(www.villagehistoriqueacadien.com; 14311 Hwy 11; adult/student/family $20/16/45; ⊙10am-6pm Jun-Sep) Acadian Historic Village, 15km west of Caraquet, is a major historical reconstruction set up like a village of old. Thirty-three original buildings have been relocated to the site, and animators in period costumes reflect life from 1780 to 1880. Several hours are required to have a good look, and then you'll definitely want to eat. For that, there

are old-fashioned sit-down Acadian meals at La Table des Ancêtres, the 1910 historical menu at the Château Albert dining room and several snack bars.

The village has a program for kids ($35), which provides them with a costume and seven hours of supervised historical activities.

🛏 Sleeping & Eating

★ Maison Touristique Dugas   INN, CAMPGROUND $

(☑506-727-3195; www.maisontouristiquedugas.ca; 683 Blvd St-Pierre W; campsites/r from $25/89, cabins $119) Five generations of the ultrafriendly Dugas family have run this rambling, something-for-everyone property, 8km west of Caraquet. The homey, antique-filled 1926 house has 11 rooms, four with shared bathrooms. There are five clean, cozy cabins with private bathrooms and cooking facilities, a small field for RVs beyond that, and a quiet, tree-shaded campground with access to the water for tenters.

★ Hotel Paulin   HOTEL $$

(☑506-727-9981, 866-727-9981; www.hotelpaulin.com; 143 Blvd St-Pierre W; r incl breakfast $149-289; P🐾) Scrimp elsewhere and splurge on a night at the exquisite Hotel Paulin. This vintage seaside hotel overlooking the bay was built in 1891 and has been run by the Paulin family since 1905. Good old-fashioned service remains and the rooms are sunny and polished, done up in crisp white linens, lace and quality antiques.

Château Albert   INN $$$

(☑506-726-2600; www.villagehistoriqueacadien.com/chateauanglais.htm; Acadian Historic Village; d incl dinner & site visit $150; P🐾) For complete immersion in the Acadian Historic Village, spend the night in early 20th-century style – no TV and no phone, just a charming, quiet room restored to its original 1909 splendor (with a modern bath). The original Albert stood on the main street in Caraquet until it was destroyed by fire in 1955. Packages are available that include breakfast and a site visit.

Mitchan Sushi   JAPANESE $$

(www.mitchansushi.com; 114 Blvd St-Pierre West; sushi $6-10, mains $8-14; ⊙5-8pm Wed-Sat) A tasteful, ordered experience where beautifully concocted Japanese morsels comprise fresh local seafood. Unfortunately, it's not open daily; check hours.

Le Caraquette   CANADIAN $$

(89 Blvd St-Pierre Est; mains $8-15; ⊙6-9pm Mon-Sat, 7-9pm Sun) Overlooking the harbor, this no-fuss, family diner-style restaurant serves Maritime provinces standards including fried clams and mayonnaise shrimp salad, along with French Canadian specialties like poutine and smoked-meat sandwiches.

ℹ Information

Visitor Information Centre (☑202-726-2676; www.caraquet.ca/en/tourism/discover-caraquet; 39 Blvd St-Pierre West; ⊙9am-5pm Jun-Sep) Information on all things local, and the Acadian Historic Village.

ℹ Getting There & Away

Public transportation around this part of the province is very limited, as Maritime Bus services don't pass this way. Local residents wishing to connect with the bus or train in Miramichi or Bathurst use a couple of van shuttles; ask for details at the **visitor information centre**.

Bathurst

A former mining town, the tranquil, pretty city of Bathurst is situated on Bathurst Harbour, and enclosed by two peninsulas: Carron Point and Alston Point. The town itself is joined by a bridge that spans the harbor, with most things of interest for the tourist on the southern side.

Several historic buildings were damaged by fire in 2015, but the streets still are a pleasant place for a stroll and to stretch your legs. The revamped harborfront is where you'll find the tourist office and a couple of restaurants. There's not a lot to do here, but it's a good jumping-off point to nature-based activities around the town and wider Chaleur Bay area: Youghall Beach (near Alston Point), the lovely Daly Point Nature Reserve, and the Pabineau Falls.

Bathurst's original name was Nepisiquit, a Mi'qmaq word meaning 'Rough Waters'.

◉ Sights

Point Daly Reserve   NATURE RESERVE

(Carron Dr) Located 5.5km east of Bathurst, this lovely nature reserve has various marked trails, all courtesy of a former mining company. In fall you can see the Canada geese on their migratory voyage. There are also eagles, osprey and lovely trees and shrubs. Informative boards are located throughout the trails.

Bathurst Heritage Museum   MUSEUM
(☑506-546-9449; 360 Douglas Ave; ⊙8:30am-4:30pm late Jun–mid-Aug) Bathurst's history is proudly displayed here with artifacts galore, from photos to documents.

🛏 Sleeping & Eating

Auberge & Bistro l'Anjou   B&B $$
(http://aubergedanjou.com; 587 Principale St, Petit Rocher; r $89-108) Located 30km northwest of Bathurst in the small village of Petit-Rocher, this is the perfect spot for anyone wishing to stay in the region. It's both a comfortable B&B and smart bistro in one. Locals rave about its cuisine (with instructions not to miss the sugar pie). The bistro is open are Wednesday to Sunday; check website for hours.

L'Étoile du Havre B&B   B&B $$
(☑506-545-6238; www.etoileduhavre.com; 405 Youghall Dr; r $125; P ❄ 🕾) Situated in a tranquil location opposite a golf course, and en route to Youghall Beach, this designer-sleek, open-plan, ultracontemporary B&B with six rooms looks like it's out of the pages of an LA showroom magazine. Cooked breakfasts (the likes of pancakes) are served to all in the massive open-plan kitchen-lounge room. It's gay friendly.

Pabineau Seafood Restaurant   SEAFOOD $
(☑506-546-5150; www.facebook.com/pabineau-seafood; 1295 Pabineau Falls Rd, Pabineau First Nation; mains $8-20; ⊙11am-8pm Thu-Sun May-Sep) Located near the site of the **Pabineau Falls** (Pabineau Falls Rd, Pabineau First Nation), this small eatery, run by the local First Nations

group, is the spot to pick up your picnic supplies before heading to the rapids. Lobster rolls and fried shrimp, scallops and clams are on the menu. Call ahead to check it's open.

Nectar   INTERNATIONAL $$$
(www.facebook.com/nectarcuisineinternationale; 50 Douglas Ave; mains $26-36; ⊙9am-8pm Mon-Sat) Perched over the Bathurst Harbour, Nectar caters to everyone from cafe-goers (downstairs) to those after a light lunch to heftier (and pricier) fine-dining options (upstairs). The ambitious menu includes everything from lobster sandwiches to salmon dishes and a variety of salads. A smart martini lounge is on the premises too. Popular among the local businesspeople and a safe option.

ℹ Information

Tourist office (☑506-548-0412; www.bathurst.ca; Bathurst Harbor; ⊙9am-4pm Mon-Fri Sep-Apr, to 5pm May, to 8pm Jun-Aug) This helpful office will direct you to nature-based activities around Bathurst.

ℹ Getting There & Away

Maritime Bus (www.maritimebus.com) services Bathurst. Handy links include Fredericton ($68.50, six hours, one daily), Campbellton ($25.50, 1½ hours, one daily), Saint John ($63.50, 6¼ hours, one daily) and Moncton ($46, 3¼ hours, one daily). Note: for Shediac ($41.75, 2¾ hours, one daily) you must book 24 hours ahead. See the website for services to Sydney, Nova Scotia.

WORTH A TRIP

SCENIC DRIVE: THE ACADIAN PENINSULA

Take a run out to the very northeastern tip of the province – a chain of low, flat islands pointing across the Gulf of St Lawrence to Labrador. Rte 113 cuts across salt marsh and scrub arriving first in **Shippagan**, home of the province's largest fishing fleet, where crab is king. Hop the bridge to **Lamèque**, a tidy fishing village that has hosted the **Lamèque International Baroque Festival** (☑506-344-5846; www.festivalbaroque.com; ⊙late Jul) for over 30 years. Note the red, white and blue Acadian flags flying from nearly every porch. Grab a light lunch at the excellent **Aloha Café-Boutique** (41 Rue Principale, Lamèque; mains $7-9; ⊙7am-4pm Mon-Thu, to 9pm Fri, 8:30am-4pm Sat & Sun; 🕾). Rte 113 continues north to **Miscou Island**. The road dead-ends at a beautiful lighthouse. On the way back, just before you cross the bridge, at the quay, gorge yourself on lobster and seafood at **La Terrasse à Steve** (Rte 113, Quai de Miscou, Miscou Island; mains from $20, seafood platter $130; ⊙8am-8pm May-Sep). The good news? Fresh fish and not a skerrick of frying.

Campbellton

Campbellton is a pleasant but unremarkable mill town on the Québec border. The lengthy Restigouche River, which winds through northern New Brunswick and then forms the border with Québec, empties to the sea here. The Bay of Chaleur is on one side and dramatic rolling hills surround the town on the remaining sides. Across the border is Matapédia and Hwy 132 leading to Mont Joli, 148km into Québec.

The last naval engagement of the Seven Years' War was fought in the waters off its coast in 1760. The Battle of Restigouche marked the conclusion of the long struggle for Canada by Britain and France.

These days, there are really only two reasons to come here: to transit to/from Québec, or to hike, ski and camp at **Sugarloaf Provincial Park** (www.parcsugarloafpark.ca; 596 Val d'Amours Rd, Atholville). Dominated by Sugarloaf Mountain, which rises nearly 400m above sea level and looks vaguely like one of its other namesakes in Rio, the park is off Hwy 11 at Exit 415. From the base, it's just a half-hour walk to the top – well worth the extensive views of the town and part of the Restigouche River. Another trail leads for 4.2km around the bottom of the hill.

🛏 Sleeping

Campbellton Lighthouse Hostel HOSTEL $
(☑ 506-759-7044; www.hihostels.com/hostels/hi-campbellton; 1 Ritchie St; dm $16.50; ☉ Jun-Aug; 🛜) The Campbellton Lighthouse Hostel, a converted lighthouse by the Restigouche River, makes for an illuminatingly novel stay. Dorms are clean and separate male and female arrangements apply. It's near the Maritime bus stop and Campbellton's 8.5m salmon sculpture.

Dans les Draps de Morphée B&B $
(☑ 506-329-0274; www.drapsdemorphee.com; 7 Ritchie St; r $75-100) A spotless B&B with four rooms (plus loft apartment) in a pleasant house and in a central location near the lighthouse. The hearty cooked breakfast is served in the owners' kitchen.

Sugarloaf Provincial Park CAMPGROUND $
(☑ 506-789-2366; www.parcsugarloafpark.ca; 596 Val d'Amours Rd; campsites/RV sites $28/36, yurts $43; ☉ end May-end Sep) Four kilometers from downtown Campbellton, Sugarloaf Provincial Park has 76 campsites in one of the most beautiful nonwild camping areas around. RVs have separate areas, though you may still hear generator noise. If you don't have a tent you can opt for a yurt. The communal kitchen has a wood stove for baking.

Maison McKenzie House B&B B&B $$
(☑ 506-753-3133; www.bbcanada.com/4384.html; 31 Andrew St; r with shared bath incl breakfast $75-100; 🅿🖨🛜) Maison McKenzie B&B is a homey 1910 house handy to downtown. For $60, the folks here will rent you a kayak and drop you off upriver.

ℹ Information

Provincial tourist office (☑ 506-789-2367; www.tourismnewbrunswick.ca; 56 Salmon Blvd; ☉ 9am-5:30pm May & Jun, 9am-7pm Jul & Aug, 9:30am-6pm Sep & Oct) This helpful office is next to City Centre Mall and near the 8.5m giant salmon feature.

ℹ Getting There & Away

Maritime Bus (☑ 506-753-6714; www.maritimebus.com; 157 Roseberry St; ☉ 6am-9pm) services stop at the Pik-Quik convenience store, near Prince William St. Buses departs daily for Fredericton ($82, 7½ hours) and Moncton ($59, five hours). Twice a day (morning and afternoon), an **Orléans Express** (www.orleansexpress.com) bus leaves from the Pik-Quik for Gaspé ($41, six hours) and Québec City ($91, seven hours).

The **VIA Rail station** (www.viarail.ca; 99c Roseberry St) is conveniently central. Trains depart three times weekly to Québec City ($95 including tax, eight hours).

Prince Edward Island

Best Places to Eat

➡ Inn at Bay Fortune (FireWorks) (p157)

➡ New Glasgow Lobster Supper (p163)

➡ Landmark Café (p158)

➡ Harbourview Restaurant (p154)

➡ Water Prince Corner Shop & Lobster Pound (p152)

Best Places to Sleep

➡ Fairholm National Historic Inn (p150)

➡ Dalvay by the Sea (p159)

➡ Barachois Inn (p162)

➡ Great George (p150)

➡ Around the Sea (p162)

Why Go?

Prince Edward Island (PEI) is as pretty as a storybook: Lucy Maud Montgomery's classic *Anne of Green Gables,* to be exact. Like Anne Shirley, the book's heroine, loved the world over, the island too is a redhead – from coast to coast, rich, sienna-colored soil nourishes luminous green pastures and shores are lined with rose and golden sand. Anne's beloved landscape, a patchwork of lush rolling fields, tidy gabled farmhouses and seaside villages has barely changed.

The island is, as far as islands go, largely self-sufficient and has gained a reputation as a farm- and ocean-to-table culinary destination. Its size makes it easy to explore by car or bike – the island's Confederation Trail is one of the world's best cycling destinations. And, like the rest of the Maritime provinces, its people are warm and inviting.

When to Go
Charlottetown

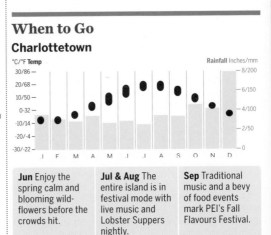

Jun Enjoy the spring calm and blooming wildflowers before the crowds hit.

Jul & Aug The entire island is in festival mode with live music and Lobster Suppers nightly.

Sep Traditional music and a bevy of food events mark PEI's Fall Flavours Festival.

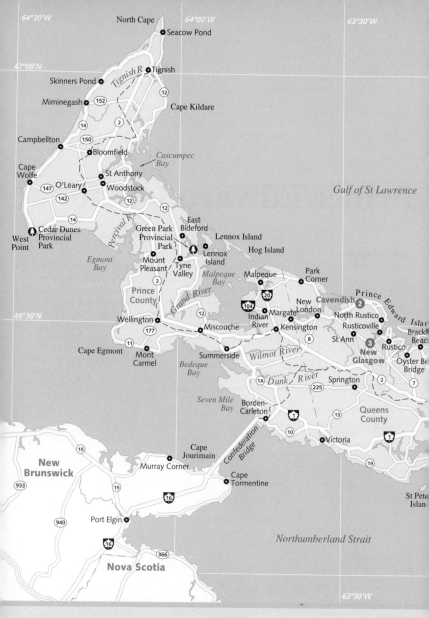

Prince Edward Island Highlights

1 Charlottetown (p146) Staying in a heritage B&B, walking the scenic waterfront and enjoying fine dining.

2 Green Gables Heritage Place (p164) Finding yourself among the pages of *Anne of Green Gables*, in Cavendish.

3 New Glasgow Lobster Supper (p163) Gorging yourself on lobster at PEI's original crustacean extravaganza.

4 Greenwich Interpretation Centre (p157) Walking the floating boardwalk into the undulating dunes.

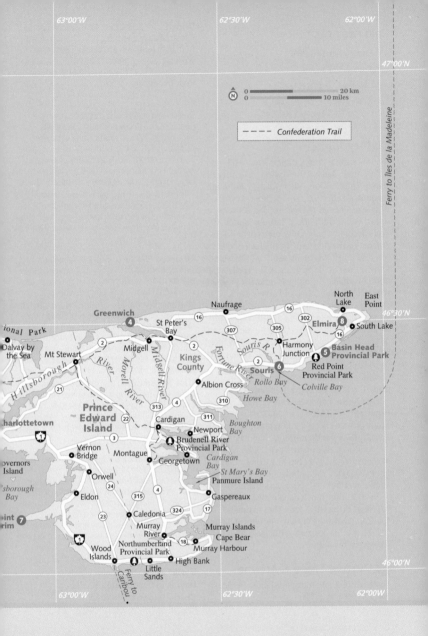

5 **Basin Head Provincial Park** (p156) Listening to the sounds of the singing sands beneath your feet before taking a dip.

6 **Inn at Bay Fortune** (p157) Indulging in this dining sensation, near Souris.

7 **Point Prim Lighthouse** (p151) Imagining yourself as a lonely lighthouse keeper from another time.

8 **Elmira Railway Museum** (p156) Reliving childhood and taking ownership of your inner train-spotter.

PEI FAST FACTS

➡ Population: 146,283

➡ Area: 5700 sq km

➡ Capital: Charlottetown

➡ Quirky fact: Kilos of potatoes produced per year – 1.3 billion

History

Its Aboriginal inhabitants, the Mi'kmaq (mig-*maw*), knew the island as Abegeit (Land Cradled on the Waves). Although Jacques Cartier of France first recorded PEI's existence in 1534, European settlement didn't begin until 1603. Initially small, the French colony only grew after Britain's expulsion of the Acadians from Nova Scotia in the 1750s. In 1758 the British took the island, known then as Île St Jean, and expelled the 3000 Acadians. Britain was officially granted the island in the Treaty of Paris of 1763.

To encourage settlement, the British divided the island into 67 lots and held a lottery to give away the land. Unfortunately, most of the 'Great Giveaway' winners were speculators and did nothing to settle or develop the island. The questionable actions of these absentee landlords hindered population growth and caused unrest among islanders.

One of the major reasons PEI did not become part of Canada in 1867 was because union did not offer a solution to the land problem. In 1873 the Compulsory Land Purchase Act forced the sale of absentee landlords' land and cleared the way for PEI to join Canada later that year. The population has remained stable, at around 140,000, since the 1930s.

In 1997, after much debate, PEI was linked to New Brunswick and the mainland by the Confederation Bridge – at almost 13km, it's the world's longest artificial bridge over ice-covered waters.

ℹ Getting There & Around

There is little public transportation on PEI. Most visitors rent a car or bike.

AIR

Charlottetown Airport (p154) Located 8km from town and serves all flights entering and leaving the province.

Air Canada (AC; ☎ 888-247-2262; www. aircanada.com) Has daily flights to Charlottetown from Halifax and Toronto, and from Montréal in the high season (June to September).

Delta (DL; ☎ 800-241-4141; www.delta.com) Runs one daily direct flight to Charlottetown from both New York and Boston, in season.

WestJet (WS; ☎ 888-937-8538; www.westjet. com) Offers direct flights to Charlottetown from Toronto and Ottawa.

BICYCLE

Cyclists and pedestrians are banned from the Confederation Bridge and must use the 24-hour, demand-driven shuttle service (bicycle/pedestrian $8.75/4.25). On the PEI side, go to the bridge operations building at Gateway Village in Borden-Carleton; on the other side, pickup is at the Cape Jourimain Nature Centre at exit 51 on Rte 16.

The flat and well-maintained Confederation Trail runs the length of the island through some beautiful countryside and small towns. For details, check out: www.tourismpei.com/pei-confederation-trail.

BUS

Advanced Shuttle (p154) A convenient service from Charlottetown or Summerside to Halifax or any point along the way (adult one-way $69). The van has a bicycle carrier.

Maritime Bus (☎ 800-575-1807; www.maritime bus.com) Has services to Charlottetown from Moncton, New Brunswick (one way $41.75, three hours, twice daily), with stops at Borden-Carleton and Summerside en route. There are two buses a day to Halifax (one way $58.25, 5½ hours), with a transfer in Amherst, Nova Scotia.

Trius Transit (p154) Runs local services within Charlottetown and Summerside and its County Line Express runs between the two (each way $9) three times a day via Rte 2. Schedules are available on its website.

CAR & MOTORCYCLE

The **Confederation Bridge** is the quickest way to get to PEI from New Brunswick and east central Nova Scotia. Unfortunately, the 1.1m-high guardrails rob you of any hoped-for view. The toll is only charged on departure from PEI, and includes all passengers. If you're planning to travel one way on the bridge and the other way by ferry, it's cheaper to take the ferry to PEI and return via the bridge.

Regional driving distances are as follows:

North Cape to East Point 273km

Halifax to Charlottetown 227km

Charlottetown to Montréal 1199km

CHARLOTTETOWN

POP 34,562 / ☎ 902

If it weren't for its isolation and inhospitable winters, charming Charlottetown might just be one of the loveliest, affordable places to live, anywhere. Failing that, a visit is recommended. This little city is the perfect size with big-city benefits minus the unpleasant stuff like overcrowding, pollution and the need for public transportation.

Historically, in 1864, it was here that the Confederation Conference set in motion a series of events that led to the birth of the nation of Canada.

There is, however, a burgeoning restaurant scene capitalizing on the island's abundant seafood and fresh produce, combined with its wealth of talented graduates from the Culinary Institute of Canada. Add a lively cultural scene and you have a capital city oozing small-town feel and appeal.

History

Charlottetown is named after the exotic consort of King George III. Her African roots, dating back to Margarita de Castro Y Sousa and the Portuguese royal house, are as legendary as they are controversial.

While many believe the city's splendid harbor was the reason Charlottetown became the capital, the reality was less glamorous. In 1765 the surveyor-general decided on Charlottetown because he thought it prudent to bestow the poor side of the island with some privileges. Thanks to the celebrated 1864 Confederation Conference, however, Charlottetown is etched in Canadian history as the country's birthplace.

◎ Sights

Charlottetown isn't top-heavy on sights. That said, think of the whole of the downtown area (known as Old Charlottetown), with its beautifully preserved and colorful colonial buildings, and the wealth of boutiques, bistros and bars they contain, as the main event.

★ Victoria Park   PARK
(www.city.charlottetown.pe.ca/victoriapark.php) Dedicated in 1873, Charlottetown's most popular and beautiful waterfront green space has 16 hectares of loveliness for you to enjoy on a fine day.

COWS Creamery   FACTORY
(☑ 902-566-5558; www.cowscreamery.ca/tours; 397 Capital Dr; ⊙ 10am-6pm) **FREE** Who doesn't love a self-guided, buttery, *fromagerie* and ice-creamery tour that spits you out in the mecca retail store that is this PEI institution's award-winning dairy heaven, hmm?

St Dunstan's Basilica   NOTABLE BUILDING
(☑ 902-894-3486; www.stdunstanspei.com; 45 Great George St; ⊙ 9am-5pm) **FREE** Rising from the ashes of a 1913 fire, the three towering stone spires of this Catholic, neo-Gothic basilica are now a Charlottetown landmark. The marble floors, Italianate carvings and decoratively embossed ribbed ceiling are surprisingly ornate.

Government House   NOTABLE BUILDING
(☑ 902-368-5480; 165 Richmond St; ⊙ 10am-4pm Mon-Fri Jul & Aug) **FREE** This striking colonial mansion, with its grand hall, Palladian window and Doric columns, has been home to PEI's lieutenant governors since 1835. As it is a private residence, the house is not open to the public outside the months of July and August when guided tours are conducted.

Beaconsfield
Historic House   NOTABLE BUILDING
(☑ 902-368-6603; www.peimuseum.com; 2 Kent St; adult/student/family $5/4/14; ⊙ 10am-5pm) With its crowning belvedere, intricate gingerbread trim and elegant 19th-century furnishings, Beaconsfield House is the finest Victorian mansion in Charlottetown. Have a wander or sit on the verandah and be stunned by the view.

☞ Tours

Self-guided walking-tour booklets are available at the visitor center (p153).

★ Happy Clammers   FISHING
(☑ 866-887-3238; www.experiencepei.ca/happyclammers; Rte 1, Pinette; adult/child $100/25, minimum 4 people; ⊙ Mon-Sat Jul-Oct , times vary with tides) Many folks come out this way to dig razor, soft-shell, bar and quahog clams. Once you've filled your buckets, go home to Gilbert and Goldie's house to steam up your catch and dine on other treats cooked up by this charming local family.

★ Confederation Players
Walking Tours   WALKING
(☑ 800-565-0278; www.confederationcentre.com; 6 Prince St; adult/child $15/8; ⊙ daily Jul-Aug) There is no better way to tour Charlottetown. Playing the fathers and ladies of Confederation, actors garbed in 19th-century dress educate and entertain through the town's historic streets. Tours leave from Founders' Hall, with a variety of themes and itineraries to choose from.

Charlottetown

PRINCE EDWARD ISLAND CHARLOTTETOWN

N
0   400 m
0   0.2 miles

Papa Joe's (700m);
Upstreet Brewery (1km);
Farmers Market (2km)

Maritime Bus
(900m)

Peake's
Wharf

East
(Hillsborough)
River

Victoria
Park

Grafton St

Great George St

Euston St

Charlottetown

◉ Top Sights
1 Victoria Park A4

◉ Sights
2 Beaconsfield Historic House B4
3 Government House A4
4 St Dunstan's Basilica............................. D3

✚ Activities, Courses & Tours
5 Confederation Players Walking
   Tours F3
6 Harbour Hippo Hippopotabus F4
7 Peake's Wharf Boat Cruises..................E4

🛏 Sleeping
8 Aloha Tourist Home F2
9 Charlotte's Rose Inn B4
10 Charlottetown Backpackers Inn E2
11 Delta Prince Edward...............................E4
12 Fairholm National Historic Inn D1
13 Fitzroy Hall B&B..................................... B2
14 Great George E3
15 Holman Grand Hotel............................. D2
16 Rodd Charlottetown C3
17 Spillett House B&B E1

✖ Eating
18 Brickhouse Kitchen & Bar D3

19 Cedar's.. C2
20 Churchill Arms D3
21 Claddagh Oyster House D3
22 Kettle Black D4
23 Leonhard's D2
24 Local 343 .... E4
25 Pilot House C3
26 Splendid Essence D1
27 Terre Rouge... D3
28 Water Prince Corner Shop &
    Lobster Pound E3

🍷 Drinking & Nightlife
29 Brakish... E4
30 Gahan House... D3
31 Hopyard C2
   Marc's Studio ....(see 18)
32 Merchantman E4
33 Old Triangle C2

🎭 Entertainment
   Baba's Lounge ....(see 19)
34 City Cinema... D4
35 Confederation Centre of the
    Arts... D3
36 Mack... D2
   Olde Dublin Pub ....(see 21)
37 Peake's Quay E4

PRINCE EDWARD ISLAND CHARLOTTETOWN

Peake's Wharf Boat Cruises CRUISE
(📞 902-566-4458; www.charlottetownboattours. com; 1 Great George St; tours from $34; ⏱ 2:30pm, 6:30pm & 8pm Jun-Aug) Observe sea life, hear interesting stories and witness a wonderfully different perspective of Charlottetown from the waters of its harbor aboard the 45ft good ship *Fairview*. A variety of itineraries of varying durations is available.

Harbour Hippo Hippopotabus TOURS
(📞 902-628-8687; www.harbourhippo.com; 2 Prince St; 1hr tour adult/child $26/19) Want to explore historic Charlottetown but afraid the kids will get bored? Hop on this amphibious bus that takes you to all the sights on land, then floats in the water.

✨ Festivals & Events

PEI Burger Love FOOD & DRINK
(www.peiburgerlove.ca; ⏱ Mar) This monthlong celebration of the humble burger has gained cultlike status in the restaurants of Charlottetown, which try to outdo each other for the title of PEI's most-loved burger.

Festival of Small Halls MUSIC
(www.smallhalls.com; ⏱ mid-Jun) Island musicians, dancers and storytellers who have

'made it' out of the province return to their homeland to perform in rural community halls around PEI during this popular festival.

Charlottetown Festival PERFORMING ARTS
(📞 800-565-0278; www.confederationcentre.com; ⏱ Jun-Sep) This long-running festival organized by the Confederation Centre of the Arts (p153) features free outdoor performances, a children's theater and dance programs.

Old Home Week CULTURAL
(📞 902-629-6623; www.oldhomeweekpei.com; ⏱ mid-Aug) Held at the Provincial Exhibition grounds, this 10-day event features carnival rides, musical entertainment, games of chance, harness racing and livestock shows.

Fall Flavours FOOD & DRINK
(📞 866-960-9912; www.fallflavours.ca; ⏱ Sep) Now one of the island's largest festivals, this massive, monthlong kitchen party merges traditional music with incredible cuisine. Don't miss the oyster-shucking championships or the chowder challenge.

🛏 Sleeping

Old Charlottetown's charms and proximity to major sights and restaurants makes it the most enviable area to rest your head. During summer, Charlottetown hums with activity, so it's wise to book ahead. In the off-season, accommodations are plentiful and most places reduce their rates. Parking is freely available at, or close to, all accommodations.

Charlottetown Backpackers Inn   HOSTEL $
(☑ 902-367-5749; www.charlottetownbackpack ers.com; 60 Hillsborough St; dm/r incl breakfast $33/80; ☎) Impossible to miss with its bright red-and-white paint job and happy hostellers milling about on the lawn, this superbly happening backpackers has cozy single-sex or mixed dorms, a good kitchen, and a quirky common room with a turntable and a rather epic vinyl collection. Be prepared for spontaneous barbecues and pub outings.

Spillett House B&B   B&B $
(☑ 902-892-5494; www.spilletthouse.pe.ca; 157 Weymouth St; d from $70; ☎) This lovely heritage home is scrupulously clean, with polished hardwood floors and antique furnishings, homemade quilts on the beds and lace curtains on the windows. Kids are welcome and there are storage facilities for bicycles. Shared bathrooms.

Aloha Tourist Home   B&B $
(☑ 902-892-5642; www.alohaamigo.com; 234 Sydney St; d/ste from $65/140; ☎) A central, welcoming choice that's really a heritage B&B complete with antiques and comfy beds, but without the hefty price tag: three of the six rooms have shared bathrooms and there's a two-bedroom family suite. Breakfast is a tasty serve-yourself affair.

Holman Grand Hotel   HOTEL $$
(☑ 877-455-4726; www.theholmangrand.com; 123 Grafton St; d/ste from $119/189) This modern, minimalist private hotel has a neat selection of simple, stylish rooms incorporating some unique features like sun-drenched terraces and lofty nooks. The indoor-pool and gym area is one you might actually want to use!

Great George   BOUTIQUE HOTEL $$
(☑ 902-892-0606; www.thegreatgeorge.com; 58 Great George St; d/ste from $179/219; ❋☎) This colorful collage of celebrated buildings along Charlottetown's most famous street has rooms ranging from plush and historic to bold and contemporary – but all are simply stunning. It's both gay- and family-friendly. A babysitting service is available, as is a fitness room.

Rodd Charlottetown   HISTORIC HOTEL $$
(☑ 902-894-7371; 75 Kent St; d from $149; P ⊖ ❋@❋) Built by Canadian Pacific Railways in 1931, this once-grand hotel hasn't changed much over the years. Many would say it's due for a revamp, but others will love the gently jaded rooms, antique bathrooms, solid doors and opening windows. It's age and the competition in town means bargain rates can be found if you keep your eyes peeled.

Fitzroy Hall B&B   B&B $$
(☑ 866-627-9766; www.fitzroyhall.com; 45 Fitzroy St; d/ste from $165/219; ☎) A perfect blend of elegance and comfort, this house is as grand as they come, while the welcome is warm and down to earth. The innkeepers have put serious thought into how to make their guests comfortable, with refined antiques, muted color schemes, and details like hidden alcoves with fridges to keep cold drinks and hot pots to make tea.

Charlotte's Rose Inn   INN $$
(☑ 902-892-3699; www.charlottesrose.ca; 11 Grafton St; apt from $150, d from $165; ❋☎❋) Miss Marple must be around here somewhere. This decadent Victorian has true English flair with bodacious rose-printed wallpaper, lace canopies, big fluffy beds and grand bathrooms. There's a fire in the parlor for guests to enjoy along with complimentary tea and cakes. A modern loft apartment can accommodate five and has its own private rooftop deck. Two-night minimum stay.

★ Fairholm National Historic Inn   INN $$$
(☑ 902-892-5022; www.fairholminn.com; 230 Prince St; d/ste from $129/289; ☎) This historic inn was built in 1838 and its rooms feature luxurious fabrics, beautiful local art and grand antiques. Out back are brilliantly designed, well-appointed, self-contained apartments. At the time of writing, the inn's fabulously intelligent, resourceful and friendly owner was expanding his empire to his equally beautiful neighboring properties. Be sure to check the website for the full scoop.

★ Delta Prince Edward   HOTEL $$$
(☑ 902-566-2222; www.marriott.com; 18 Queen St; d/ste from $169/269; P ⊖ ❋☎❋) You can't beat the Delta's prime waterfront location in the heart of Old Charlottetown's vibrant restaurant district. It's also hard to fault its selection of comfy, freshly updated rooms with their crisp, clean lines, modern styling and (for many) harbor views.

ORWELL CORNER & POINT PRIM

If you're looking for a sweet, kid-friendly, half-day trip from Charlottetown and have had your fill of Anne of Green Gables action, head east on Rte 1. After about 30km, you'll come to Orwell Corner Historic Village (☑902-651-8510; www.peimuseum.com; Resource Rd 2, Vernon Bridge; adult/child $9/4.50; ⊙9am-4:30pm Jul-Sep, 9:30am-4:30pm Mon-Fri Jun & Sep-Nov), a recreation of a rustic 19th-century farming community with animals, antiques and costumed locals. Further down the road, the Sir Andrew MacPhail Homestead (☑902-651-2789; www.macphailhomestead.ca; 271 MacPhail Park Rd, Vernon Bridge; ⊙10am-5pm Wed-Sun Jul-Sep) is open for tea on summer afternoons.

The real delight of the excursion is found continuing south on Rte 1 for a further 11km, where you'll come to signs for Point Prim. This skinny bucolic spit of land is covered in wild rose, Queen Anne's lace and wheat fields through summer and has views of red sand shores on either side. At the tip is the Point Prim Lighthouse (☑902-659-2768; www.pointprimlighthouse.com; 2147 Point Prim Rd, Belfast; adult/child $3.50/2; ⊙10am-6pm Jul & Aug, 10am-6pm Wed-Sun Jun & Sep): the province's oldest and, we think, prettiest. If you're lucky, you'll be able to climb to the top to pump the foghorn.

If you need more to do, get in touch with the friendly folks at Happy Clammers (p147), who'll take you searching for soft-shell, bar and quahog clams, then take you home and show you how to turn your briny catch into a fantastic feast.

Round out your day with a cup of chowder by the ocean at Point Prim Chowder House (☑902-659-2187; www.chowderhousepei.com; 2150 Point Prim Rd, Belfast; mains $8-25; ⊙11am-7pm Jun-Oct), then head back to Charlottetown, or continue south to Wood Islands (30km) for your ferry to Nova Scotia.

✖️ Eating

Thanks largely to the Culinary Institute of Canada, which keeps churning out talented chefs, the city has a heaped helping of fine eateries. During summer, Victoria Row's pedestrian mall and the waterfront are hot spots for diners and drinkers. Pubs are also a great place to go for good-value eating.

Cedar's   LEBANESE $
(☑902-892-7377; 181 Great George St; mains $10-25; ⊙11am-11pm Mon-Sat, to 4pm Sun; ✔️) Cedar's has been serving the home-style flavors of Lebanon to the people of Charlottetown since 1979 and it still rates as one of the best places for a cheap, tasty and healthy feed in town. Nightly specials every day.

Leonhard's   CAFE $
(www.leonhards.ca; 142 Great George St; sandwiches from $8; ⊙9am-5pm Tue-Sat) Find absolute comfort in this little cafe full of cushioned seating and soothing country-style muted hues. Treat yourself to excellent German pastries, salads and creative sandwiches, as well as all-day breakfasts made with free-range eggs, a great cheese selection and cold cuts like Black Forest ham. Wash it down with farmers-market teas and espresso.

Splendid Essence   TAIWANESE $
(☑902-566-4991; www.splendidessence.com; 186 Prince St; mains $7-14; ⊙11:30am-3pm & 5-8pm; ✔️) Savory Taiwanese vegetarian dishes are served in this cozy Victorian, fitted out with warm wood paneling and intimate booths upholstered in red, green and gold and accented with Chinese art. Recommended are the spicy vegetables and fried rice chased with a steaming mug of hot almond milk.

Maid Marian's   DINER $
(☑902-566-4641; 7 Ellis Rd; meals $5-9; ⊙7am-8pm) This old-school local hot spot is always hopping. It's not downtown, but it is a great spot to stop for a quick, cheap breakfast on your way to the airport. There's nothing fancy here: just awesome 1980s green-vinyl booths, PEI people watching, nightly specials including scallop dinners, and plenty of basic, hearty meals for under $10.

Papa Joe's   CANADIAN $
(☑902-566-5070; www.papajoespei.ca; 345 University Ave; mains $10-18; ⊙11am-9pm) This family-style restaurant is super popular with locals. Here all pretensions are checked at the door as you dine on bacon-wrapped meatloaf, turkey pot pie or a steak sandwich. Wednesdays go exotic with Indian cuisine served all day.

Kettle Black CAFE $
(☑902-370-0776; 45 Queen St; light lunches $9;
⊘7am-7pm) A cozy bakery and cafe that feels
like a mix between a rural farmhouse and an
urban art gallery. Enjoy great coffee, breakfasts and light lunches.

★**Water Prince Corner**
Shop & Lobster Pound SEAFOOD $$
(☑902-368-3212; http://waterprincelobster.ca; 141
Water St; mains $12-36; ⊘9:30am-8pm) When
locals want seafood they head to this incon-
spicuous, sea-blue eatery near the wharf. It
is deservedly famous for its scallop burgers,
but it's also the best place in town for fresh
lobster. You'll probably have to line up for a
seat, otherwise order take-out lobster, which
gets you a significant discount.

★**Claddagh Oyster House** SEAFOOD $$
(☑902-892-6992; http://claddaghoysterhouse.
com; 131 Sydney St; mains $13-32; ⊘5-9pm) Lo-
cals herald the Claddagh Room as one of the
best seafood restaurants in Charlottetown.
Trust 'em! The Irish-inspired Galway Bay Delight features a coating of fresh cream and
seasonings over scallops and shrimp that
have been sautéed with mushrooms and onions, then flambéed with Irish Mist liqueur.

Terre Rouge CANADIAN $$
(☑902-892-4032; www.terrerougepei.ca; 72 Queen
St; mains $12-32; ⊘11am-3pm & 5-10pm Tue-Sun)
Self billed as a craft kitchen, Terre Rouge is
the place where healthy eating meats com-
fort and fun. Only the most boring of eat-
ers will struggle to find something on the
menu to get excited about: beet salad, fish
cakes, chowder, lentil burgers and tacos are
all presented here in happy, hipster-friendly
environs.

Local 343 CAFE $$
(☑902-569-9343; 98 Water St; ⊘11:30am-8pm;
☑) This fabulous deli-cum-cafe was a local
secret until we let the cat out of the bag.
Swing by for tasty home-style soups, salads,
sandwiches, quiches, meatloaf, crab cakes...
you get the gist. There's plenty you can order
and go for those perfect PEI picnic days, or
if you're feeling like laying low and enjoying
the comforts of your swanky digs.

Brickhouse Kitchen
& Bar MODERN CANADIAN $$
(☑902-566-4620; http://brickhousepei.com; 125
Sydney St; mains $16-36; ⊘11am-10pm) The
chic ambience of this heritage brick build-
ing is matched by creative dishes inspired
by island culture and made with local in-
gredients. Try the lobster poutine, seafood
bouillabaisse, Thai curry chicken or just a
good PEI beef burger. Don't leave without
enjoying a cocktail or dessert in the upstairs
lounge.

Churchill Arms PUB FOOD $$
(☑902-367-3450; www.churchillarms.ca; 75 Queen
St; mains $10-22; ⊘11:30am-9pm Mon-Sat)
Equally worthy as a standalone drinking
haunt, this lively, quintessentially British pub
makes the grade for heavy, authentic Brit-
pub food: curries, shepherd's pies, bangers
and mash, killer fish-and-chips (sourced locally) and bubble and squeak, for those times
when, well, nothing else will do.

Pilot House MODERN CANADIAN $$$
(☑902-894-4800; http://thepilothouse.ca; 70
Grafton St; mains $24-39; ⊘11am-10pm Mon-
Sat) The oversized wood beams and brick
columns of the historic Roger's Hardware
building provide a bold setting for fine din-
ing or light pub fare. A loyal clientele tucks
into lobster-stuffed chicken, vegetarian pizza
or seafood torte. Lunch specials start at $10.

🍷 **Drinking & Nightlife**

Charlottetown has an established and bur-
geoning drinking scene. Historic pubs dot the
old part of town. Most bars and pubs have a
small cover charge (about $5) on weekends,
or when there is live music. People spill into
the streets at 2am when things wrap up.

★**Gahan House** PUB
(☑902-626-2337; http://charlottetown.gahan.ca;
126 Sydney St; ⊘11am-midnight) Within these
homey, historic walls the pub owners brew
PEI homegrown ales. Sir John A's Honey
Wheat Ale is well worth introducing to your
insides, as is the medium- to full-bodied Syd-
ney Street Stout. The food here is also great –
enjoy with friends old and new.

Hopyard BAR
(☑902-367-2599; 131 Kent St; ⊘11am-midnight)
Beer, food and vinyl: that's the promise of
these newcomers to the growing Charlotte-
town bar scene...and the locals are loving it!

Upstreet Brewery BREWERY
(☑902-894-0543; www.upstreetcraftbrewing.com;
41 Allen St; ⊘noon-midnight) This original craft
brewer is fast becoming Charlottetown's fa-
vourite drinking haunt with a fun vibe and
great beer.

Old Triangle IRISH PUB
(✐ 902-892-5200; www.oldtrianglecharlottetown.com; 189 Great George St; ⊙ 11am-10pm) This lively Irish Pub has regular live music and the Guinness just keeps on flowing.

Merchantman BAR
(✐ 902-892-9150; www.merchantman.ca; 23 Queen St; ⊙ 11am-9pm) Merchantman wears many hats; it's a bar, it's a restaurant, it's a take-out. In summer months, the patio tables are a great place to soak up the sun and enjoy a drink while you work up your appetite for fresh PEI oysters, seafood or all manner of upscale pub grub.

Brakish BAR
(✐ 902-894-1112; www.brakish.com; 2 Lower Water St; ⊙ noon-11pm) This joint comes alive in the summer months when it's known for having Charlottetown's best waterfront patio, perfect for drinking the long sunny days away, but if you must stop to eat, there's plenty of fresh local seafood on the menu.

Marc's Studio BAR
(✐ 902-566-4620; http://brickhousepei.com/marcs-studio.html; 125 Sydney St; ⊙ 4:30pm-midnight) Climb the stairs for a cocktail or a nightcap. Think plenty of art by the late, local artist Marc Gallant (who restored this building in the 1980s) and cozily grouped sofas set against exposed brick walls. It usually closes around midnight, but will stay open until the crowd thins out.

☆ Entertainment

Charlottetown serves up a great mix of theater, music, island culture and fun. Throughout the city, various venues host traditional ceilidhs (kay-lees), sometimes referred to as 'kitchen parties.' These lively community gatherings almost always feature gleeful Celtic music and dance. The Friday edition of the *Guardian* newspaper and the free monthly *Buzz* list times and locations of upcoming ceilidhs, along with other details of what's on when and where.

★ Confederation Centre of the Arts THEATER
(✐ 902-566-1267; www.confederationcentre.com; 145 Richmond St) This modern complex's large theater and outdoor amphitheater host concerts, comedic performances and elaborate musicals. *Anne of Green Gables – The Musical* has been entertaining audiences here as part of the Charlottetown Festival since 1964, making it Canada's longest-running musical.

You'll enjoy it, and your friends will never have to know.

Peake's Quay LIVE MUSIC
(✐ 902-368-1330; www.peakesquay.com; 11 Great George St; ⊙ noon-midnight) It's actually more of a bar-restaurant (with the largest patio on the island) but this venue is the closest thing to a nightclub Charlottetown has to offer, with guest DJs and special events.

Mack THEATER
(128 Great George St) An intimate venue where guests sit at round tables for predominantly comedy gigs.

City Cinema CINEMA
(✐ 902-368-3669; http://citycinema.net; 64 King St) A small independent theater featuring Canadian and foreign-language films.

Benevolent Irish Society LIVE MUSIC
(✐ 902-963-3156; 582 North River Rd; $10; ⊙ 8pm Fri) On the north side of town, this is a great place to catch a ceilidh. Come early, as seating is limited.

Olde Dublin Pub LIVE MUSIC
(✐ 902-892-6992; 131 Sydney St; $8) A traditional Irish pub with a jovial spirit and live entertainment nightly during the summer months. Celtic bands and local notables take to the stage and make for an engaging night out.

Baba's Lounge LIVE MUSIC
(✐ 902-892-7377; 81 University Ave; ⊙ noon-midnight) Located above Cedar's Eatery, this welcoming, intimate venue hosts great local bands playing their own tunes. Occasionally there are poetry readings.

🛍 Shopping

Farmers Market MARKET
(✐ 902-626-3373; http://charlottetownfarmersmarket.weebly.com; 100 Belvedere Ave; ⊙ 9am-2pm Sat, also Wed Jul & Aug) Come hungry and empty-handed. Enjoy some prepared island foods or peruse the cornucopia of fresh organic fruit and vegetables. The market is north of the town center off University Ave.

ℹ Information

Charlottetown Visitor Information Centre
(✐ 902-368-4444; 178 Water St; ⊙ 9am-5pm May-Oct) The island's main tourist office has all the answers, a plethora of brochures and maps, and free internet access.

Main Post Office (📞 902-628-4400; 101 Kent St; 🕓 9am-5pm Mon-Fri.) Central post office.

Polyclinic Professional Centre (📞 902-629-8810; polycliniconline.com; 199 Grafton St; 🕓 5:30-8pm Mon-Fri, 9:30am-noon Sat) Charlottetown's after-hours, walk-in medical clinic.

Queen Elizabeth Hospital (📞 902-894-2111; 60 Riverside Dr; 🕓 24hr) Emergency room.

Royal Canadian Mounted Police (📞 902-368-9300; 450 University Ave) Nonemergencies only.

❶ Getting There & Around

Charlottetown Airport (YYG; 📞 902-566-7997; www.flypei.com; 250 Maple Hills Ave) is 8km north of the city center. A taxi to/from town costs $12, plus $3.50 for each additional person.

Rental cars, available from a variety of providers with city and airport depots, are the preferred method of transportation. During summer cars are in short supply, so be sure to book ahead.

Limited public transportation is provided by **Trius Transit** (T3 Transit; 📞 902-566-9962; www.triustransit.ca/), but walking or renting a bike are both great ways to get around this compact city.

Advanced Shuttle (📞 877-886-3322; www.advancedshuttle.ca) Offers shuttle services between PEI and Nova Scotia.

City Taxi (📞 902-892-6567; www.citytaxipei.com) Operates taxi services.

MacQueen's Bicycles (📞 902-368-2453; www.macqueens.com; 430 Queen St; rental per day/week $25/125) Rents a variety of quality bikes. Children's models half price.

Smooth Cycle (📞 902-566-5530; www.smoothcycle.com; 330 University Ave; rental per day/week $26/115) Offers well-priced bike rentals and sales.

Yellow Cab PEI (📞 902-566-6666; www.yellowcabpei.com)

EASTERN PRINCE EDWARD ISLAND

You can make your own tracks across Kings County, the eastern third of the province and PEI's most under-touristed region. From stretches of neatly tended homesteads to the sinuous eastern shore with its protected harbors, sweeping beaches and country inns, majestic tree canopies seem to stretch endlessly over the scenic heritage roads. The 338km Points East Coastal Drive winds along the shore, hitting the highlights.

Wood Islands

Wood Islands is the jumping-off point for ferries to Nova Scotia.

If you'll be waiting a while at the terminal, Wood Islands Provincial Park and its 1876 lighthouse are well worth the short walk.

From Wood Islands, Rte 4 heads east along the Northumberland Strait, veering inland at High Bank toward the lively and surprisingly artsy fishing settlement of Murray River. The coastal road becomes Rte 18, keeping the sea in view as it rounds Cape Bear, passing the lighthouse before looping back through the village of Murray Harbour and into Murray River. This stretch of flat, empty road offers superbly serene scenery and excellent cycling possibilities. Cyclists can follow the coastal road from Murray River, then loop back on the extension of the Confederation Trail at Wood Islands.

◉ Sights

Newman Estate Winery　　　　　　WINERY
(📞 902-962-4223; www.newmanestatewinery.com; 9404 Gladstone Rd, Gladstone; 🕓 by appointment) Head toward the coast from Murray River along Rte 348 (Gladstone Rd) to find Newman Estate Winery. This lovely place specializes in blueberry wines, but has recently begun making white wine from grapes.

Rossignol Estate Winery　　　　　　WINERY
(📞 902-962-4193; www.rossignolwinery.com; 11147 Shore Rd, Murray River; 🕓 10am-5pm Mon-Sat, 1-5pm Sun May-Oct) For wine tasting on a grand scale, cruise over to Little Sands, 9km from the Wood Islands Ferry, where Rossignol Estate Winery has free tastings and specializes in fruit wines. The divine Blackberry Mead has won a string of gold medals and the Wild Rose Liquor made from rose hips is also well worth a try; call ahead for winter hours.

✗ Eating

Crabby's Seafood　　　　　　SEAFOOD $
(📞 902-962-3228; 84 Lighthouse Rd, Wood Islands; items from $5; 🕓 noon-6pm Jun-Sep) Munch on a rock-crab sandwich or a lobster roll at Crabby's Seafood near the ferry terminal.

★ **Harbourview Restaurant**　　　CANADIAN $$
(📞 902-962-3141; www.harbourviewrestaurant.ca; 7 Mariners Lane, Murray Harbour; mains $8-24; 🕓 8am-9pm Mon-Sat, 11am-9pm Sun) When the owners of this popular restaurant formerly known as Brehaut's retired, some of the

staff decided they'd step up and take over, renaming it and keeping tried-and-true local favorites alongside new items. Dine in cozy, country-cute booths on the island's best chowder and other casual eats. They make a mean milkshake too! Murray Harbour is 21km east of Wood Islands.

ℹ️ Information

Wood Islands Visitor Information Centre
(☑ 902-962-7411; 13054 Shore Rd; ⊙ 10:30am-9pm) This is the main visitor center for those arriving on PEI by ferry.

ℹ️ Getting There & Away

Wood Islands is 51km southeast of Charlottetown and the boarding point for **Bay Ferries** (p41) services to Caribou, Nova Scotia (adult/child $19/free, 1¼ hours). A standard vehicle costs $81.

Montague & Georgetown

The fact that Montague isn't flat gives it a unique, inland feel. Perched on either side of the Montague River, the busy little town is the service center for Kings County; its streets lead from the breezy, heritage marina area to modern shopping malls, supermarkets and fast-food outlets.

Around the peninsula, the many heritage buildings in Georgetown are testament to the town's importance as a shipbuilding center in the Victorian era. Today, it's a sleepy village cum tourist spot thanks to its great places to eat and waterfront setting.

👁 Sights & Activities

Panmure Head Lighthouse LIGHTHOUSE
(☑ 902-838-3568; 62 Lighthouse Rd, Panmure Island; tours $5; ⊙ 9:30am-5pm Jul & Aug, hours vary Jun & Sep) Needing a little TLC, this is the island's first octagonal and oldest wooden lighthouse.

Garden of the Gulf Museum MUSEUM
(☑ 902-838-2467; www.montaguemuseumpei.com; 564 Main St, Montague; adult/child under 12yr $3/free; ⊙ 9am-5pm Mon-Fri Jun-Sep) On the southern side of the river, the statuesque former post office and customs house (1888) overlooks the marina, and houses the Garden of the Gulf Museum. Inside are several artifacts illustrating local history.

Tranquility Cove Adventures FISHING
(☑ 902-969-7184; www.tranquilitycoveadventures.com; Fisherman's Wharf, 1 Kent St, Georgetown; half-/full-day tours from $60/100) Tranquility Cove Adventures leads excellent fishing and clamming trips, as well as kundalini yoga on a deserted island. Check the website for details on other packages.

Brudenell Riding Stables HORSEBACK RIDING
(☑ 902-652-2396; www.brudenellridingstables.com; 1hr ride $35; ⊙ Jun-Sep) You can take a one-hour horseback trail ride through the sun-dappled forest and onto the beach with Brudenell Riding Stables.

⭐ Festivals & Events

Panmure Island Powwow CULTURAL
(☑ 902-892-5314; ⊙ mid-Aug) There's a powwow held each year with drumming, crafts and a sweat tent – it attracts around 5000 visitors, so don't expect any secluded beaches!

🛏 Sleeping

⭐ **Maplehurst** B&B $$
(☑ 902-838-3959; www.maplehurstproperties.com; 1220 Route 347; d from $145; ⊙ May-Nov; 🛜) For luxury, stay at the grand Maplehurst B&B. Marsha Leftwich has mustered every glimmer of her native Southern hospitality to create this exceptional B&B illuminated by gorgeous chandeliers and furnished with the utmost attention to detail.

Georgetown Inn & Dining Room INN $$
(☑ 902-652-2511; www.peigeorgetownhistoricinn.com; 62 Richmond St, Georgetown; d from $105; 🛜) Right in the center of Georgetown, this place is as equally well known for its PEI-themed rooms (including a Green Gables room) as for its fine casual island-fare dining.

Brudenell River Provincial Park CAMPGROUND
(☑ 902-652-8966; www.tourismpei.com/provincial-park/brudenell-river; off Rte 3, Cardigan; tent sites $21, RV sites $24-28; ⊙ May-Oct) Just north of town, development meets nature at Brudenell River Provincial Park, which is a park and resort complex. Tent and RV sites are available, as well as cottages and motel-style accommodation. Activities range from kayaking to nature walks and golf on two championship courses.

Panmure Island Provincial Park CAMPGROUND
(☑ 902-838-0668; www.tourismpei.com/provincial-park/panmure-island; Hwy 347; tent & RV sites from $27; ⊙ Jun-Sep) Bring a picnic for the supervised beach at Panmure Island Provincial Park. The park campground has every amenity for its 44 sites (most unserviced) tucked under the trees and along the shore.

✕ Eating

Cardigan Lobster Suppers SEAFOOD **$$**
(☑ 902-583-2020; www.peicardiganlobstersuppers.com; 4557 Wharf Rd, Cardigan; adult/child $39/26; ☺ 5-9pm Jun-Oct) In tiny Cardigan, enjoy a five-course Lobster Supper in a heritage building on Cardigan Harbor.

Famous Peppers PIZZA **$$**
(☑ 902-361-6161; www.famouspeppers.ca; 3 Rink St, Montague; pizzas from $10) Quite simply, the best pizza in town – not that there's much competition.

Clamdigger's Beach House & Restaurant SEAFOOD **$$**
(☑ 902-652-2466; 7 West St, Georgetown; mains $12-37; ☺ 11am-9pm) Some claim this place serves PEI's best chowder, but no matter what your opinion, you can't help but ooh and aah about the water view from the deck or through the dining room's giant windows.

Windows on the Water Café MODERN CANADIAN **$$**
(☑ 902-838-2080; cnr Sackville & Main Sts; mains $9-17; ☺ 11:30am-9:30pm May-Oct) Enjoy a flavorful array of seafood, chicken and vegetarian dishes on the deck overlooking the water and, sort of, the road. Try the lobster quiche and leave room for a freshly baked dessert.

ⓘ Information

Island Welcome Center (☑ 902-838-0670; cnr Rtes 3 & 4; ☺ 9am-6pm May-Oct) In the old train station on the riverbank there's an Island Welcome Center, which is a font of knowledge about this corner of the island.

Souris

Wrapped around the waters of Colville Bay is the bustling fishing community of Souris (*sur*-rey). It owes its name to the French Acadians and the gluttonous mice who repeatedly ravaged their crops. It's now known more for its joyous annual music festival than for the hungry field rodents of old.

This is a working town that's a friendly jumping-off point for cycling the coastal road (Rte 16) and the Confederation Trail, which comes into town. Souris is also the launching point for ferries to the Îles de la Madeleine in Québec. The wooded coast and lilting accents along this stretch of coastline offer some welcome variety from the patchwork of farms found inland. Giant white windmills march

BASIN HEAD PROVINCIAL PARK

The star attraction of **Basin Head Provincial Park** (www.tourismpei.com/provincial-park/basin-head; Basin Head) is the sweeping sand of golden **Basin Head Beach**. Many islanders rank this as their favorite beach and we have to agree. The sand is also famous for its singing – well, squeaking – when you walk on it. Unfortunately, the sand only performs when dry, so if it's been raining, it's no show. Five minutes of joyous 'musical' footsteps south from the museum and you have secluded bliss – enjoy!

across the landscape. North Lake and Naufrage harbors are intriguing places to stop and, if you feel so inclined, join a charter boat in search of a monster 450kg tuna.

◉ Sights

Elmira Railway Museum MUSEUM
(☑ 902-357-7234; Rte 16A; adult/student/family $5/4/10; ☺ 10am-6pm Jun-Sep) The railway museum in Elmira includes a quirky miniature train ride (adult/student/family $6/4/15) that winds through the surrounding forest. The station marks the eastern end of the Confederation Trail.

East Point Lighthouse LIGHTHOUSE
(☑ 902-357-2106; adult/child $4/2; ☺ 10am-6pm Jun-Aug) Built the same year Canada was unified, the East Point Lighthouse still stands guard over the northeastern shore of PEI. After being blamed for the 1882 wreck of the *British Phoenix,* the lighthouse was moved closer to shore. The eroding shoreline is now chasing it back. There's a gift shop and a little cafe next to the lighthouse that serves lobster rolls ($9.50), chowder and sandwiches.

Basin Head Fisheries Museum MUSEUM
(☑ 902-357-7233; adult/student $4.50/2; ☺ 9am-6pm Jun-Sep) This small museum explores the history of the fishing industry in PEI.

✦ Festivals & Events

PEI Bluegrass & Old Time Music Festival MUSIC
(☑ 902-569-3153; http://peibluegrass.tripod.com; ☺ early Jul) Draws acts from as far away as Nashville. Come for just a day, or camp out for all three.

🛏️ Sleeping & Eating

Johnson Shore Inn INN $$
(☑ 902-687-1340; www.jspei.com; 9984 Northside Rd, Hermanville; r from $175; ⊙ May-Feb; 🛜) Treat yourself to a little luxury at this impeccably managed inn blessed with a stunning setting on a red bluff that looks over endless sea.

★ Inn at Bay Fortune INN $$$
(☑ 902-687-3745; www.innatbayfortune.com; 758 Rte 310, Bay Fortune; r from $225; ❄️🛜) Returning to the inn where he spent seven formative years of his training, celebrated chef Michael Smith and his wife Chastity have returned to their roots and reimagined this fabulous property and its restaurant, FireWorks, to be one of Canada's hottest culinary destinations. You come for the epic interactive dining experience 'The Feast' (from $95) then enjoy the inn.

21 Breakwater CANADIAN $$
(☑ 902-687-2556; 21 Breakwater St; mains $12-28; ⊙ 11:30am-8pm Mon-Sat) Patrons come for casual fine dining in this historic mansion overlooking the industrial waterfront. The menu focuses on the usual suspects, such as burgers, pasta with scallops, steamed mussels or chowder, but the preparation is top notch, as is the service.

ℹ️ Getting There & Away

Souris is 72km east of Charlottetown and located in the northeast corner of the island. Souris is also the boarding point for the **CTMA Ferr** (traversierctma.ca/en)y to Quebec's Îles de la Madeleine (from $52, five hours).

Saint Peter's Bay to Mt Stewart

The area between the villages of St Peter's Bay and Mt Stewart is a hotbed for cycling. The section of the Confederation Trail closest to Saint Peter's Bay flirts with the shoreline and rewards riders with an eyeful of the coast. In Mt Stewart three riverside sections of the Confederation Trail converge, giving riders and hikers plenty of attractive options

👁️ Sights

Greenwich
Interpretation Centre NATURE RESERVE
(☑ 902-961-2514; Rte 13; ⊙ 9:30am-7pm Jul & Aug, to 4:30pm May, Jun, Sep & Oct) Avant-garde meets barn at the Greenwich Interpretation Centre, where an innovative audiovisual presentation details the ecology of the dune system and the archaeological history of the site. The highlight, though, is getting out into the tree-eating dunes. Four walking trails traverse the park; the Greenwich Dunes Trail (4.5km return, 1½ hours) is especially scenic.

🛏️ Sleeping & Eating

There are only a handful of accommodations in the area, mostly centered around the Confederation Trail. Dining in both St Peter's Bay and Mt Stewart is of the casual takeout and diner variety at best. Nearby Souris has a better selection for food-lovers.

Inn at St Peters Village INN $$$
(☑ 902-961-2135, 800-818-0925; www.innat stpeters.com; 1168 Greenwich Rd; d $125-265; 🛜) Even with its large, comfortable rooms and stunning water views, the main reason to come to this inn is to dine on some of PEI's finest fare at the sunset-facing restaurant (lunch/dinner mains from $17/22). Rooms are simply and elegantly decorated with antique furniture, but if you don't stay here, we still highly recommend stopping in for a meal (even you, sweaty bikers).

★ Trailside Cafe & Inn CAFE $$
(☑ 902-628-7833; www.trailside.ca; 109 Main St, Mt Stewart; mains $12-17; r $89) It's a cafe, it's a music venue, it's an inn. In all ways this place exudes the best of PEI. Grab a pot of mussels or a taster plate of local cheeses and a beer and let the live local music tingle your spine. Check the website for showtimes and tickets.

ℹ️ Information

Provincial Tourist Office (☑ 902-961-3540; Rte 2; ⊙ 8am-7pm Jul & Aug, 9am-4:30pm Jun, Sep & Oct) Both the Confederation Trail and a tourist office are found next to the bridge in St Peter's.

WORTH A TRIP

GREENWICH

Massive, dramatic and ever-shifting sand dunes epitomize the amazing area west of Greenwich. These rare parabolic giants are fronted by an awesome, often empty beach – a visit here is a must. Preserved by Parks Canada in 1998, this 6km section of shore is now part of Prince Edward Island National Park. Learn about it all in the Greenwich Interpretation Centre.

CENTRAL PRINCE EDWARD ISLAND

Central PEI contains a bit of all that's best about the island: verdant fields, quaint villages and forests undulating north to the dramatic sand-dune-backed beaches of Prince Edward Island National Park. Anne of Green Gables, the engaging heroine of Lucy Maud Montgomery's 1908 novel, has spawned a huge global industry focused on the formerly bucolic hamlet of Cavendish. However, this being PEI, even its most savagely developed patch of tourist traps and commercial detritus is almost quaint – freshly painted bedecked with flowers.

For those entering central PEI via the Confederation Bridge, it's worth stopping at the **Gateway Village Visitors Information Centre** (☑ 902-437-8570; Hwy 1; ⊙ 8:30am-8pm), just off the bridge on the PEI side, for its free maps, brochures, restrooms and an excellent introductory exhibit called 'Our Island Home' (open May to November). Staff can point you to the Confederation Trail, which starts nearby.

Victoria

A place to wander and experience more than 'see,' the shaded, tree-laden lanes of this lovely little fishing village scream character and charm. The entire village still fits neatly in the four blocks laid out when the town was formed in 1819. Colorful clapboard and shingled houses are home to more than one visitor who was so enthralled by the place they decided to stay. There's a profusion of art, cafes and eateries, as well as an excellent summer theater festival.

⊙ Sights & Activities

Victoria Seaport Lighthouse Museum   MUSEUM
(Water St; entry by donation; ⊙ 9am-5:30pm Jun-Aug) This museum has an interesting exhibit on local history. If it's closed, get the key from the shop across the road.

By the Sea Kayaking   KAYAKING
(☑ 902-658-2572; www.bytheseakayaking.ca; 1 Water St; kayak rentals per hour/day from $25/50) Paddle round on your own or on a guided tour, then take a dip at the beach, where change rooms are available. The outfit also operates popular 'I Dig Therefore I Clam' expeditions ($8) and offers bike rentals (per hour $15).

🛏 Sleeping & Eating

Orient Hotel B&B   B&B $$
(☑ 902-658-2503; www.theorienthotel.com; 34 Main St; d/ste from $95/135; 🕾) A delightful Victorian confection of buttercup yellow, red and blue, this historic inn is a perfect jewel.

★ **Landmark Café**   CAFE $$
(☑ 902-658-2286; www.landmarkcafe.ca; 12 Main St; mains $12-28; ⊙ 11:30am-10pm May-Sep) Diners come from miles around for the imaginative food at this family-run cafe. Prepared with wholesome ingredients, every colorful menu item from lasagnas and homemade soups to Cajun stir-fries and feta-stuffed vine leaves is a winner.

🍷 Drinking & Entertainment

Lobster Barn Pub and Eatery   PUB
(☑ 902-658-2722; 19 Main St; ⊙ noon-10pm) This gorgeous little pub in an old barn is a great place for a beer, but the food's pretty special too – and yes, there's lobster on the menu!

Victoria Playhouse   THEATER
(☑ 902-658-2025; www.victoriaplayhouse.com; 20 Howard St; ticket prices vary; ⊙ 8pm Jun-Sep) This ornate theater presents a series of plays over summer, and concerts from some of the region's finest musicians on Monday nights.

Prince Edward Island National Park

Heaving dunes and red sandstone bluffs provide startling backdrops for some of the island's finest stretches of sand; welcome to **Prince Edward Island National Park** (☑ 902-672-6350; www.pc.gc.ca; day pass adult/child $7.80/3.90). This dramatic coast, and the narrow sections of wetland and forests behind it, is home to diverse plants, animals and birdlife, including the red fox and endangered piping plover.

The park is open year-round, but most services only operate between mid-May and mid-October, with full services operational for the months of July and August. Entrance fees (charged when the picnic grounds and beaches are open, from mid-June to mid-September) admit you to all park sites, except Green Gables Heritage Place (p164). If you're planning to stay longer than five days, look into a seasonal pass. The park maintains an information desk at the Cavendish Visitor Information Centre (p165).

DISTILLERIES

Two distinctly different distilleries operate on PEI, echoing the province's fame for bootlegging during Prohibition. Even today many families distill their own moonshine (which is technically illegal) which is often mixed in punch and cocktails at weddings and parties.

Prince Edward Distillery (☑ 902-687-2586; www.princeedwarddistillery.com; Rte 16, Hermanville; ⊙11am-6pm) specializes in potato vodka that, even in its first year of production, has turned international heads (some calling it among the finest of its class). Stop in for tours of the immaculate distillery and to taste the different vodkas (potato, grain and blueberry) as well as the newer products, such as bourbon, rum, whiskey, pastis, and a very interesting and aromatic gin.

Myriad View Distillery (☑ 902-687-1281; www.straitshine.com; 1336 Rte 2, Rollo Bay; ⊙11am-6pm Mon-Sat, 1-5pm Sun) produces Canada's first and only legal moonshine. The hard-core Straight Lightning Shine is 75% alcohol and so potent it feels like liquid heat before it evaporates on your tongue. Take our advice and start with a micro-sip! A gulp could knock the wind out of you. The 50% alcohol Straight Shine lets you enjoy the flavor a bit more. Tours and tastings are free and the owner is happy to answer any questions.

It's about a 10-minute drive on Rte 307 between the two places.

⊙ Sights & Activities

Beaches lined with marram grasses and wild rose span almost the entire length of the park's 42km coastline. In most Canadians' minds, the park is almost synonymous with these strips of sand. Dalvay Beach sits to the east, and has some short hiking trails through the woods. The landscape flattens and the sand sprawls outward at Stanhope Beach. Here, a boardwalk leads from the campground to the shore. Backed by dunes, and slightly west, is the expansive and popular Brackley Beach. On the western side of the park, the sheer size of Cavendish Beach makes it the granddaddy of them all. During summer this beach sees copious numbers of visitors beneath its hefty dunes. If crowds aren't your thing, there are always the pristine sections of sand to the east. Lifeguards are on duty at Cavendish, Brackley and Stanhope beaches in midsummer. A beautiful bike lane runs all the way along this coast.

🛏 Sleeping

Parks Canada operates three highly sought-after campgrounds (☑ 800-414-6765; www.pc.gc.ca/eng/pn-np/pe/pei-ipe/visit. aspx; tent/RV sites $28/36; ⊙ Jun-Aug), which are spread along the park's length. Reservations can be made online. You can request a campground, but not a specific site; you must accept whatever is available when you arrive. While 80% of sites can be booked in advance, the remaining sites are first-come, first-served, so it's wise to arrive early.

Stanhope Campground (Gulfshore East Pkwy) is nestled nicely in the woods behind the beach of the same name. There is a well-stocked store on-site. Located at the end of Brackley Point, Robinsons Island Campground (Gulfshore East Pkwy) is the most isolated of the three campgrounds. It's not too much fun if the wind gets up. The proximity of Cavendish Campground, off Rte 6, to the sights makes it the most popular. It has exposed oceanfront sites as well as sites within the shelter and shade of the trees. Don't be lured by the view – it's nice, but sleep is better.

Andy's Surfside Inn   INN $
(☑ 902-963-2405; 469 Gulfshore Pkwy W; d from $50; 🛜) Inside Prince Edward Island National Park, 2.7km toward Orby Head from North Rustico, is this very rambling, ramshackle house overlooking beautiful Doyle's Cove. It has been a salty-dog inn since the 1930s. Sit back on the porch, put your feet up and thank your lucky stars. Basic accommodations with shared bathroom.

★ Dalvay by the Sea   HISTORIC HOTEL $$$
(☑ 902-672-2048; www.dalvaybythesea.com; 16 Cottage Cres, Dalvay; d/cottages from $199/379; ⊙ May-Oct; ❄🛜🏊) Overlooking its eponymous beach, this majestic 1895 historic mansion has a fascinating history. Aside from the main inn with its gorgeous woods and country-lodge luxury, a range of high-end cabins are dotted around the grounds. The drawing-room bar is a wonderful place for a beverage or casual eats, while the public dining room is a fancy affair.

Around PEI National Park

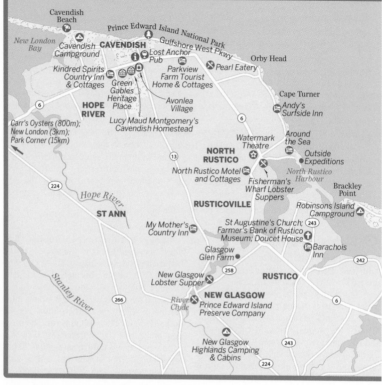

Brackley Beach

Brackley Beach isn't so much a town as a rural area, with a few scattered amenities and the main beach access to the central eastern beaches of Prince Edward Island National Park.

🛏 Sleeping & Eating

Brackley Beach Hostel　　　HOSTEL **$**
(☏ 902-672-1900; www.brackleybeachhostel.com; 37 Britain Shore Rd; dm/q from $27/59; ☎) For near-the-beach budget digs you won't find better than this clean and super-friendly hostel housed in a big barn about 2km from the shoreline. There are several eight-bed dorm rooms and a few quads, as well as plenty of showers and an equipped kitchen.

Shaw's Hotel & Cottages　　　COTTAGE **$$**
(☏ 902-672-2022; www.shawshotel.ca; 99 Apple Tree Rd; d/cottages from $95/175; ❋☎) Shaw's

Hotel & Cottages, open since 1860, is Canada's oldest family-operated inn. The hotel occupies 30 hectares of the family farm, with a private lane leading to Brackley Beach, a 600m walk away. Rooms in the inn have old-fashioned simplicity. One- to four-bedroom cottages, ranging from rustic to modern, are scattered around the property.

The dining room is open to outside guests (mains $18 to $28); reservations are recommended for the popular Sunday-evening buffet ($45; held in July and August).

Dunes Café & Gallery　　　FUSION **$$**
(☏ 902-672-2586; www.dunesgallery.com; 3622 Brackley Point Rd; dinner mains $16-28; ⊙ 11:30am-10pm) While over-the-top springs to mind, Dunes Café & Gallery is a nice change of pace. Where else on the island can you enjoy Vietnamese rice-noodle salad in the shade of a giant Buddha? Come for coffee, a meal or to roam the eclectic mix of Asian and island art in the sprawling glass gallery and garden.

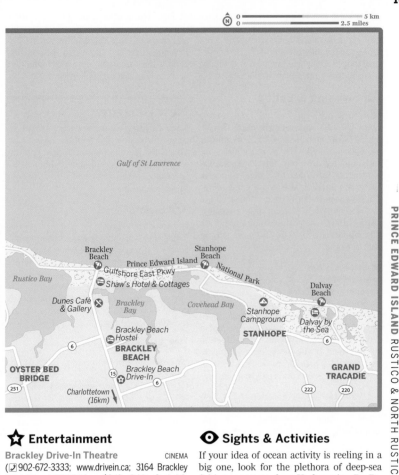

☆ Entertainment

Brackley Drive-In Theatre   CINEMA
(☏ 902-672-3333; www.drivein.ca; 3164 Brackley
Point Rd; adult/child from $9/6; ⊙ May-Sep) It's
fun to catch a movie at this long-standing
drive-in. Check the website for what's on.

Rustico & North Rustico

The seafront Acadian settlement at Rustico
dates back to 1700, and several fine historic
buildings speak of this tiny village's former
importance.

Just 5km further along Rte 6, North Rustico feels less like a tourist town with its
rickety, boxy fisher's houses painted in na-
vies, brick reds and beiges. A walk east from
the pier along the boardwalk is a great way
to take this atmospheric little village and its
busy harbor packed with fishing boats.

◉ Sights & Activities

If your idea of ocean activity is reeling in a
big one, look for the plethora of deep-sea
fishing operators along Harbourview Dr. Expect to pay around $50 per person.

Farmer's Bank of Rustico Museum   MUSEUM
(☏ 902-963-2194; www.farmersbank.ca; Church Rd,
Rustico; adult/student $4/2; ⊙ 9:30am-5:30pm
Mon-Sat, 1-5pm Sun) The solid red-stone Farmer's Bank of Rustico operated here between
1864 and 1894. Nextdoor is Doucet House,
an old Acadian dwelling that was relocated
here. This museum describing the settlement
of the community and the establishment of
the bank is now housed in the two secular
buildings.

Outside Expeditions   OUTDOORS
(☏ 902-963-3366; www.getoutside.com; 374 Harbourview Dr; tours from $45; ⊙ May-Oct) Situated
at the far end of the harbor in a bright-yellow

fishing shed, this company's 1½-hour introductory 'Beginner Bay' course starts with a lesson in kayaking techniques. The most popular trip is the three-hour 'Harbour Passage' tour ($65), which operates twice daily. Bike and kayak rentals are available.

🍽 Sleeping & Eating

★ Around the Sea   APARTMENT $$
(📞866-557-8383; www.aroundthesea.ca; 130 Lantern Hill Dr; apt from $125; 🕑🛜) Truly unique and one of a kind, this two-story home 'in-the-round' features four fully self-contained apartments furnished to a high standard. The entire building sits atop a giant motor that slowly and silently rotates the structure so the ocean view is constantly changing. Tours of the basement mechanics are available. There's a two-night minimum stay in peak season.

★ Barachois Inn   B&B $$
(📞902-963-2906; www.barachoisinn.com; 2193 Church Rd, Rustico; r from $145; ❄🛜) This grand, historic Acadian-style mansion is decorated with an eclectic selection of sublime antiques and paintings. Bathrooms are nearly equal in size to the enormous rooms, and hidden in the basement of the newer annex (built to copy the older building to perfection) is an exercise room, sauna and conference area.

North Rustico Motel & Cottages   MOTEL $$
(📞902-963-2253; www.cottages-pei.ca; 7103 Cavendish Rd; r/cottages from $89/125) The best feature of this updated 1980s-style vacation property with a variety of accommodation types is its charming, wood-paneled, self-contained cottages scattered about the leafy grounds.

Fisherman's Wharf
Lobster Suppers   SEAFOOD $$$
(📞902-963-2669; http://fishermanswharf.ca; 7230 Rustico Rd; lobster dinners from $32; 🕑noon-9pm) During the dinner rush in July and August this huge place has lines of people out the door. Come hungry, as there are copious servings of chowder, tasty local mussels, rolls and a variety of desserts to go with your pound of messy crustacean. If things go your way, you may get a table with an ocean view.

☆ Entertainment

Watermark Theatre   THEATER
(📞902-963-3963; www.watermarktheatre.com; North Rustico Village; ticket prices vary) Opened in 2008 in honor of the 100th anniversary of the publication of *Anne of Green Gables,* this theater presents plays from the life and times of Lucy Maud Montgomery. Performances are in a renovated 19th-century church that Montgomery herself attended. Seats sell out fast, so book in advance!

New Glasgow

New Glasgow is a quiet town that spreads elegantly across the shores of the River Clyde. This is the favorite Lobster Supper getaway for folks from Charlottetown, although it's becoming equally respected for its luscious preserves.

⊙ Sights

Glasgow Glen Farm   FARM
(📞902-963-2496; http://glasgowglenfarm.ca; 190 Lower New Glasgow Rd; 🕑9am-5pm Tue-Sat May-Oct) Blessed are the cheesemakers, or so they say. This one produces numerous variants of Gouda, which makes the perfect addition to any picnic hamper. Otherwise, the cheesy goodness is liberally applied to the island's most delicious pizzas.

🍽 Sleeping

★ New Glasgow Highlands
Camping & Cabins   CAMPGROUND $
(📞902-964-3232; www.newglasgowhighlands.com; 2499 Glasgow Rd, Hunter River; tent/RV sites from $36/42, cabins from $65; 🕑Apr-Nov; 🛜🏊) In Hunter River, 7km south of New Glasgow, you'll find this lovely campground with well-spaced sites that each have a fire pit. For rainy days there are simple cooking facilities in the lodge. There are also bright cabins, each with two bunks, a double bed, a sofa and a picnic table, but no linen or pillows; bathrooms are shared. Be sure to book ahead and don't even think about making late-night noise. It's all about peace and quiet. There's a laundry, a small store and a mystifying absence of bugs.

My Mother's Country Inn   B&B $$
(📞902-964-2508; www.mymotherscountryinn. com; 6123 Hwy 13; r/cottages from $110/135; 🛜) An oasis within 20 hectares of rolling hills, brisk streams and enchanting woodlands, this is a pure, rural delight. The house is the essence of country style with sea-green and ochre painted walls, bright pastel quilts, wood floors and plenty of light. A big red barn just begs to be photographed beside a storybook brook.

✖ Eating

Tucking in to one of New Glasgow's spectacular Lobster Suppers is something you must do when you come to PEI. You're in for a real treat if you've not experienced this Maritime way of dining before.

Their popularity with visitors has given rise to a nice bunch of locavore dining establishments in the surrounding area, catering to those who aren't so keen on these communal crustacean cook-offs.

★**New Glasgow Lobster Supper** SEAFOOD **$$**
(☑ 902-964-2870; http://peilobstersuppers.com; 604 Rte 258; lobster dinners from $35; ⊙ 4-8pm Jun-Oct) You can make a right mess with the lobster here at the home of the original PEI Lobster Suppers (since 1958), while also gorging on an endless supply of great chowder, mussels, salads, breads and homemade desserts. Finish the feast with a mile-high lemon pie...if you possibly can.

★**Prince Edward Island
Preserve Company** CAFE **$$**
(☑ 902-964-4300; http://preservecompany.com; 2841 New Glasgow Rd; mains $12-26; ⊙ 9am-8pm; ♫) Try free samples of delicious, though pricey, local preserves (such as raspberry champagne and orange ginger) before enjoying a casual meal overlooking the River Clyde. Hopefully your arrival won't coincide with a tour bus, which can take the edge off the serenity a little. Vegetarians are well catered for and the house specialty, raspberry cream cheese pie, is the bomb.

New London

New London is Green Gables country, with strong ties to Lucy Maud Montgomery. Of course, the town remains forever entwined with all things Anne.

◉ Sights

Lucy Maud Montgomery Birthplace MUSEUM
(☑ 902-886-2099; www.lmmontgomerybirthplace. ca; cnr Rtes 6 & 20; $4; ⊙ 9am-5pm) This house is now a museum that contains some of Lucy Maud's personal belongings, including her wedding dress.

Anne of Green Gables Museum MUSEUM
(☑ 902-886-2884; www.annemuseum.com; 4542 Rte 20; adult/child $5/1; ⊙ 9am-6pm May-Oct) Surrounded by a luscious 44-hectare property, this is the charming home Lucy Maud called

Silver Bush. It was always dear to her and she chose the parlor for her 1911 wedding. The museum contains such items as her writing desk and autographed 1st-edition books.

♨ Courses

★**Table** COOKING
(☑ 902-314-9666; thetablepei.com; 4295 Graham's Rd; 2hr course from $65) Formerly the extremely popular Annie's Table, this unique outfit continues to operate in a similar vein under the new tutelage of Chef Derrick. Learn the secrets of local lavender, discover how to make PEI spuds spectacular and wrangle seafood into deliciousness at a cookery course in this gorgeous historic church that has been remodeled into a chef's kitchen.

✖ Eating & Drinking

★**Blue Winds Tea Room** TEAHOUSE **$$**
(☑ 902-886-2860; http://bluewindstearoom.blog-spot.com; 10746 Rte 6, New London; meals $10-14; ⊙ 11am-6pm Mon-Thu, to 8pm Fri-Sun) This most charming place to stop for a bite and a cup of tea is surrounded by English gardens. Like everything else in this region, the fare can be very 'Anne'-centric. Order a raspberry cordial or some New Moon Pudding – both recipes have been taken from Lucy Maud's journals.

Sou'west Bar and Grill BAR
(☑ 902-886-3000; http://souwestbargrill.com; 6457 Rte 20; ⊙ noon-11pm May-Oct) This modern joint with its sunny waterfront beer deck, sports on the big screen and weekly live music looks a little out of place in the bucolic countryside.

🛍 Shopping

★**Village Pottery** CERAMICS
(☑ 902-886-2473; www.villagepottery.ca; 10567 Rte 6; ⊙ 10am-5pm) PEI's longest-running pottery studio is a family affair and a labor of love. Come in and meet Suzzane (she's tops!) for a chat or demonstration. We doubt you'll be able to leave without taking home one of the beautiful and colorful original works, which make great souvenirs.

Kensington

Kensington is a busy market town about halfway between Cavendish and Summerside. It's a good place to replenish supplies and the closest service center for those attending the popular Indian River Festival.

☞ Tours

Malpeque Bay Kayak Tour Ltd   KAYAKING
(☑866-582-3383; www.peikayak.ca; 3hr kayak tour $55) Just 15km from Kensington, this outfitter will kit you up and get you on the water above those famous oysters. Both kayak and stand-up paddleboard tours are available.

🎆 Festivals & Events

Indian River Festival   MUSIC
(www.indianriverfestival.com; ⊙Jul-Sep) The Indian River Festival features a full season of performances by some of Canada's finest musicians (from Celtic to choral) in the wonderfully acoustic St Mary's Church.

🛏 Sleeping & Eating

Home Place Inn & Restaurant   INN $
(☑902-836-5686; www.thehomeplace.ca; 21 Victoria St E; d/ste from $89/149; ⊙May-Oct; 🛜) Home Place Inn & Restaurant exudes country elegance at its finest. In the morning you may be awakened with scents of freshly baking cinnamon rolls, and there's a licensed pub and restaurant on the premises.

★**Malpeque Oyster Barn**   SEAFOOD $$
(☑902-836-3999; King St, Malpeque Bay; 6 oysters $14; ⊙11am-9pm Mon-Sat, noon-9pm Sun) The hamlet of Malpeque Bay is where PEI's famous eponymous oysters come from, renowned for their briny taste that's perfect with a beer. This atmospheric cafe sits in the top of a fisher's barn overlooking the bay.

Shipwright's Café   MODERN CANADIAN $$$
(☑902-836-3403; http://shipwrightspei.com; 11869 Hwy 6, Margate; mains $18-28; ⊙11:30am-8:30pm Mon-Fri, from 5pm Sat & Sun) In Margate, 5km from Kensington, the Shipwright's Café is housed in an 1880s farmhouse overlooking rolling fields and flower gardens. It earns rave reviews for its seafood dishes and vegetarian fare concocted from organic herbs and vegetables from the gardens.

Cavendish

Anyone familiar with *Anne of Green Gables* might have lofty ideas of finding Cavendish as a quaint village bedecked in flowers and country charm; guess again. While the Anne and Lucy Maud Montgomery sites are right out of the imagination-inspiring book pages, Cavendish itself is a mishmash of manufactured attractions with no particular center.

The junction of Rtes 6 and 13 is the tourist center and the area's commercial hub. When you see the service station, wax museum, church, cemetery and assorted restaurants, you know you're there. This is the most-visited community on PEI outside of Charlottetown and, although an eyesore in this scenic region, it is a kiddie wonderland.

◉ Sights

Green Gables Heritage Place   HISTORIC SITE
(☑902-672-7874; www.pc.gc.ca/eng/lhn-nhs/pe/greengables/visit.aspx; 8619 Hwy 6; adult/child $8/4; ⊙10am-5pm Mon-Sat) Cavendish is the home town of Lucy Maud Montgomery (1874–1942), author of *Anne of Green Gables*. Here she is simply known as Lucy Maud or LM. Owned by her grandfather's cousins, the now-famous House of Green Gables and its Victorian surrounds inspired the setting for her fictional tale. A variety of combination tickets and packages are available.

In 1937 the house became part of the national park and it's now administered as a national heritage site, celebrating Lucy Maud and Anne with exhibits and audiovisual displays.

Cavendish Beach   BEACH
(http://cavendishbeachpei.com) Beautiful Cavendish Beach gets crowded during summer months, but with perfect sand and a warm (ish) ocean in front, you won't really care

Lucy Maud Montgomery's Cavendish Homestead   HISTORIC SITE
(☑902-963-2231; www.peisland.com/lmm; 8523 Cavendish Rd; adult/child $3/1; ⊙9am-5pm) This is considered hallowed ground to Anne fans Raised by her grandparents, Lucy Maud lived in this house from 1876 to 1911 and it is here that she wrote *Anne of Green Gables*. You'll find the old foundation of the house, many interpretive panels about Lucy Maud, a small on-site museum and a bookshop.

🎆 Festivals & Events

Cavendish Beach Music Festival   MUSIC
(www.cavendishbeachmusic.com; ⊙early Jul) This hugely popular weekend festival attracts the biggest names in the US country scene and revelers from across the Maritime provinces.

🛏 Sleeping & Eating

While accommodations are numerous, remember that this is the busiest and most expensive area you can stay. There are more

WALKING LUCY MAUD MONTGOMERY'S CAVENDISH

If you haven't read the 1908 novel, this is the place to do it – not just to enjoy it, but to try and understand all the hype. The story revolves around Anne Shirley, a spirited 11-year-old orphan with red pigtails and a creative wit, who was mistakenly sent from Nova Scotia to Prince Edward Island. The aging Cuthberts (who were brother and sister) were expecting a strapping boy to help them with farm chores. In the end, Anne's strength of character wins over everyone in her path.

To really get a feel for the *Anne of Green Gables* scenery, get out and walk the green, gentle creek-crossed woods that Lucy Maud herself knew like the back of her hand. The best way is to start at the Lucy Maud Montgomery's Cavendish Homestead, then walk the 1.1km return trail to the Green Gables Heritage Place through the 'Haunted Wood.' In this way you arrive to a magical view from below the house rather than via a big parking lot and modern entrance. Once you're at the House of Green Gables you can enjoy the site plus many other surrounding trails, including 'Lover's Lane,' before hoofing it back to the Homestead.

bargains and more bucolic settings east, toward North Rustico, or just stay in Charlottetown (37km) and visit as a day trip.

Parkview Farms Tourist
Home & Cottages GUESTHOUSE **$**

(✆902-963-2027; www.parkviewfarms.com; 8214 Cavendish Rd; r/cottages from $65/170; 🛜📶) This fine choice is set on a working dairy farm, 2km east of Cavendish. Ocean views, bathrooms and flowered wallpaper and frills abound in this comfortable and roomy tourist home. Each of the seven cottages contains a kitchen and a barbecue, plus a balcony to catch the dramatic comings and goings of the sun. The cottages are available May to mid-October; the B&B is open year-round.

Kindred Spirits Country
Inn & Cottages INN **$$**

(✆902-963-2434; www.kindredspirits.ca; 46 Memory Lane; r/cottages from $95/120; ❄🛜📶) A huge, immaculate complex, this place has something for everyone from a storybook-quality inn-style B&B to deluxe suites. Rooms are every Anne fan's dream, with dotty floral prints, glossy wood floors and fluffy, comfy beds. Downstairs the lounge has a fireplace that will make you wish it would snow.

Carr's Oysters SEAFOOD **$$**

(✆902-886-3355; www.carrspei.ca; 32 Campbellton Rd, Stanley Bridge; mains $14-32; ⊙10am-7pm) Dine on oysters straight from Malpeque Bay, or lobster, mussels and seafood you've never even heard of, like quahogs. There is also plenty of fish on offer, from salmon to trout. The setting is sociable and bright, and there's also an on-site seafood market.

★ **Pearl Eatery** MODERN CANADIAN **$$$**

(✆902-963-2111; http://pearleatery.com; 7792 Cavendish Rd, North Rustico; brunch $8-12, mains $22-32; ⊙from 4:30pm daily, 10am-2pm Sun) This shingled house just outside Cavendish is surrounded by flowers and is an absolutely lovely place to eat. There are plenty of unusual and seasonally changing options like ice-wine-infused chicken-liver pâté on a Gouda brioche and locally inspired mains, such as delicious butter-poached scallops.

🍷 Drinking & Nightlife

Lost Anchor Pub PUB

(✆902-388-0118; 8572 Cavendish Rd; ⊙noon-9pm) If all this talk of Anne is driving you to drink, here's where to come. Simple but hearty pub meals are available.

🛍 Shopping

Avonlea Village MALL

(✆902-963-3050; www.avonlea.ca; Rte 6; adult/family $19/70; ⊙10am-5pm Jun-Sep) What was once a theme park has wound down into a glorified shopping mall. Still, costumed actors portray characters from the book and perform dramatic moments and scenes from its chapters. You might see a cow being milked, or ride on a wagon.

ℹ Information

Cavendish Visitor Information Centre (✆902-963-7830; cnr Rte 6 & Hwy 13; ⊙9am-5pm) Anne fans will want to chat with the friendly staff who really know their stuff about all things PEI.

WESTERN PRINCE EDWARD ISLAND

Malpeque and Bedeque Bays converge to almost separate the western third of PEI from the rest of the province. This region sits entirely within the larger Prince County, and it combines the sparse pastoral scenery of Kings County's interior with some of Queens County's rugged coastal beauty.

The cultural history here stands out more than elsewhere on the island. On Lennox Island a proud Mi'kmaq community is working to foster knowledge of its past, while French Acadians are doing the same in the south, along Egmont and Bedeque Bays.

PEI's second-largest city, Summerside, is located on the region's southern shore.

Summerside

📞 902 / POP 14,751

While it lacks the elegance and cosmopolitan vibe of Charlottetown, Summerside is a simpler, seaside-oriented place with everything you need in one small, tidy package. Recessed deep within Bedeque Bay and PEI's second-largest 'city,' this tiny seaside village possesses a modern waterfront and quiet streets lined with leafy trees and grand old homes. The two largest economic booms in the province's history, shipbuilding and fox breeding, shaped the city's development in the 19th and early 20th centuries. Like Charlottetown, its outskirts are plagued by unsightly development – you'll find most of Summerside's interesting bits along, or near to, Water St, which runs parallel to the waterfront.

◉ Sights

Acadian Museum   MUSEUM
(📞 902-432-2880; http://museeacadien.org; 23 Maine Dr E, Miscouche; $5; ⊙9:30am-7pm) The very worthwhile Acadian Museum, in Miscouche, uses 18th-century Acadian artifacts, texts, visuals and music to enlighten visitors about the tragic and compelling history of the Acadians on PEI since 1720. The introspective video introduces a fascinating theory that the brutal treatment of the Acadians by the British may have backhandedly helped preserve a vestige of Acadian culture on PEI.

Bottle Houses   ARCHITECTURE
(📞 902-854-2987; Rte 11, Cape Egmont; adult/child $5/2; ⊙9am-8pm) The artful and monumental recycling project of Edouard Arsenault, this islander favorite features over 25,000 bottles of all shapes and sizes, stacked in white cement to create a handful of buildings with light-filled mosaic walls.

Spinnaker's Landing   WATERFRONT
This redeveloped waterfront is the highlight of Summerside. A continually expanding boardwalk allows you to wander and enjoy the harbor and its scenic surrounds. There are some very nice eateries, a stage for live music in the summer and numerous shops. A mock lighthouse provides an attractive lookout and some local information, while a large model ship is a dream playground for kids.

Eptek Exhibition Centre   GALLERY
(📞 902-888-8373; 130 Harbour Dr; entry by donation; ⊙10am-4pm) The modern Eptek Exhibition Centre features local and traveling art exhibitions.

🛏 Sleeping & Eating

Cedar Dunes Provincial Park CAMPGROUND $
(📞 902-859-8785; www.tourismpei.com/provincialpark/cedar-dunes; tent sites $23-25, RV sites $26-27) Has tent space in an open grassy field adjacent to West Point Lighthouse. Its redsand beach is an island gem.

Willowgreen Farm   B&B $
(📞 902-436-4420; www.willowgreenfarm.com; 117 Bishop Dr; r from $65; 🐾) With the Confederation Trail at its back door, this rambling farmhouse is an incredibly great-value place to stay; you feel like you're in the country, but actually you're in central Summerside. Rooms are bright, and the bold country interior is a refreshing change from busy period decors. Read beside the woodstove, or check out some of the interesting farm animals.

Summerside Bed & Breakfast   B&B $$
(📞 902-620-4993; www.summersideinnbandb.com; 98 Summer St; r from $115; ❄🐾) Poetically located on the corner of Summer and Winter Sts, the room you should obviously angle for is the bright and spacious Spring Room. This fine heritage building has been home to two Canadian premiers and boasts plenty of sitting areas and charm. Your friendly hosts prepare delicious hot breakfasts.

Five Eleven West   CANADIAN $$
(http://fiveelevenwest.com; 511 Notre Dame St; mains $12-24; ⊙11:30am-2pm Mon-Fri, 5-8pm daily) Summerside's most modern eatery is tucked into a very unlikely corner of the town's multipurpose sports complex. Once you find it (to the left of the snack bar) be

Summerside

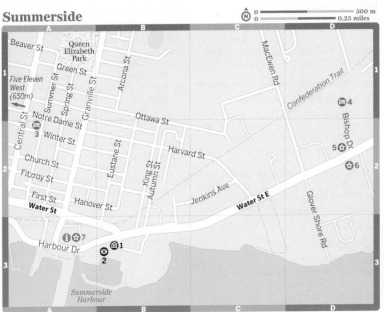

prepared to be impressed. Everything from the massive portion of beer-battered fish-and-chips to Madras chicken over rice, steamed mussels and prime rib is beautifully prepared, and the ambience is chic.

☆ Entertainment

**College of Piping & Celtic
Performing Arts** LIVE MUSIC
(☑ 902-436-5377; http://collegeofpiping.com; 619 Water St E; ceilidhs adult/student $12/7; ⊙ 9am-9pm, ceilidhs 7pm) In celebration of Celtic dance and music, this school provides visitors with free 20-minute miniconcerts from Monday to Friday at 11:30am, 1:30pm and 3:30pm – expect bagpipes, singing and dancing. Inspired? Then get yourself out to the 'Highland Storm,' a Celtic music and dance extravaganza with a cast of 30 of the island's best performers. It's performed three days a week through summer.

Feast Dinner Theatres THEATER
(☑ 902-888-2200; http://feastdinnertheatres.com; 618 Water St E; dinner & show from $40; ⊙ 6:30pm Mon-Sat Jun-Dec) Most locals giggle when they speak of their last time at Feast Dinner Theatres, the longest-running theater restaurant in Atlantic Canada. Music, script and improvisation combine with audience participation

to make for a truly memorable evening. And the food's not too shabby either.

Harbourfront Theatre THEATER
(☑ 902-888-2500; www.harbourfronttheatre.com; 124 Harbour Dr) This modern theater is the venue for a changing series of plays, comedy and more.

❶ Information

Visitor Information Centre (☑ 902-888-8364; 124 Harbour Dr; ⊙ 9am-7pm Jul & Aug, reduced hours May, Jun, Sep & Oct) Pick up a copy of the useful walking-tour pamphlet, which details the town's finer 19th-century buildings.

❶ Getting There & Away

Summerside is 61km west of Charlottetown on Rte 2.

Maritime Bus (p146) runs between Summerside and Charlottetown ($21, 1½ hours).

Tyne Valley

This area, famous for its Malpeque oysters, is one of the most scenic in the province. The village, with its cluster of ornate houses, gentle river and art studios, is definitely worth a visit.

Set in the mouth of Malpeque Bay, sheltered behind Hog Island, is Lennox Island and its 250 Mi'kmaq people. The island is connected by a causeway, making it accessible from the town of East Bideford off Rte 12.

◉ Sights

Canadian Potato Museum   MUSEUM
(☑ 902-859-2039; www.canadianpotatomuseum. info; 1 Dewar Lane, O'Leary; $8; ☺ 9am-5pm Mon-Sat, 1-5pm Sun May-Oct) Located inland at O'Leary. It's a bit like a giant school science fair project with hallways of information panels and pictures on the walls.

**Lennox Island Aboriginal
Ecotourism Complex**   NOTABLE BUILDING
(☑ 866-831-2702; 2 Eagle Feather Trail, Lennox Island; adult/student $4/3; ☺ 10am-6pm Mon-Sat Jun-Sep) Small, changing exhibits and information about the two excellent interpretive trails around the island. These trails consist of two loops, forming a total of 13km, with the shorter one (3km) being accessible to people in wheelchairs – if you're lucky and someone's around, a local will guide you for a small fee. Also ask at the information desk if anything else is on offer, as the complex's program changes frequently

Green Park Shipbuilding Museum MUSEUM
(☑ 902-831-7947; 360 Green Park Rd; adult $5; ☺ 9am-5pm) This museum and restored Victorian home, **Historic Yeo House**, along with a recreated shipyard and partially constructed 200-tonne brigantine, combine to tell the story of the booming shipbuilding industry in the 19th century.

✦ Festivals & Events

Tyne Valley Oyster Festival   FOOD & DRINK
(www.tvoysterfest.ca; ☺ Aug) Four days of shucking and slurping slimy oysters. Not for everyone. A must for lovers of the bivalve.

🛏 Sleeping & Eating

Green Park Campsites   CAMPGROUND $
(☑ 902-831-7912; www.greenparkcampground.com; 364 Green Park Rd; tent sites $23-25, with hookups $30, cabins without bath $45; ☺ Jun-Sep) The park has 58 campsites spread within a mixed forest. The dozen cabins just beyond the campground are a steal.

Landing Oyster House & Pub   SEAFOOD
(☑ 902-831-3138; www.thelandingpei.com; 1327 Port Hill Station Rd; mains $9-16; ☺ 11am-9pm Mon & Tue, to 11pm Wed, to midnight Thu-Sat, 8am-8pm Sun) Not surprisingly, the specialty here is deep-fried oysters – definitely indulge. Live bands (cover $4 to $8) play here on Friday night, and on Saturday during summer.

Tignish & North Cape

Tignish is a quiet town tucked up near the North Cape; it sees only a fraction of PEI's visitors. The towering **Church of St Simon & St Jude** (1859) was the first brick church built on the island. Have a peek inside – its ceiling has been restored to its gorgeous but humble beginnings, and the organ (1882) is of gargantuan proportions.

The narrow, windblown North Cape home to the Atlantic Wind Test, and to the longest natural rock reef on the continent. At low tide, it's possible to walk out 800m to explore tide pools and search for seals.

Tignish Cultural Centre   NOTABLE BUILDING
(☑ 902-882-1999; 305 School St, Tignish; ☺ 8am-4pm Mon-Fri) FREE The Confederation Trail begins two blocks south of the church on School St. The Tignish Cultural Centre, near the church, has a good exhibition of old maps and photos and tourist information.

Interpretive Center   MUSEUM
(☑ 902-882-2991; Rte 12, North Cape; $6; ☺ 9:30am-8pm) Provides high-tech displays dedicated to wind energy, and informative displays on the history of the area. The aquarium is always a hit with kids. The Black Marsh Nature Trail (2.7km) leaves the interpretive center and takes you to the west side of the cape – at sunset these crimson cliffs simply glow against the deep-blue waters.

Wind & Reef Restaurant & Lounge SEAFOOD
(☑ 902-882-3535; mains $9-29; ☺ noon-9pm) The menu and view are equally vast and pleasing at this atmospheric restaurant, lcoated above the Interpretive Center.

Newfoundland & Labrador

Best Places to Eat

➡ Merchant Tavern (p180)

➡ Bonavista Social Club (p193)

➡ Chafe's Landing (p185)

➡ Norseman Restaurant (p207)

➡ Adelaide Oyster House (p179)

Best Places to Sleep

➡ Fogo Island Inn (p200)

➡ Tuckamore Lodge (p208)

➡ Artisan Inn (p191)

➡ Skerwink Hostel (p191)

➡ Quirpon Lighthouse Inn (p207)

Why Go?

With rocky crags, drifting icebergs and puffins flapping by, Canada's easternmost province – and historically its most rebellious – floats in a stunning world of its own. The island that has long moved to its own beat maintains its own time zone (a half-hour ahead of the mainland) and lilting old-world dialect (the *Dictionary of Newfoundland English* provides translation).

St John's, with its buoyant music, modern dining scene and steep, foggy streets, abounds with entertainment. Outside of the good-time capital, wee fishing villages freckle the coast and isolated outer isles. Here the natural world is your oyster. Set off for woodland hikes, berry picking and sea kayaking with glittering views. Don't miss the Viking vestiges, plates of cod tongue and partridgeberry pie, or the rum-soaked tales that color this remote hunk of northern rock.

When to Go
St John's

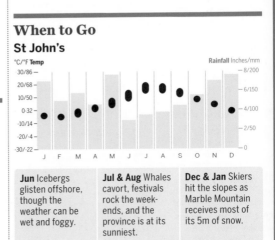

Jun Icebergs glisten offshore, though the weather can be wet and foggy.

Jul & Aug Whales cavort, festivals rock the weekends, and the province is at its sunniest.

Dec & Jan Skiers hit the slopes as Marble Mountain receives most of its 5m of snow.

Newfoundland & Labrador Highlights

1 St John's (p172)
Hoisting a drink, taking a ghost tour and soaking up the history of North America's oldest city.

2 Witless Bay Ecological Reserve (p185)
Sharing the waves with whales and puffins.

3 L'Anse aux Meadows National Historic Site (p206) Exploring Leif Eriksson's sublime 1000-year-old Viking pad.

4 Gros Morne National Park (p202) Hiking the ridges and kayaking the fjord-like lakes.

5 Fogo (p200) Trying out the modern outport life.

6 Twillingate (p198)
Ogling icebergs, hiking and sipping Moose Joose.

7 St-Pierre (p194)
Getting your French fix – wine, éclairs and baguettes.

8 Red Bay (p219)
Learning Basque whaling history then walking alongside ancient whale bones.

History

The Paleo-Indians walked into Labrador 9000 years ago. They hunted seals, fished for salmon and tried to stay warm. The Vikings, led by Leif Eriksson, washed ashore further south at L'Anse aux Meadows in Newfoundland in AD 1000 and established North America's first European settlement.

John Cabot (Italian-born Giovanni Caboto) sailed around the shores of Newfoundland next. It was 1497, and he was employed by England's Henry VII. Cabot's stories of cod stocks so prolific that one could nearly walk on water spread throughout Europe. Soon the French, Portuguese, Spanish and Basques were also fishing off Newfoundland's coast.

The 1713 Treaty of Utrecht ceded all of Newfoundland to England. The land remained a British colony for most of the next two centuries, with life revolving around the booming fishing industry. Newfoundland's Aboriginal people, the Beothuk, did not fare well after settlement began. Diseases and land conflicts contributed to their demise by 1829.

Ever true to its independent spirit, Newfoundland was the last province to join Canada, doing so in 1949. While Labrador was always part of the package, it wasn't until 2001 that it became part of the provincial name.

Language

Two hundred years ago, coastal fishing families from Ireland and England made up almost the entire population. Since then, as a result of living in isolated outposts, their language has evolved into almost 60 different dialects. Strong, lilting inflections, unique slang and colorful idioms pepper the language, sometimes confounding even residents.

The authoritative source is the *Dictionary of Newfoundland English* (www.heritage.nf.ca/dictionary).

Land & Climate

They don't call it the Rock for nothing. Glaciers tore through, leaving behind a rugged landscape of boulders, lakes and bogs. Newfoundland's interior remains barren, while the island's cities and towns congregate at its edges near the sea.

Labrador is sparser than Newfoundland, puddled and tundra-like, with mountains thrown in for good measure.

Temperatures peak in July and August, when daytime highs average 20°C. These are also the driest months; it rains or snows about 15 out of every 30 days. Wintertime

> ## ℹ PLANNING YOUR TRIP
>
> ⇒ Book ahead for rental cars and accommodations. If you're arriving during the mid-July to early August peak, secure a car by April or May and don't wait much longer to book a room. **Newfoundland & Labrador Tourism** (☑ 800-563-6353; www.newfoundlandlabrador.com) has listings.
>
> ⇒ Driving distances are lengthy so have realistic expectations of what you can cover. For instance, it's 708km between St John's and Gros Morne National Park. The **Road Distance Database** (www.stats.gov.nl.ca/DataTools/RoadDB/Distance) is a good reference.
>
> ⇒ Know the seasons for puffins (May to August) and whales (July to August). Icebergs (June to early July) can be tricky to predict. Check **Iceberg Finder** (www.icebergfinder.com) to get the drift.

temperatures hover at 0°C. Fog and wind plague the coast much of the year (which makes for a lot of canceled flights).

Parks & Wildlife

Whales, moose and puffins are Newfoundland's wildlife stars, and most visitors see them all. Whale-watching tours depart from all around the province and will take you close to the sea mammals (usually humpback and minke). Puffins – the funny-looking love child of the penguin and parrot – flap around Witless Bay and Elliston. Moose nibble shrubs near roadsides throughout the province, so keep an eye out while driving. Some visitors also glimpse caribou near the Avalon Wilderness Reserve, which is special because usually these beasts can only be seen in the High Arctic. Caribou herds also roam in Labrador, though their numbers have been declining sharply in recent years.

ℹ Getting There & Around

AIR

St John's International Airport (p183) is the main hub for the region, though **Deer Lake Airport** (p202) is an excellent option for visitors focusing on the Northern Peninsula. Airlines flying in include **Air Canada** (☑ 888-247-2262; www.aircanada.com), **PAL Airlines** (☑ 709-576-1666; www.palairlines.ca), **Porter** (☑ 888-619-8622; www.flyporter.com) and **United** (☑ 800-864-8331; www.united.com).

NEWFOUNDLAND ITINERARIES

Five Days

Start in **St John's** by visiting **Signal Hill** (p173) and **Cape Spear** (p183). Both are historic sites, but they also offer walking trails and views where you just may see an iceberg, a whale or both. At night sample St John's eateries, funky shops and music-filled pubs.

After a couple of days of 'big city' life, move onward through the **Avalon Peninsula**. Cruise to see whales and puffins at **Witless Bay Ecological Reserve** (p185), plan a picnic in **Ferryland** (p186) or visit the birds at **Cape St Mary's Ecological Reserve** (p189). Spend the last day or two soaking up the historic eastern communities of **Trinity** (p190) and **Bonavista** (p192) and the cliffside hikes in between.

Ten Days

Do the five-day itinerary and then go west, possibly via a quick flight to **Deer Lake** (p202), and reap the reward of viewing the mighty fjords of **Gros Morne National Park** (p202) and the monumental Viking history at **L'Anse aux Meadows National Historic Site** (p206). With a few extra days you could sail across the **Strait of Belle Isle** and slow way down among the wee towns and bold granite cliffs of the **Labrador Straits** (p216).

BOAT

Marine Atlantic (☑ 800-341-7981; www. marine-atlantic.ca) operates two massive car/passenger ferries between North Sydney (NS) and Newfoundland. There's a daily, six-hour crossing to Port aux Basques (western Newfoundland) year-round, and a thrice-weekly, 14-hour crossing to Argentia (on the Avalon Peninsula) in summer. Reservations are recommended, especially to Argentia.

Provincial Ferry Service (www.gov.nl.ca/ferryservices) runs the smaller boats that travel within the province to various islands and coastal towns. Each service has its own phone number with up-to-the-minute information; it's wise to call before embarking.

BUS

DRL (☑ 709-263-2171; www.drl-lr.com) sends one bus daily each way between St John's and Port aux Basques (13½ hours), making 25 stops en route. Other than DRL, public transportation consists of small, regional shuttle vans that connect with one or more major towns. Although not extensive, the system works pretty well and will get most people where they want to go.

CAR & MOTORCYCLE

The Trans-Canada Hwy (Hwy 1) is the main cross-island roadway. Driving distances are deceptive, as travel is often slow going on heavily contorted, single-lane roads. Watch out for moose, especially at dusk.

Be warned: rental-car fleets are small (thanks to the island's remoteness and short tourist season), which means loads of visitors vie for limited vehicles in midsummer. Costs can rack up to $100 per day (including taxes and mileage fees). Reserve well in advance – April or May is recommended if you're traveling during the

mid-July-to-early-August peak – and confirm the booking before you arrive.

Driving distances include the following:
St John's to Port aux Basques 905km
St John's to Gros Morne 708km
Gros Morne to St Anthony 372km

ST JOHN'S

POP 106,200

North America's oldest city sits on the steep slopes of a snug and sheltered harbor. With jelly-bean-colored row houses lining the hilly streets, the city begs comparisons to San Francisco – though in miniature. It too is home to artists, musicians, cutting-edge eateries, inflated real estate and young, iPhone-using denizens. Yet the vibe of Newfoundland's largest city and capital remains refreshingly small-town.

Highlights include a jaunt up Signal Hill, with its sweeping views of the harbor, and listening to live music and hoisting a pint (or shot of rum) in pubs along George St. Many visitors take advantage of the city's excellent dining and lodging options by making St John's their base camp for exploring the Avalon Peninsula. Cape Spear, Witless Bay Ecological Reserve and Ferryland are among the easy day trips.

History

St John's excellent natural harbor, leading out to what were once seething seas of cod, prompted the first European settlement here in 1528. During the late 1600s and much of the 1700s, St John's was razed and taken over several times as the French, English and Dutch fought for it. Britain won the ultimate victory on Signal Hill in 1762.

The harbor steadfastly maintained its position as the center of world trade for salted cod well into the 20th century. By midcentury, warehouses lined Water St, and the merchants who owned them made a fortune. Come the early 1960s, St John's had more millionaires per capita than any other city in North America.

Today the city's wharves still act as service stations to fishing vessels from around the world and the occasional cruise ship, though the cod industry suffered mightily after a 1992 fishing moratorium. The offshore oil industry now drives the economy.

⊙ Sights

Most sights are downtown or within a few kilometers, though be prepared for some serious uphill walking.

★Rooms   MUSEUM
(☑709-757-8000; www.therooms.ca; 9 Bonaventure Ave; adult/child $7.50/4, 6-9pm Wed free; ☺10am-5pm Mon, Tue & Thu-Sat, to 9pm Wed, noon-5pm Sun) Not many museums offer the chance to see a giant squid, hear avant-garde sound sculptures and peruse ancient weaponry all under one roof. But that's the Rooms, the province's all-in-one historical museum, art gallery and archives. The building itself, a massive stone-and-glass complex, is impressive to look at, with views that lord it over the city. Has an on-site cafe and excellent restaurant.

Quidi Vidi   HISTORIC SITE
Over Signal Hill, away from town, is the tiny picturesque village of Quidi Vidi. Check out the 18th-century battery and the lakeside regatta museum, but make your first stop Quidi Vidi Brewery (p176). The fee includes ample tastings and a bottle to sip while touring. Be sure to try the Iceberg brand, made with water from the big hunks.

Nearby you'll find the oldest cottage in North America, the 1750s-era Mallard Cottage (p180). At press time it was being converted into a restaurant serving Newfoundland comfort foods.

The 1762 **Quidi Vidi Battery**, atop the hill end of Cuckhold's Cove Rd, was built by the French after they took St John's. The British

quickly claimed it, and it remained in military service into the 1800s.

Inland from the village, **Quidi Vidi Lake** is the site of the city-stopping St John's Regatta. The **Royal St John's Regatta Museum** (☑709-576-8921; cnr Lakeview Ave & Clancy Dr, off Forest Rd; ☺by appointment) FREE is on the 2nd floor of the boathouse. A popular walking trail leads around the lake.

Quidi Vidi is about 2km from the northeast edge of downtown. Take Plymouth Rd, go left on Quidi Vidi Rd, then right on Forest Rd (which becomes Quidi Vidi Village Rd). For the brewery, bear right onto Barrows Rd. For the battery, veer off on Cuckold's Cove Rd. For the regatta museum, take a left off Forest Rd onto Lakeview Ave. You can also walk from Signal Hill via the Cuckold's Cove Trail, which takes about 30 minutes.

Signal Hill National
Historic Site   HISTORIC SITE
(☑709-772-5367;   www.pc.gc.ca/signalhill;
☺grounds 24hr) The city's most famous landmark is worth it for the glorious view alone, though there's much more to see. The tiny castle atop the hill is **Cabot Tower** (☺8:30am-5pm Apr-Nov) FREE, built in 1900 to honor both John Cabot's arrival in 1497 and Queen Victoria's Diamond Jubilee. In midsummer soldiers dressed as the 19th-century Royal Newfoundland Company perform a tattoo (p182) and fire cannons.

The Signal Hill Visitor Centre (p176) features interactive displays on the site's history. The last North American battle of the Seven Years' War took place here in 1762, and Britain's victory ended France's renewed aspirations for control of eastern North America. The tattoo takes place next to the center at O'Flaherty Field.

You can see cannons and the remains of the late 18th-century British battery at **Queen's Battery & Barracks** further up the hill. Inside Cabot Tower, educational displays relay how Italian inventor Guglielmo Marconi received the first wireless transatlantic

NEWFOUNDLAND FAST FACTS

→ Population: 527,000

→ Area: 405,212 sq km

→ Capital: St John's

→ Quirky fact: Newfoundland has 82 places called Long Pond, 42 called White Point and one called Jerry's Nose

St John's

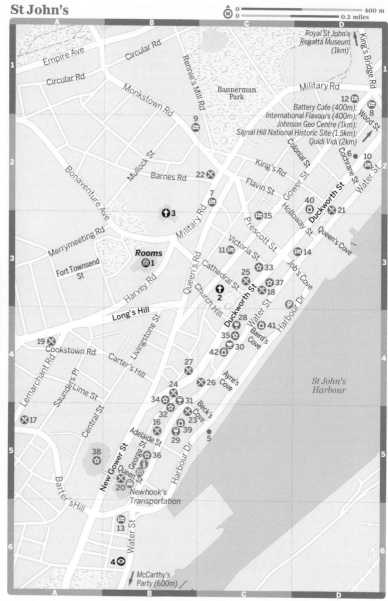

message from Cornwall, England at the site in 1901. An amateur radio society operates a station in the tower in July and August.

Signal Hill also offers guided tours around the grounds, Thursday lunches where you eat like an 18th-century soldier and sunset concerts. Check the website's 'Activities' section for details and costs.

An awesome way to return to downtown is along the 1.7km North Head Trail (p177).

The site sits 1.5km from downtown, up Signal Hill Rd.

St John's

NEWFOUNDLAND & LABRADOR ST JOHN'S

CA Pippy Park PARK
(www.pippypark.com) Full of features, 1343-hectare CA Pippy Park coats downtown's northwestern edge. Recreational facilities include walking trails, picnic areas, playgrounds, a golf course and a campground. **Memorial University**, the province's only university, is here too. The university's botanical garden (p176) is at Oxen Pond, at the park's western edge off Mt Scio Rd.

Cultivated areas and a nature reserve fill the botanical landscape. Together, these and the park's **Long Pond** marsh give visitors an excellent introduction to Newfoundland's flora, habitats (including boreal forest and bogs) and animals (look for birds at Long Pond and the occasional moose). Take the 3km **Long Pond Walk** for the full effect.

The **Fluvarium** (☑709-754-3474; www.fluvarium.ca; 5 Nagle's Pl; adult/child/family $8/6/25; ☺9am-5pm Mon-Fri, from 10am Sat & Sun Jul & Aug, reduced hours Sep-Jun), a glass-sided cross-section of a 'living' river, is located across the street from the campground. Viewers can peer through large windows to observe the undisturbed goings-on beneath the surface of Nagle's Hill Brook. Numerous brown trout and the occasional eel can be seen. If there has been substantial rain or high winds, all visible life is completely lost in the murkiness.

To get here from downtown, take Bonaventure Ave north to Allandale Rd and follow the signs; it's about 2km.

Johnson Geo Centre MUSEUM
(☑709-737-7880; www.geocentre.ca; 175 Signal Hill Rd; adult/child $12/6; ☺9:30am-5pm) Nowhere in the world can geo-history, going back to the birth of the earth, be accessed so easily as in Newfoundland, and the Geo Centre does a grand job of making snore-worthy geological information perk up with appeal via its underground, interactive displays.

The center also has an exhibit on the *Titanic,* and how human error and omission, not just an iceberg, caused the tragedy. For instance, the ship's owners didn't supply her with enough lifeboats so as not to 'clutter the deck,' and the crew ignored myriad ice warnings. What any of this has to do with geology remains unclear, but who cares? It's fascinating.

Trails with interpretive panels wind around outside. The Geo Centre is up Signal Hill Rd, about 1km beyond downtown.

Memorial University Botanical Garden
GARDENS

(☑709-737-8590; www.mun.ca/botgarden; adult/child $8/3; ☺10am-5pm May-Aug, reduced hours Sep-Apr) The premier botanical garden of the province, with nature trails, a large cultivated garden and a greenhouse within a 100-acre nature reserve.

Newman Wine Vaults
HISTORIC SITE

(☑709-739-7870; www.seethesites.ca; 436 Water St; admission by donation; ☺by appointment) Dating from the 1780s, these dark, cool wine vaults are where the Newman company aged its port until 1996 (when EU regulations forced the process back to Portugal). Guides used to give tours, but at press time they were on hold. The vaults often host music, literary and foodie events.

Quidi Vidi Brewery
BREWERY

(☑709-738-4040; www.quidividibrewery.ca; 35 Barrows Rd; tasting or tour $10; ☺10am-4pm) Quidi Vidi Brewing is a microbrewery located in an old fish-processing plant on the tiny wharf. It's a swell place to slake one's thirst. By car, take Forest Rd from the city and follow it past the lake until it turns into Quidi Vidi Village Rd. Locals prefer you to park on the outskirts of town and walk in.

Anglican Cathedral of St John the Baptist
CHURCH

(☑709-726-5677; www.stjohnsanglicancathedral.org; 16 Church Hill; high tea $9; ☺9:30am-4pm) Serving Canada's oldest parish (1699), the Anglican cathedral is one of the finest examples of ecclesiastical Gothic architecture in North America. Although originally built in the 1830s, all but its exterior walls were reduced to ashes by the Great Fire of 1892. Rebuilt in 1905, its Gothic ribbed ceiling, graceful stone arches and long stained-glass windows are timeless marvels. **High tea** is offered in the crypt on weekday afternoons in July and August.

Harbourside Park
PARK

With iconic statues of a Newfoundland dog and a Labrador retriever, this park hosts the City of St John's free Music at Harbourside lunchtime concert series, on Fridays at 12:30pm throughout the summer.

Bowring Park
PARK

(www.bowringpark.com; Waterford Bridge Rd) A beautiful 200-acre city park with a duck pond, tennis courts, swimming pool and playground.

Signal Hill Visitor Centre
MUSEUM

(adult/child $3.90/1.90; ☺10am-6pm May-Oct) Features interactive displays on the site's history. The last North American battle of the Seven Years' War took place here in 1762, and Britain's victory ended France's renewed aspirations for control of eastern North America.

Basilica of St John the Baptist
CHURCH

(☑709-754-2170; www.thebasilica.ca; 200 Military Rd; ☺9:30am-5pm) Built in 1855, the soaring twin spires of the basilica pierce the sky and are visible all the way from Signal Hill. Its design marks the revival of classical architecture in North America. Inside, 65 stained-glass windows illuminate the remarkable polychromatic Italianate ceiling and its gold-leaf highlights.

ST JOHN'S FOR CHILDREN

St John's will keep the wee ones entertained, rain or shine.

Boat Tours (right) The various boat tours are also a great bet, but inquire if there are icebergs and whales in the area first.

Bowring Park (p176) The ever-hungry ducks at the pond love company.

CA Pippy Park (p175) A kids' haven, with a huge playground, lots of trails and, of course, the Fluvarium.

Johnson Geo Centre (p175) While geology may not initially spark their interest, the fact that this center is underground may do the trick.

Ocean Sciences Centre (p216) Check out the sea creatures.

Signal Hill Tattoo (p182) Just knowing a cannon will blast at the end of the tattoo should keep kids riveted.

St John's Haunted Hike (p177) Older kids will enjoy the ghostly tales.

✦ Activities

★ North Head Trail — WALKING

An awesome way to return to downtown from Signal Hill is along the North Head Trail (1.7km) that connects Cabot Tower with the harborfront Battery neighborhood. The walk departs from the tower's parking lot and traces the cliffs, imparting tremendous sea views and sometimes whale spouts. Because much of the trail runs along the bluff's sheer edge, it isn't something to attempt in icy, foggy or dark conditions.

Grand Concourse — WALKING

(www.grandconcourse.ca) The Grand Concourse is an ambitious 160km-long network of trails all over town and linking St John's with nearby Mt Pearl and Paradise via downtown sidewalks, trails, river corridors and old railway beds.

☞ Tours

★ St John's Haunted Hike — WALKING

(www.hauntedhike.com; adult/child $10/5; ⊙9:30pm Sun-Thu Jun-Sep) The black-caped Reverend Thomas Wyckham Jarvis Esq leads these super-popular explorations of the city's dark corners. He'll spook you with tales of headless captains, murderers and other ghosts. Departure is from the Anglican Cathedral's west entrance. On midsummer Fridays and Saturdays, the spine-tingling action moves to Signal Hill for a seated, indoor show of ghost stories (8pm, tickets $15).

Outfitters — KAYAKING

(☑709-579-4453; www.theoutfitters.nf.ca; 220 Water St; half-/full-day tour $69/169; ⊙10am-6pm Mon-Wed, to 9pm Thu & Fri, 10am-6pm Sat, noon-5pm Sun) Popular kayak tours at Bay Bulls, with shuttle service (round-trip $30) from Outfitters' store downtown. It also rents outdoor equipment and has good information on the East Coast Trail (p184).

McCarthy's Party — BUS

(☑709-579-4480; www.mccarthysparty.com; 566 Water St; 3hr tour $55) A seasoned tour company with wonderful guides that will give you a true sense of local culture. Offerings range from half-day tours of St John's and Cape Spear to 12-day trips around the island.

Iceberg Quest — BOATING

(☑709-722-1888; www.icebergquest.com; Pier 6; 2hr tour adult/child $65/28) Departs from St John's harbor and makes a run down to Cape Spear in search of icebergs in June and whales in July and August. There are multiple departures daily in a new 100-person boat.

O'Brien's — BOATING

(☑709-753-4850; www.obriensboattours.com; 126 Duckworth St; 2hr tour adult/child $58/30) See whales, puffins and icebergs at Witless Bay. Boats launch from Bay Bulls 31km south, but O'Brien's has a shuttle service (round-trip $25) that picks up from hotels throughout St John's. Buy tickets at the O'Brien's shop.

Legend Tours — BUS

(☑709-753-1497; www.legendtours.ca; 3hr tour $59-69) This award-winning operator covers St John's, Cape Spear and the northeast Avalon Peninsula. The commentary is richly woven with humor and historical tidbits. Call to reserve; they'll pick you up at your hotel or B&B.

✦ Festivals & Events

Sound Symposium — PERFORMING ARTS

(www.soundsymposium.com; tickets from $10; ⊙early Jul) Held in even-numbered years, it's a big, avant-garde week of concerts, workshops, dance, theater and film experiments.

Shakespeare by the Sea Festival — THEATER

(☑709-722-7287; www.shakespearebytheseafestival.com; tickets $20-25; ⊙early Jul–mid-Aug) Live outdoor productions are presented at Signal Hill, local parks and other venues. Buy all tickets on-site; cash only. Some performances are free.

George Street Festival — MUSIC

(www.georgestreetlive.ca; tickets from $20; ⊙late Jul/early Aug) The mighty George St becomes one big nightclub for a fabulous week of daytime and nighttime musical performances.

Downtown Busker Festival — CARNIVAL

(www.downtownstjohns.com; ⊙early Aug) Jugglers, magicians, acrobats, comedians and more take their performances to the streets for a long weekend.

Newfoundland & Labrador Folk Festival — MUSIC

(www.nlfolk.com; ⊙early Aug) This three-day event celebrates traditional Newfoundland music, dancing and storytelling. It's held the weekend after the regatta.

Royal St John's Regatta — SPORTS

(www.stjohnsregatta.org; ⊙1st Wed Aug) The streets are empty, the stores are closed and everyone migrates to the shores of Quidi Vidi Lake. This rowing regatta officially began in

1825 and is now the oldest continuously held sporting event in North America. Postponed if the rowing conditions are poor.

Doors Open CULTURAL
(www.doorsopendays.com; ☉ early Sep) Every year in the second week of September, normally private businesses and buildings open their doors to the public for an inside look. Venues change, but have featured warehouses, churches and old museums.

🛌 Sleeping

Scores of B&Bs offer a place to rest your head in the heart of St John's; they're usually better value than the hotels and motels. They fill fast, so book ahead. Many have a two-night minimum-stay requirement. The ones listed here all serve a hot breakfast. The city's 17% tax is not included in prices listed here. Parking is available at or near all accommodations.

Memorial University Rooms ACCOMMODATION SERVICES $
(☑ 877-730-7657; www.mun.ca/conferences; r with shared bath $59-72; ☉ late Jun-Aug; 🖥) One of the best deals in town, the local university offers summer accommodations in its dormitory housing with shared washroom facilities. There's the option of twin or double beds in modern, pleasant rooms. Guests have access to kitchen facilities, a pool and fitness center. There are no TVs, and it's BYO toiletries.

HI St John's HOSTEL $
(☑ 709-754-4789; www.hihostels.ca; 8 Gower St; dm $38, r 89-103; ☺ 🖥 🛜) It's everything a good hostel should be: well located near the action, spick-and-span facilities, not too big (16

beds in all), and helpful. Doubles are less of a deal, with rooms that seem pretty worn out for the price. A whiteboard lists everything of interest happening in town each day. The hostel also books reasonably priced tours.

JAG BOUTIQUE HOTEL $$
(☑ 709-738-1524; www.steelehotels.com; 115 George St W; r from $236; 🖥 🛜) What's not to like about a hotel that blasts the Stones or Dylan in the lobby? This rock-and-roll-themed boutique hotel occupies a tall multistory building with harbor views. Spacious rooms have a sleek look of muted colors with pleated leather headboards and oversized windows (double-paned with blackout curtains specially made for rock stars). The on-site restaurant and bar are excellent.

Cabot House B&B $$
(☑ 709-754-0058; www.abbainn.com; 26 Monkstown Rd; s/d $209/219; 🅿 🛜) A stunning 1904 Queen Anne revival mansion, this sprawling house full of antiques and stained-glass windows makes for a subdued stay. Gorgeous, spacious rooms are mostly restored to their original layout, with the addition of bathrooms and a Jacuzzi suite. With no on-site host, the experience is more hotel-like.

Leaside Manor B&B $$
(☑ 709-722-0387; www.leasidemanor.com; 39 Topsail Rd; r $179-229; ☺ 🖥 @ 🛜) The higher-end rooms in this old merchant's home have a canopied bed, fireplace and Jacuzzi, which explains why the *Globe and Mail* designated Leaside one of Canada's 'most romantic destinations.' It's about a half-hour walk from downtown; to be closer, inquire about the downtown apartments.

Gower House B&B $$
(☑ 709-754-0058; www.abbainn.com; 180 Gower St; s/d $149/159; 🖥 🛜) Gower House is more like a boarding house than a frilly B&B. Rooms are small, but with restful bedding, a flat-screen TV and amenity-laden en suite bathroom. An on-site manager cooks the egg-filled breakfast.

At Wit's Inn B&B $$
(☑ 709-739-7420; www.atwitsinn.ca; 3 Gower St; r $160; ☺ 🖥 @ 🛜) Polished floorboards, plasterwork ceilings, ornate fireplaces, brightly colored walls, and beds you'll have trouble leaving make this B&B memorable. The living and dining rooms are as swank as they are comfy. It's also in a convenient location.

SCRUNCHEONS, TOUTONS & FLIPPER PIE: A GASTRONOMIC GUIDE

Get ready for a whole new culinary vocabulary when you enter Newfoundland. Lesson number one: having a 'scoff' is local parlance for eating a big meal.

Two of Newfoundland's favorite dishes are fish 'n' brewis and Jiggs dinner. Fish 'n' brewis is a blend of salted fish, onions, scruncheons (aka fried pork fat) and a near-boiled bread. Jiggs dinner is a right feast comprising a roast (turkey or possibly moose) along with boiled potatoes, carrots, cabbage, salted beef and pea-and-bread pudding. A touton is fried dough that you dip in gooey molasses.

Cod tongues are the tender, fleshy bits between the lower jaws served battered and fried, while cod cheeks are just that: cheeks from the fish. Fishcakes are a blend of cod, potato and onion mashed together and fried – delicious. Seal flipper pie, on the other hand, is for the brave; the strong flavor of seal meat is definitely an acquired taste.

To finish off your meal, try figgy duff, a thick fig pudding boiled in a cloth bag.

Balmoral House
B&B **$$**

(☑ 709-754-5721; www.balmoralhouse.com; 38 Queen's Rd; r $149-199; ☞ ✳ @) While the Balmoral is a typical B&B in many ways (cherub statues, long wooden antique tables), its owners live off-site and breakfast is self-serve, so it's more relaxed and private than many B&Bs. The beds have super-comfy mattresses.

Abba Inn
B&B **$$**

(☑ 709-754-0058; www.abbainn.com; 36 Queen's Rd; s/d $159/169; ☞ ✳ @ 🕿) The Abba shares a building with Balmoral House (p179), and both B&Bs have similar amenities and ambience. If Abba is full, the owner also has nearby Gower House and Cabot House. There's often no on-site host; guests let themselves in with a lock code.

Narrows B&B
B&B **$$**

(☑ 709-739-4850; www.thenarrowsbb.com; 146 Gower St; s/d $135/170; ☞ 🕿) Warm colors mix with elegant trims and large wooden beds in the rooms of this welcoming B&B. Some rooms are on the slim side. There are modern amenities throughout and a gorgeous sitting room and balcony where guests can mingle and swap whale stories.

Courtyard St John's
HOTEL **$$**

(☑ 709-722-6636; www.marriott.com/yytcy; 131 Duckworth St; r $189-244; P ✳ @ 🕿) It's the Marriott chain's typical property, with comfy beds. Some rooms have harbor views (about $20 extra).

★ Luxus
BOUTIQUE HOTEL **$$$**

(☑ 844-722-8899; www.theluxus.ca; 128 Water St; r $379-579; 🕿) Opened by a businessman originally from the area, the Luxus' amenities read like a wishlist of those who travel for a living. Bose speakers, check. Dual jet shower and freestanding tub, check. Electronic Japanese toilet, check. All six luxurious rooms boast harbor views, minibar and a whopping 70-inch (178cm) flat-screen TV. Don't miss happy hour at the ambient cocktail bar. Parking is off-site in a garage.

✖ Eating

★ Adelaide Oyster House
INTERNATIONAL **$**

(☑ 709-722-7222; 334 Water St; small plates $8-17; ⊙5-10pm) For a boisterous, busy happy hour it would be hard to do better than the Adelaide, a stylish sliver of a bar and restaurant in the thick of things. Its specialty is small plates such as fish tacos, Kobe beef lettuce wraps topped with spicy kimchi, and, of course, fresh oysters from both coasts. With lovely cocktails. It's good for singles too.

★ Battery Cafe
CAFE **$**

(☑ 709-722-9167; 1 Duckworth St; snacks $3-9; ⊙6:30am-6:30pm Mon-Fri, 7:30am-6:30pm Sat & Sun) This Aussie-run espresso bar and cafe brews the finest cup in town; there are also good sandwiches and baked goods. Has outdoor picnic-table seating in good weather.

Piatto
PIZZA **$**

(☑ 709-726-0709; www.piattopizzeria.com; 377 Duckworth St; mains $12-19; ⊙11:30am-10pm Mon-Thu, to 11pm Fri & Sat, to 9pm Sun) Offering a great night out without breaking the bank, cozy brick Piatto wood-fires pizza like nobody's business. Go trad or try a thin-crust pie topped with proscuitto, figs and balsamic. It's all good. There are nice fresh salads too, wine and Italian cocktails.

Fixed Coffee & Baking
CAFE **$**

(www.fixedcoffee.com; 183 Duckworth St; baked goods $3-8; ⊙7am-6pm Mon-Fri, from 9am Sat & Sun; 🕿) Hipster haven Fixed pours the city's best hot chocolate and mighty fine coffee and chai, plus it's cheaper than elsewhere. Housemade bagels and breads add to the divine aroma.

Rocket Bakery
BAKERY **$**

(www.rocketfood.ca; 272 Water St; mains $3-10; ☺7:30am-9pm Mon-Sat, to 6pm Sun; 🛜) Cheery Rocket is the perfect spot for a cup o' joe, groovy sandwich or sweet treat. Try the hummus on crusty homemade multigrain bread, or maybe a croissant with lemon curd. The fish cakes also win raves. Order at the counter, then take your goodies to the tables in the adjoining room.

Hungry Heart
CAFE **$**

(☑709-738-6164; www.hungryheartcafe.ca; 142 Military Rd; mains $13-16; ☺10am-2pm Mon-Sat) Eat in this warm-toned cafe and you're helping abused women and others in need to train in food service. Try the curry mango chicken or pulled-pork sandwiches. Saturday brunch brings out the cheese scones with crisp, house-cured bacon and cherry bread pudding. Lots of baked goodies too. Attentive service.

Sprout
VEGETARIAN **$**

(☑709-579-5485; www.thesproutrestaurant.com; 364 Duckworth St; mains $10-15; ☺11:30am-9pm Mon-Fri, from 10am Sat; 🖋) Full-on vegetarian food is almost unheard of in Newfoundland. Sprout offers both vegan and gluten-free options. So take a seat in this small cafe and savor your marinated tofu burger, walnut-pesto-melt sandwich and brown rice poutine (fries served under miso gravy) before leaving town. Sandwiches feature thick slices of homemade bread.

International Flavours
PAKISTANI **$**

(☑709-738-4636; 4 Quidi Vidi Rd; mains $11-14; ☺noon-7pm Tue-Sat; 🖋) A popular choice for locals on their lunch break, this Middle Eastern restaurant provides a welcome respite from fish-and-chips. Pakistani owner Talat ladles out a whopping spicy plateful of dal or curry with basmati rice for her daily set meal, also available vegetarian. It's in a small room at the bottom of Signal Hill Rd.

Ches's
FAST FOOD **$**

(☑709-726-2373; www.chessfishandchips.ca; 9 Freshwater Rd; mains $8-15; ☺11am-2am Sun-Thu, to 3am Fri & Sat) Ches's and its fish-and-chips are an institution in Newfoundland. No frills, just cod that will melt in your mouth.

★ Merchant Tavern
CANADIAN **$$$**

(☑709-722-5050; http://themerchanttavern.ca; 291 Water St; mains $15-45; ☺11:30am-2pm & 5:30pm-midnight Tue-Thu, to 2am Fri, 10:30am-2am Sat, 10:30am-3pm Sun) An elegant tavern housed in a former bank building, Merchant shares its chef with Canadian top-tier restaurant Raymond's, but without the $400 price tag. Gorgeous seafood stews, grilled local lamb sausage and cod with smoked bacon near perfection. For happy endings, the salted-caramel soft serve is a must. Some seating faces the open-view kitchen – good for chatting with the cooks.

Chinched
MODERN CANADIAN **$$$**

(☑709-722-3100; www.chinchedbistro.com; 7 Queen St; mains $14-35; ☺5:30-9:30pm Mon-Sat) 🖋 Quality dishes without the white-table-cloth pretense – think octopus tacos or Newfoundland wild mushroom risotto served in a warm, dark-wood room. On an ever-changing menu, meat figures prominently – don't skip the charcuterie boards or homemade pickles. The young chefs' creativity extends to the singular desserts (say, wild-nettle ice cream) and spirits (partridgeberry vodka) made in-house.

Reluctant Chef
MODERN CANADIAN **$$$**

(☑709-754-6011; www.thereluctantchef.ca; 281 Duckworth St; set menu $60; ☺5-9:30pm Tue-Sun) 🖋 The reluctant-but-passionate Jonathan Schwartz creates lovingly prepared, five-course meals for an intimate room. The dishes always vary, but may include originals like duck in dandelion broth or a rhubarb and sorrel dessert. There's also weekend brunch ($18). Check the Facebook page menu and reserve ahead. Then plan on a three-hour flavorgasm. Those with special dietary needs should advise ahead.

Bacalao
MODERN CANADIAN **$$$**

(☑709-579-6565; www.bacalaocuisine.ca; 65 Lemarchant Rd; mains $26-36; ☺noon-2:30pm Tue-Fri, from 11am Sat & Sun, 6-10pm Tue-Sun) 🖋 Cozy Bacalao sources local, sustainable ingredients for its 'nouvelle Newfoundland cuisine.' Dishes include salt cod du jour and caribou in partridgeberry sauce, washed down by local beer and wines. It's located 1.5km west of downtown; take Water St south to Waldegrave St, then Barters Hill Rd.

Mallard Cottage
CANADIAN **$$$**

(☑709-237-7314; www.mallardcottage.ca; 2 Barrows Rd; mains $19-35; ☺10am-2pm Wed-Sat, 5:30-9pm Tue-Sat, 10am-5pm Sun) A lot of restaurants give lip service to local and sustainable, but this one is spot on and devilishly good. The blackboard menu changes daily. Think turnips with yogurt and crispy shallots or brined duck with spaetzle and fried rosemary. The adorable Mallard Cottage, which dates from the 1750s, is a historic site.

Basho SUSHI $$$

(☎ 709-576-4600; www.bashorestaurant.com; 283 Duckworth St; mains $22-36; ⊗ 6pm-late Mon-Sat) This trendy newcomer is St John's best bet for high-grade, traditional sushi, Nobu-style sashimi and crisp tempura with sea salt. Basho is also known for exceptional cocktails. The popular lounge opens up an hour before dinner on Fridays.

🍷 Drinking & Nightlife

George St is the city's famous party lane. Water and Duckworth Sts also have plenty of places to drink, but the scene is slightly more sedate. Bars stay open until 2am (3am on weekends). Expect many places to charge a small cover (about $5) on weekends or when there's live music. Don't forget to try the local Screech rum.

★ Duke of Duckworth PUB

(www.dukeofduckworth.com; McMurdo's Lane, 325 Duckworth St; ⊗ noon-late; 🛜) 'The Duke,' as it's known, is an unpretentious English-style pub that represents all that's great about Newfoundland and Newfoundlanders. Stop in on a Friday night and you'll see a mix of blue-collar and white-collar workers, young and old, and perhaps even band members from Great Big Sea plunked down on the well-worn red-velour bar stools.

Mochanopoly CAFE

(☎ 709-576-3657; 204 Water St; per hour boardgames $2.50; ⊗ noon-midnight Mon-Thu, to 1am Fri & Sat, to 11pm Sun) Welcome to Newfound-

land's first boardgame cafe. Inspired by counterparts in South Korea, young brothers and game gurus Erich and Leon opened this welcoming branch with over 300 games, ranging from classics like Battleship to Pandemic and Exploding Kittens. It's usually packed after 7pm. It also serves small bites and coffee drinks. Kids under six can play free.

Yellow Belly Brewery PUB

(☎ 709-757-3784; www.yellowbellybrewery.com; 288 Water St; ⊗ 11:30am-2am Mon-Fri, to 3am Sat & Sun) Refreshing brews crafted on-site are front and center at this casual meeting spot, a brick behemoth dating back to 1725. Everyone's having a good time and there's decent pub grub to soak up the brews. For extra ambience descend to the underbelly – a dark basement bar with a speakeasy feel.

Velvet CLUB, GAY & LESBIAN

(http://twitter.com/Velvetniteclub; 208 Water St; ⊗ 11pm-3am Fri & Sat) This is the premier gay dance bar in Newfoundland. Straights are equally welcome to soak up the fun energy. Located above Rose & Thistle; the entrance is via McMurdo's Lane.

Gypsy Tea Room BAR

(☎ 709-739-4766; www.gypsytearoom.ca; 315 Water St; ⊗ 11:30am-3pm & 5:30-11pm Mon-Fri, from 11am Sat & Sun) It holds a well-regarded Mediterranean restaurant and chic lounge, but the courtyard is where you want to be, sipping wine, cocktails and other refreshing beverages under the stars.

☆ Entertainment

The Overcast (www.theovercast.ca) has the daily lowdown. Perhaps because this is such an intimate city, word of mouth and flyers slapped on light poles are also major vehicles for entertainment information. Venues are close together – have a wander and enjoy.

GETTING SCREECHED IN

Within a few days of your arrival in St John's, you'll undoubtedly be asked by everyone if you've been 'screeched in,' or in traditional Newfoundland slang, 'Is you a screecher?' It's not as painful as it sounds, and is, in fact, locals' playful way of welcoming visitors.

Screeching derives from the 1940s when new arrivals were given their rites of passage, and from pranks played on sealers heading to the ice for the first time. Today the ceremony takes place in local pubs, where you'll gulp a shot of rum (there's actually a local brand called Screech), recite an unpronounceable verse in the local lingo, kiss a stuffed codfish and then receive a certificate declaring you an 'Honorary Newfoundlander.' Sure it's touristy, but it's also good fun. The more the merrier, so try to get screeched in with a crowd.

Cover charges for live music range from $5 to $10. **Mighty Pop** (www.mightypop.ca) lists cool upcoming shows.

Ship Pub   LIVE MUSIC
(☑709-753-3870; 265 Duckworth St; ⊘noon-late) Attitudes and ages are checked at the door of this little pub, tucked down Solomon's Lane. You'll hear everything from jazz to indie, and even the odd poetry reading. Wednesday is folk-music night.

Shamrock City   LIVE MUSIC
(www.shamrockcity.ca; 340 Water St; ⊘noon-late) Bands, most playing Irish and Newfoundland-style music, take the stage nightly at this all-ages pub.

Rose & Thistle   LIVE MUSIC
(☑709-579-6662; 208 Water St; ⊘9am-late) Pub where well-known local folk musicians strum.

Fat Cat   BLUES
(www.fatcatbluesbar.com; George St; ⊘8pm-late Tue-Sun) Blues radiates from the cozy Fat Cat nightly during the summer months.

Rock House   LIVE MUSIC
(☑709-579-6832; 8 George St) When indie bands visit town, they plug in here.

Signal Hill Tattoo   MILITARY PERFORMANCE
(www.rnchs.ca/tattoo; $10; ⊘11am & 3pm Wed-Thu, Sat & Sun Jul & Aug) An award-winning historical animation program that brings back British 19th-century military might with cannon fire, mortars and muskets backed by a fife and drum band. It's set atop Signal Hill.

Resource Centre for the Arts   PERFORMING ARTS
(☑709-753-4531; www.rca.nf.ca; 3 Victoria St) Sponsors indie theater, dance and film by Newfoundland artists, all of which play downtown in the former longshoremen's union hall (aka LSPU Hall). Box office is on the website.

St John's IceCaps   HOCKEY
(www.stjohnsicecaps.com; 50 New Gower St; ⊘Oct-May) The popular IceCaps, part of the American Hockey League, slap the puck at Mile One Centre.

🛍 Shopping

You'll find traditional music, berry jams and local art in the nooks and crannies of Water and Duckworth Sts.

Outfitters   SPORTS & OUTDOORS
(☑709-579-4453; www.theoutfitters.nf.ca; 220 Water St; ⊘10am-6pm Mon-Wed & Sat, to 9pm Thu & Fri, noon-5pm Sun) A camping and gear shop where you can get the local outdoorsy lowdown (check the bulletin board) and good rentals. For hikers, it sells East Coast Trail (p184) maps and butane canisters.

Fred's   MUSIC
(☑709-753-9191; www.fredsrecords.com; 198 Duckworth St; ⊘9:30am-9pm Mon-Fri, to 6pm Sat, noon-5pm Sun) This is the premier music shop in St John's. It features local music such as Hey Rosetta, Buddy Wasisname, Ron Hynes, Amelia Curran, The Navigators and Great Big Sea.

Living Planet   GIFTS & SOUVENIRS
(☑709-739-6810; www.livingplanet.ca; 181 Water St; ⊘10am-5pm Mon-Sat, noon-5pm Sun) For quirky tourist T-shirts and buttons even locals are proud to wear.

Downhome   GIFTS & SOUVENIRS
(☑709-722-2070; 303 Water St; ⊘10am-5:30pm Mon-Sat, noon-5pm Sun) It's touristy, but it does have a fine selection of local goods such as jams, woolen wear, moose cookbooks and the coveted *How to Play the Musical Spoons* CD.

ℹ Information

MEDICAL SERVICES
Health Sciences Complex (☑709-777-6300; 300 Prince Phillip Dr; ⊘24hr) A 24-hour emergency room.

MONEY
Banks stack up near the Water St and Ayre's Cove intersection.
CIBC (215 Water St; ⊘9:30am-5pm Mon-Fri)
Scotia Bank (245 Water St; ⊘10am-5pm Mon-Fri)

POST
Central Post Office (☑709-758-1003; 354 Water St)

TOURIST INFORMATION
Quidi Vidi Visitors Centre (☑709-570-2038; tourism@stjohns.ca; 10 Maple View Pl, Quidi Vidi Village Plantation; ⊘11am-5pm Tue-Sun) An outpost of the St John's visitor center, with good information on local happenings. Open year-round.

Visitors Centre (☑709-576-8106; www.stjohns.ca; 348 Water St; ⊘10am-4:30pm May-early Oct) Excellent resource with free provincial and city road maps, and staff to answer questions and help with bookings.

ℹ Getting There & Away

AIR

St John's International Airport (YYT; ☑ 709-758-8500; www.stjohnsairport.com; 100 World Pkwy; 📶) is 6km north of the city on Portugal Cove Rd (Rte 40).

Air Canada offers a daily direct flight to and from London, WestJet goes direct to Dublin and Gatwick. **United Airlines** (p171) flies to the USA. The main carriers:

Air Canada (p171)

PAL Airlines (p171)

Porter Airlines (p171)

WestJet (☑ 888-937-8538; www.westjet.com)

BUS

DRL (p172) sends one bus daily each way between St John's and Port aux Basques ($126, cash only, 13½ hours) via the 905km-long Hwy 1, making 25 stops en route. It leaves at 7:30am from Memorial University's Student Centre, in CA Pippy Park.

CAR & MOTORCYCLE

Avis, Budget, Enterprise, Hertz, National and Thrifty have offices at the airport. Rent RVs and motorhomes from **Islander RV** (☑ 709-364-7368; www.islanderrv.com; Paddy's Pond, Exit 40, Trans Canada Hwy).

SHARE TAXIS

These large vans typically seat 15 and allow you to jump on or off at any point along their routes. You must call in advance to reserve. They pick up and drop off at your hotel. Cash only.

Foote's Taxi (☑ 709-832-0491) Travels daily down the Burin Peninsula as far as Fortune ($45, 4½ hours).

Newhook's Transportation (☑ 709-682-4877, in Placentia 709-227-2552) Travels down the southwestern Avalon Peninsula to Placentia ($35, two hours), in sync with the Argentia ferry schedule.

Shirran's Taxi (☑ 709-468-7741) Plies the Bonavista Peninsula daily, making stops at Trinity ($50, 3½ hours) and Bonavista ($40, four hours), among others.

ℹ Getting Around

BUS

The **Metrobus** (☑ 709-722-9400; www.metrobus.com; 25 Messenger Dr) system covers most of the city (fare $2.25). Maps and schedules are online and in the visitor center. Bus 3 is useful; it circles town via Military Rd and Water St before heading to the university. The new 'trolley line' (it's actually a bus) loops around the main tourist sights, including Signal Hill. It costs $5/20 per person/family per day.

CAR & MOTORCYCLE

The city's one-way streets and unique intersections can be confounding. Thankfully, citizens are incredibly patient. The parking meters that line Water and Duckworth Sts cost $1.50 per hour. **Sonco Parking Garage** (☑ 709-754-1489; cnr Baird's Cove & Harbour Dr; ⊙ 6:30am-11pm) is central, but there are several others; most charge around $2 per hour.

TAXI

Except for the trip from the airport, all taxis operate on meters. A trip within town should cost around $8. **Jiffy Cabs** (☑ 709-722-2222; www.jiffycab.com) provides dependable service.

AVALON PENINSULA

The landscape along the coastline's twisting roads is vintage fishing-village Newfoundland. Many visitors make day trips to the peninsula's sights from St John's, which is easily doable, but there's something to be said for burrowing under the quilt at night, with the sea sparkling outside your window, in Cupids or Branch. Four of the province's six seabird ecological reserves are in the region, as are 28 of its 41 national historic sites.

Much of the East Coast Trail (p184) runs through the area. The ferry to Nova Scotia leaves from Argentia.

Southeastern Avalon Peninsula

This area, sometimes called the South Shore, is known for its wildlife, archaeology, boat and kayak tours, and unrelenting fog. Scenic Rtes 10 and 90, aka the Irish Loop (p187), lasso the region. For a quick taste, visit the Cape Spear Lighthouse and the fishing village of Petty Harbour, though sites further south are well worth exploring. Highlights include watching the puffins and whales in Witless Bay, exploring La Manche Provincial Park and hiking the East Coast Trail.

Cape Spear

A 15km drive southeast of St John's leads you to the most easterly point in North America, with spectacular coastal scenery and whale-watching during much of the summer. A **trail** leads along the edge of the headland cliffs, past 'the most easterly point' observation deck and up to the lighthouse. You can continue all the way to Maddox Cove and

NEWFOUNDLAND & LABRADOR SOUTHEASTERN AVALON PENINSULA

Petty Harbour along the East Coast Trail; even walking it a short way is tremendously worthwhile.

Heed all signs warning visitors off the coastal rocks, as rogue waves have knocked people into the water.

⊙ Sights & Activities

★ **Cape Spear Lighthouse**   LIGHTHOUSE
(entry incl with Cape Spear National Historic Site; ⊙10am-6pm Jun-Aug, reduced hours May, Sep & Oct) Constructed in 1835, the oldest surviving lighthouse in the province sits on the dramatic headlands of the continent's most easterly point.

Cape Spear Interpretive Center   MUSEUM
(entry incl with Cape Spear National Historic Site; ⊙10am-6pm May-Oct) Offers exhibits on lighthouse technology and its changes throughout time.

Cape Spear National Historic Site   HISTORIC SITE
(⎘709-772-5367; www.pc.gc.ca/capespear; Blackhead Rd; adult/child $3.90/1.90; ⊙grounds year-round) In a stunning windswept setting, Cape Spear National Historic Site includes an interpretive center, the refurbished 1835 lighthouse and the heavy gun batteries and magazines built in 1941 to protect the harbor during WWII. Hikers can also join up with the East Coast Trail here.

❶ Getting There & Away

Many St John's day tours include Cape Spear. Otherwise, it's possible to come by private vehicle or taxi from St John's.

You reach the cape from Water St by crossing the Waterford River south of town and then following Blackhead Rd for 11km.

Goulds & Petty Harbour

Backed against steep slopes, beautiful, pocket-sized Petty Harbour shelters weathered boats in an active port filled with wharves and sheds. It has a lively sense of community and plenty to do. Nearby Goulds is a useful stop for groceries.

⊙ Sights & Activities

Petty Harbour Mini Aquarium   AQUARIUM
(⎘709-330-3474; www.miniaqua.org; Main Rd, Petty Harbour; adult/child $8/5; ⊙10am-6pm Jun-Oct) This small attraction is perfect for kids, who will love the touch tanks filled with sea life. Animals are re-released into the ocean at season's end. The big attractions are the wolf fish and golden lobster.

★ **Fishing for Success**   FISHING
(www.islandrooms.org; 10d Main Rd, Petty Harbour; adult/child $99/50) ✿ Run by Kimberly and Leo, a local fishing family, this new nonprofit organization seeks to rescue the local fishing traditions by teaching them to local kids and visitors. Dory trips include rowing lessons in traditional wood boats and cod jigging. For $50 extra they can cook up your catch and serve it to you Newfoundland-style right on the pier. There's also a full-day option that includes net-knitting, rope work and a historical wharf tour.

North Atlantic Zip Lines   ADVENTURE SPORTS
(⎘709-368-8681; www.zipthenorthatlantic.com; 62 Main Rd, Petty Harbour; adult/child $130/95) Canada's longest zip-line course has 10 zip lines at its family adventure center ranging from 300ft to 2200ft in length. Tours run at 11am, 3pm and 6pm.

HIKING THE EAST COAST TRAIL

Skirting gaping cliffs, fairy-tale forests and fields of edible berries, the world-class **East Coast Trail** (⎘709-738-4453; www.eastcoasttrail.ca) is a through-hiker's delight. It stretches 265km from Cape St Francis (north of St John's) south to Cappahayden with an additional 275km still underway.

Its 26 sections range in difficulty from easy to challenging, but most make good day hikes. For a sample, try the scenic 9.3km path between Cape Spear and Maddox Cove (near Petty Harbour), it should take between four and six hours.

For seasoned hikers, the ECT can also be walked as a through-hike, combining camping with lodging in villages along the way. Campsites generally feature pit toilets and a good water source nearby. Fires are prohibited. A local taxi service operates at the trailheads and can bring you to nearby lodging or your vehicle.

Topographical maps are available in St John's at Outfitters (p177) or Downhome (p182). Visit the trail website for detailed information and the lowdown on guided hikes.

✗ Eating

WaterShed CAFE $
(☎ 709-747-0500; 24a Main Rd, Petty Harbour; ⏱10am-4pm Jun-Sep, Sat & Sun only in winter; 🛜) Joy is here: real espresso drinks at a refurbished waterfront shed. Owner Karen loves talking local lore, she also makes a mean hiker cookie, packed with seeds. It also has great baked treats and sandwiches. If you have an extra few hours to chill out, spend them on the deck.

★ Chafe's Landing SEAFOOD $$
(☎ 709-747-0802; www.chafeslanding.com; 11 Main Rd, Petty Harbour; mains $9-19; ⏱11am-8pm Mon-Thu, to 9pm Fri & Sat, 2-9pm Sun) Most folks here day trip from St John's specifically for these fish-and-chips, the freshest you can find. Lines get long and parking might be impossible, but it's worth it. It also serves locally made moose sausage, beer-steamed mussels, and salads.

🛍 Shopping

Bidgood's FOOD
(www.bidgoods.ca; Bidgood's Plaza, Goulds; ⏱9am-7pm Mon-Sat, 10am-5pm Sun) Just a normal supermarket, except for the fresh seal flipper (in pies, jars or jerky-like strips) and caribou steak. Partridgeberry and bakeapple jams are the other Newfoundland specialties on hand. In Goulds, at the junction of Rte 10 and the road to Petty Harbour.

Witless Bay Ecological Reserve & Around

This is a prime area for whale-, iceberg- and puffin-watching, and several boat tours will take you to see them from the towns of **Bay Bulls** (31km south of St John's) and **Mobile** (10km south of Bay Bulls). Midway between the towns, there's lodging in **Witless Bay**.

Four islands off Witless Bay and southward are preserved as the **Witless Bay Ecological Reserve** (www.env.gov.nl.ca/parks) and represent one of the top seabird breeding areas in eastern North America. The reserve is North America's largest Atlantic puffin colony, with over 260,000 pairs nesting here during the late spring and summer. In fact, every summer, more than a million pairs of birds gather here, including puffins, kittiwakes, storm petrels and the penguin-like murres. Tour boats sail to the islands, hugging the shore beneath sheer cliffs and giving you a shrieking earful as well as an eyeful.

The best months for trips are late June and July, when the humpback and minke whales arrive to join the birds' capelin (a type of fish) feeding frenzy. If you really hit the jackpot, in early summer an iceberg might be thrown in too.

👉 Tours

Tours from Bay Bulls visit Gull Island, which has the highest concentration of birds in the Witless Bay Ecological Reserve. Tours that depart to the south around Bauline East head to nearby Great Island, home to the largest puffin colony. Bauline East is closer to the reserve, so less time is spent en route, but you see the same types of wildlife on all of the tours.

Also popular, kayaking provides a special perspective on wildlife. After all, you don't just see a whale while paddling, you feel its presence.

You can't miss the boat operators – just look for signs off Rte 10. Sometimes the smaller companies cancel tours if there aren't enough passengers; it's best to call ahead to reserve and avoid such surprises. They operate from mid-May through mid-September. Most depart several times daily between 9:30am and 5pm.

★ Captain Wayne's WHALE-WATCHING
(☎ 709-763-8687; www.captwaynes.com; Northside Rd, Bay Bulls; tour $80) Descended from generations of Newfoundland fishers, Captain Wayne really knows his coast and his enthusiasm proves contagious. Best of all, he only does small, 12-person tours in his custom boat. The three-hour tour includes puffin- and whale-watching. There are several departures daily, but photographers should go at 5pm for best light.

Molly Bawn Tours BOATING
(☎ 709-334-2621; www.mollybawn.com; Rte 10, Mobile; 1hr tour adult/child $45/40) These popular tours cruise over the waves on a small, 35ft boat. Mobile is halfway between Bay Bulls and Bauline East.

Outfitters KAYAKING
(☎ 709-579-4453; www.theoutfitters.nf.ca; Bay Bulls; half-/full-day tour $69/169) Popular half-day kayak tours leave at 9am and 2pm; full-day tours depart at 9:30am and travel beyond the inner bay of Bay Bulls to the top of the eco reserve. There is a shuttle service (round-trip $25) from St John's that leaves from Outfitters at 220 Water St.

NEWFOUNDLAND & LABRADOR SOUTHEASTERN AVALON PENINSULA

RUNNING THE GOAT

This active **printing press** (☑709-334-3239; http://runningthegoat.com; Cove Rd, Tors Cove; ☺10:30am-5:30pm Thu-Tue mid-May–Oct) is a bibliophile's dream. Owner Marnie Parsons gives tours of her presses, one from 1830s London. In addition to handmade poetry chapbooks and manifestos, there's a wonderful selection of local artists' prints and good books for adults and children authored by Newfoundlanders.

O'Brien's BOATING

(☑709-753-4850; www.obriensboattours.com; 2hr tour adult/child $55/25) O'Brien's, on the south side of Bay Bulls, is the granddaddy of tours and includes storytelling, music and more on its nice, big boat. A more expensive but exhilarating option is the two-hour tour in a high-speed Zodiac ($85). There's a shuttle service from St John's (round-trip $25).

Gatherall's BOATING

(☑800-419-4253; www.gatheralls.com; Northside Rd, Bay Bulls; 1½hr tour adult/child $57/38) A large, fast catamaran. A good choice for people prone to seasickness.

🛏 Sleeping

Armstrong's Suites MOTEL $

(☑709-334-2201; 236 Main Hwy, Witless Bay; r $80) Though this is just your run-of-the-mill roadside motel, it's unlikely that even your own grandmother could better receive your visit. The kind owner thinks nothing of going the extra mile, providing extra cots and towels and breakfast fixings to East Coast Trail through-hikers.

Bread & Cheese B&B $$

(☑709-334-3994; 22a Bread & Cheese Rd, Bay Bulls; r incl breakfast $149; ☎) This gorgeous country house with a wraparound porch and sprawling lawn is a sight for sore feet, located a short stroll from the East Coast Trail. Rooms are smart and modern, with one handicapped-accessible option. Our only wish is for a cheerier welcome.

Bears Cove Inn B&B $$

(☑709-334-3909; www.bearscoveinn.com; 15 Bears Cove Rd, Witless Bay; d with ocean/forest view $149/129; ☎) A pleasant place to stay, this seven-room B&B has all the amenities you could want, including water views and

a lovely garden and barbecue area. Rooms feature country decor and flat-screen TVs. The helpful owners also run a local pub and speak French.

La Manche Provincial Park

Diverse birdlife, along with beavers, moose and snowshoe hare, can be seen in this lush **park** (www.env.gov.nl.ca) FREE only 53km south of St John's. A highlight is the 1.25km trail to the remains of La Manche, a fishing village that was destroyed in 1966 by a fierce winter storm. Upon arrival, you'll see the beautiful newly built suspension bridge dangling over the narrows – it's part of the East Coast Trail (p184). The trailhead is situated at the park's fire-exit road, past the main entrance.

There is excellent camping at **La Manche Provincial Park Camping** (☑709-685-1823; www.nlcamping.ca; Rte 10; campsites $18-26, per vehicle $5; ☺May-Sep). Lovely and shaded, it has 83 campsites, picnic tables, fire pits, water taps and pit toilets. Firewood is available at the checkpoint.

Ferryland

Ferryland, one of North America's earliest settlements, dates to 1621, when Sir George Calvert established the Colony of Avalon. A few Newfoundland winters later he was scurrying for warmer parts. He settled in Maryland and eventually became the first Lord Baltimore. Other English families arrived later and maintained the colony despite it being razed by the Dutch in 1673 and by the French in 1696.

For gorgeous windswept panoramas, don't miss the 2km walk out to the lighthouse.

⊙ Sights

Colony of Avalon ARCHAEOLOGICAL SITE

(☑709-432-3207, 709-432-3200; www.colonyof avalon.ca; Rte 10; adult/child $12.70/10.20; ☺10am-6pm Jun-Sep) The seaside surrounds of the Colony of Avalon archaeological site only add to the rich atmosphere, where you'll see archaeologists unearthing everything from axes to bowls. The worthwhile interpretation center houses beautiful displays and many of the artifacts that have been recovered. Guided 45-minute tours are offered upon request.

Historic Ferryland Museum MUSEUM

(☑709-432-2711; www.manl.nf.ca/ferryland museum; Baltimore Dr; $3; ☺10am-4pm Mon-Sat,

1-4pm Sun Jun–Aug) The village's former courthouse is now the small Historic Ferryland Museum. The towering hill behind the museum was where settlers climbed to watch for approaching warships, or to escape the Dutch and French incursions. After seeing the view, you'll understand why the settlers named the hill 'the Gaze.'

Tours

Stan Cook Adventures   ADVENTURE

(☑709-579-6353; www.wildnfld.ca; Harbour Rd, Cape Broyle; 2½hr kayak tour from $59) Located near Ferryland, this company offers great guided kayak tours for beginners and advanced paddlers as well as mountain biking and hiking options.

✖ Eating

★**Lighthouse Picnics**   SANDWICHES $$

(☑709-363-7456; www.lighthousepicnics.ca; Lighthouse Rd; per person $26; ⊙11:30am-4:30pm Wed-Sun Jun-Sep; ☻; ◢) Lighthouse Picnics has hit upon a winning concept: it provides a blanket and organic picnic meal (say, a curried chicken sandwich, mixed-green salad and lemonade from a Mason jar) that visitors wolf down while sitting in a field overlooking explosive ocean views. It's at Ferryland's old lighthouse, off Rte 10; you have to park and hike 2km to reach it, but ooh is it worth it. Reserve in advance.

Mistaken Point Ecological Reserve

Designated a World Heritage site in 2016, this **ecological reserve** (www.env.gov.nl.ca/parks) **FREE** protects 575-million-year-old multicelled marine fossils – the oldest in the world. The only way to reach it is via a free, ranger-guided, 45-minute hike from the **Edge of Avalon Interpretive Centre** (☑709-438-1100; www.edgeofavalon.ca; Rte 10; adult/child $8/5; ⊙10am-6pm mid-May–Oct) in Portugal Cove South. This center offers information and interesting exhibits on the reserve's history.

You can also drive the bumpy gravel road between here and Cape Race. At the end, a lighthouse rises up beside an artifact-filled, replica 1904 Marconi wireless station. It was the folks here who received the fateful last message from the *Titanic*.

The 'Mistaken Point' name, by the way, comes from the blinding fog that blankets the area and has caused many ships to lose their way over the years.

AVALON WILDERNESS RESERVE

Dominating the interior of the region is the 1070-sq-km Avalon Wilderness Reserve. Illegal hunting dropped the region's caribou population to around 100 in the 1980s. Thirty years later, a couple of thousand now roam the area. Permits for hiking, canoeing and bird-watching in the reserve are available at La Manche Provincial Park.

Even if you don't trek into the wilds, you still might see caribou along Rte 10 between Chance Cove Provincial Park and St Stevens.

Along Route 90

The area from St Vincent's to St Mary's provides an excellent chance of seeing whales, particularly humpbacks, which feed close to shore. The best viewing is from **St Vincent's beach**. Halfway between the two villages is **Point La Haye Natural Scenic Attraction**, a dramatic arm of fine pebbles stretching across the mouth of St Mary's Bay – it's perfect for a walk.

Salmonier National Park (☑709-229-7189; www.env.gov.nl.ca/snp; Rte 90; ⊙10am-5pm Jun-Aug, to 3pm Sep & Oct) **FREE** is an animal rehabilitation center for injured and orphaned animals with an interpretive center and touch displays for children. A 2.5km trail through pine woods takes you past indigenous fauna and natural enclosures with moose, caribou and cavorting river otters. The park is on Rte 90, 12km south of the junction with Hwy 1.

Settled by Irish, scenic Rte 90 makes up part of the aptly named **Irish Loop** (www.theirishloop.com), a lovely driving route in the Avalon Peninsula.

Baccalieu Trail

The Bay de Verde Peninsula has a scenic driving route known as the Baccalieu Trail. Fishing villages and pirate haunts stretch endlessly along Conception Bay's scenic western shore, a mere 80km from St John's. Highlights include Brigus, in all its Englishy, rock-walled glory combined with North Pole history, and Cupids, a 1610 settlement complete with an archaeological dig to explore.

Brigus

Resting on the water and surrounded by rock bluffs is the heavenly village of Brigus. Its idyllic stone-walled streams meander slowly past old buildings and colorful gardens before emptying into the serene Harbour Pond.

During WWI, American painter Rockwell Kent lived here, before his eccentric behavior got him deported on suspicion of spying for the Germans in 1915. The path toward his old cottage makes a great walk.

Captain Robert Bartlett, the town's most famous son, is renowned as one of the foremost Arctic explorers of the 20th century. His house, **Hawthorne Cottage** (☑709-753-9262; www.pc.gc.ca/hawthornecottage; cnr Irishtown Rd & South St; adult/child $4/2; ☉10am-6pm Jul & Aug, Wed-Sun Jun), is a national historic site and museum.

On the waterfront, below the church, **Brigus Tunnel** was cut through rock in 1860 so Robert Bartlett could easily access his ship in the deep cove on the other side.

Every perfect village needs a perfect eatery. At **North St Cafe** (☑709-528-1350; 29 North St; light meals $6-14; ☉11am-6pm May-Oct), quiche, fish cakes, scones and afternoon tea are all on order.

Cupids

This atmospheric village is imbued with rich history. Merchant John Guy sailed here in 1610 and staked out England's first colony in Canada, now **Cupids Cove Plantation Provincial Historic Site** (☑709-528-3500; www.seethesites.ca; Seaforest Dr; adult/child $6/3; ☉9:30am-5pm May-Oct). It features an ongoing archaeological dig that's worth touring. A stone's throw down the road is the **Cupids Legacy Centre** (www.cupidslegacycentre. ca; Seaforest Dr; adult/child $8/4; ☉9:30am-5pm Jun-Oct), with fascinating exhibits.

Afterward, head to the town's northern edge and hike the **Burnt Head Trail**. Climb to the rocky headlands, past blueberry thickets and stone walls that once fenced settlers' gardens, and look out over the same sea-buffeted coast that drew Guy. The trail departs from **Cupid's Haven B&B and Tea Room** (☑709-528-1555; www.cupidshaven.ca; 169 Burnt Head Loop; r $119-169; ☺☏), an old Anglican church that has been converted into a divine B&B. Each of the four rooms has a private bathroom, vaulted ceilings and Gothic arched windows that let light stream in.

Harbour Grace & Around

Notable historic figures have paraded through Harbour Grace over the past 500 years, including the pirate Peter Easton and aviator Amelia Earhart. Their stories are told at **Conception Bay Museum** (☑709-596-5465; www.hrgrace.ca; Water St; adult/child $3/2; ☉10am-6pm Jun-Aug). Nearby **Harbour Grace Airfield** (www.hrgrace.ca/air.html; Earhart Rd) is the site where Earhart launched her historic solo Atlantic flight from in 1932.

It's hard to miss the large ship beached at the mouth of the harbor. This is the **SS Kyle** (1913), wrecked during a 1967 storm. Locals liked the look of it so much they paid to have it restored instead of removed.

Clinging to cliffs at the northern end of the peninsula are the remote and striking villages of Bay de Verde and Grates Cove. Hundreds of 500-year-old **rock walls** line the hills around Grates Cove and have been declared a national historic site.

Further offshore, in the distance, is the inaccessible **Baccalieu Island Ecological Reserve**, which is host to three million pairs of Leach's storm petrel, making it the largest such colony in the world.

Heart's Content

The **Cable Station Provincial Historic Site** (☑709-583-2160; www.seethesites.ca; Rte 80; adult/child $6/3; ☉10:30am-5:30pm May-Oct) tells the story of the first permanent transatlantic cable that was laid here in 1866. The word 'permanent' is significant, because the first successful cable (connected in 1858 to Bull Arm, on Trinity Bay) failed shortly after Queen Victoria and US President James Buchanan christened the line with their congratulatory messages.

Dildo

Oh, go on – take the obligatory sign photo. For the record, no one knows definitively how the name came about; some say it's from the phallic shape of the bay, others think it named for an oar pin. Nevertheless, proud and stalwart locals have denied several campaigns to change the town name.

Joking aside, Dildo is a lovely village and its shore is a good spot for whale-watching.

The **Dildo Interpretation Centre** (☑709-582-3339; Front Rd; adult/child $2/1; ☉10am-4:30pm Jun-Sep) features a whale skeleton and exhibits on the ongoing Dorset Eskimo archaeological dig on Dildo Island. It's not terribly exciting, but outside are excellent photo opportunities with Captain Dildo and a giant squid.

The many 'Dildo' logoed items sold at **Kountry Kravins 'n' Krafts** (☑709-582-3888; ⊙9am-8pm Mon-Sat, 10am-6pm Sun Jun-Sep) may be a fine souvenir for folks back home.

Cape Shore

The ferry, French history and lots of birds fly forth from the Avalon Peninsula's southwesterly leg.

Argentia

Formerly a US Naval Station during WWII, Argentia's main purpose today is to play host to the ferry from Nova Scotia.

A provincial **Visitors Centre** (☑709-227-5272; Rte 100) is 3km from the ferry on Rte 100. Its opening hours vary to coincide with ferry sailings.

The **Marine Atlantic ferry** (☑800-341-7981; www.marine-atlantic.ca; adult/child $115/54, car/motorcycle $225/113; ⊙mid-Jun–late Sep) links Argentia with North Sydney in Nova Scotia, a 14-hour trip. It's 134km to St John's.

Placentia

In the early 1800s, Placentia – then Plaisance – was the French capital of Newfoundland, and the French attacks on the British at St John's were launched from here. Today, it's a useful hub for those sailing to Nova Scotia on the ferry.

◎ Sights

Near town, lording over the shores, is **Castle Hill National Historic Site** (☑709-227-2401; www.pc.gc.ca/castlehill; adult/child $3.90/1.90; ⊙10am-6pm Jun-Aug), where remains of French and British fortifications from the 17th and 18th centuries provide panoramic views over the town.

The fascinating **graveyard** next to the Anglican church holds the remains of people of every nationality who have settled here since the 1670s. For local history, visit **O'Reilly House Museum** (☑709-227-5568; 48 Orcan Dr; adult/child $5/2; ⊙9am-5pm Jun-Aug) and other notable buildings, including the Roman Catholic church and the stone convent. A boardwalk runs along the stone-skipper's delight of a beach.

🛏 Sleeping & Eating

Rosedale Manor B&B   B&B $$
(☑877-999-3613; www.rosedalemanor.ca; 40 Orcan Dr; r $109-139; ❄🐾) A beautiful heritage B&B that has flower gardens and romantic rooms with claw-foot tubs.

Philip's Cafe   CAFE $
(170 Jerseyside Hill; mains $3-12; ⊙7:30am-3:30pm Tue-Sat; 🐾) A must pre- or post-ferry ride for yummy baked goods and creative sandwiches like apple and sharp cheddar on molasses-raisin bread. The breakfasts are well known; come early and skip the wait.

Three Sisters   PUB FOOD $$
(☑709-227-0124; 2 Orcan Dr; mains $8-30; ⊙8am-9pm Mon-Fri, 10am-9pm Sat & Sun) Lovely pub grub and chilly pints of beer are served in this atmospheric Placentia house. It's usually busy.

Cape St Mary's Ecological Reserve & Around

At the southwestern tip of the peninsula is Cape St Mary's Ecological Reserve, one of the most accessible bird colonies on the continent, with 70,000 specimens, including gannets, kittiwakes, murres and razorbills. Birders swoon over it, and it's impressive even for those who aren't bird crazy.

There's food and lodging in the wee town of Branch 22km away.

◎ Sights

Stop at the Interpretive Centre (p190) for directions for the 1km trail to Bird Rock.

Bird Rock   VIEWPOINT
Bird Rock is reached by an easy footpath through fields of sheep and blue irises, and then suddenly you're at the cliff's edge facing a massive, near-vertical rock swarmed by squawking birds.

Cape St Mary's Ecological Reserve   PARK
(☑709-277-1666; www.env.gov.nl.ca/parks) **FREE** A major seabird colony, with breeding-season populations of tens of thousands of northern gannet, black-legged kittiwake and common murre. Viewing is easy, with land sightings as close as 10m. There are also thick-billed murres, razorbills, black guillemots, double-crested and great cormorants, and northern fulmars. Call ahead to reserve a free guided tour.

Interpretive Centre
MUSEUM

(☑ 709-277-1666; ☺ 9am-5pm May-Oct) With information on nesting seabirds and displays on local ecology.

🍴 Sleeping & Eating

Driftwood Cottage
COTTAGE $$

(☑ 709-338-2133; www.driftwoodcottagebranch. com; Branch; r incl breakfast $120; ☎) A wonderful little spot to stay near the reserve. It's well-kept and painted in brilliant, happy tones with a deck overlooking the water.

Loft
SEAFOOD $

(☑ 709-338-2090; Main Rd, Branch; mains $10-12; ☺ 11am-8pm) Overlooking the water (on the 2nd floor of a convenience store), this little spot has great fresh fish and moose burgers.

EASTERN NEWFOUNDLAND

Two peninsulas stretched out from the heartland comprise the sliver of eastern Newfoundland. The beloved, well-touristed Bonavista Peninsula projects northward. Historic fishing villages freckle its shores, and windblown walking trails swipe its coast. Clarenville (www.clarenville.net) is the Bonavista Peninsula's access point and service center, though there's not much for sightseers.

To the south juts the massive but less-traveled Burin Peninsula, with fishing villages struggling to find their way in the post-cod world. You will need your passport to hop the ferry from Fortune to the nearby French islands of St-Pierre and Miquelon, a regional highlight complete with wine, éclairs and Brie.

Trinity

Let's set the record straight: Trinity is the Bonavista Peninsula's most popular stop, a historic town of crooked seaside lanes, storybook heritage houses and gardens with white picket fences. Trinity Bight, however, is the name given to the 12 communities in the vicinity, including Trinity, Port Rexton and New Bonaventure.

If it all looks familiar, it may be because *The Shipping News* was partly filmed here. While the excitement has faded, there are still historic buildings, stunning hiking and theater along with whale-watching.

First visited by Portuguese explorer Miguel Corte-Real in 1500 and established as a town in 1580, Trinity is one of the oldest settlements on the continent.

⊙ Sights

Trinity's Historic Buildings
HISTORIC SITE

(7-site admission adult/child $20/free; ☺ 9:30am to 5pm, May to mid-October) One admission ticket lets you gorge on seven buildings scattered throughout the village of Trinity. They are run by both the **Trinity Historical Society** and the provincial government (www.seethesites.ca).

➡ **Interpretation Centre**

(☑ 709-464-2064; www.seethesites.ca; West St) Worth a stop if you're interested in a comprehensive history of Trinity.

➡ **Lester Garland Premises**

(☑ 709-464-2064; www.seethesites.ca; West St) Lester Garland Premises depicts an 1820s general store with costumed interpreters.

➡ **Trinity Museum**

(www.trinityhistoricalsociety.com; Church Rd) Displays more than 2000 pieces of historical relics, including North America's second-oldest fire wagon.

➡ **Cooperage**

(☑ 709-464-3599; www.trinityhistoricalsociety.com; West St) A historical site used for fisheries and shipping-related activities. First a seasonal 'fishing room' for drying codfish, it later housed an expanding mercantile business, with a real live barrel-maker.

➡ **Hiscock House**

(☑ 709-464-2064; www.seethesites.ca; Church Rd) A restored merchant's home from 1910.

➡ **Green Family Forge**

(☑ 709-464-3599; www.trinityhistoricalsociety. com; West St) An iron-tool-filled blacksmith museum.

➡ **Lester Garland House**

(☑ 709-464-3599; www.trinityhistoricalsociety. com; West St) This historic home was rebuilt to celebrate cultural links between Trinity and Dorset, England – major trading partners in the 17th, 18th and 19th centuries.

Fort Point
HISTORIC SITE

FREE At Fort Point (aka Admiral's Point) there's a pretty lighthouse and four cannons, the remains of the British fortification from 1745. There are 10 more British cannons in the water, all compliments of the French in

1762. An interpretive center and trail tell the tale. It's accessible from Dunfield, a few kilometers south on Rte 239.

Activities

Skerwink Trail   HIKING
(www.theskerwinktrail.com) This 5km loop is well worth the effort, with dramatic coastal vistas of sea stacks, early summer icebergs and a lighthouse. Be on guard for moose. The trailhead is near the church in Trinity East, off Rte 230.

Tours

Rugged Beauty Tours   WILDLIFE
(709-464-3856; www.ruggedbeautyboattours. net; 3hr tour adult/child $90/60; ⊙10am & 2pm May-Oct) Unique trips with Captain Bruce, who takes you to abandoned outports and makes their history come alive. You might even see an eagle along the way.

Sea of Whales   BOATING
(709-464-2200; www.seaofwhales.com; 1 Ash's Lane; 3hr tour adult/child $80/50) Zodiac boats head out in search of whales three times per day.

Trinity Historical Walking Tours   WALKING
(709-464-3723; www.trinityhistoricalwalking tours.com; Clinch's Lane; adult/child $15/free; ⊙10am Mon-Sat Jul & Aug) These entertaining and educational tours start behind Hiscock House.

Sleeping & Eating

There are numerous fine inns and B&Bs. Space gets tight in summer, so book ahead.

★Skerwink Hostel   HOSTEL $
(709-436-3033; www.skerwinkhostel.com; dm/r $34/69; ⊙May-Oct; ☎) Travelers of all ages stay at homey, community-oriented Skerwink. With two six-bed dorms (with squishy, plastic-coated mattresses) and two private rooms, it's part of Hostelling International. Lots of locals drop by to chat and play guitar with the staff. Fresh bread and weak coffee are included for breakfast, and the fabulous Skerwink Trail (p191) is across the street.

It's off Rte 230, about 500m from the Skerwink Trail.

★Artisan Inn & Campbell House   INN $$
(709-464-3377; www.trinityvacations.com; 57 High St; r incl breakfast $125-179; ⊙mid-May-Oct; ☎) A fantasy coastal getaway, these gorgeous properties are adjacent to each other and managed by the same group. Both have ocean vistas. The three-room inn hovers over the sea on stilts; set further back, Campbell House has lush gardens.

Fishers' Loft   INN $$
(709-464-3240; http://fishersloft.com; Port Rexton; r incl breakfast $145-218; ☎) Featuring traditional 19th-century local architecture, this colonial is a favorite of return travelers. Rooms and suites are bright and spacious with fluffy duvets and down pillows; the treetop rooms offer stunning views of the bay. It's kitted out perfectly, with iPod docks, hiking poles and binoculars.

Eriksen Premises   B&B $$
(709-464-3698; www.newfoundlandexperience. com; 8 West St; r $130-190; ⊙mid-May–mid Oct; ☎☎) This 19th-century merchant home offers elegance in accommodations and dining (mains $20 to $30, open lunch and dinner). It also books two nearby B&Bs: Kelly's Landing (four rooms) and Bishop White Manor (nine rooms).

Trinity Mercantile   CAFE $
(www.trinitymercantile.ca; 24 West St; mains $6-15; ⊙8am-6pm; ☎) Grab coffee and a bagel topped with salmon smoked on-site and eavesdrop on the local gossip mill. There are also baked goods, sandwiches, chowder, salt cod and beer.

★Twine Loft   CANADIAN $$$
(709-728-1805; 57 High St; prix-fixe $46) The upscale restaurant of the Artisan Inn serves a three-course, prix-fixe meal of local specialties, with wonderful seafood and wine selections guided by an in-house sommelier. Reservations are necessary, but you can also stop by for a sunset drink on the deck. Check the daily menu posted out front.

Drinking & Entertainment

Two Whales Cafe   COFFEE
(709-464-3928; http://twowhales.com; 99 Main Rd, Port Rexton; ⊙10am-6pm) An adorable coffee shop serving the full-octane variety and lemon blueberry cake that's off the charts. It also does good vegetarian fare and organic salads.

Trinity Pageant   THEATER
(adult/child $27/free; ⊙2pm Wed & Sat) An entertaining outdoor drama on Trinity's history held at the Rising Tide Theatre.

Rising Tide Theatre
THEATER

(☎709-464-3232; www.risingtidetheatre.com; Water St; ⊙Jun-Sep) Alongside the Lester Garland Premises is the celebrated Rising Tide Theatre, which hosts the 'Seasons in the Bight' festival and the Trinity Pageant.

Rocky's Place Lounge
LIVE MUSIC

(☎709-464-3400; High St; ⊙from 7pm) Rocky's hosts bands from time to time, but even if the mikes are quiet, it's a friendly place to hoist a brew.

ℹ Information

The town website (www.townoftrinity.com) has tourism information.

RBC Royal Bank (West St; ⊙10:30am-2pm Mon-Thu, to 5pm Fri) No ATM.

ℹ Getting There & Away

Trinity is 259km from St John's and is reached via Rte 230 off Hwy 1. **Shirran's Taxi** (☎709-468-7741) offers a daily taxi service to St John's.

Bonavista

'O buona vista!' (Oh, happy sight!), shouted John Cabot upon spying the New World from his boat on June 24, 1497. Or so the story goes. From all accounts, this pretty spot is where he first set foot in the Americas. Today, Bonavista's shoreline, with its lighthouse, puffins and chasms, continues to rouse emotions.

◉ Sights

Cape Bonavista Lighthouse
LIGHTHOUSE

(☎709-468-7444; www.seethesites.ca; Rte 230; adult/child $6/3; ⊙9:30am-5pm May-Oct) A brilliant red-and-white-striped lighthouse dating from 1843. The interior has been restored to the 1870s, and it is now a provincial historic site. A puffin colony lives just offshore; the birds put on quite a show around sunset.

Dungeon Park
PARK

(Cape Shore Rd, off Rte 230) Nowhere is the power of water more evident than at the Dungeon, a deep chasm 90m in circumference that was created by the collapse of two sea caves, through which thunderous waves now slam the coast.

Ye Matthew Legacy
HISTORIC SITE

(☎709-468-1493; www.matthewlegacy.com; Roper St; adult/child $7.25/3; ⊙9:30am-4:45pm Jun-Sep) A 15th-century replica of *The Matthew*, which Cabot sailed into Bonavista.

Ryan Premises National Historic Site
HISTORIC SITE

(☎709-468-1600; www.pc.gc.ca/ryanpremises; Ryans Hill Rd; adult/child $3.90/1.90; ⊙10am-6pm Jun-Sep) Ryan Premises National Historic Site is a restored 19th-century saltfish mercantile complex. The slew of white clapboard buildings honors five centuries of fishing in Newfoundland via multimedia displays and interpretive programs.

🛏 Sleeping

The cute town options fill up in high season. Check www.bonavista.net for other lodgings.

White's B&B
B&B $

(☎709-468-7018; www.bbcanada.com/3821.htm; 21 Windlass Dr; s/d $95/100; ☯@🛜) Low-key White's has three rooms to choose from, all with either private bathroom or en suite. Enjoy the bike rentals, barbecue use and ocean view.

HI Bonavista
HOSTEL $

(☎709-468-7741; www.hihostels.ca; 40 Cabot Dr; dm $26-30, r $79-120; @🛜) This tidy white-clapboard hostel offers four private rooms, two shared dorm rooms, free bike use, and kitchen and laundry facilities. It's a short walk from the center.

Harbourview B&B
B&B $$

(☎709-468-2572; www.harbourviewgetaway.com; 21 Ryans Hill Rd; r $115; ⊙Jun-Sep; ☯🛜) The name doesn't lie: you get a sweet view at this simple, four-room B&B, plus an evening snack (crab legs) with owners Florence and Albert. Breakfast has a gluten-free option.

🍴 Eating

Bonavista has one of the best restaurant scenes in the province.

Boreal Diner
CAFE $

(☎709-476-2330; 61 Church St; mains $6-15; ⊙11am-7pm Tue-Sat; 🌱) In a bright-red colonial house, this mom-and-pop cafe offers great alternative eats. Crab pot stickers, cod in tarragon sauce, and burgers with toasted buns are some of the scrumptious offerings. It also does vegan and gluten free. Real espresso drinks keep you wired.

Neil's Yard
CAFE $

(www.neilsyard.org; Mockbeggar Plantation, Mockbeggar Rd; mains $5-12; ⊙10am-8pm May-Oct; 🛜) Get comfortable. Here, the gregarious English owner will set you up with a steaming mug of exotic tea, while his wife cooks

WORTH A TRIP

ELLISTON: ROOT CELLARS & PUFFINS

The Root Cellar Capital of the World, aka Elliston, lies 6km south of Bonavista on Rte 238. The teeny town was struggling until it hit upon the idea to market its 135 subterranean veggie storage vaults, and then presto – visitors came a knockin'. Actually, what's most impressive is the **puffin colony** just offshore and swarming with thousands of chubby-cheeked, orange-billed birds from mid-May to mid-August. A quick and easy path over the cliffside brings you quite close to them and also provides whale and iceberg views.

Stop at the **Elliston Visitors Centre** (☑ 709-468-7117; www.townofelliston.ca; Main St; ⊙ 10am-5pm) as you enter town, and the kindly folks will give you directions to the site along with a map of the cellars (which you're welcome to peek inside).

Work up an appetite while you're here, because **Nanny's Root Cellar Kitchen** (☑ 709-468-7998; Orange Hall; mains $7-15; ⊙ 8am-10pm) in historic Orange Hall cooks a mighty fine lobster, Jiggs dinner (roast meat with boiled potatoes, carrots, cabbage, salted beef and pea-and-bread pudding) and other traditional foods, plus she's licensed.

The **Roots, Rants and Roars Festival** (www.rootsrantsandroars.ca; ⊙ mid-Sep) celebrates the province's top chefs, who prepare outdoor feasts in a dramatic setting.

From the adjoining hamlet of **Maberly** a gorgeous 17km coastal hiking trail winds over the landscape to Little Catalina.

up buckwheat crepes, carrot ginger soup, cheesecake with local berries and other healthy fare. Service can be slow, but there's plenty to look at in the attached craft shop.

Walkham's Gate   CAFE $
(☑ 709-468-7004; www.walkhamsgatepub.ca; mains $5-12; ⊙ 24hr; ☎) One side is a coffee shop with whopping pies and hearty soups, the other side a congenial pub tended by music-lover Harvey. Located in the town center, near the courthouse.

★ **Bonavista Social Club** MODERN CANADIAN $$
(☑ 709-445-5556; www.bonavistasocialclub.com; Upper Amherst Cove; mains $12-23; ⊙ 11am-8pm Tue-Sun) 🍃 Social Club's innovative meals are sourced on-site and served with a view. From incredible wood-fired breads and piz-zas to rhubarb lemonade and local moose burgers with partridgeberry ketchup, the kitchen churns out satisfying fare. Tables are few for the demand. The goats roaming the grounds provide milk for cheese, while the chickens lay the eggs. Reserve ahead.

The rustic restaurant is about 15 minutes from Bonavista via Rte 235 (turn left when you see the sign for Upper Amherst Cove). The chef's dad carved all the beautiful wood decor in his workshop next door.

☆ **Entertainment**

Garrick Theatre   THEATER
(www.garricktheatre.ca; 18 Church St) The artfully restored Garrick shows mainstream and in-die films and hosts live-music performances.

ℹ Information

MONEY
There's several bank branches, including **Scotiabank** (☑ 709-468-1070; 1 Church St; ⊙ 9:30am-4pm Mon-Thu), in town.

MEDICAL SERVICES
Bonavista Community Health Centre (☑ 709-468-7881; Hospital Rd)

TOURIST INFORMATION
The town website (www.townofbonavista.com) has tourism information.

ℹ Getting There & Away

Bonavista is a scenic 50km drive north of Trinity along Rte 230. **Shirran's** (☑ 709-468-7741; $40) offers a daily shuttle service from St John's.

Burin Peninsula

It's not exactly lively on the Burin Peninsu-la, due to the effects of the besieged fishing economy. Still, the coastal walks inspire, and the region is a low-key place to spend a day or two before embarking toward the baguettes of France (aka St-Pierre).

Marystown is the peninsula's largest town; it's jammed with big-box retailers but not much else. **Burin** is the area's most attractive town, with a gorgeous elevated boardwalk over the waters of its rocky shore-line. **St Lawrence** is known for fluorite mining and scenic coastal hikes. In **Grand Bank**, there's an interesting self-guided walk through the historic buildings and along the waterfront. Just south is fossil-rich **Fortune**, the jump-off point for St-Pierre.

◉ Sights

Fortune Head Ecological Reserve   PARK

(www.env.gov.nl.ca/parks; off Rte 220; ⊘24hr) The reserve protects fossils dating from the planet's most important period of evolution, when life on earth progressed from simple organisms to complex animals some 550 million years ago. The reserve is about 3km west of Rte 220, by the Fortune Head Lighthouse.

Fortune Head Geology Centre   MUSEUM

(✆709-832-3031; www.fortunehead.com; Bunker Hill Rd, Fortune; adult/child $7.50/5; ⊘8am-8pm Jun-Aug) New exhibits examine the geology of the Burin Peninsula, minerals and rocks, the 1929 Grand Banks tsunami and prehistoric animals. Kids will appreciate this interactive center with fossils to touch from Fortune Head Ecological Reserve; it's in town by the St-Pierre ferry dock. It also offers children's day camp with a daily rate. Daily tours go to the reserve ($25).

Burin Heritage Museums   MUSEUM

(✆709-891-2217; Seaview Dr, Burin; ⊘9am-6pm Mon-Fri, 10:30am-6pm Sat & Sun Apr-Sep) FREE Displays in two historic homes tell of life's highs and lows in remote outports.

Provincial Seamen's Museum   MUSEUM

(✆709-832-1484; www.therooms.ca/museum; Marine Dr, Grand Bank; $2.50; ⊘9:30am-4:45pm May-Oct) The impressive-looking Seamen's Museum depicts both the era of the banking schooner and the changes in the fishery over the years.

⚡ Activities

Ask at the Burin Heritage Museum about locating the **Cook's Lookout** trailhead. It's a 20-minute walk from town to the panoramic view. Off Pollux Cres in St Lawrence, the rugged, breath-draining **Cape Trail** (4km) and **Chamber Cove Trail** (4km) shadow the cliff edges and offer amazing vistas to rocky shores and some famous WWII shipwrecks. Another good (and easier) trail is the **Marine Hike** (7km), which traces Admiral's Beach near Grand Bank. It leaves from Christian's Rd off Rte 220.

⌕ Sleeping & Eating

Options are spread thinly. For those heading to St-Pierre, Grand Bank and Fortune are the best bases. Grand Bank has better lodging, but at 8km from the ferry dock it's further from St-Pierre. Fortune has a sweet bakery by its dock. For more choices check the **Heritage Run** (www.theheritagerun.com).

Thorndyke B&B   B&B $$

(✆709-832-0820; www.thethorndyke.ca; 33 Water St, Grand Bank; r $130; ⊘May-Oct; ☞) This handsome old captain's home overlooks the harbor. Antique wood furnishings fill the four light and airy rooms (each with private bathroom). The hosts will provide dinner with advance notice.

Fortune Harbourview B&B   B&B $$

(✆709-832-7666; www.fortuneharbourview.com; 74 Eldon St, Fortune; r $119-159; ☎) The five rooms aren't fancy, and they're perched on top of a beauty salon, but they're tidy and, best of all, located near the ferry to St-Pierre. It's a serve-yourself, continental-style breakfast.

Stage Head Cafe   CAFE $

(✆709-832-5796; 18 Bayview St, Fortune; mains $6-14; ☎) Attached to the ferry office in Fortune, this small restaurant does a bustling business in quick breakfasts, lunch sandwiches and fish-and-chips. The set dinners ($30) with fresh-caught seafood are well worth it.

Sharon's Nook & the Tea Room   CAFE $

(✆709-832-0618; 12 Water St, Grand Bank; mains $7-12; ⊘7:30am-9pm Mon-Sat, 11am-7:30pm Sun) This kitschy and countrified eatery serves up lasagna, chili, sandwiches and over a dozen varieties of heavenly cheesecake.

❶ Getting There & Away

The Burin Peninsula is accessed via Rte 210 off Hwy 1. The drive from St John's to Grand Bank is 359km and takes just over four hours. Several shuttle services, including **Foote's Taxi** (✆709-832-0491) and **Matthew's Taxi** (✆709-832-4633), go from St John's down the peninsula as far as Fortune.

ST-PIERRE & MIQUELON

POP 6100

Twenty-five kilometers offshore from the Burin Peninsula floats a little piece of France. The islands of St-Pierre and Miquelon aren't just French-like with their berets, baguettes and Bordeaux, they *are* France, governed and financed by the *tricolore*.

Locals kiss their hellos and pay in euros, while sweet smells waft from the myriad pastry shops, and French cars crowd the tiny one-way streets. It's a world away from Newfoundland.

St-Pierre is the more populated and developed island, with most of its 5500 residents living in the town of St-Pierre. Miquelon is larger geographically but has only 600 residents overall.

Jacques Cartier claimed the islands for France in 1536, after they were discovered by the Portuguese in 1520. At the end of the Seven Years' War in 1763, the islands were turned over to Britain, only to be given back to France in 1816. And French they've remained ever since.

◉ Sights

Miquelon & Langlade
ISLAND

(adult/child 3hr tour €35/18; ⊙ Jun-Sep) The island of Miquelon is less visited and less developed than St-Pierre. The village of Miquelon, centered on the church, is at the northern tip of the island. From nearby l'Étang de Mirande a walking trail leads to a lookout and waterfall. From the bridge in town, a scenic 25km road leads across the isthmus to the wild and uninhabited island of Langlade. There are some wild horses, and around the rocky coast you'll see seals and birds. Tours are operated by the Comite Regional de Tourisme.

Île aux Marins
HISTORIC BUILDING

(3hr tour adult/child €24/16; ⊙ 9am & 1:30pm May-Sep) The magical Île aux Marins is a beautiful abandoned village on an island out in the St-Pierre harbor. A bilingual guide will walk you through colorful homes, a small schoolhouse museum and the grand church (1874). Book tours at the visitor center. You can also go over on the boat (€6) sans guide, but be aware most signage is in French. Outside of July and August boats must be pre-arranged (see the tourism office).

Les Salines
AREA

(Rue Boursaint & the waterfront) Old-timers hang out around this scenic cluster of multi-hued fishing shacks.

L'Arche Museum
MUSEUM

(☑ 508-410-435; www.arche-musee-et-archives. net; Rue du 11 Novembre; adult/child €5/3; ⊙ 10am-noon & 2-6pm Tue-Sun Jun-Sep) The well-done exhibits cover the islands' history, including Prohibition times. The showstopper is the guillotine – the only one to slice in North America. Islanders dropped the 'timbers of justice' just once, in 1889, on a murderer. The museum also offers bilingual architectural walking tours (€7).

☆ Activities

In St-Pierre, the best thing to do is just walk around and soak it up – when you're not eating, that is. Pop into stores and sample goods you'd usually have to cross an ocean for. Or conduct research as to the best chocolate-croissant maker. A couple of walking trails leave from the edge of town near the power station and loop between the far coast and inland lakes.

Zodiac Tours
BOATING

(adult/child €41/35) Full-day, bilingual tours by Zodiac cover both Miquelon and Langlade. Book at the visitor center. Rates include snack.

Fronton
PELOTE

(Rues Maître Georges Lefèvre & Gloanec) Watch locals play the Basque game of *pelote* (a type of handball) at the outdoor court here.

✦ Festivals & Events

From mid-July to the end of August, folk dances are often held in St-Pierre's square.

Basque Festival
CULTURAL

(⊙ mid-Aug) A weeklong festival with music, marching and invigorating street fun.

Bastille Day
CULTURAL

(⊙ Jul 14) The largest holiday of the year.

⊨ Sleeping

There are about a dozen accommodations on St-Pierre; most include continental breakfast. Book ahead in summer.

Auberge Quatre Temps B&B
B&B $

(☑ 508-414-301; www.quatretemps.com; s/d €78/82; ❀ ⊛) Quatre Temps is a 15-minute schlep from the ferry dock, but don't let that deter you. All six rooms have their own bathroom. There's a fine terrace where you can buy drinks and sip alfresco. The owner also runs the Saveurs des Îles restaurant.

Bernard Dodeman B&B
B&B $

(☑ 508-413-060; www.pensiondodeman.com; 15 Rue Paul Bert; r €55; ⊜ ⊛) The Dodeman's three simple rooms share two bathrooms and a communal TV parlor. It's a 15-minute walk from the ferry, on a hill above town.

NEWFOUNDLAND & LABRADOR ST-PIERRE & MIQUELON

★ **Auberge St Pierre**   B&B $$

(📱508-414-086; www.aubergesaintpierre.fr; 16 Rue Georges Daguerre; d €88-176; 📶) Guests rave about the warm service and lovely atmosphere of this family-run island B&B. Arrive to chilled wine and cheese. Remodeled rooms feature flat-screen TVs and hydromassage showers; they're also stocked with robes and extra towels. Transportation to and from the ferry and island tours included.

Nuits St-Pierre   B&B $$

(📱508-412-720; www.nuits-saint-pierre.com; 10 Rue du Général Leclerc; r €130-175; 🛏📶) An upscale lodging aimed at the honeymoon crowd. The five rooms, each with private bathroom and blissful, downy beds, are named after famous French authors. There's free pickup from the airport or ferry. The attached tea salon is open every afternoon from 2pm to 6pm and is a must for a restorative beverage and slice of cake. It also boasts a fitness center.

Hotel Robert   HOTEL $$

(📱508-412-419; www.hotelrobert.com; 2 Rue du 11 Novembre; d €90-118; 📶) Most visitors end up in this decent-value hotel, the largest on the island. Rooms are pleasant, with crisp white sheets and powerful showers. Some are dated. A downstairs restaurant serves breakfast (not included) but be warned: there's only one waiter serving two clamoring, hungry rooms. It's within close walking distance of the ferry.

✖ Eating

The few island restaurants can barely meet demand in summer, so be sure to make dinner reservations well in advance if you plan on eating out. It's not unusual for all restaurants to be fully booked.

★ **Guillard Gourmandises**   BAKERY $

(31 Rue Boursaint; pastries €1-3; ⊙7am-noon & 2-5:30pm Tue-Sat, to 4:30pm Sun) It's worth memorizing the complicated schedule to make good on this slice of *la belle* France. After all, these cream-plumped chocolate éclairs, macarons, piping-hot pastries and gateaux are the reason you came, right?

Le Cafe du Chat Luthier   SUSHI, PIZZA $$

(www.lecafeduchatluthier.com; 6 Rue Amiral Muselier; mains €9-22; ⊙noon-1:30pm Tue-Fri, 6-10pm Tue-Sun) An apt response to everything St-Pierre lacks, this amicable hipster hideout serves wonderful sushi rolls, crisp, wood-fired, wafer-thin pizzas and gourmet burgers. If you are stuck without a dinner reservation, the takeout is a godsend. Offers set lunches on weekdays.

L'Atelier Gourmand   FRENCH $$$

(📱508-415-300; www.lateliergourmandspm.com; 12 Rue du 11 Novembre; mains €18-25; ⊙noon-2pm & 6-10:30pm; 📶) Crowds of diners tuck into classic French fare at this cozy restaurant with a streetfront patio. Yet the prix-fixe menu can be hit or miss and service is painfully slow. However, you can't go wrong with a heaping bowl of mussels served with a nice vintage and topped off with white chocolate crème brûlée.

❶ Information

Americans, EU citizens and all visitors except Canadians need a passport for entry. Those staying longer than 30 days also need a visa. Other nationalities should confirm with their French embassy if a visa is needed prior to arrival. Canadians can enter with a driver's license.

BUSINESS HOURS

Most shops and businesses close between noon and 1:30pm. Some stores also close on Saturday afternoons, and most are closed on Sunday.

ST-PIERRE'S BOOZY BACKSTORY

When Prohibition dried out the USA's kegs in the 1920s, Al Capone decided to slake his thirst – and that of the nation – by setting up shop in St-Pierre.

He and his mates transformed the sleepy fishing harbor into a booming port crowded with warehouses filled with imported booze. Bottles were removed from their crates, placed in smaller carrying sacks and taken secretly to the US coast by rum runners. The piles of Cutty Sark whiskey crates were so high on the docks that clever locals used the wood both to build and heat houses. At least one house remains today and is known as the 'Cutty Sark cottage'; most bus tours drive by.

The tourist information center offers a special two-hour Prohibition tour (adult/child €20/10) that covers sites related to the theme. If nothing else, drop by the Hotel Robert near the tourist information center and check out Al Capone's hat; it hangs in the gift shop.

CUSTOMS

To merit the duty-free waiver on alcohol, you must stay on the islands at least 48 hours.

LANGUAGE

French is the language, but many people also speak English.

MONEY

Most vendors accept credit cards. Some accept the loonie, though they return change in euros. If you're staying more than an afternoon, it's probably easiest to get euros from the local ATMs.

TELEPHONE

Calling the islands is an international call, meaning you must dial ☑ 011 in front of the local number. Phone service links in to the French system, so beware of roaming charges on your mobile.

TIME

Half an hour ahead of Newfoundland Time.

TOURIST INFORMATION

The **visitor center** (www.st-pierre-et-miquelon. com; ⊙8:30am-6:30pm; ☎), near the ferry dock, has a map showing all the banks, restaurants etc. Staff also provides info on the islands' hotels and tours and makes bookings for free.

❶ Getting There & Away

AIR

Air St-Pierre (www.airsaintpierre.com; roundtrip $353) flies to St John's, Montréal and Halifax. There are two to three flights weekly to each city. Taxis to/from the airport cost around €5.

BOAT

From Fortune on Newfoundland, the **St-Pierre Ferry** (☑709-832-3455; www.saintpierreferry. ca; 14 Bayview St, Fortune; adult/child return $93/58) makes the hour-long trip to and from the island once daily (twice on Wednesdays) in July and August. It runs less often the rest of the year. Departure times vary, so check the website. Boats carry foot passengers only, though there are plans for two car ferries. Staff coordinate Fortune parking in lots near the dock (per day $10). Buy tickets in advance and arrive 30 minutes early or one hour before departure if you need to leave a car.

❶ Getting Around

Much can be seen on foot. Roads are steep, so prepare to huff and puff. Car-rental agencies are resistant to renting to tourists, who admittedly have difficulty navigating the unsignposted, narrow, one-way streets.

The visitor center rents bicycles (per day €13) and there are also motorized bicycles for rent. Local ferries head to Miquelon and Langlade; check with the visitor center for schedules and costs.

CENTRAL NEWFOUNDLAND

Central Newfoundland elicits fewer wows per square kilometer than the rest of the province, but that's because huge chunks of the region are pure bog land and trees. The islands of Notre Dame Bay – particularly Twillingate, when icebergs glide by – are the exceptions.

Terra Nova National Park

Backed by lakes, bogs and hilly woods, and fronted by the salty waters of Clode and Newman Sounds, Terra Nova National Park is spliced by Hwy 1 running through its interior.

◉ Sights

Burnside Archaeology Centre   MUSEUM
(☑709-677-2474; www.digthequarry.com; Main St; adult/child $3/1; ⊙9am-6pm Jul-Oct) About 15km from the western gate of Terra Nova National Park, the Burnside Archaeology Centre catalogs artifacts found at local Beothuk sites.

Terra Nova National Park   PARK
(☑709-533-2801; www.pc.gc.ca/terranova; adult/child/family per day $5.80/2.90/14.70) Though not nearly as dramatic as the province's other national parks, it does offer moose, bears, beavers and bald eagles, as well as relaxed hiking, paddling, camping and boat tours.

🏃 Activities

Terra Nova's 14 hiking trails total almost 100km; pick up maps at the Visitors Centre (p198). Highly recommended is the **Malady Head Trail** (5km), which climaxes at the edge of a headland cliff offering stunning views of Southwest Arm and Broad Cove. **Sandy Pond Trail** (3km) is an easy loop around the pond – your best place to spot a beaver. The area is also a favorite for **swimming**, with a beach, change rooms and picnic tables. In winter the park grooms trails here for cross-country skiing.

The epic **Outport Trail** (48km) provides access to backcountry campgrounds and abandoned settlements along Newman Sound. The loop in its entirety is rewarding, but be warned: parts are unmarked, not to mention mucky. A compass, a topographical map and ranger advice are prerequisites for this serious route.

Kayak rentals are available at the kiosk by the visitor center. Inquire about the **Sandy Pond–Dunphy's Pond Route** (10km), a great paddle with only one small portage.

Also in the region is **Salvage**, a photogenic fishing village with well-marked walking trails. It's near the park's north end on Rte 310, about 26km from Hwy 1.

👉 Tours

Boat Tours   BOATING
(per adult/child $45/30) Interesting boat tours reach the more far-flung settlements. Ask at the Terra Nova National Park Visitors Centre or the Burnside Archaeology Centre for information.

Coastal Connections   BOATING
(☑709-533-2196;   www.coastalconnections.ca; 2½hr tours adult/child $85/35; ⏱10am & 2pm May-Oct) Climb aboard for a trip through Newman Sound, where you'll pull lobster pots, examine plankton under a microscope and engage in other hands-on activities. It's common to see eagles, less so whales.

🛌 Sleeping

Camping is the only option within the park itself. Those with aspirations of a bed should head to Eastport; it's near the park's north end on Rte 310, about 16km from Hwy 1. For camping reservations (recommended on summer weekends), call **Parks Canada** (☑877-737-3783; www.pccamping.ca; reservation fee $10.80) or go online.

Backcountry Camping   CAMPGROUND $
(free permit required, tent sites $16) There are several backcountry sites around the Outport Trail, Beachy Pond, Dunphy's Island and Dunphy's Pond, reached by paddling, hiking or both. Register at the visitor center.

Newman Sound Campground   CAMPGROUND $
(campsites $26-30) This is the park's main (noisier) campground, with 343 sites, a grocery store and a laundromat. It has electricity, toilets and showers. It's open for winter camping too.

ℹ Information

Make your first stop the **Terra Nova National Park Visitors Centre** (☑709-533-2942; Hwy 1; ⏱10am-6pm Jul & Aug, to 4pm May, Jun & Sep), which has oodles of park information, ranger-guided programs and marine displays with touch tanks and underwater cameras. It's 1km off Hwy 1 at Salton's Day-Use Area, 80km east of Gander.

Gander

Gander sprawls across the juncture of Hwy 1 and Rte 330, which leads to Notre Dame Bay. It is a convenient stopping point and offers a couple of sights for aviation buffs. Big-box retailers are everywhere, as this is the region's main town. If you need to stock up on anything, do it here.

For aviation fanatics, the **North Atlantic Aviation Museum** (☑709-256-2923; www.northatlanticaviationmuseum.com; Hwy 1; adult/child $6/5; ⏱9am-7pm Jul & Aug, to 4pm Mon-Fri Sep-Jun) is a drawcard. Just east on Hwy 1 is the sobering **Silent Witness Monument**, a tribute to 248 US soldiers whose plane crashed here in December 1985.

Though expensive for the location, the hotel rooms at **Sinbad's Hotel & Suites** (☑709-651-2678; www.steelehotels.com; Bennett Dr; r $129-147) in the center of Gander are clean and welcoming for a rest from highway driving.

There is a **Visitors Centre** (www.gandercanada.com; ⏱8am-8pm Jun-Sep, 8:30am-5pm Oct-May) on Hwy 1 at the central entry into town.

The **Gander Airport** (YQX; ☑709-256-6666; www.ganderairport.com) gets a fair bit of traffic. **DRL** (☑709-263-2171; www.drl-lr.com) buses stop at the airport en route to St John's (four hours) and Port aux Basques (nine hours).

Twillingate Island & New World Island

This area of Notre Dame Bay gets ample attention thanks to an influx of whales and icebergs every summer. Twillingate (comprised of two barely separated islands, North and South Twillingate) sits just north of New World Island. The islands are reached from the mainland via short causeways. On a summer day it can be touristy, though stunning. Every turn of the road reveals new ocean vistas, fishing wharves or outcrops of tidy pastel houses.

👁 Sights

⭐**Prime Berth Fishing Museum**   MUSEUM
(☑709-884-2485;   www.primeberth.com; Main Tickle Causeway; $5, tour $8; ⏱10am-5pm Jul & Aug) Make this your first stop. Run by an engaging fisherman, the private museum, with its imaginative and deceptively simple

concepts (a cod splitting show!), is brilliant, and fun for mature scholars and schoolkids alike. It's the first place you see as you cross to Twillingate.

Long Point Lighthouse LIGHTHOUSE
(☑709-884-2247; ⊘10am-6pm) **FREE** Long Point provides dramatic views of the coastal cliffs. Travel up the winding steps, worn from lighthouse-keepers' footsteps since 1876, and gawk at the 360-degree view. Located at the tip of the north island, it's an ideal vantage point for spotting icebergs in May and June.

Auk Island Winery WINERY
(☑709-884-2707; www.aukislandwinery.com; 29 Durrell St; tastings $3, with tour $5; ⊘9am-9pm Jul & Aug, reduced hour Sep-Jun) Visit the grounds that produce Moose Joose (blueberry-partridgeberry), Funky Puffin (blueberry-rhubarb) and other fruity flavors using iceberg water and local berries. There's also ice cream made from iceberg water.

Little Harbour WATERFRONT
In Little Harbour, en route to the town of Twillingate, a 5km trail leads past the vestiges of a resettled community and rock arch to secluded, picturesque Jone's Cove.

Twillingate Museum MUSEUM
(☑709-884-2825; www.tmacs.ca; admission by donation; ⊘9am-5pm May-Sep) Housed in a former Anglican rectory off Main St, the museum tells the island's history since the first British settlers arrived in the mid-1700s. One room delves into the seal hunt and its controversy. There's a historic church next door.

Durrell Museum MUSEUM
(☑709-884-2780; Museum St; adult/child $3/1.50; ⊘9am-5pm Jun-Sep) Don't neglect to see scenic Durrell and its museum, dwelling off Durrell St atop Old Maid Hill. The polar bear is a bonus. Bring your lunch; there are a couple of picnic tables and a spectacular view.

👉 Tours

Fun two-hour tours to view icebergs and whales depart daily from mid-May to early September.

Iceberg Man Tours BOATING
(☑800-611-2374; www.icebergtours.ca; Southside; adult/child $50/25) Captain Cecil's popular two-hour tour departs at 9:30am, 1pm and 4pm. Guests rave about the service.

Twillingate Adventure Tours BOATING
(☑888-447-8687; http://twillingateadventuretours.com) Depart from Twillingate's wharf off Main St at 10am, 1pm and 4pm (and sometimes 7pm).

🎊 Festivals & Events

Fish, Fun & Folk Festival MUSIC
(www.fishfunfolkfestival.com; ⊘late Jul) Traditional music and dance, some of which goes back to the 16th century, merrily take over Twillingate during this weeklong festival.

🛌 Sleeping & Eating

Despite having about 20 lodging options, Twillingate gets very busy in the summer. Book early.

Paradise B&B B&B $
(☑709-884-5683; www.capturegaia.com/paradiseb&b.html; 192 Main St; r incl breakfast $90-110; ⊘May-Sep; ➡🛜) Set on a bluff overlooking Twillingate's harbor, Paradise offers the best view in town. You can wander down to the beach below, or relax on a lawn chair and soak it all up. Oh, the three rooms are comfy too. Angle for room 1. Cash only.

Anchor Inn Hotel HOTEL $$
(☑709-884-2777; www.anchorinntwillingate.com; 3 Path End; r $135-165; ⊘Mar-Dec; 🛜) The waterfront Anchor has rooms with deliciously soft beds. Amenities include the hotel's view-worthy deck and the barbecue grill for do-it-yourself types. There's also an excellent on-site restaurant.

Captain's Legacy B&B B&B $$
(☑709-884-5648; www.captainslegacy.com; Hart's Cove; r $110-140; ⊘May-Oct; ➡🛜) A real captain named Peter Troake once owned this historic 'outport mansion,' now a gracious four-room B&B overlooking the harbor.

R&J Restaurant SEAFOOD $
(☑709-884-2212; 110 Main St; mains $8-14; ⊘8am-11pm) A greasy spoon popular with families – probably because it serves pizza and burgers alongside fish 'n' brewis (a blend of salted fish, onions, fried pork fat and a near-boiled bread).

⭐ Doyle Sansome & Sons SEAFOOD $$
(www.sansomeslobsterpool.com; 25 Sansome's Place, Hillgrade; mains $8-24; ⊘10am-9pm) It's well worth veering out of your way for this classic fish shack serving crisp cod, fish cakes with rhubarb relish and fresh lobster. If it's a nice day, the dock seating provides a fine

view. Don't be fooled by the name – a slew of friendly women cook here. The village of Hillgrade is 17km before Twillingate on the left.

☆ Entertainment

Twillingate/NWI Dinner Theatre THEATER
(☑709-884-2300; Crow Head; adult/child $32/16; ☺5:30pm Mon-Sat Jun-Sep) Six of Newfoundland's best will not only cook you a traditional meal, they'll also leave you in stitches with their talented performances. It's just south of the Long Point Lighthouse.

Fogo Island & Change Islands

POP 2400

Settled in the 1680s, Fogo is an intriguing and rugged island to poke around. Keep an eye on this place: it has embarked on an ambitious, arts-oriented sustainable tourism plan that's quite progressive for the region. The rare Newfoundland pony roams the Change Islands, which float to the west.

◎ Sights & Activities

On Fogo, the village of **Joe Batt's Arm**, backed by rocky hills, is a flashback to centuries past – though it now has a mod twist thanks to the luxe new Fogo Island Inn. A **farmers market** takes place at the ice rink on Saturday mornings.

Nearby **Tilting** is perhaps the most engaging village on the island. Irish roots run deep here and so do the accents. The inland harbor is surrounded by picturesque fishing stages and flakes, held above the incoming tides by weary stilts. There's also the great coastal **Turpin's Trail** (9km), which leaves from Tilting, near the beach at **Sandy Cove**.

On the opposite end of the island is the village of **Fogo** and the indomitable **Brimstone Head**. After you take in the mystical rock's view, do another great hike in town: the **Lion's Den Trail** (5km), which visits a Marconi radio site. Keep an eye out for the small group of caribou that roams the island.

As part of the development plan, the island has built **art studios** along its walking trails, and invites painters, filmmakers and photographers from around the world for residencies.

The Change Islands are home to the **Newfoundland Pony Sanctuary** (☑709-621-6381; www.nlponysanctuary.com; 12 Bowns Rd; admission by donation; ☺by appointment), established to increase numbers of the native,

endangered Newfoundland pony. Less than 100 registered beasts of breeding age remain in the province.

☆✦ Festivals & Events

Brimstone Head Folk Festival MUSIC
(www.brimstoneheadfestival.com; ☺mid-Aug) A three-day hootenanny; Irish and Newfoundland music.

Great Fogo Island Punt Race CULTURAL
(www.fogoislandregatta.com; ☺late Jul) Locals row traditionally built wooden boats (called punts) 16km across open sea to the Change Islands and back.

🛏 Sleeping & Eating

Accommodations range from B&Bs to the most exclusive hotel in Newfoundland. Reserve ahead as Fogo is wildly popular in summer.

★**Tilting Harbour B&B** B&B $
(☑709-658-7288; www.tiltingharbourbnb.ca; 10a Kelley's Island Rd, Tilting; r $98-110; ☻🖱) Outstanding in hospitality, this traditional, 100-year-old home has four spotless rooms with renovated bathrooms. While angles are sharp, it's comfortable and cozy. Best of all, the owner Tom is an accomplished chef who offers wonderful, social dinners ($35) with fresh local seafood. Breakfast scones are also a big hit.

Peg's B&B B&B $
(☑709-266-2392; www.pegsbb.com; 60 Main St, Fogo; r $85-105; ☺May-Oct; ☻🖱) In the heart of Fogo village, Peg's four-room place offers up a friendly atmosphere and harbor views.

Quintal House INN $$
(www.quintalhouse.ca; 153 Main Rd, Joe Batt's Arm; d $130-150; 🖱) Open year-round, this colorful heritage house has just three guest rooms adorned with works from local artisans. Guests have kitchen and laundry access. If there's a disadvantage, it's being right on the main road close to traffic. Reservations only.

★**Fogo Island Inn** INN $$$
(☑709-658-3444; www.fogoislandinn.ca; Joe Batt's Arm; 2-night stay incl meals $1775-2875; 🅿🖱) ◢ With modern, minimalist design and sterling service, this 29-room inn is an architectural wonder clasping the edge of the world. Canada's Prime Minister Justin Trudeau vacations here. Rooms have king-sized beds draped with quilts, plus binoculars and phenomenal sea views. The chef

sources ingredients from island forages. In July nonguests can tour the ecofriendly facilities daily at 11am and 2:30pm.

Growler's ICE CREAM $

(Joe Batt's Arm; cones $5; ☺12:30-7pm Wed-Sun) It would be a pity to miss this seaside stop, serving homemade partridgeberry-pie ice cream flecked with cinnamon and salty crumbs of crust.

Nicole's Cafe CAFE $$

(☑709-658-3663; www.nicolescafe.ca; 159 Main Rd, Joe Batt's Arm; mains $16-22; ☺10:30am-8pm Mon-Sat) ✔ Nicole uses ingredients from the island – sustainably caught seafood, root vegetables and wild berries – for her contemporary take on dishes like Jiggs dinner, caribou pâté and the daily vegetarian plate. It's a sunny spot with big wood tables and local artwork and quilts on the walls.

Fogo Island Inn Restaurant CANADIAN $$$

(☑709-658-3444; www.fogoislandinn.ca; Joe Batt's Arm; lunch mains $20-45, prix-fixe dinner $115; ☺7-10am, noon-3pm & 6-9pm, by reservation only) ✔ With sparkling sea views, this tiny gourmet eatery dishes up innovative three-course dinners sourced as locally as possible. The menu changes daily. Think delicate preparations of snow crab with sea salt, Prince Edward Island grass-fed beef and rye ice cream with nettles. Drinks extra. Nonguests should reserve at least three days ahead and park roadside, a five-minute walk from the inn.

❶ Getting There & Away

Rte 335 takes you to the town of Farewell, where the ferry sails to the Change Islands (20 minutes) and then onward to Fogo (45 minutes). Demand is heavy in summer – it is worth arriving two hours before your departure to ensure a spot for your vehicle.

Five boats leave between 7:45am and 8:30pm. Schedules vary, so check with **Provincial Ferry Services** (☑709-627-3492; www.gov.nl.ca/ferryservices; round-trip Fogo vehicle/passenger $18/6). Note it is about 25km from Fogo's ferry terminal to Joe Batt's Arm.

Grand Falls-Windsor

POP 13,700

The sprawl of two small pulp-and-paper towns has met and now comprises the community of Grand Falls-Windsor. The historic Grand Falls portion, south of Hwy 1 and near the Exploits River, is more interesting for visitors.

◉ Sights

Mary March Provincial Museum MUSEUM

(☑709-292-4522; http://manl.nf.ca; 24 St Catherine St; adult/child $2.50/free; ☺9am-4:30pm Mon-Sat, from noon Sun May-Oct) Worth visiting with exhibits on the recent and past histories of Aboriginal peoples in the area, including the extinct Beothuk tribe. Take exit 18A south to get here. Admission includes the loggers' museum.

Salmonid Interpretation Centre PARK

(☑709-489-7350; www.exploitsriver.ca; adult/child $6.50/3; ☺8am-8pm Jun-Sep) Watch Atlantic salmon start their mighty struggle upstream to spawn. Unfortunately, they do so under the pulp mill's shadow. To get there, cross the river south of High St and follow the signs.

✪ Festivals & Events

Salmon Festival MUSIC

(www.evsalmonfestival.com; ☺mid-Jul) The five-day Salmon Festival rocks with big-name Canadian bands.

⛌ Sleeping & Eating

Hill Road Manor B&B B&B $$

(☑709-489-5451; www.hillroadmanor.com; 1 Hill Rd; r $119-129; ❖) Elegant furnishings, cushiony beds that will have you gladly oversleeping and a vibrant sunroom combine for a stylish stay. Kids are welcome.

Kelly's Pub BURGERS $

(☑709-489-9893; 18 Hill Rd; mains $8-14; ☺9am-2am) Hidden neatly behind the smoky pub is this great countrified spot. It makes the best burgers in town and the stir-fries are not too shabby either.

❶ Getting There & Away

DRL (☑709-263-2171; www.drl-lr.com) has its bus stop at the Highliner Inn on the Hwy 1 service road. Buses go 430km to St John's ($72) and to 477km Port aux Basques ($124).

Central South Coast

Rte 360 runs 130km through the center of the province to the south coast. It's a long way down to the first settlements at the end of **Bay d'Espoir**, a gentle fjord. Note there is no gas station on the route, so fill up on Hwy 1. **St Alban's** is on the west side of the fjord. You'll find a few motels with dining rooms and lounges around the end of the bay.

Further south is a concentration of small fishing villages. The scenery along Rte 364 to **Hermitage** is particularly impressive, as are the landscapes around **Harbour Breton**. The largest town (population 1700) in the region, it huddles around the ridge of a gentle inland bay.

🛏 Sleeping & Eating

Southern Port Hotel   HOTEL $$
(☑709-885-2283; www.southernporthotel.ca; Rte 360, Harbour Breton; r $110-129; ☎) Provides spacious, standard-furnished rooms; even-numbered ones have harbor views.

Scott's Snackbar   BURGERS $
(☑709-885-2406; Harbour Breton; mains $7-15; ☉10:30am-11pm Sun-Thu, to 1am Fri & Sat) Near lodgings, Scott's Snackbar serves burgers and home-cooked dishes; it's licensed.

❶ Getting There & Away

To access this remote area it's best to go by private vehicle, though **Thornhill Taxi Service** (☑709-885-2144) also runs between Grand Falls and Harbour Breton. **Provincial Ferry Services** (☑709-292-4302; www.tw.gov.nl.ca/ferryservices) serve Hermitage, making the western south-coast outports accessible from here.

NORTHERN PENINSULA

The Northern Peninsula points upward from the body of Newfoundland like an extended index finger, and you almost get the feeling it's wagging at you saying, 'Don't you dare leave this province without coming up here.'

Heed the advice. Two of the province's World Heritage–listed sites are here: Gros Morne National Park, with its fjord-like lakes and geological oddities, rests at the peninsula's base, while the sublime, 1000-year-old Viking settlement at L'Anse aux Meadows stares out from the peninsula's tip. Connecting these two famous sites is the Viking Trail (www.vikingtrail.org), aka Rte 430, an attraction in its own right that holds close to the sea as it heads resolutely north past the ancient burial grounds of Port au Choix and the ferry jump-off point to big, brooding Labrador.

The region continues to gain in tourism, yet the crowds are nowhere near what you'd get at Yellowstone or Banff, for example.

Deer Lake

There's little in Deer Lake for the visitor, but it's an excellent place to fly into for trips up the Northern Peninsula and around the west coast.

For B&B comfort, hunker down at plain-and-simple **Auntie M's Lucas House** (☑709-635-3622; www.lucashouse.net; 22 Old Bonne Bay Rd; r $75-85; ☉May-Sep; @☎); it's a five-minute ride from the airport.

The **visitors center** (☑709-635-2202; dlvic@gov.nl.ca; Hwy 1; ☉9am-7pm) and the **DRL** (☑709-263-2171; www.drl-lr.com) bus stop at the Irving gas station sit beside each other on Hwy 1. A taxi from the airport to any of these spots costs about $10.

Visitors to Gros Morne National Park usually fly into the **Deer Lake Airport** (YDF; ☑709-635-3601; www.deerlakeairport.com; 1 Airport Rd; ☎). Long-distance DRL buses transit the Trans Canada Hwy.

Gros Morne National Park

The stunning flat-top mountains and deeply incised waterways of this **national park** (☑709-458-2417; www.pc.gc.ca/grosmorne; per day adult/child/family $9.80/4.90/19.60) are simply supernatural playgrounds. Designated a World Heritage Site in 1987, the park offers special significance to geologists as a blueprint for the planet. The bronze-colored Tablelands feature rock from deep within the earth's crust, supplying evidence for theories such as plate tectonics. Nowhere else in the world is such material as easily accessed as it is in Gros Morne.

Several small fishing villages dot the shoreline and provide amenities. Bonne Bay swings in and divides the area: to the south is Rte 431 and the towns of **Glenburnie**, **Woody Point** and **Trout River**; to the north is Rte 430 and **Norris Point**, **Rocky Harbour**, **Sally's Cove** and **Cow Head**. Centrally located Rocky Harbour is the largest village and most popular place to stay. Nearby Norris Point and further-flung Woody Point also make good bases.

◉ Sights

The park is quite widespread – it's 133km from Trout River at the south end to Cow Head in the north – so it takes a while to get from sight to sight. Don't forget to stop at the park's visitor centers, which have interpretive programs and guided walks.

THE SEAL HUNT DEBATE

Nothing ignites a more passionate debate than Canada's annual seal hunt, which occurs in March and April off Newfoundland's northeast coast and in the Gulf of St Lawrence around the Îles de la Madeleine and Prince Edward Island. The debate pits animal-rights activists against sealers (typically local fishers who hunt in the off-season). The main issues revolve around the following questions.

Are baby seals being killed? Yes and no. Whitecoats are newborn harp seals, and these are the creatures that have been seen in horrifying images. But it has been illegal to hunt them for decades. After seals lose their white coats at 12 to 14 days old, they're considered fair game.

Are the animals killed humanely? Sealers say yes, that their guns and/or clubs kill the seals humanely. Animal activists dispute this, saying seals are injured and left on the ice to suffer until the sealers come back later and finish the job.

Is the seal population sustainable? The Canadian government says yes, and sets the yearly quota based on the total seal population in the area (estimated at 7.3 million). For 2015, the harp-seal quota was 468,000, despite market decline.

Is the seal hunt really an important part of the local economy? Activists say no, that it represents a fraction of Newfoundland's income. The province disagrees, saying for some sealers it represents up to one-third of their annual income. And in a province with unemployment near 12%, that's significant.

In 2009 the EU banned the sale of seal products, which hurt the industry considerably. For more on the two perspectives, see the Canadian Sealers Association (www.sealharvest.ca) and the Humane Society of the United States (www.protectseals.org).

Tablelands GEOLOGICAL FEATURE

Dominating the southwest corner of the park, near Trout River, are the unconquerable and eerie Tablelands. This huge flat-topped massif was part of the earth's mantle before tectonics raised it from the depths and planted it squarely on the continent. Its rock is so unusual that plants can't even grow on it. You can view the barren golden phenomenon up close on Rte 431, or catch it from a distance at the stunning photography lookout above Norris Point. West of the Tablelands, dramatic volcanic sea stacks and caves mark the coast at **Green Gardens**.

Bonne Bay Marine Station AQUARIUM

(✆709-458-2550; www.bonnebay.ca; Rte 430, Norris Point; adult/child/family $6.25/5/15; ⊘9am-5pm Jun-Aug) At the wharf in Norris Point is this research facility, which is part of Memorial University. Every half-hour there are interactive tours, and the aquariums display the marine ecological habitats in Bonne Bay. For children, there are touch tanks and a rare blue lobster lurking around.

Arches Provincial Park PARK

These scenic arched rocks on Rte 430 north of Parsons Pond are formed by pounding waves and worth a look-see.

Shallow Bay BEACH

This gentle, safe, sand-duned beach seems out of place, as if transported from the Caribbean. The water, however, provides a chilling dose of reality, rarely getting above 15°C.

Broom Point Fishing Camp HISTORIC SITE

(Rte 430, Broom Point; ⊘10am-5:30pm May-Oct) **FREE** This restored fishing camp sits a short distance north of Western Brook Pond. The three Mudge brothers and their families fished here from 1941 until 1975, when they sold the entire camp, including boats, lobster traps and nets, to the national park. It's staffed by guides.

SS Ethie SHIPWRECK

(Rte 430, past Sally's Cove) Follow the sign off the highway to where waves batter the rusty and tangled remains of the SS *Ethie*. The story of this 1919 wreck, and the subsequent rescue, was inspiration for a famous folk song.

🏃 Activities

Hiking

Twenty maintained trails of varying difficulty snake through 100km of the park's most scenic landscapes. The gem is the 16km **Gros Morne Mountain Trail** to the peak of Gros Morne, the highest point at 806m. A good alternative in poor weather, the 16km **Green Gardens Trail** is almost as scenic and challenging.

Shorter scenic hikes are **Tablelands Trail** (4km), which extends to Winterhouse Brook Canyon; **Lookout Trail** (5km), which starts behind the Discovery Centre and loops to the site of an old fire tower above the tree line; **Lobster Cove Head Trail** (2km), which loops through tidal pools; and **Western Brook Pond Trail** (Rte 430), the most popular path.

The granddaddies of the trails are the **Long Range Traverse** (35km) and **North Rim Traverse** (27km), serious multiday treks over the mountains. Permits and advice from park rangers are required.

If you plan to do several trails, invest $20 in a copy of the *Gros Morne National Park Trail Guide*, a waterproof map with trail descriptions on the back, which is usually available at the visitor centers.

Kayaking & Boating

Kayaking in the shadow of the Tablelands and through the spray of whales is truly something to be experienced.

★ **Western Brook Pond Boat Tour** BOATING
(2hr trip per adult $58-65, child $26-30) With dramatic views second to none, this acclaimed tour is run by Bon's Tours. Prices are cheapest for morning tours. It's about a 25-minute drive from Bon's office to the trailhead. The dock is a 3km walk from Rte 430 via the easy Western Brook Pond Trail.

Gros Morne Adventures TOURS
(☑ 709-458-2722; www.grosmorneadventures. com; Norris Point wharf; 2hr kayak tour adult/child $55/45) A great way to experience Bonne Bay is through this outfitter's daily sea-kayak tours. It also offers full-day and multiday kayak trips and various hiking tours. Also provides kayak rentals (single/double per day $55/65) for experienced paddlers.

Bon Tours BOATING
(☑ 709-458-2016; www.bontours.ca; Ocean View Motel, Main St, Rocky Harbour) Bon runs the phenomenal Western Brook Pond boat tour every hour between 10am and 5pm and boat tours of Bonne Bay. If you haven't purchased a park pass, you must do so before embarking. Reserve in advance, either online or at Bon's office in the Ocean View Hotel.

Bonne Bay Boat Tours BOATING
(2hr trip adult/child $45/19) Bonne Bay boat tours depart from Norris Point wharf, as does a water taxi (adult/child $14/10 round-trip, foot passengers and bikes only) from Norris Point to Woody Point. Both taxi and tour are run by Bon Tours.

Skiing

Many trails in the park's impressive 55km cross-country ski-trail system were designed by Canadian Olympic champion Pierre Harvey. Contact the Main Visitor Centre (p205) for trail information and reservations for backcountry huts.

Cycling

The Corner Brook–based **Cycle Solutions** (☑ 709-634-7100; www.cyclesolutions.ca; Rte 430, Rocky Harbour) offers mountain biking and cycling tours through Gros Morne, from easy half-day rides to hard-core, multiday trips. Prices vary. The office is next to Rocky Harbour's town information center.

✦✦ Festivals & Events

Writers at Woody Point Festival LITERATURE
(☑ 709-453-2900; www.writersatwoodypoint.com; tickets from $20; ☺ mid-Aug) Authors from across Newfoundland, Canada and the world converge at the Woody Point Heritage Theatre for readings. There's also live-music

Gros Morne Theatre Festival THEATER
(☑ 709-243-2899; www.theatrenewfoundland. com; tickets $15-35; ☺ late May–mid-Sep) Eight productions of Newfoundland plays, staged both indoors and outdoors at various locations throughout the summer.

🛏 Sleeping

Rocky Harbour has the most options. Woody Point and Norris Point are also good bets. Places fill fast in July and August.

For backcountry campsites reachable by hiking, inquire at the Main Visitor Centre (p205). Four developed **campgrounds** (☑ 877-737-3783; www.pccamping.ca) lie within the park: Berry Hill (campsites $19-26, oTENTik per night $120, reservation fee $11; ☺ Jun-Sep), Lomond (campsites $19-26, reservation fee $11; ☺ Jun-Oct), Trout River (campsites $19-26, reservation fee $11; ☺ Jun-Sep) and Shallow Bay (campsites $19-26, oTENTik per night $120, reservation fee $11; ☺ Jun-Sep).

Gros Morne Accommodations & Hostel HOSTEL $
(☑ 709-458-3396; www.grosmorneaccommodations andhostel.com; 8 Kin Pl, Rocky Harbour; dm/r $30/70; ☺ 🛜) At this well-kept, newish hostel,

dorms have pinewood bunk beds with thin plastic-covered mattresses. It offers cable TV, a shared kitchen and towels for a small fee. There's no reception on-site. Check in at the Gros Morne Wildlife Museum at 76 Main St, which is a bit of a walk if you're without a car.

Aunt Jane's B&B B&B $
(☑709-453-2485; www.grosmorneescapes.com; Water St, Woody Point; d $70-90; ⏾May-Oct; ♿) This historic house oozes character. Cheaper rooms share a bathroom. It sits beachside, so you may be woken early in the morning by the heavy breathing of whales.

Gros Morne Cabins CABIN $$
(☑709-458-2020; www.grosmornecabins.ca; Main St, Rocky Harbour; cabins $149-209; 🛜) While backed by tarmac, most of these beautiful log cabins are fronted by nothing but ocean (ask when booking to ensure a view). Each has a full kitchen, TV and pullout sofa for children. Bookings can be made next door at Endicott's variety store.

Anchor Down B&B B&B $$
(☑709-458-2901; www.theanchordown.com; Pond Rd, Rocky Harbour; r $100-110; ♿@) The home and its five rooms are pretty simple, but guests have raved about excellent hospitality and cooking from the friendly hosts. Rooms with the higher rate have a Jacuzzi tub.

Middle Brook Cottages CABIN $$
(☑709-453-2332; www.middlebrookcottages.com; off Rte 431, Glenburnie; cabins $99-149; ⏾Mar-Nov; ♿🛜) These all-pinewood, spick-and-span cottages are both perfectly romantic and perfectly kid friendly. They have kitchens and TVs, and you can splash around in the swimming hole and waterfalls behind the property.

✖ Eating

Java Jack's CAFE $
(☑709-458-3004; www.javajacks.ca; Main St, Rocky Harbour; mains $9-19; ⏾7:30am-8:30pm Wed-Mon May-Sep; 🖉) To escape the tyranny of fried food, head to Jack's. This popular artsy outpost offers Gros Morne's best coffees, wraps and soups by day. By night, the upstairs dining room fills hungry, post-hike bellies with fine seafood, caribou and vegetarian fare. Greens come fresh from the property's organic garden.

Earle's CANADIAN $
(☑709-458-2577; Main St, Rocky Harbour; mains $8-14; ⏾9am-11pm) Earle is an institution in

Rocky Harbour. Besides selling groceries and renting DVDs, he has great ice cream, pizza, moose burgers and traditional Newfoundland fare that you can chomp on the patio.

Old Loft SEAFOOD $$
(☑709-453-2294; www.theoldloft.com; Water St, Woody Point; mains $10-21; ⏾11:30am-9pm Jul & Aug, to 7pm May, Jun & Sep) Set on the water in Woody Point, this tiny place is popular for its traditional Newfoundland meals and seafood. Try the crisp onion rings.

ℹ Information

Park admission includes the trails, the Discovery Centre and all day-use areas.

Discovery Centre (☑709-453-2490; Rte 431, Woody Point; ⏾9am-6pm May-Oct) Has interactive exhibits and a multimedia theater explaining the area's ecology and geology. There's also an information desk with maps, daily interpretive activities and a small cafe.

Main Visitor Centre (☑709-458-2066; Rte 430; ⏾8am-8pm May-Oct) As well as issuing day and backcountry permits, it has maps, books, Viking Trail materials and an impressive interpretive area.

Park Entrance Kiosk (Rte 430; ⏾10am-6pm May-Oct) Near Wiltondale.

Rocky Harbour (www.rockyharbour.ca) Online information about lodging, restaurants and attractions in Rocky Harbor.

Western Newfoundland Tourism (www.gowesternnewfoundland.com)

ℹ Getting There & Away

Deer Lake Airport is 71km south of Rocky Harbour. There are shuttle-bus services (p212) from the airport to Rocky Harbour, Woody Point and Trout River.

Port au Choix

Port au Choix, dangling on a stark peninsula 13km off the Viking Trail, houses a large fishing fleet, a quirky museum and a worthy archaeological site that delves into ancient burial grounds.

◉ Sights

Port au Choix
National Historic Site HISTORIC SITE
(☑709-861-3522; www.pc.gc.ca/portauchoix; Point Riche Rd; adult/child $3.90/1.90; ⏾9am-6pm Jun-Sep) These ancient burial grounds of three different Aboriginal groups date back 5500 years. The modern **visitors center** tells of these groups' creative survival in

the area and of one group's unexplained disappearance 3200 years ago. Several good trails around the park let you explore further. Reached by walking, **Phillip's Garden**, a site with vestiges of Paleo-Eskimo houses, is a highlight.

Two trails go to Phillip's Garden. One is the **Phillip's Garden Coastal Trail** (4km), which leaves from Phillip Dr at the end of town. From here you hopscotch your way over the jigsaw of skeletal rock to the site 1km away.

If you continue, it's another 3km to the **Point Riche Lighthouse** (1871), also accessible via the visitors-center road.

Another way to Phillip's Garden is the **Dorset Trail** (8km). It leaves the visitors center and winds across the barrens past stunted trees, passing a Dorset Paleo-Eskimo **burial cave** before finally reaching the site and linking to the Coastal Trail.

Ben's Studio GALLERY
(☑709-861-3280; www.bensstudio.ca; 24 Fisher St; ◷9am-5pm Mon-Fri, 9am-5pm every other weekend Jun-Sep) **FREE** At the edge of town is Ben Ploughman's capricious studio of folk art. Pieces like *Crucifixion of the Cod* are classic and the artist himself welcomes conversation.

🛏 Sleeping & Eating

Jeannie's Sunrise B&B B&B $
(☑709-861-2254; www.jeanniessunrisebb.com; Fisher St; r $79-99; ◷❀) Jeannie radiates hospitality through her spacious rooms, bright reading nook and demeanor as sweet as her muffins. Guests rave about the big breakfasts with homemade jam. Rooms at the lower end of the price spectrum share a bathroom.

Anchor Cafe SEAFOOD $
(☑709-861-3665; Fisher St; mains $12-18; ◷11am-9pm) You can't miss this place – the front half is the bow of a boat – and don't,

because it has great service and the best meals in town. Perfect fries and cod, rich moose stew and original salads are served in cozy leather booths. Lunch specials offer good value and the dinner menu features a wide array of seafood.

St Barbe to L'Anse aux Meadows

As the Viking Trail nears St Barbe, the waters of the gulf quickly narrow and give visitors their first opportunity to see the desolate shores of Labrador. Ferries take advantage of this convergence and ply the route between St Barbe and the Labrador Straits. At Eddies Cove, the road leaves the coast and heads inland.

As you approach the northern tip of the peninsula, Rte 430 veers off toward St Anthony, and two new roads take over leading to several diminutive fishing villages that provide perfect bases for your visit to L'Anse aux Meadows National Historic Site. Route 436 hugs the eastern shore and passes through (from south to north) St Lunaire-Griquet, Gunners Cove, Straitsview and L'Anse aux Meadows village.

L'Anse aux Meadows has a stunning end-of-the-road ambience, surrounded by gemstone isles and bergs. Route 437 heads in a more westerly direction through Pistolet Bay, Raleigh and Cape Onion.

⊙ Sights

★**L'Anse aux Meadows**
National Historic Site HISTORIC SITE
(☑709-623-2608; www.pc.gc.ca/lanseauxmeadows; Rte 436; adult/child/family $11.70/5.80/29.40; ◷9am-6pm Jun-Sep) Leif Eriksson and his Viking friends lived here circa AD 1000. Visitors can see the remains of their waterside settlement: eight wood-and-sod buildings,

---

THE VIKINGS

Christopher Columbus gets the credit for 'discovering' North America, but the Vikings were actually the first Europeans to walk upon the continent. Led by Leif Eriksson, they sailed over from Scandinavia and Greenland some 500 years before Columbus and landed at L'Anse aux Meadows. They settled, constructed houses, fed themselves and even smelted iron out of the bog to forge nails, attesting to their ingenuity and fortitude. That it was all accomplished by a group of young-pup twenty-somethings is even more impressive.

Norse folklore had mentioned a site called 'Vinland' for centuries. But no one could ever prove its existence – until 1968, when archaeologists found a small cloak pin on the ground at L'Anse aux Meadows. Archaeologists now believe the site was a base camp, and that the Vikings ranged much further along the coast.

now just vague outlines left in the spongy ground, plus three replica buildings inhabited by costumed docents. The latter have names such as 'Thora' and 'Bjorn' and simulate Viking chores such as spinning fleece and forging nails. Allow two or three hours to walk around and absorb the ambience.

The premise may seem dull – visiting a bog in the middle of nowhere and staring at the spot where a couple of old sod houses once stood – but somehow this site lying in a forlorn sweep of land turns out to be one of Newfoundland's most stirring attractions.

Be sure to browse the interpretive center and watch the introductory film, which tells the captivating story of Norwegian explorer Helge Ingstad, who rediscovered the site. Also worthwhile is the 3km trail that winds through the barren terrain and along the coast surrounding the interpretive center.

Norstead HISTORIC SITE

(☑709-623-2828; www.norstead.com; Rte 436; adult/child/family $10/6.50/30; ☉9:30am-5:30pm Jun-Sep) Can't get enough of the long-bearded Viking lifestyle? Stop by Norstead, just beyond the turnoff to the national historic site. This re-created Viking village features costumed interpreters smelting, weaving, baking and telling stories around real fires throughout four buildings. Sounds cheesy, but they pull it off with class. There's also a large-scale replica of a Viking ship on hand.

🏃 Activities

★Quirpon

Lighthouse Inn ADVENTURE SPORTS

(☑709-634-2285; www.linkumtours.com; Main Rd; per person package incl boat transfer $250-400; ☉May-Sep) Whales and icebergs skim by this deserted island located 9km west of L'Anse aux Meadows. As remote getaways go, it would be hard to beat this 10-room inn, close by a working lighthouse with an indoor whale-watching station. Package stays include hiking, Zodiac tours and guided kayaking.

🛏 Sleeping & Eating

Hillsview B&B B&B $

(☑709-623-2424; Gunner's Cove; r from $80; ☎) Ina Hill hosts this lovely B&B set in a large modern home with bay views. Rooms have granny-style charm, with comfortable quilt-covered beds. Breakfast features homemade jams.

Viking Village B&B B&B $

(☑709-623-2238; www.vikingvillage.ca; Hay Cove, L'Anse aux Meadows village; s/d from $65/88; ☻☎) A timbered home with ocean views, Viking Village offers comfy, quilted rooms just 1km from the Viking site. Ask for one of the rooms with balcony access and watch the sun rise.

Valhalla Lodge B&B B&B $$

(☑709-623-2018; www.valhalla-lodge.com; Rte 436, Gunners Cove; r $95-115; ☉May-Sep; ☻☎) Sea views from this hilltop location inspired Pulitzer Prize–winning author E Annie Proulx, who penned *The Shipping News* here. Sleep in a simple cottage or in the more modern main lodge with a cozy living-room fireplace and a deck to watch icebergs in comfort. The five-room Valhalla is only 8km from the Viking site.

Snorri Cabins CABIN $$

(☑709-623-2241; www.snorricabins.com; Rte 436, Straitsview; cabins $119; ☉Jun-Sep; ☎) These modern cabins offer simple comfort and great value. They're perfect for families, with a full kitchen, sitting room and a pullout sofa. There's a convenience store on-site.

Northern Delight SEAFOOD $

(☑709-623-2220; Rte 436, Gunners Cove; mains $10-16; ☉8am-9pm) Dine on local favorites such as turbot cheeks and pan-fried cod, fresh lobster and mussels, or just have a 'Newfie Mug-up' (bread, molasses and a strong cup of tea). There's live music on some evenings.

Daily Catch SEAFOOD $$

(☑709-623-2295; 112 Main St, St Lunaire-Griquet; mains $10-26; ☉11am-9pm) A stylish little restaurant serving finely prepared seafood and wine. The basil-buttered salmon gets kudos. Fish cakes, crab au gratin and cod burgers also please the palate.

★Norseman Restaurant & Art Gallery SEAFOOD $$$

(☑709-623-2018; www.valhalla-lodge.com; Rte 436, L'Anse aux Meadows village; mains $20-38; ☉noon-9pm May-Sep) This lovely waterfront outpost ranks among Newfoundland's best. Emphasizing local products and creative preparations, the menu will have you wavering between tantalizing options. Relish a kale Caesar salad with Arctic char, seared scallops or tender Labrador caribou tenderloin. Espresso drinks are served and cocktails come chilled with iceberg ice.

ROUTE 432 & THE FRENCH SHORE

Surprises await along lonely Rte 432. Follow the moose to **Tuckamore Lodge** (☑ 709-865-6361; www.tuckamorelodge.com; Main Brook; r incl breakfast $150-180; @ 🤶), a wood-hewn, lakeside retreat with heavenly beds and home-cooked meals, located smack in the middle of nowhere. Owner Barb Genge arranges fishing, bird-watching, hunting and photography classes with first-rate guides.

The little towns along the coast are known as the **French Shore** (www.frenchshore.com) for the French fishers who lived in the area from 1504 to 1904. Top of the heap is **Conche** with its intriguing sights: a **WWII airplane** that crashed in town in 1942, the seaside **Captain Coupelongue walking trail** past old French grave markers, and a crazy-huge **tapestry** in the local interpretation center.

A woman named Delight runs the sunny **Bits-n-Pieces Cafe** (☑ 709-622-5400; 9 Stage Cove Rd, Conche; mains $10-15; ⊗ 8am-8pm, to 9pm Thu-Sat), ladling out cod cakes, Thai chicken and other satisfying fare. It's about 68km from Tuckamore Lodge; take Rte 433 to unpaved Rte 434.

❶ Getting There & Away

The road to the Northern Peninsula is narrow and potholed. Travel extra slow in the rain. Access by private vehicle.

A ferry travels between St Barbe and Blanc Sablon, Québec (near the Labrador border) daily. The two-hour trip across the Strait of Belle Isle is run by **Labrador Marine** (☑ 866-535-2567; www.labradormarine.com; adult/child/vehicle $8.25/6.60/25); see the website for schedules.

St Anthony

Congratulations. You've made it to the end of the road, your windshield has culled the insect population and you have seen two World Heritage Sites. After such grandeur, St Anthony may be a little anticlimactic. Though not pretty, it possesses a rough-hewn charm and inspiring hiking and whale- and iceberg-watching.

Grenfell is a big name around here. Sir Wilfred Grenfell was a local legend and, by all accounts, quite a man. This English-born and educated doctor first came to Newfoundland in 1892 and, for the next 40 years, traveling by dogsled and boat, built hospitals and nursing stations and organized much-needed fishing cooperatives along the coast of Labrador and around St Anthony.

◉ Sights

Fishing Point Park   PARK

The main road through town ends at Fishing Point Park, where a lighthouse and towering headland cliffs overlook the sea. The **Iceberg Alley Trail** and **Whale Watchers**

Trail both lead to cliff-top observation platforms – the names say it all.

There's also a visitor center–cafe and an adjacent craft shop; in the side room there's a polar bear display. Creatures like this guy have been known to roam St Anthony from time to time as pack ice melts in the spring.

Grenfell Interpretation Centre   HISTORIC BUILDING

(www.grenfell-properties.com; West St; multi-site admission adult/child/family $10/3/22; ⊗ 8am-5pm Jun-Sep) A number of local sites pertaining to pioneering doctor Wilfred Grenfell are subsumed under Grenfell Historic Properties. The Interpretation Centre, opposite the hospital, is a modern exhibit recounting the historic and sometimes dramatic life of Grenfell. Its **handicraft shop** has some high-quality carvings and artwork, as well as embroidered parkas made by locals – proceeds go to maintenance of the historic properties.

Grenfell Museum   MUSEUM

(www.grenfell-properties.com; multi-site admission adult/child/family $10/3/22; ⊗ 9am-6pm Jun-Sep) Admission to the Grenfell Historic Properties also includes Grenfell's beautiful mansion, now the Grenfell Museum. It's behind the hospital, about a five-minute walk from the waterfront. Dyed burlap walls and antique furnishings envelop memorabilia, including a polar-bear rug and, if rumors are correct, the ghost of Mrs Grenfell.

☞ Tours

Northland Discovery Tours   BOATING

(☑ 709-454-3092; www.discovernorthland.com; 2½hr tour adult/child $60/32; ⊗ 9am, 1pm & 4pm

Jun-Sep) Northland offers highly recommended cruises for whale- or iceberg-viewing that leave from the dock behind the Grenfell Interpretation Centre on West St. If you tend to get seasick, medicate before this one.

🛏 Sleeping & Eating

Fishing Point B&B   B&B $$
(☎709-454-3117; www.bbcanada.com/6529.html; Fishing Point Rd; r $110; ❀🛜) This teensy place clings to the rocks en route to the lighthouse and offers the best harbor view in St Anthony. Get up early, enjoy a bountiful breakfast and watch the boats head out to sea. The three rooms each have their own bathroom.

Lightkeeper's
Seafood Restaurant   SEAFOOD $$
(☎709-454-4900; Fishing Point Park; mains $12-20; ⏱11:30am-8pm Jun-Sep) Smack in the shadow of the lighthouse, this restaurant gazes out on icebergs and whales. Unfortunately, you're shelling out for the view, not the rather ordinary food. Fat fish burgers with fries beat out the bland cod and mashed potato dinner.

ℹ Getting There & Away

The St Anthony Airport is 22 miles northwest of town. **PAL Airlines** (☎800-563-2800; www.provincialairlines.ca; St Anthony Airport) makes the trip from St John's daily.

If you're leaving St Anthony by car, you have two options: backtrack entirely along Rte 430, or take the long way via Rte 432 along the east coast and Hare Bay. This will meet up with Rte 430 near Plum Point, between St Barbe and Port aux Choix.

WESTERN NEWFOUNDLAND

Western Newfoundland presents many visitors with their first view of the Rock, thanks to the ferry landing at Port aux Basques. It's big, cliffy, even a bit forbidding with all those wood houses clinging to the jagged shoreline against the roaring wind. From Port aux Basques, poky fishing villages cast lines to the east, while Newfoundland's second-largest town, Corner Brook, raises its wintry head (via its ski mountain) to the northeast.

Corner Brook

POP 19,900

Newfoundland's number-two town is pretty sleepy, though skiers, hikers and anglers will find plenty of action. The handsome Humber Valley, about 10km east, is where it's going on. Centered on the Marble Mountain ski resort, the area experienced a huge development boom until the bottom fell out of the international economy. But now the area is heating up again. The valley offers adventure-sport junkies places to play, while the city itself sprawls with big-box retailers and a smoke-belching pulp and paper mill.

◉ Sights

Captain James Cook Monument   MONUMENT
(Crow Hill Rd) While this cliff-top monument is admirable – a tribute to James Cook for his work in surveying the region in the mid-1760s – it's the panoramic view over the Bay of Islands that is the real payoff.

Railway Society of Newfoundland   MUSEUM
(☎709-634-2720; Station Rd, off Humber Rd; admission $3; ⏱9am-8pm Jun-Aug) Within historic Humbermouth Station, it has a good-looking steam locomotive and some narrow-gauge rolling stock that chugged across the province from 1921 to 1939.

🏃 Activities

Marble Mountain   SKIING
(☎709-637-7616; www.skimarble.com; Hwy 1; day pass adult/child $60/35; ⏱10am-4:30pm Sat-Thu, 9am-9:30pm Fri Dec-Apr) Marble Mountain is the lofty reason most visitors come to Corner Brook. With 35 trails, four lifts, a 488m vertical drop and annual snowfall of 5m, it offers Atlantic Canada's best skiing. There are snowboarding and tubing parks, as well as night skiing on Friday, plus there's Oh My Jesus (you'll say it when you see the slope).

When the white stuff has departed, the **Steady Brook Falls Trail** (500m) leads from the ski area's rear parking lot, behind the Tim Hortons, to a cascade of water that tumbles more than 30m.

Cycle Solutions   CYCLING
(☎709-634-7100; www.cyclesolutions.ca; 35 West St; ⏱9am-6pm Mon-Wed & Sat, to 8:30pm Thu & Fri) This sweet bike shop runs local cycling and caving tours; it's attached to the Brewed Awakening coffee shop.

Corner Brook

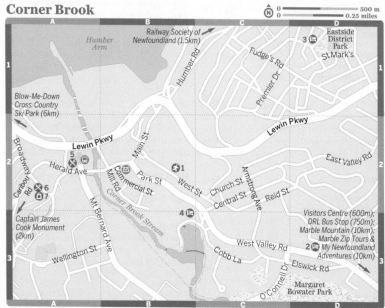

Corner Brook

⊙ Activities, Courses & Tours

1 Cycle Solutions B2

⬤ Sleeping

2 Brookfield Inn D3
3 Garden Hill Inn D1
4 Glynmill Inn B3

✕ Eating

Brewed Awakening .... (see 1)
5 Gitano's A2
6 Taste of Jamaica A2
Thistle's Place .... (see 5)

⬤ Shopping

7 Newfoundland Emporium A2

Blow-Me-Down
Cross-Country Ski Park SKIING

(☑ 709-639-2754; www.blowmedown.ca; Lundi-gran Dr; day pass $20; ⊙ sunrise-9pm Dec-Apr) It has 50km of groomed trails; ski rentals (per day $15) are available. It's about 6km southwest of downtown.

Marble Zip Tours ADVENTURE SPORTS

(☑ 709-632-5463; www.marbleziptours.com; Thistle Dr; 2hr tour adult/child $99/89) It's the highest zip line in eastern Canada. Strap in near the mountaintop, and zigzag platform to platform down a gorge traversing Steady Brook Falls. It'll take your breath away. Tours depart four to five times daily. The office is past Marble Mountain's lodge.

My Newfoundland
Adventures ADVENTURE SPORTS

(☑ 709-638-0110; www.mynewfoundland.ca) If skiing doesn't get the adrenaline flowing, you must try snow-kiting (a windsurfing-meets-snowboarding endeavor). Or there's snowshoeing, ice fishing and even ice climbing. Canoeing, salmon fishing and caving all take place in the warmer seasons. Pretty much anything is possible with these patient folks; no experience is required. The office is at Marble Mountain's base by the Tim Hortons.

🛏 Sleeping & Eating

Brookfield Inn B&B **$**

(☑ 709-639-3111; brookfieldinn@gmail.com; 2 Brookfield Ave; r $60-90; ⊕ 🛜) A cool couple runs this B&B. The white-frame house has homey rooms, with hardwood floors and plump beds. In the morning make your own breakfast from the eggs, bacon, cheeses and breads in the well-stocked kitchen. In the evening watch the sun set from the deck. The house dogs will amble up for a scratch if you want.

Glynmill Inn   HOTEL $$
(☑709-634-5181; www.steelehotels.com; 1 Cobb Lane; r incl breakfast $135-165; ✻@🛜) Lawns and gardens surround the gracious Tudor-style Glynmill. It was built originally for the engineers supervising the pulp mill's construction in the 1920s, at that time the largest project in the history of paper making. The inn retains an elegant if somewhat faded ambience.

Garden Hill Inn   B&B $$
(☑709-634-1150; www.gardenhillinn.ca; 2 Ford's Rd; r $95-120; ⊖🛜) Gordon Bell's rambling green house tops a hill that's a 15-minute walk from downtown. The eight smallish, comfy rooms all have private bathroom; rooms 1 and 4 have harbor views. Breakfast includes coffee, fruit and blueberry pancakes.

★ Taste of Jamaica   JAMAICAN $
(www.tasteofjamaica.ca; 33 Broadway; mains $8-16; ⊗11:30am-10pm Tue-Sun) Get instantly transported to the Caribbean with these mouth-watering preparations of jerk chicken, stuffed avocados and spiced kabobs. Chef Kirk Myers, a native islander, does his best with the local selection of produce.

Brewed Awakening   COFFEE $
(www.brewedawakening.ca; 35 West St; baked goods $3-7; ⊗7am-9pm Mon-Fri, 8am-9pm Sat, 9am-6pm Sun; 🛜) This small, funky, art-on-the-wall coffee shop pours fair-trade, organic java done right. It's attached to the groovy bike shop Cycle Solutions.

Thistle's Place   CAFE $
(☑709-634-4389; www.thistledownflorist.com; Millbrook Mall, Herald Ave; sandwiches $6-11; ⊗9am-5pm Mon-Sat; 🛜) Walk through the front flower shop to reach the smoked meat, curried chicken and whole-wheat vegetable wraps at the wee cafe out the back.

Gitano's   MEDITERRANEAN $$
(☑709-634-5000; www.gitanos.ca; Millbrook Mall, Herald Ave; tapas $8-14, mains $22-45; ⊗11:30am-2pm Mon-Fri, 5-9pm Sun-Thu, to 10pm Fri & Sat; 🛜) 🍃 Behind Thistle's Place and owned by the same family, Gitano's dishes up *estofado* (stewed sweet potatoes, chickpeas and figs over couscous), pastas and locally sourced tapas (try the saltfish cakes). Live jazz wafts through the supper-club-esque room on weekends.

🛍 Shopping

Newfoundland Emporium   GIFTS & SOUVENIRS
(☑709-634-9376; 11 Broadway; ⊗9am-5pm Mon-Sat) A trove of local crafts, music, antiques and books.

ℹ Information

CIBC Bank (☑709-637-1700; 9 Main St; ⊗10am-5pm Mon-Fri)

Post Office (14 Main St; ⊗9am-5pm Mon-Fri)

Visitors Centre (☑709-639-9792; www.cornerbrook.com; 15 Confederation Dr; ⊗9am-5pm) Just off Hwy 1 at Exit 5. Has a craft shop.

Western Memorial Regional Hospital (☑709-637-5000; 1 Brookfield Ave)

ℹ Getting There & Away

Corner Brook is a major hub for bus services in Newfoundland. **DRL** (☑709-263-2171; www.drl-lr.com; Confederation Dr) stops on the outskirts of town at the Irving Gas Station, just off Hwy 1 at exit 5 across from the visitor center.

All other operators use the **bus station** (☑709-634-7777; Herald Ave, Millbrook Mall) in the Millbrook Mall building. The following are shuttle vans. Prices are one way. You must make reservations.

Burgeo Bus (☑709-634-7777, reservations 709-886-6162; bus station, Millbrook Mall) Runs to Burgeo ($40 cash only, two hours) departing at 3pm Monday through Friday. Leaves Burgeo between 8am and 9am.

Deer Lake Airport Shuttle (☑709-634-4343) Picks up from various hotels en route to Deer Lake Airport ($22, 45 minutes) three to five times daily.

Eddy's (☑709-643-2134; bus station, Millbrook Mall) Travels to/from Stephenville ($25, 1¼ hours) twice daily on weekdays, once daily on weekends.

Gateway (☑709-695-9700; bus station, Millbrook Mall) Runs to Port aux Basques ($40,

---

OFF THE BEATEN TRACK

STEPHENVILLE ON STAGE

As the drive into town past deserted hangars, piles of rusted pipes and tract housing portends, Stephenville is hardly a tourism hub. Yet it's well worth a detour for the **Stephenville Theatre Festival** (☑709-643-4553; www.stephenvilletheatrefestival.com; Stephenville; ⊗Jul & Aug). Featuring cutting-edge Newfoundland plays, it also stirs the pot with a good dose of the Bard and Broadway.

ⓘ APPALACHIAN TRAIL

Think the **International Appalachian Trail** ends in Québec? Think again. It picks up in Newfoundland, where another 1200km of trail swipes the west coast from Port aux Basques to L'Anse aux Meadows. The province has linked existing trails, logging roads and old rail lines through the Long Range Mountains, part of the Appalachian chain. It's a work in progress, but some of the most complete sections are around Corner Brook and the Blomidon Mountains. See www.iatnl. com for trail details.

three hours) on weekdays at 3:45pm. Departs Port aux Basques at 7:45am.

Martin's (☑ 709-453-2207, 709-458-7845; bus station, Millbrook Mall) Operates weekdays, departing for Woody Point ($18, 1½ hours) and Trout River ($20, two hours) at 4:30pm. Returns from Trout River at 9am.

Pittman's (☑ 709-458-2486; bus station, Millbrook Mall) Runs to Rocky Harbour ($35, two hours) via Deer Lake on weekdays at 4:30pm. Departs Rocky Harbour at noon.

Blomidon Mountains

The Blomidon Mountains (aka Blow Me Down Mountains), heaved skyward from a collision with Europe around 500 million years ago, run along the south side of the Humber Arm, west of Corner Brook. They're tantalizing for hikers, providing many sea vistas and glimpses of the resident caribou population. Some of the trails, especially ones up on the barrens, are not well marked, so topographical maps and a compass are essential for all hikers. Further on, Blow Me Down Provincial Park has beaches and scenery.

🏃 Activities

Many trails are signposted off Rte 450, which runs west from Corner Brook along the water for 60km.

Copper Mine Trail   HIKING
(York Harbour) This moderately difficult 7km trail by York Harbour provides awesome views of the Bay of Islands and also links to the International Appalachian Trail (IAT).

Blow Me Down Brook Trail   HIKING
(Frenchman's Cove) One of the easiest and most popular trails in the Blomidon range, this 5km trail begins west of Frenchman's Cove at a parking lot. The trail can be followed for an hour or so; for more avid hikers it continues well into the mountains, where it becomes part of the IAT.

🛌 Sleeping

The only accommodations is a provincial-park campground.

Blow Me Down Provincial Park CAMPGROUND $
(☑ 709-681-2430; www.nlcamping.ca; Rte 450; campsites $18, per vehicle $5; ☉ Jun-Aug) Nice campsites in a beach setting.

Port au Port Peninsula

The large peninsula west of Stephenville is a French-speaking area, a legacy of the Basque, French and Acadians who settled the coast starting in the 1700s. Today, the culture is strongest along the western shore between **Cape St George** and **Lourdes**. Here children go to French school, preserving their dialect, which is now distinct from the language spoken in either France or Québec.

In Port au Port West, near Stephenville, the gorgeous Gravels Trail (3km) leads along the shore, passing secluded beach after secluded beach. Nearby in Felix Cove, stop at **Alpacas of Newfoundland** (www.alpacasof nfld.ca; Rte 460, Felix Cove; ☉ 9am-6pm) FREE for an entertaining farm tour.

Port Aux Basques

POP 4170

Traditional wood houses painted aqua, scarlet and sea green clasp the stony hills, but it's all about the ferry in Port aux Basques. Most visitors come here to jump onto the Rock from Nova Scotia, or jump off for the return trip. That doesn't mean the town isn't a perfectly decent place to spend a day or night. Laundry blows on the clotheslines, boats moor in backyard inlets and locals never fail to wave hello to newcomers.

Port aux Basques (occasionally called Channel-Port aux Basques) was named in the early 16th century by Basque fishers and whalers who came to work the waters of the Strait of Belle Isle. The town is a convenient place to stock up on food, fuel and money before journeying onward.

Port aux Basques

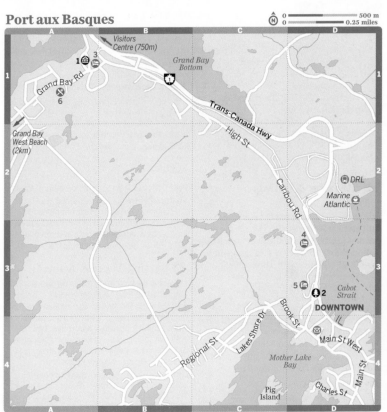

◉ Sights

Several scenic fishing villages lie to the east.

Grand Bay West Beach BEACH
(Kyle Lane) Located a short distance west of town, the long shore is backed by grassy dunes, which are breeding grounds for the endangered piping plover. The **Grand Bay West Trail** leaves from here and flirts with the coast for 10km.

Railway Heritage Centre MUSEUM
(☑709-695-5775; off Hwy 1; museum $2, railcars $5; ⊙10am-8pm Jul & Aug) The center has two things going on. One is a museum stuffed with shipwreck artifacts. Its showpiece is the astrolabe, a striking brass navigational instrument made in Portugal in 1628. The device is in remarkable condition and is one of only about three dozen that exist in the world. Restored railway cars are the center's other drawcard.

Port aux Basques

Scott's Cove Park PARK
(Caribou Rd) This park, with its restored boardwalk, candy-colored snack shacks and boat-shaped amphitheater, is the place to mingle with townsfolk and listen to live music.

WORTH A TRIP

CAPE ANGUILLE

The westernmost point of Newfoundland is Cape Anguille, located 58km north of Port aux Basques. Drive out to explore the windswept lighthouse, where you can watch blue whales and stay in an adjoining lightkeeper's cottage.

Cape Anguille Lighthouse Inn (☑709-634-2285; www.linkumtours.com; 1 Lighthouse Rd; r incl breakfast $100-120; ⊙May-Sep) is a restored but rustic century-old lighthouse with comfortable rooms in homespun style. Don't expect phones or TVs – the idea is to get away here. Seasonal blue-whale-watching and bird-watching can be done on-site. Spring 10 extra bucks for an ocean view. Dinner with locally sourced fish and berries is available ($30). It's 45 minutes north of Port aux Basques in moose country; pay particular attention if driving at dusk or at night.

🛏 Sleeping & Eating

Radio Station Inn   B&B $
(☑709-695-2906; jggillam@hotmail.com; 100 Caribou Rd; r from $69; ⊙May-Oct) Up on the bluff overlooking the harbor, the five-room Radio Station is one of the closest lodgings to the ferry (a 10-minute walk). Three rooms have their own bathroom, the other two share, and there's a kitchen for guest use.

Hotel Port aux Basques   HOTEL $$
(☑709-695-2171; www.hotelpab.com; 1 Grand Bay Rd; r $85-170; ☀☎) A runner-up to the most popular hotel in town, this one is older but has more character. An executive suite features Jacuzzi tub. Kids stay for free.

St Christopher's Hotel   HOTEL $$
(☑709-695-3500; www.stchrishotel.com; Caribou Rd; r $121-146; ☀☎) This is the most professional digs in town, with a small fitness room and a seafood restaurant called the Captain's Room (p214). Odd-numbered rooms have harbor views.

Alma's   CANADIAN $
(☑709-695-3813; Mall, Grand Bay Rd; mains $7-15; ⊙8am-8pm Mon-Sat) Follow the locals into this no-frills family diner for heaping portions of cod, scallops, fish cakes and berry pies. Your best bet for a good meal in town, it serves breakfasts, burgers and sandwiches too.

Captain's Room   SEAFOOD $
(☑709-695-3500; St Christophers Hotel, Caribou Rd; mains $10-17; ⊙7am-1:30pm & 5-10pm) A mixed bag for fine dining with a nautical theme. Think seafood and moose burgers. The authentic potato skins beat the fries.

❶ Information

Bank of Montréal (83 Main St; ⊙10am-5pm Mon-Fri)

Hospital (☑709-695-2175; Grand Bay Rd)

Post Office (3 Main St; ⊙8:30am-5pm Mon-Fri)

Visitors Centre (☑709-695-2262; www.port auxbasques.ca; Hwy 1; ⊙9am-5pm Mon-Fri May-Oct) Information on all parts of the province; sometimes open later to accommodate ferry traffic.

❶ Getting There & Away

Marine Atlantic (☑800-341-7981; www. marine-atlantic.ca; adult/child/car $42/20/110) The Marine Atlantic Ferry connects Port aux Basques with North Sydney in Nova Scotia. It operates year-round, typically with two sailings daily during winter and three or four sailings between mid-June and mid-September. Crossings take about six hours.

DRL (☑709-263-2171; www.drl-lr.com) Bus stops at the ferry terminal. Buses leave at 8am for Corner Brook ($42, 3½ hours) and St John's ($124, 13½ hours); cash only.

Cape Ray

Adjacent to John T Cheeseman Provincial Park and 19km north of Port aux Basques is Cape Ray. The coastal scenery is engaging, and the road leads up to the windblown **Cape Ray Lighthouse** (⊙8am-8pm Tue-Sun Jul & Aug) FREE. After the original 1871 lighthouse was struck by lightning and burned in 1885, it was replaced by the current version. This area is the southernmost known Dorset Paleo-Eskimo site, dating from 400 BC to AD 400. Thousands of artifacts have been found here and some dwelling sites can be seen.

John T Cheeseman Provincial Park (www.env.gov.nl.ca/env/parks; Rte 408) rests next to the beach and has top-notch facilities.

There are some fine hikes in the area. **Table Mountain Trail** (Hwy 1) is more like a rugged road (but don't even think about driving up it) and begins on Hwy 1 opposite the exit to Cape Ray. The hike leads to a

518m plateau, where there are ruins from a secret US radar site and airstrip from WWII. It's not a hard hike, but it's 12km long so allow three or four hours.

If you're looking for somewhere to camp, **John T Cheeseman Provincial Park Campground** (709-695-7222; www.nlcamping.ca; Rte 408; campsites $18-28, per vehicle $5; Jun-Sep) has 92 campsites featuring picnic table and fire pit. Water and pit toilets are available.

South Coast

Visitors often ignore Rte 470, and that's a shame because it's a beauty. Heading east out of Port aux Basques for 45km and edging along the shore, the road rises and falls over the eroded, windswept terrain, looking as though it's following a glacier that plowed through yesterday.

Isle aux Morts (Island of the Dead) got its label compliments of the many shipwrecks that occurred just offshore over some 400 years. Named after a family famous for daring shipwreck rescues, the **Harvey Trail** (7km) twists along the rugged shore and makes a stirring walk. Look for the signs in town.

Another highlight is the last settlement along the road, **Rose Blanche**, an absolutely splendid, traditional-looking village nestled in a cove with a fine natural harbor – a perfect example of the classic Newfoundland fishing community. From here follow the signs to the restored **Rose Blanche Lighthouse** (709-956-2052; www.roseblanchelighthouse.ca; admission $6; 9am-9pm May-Oct). Built in 1873, it's the last remaining granite lighthouse on the Atlantic seaboard.

If you think Rose Blanche is too pretty to leave, stay the night at the **Rose Sea Guest House** (709-956-2872; www.roseblanche.ca; r $95-110; Jun-Oct). It offers five rooms in a recently refurbished traditional home right on the water. It also offers workshops on craft-making or geology.

KILLICK COAST

The peninsula just north and west of St John's is known as the Killick Coast, a 55km one-way journey that makes a good day trip. About 8km north of St John's, Memorial University's Ocean Sciences Centre (p216) has outdoor exhibits in summer. Secluded and rocky, **Middle Cove** and **Outer Cove** are a bit further north on Rte 30 – they're perfect for a beach picnic.

North at the head of **Torbay Bight** is the enjoyably short **Father Troy Path**, which hugs the shoreline. The view from **Cape St Francis** is worth the bumpy gravel road from Pouch Cove. There's an old battery and you may see a whale or two.

OFF THE BEATEN TRACK

SOUTH COAST OUTPORTS

If you have the time and patience, a trip across the south coast with its wee fishing villages – called outports – is the best way to witness Newfoundland's unique culture. These little communities are some of the most remote settlements in North America, reachable only by boat as they cling to the convoluted shore. An anomaly is Burgeo (population 1460), connected by an easy road trip; it has an unspoiled, isolated feel, yet good amenities for travelers. **Ramea** (population 525) is another uncomplicated option. It's an island just offshore from **Burgeo** with lodging and activities.

When the sun is out and the sea shimmers between endless inlets and islands, Burgeo is a dream. Climb the stairs to Maiden Tea Hill and look out in admiration. The 7km of white-sand beaches at Sandbanks Provincial Park may be the best in the entire province (at least the piping plover who dawdle there think so).

Author Farley Mowat lived in Burgeo for several years, until he penned A Whale for the Killing and irked the locals. The book tells the story of how Burgeo's townsfolk treated an 80-tonne fin whale trapped in a nearby lagoon. Let's just say the outcome was not a happy one for the whale. Locals can point out the lagoon and Mowat's old house, though expect to get an earful about it.

Ramea Retreat (709-625-2522; www.easternoutdoors.com; 2 Main St, Ramea; dm/r $39/89; May-Nov;) is an adventure lodge with 10 hostel beds and options for kayaking, bird-watching, hiking and fishing tours. In addition, the lodge owners rent rooms in various vintage clapboard houses scattered around Ramea.

West of St John's on Topsail Rd (Rte 60), just past Paradise, is **Topsail Beach**, with picnic tables, a walking trail and panoramic views of Conception Bay and its islands.

To reach Bell Island, go 14km northwest from St John's to Portugal Cove and the ferry.

⊙ Sights

Bell Island Community Museum   MUSEUM
(☑ 709-488-2880; adult/child $12/5; ⊙ 11am-6pm Jun-Sep) Miners here used to work in shafts under the sea at the world's largest submarine iron mine. Conditions were grim: the museum tells tales of adolescents working 10-hour days by candlelight. Visitors can also go underground; dress warmly.

Ocean Sciences Centre   AQUARIUM
(☑ 709-864-2459; www.mun.ca/osc; ⊙ 10am-5pm Jun-Aug) **FREE** Right out of *20,000 Leagues Under the Sea*, this university center examines the salmon life cycle, seal navigation, ocean currents and life in cold oceanic regions. The outdoor visitors area consists of local sea life in touch tanks. It's about 8km north of St John's, just before Logy Bay.

From the city, take Logy Bay Rd (Rte 30), then follow Marine Dr to Marine Lab Rd and take it to the end.

Bell Island   ISLAND
(www.tourismbellisland.com) The largest of Conception Bay's little landmasses makes an interesting day trip from St John's. It was the only place on the continent hit by German forces in WWII. U-boats torpedoed the pier and 80,000 tonnes of iron ore in 1942. At low tide, you can still see the aftermath. The island sports a pleasant mélange of beaches, coastal vistas, lighthouses and trails.

ⓘ Getting There & Away

Visitors will need a car to explore the Killick Coast. The **Bell Island Ferry** (☑ 709-895-6931; www.tw.gov.nl.ca; per passenger/car $2.50/7; ⊙ hourly 6am-10:30pm) provides quick transit between Portugal Cove and the island.

LABRADOR

POP 26,700

Undulating, rocky, puddled expanses form the sparse, primeval landscape of Labrador. Home to Inuit and Innu, its 293,000 sq km sprawl toward the Arctic Circle. If you ever wanted to imagine the world before humans, this is the place.

Inuit and Innu have occupied Labrador for thousands of years. Until the 1960s they were the sole inhabitants, alongside a few longtime European descendants known as 'liveyers,' who eked out an existence by fishing and hunting from tiny villages that freckled the coast. The interior was virgin wilderness.

The simplest way to take a bite of the Big Land is via the Labrador Straits region, which connects to Newfoundland via a daily ferry. From there, a solitary road connects the interior's main towns. The aboriginal-influenced northern coast is accessible only by plane or supply ferry. Here, the newly designated Torngat Mountains National Park offers a privileged glimpse into ultra-remote wilderness.

Labrador is cold, wet and windy, and its bugs are murderous. Facilities are few and far between throughout the behemoth region, so planning ahead is essential.

Labrador Straits

And you thought the Northern Peninsula was commanding? Sail the 28km across the Strait of Belle Isle and behold a landscape even more windswept and black-rocked. Clouds rip across aqua-and-gray skies, and the water that slaps the shore is so cold it's purplish. Unlike the rest of remote Labrador, the Straits region is easy to reach and exalted with sights such as Red Bay and a slew of great walking trails that meander past shipwreck fragments and old whale bones. 'Labrador Straits' is the colloquial name for the communities that make up the southern coastal region of Labrador.

Blanc Sablon to L'Anse au Clair

After arriving by ferry or plane in Blanc Sablon, Québec, and driving 6km northeast on Rte 510 you come to Labrador and the gateway town of L'Anse au Clair. The town makes a good pre-ferry base, with sleeping and basic dining options and a useful visitor center.

🛏 Sleeping & Eating

Northern Light Inn   HOTEL **$$**
(☑ 709-931-2332; www.northernlightinn.com; 56 Main St, L'Anse au Clair; campsites $25-35, d $115-129; ❄ 🐾) The modern, well-kept Northern Light Inn is a tour-bus favorite, with a dining room that serves the best meals in town. Even-numbered rooms have harbor views. The campground has showers and laundry.

Labrador

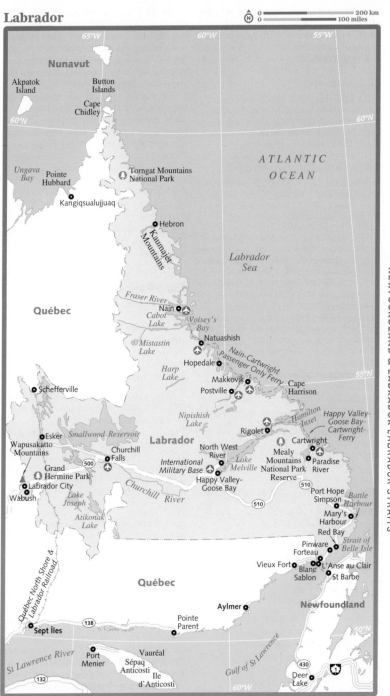

Northern Light Inn Dining Room CANADIAN $$
(☑709-931-2332; 56 Main St, L'Anse au Clair; mains $12-27; ⊙7am-9pm Sun-Thu, to 10pm Fri & Sat) Your best bet for food in town, it serves classic fare and seafood.

ℹ Information

Visitors Centre (☑709-931-2013; www.labra dorcoastaldrive.com; Rte 510, L'Anse au Clair; ⊙9am-5pm Jun-Oct) The Straits' excellent visitor center is in an old church that doubles as a small museum.

ℹ Getting There & Around

The **MV Apollo** (☑709-535-0810; www.labrador marine.com; adult/child/car $8.25/6.60/25; ⊙May-early Jan) sails the two hours between St Barbe in Newfoundland and Blanc Sablon from May to early January. The boat runs one to three times daily (8am and 6pm). Schedules vary from day to day. In July and August, it's not a bad idea to reserve in advance (though there's a $10 fee). Note that the ferry terminal in Blanc Sablon operates on Newfoundland Time and not Eastern Time (as in the rest of Québec).

PAL Airlines (☑800-563-2800; www.palairlines.ca) flies to Blanc Sablon from St John's and St Anthony. Just to confuse you, departure times from the airport are on Eastern Time versus Labrador Straits (ie Newfoundland) Time.

Rental cars are available at the airport from **Eagle River Rent-a-Car** (☑709-931-3300, 709-931-2352).

Forteau to Pinware

Heading northeast on Rte 510 you'll pass Forteau, L'Anse Amour, L'Anse au Loup, West St Modeste and Pinware. In Forteau, the **Overfall Brook Trail** (4km) shadows the coast and ends at a 30m waterfall. Six houses comprise the village of **L'Anse Amour**; among its many attractions, **L'Anse Amour Burial Mound** (L'Anse Amour Rd) is the oldest burial monument in North America. A small roadside plaque marks the 7500-year-old site.

LABRADOR FAST FACTS

➡ Population: 26,700

➡ Area: 294,330 sq km

➡ Biggest town: Labrador City

➡ Time zones: Labrador Straits are on Newfoundland Time, while the rest of Labrador (starting at Cartwright) is on Atlantic Time, ie 30 minutes behind Newfoundland.

On the same road, **Point Amour Lighthouse** (☑709-927-5825; www.pointamourlighthouse.ca; L'Anse Amour Rd; adult/child $6/4; ⊙9:30am-5pm May-Oct) is well worth climbing for the outrageous panoramas up top. The **Raleigh Trail** (2km) takes you by the site and warship fragments on the beach.

Past L'Anse au Loup, the **Battery Trail** (4km) meanders through tuckamore forest to the summit of the Battery, unfurling sweeping sea views. The road veers inland at Pinware, crisscrossing the Pinware River. The white water after the one-lane bridge is renowned for its salmon fishing.

⟳ Tours

Labrador Adventures TOURS
(☑709-931-2055; www.tourlabrador.ca) Provides knowledgeable guides for Straits-oriented hikes or day tours by SUV. Arranges all-inclusive overnight packages. A terrific way to see the area.

🛏 Sleeping & Eating

Pinware River Provincial Park CAMPGROUND $
(☑709-927-5516; www.nlcamping.ca; Rte 510; campsites $18; ⊙Jun-Sep) A 22-site campground with drinking water, pit toilets, showers and dumping station. Good fishing and trails are nearby. Located 53km from the Blanc Sablon ferry.

Grenfell Louie A Hall B&B B&B $$
(☑709-931-2916; www.grenfellbandb.ca; Willow Ave, Forteau; r $95-110, cottages $165; ⊙May-Oct) This charming B&B is in the old nursing station where generations of Labrador Straits folk were born – there's also rumor of a few ghosts floating around. With quilts and country decor, the five simple rooms share two bathrooms. Some have sea views.

Max's House HISTORIC HOTEL $$$
(Point Amour Lighthouse; ☑709-931-2840; www.tourlabrador.ca; Point Amour Lighthouse; cottage $256; ⊙Jun-early Oct; 🛜) On the grounds of the Point Amour Lighthouse, this historic building was the residence of lighthouse keeper Max Sheppard. The house features five guest rooms with a well-stocked kitchen and two bathrooms, sleeping 10. Dinner is served in the lighthouse, there's also whale- and iceberg-viewing. No phones on-site.

Dot's Bakery BAKERY $
(☑709-927-5311; Rte 510, L'Anse au Loup; snacks $4-8; ⊙7am-11pm Mon-Sat) Fresh doughnuts, pies, and pizzas are served at this small bakery.

TORNGAT MOUNTAINS NATIONAL PARK

With otherworldly scenery of spindle peaks and rocky headlands that plunge to a turquoise river basin, **Torngat Mountains National Park** (☑ 709-922-1290; www.pc.gc.ca/torngat) is nature at its wildest. It's also an important area for scientific research, with some of the world's oldest rock (3.9 billion years) and a rare population of seals in a freshwater lake habitat. The **Kaumajet Mountains**, south of the park, also make for an out-of-this-world hiking experience.

Sitting at Labrador's wintry tip, access is by charter flight, private vessel or cruise ship only. Healthy polar-bear numbers means that armed bear guards are required for visitors. The Inuit-run Torngat Mountains Base Camp and Research Station (p220) offers package tours. The park headquarters is in Nain, where staff can direct you to local Inuit guides.

Seaview Restaurant   CANADIAN **$$**
(Rte 510, Forteau; mains $10-25; ⊘ 11am-9pm) Enjoy some fresh seafood or chow down on the famous fried chicken and tender caribou. A grocery store and jam factory are also on-site.

Red Bay

Spread between two venues, Red Bay National Historic Site (declared a Unesco World Heritage site in 2013) chronicles the discovery of three 16th-century Basque whaling galleons on the seabed here. Well preserved in the ice-cold waters, the vestiges of the ships tell a remarkable story of what life was like here some four centuries ago.

In the 16th century Red Bay was the largest whaling port in the world, with more than 2000 residents. Have a look at the reconstructed *chalupa* (a small Basque dingy used for whale hunting) and some of the other relics in the museum. Then hop in a small boat ($2) to nearby **Saddle Island**, where there is a self-guided interpretive trail around the excavated land sites. Allow at least two or three hours for the museum and island.

◉ Sights & Activities

Across the bay, the amazing **Boney Shore Trail** (2km) skirts along the coast and passes ancient whale bones (they pretty much look like rocks) scattered along it. **The Tracey Hill Trail** climbs a boardwalk and 670 steps to the top of American Rockyman Hill for a bird's-eye view of the harbor; it takes about 20 minutes each way.

Red Bay National Historic Site   HISTORIC SITE
(☑ 709-920-2051; www.pc.gc.ca/redbay; Rte 510; adult/child/family $7.80/3.90/19.60; ⊘ 9am-5pm Jun-Sep) In the mid-16th century, Basque whalers came to the Strait of Belle Isle to hunt large numbers of right and bowhead whales and harvest their oil to light lamps

all around Europe. The major whaling port of Red Bay is now a national historic site and World Heritage Site. View the original Basque artifacts, remains, and a restored *chalupa* (whaling boat) on-site.

Selma Barkham Town Centre   MUSEUM
($2; ⊘ 9am-5pm Jul-Sep) Selma Barkham was a tireless investigator of local history. Check out the stories she uncovered in this pleasant museum, which also features a 15m, 400-year-old North Atlantic right whale skeleton.

🛏 Sleeping & Eating

Basinview B&B   B&B **$**
(☑ 709-920-2002; blancheearle@hotmail.com; 145 Main St; s/d with shared bath $60/70, d $90) Basinview B&B is a simple four-room, shared bathroom home right on the water.

Whaler's Station   INN **$$**
(☑ 709-920-2156; www.redbaywhalers.ca; 72-76 West Harbour Dr; r $95-135) Divided between several buildings, these rustic but comfortable lodgings provide a central base for visits to the historic site. Some rooms offer water views. They all have private bathrooms, TV, a microwave and refrigerator. There's also an on-site restaurant.

Whaler's   SEAFOOD **$$**
(mains $9-20; ⊘ 8am-8pm) For fish-and-chips with partridgeberry pie, look no further than this friendly restaurant, a focal point for visitors to the bay. It also serves substantial breakfasts, and picnickers can order boxed lunches.

Battle Harbour

Sitting on an island in the Labrador Sea is the elaborately restored village and saltfish premises of Battle Harbour. Now a national historic district, it used to be the unofficial 'capital' of Labrador during the early 19th century, when fishing schooners lined its docks. Another claim to fame: Robert E Peary gave his first news conference here after reaching the North Pole in 1909.

⭐**Battle Harbour**
Heritage Properties INN $$
(☎709-921-6325; http://battleharbour.com; r $75-245, package with 3 meals, tour & transport from $545; ⊙Jun-Sep; 🛜) In addition to a classic inn, there are adorable heritage homes and cottages throughout the settlement. Think decks with sea views and little distraction: there are no cars, cell signal or TVs on the island. Instead you will find hiking trails with good berry-picking prospects and boat rides. Wi-fi is available in a common lounge area of the inn, which also serves meals.

Battle Harbour Dining Room CANADIAN $$
(Battle Harbour Inn; meals incl with lodgings; ⊙8am-6pm) Gourmet dining with set serving times; it's part of a package deal with lodging on the island.

ℹ️ Getting There & Away

Battle Harbour is accessed by boat from Mary's Harbour (departure at 11am, one hour). The passenger ferry is included with accommodations.

Northern Coast

North of Cartwright up to Ungava Bay there are a half-dozen small, semitraditional Inuit communities accessible only by sea or air along the rugged, largely unspoiled mountainous coast. Torngat Mountains National Park is the (literal) high point.

In 1993, geologists discovered copper, cobalt and large quantities of nickel on the shores of Voisey's Bay near Nain. Mining could pump billions into the provincial economy over the next few decades, but it also compromises both the environment and the way of life of native Innu and Inuit people.

⊙ Sights

The first port of call on the northern coast is **Makkovik**, an early fur-trading post and a traditional fishing and hunting community. Both new and old-style crafts are sold here.

Further north in **Hopedale** visitors can look at the old wooden Moravian mission church (1782). This national historic site (☎709-933-3864; $5; ⊙8:30am-7pm Jul-Oct)

also includes a store, residence, some huts and a museum collection.

Natuashish is a new town that was formed when the troubled village of Utshimassit (Davis Inlet) was relocated to the mainland in 2002. The move was made after a 2000 study showed that 154 of 169 youths surveyed had abused solvents (ie sniffed gasoline) and that 60 of them did it on a daily basis.

The last stop on the ferry is **Nain**. Fishing has historically been the town's main industry, but this is changing due to the Voisey's Bay nickel deposit. It's the last town of any size as you go northward.

🛏️ Sleeping

Most travelers use the ferry as a floating hotel. For those wishing to get off and wait until the next boat, it usually means winging it for a room, as only Postville, Hopedale and Nain have official lodging.

Amaguk Inn HOTEL $$
(☎709-933-3750; www.amagukinn.ca; 3 Harbour Dr, Hopedale; s/d $130/155; 🛜) This 18-room inn also has a dining room (meals $15 to $20), and a lounge where you can get a cold beer. Airport transfers are also available.

Atsanik Lodge HOTEL $$
(☎709-922-2910; atsaniklabrador@msn.com; Sand Banks Rd, Nain; r $125-180; 🛜) This large, 25-room lodge and its restaurant (meals $15 to $22) are your best bet in Nain.

⭐**Torngat Mountains Base**
Camp & Research Station LODGE $$$
(☎855-867-6428; www.thetorngats.com; Torngat Mountains National Park; 4-night all-inclusive packages from $5200; ⊙Jul & Aug) The only way to enjoy Torngat Mountains National Park overnight is at this well-heeled base camp in the park. Guests sleep in comfortable yurts or more luxuriant dome tents with heat and electricity. There are also showers and chef-made meals. At camp, activities include hiking, boating and heli-tour options. An electrified fence keeps out polar bears.

ℹ️ Getting There & Away

Daily flights to North Coast communities leave from Happy Valley-Goose Bay with air carriers **Air Labrador** (☎800-563-3042; www.airlabrador.com) and **PAL Airlines** (Provincial Airlines; ☎800-563-2800; www.palairlines.ca).

The passenger-only **MV Northern Ranger** (www.labradorferry.ca; 1-way adult/child $157/78) plies this section of coast from mid-June to mid-November. It leaves once per week, making the three-day (one way) journey between Happy Valley-Goose Bay and Nain, stopping in Makkovik, Hopedale and Natuashish along the way. Check online for the ever-evolving schedule and fares.

Central Labrador

Making up the territorial bulk of Labrador, the central portion is an immense, sparsely populated and ancient wilderness. Paradoxically, it also has the largest town in Labrador, Happy Valley-Goose Bay, home to a military base. The town (population 7600) has all the usual services, but unless you're an angler or hunter, there isn't much to see or do.

Goose Bay was established during WWII as a staging point for planes on their way to Europe. The airport is also an official NASA alternate landing site for the space shuttle.

⊙ Sights

Labrador Interpretation Centre   MUSEUM
(☎709-497-8566; www.therooms.ca/exhibits/regional-museums; 2 Portage Rd, North West River; ☉9am-4:30pm Mon-Sat, 1-4:30pm Sun) **FREE** This is the provincial museum, which holds some of Labrador's finest works of art. It's in North West River, via Rte 520.

Northern Lights Building   MUSEUM
(☎709-896-5939; 170 Hamilton River Rd, Happy Valley-Goose Bay; ☉10am-5:30pm Tue-Sat) **FREE** Hosts a military museum, interesting lifelike nature scenes and simulated northern lights.

🛏 Sleeping & Eating

Big Land B&B   B&B $
(☎709-896-2082; http://biglandbedandbreakfast.com; 34b Palliser Cres, Happy Valley-Goose Bay; r $85; ☎⊛⊛) Friendly family-run B&B that also welcomes pets. Rooms are well-equipped and continental breakfasts with homemade bread and regional jam are served.

Royal Inn & Suites   HOTEL $$
(☎709-896-2456; www.royalinnandsuites.ca; 5 Royal Ave, Happy Valley-Goose Bay; s/d/ste from $120/130/150; ⊛☎) The Royal has a variety of rooms to choose from; many have kitchens. It also loans out satellite phones to drivers through the region-wide safety program.

Davis' B&B   B&B $$
(☎709-896-5077; valleybb5077@gmail.com; 14 Cabot Cres, Happy Valley-Goose Bay; s/d $100/120; ☎) Family atmosphere and caribou sausages await you at Davis' four-room home.

El Greco   PIZZA $
(☎709-896-3473; 133 Hamilton River Rd, Happy Valley-Goose Bay; mains $9-18; ☉4pm-1am Sun-Wed, to 3am Thu-Sat) Popular for pizzas and takeout, El Greco also serves pasta and Greek-style kabobs. It's near the Royal Inn.

Mariner's Galley   SEAFOOD $$
(☎709-896-9301; 25 Loring Dr, Happy Valley-Goose Bay; mains $7-24; ☉6am-9pm) Come here for fried cod tongues with scruncheons (pork rind) or crab cocktail. Visitors rave about the friendly service and buffet options.

❶ Information

Visitor Information Centre (www.tourismlabrador.com; 6 Hillcrest Rd, Happy Valley-Goose Bay; ☉8:30am-8pm Mon-Fri, 9am-5pm Sat & Sun; ☎) Provides information on Central Labrador, plus brochures and maps. Events are announced on the Facebook page. There's also a useful town website (www.happy-valley-goosebay.com).

❶ Getting There & Away

AIR

Daily flights are available to Happy Valley-Goose Bay from St John's via Deer Lake and Halifax. Montréal has daily flights to Wabush. The following offer services:

Air Canada (☎888-247-2262; www.aircanada.com)

PAL Airlines (Provincial Airlines; ☎800-563-2800; www.palairlines.ca)

BOAT

You can reach Happy Valley-Goose Bay by the seasonal passenger-only ferry **MV Northern Ranger** (☎709-896-2262; www.labradorferry.ca; adult/child to Nain $157/78; ☉Jul-Aug).

CAR & MOTORCYCLE

From Happy Valley-Goose Bay you can take the mostly gravel Rte 500 west to Churchill Falls and then on to Labrador City. The drive to Labrador City takes about seven hours. There are no services until Churchill Falls, so stock up. The Royal Inn & Suites has free satellite phones you can take on the road (part of a region-wide safety program).

The partially paved Rte 510 heads toward Cartwright (383km) and L'Anse au Clair (623km).

Before leaving, contact the Department of Transportation & Works (www.roads.gov.nl.ca) for the latest conditions. Many rental-car agreements prohibit driving on the Trans Labrador Hwy or will not provide insurance, some have vehicles specifically designated for the route. You can hire cars from **National** (☎709-896-5575), among others.

Labrador West

Just 5km apart and 15km from Québec, the twin mining towns of Labrador City (population 9400) and Wabush (population 1900) are referred to collectively as Labrador West, and this is where the western region's population is concentrated. The largest open-pit iron ore mine in the world is in Labrador City, though the nearby Wabush mine closed in 2014 due to a slump in steel demand. The landscape is massive and the celestial polychromatic artwork can expand throughout the entire night sky.

⊙ Sights & Activities

Grande Hermine Park   PARK
(☑709-282-5369; ⊙Jun-Sep) From Wabush, 39km east on Rte 500 is Grande Hermine Park, which has a beach and some fine scenery. The **Menihek hiking trail** (15km) goes through wooded areas with waterfalls and open tundra. Outfitters can take anglers to excellent fishing waters.

Gateway Labrador   MUSEUM
(☑709-944-5399; 1365 Rte 500; ⊙9am-4pm Mon-Fri, 10am-5pm Sat) FREE In the same building as the visitor center is Gateway Labrador and its Montague Exhibit Hall, where 3500 years of human history and culture, including the fur trade, are represented with intriguing artifacts and displays.

🏃 Activities

The Wapusakatto Mountains are 5km from town, popping up off the vast landscape interspersed with flat northern tundra. A good, cold dry snow falls from late October to late April, so the ski season here is much longer than anywhere else in Canada.

Menihek Nordic Ski Club   SKIING
(☑709-944-5842; www.meniheknordicski.ca; day pass adult/child $20/15) Offers 30km of trails with world-class cross-country skiing. The Canadian national team trains here, but novices are also welcome. There are lessons, skate skiing, night skiing options and rentals for skis and snowshoes.

Smokey Mountain Ski Club   SKIING
(☑709-944-2129; www.smokeymountain.ca; Smokey Mountain Rd; ⊙Nov-Apr) There's still some steeps at this small snow-sports resort with 845m of vertical. It's serviced by a double chairlift and poma lift with a quad chairlift in the works. It's 5km from Labrador City.

🛏 Sleeping & Eating

Ptarmigan's Nest   B&B $
(☑709-944-3040; theptarmigansnest@gmail.com; 28 Snow's Dr; r $98; 🐾) A lakeside retreat located in a quiet area 10 minutes from Labrador City with elegant, classic decor. Includes continental breakfast.

Wabush Hotel   HOTEL $$
(☑709-282-3221; www.wabushhotel.com; 9 Grenville Dr, Wabush; r $165-175; ❋🐾) Centrally located in Wabush, this chalet-style 68-room hotel has spacious and comfortable rooms. The dining room has a popular buffet. Also the place to get free satellite phones on loan for driving the remote regions of the province.

Carol Inn   MOTEL $$
(☑709-944-7736; www.carolinn.ca; 215 Drake Ave, Labrador City; s/d $140/165; ❋🐾) All 20 rooms here have a kitchenette. There's also a dining room with proper meals and a pub.

Sushi Lab   SUSHI $
(☑709-944-4179; 118 Humphrey Rd, Labrador City; mains $6-16; ⊙11am-2pm & 5-11pm Mon-Fri, 5-11pm Sat & Sun) This pleasant dining experience is nouveau-Labrador all the way. Order from a selection of dozens of sushi rolls with an iPad, and you will be pleasantly rewarded. For less adventurous diners, there's also Chinese food or pizza.

ℹ Information

Destination Labrador (www.destinationlabrador.com) is comprehensive tourism website with special events, services and tips, and there's a **visitors centre** (☑709-944-5399; www.labradorwest.com; 1365 Rte 500) just west of Labrador City, in the Gateway Labrador building.

ℹ Getting There & Away

AIR

Air Canada (☑888-247-2262; www.aircanada.com), **PAL Airlines** (Provincial Airlines; ☑800-563-2800; www.palairlines.ca), **Air Inuit** (☑800-361-2965; www.airinuit.com) and **Air Labrador** (p220) fly into Happy Valley-Goose Bay and Wabush, with some other destinations.

CAR & MOTORCYCLE

Fifteen kilometers west from Labrador City along Rte 500 is Fermont, Québec. From there, Rte 389 is mainly paved (with some fine gravel sections) and continues south 581km to Baie Comeau.

Happy Valley-Goose Bay is a seven-hour drive east on Rte 500, considered a good gravel road.

Budget (☑709-282-1234) has an office at the airport; rental cars may not be driven on Rte 500.

Understand Nova Scotia, New Brunswick & Prince Edward Island

Nova Scotia, New Brunswick & Prince Edward Island Today

Should they stay or should they go? These provinces with their scenic coastlines, strong family traditions and low cost of living are enticing places for winter-hardy folks to live and raise a family, but recent years have seen a marked decline in professional opportunities that often leaves ambitious youth little choice but to move away. It takes a certain amount of creativity to survive in Atlantic Canada without living the hard and uncertain life of a fisher.

Best on Film

Children of a Lesser God (1986) An award-winning romance between a young deaf woman working as a school custodian and a handsome new teacher. Filmed in New Brunswick.

Titanic (1997) James Cameron's Hollywood blockbuster successfully embellishes on the *Titanic*'s fateful voyage.

The River King (2004) An investigator into the apparent suicide of a young boy at an exclusive school suspects there is more to the story than meets the eye.

Best in Print

The Shipping News (E Annie Proulx) A series of tragic events sees an upstate New York reporter relocate to his ancestral home in Newfoundland.

Anne of Green Gables (Lucy Maud Montgomery) The famous series featuring a shy, red-haired orphan who was mistakenly sent to a farm on PEI.

A Whale for the Killing (Farley Mowat) A moving exposé of the cruelty of the centuries-old whaling industry.

Fall on Your Knees (Anne-Marie MacDonald) Four sisters and five generations of family secrets.

There's No Place Like Home

Until recently, you could sit down at any dinner table in Atlantic Canada and hear the same thing:

'My ___ [fill in the blank: sister, cousin, neighbor] just left for Alberta to work in the oil fields.'

Outward migration has been the single biggest issue facing the Atlantic provinces during the past 15 to 25 years, but the region is finally experiencing a small rebound. As the provinces' traditional industries – fishing, logging and mining – continue to fall deeper into decline, a glimmer of hope is coming from newer industries, particularly gypsum mining and offshore oil and natural gas. Although Alberta's oil fields offer high-paying industrial jobs, and plenty of people still leave to make their living where it makes economic sense, the quality of life, low cost of living and hope of finding work closer to home is keeping an increasing number of folks on the Atlantic coasts.

Nova Scotia has been the mover and shaker of the crowd by becoming a hub for Canada's defense and aerospace sector (which also tips into Prince Edward Island). In fact, a surprising 40% of the country's military assets are found in this low-key province. Halifax was also given a massive $25 billion, 30-year military shipbuilding contract in 2011 from the Canadian government; this will theoretically create more than 10,000 jobs during its time span. While some locals complain that most of the jobs go to skilled workers brought in from other provinces, the economic impact of so many paid employees can only be positive on local businesses.

Getting Creative

Canada's Atlantic provinces have some of the nation's highest unemployment rates, with Newfoundland leading the pack at around 12%. In an apparent backlash towards the area's historically conservative bent and the perceived inability of the formerly governing center-right parties to deal with the situation, the four maritime provinces are, at the time of writing, newly led by recently installed Liberal governments.

This a region that embraces an independent and entrepreneurial spirit, one that is born of generations of battlers and survivors. Plenty of creative folks recognize the decline of traditional industries as opportunity for growth and change: they refurbish fishing boats into whale-watching boats, or turn mines into attractions that teach about ecology. Meanwhile, Halifax's arts culture has helped create the fourth-largest film industry in the nation, and small businesses, manufacturing and technology are all growing sectors that are keeping more and more young graduates from the city's universities employed. In other provinces, small-scale businesses add to the ever-plodding agricultural economy.

The region's abundant natural resources remain, but the resources that are most valuable economically are undergoing a transformation: cod fishing may be on its way out, for example, but offshore oil drilling has arrived to take its place. Fracking, a controversial method of natural gas extraction, is growing, particularly in out-of-the-way areas in Newfoundland and Labrador. While this is great for creating local jobs, opponents state that the chemicals used in the process could contaminate the soil, groundwater and eventually the oceans, as well as cause small earthquakes.

What remains to be seen is how these resources will be developed. Has the region learned enough from past mistakes to move forward responsibly and sustainably? It's this struggle that will loom largest over Atlantic Canada in the coming years.

POPULATION: **1.84 MILLION**

UNEMPLOYMENT: **9.8%**

MEDIAN INCOME: **$69,210**

LIFE EXPECTANCY: **80 YEARS**

- - - - - - - - - - - - - - - - - - - -

if Atlantic Canada were 100 people

32 would be Scottish   14 would be French
28 would be English   2 would be Aboriginal
23 would be Irish   1 would be African

- - - - - - - - - - - - - - - - - - - -

belief systems
(% of population)

Roman Catholic	United Church
65	13

Anglican	Other	No religion
9.5	8	3.5

- - - - - - - - - - - - - - - - - - - -

population per sq km

CANADA   USA   FRANCE

≈ 4 people

History

The history of this long-inhabited region, which has had its fair share of hardship, colonization, enforced exodus, genocide and disaster, is a complicated one, with a number of disparate cultures at different times each laying claim to land that was inhabited for millennia by aboriginal tribes. Add to that an environment whose beauty can be outweighed by its brutality and you begin to get a sense of the resilient people who have chosen to call Eastern Canada home.

The First Fishers

Atlantic Canada's first inhabitants, the Paleoindians, walked into Labrador 9000 years ago. The harsh, frozen land didn't make life easy or lengthy for these folks. Next came the Maritime Archaic Indians, hunters and gatherers who survived on the sea's bountiful fish-and-seal dinners. They ranged throughout Atlantic Canada, Maine and into parts of Labrador between 7500 and 3500 years ago and are known for their ceremonial burials and other religious and magical practices, evidenced at sites such as Newfoundland's Port au Choix. They mysteriously disappeared around 1000 BC.

The next to tend the land were the Mi'kmaq and Maliseet peoples in the Maritimes and the Beothuk people in Newfoundland – all members of the Algonquin-speaking eastern woodlands tribes. The Mi'kmaq and Maliseet practiced agriculture and lived in fairly permanent settlements. The Beothuk were seminomadic and paddled the area in their birch-bark canoes. It was the Beothuk and their ceremonially ocher-coated faces who were dubbed 'red men' by the arriving Europeans, a name soon applied to all of North America's indigenous groups.

None of these people fared well once Europeans arrived and introduced diseases, land conflict and war to the mix. While the Mi'kmaq and Maliseet still occupy parts of Atlantic Canada, the last person of Beothuk ethnicity died in 1829, and a unique language and culture was lost forever.

Age of European Discovery

Viking celebrity Leif Erikson and his tribe of adventurous seafarers from Iceland and Greenland were the first Europeans in North America.

First Nations Culture

Lennox Island First Nation, Price Edward Island

Port au Choix National Historic Site, Newfoundland

Bear River First Nation Heritage & Cultural Centre, Nova Scotia

TIMELINE	1000 BC	AD 1000	1492
	After hanging around for a few thousand years eating fish and seals and developing complex ceremonial practices, the Maritime Archaic Indians inexplicably disappear.	Viking Leif Erikson and crew wash up at L'Anse aux Meadows, create the New World's first European settlements, repair their ships and smelt iron.	Christopher Columbus, under the crown of Spain, stumbles upon the Bahamas and gets credit for 'discovering' America; John Cabot sails five years later and lands on Cape Breton and Newfoundland.

Around AD 1000, they poked around the eastern shores of Canada, establishing winter settlements and way stations for repairing ships and restocking supplies, such as at L'Anse aux Meadows in Newfoundland. The local Canadian Aboriginal tribes did not exactly roll out the welcome mat for these intruders, who eventually tired of the hostilities and withdrew.

The action didn't heat up again until after 1492 when Christopher Columbus stumbled upon some small islands in the Bahamas. Other European monarchs, excited by his 'discovery', quickly sponsored expeditions of their own. In 1497 Giovanni Caboto, better known as John Cabot, sailed under a British flag as far west as Newfoundland and Cape Breton. Although there's no evidence of where he first made landfall, the village of Bonavista in eastern Newfoundland usually gets the nod.

Cabot didn't find a passage to China but he did find cod, then a much-coveted commodity in Europe. Soon, hundreds of boats were shuttling between Europe and the fertile new fishing grounds. Several were based at Red Bay in Labrador, which became the world's biggest whaling port during the 16th century.

AVAST! PIRATES ON THE HORIZON

Pirates began to ply and plunder Atlantic Canada's waters soon after Europeans arrived to colonize the area. Peter Easton was one of the region's most famous pirates. He started out as an English naval officer in 1602. But when King James downsized the Royal Navy the next year, stranding Easton and his men in Newfoundland without any money, they understandably got pissed off and decided to use the resources at hand (ie boats and a bad attitude) to become pirates. By 1610 Easton was living large in Harbour Grace, commanding a fleet of 40 ships and a crew of 5000 men. The money piled in for several more years, until he eventually retired to France, married a noblewoman and became the Marquis of Savoy.

Black Bart, aka Bartholomew Roberts, was another boatsman who made quite a splash in the local plundering business. He became a pirate after being captured by another, and he took to the lifestyle. Sort of. He liked the booty and the clothing it enabled (crimson waistcoat, scarlet plumed hat, gold necklaces), but he disliked booze and gambling. He also encouraged prayer among his employees. No one mutinied though, because his pirating prowess was legendary. For example, in 1720 he sailed into Newfoundland's Trepassey Bay aboard a 10-gun sloop with a crew of 60 men, where they were able to capture 21 merchant ships manned by 1200 sailors.

Halifax put a unique spin on its pirate history when the local government began sponsoring the plunder. The pirates were called privateers, and during the War of 1812 the government sanctioned them to go out and get the goods and then provided them with waterfront warehouses to store it all. You can see where the action took place at the Privateer's Warehouse. The South Shore town of Liverpool commemorates the era by hosting a rollicking Privateer Days festival.

1528	1755	1763	1769
Fishing village of St John's bobs up as North America's first European settlement but belongs to no nation; instead it serves fishing fleets from around the world.	English round up and deport thousands of French Acadians from Bay of Fundy region for not pledging allegiance to the Crown. Many move to Louisiana to become known as Cajuns.	Treaty of Paris boots France out of Canada after France loses the Seven Years' War. France retains St Pierre and Miquelon, however, which remain an overseas French territory to this day.	The colony of Prince Edward Island is created from the larger Nova Scotia and will one day become Canada's smallest province; English is the official language.

Early European Settler Sites

·····················

Highland Village Museum (Scottish), Cape Breton, Nova Scotia

·····················

Colony of Avalon Historic Site (British), Ferryland, Newfoundland

·····················

Cupids (British), Avalon Peninsula, Newfoundland

·····················

Port Royal National Historic Site (French), Annapolis Royal, Nova Scotia

About this time, French explorer Jacques Cartier also was sniffing around Labrador. He was looking for gold and precious metals, but found only 'stones and horrible rugged rocks,' as he wrote in his journal in 1534. So he moved on to Québec – but not before bestowing Canada with its name. Scholars say it comes from *kanata*, a Huron-Iroquois word for village or settlement, which was written in Cartier's journal and later transformed by mapmakers to Canada.

Settlers Move In

So we've got fish, furs and nice juicy chunks of land – is it any wonder Europe started salivating?

St John's lays claim to being the oldest town in North America, first settled around 1528. It belonged to no nation; rather it served fishing fleets from all over Europe. By 1583 the British claimed it, and St John's had the distinction of being the first colony of the empire.

The French weren't just sitting on their butts during this time. In 1604 explorer Samuel de Champlain and his party spent the winter on St Croix Island, a tiny islet in the river on the present international border with Maine. The next year Champlain and his fur-trader patron Sieur de Monts moved their small settlement to Port Royal in the Annapolis Valley, which would soon become an English–French flashpoint.

The French revved up their colonization in 1632 by bringing in a load of immigrants to LaHave on Nova Scotia's south shore. More settlers arrived in 1635, and soon the French had spread throughout the Annapolis Valley and the shores of the Bay of Fundy – a rich farming region they called Acadia.

French & English at War

The French were galling the English, and the English were infuriating the French. Both had claims to the land – hadn't Cabot sailed here first for England? Or was it Cartier for France? – but each wanted regional dominance. They skirmished back and forth in hostilities that mirrored those in Europe, where wars raged throughout the first half of the 18th century.

Things came to head in 1713 with the Treaty of Utrecht, which ended Queen Anne's war (1701–13) overseas. Under its provisions the majority of Nova Scotia and Newfoundland went to the British, and Cape Breton Island, Prince Edward Island and what is today New Brunswick went to the French. That Acadia was now British was a particularly bitter spoonful for the French; the Brits had even overtaken Port Royal and renamed it Annapolis Royal, after Queen Anne.

The French reorganized and decided to give regional dominance another shot. In 1719 they began construction of a fortress at Louisbourg on Cape Breton Island to protect their interests. Bit by bit the fortified town grew.

1784	**1812**	**1840**	**1864**
New Brunswick is created as a separate province from Nova Scotia in order to appease the tension between the huge influx of Loyalists from the USA with the original settlers.	Halifax's local government takes advantage of the War of 1812 by sponsoring 'privateers' to plunder ships then store it all along the city's waterfront.	Cunard Line shipping company founded in Halifax providing the fastest link to England and boosting the region's economy; immigrants from around Europe and the UK arrive in droves.	Fathers of the Confederation meet in Charlottetown and create the framework for a new country called Canada. The deal is sealed by the *British North America Act* in London three years later.

The British took note and in 1745 sent out a colonial army from Massachusetts to capture Louisbourg. It fell after a 46-day siege. A treaty a few years later returned it to France.

And so it went, with control of the region ping-ponging, until 1754 when the French and Indian Wars (sometimes called the Seven Years' War) began and ramped up the fighting to a new level.

Memo to Acadians: Get Out

Charles Lawrence, the security-conscious British governor of Nova Scotia, had had enough. A war was going on and when the French Acadian citizens in his territory refused to swear allegiance to Britain, his suspicions mounted to fever pitch. In 1755, he ordered the Acadians to be rounded up and deported.

In a tragic chapter of history known as the Great Expulsion, the British burned villages and forced some 14,000 men, women and children onto ships. Grand Pré was the heart of the area from which the Acadians were removed. Many headed for Louisiana and New Orleans; others went to various Maritime points, the Caribbean or back to Europe.

The government gave their lands in the Annapolis Valley to 12,000 New England colonists called 'planters.' After peace was restored, some Acadians chose to return from exile but they were forced to settle on the less favorable 'French Shore' between Yarmouth and Digby.

LOYALIST COLONIES IN THE MARITIMES

Some Acadians returned to Canada but *merde alors,* they hadn't seen the end of English-speaking colonization. Many American colonists who remained loyal to the King of England during the American Revolutionary War fled or were driven out of the USA once the British were defeated; these families resettled throughout the British Empire, including the Maritime provinces while others went to the British West Indies.

Loyalists were offered free land by the British and their arrival meant an influx of English speakers west and east of Québec. This new division of language and culture divided the country into British 'Upper Canada' and French 'Lower Canada.' It also led to the division of Nova Scotia into two provinces, modern-day Nova Scotia and New Brunswick.

Meanwhile, many Loyalists from the American south brought their slaves as they were assured by law that their slaves would remain their property. However, there were also freed black Loyalists who had been granted their freedom by fighting for the British during the Revolution. The government helped these ex-slaves resettle in Canada but they were met far less kindly than their white compatriots.

Ultimately, the influx of Loyalists to Canada helped strengthen ties with Britain and increased antipathy to the United States, which contributed to keeping Canada an independent country in North America.

1912	1917	1925	1942
Titanic sinks off the southern coast of Newfoundland and rescue ships are sent from Halifax – most of the recovered bodies are buried in Halifax.	A munitions ship collides with another ship in Halifax Harbour creating the 'Halifax explosion,' the largest man-made explosion before the A-bomb, killing some 1900 people.	Fed up and hungry Cape Breton coal miners stage a 155-day strike and end up with a 7% pay cut. The industry continues to decline from here on.	Bell Island, Newfoundland, is torpedoed by German forces and 69 people are killed; this is the only location on the American continent to receive a German hit during WWII.

Ultimately, the English won the French and Indian Wars, and the French colonial era in the region ended. At the Treaty of Paris in 1763, France handed Canada over to Britain – except for two small islands off the coast of Newfoundland, named St Pierre and Miquelon, which remain staunchly French to this day.

A Perfect Union in Prince Edward Island

All through the first half of the 19th century, shipbuilding made New Brunswick and Nova Scotia wealthy, and Nova Scotia soon boasted the world's fourth-largest merchant marine. The Cunard Line was founded at Halifax in 1840, and immigration from Scotland and Ireland flourished.

In 1864 Charlottetown on Prince Edward Island served as the birthing room for modern Canada. At the town's Province House, a group of representatives from Nova Scotia, New Brunswick, Prince Edward Island, Ontario and Québec got together and hammered out the framework for a new nation. It took two more meetings – one in Québec City, the other in London – before parliament passed the *British North America Act* in 1867. And so began the modern, self-governing state of Canada. The date the act became official, July 1, is celebrated as Canada's national holiday.

Newfoundland, ever true to its independent spirit, did not join the confederation until 1949.

THE TITANIC'S CORONER, UNDERTAKER & MOURNER

When RMS *Titanic* sank in April 1912, the rescue and recovery effort started in Halifax, the nearest port city with rail connections. John Snow, owner of JA Snow Funeral Homes, sailed to the disaster site to pull bodies from the ocean, bringing with him 125 coffins, ice, iron, and all the embalming fluid in the city.

Some bodies were buried at sea (the iron ensured the coffins sank) and others were brought back to Snow's funeral home. The building now houses the Five Fishermen (p54) restaurant; the bodies were stored in today's wine cellar. Snow helped devise a system to match bodies with possessions so they could be identified and returned to their families, or buried with a marked tombstone. Eventually 150 bodies were interred in Halifax, earning the town the grim title of '*Titanic*'s coroner, undertaker and mourner.'

Five years later, the city was struck by another tragedy, known as the Halifax Explosion, when two ships collided in Halifax Harbour. Snow came out of retirement to help Halifax deal with hundreds of bodies, and ensure as many as possible got a proper burial. Snow's Funeral Home still operates out of Halifax (nowadays in the far northwest of town at 339 Lacewood Dr). It unveiled a *Titanic* memorial placard in its front garden in 2012.

By Jon Tattrie, Halifax-based author and journalist

1962	1969	1992	1997
Trans-Canada Hwy officially opens spanning 7821km from St John's to Victoria, British Columbia, and linking Canada's 13 provinces – it will be completed in 1971.	New Brunswick extends its Equal Opportunity Plan when it passes the *Official Languages Act* making it the only constitutionally bilingual province in Canada.	Cod moratorium imposed and thousands of fisherfolk lose their livelihood. While hoped to be only a temporary measure, the cod stocks do not make a comeback.	The 12.9km Confederation Bridge linking PEI and New Brunswick opens at a cost of $1 billion.

World Wars

During both world wars Atlantic Canada played a key role as a staging area for the convoys that supplied Britain. The wars also boosted local economies and helped transition the region from an agricultural to an industrial base.

Halifax was the only city in North America to suffer damage during WWI. In December 1917, the *Mont Blanc*, a French munitions ship carrying TNT and highly flammable benzol, collided with the *Imo* in Halifax Harbour. The 'Halifax Explosion' ripped through the city, leveling most of Halifax's north end, injuring 9000 and killing 1900 people.

Newfoundland had the dubious honor of being the only place in North America directly attacked by German forces during WWII. In 1942, just offshore from Bell Island near St John's, German U-boats fired on four allied ore carriers, sinking them; 69 lives were lost. The Germans fired a torpedo at yet another carrier, but the projectile missed and instead struck inland at Bell Island's loading pier – thus making it the sole spot on the continent to take a straight-on German hit. That same year, the Germans also torpedoed a Newfoundland ferry sailing in the Cabot Strait near Port aux Basques; 137 people died.

Modern Times

It wasn't until 1960 that Canada's Aboriginal people were finally granted Canadian citizenship. Even into the late 1960s, Aboriginal children were being removed from their families and sent away to residential schools to 'civilize' them; many were abused. Land-rights claims regarding the schools are still winding their way through Canadian courts, while the damage such policies inflicted continues to haunt Aboriginal communities.

Meanwhile, in Newfoundland in the 1950s, the provincial government also was enforcing a resettlement program. People living in isolated fishing communities were being strongly 'encouraged' to move inland where the government could deliver schools, health care and other services more economically. One method for encouraging villagers was to cut ferry services. Many communities had no road access so this made them inaccessible – people were squeezed out of their ancestral homes in this way.

The later 20th century was particularly harsh to the region's biggest industries: coal mining and fishing. Cape Breton's coal mines started to tank in the 1960s as its product fell out of favor in the marketplace; the mines shut for good in the 1990s. In 1992, the codfishing moratorium was put in place, and many fisherfolk and fish-plant workers – a huge percentage of the population, especially in Newfoundland – lost their livelihoods. The offshore oil and tourism industries have been trying to pick up the slack, but many people are leaving the region to find work elsewhere in Canada.

HISTORY WORLD WARS

Loyalist, French & British Holds

Louisbourg (French), Nova Scotia

King's Landing Historical Settlement (Loyalist), Upper St John River Valley, New Brunswick

Quidi Vidi (French & British), Newfoundland

Early-20th-Century Sites

Fort Amherst, St John's, Newfoundland

Cape Spear National Historic Site, St John's, Newfoundland

Titanic burial grounds, Halifax, Nova Scotia

Pier 21 Centre, Halifax, Nova Scotia

2001	2003	2005	2010
Cape Breton's last coal mine shuts down paving the way for outward migration and clean-up of Sydney Tar Ponds, Nova Scotia, North America's largest toxic-waste site.	Hurricane Juan hits Halifax, passing through central Nova Scotia and Prince Edward Island leaving extensive destruction, eight fatalities and $30 million worth of damage.	Canada legalizes gay marriage throughout the country. Most provinces and territories permitted it anyway, but now hold-out Prince Edward Island has joined the ranks.	Hurricane Igor strikes Newfoundland, causing widespread flooding, destroying bridges, homes, and roads. Damages are estimated at $200 million.

Maritimes Music

If Atlantic Canada were a bowl of chowder, music would be the stock in which everything floats. As a visitor you'll run into live performances everywhere, be they called ceilidhs (*kay*-lees), shindigs or kitchen parties. Even if you never gave fiddle music a second thought, the festive ambience will make you want to join in, sing along or tap your feet surreptitiously in time.

Aboriginal

Aboriginal cultures who populated the Atlantic coast for thousands of years are known to have sung, played music and danced, but details are few. Today, native music has been strongly influenced by the power of the fiddle. The most recent famous Mi'kmaq musician was Lee Cremo (1939–99), whose fiddle-playing talents mixing Mi'kmaq, Scottish and Irish music took him as far as Nashville and Hollywood. It's said that no one played quite like Lee, and he was ranked by many as one of the top 10 fiddle players of his time in North America.

The Mi'kmaq word that most roughly translates into the English word for music is *welta'q* which literally means 'it sounds good.' This is a wide definition that has come to encompass the poetry of Rita Joe (1932–2007), who is often referred to as the poet laureate of the Mi'kmaq people. Joe's poems are frequently set to music for school performances but even as spoken word are considered to 'sound good' and thus be as agreeable and entertaining as a song. Over her lifetime, Joe published seven books of poetry which can be found online and in bookstores around Nova Scotia.

Your best chance of hearing traditional music is at one of several pow-wows held around the region; for modern aboriginal sounds, head to music festivals that highlight the region's culture, such as Celtic Colours in Nova Scotia. One of the best acts is the Newfoundland band Tipatshimun, whose lyrics are in the Innu language.

Scottish & Irish

Bagpipes wail mysteriously from a blustery hilltop and a lone fiddler serenades you at lunch. Yes, Scottish music is the dominant influence in the region, particularly in Nova Scotia and Prince Edward Island (PEI). Highland Scots who settled here didn't leave their fiddles at home, and the lively, fun piano-and-fiddle combos were quick to catch on. To this day, these folksy sounds define the Atlantic Canadian music scene. Most modern music produced from the music-heavy regions of Cape Breton Island and Halifax still sound quite a bit like the folk music of old, blending the fiddle with some electric guitar but still little percussion. Popular Cape Breton musicians include fiddlers Ashley MacIsaac, Buddy MacMaster and Natalie MacMaster, and multi-instrumentalist JP Cormier. Banjo-strumming Old Man Luedecke, hailing from Chester, puts on an incredible show and is often touring around the region in summer.

Bagpipes might not often be found in popular music but you will hear them in the area – a lot. Between the College of Piping and Celtic

What's On

Nova Scotia: www.thecoast.ca

Newfoundland: www.the telegram.com

New Brunswick: www.musicruns throughit.com

Prince Edward Island: www. buzzon.com

Arts in PEI and the Gaelic College of Celtic Arts and Crafts on Cape Breton, bagpipers are pumped out by the dozen to play at historical sites, busk along the streets of cities and create a mysterious air in some of the most out-of-the-way places, taking you away to the Scottish Highlands.

Up Newfoundland and Labrador way, expect to hear more Irish-tinged tunes that move at a faster pace and generally tell a story, with the dialogue dominating the accompaniment – if you've ever listened to the Pogues, you know what we're talking about. This music generally emanates from Irish pubs where accents start to lilt as more beer is consumed. Singer-songwriter Ron Hynes embodies the local style and can be found strumming his guitar in St John's pubs, along with the talented folk group, the Once; the Navigators play driving Celtic tunes; the Novaks evoke Tom Petty with the whoop-ass amped up; Repartee do an excellent job of representing synth pop; and Hey Rosetta are getting uber-popular via their energetic folk rock sounds. But the band that most successfully translates this music to a larger stage is Great Big Sea. They tour throughout the United States and Canada, filling mighty venues with their Celtified rave-ups and kitchen-party enthusiasm. They are a definite must-see.

Men of the Deeps, a choral group of retired coal miners in Nova Scotia, can be found playing around the province and invariably pull a crowd.

Acadian

The Acadians are scattered in small groups that lie throughout Atlantic Canada and were often very remote and isolated before the modern advent of roads; Acadian music has therefore evolved in many different directions. Scottish influences are very apparent in areas such as Cape Breton, and, as you move up the Cabot Trail from Mabou's Scottish fiddling to Chéticamp's Acadian kitchen parties, you'll be struck by how similar the sounds are. Generally, Acadian music is a little more soulful than Scottish music, with more percussion from tricky hand-clapping, foot-tapping and the spoons. The lyrics, of course, are in French.

In southwestern Nova Scotia the local music is far more influenced by rock, bluegrass and country, as well as Cajun styles introduced by descendants of those caught up in the Great Expulsion. The most popular Acadian band today, Blou, is from this region, and they call their sound 'Acadico' – a mix of Acadian, Cajun and zydeco (American Creole

CEILIDHS AND KITCHEN PARTIES

'So, what exactly is a ceilidh?' you might ask. Well, in the broadest sense, a ceilidh is a gathering where traditional Gaelic music is played and people can dance – kind of like a rural, family-style disco with an accordion instead of heavy bass. Sometimes it's just a solo fiddle player playing during lunch hours at a restaurant; other times it can be families dressed fully in their clan tartan performing for folks in town halls, or larger, more professional groups playing in front of big audiences. Whatever the size, ceilidhs are always laid-back affairs where the musicians mingle with the audience and hold no airs of being anything more than another local who just happens to play an instrument rather well. There are usually many more locals in the audience than visitors, and everyone goes crazy when, say, Cyril and Betty's seven-year-old son Timmy gets up and step dances – and you'll be into it too because chances are little Timmy is really, really good.

The terms ceilidh and kitchen party are often used interchangeably, but the latter is a term more likely to be used by Acadians (along with the Acadian French term: 'party de cuisine'), non-Celtic folks or by anyone on Cape Breton Island in Nova Scotia. A kitchen party is also more likely to actually be at someone's house and to have food and drink, although this is not always the case.

folk music). The group's accordion-based rock tunes regularly win the East Coast Music Award title for Best Francophone recording of the year. Meanwhile, from the same region, Jacobus et Maleco, which eventually became Radio Radio, was the first Acadian rap group, and internationally renowned Grand Dérangement sings movingly of Acadian reality through its traditional tunes.

Many Acadian groups head to Montréal where there's a much stronger Francophone music scene and it's easier to get recognized. New Brunswick Acadian groups are often influenced by the traditional Québecois poetic style. Acts from Atlantic Canada that have made names for themselves include Marie-Jo Thério (soothing and lyrical from New Brunswick), Suroît (Cajun and fiddle from the Magdalen Islands), Borlico and Barachois (lively kitchen-party–style duo from PEI), and Felix and Formanger (an accordion-and-guitar group from Newfoundland).

African Influences

Just when you were getting tired of the fiddle, in come more cultures. Many Black Canadians arrived as freed slaves and Loyalists to the British Crown during the American War of Independence. Social inequalities and marginalization (Nova Scotia's racism earned it the moniker 'Mississippi of the North') stopped the black community from making a huge mark in the Maritime music scene in the past, but nowadays it's adding a lot of spice to the region's music scene. The influence had been largely gospel music, but today hip-hop, jazz, blues, R&B, pop and classical music are all holding some cultural sway.

Portia White from Truro, Nova Scotia, was one of the first African-Canadians to make it big in the region when she won a silver cup at the Nova Scotia Music Festival in 1928 at the age of 17. She went on to become a powerful and well-known contralto classical vocalist and stage presence through the early '40s. In more recent years, Nova Scotian R&B musician Gary Beals placed second in the first season of *Canadian Idol,* and Faith Nolan, a mixed-heritage African, Mik'maq and Irish jazz singer, songwriter and guitarist, has made music with powerful political statements.

FOLK & TRADITIONAL PLAYLIST

This playlist will get you in the mood for highland hills, long stretches of Atlantic coastline and perhaps a stop for some step dancing on the way. These old and new favorites are a little bit folk and a little bit country.

➡ *Guysborough Train,* Stan Rogers

➡ *The Silver Spear,* Natalie MacMaster

➡ *These Roads,* David Gunning

➡ *Rant and Roar,* Great Big Sea

➡ *Home I'll Be,* Rita MacNeil

➡ *Walk With Me,* Pogey

➡ *My Nova Scotia Home,* Hank Snow

➡ *Wrong Side of the Country,* Old Man Luedecke

➡ *Maritime Express,* Eddie LeGere

➡ *Maple Sugar,* Don Messer

➡ *Snow Bird,* Anne Murray

➡ *Sail Away to the Sea,* The Once

PARTYING AT THE PUB

Pubs are by far the best way to experience local music and, fortunately, finding a good one is about as easy as finding a public restroom. With Halifax and St John's vying for the title of most pubs per capita, you'll actually have a harder time finding a nightspot that's not hosting a live gig. The following is a list of our favorites:

Rare Bird Pub (p100) Guysborough, Nova Scotia; folk and fiddle

Red Shoe Pub (p88) Mabou, Cape Breton, Nova Scotia; folk and fiddle

Seahorse Tavern (p55) Halifax, Nova Scotia; indie, punk and metal

Benevolent Irish Society (p153) Charlottetown, PEI; Irish

O'Leary's (p126) Saint John, New Brunswick; open-mic nights

Ship Pub (p182) St John's, Newfoundland; anything and everything

Rock House (p182) St John's, Newfoundland; indie

Top Festivals

Beyond pubs and concerts, Canada's Atlantic provinces swell with music festivals, especially during the summer. The following are the most renowned:

➡ **Evolve** This three-day music and awareness festival showcases everything from grassroots music to modern, big-name performers in styles from folk to hip-hop.

➡ **Stan Rogers Folk Festival** (p100) Camp out in remote Canso for three days of live music from fine bluegrass and folk songwriters and performers.

➡ **Celtic Colours International Festival** (p87) Watch the trees turn color in several Cape Breton locations while enjoying nine days of Celtic music from around the world.

➡ **Cavendish Beach Music Festival** (p164) Big names such as Taylor Swift make it to this five-day camp-out, which features a big stage and an audience that pours in from all around Canada and the USA.

➡ **Deep Roots Music Festival** (p76) Folk and roots music are highlighted at this weekend festival, which also includes music workshops.

➡ **Indian River Festival** (p164) Classical, folk, jazz and world music resonate through the acoustically blessed St Mary's Church.

➡ **Sound Symposium** (p177) Amazing diversity from jazz, world music and classical musicians; nine days and nights of artistic jamming.

Atlantic Canadian Art

Canada's Atlantic provinces attract artists like kids to cupcakes. That ever-present sea, the blend of blues and greens on the horizon, bucolic quiet and low cost of living make the region a prime place to swipe oil paints on canvas or whittle an old log into something astonishing. Native Canadians have been taking nature's bounties, from porcupine quills to ash wood, and crafting them into beautiful daily objects for thousands of years.

Where to Find What

The Art Gallery of Nova Scotia has the largest collections with state-of-the-art galleries in both Halifax and Yarmouth. Here you'll find the stars: Alex Colville, Maud Lewis, Arthur Lismer and many more, as well as temporary shows of up and comers and renowned artists 'from away.' But there's an incredible richness to be discovered outside the museum as well. Drive around Cape Breton and it seems that every town has a shop selling arts and crafts, be that outrageous hats, forged iron sculptures, pottery or paintings hanging randomly from trees in a forest.

Other regions may not be so thickly doted with artisans but wherever you go, you'll find a plentiful array of creative folk creating beautiful works. Drive slowly, ask about local artisans at visitor centers and browse small town galleries and craft shops. If you're looking to buy something special, you'll be spoiled for choices.

Aboriginal

Many of Canada's most ancient artistic artifacts hail from the eastern subarctic areas of the country including the Atlantic provinces. The tribes that lived here were nomadic and crafted elaborate headdresses with feathers, sewed patterns of beads and porcupine quills on to clothing, and wove patterns into their basketware. Art was something that embellished practical objects or was used for religious purposes. You'll find displays full of these works of refined design at museums large and small throughout the region.

It's been argued that art for art's sake wasn't a concept in native culture until the 20th century. But even then, stereotypes of what aboriginal art should look like (prehistoric) made it difficult for modern-day artists to have their works seen, appreciated or sold. Norval Morriseau, an Ojibwa from Ontario, has been called the 'Grandfather of Canadian Native Art' for his paintings that capture Ojibwa cultural and spiritual images in a striking, colorful and modern style – his work is simply stunning. Morriseau and several other artists began to capture the art world through the late 1960s and the 1970s, paving the way for the future.

Today, Native Canadian art is an incredibly rich terrain and in the Eastern provinces, inspiration is drawn mostly from Mi'kmaq and Maliseet cultures. Some standouts in this region include Ned Bear who carves Pawakan (spirit guide) wooden masks. Recently, Bear has taken to carving living trees throughout New Brunswick – the places aren't advertised but are set up for accidental discovery. Alan Syliboy is one of the better known artists in the region and paints scenes from Mi'kmaq mythology

Big Art Museums

Art Gallery of Nova Scotia, Halifax, Nova Scotia

Art Gallery of Nova Scotia, Yarmouth, Nova Scotia

The Rooms Provincial Art Gallery, St John's, Newfoundland

Beaverbrook Art Gallery, Fredericton, New Brunswick

Confederation Centre of the Arts (PEI)

with a striking modern style; prints and note cards of David Brook's stylized animal paintings are found in many native shops; Dozay Christmas specializes in dreamlike paintings of ghostly animals or people in monocolored natural settings; Ursula Johnson takes traditional basketry to new realms, including nonfunctional colorful pieces and incorporating techniques into performance art pieces; high-realism of the natural world is painted by Nova Scotian Leonard Paul; and in Newfoundland, Jerry Evans specializes in detailed lithographs.

Folk Art

Back when roads were few and budgets were lean, many Canadians in these provinces had limited to no opportunities to visit art museums or learn about art beyond their local sphere. Folk art is the embodiment of what happens when artistic people create works without any influence from the outside world. Today the movement continues with its charming mix of simplicity and sophistication with avant-garde and tradition.

Painters include Joe Norris who depicted classic Maritime scenes from nesting ducks to sailboats in a simple colorful way; and Joseph Sleep who creates massive, childlike tableaux of animals and plants, using everything from cardboard to felt tip markers. The most famous painter, of course, was Maud Lewis.

And folk art goes far beyond paint on paper. Well-known wood artists include Ralph Boutilier, known for his lifelike human-sized wood carvings and mechanical wooden birds; Sidney Howard who made more rustic sculptures of polychrome wood of people, fish, birds and animals; Bradford Naugler who has carved life-sized wood sculptures of the Ten Fathers of the Confederation, the Obama family and British royals William and Kate among others; and Collins Eisenhauer who is considered the master of appealing, stylized poultry sculptures.

Marine-Inspired Art

Nearly any artist who has spent time in these provinces could be slotted into this category for at least some of their work. And really, how can you paint, sculpt or get creative here without getting inspiration from the surrounding sea that provides jobs, food, briny smells and a never-ending calming swish that rocks you to sleep?

Art Trails & Resources

www.halifax
artmap.com

www.capebreton
craft.com

www.artsand
heritagepei.com

MAUD LEWIS

By far the most well-known and beloved folk artist in Nova Scotia is Maud Lewis. Lewis, born in 1903, was uncommonly small, had almost no chin and suffered from juvenile rheumatoid arthritis. She spent much of her childhood alone and she never traveled beyond Yarmouth and Digby counties. After being left with no money once her parents died in the 1930s, she married Everett Lewis and the couple spent the rest of their lives in a roughly 12-foot by 12-foot house. But what a house it was! Lewis painted every surface with colorful, happy scenes of the life and community around her, making what many would have considered a place of poverty into a beautiful piece of beguiling art. In 1984, 14 years after Lewis passed away, the house was bought by the province of Nova Scotia as a landmark; it was restored in 1996. Since 2008 the entire house can be seen in the heart-wrenching Maud Lewis Room at the Art Gallery of Nova Scotia. Bring a hanky.

But Maud's artistic endeavors didn't end with her house. She began her career making Christmas cards as a child, and as an adult she was an incredibly prolific painter. The small, often 8-by-10-inch paintings she sold out of her house back in the 1950s for $2 are now sold at auction for up to $22,000. Lewis, who never sold a painting for more than $10, would have hardly believed it.

FESTIVALS

Nova Scotia Folk Art Festival (Lunenburg; www.nsfolkartfestival.com; ☉late Jul/early Aug) This fun, four-hour festival would be more aptly named the 'Folk Art Auction.' Entry ($5) to the auction includes the chance to win a lucky door prize.

Studio Rally (Nova Scotia; www.studiorally.ca; ☉end Jul) For more than 20 years, artists all over Nova Scotia have opened their doors to visitors on this special weekend.

Victoria Park Lantern Festival (St John's, Newfoundland; http://lanternfest.ca; ☉last weekend of Jul) Public lantern-making workshops are held in this popular event that concludes with a lantern-lighting ceremony featuring music, dance and theatrical performances.

Halifax native John O'Brien (1831–91) was one of the best-known artists of the region in his generation; he painted detailed, realistic seascapes that have greatly helped historians studying maritime history. Next came Edith Smith who held the position of Arts Mistress at Halifax Ladies College for nearly 40 years; she was influential in many artists' education, the shaping of the first collections for the Art Gallery of Nova Scotia (AGNS), and most importantly for her masterful realist seascape, landscape and portrait paintings. One of the artists Edith Smith chose for the AGNS collections was Arthur Lismer, another Haligonian who first made his name painting WWI camouflaged naval ships in the harbor; he also sketched the Halifax Explosion of 1917. A few years later Lismer became a part of the 'Group of Seven,' a collaboration of the seven most revered nature artists at that time in Canada who were (contentiously) promoted as Canada's national school of painters.

Other marine artists include HM Rosenberg who was the principal at the Victoria School of Art and Design (now known as NSCAD University) in Halifax from 1898 to 1910. Rosenberg took a mix of European styles from Gauguin to Sargent to create his own realistic yet stylized approach that's universally appealing. Many of his works can be seen today in the permanent collection at the AGNS.

The Maritime Museum of the Atlantic's art collection focuses on ship-related marine works, but the AGNS has a substantial collection as well.

Realism

The 20th century was dominated by the realists.

Alex Colville, whose family moved to Amherst, Nova Scotia, from Toronto when he was nine years old, is Atlantic Canada's most famous artist. While Colville is known as a realist, many of his works are reminiscent of the American Precisionist movement of the 1930s and he was greatly influenced by the American realist Edward Hopper. There's a dreamy aspect to Colville's work that make the seemingly innocuous Canadian scenes he painted a shade darker, then they become more enigmatic the longer you examine them. Colville passed away peacefully at the age of 92 in 2013 in Wolfville, Nova Scotia.

Power artist couple (although no longer married) Christopher and Mary Pratt met at Mount Allison University in Sackville, where they both studied under and were influenced by Alex Colville. While Christopher's stark, streamlined landscape pieces are nearly photographic in quality, Mary uses color and design more boldly in her still life, portrait and domestic scenes. Both of the Pratts currently live in Newfoundland and

Artisan & Gallery Hot Spots

St Ann's Bay, Nova Scotia

Lunenburg, Nova Scotia

St Andrews By-The-Sea, New Brunswick

Fogo Island, Newfoundland

Twillingate Island, Newfoundland

Charlottetown, PEI

Christopher runs a gallery featuring his works as well as other artists' work in Bay Roberts.

Another student of Colville's, Tom Forrestall, has been called a magic realist, a moniker given to many East Coast Canadian artists after WWII. Forrestall's works are very Maritime in theme (think crab traps on wood docks and ice fields).

Newfoundland painter David Blackwood takes the magic a little farther with starlit dark images of ghostly people or stormy sea vistas from the shore. In 2003 he was named Honorary Chairman of the Art Gallery of Ontario, although he still maintains a studio in Wesleyville, Newfoundland.

Food & Drink

No longer known solely for its plentiful seafood, Atlantic Canada is becoming a serious culinary destination, thanks to PEI's meteoric rise on the foodie circuit and Nova Scotia's emergence as one of the top wine-producing regions in Canada. That said, outside major cities and well-to-do tourist accommodations, dining in the Maritimes remains a simple (and delicious) affair. Main meals usually feature fish or shellfish with a veggie thrown in for good measure, and perhaps a bowl of chowder.

Bounty from the Sea

The sea defines Atlantic Canada, so it's no surprise that seafood defines the local cuisine.

Cod gets battered and fried and brought to your table as fish and chips; it's the one dish you can trust to be on every menu. The batter itself varies from a rough cornmeal coating to a big, puffy, crispy on the outside and soft on the inside beer batter. Atlantic salmon, cousin of the better-known Pacific salmon, usually arrives broiled and sauced, perhaps with dill or hollandaise. 'Nova' is lightly smoked salmon (akin to lox), for which Nova Scotia is deservedly famous.

Nova Scotia, New Brunswick and PEI boil more lobster than you can shake a pat of butter at. Crikey, even McDonald's is in on the action serving a McLobster sandwich at its regional outlets. One of the best places to get down and dirty with the crustacean is at a community-hall lobster supper. Don't eat too much; you'll need to leave room for the bulging fruit pie that'll come your way afterward.

Nova Scotia visitors should also save their appetites for Digby scallops. Those touring PEI will find succulent oysters that grow around the island's shore and have a different flavor depending on when and where they're harvested. Mussels are everywhere, although PEI is most famous for them, and up Cape Breton and Newfoundland way, look out for sweet and seasonal snow crab. Clams are another great bounty and come primarily from several beaches along Nova Scotia's east coast and Point Prim on PEI. Locals lead clamming trips where you can dig your own mollusks then help prepare them before eating to your heart's content.

Signature Sea Critters

Mussels, Prince Edward Island

Digby scallops, Nova Scotia

Malpeque oysters, Prince Edward Island

Snow crab, everywhere but particularly Newfoundland & Labrador

Lobster, everywhere

LOBSTER SUPPERS

You don't need to change out of your jeans or get the kids a babysitter to gorge yourself on the Maritime province's most delicious shellfish. The classic Nova Scotia, New Brunswick and Prince Edward Island (PEI) dining experience is a no-frills lobster supper, held in dining halls, churches and community centers. The lobster is generally unadorned with sauces and fanfare; the suppers are a place to enjoy these critters in the buff (or perhaps with a little melted butter), for their own divine flavors and texture. Kids are not only welcome, they are well catered for, with half-sized suppers and other menu options such as beef or scallops. Just to make sure no one goes hungry, there is a slew of accompaniments from chowder and mussels to potato salad and oven-fresh rolls. Held daily for dinner from roughly mid-June to mid-October, the most suppers per capita are found on PEI. The cost of dinner depends on the market price of lobster but generally hovers around $35 for an all-inclusive meal with a 1lb crustacean.

WINE FESTIVALS

Nova Scotia Fall Wine Festival (⊘mid-Sep–mid-Oct) Celebrates the grape harvest province-wide with tastings, grape stomping, chef events and food pairings.

New Festival of Wines (PEI; www.peiwinefest.com; ⊘late May) The provinces largest wine event with two evenings of tastings from vinyards around the world.

Icewine Festival (Nova Scotia; www.nsicewinefest.com; ⊘Mar) Three days sampling ice wines and food pairings at different venues.

The sea doesn't limit itself to meat either – the Maritime provinces harvest seaweeds that are eaten or used for their medicinal properties. Stop by Roland's Sea Vegetables on Grand Manan Island, New Brunswick, for a bag of dulse to eat as-is or to sprinkle on fish, or to Point Prim, PEI, for Seaweed Secrets, where you collect, learn about and eat the region's vegetables from the sea.

Earthly Delights

Eastern Canada gets much less fame for its land-based food than for its seafood, but that doesn't mean it can't cook up some tasty non-fish-based dishes. French Acadians in particular have invented several specialties throughout the centuries. In Acadian towns you might see menu items such as rappie pie (also known as *la rapure*), a potato and salted-pork dish. *Tourtière* is a meat pie. *Poutine râpée* is a mixture of grated raw and mashed potatoes wrapped around fresh pork. *Fricot* is a hearty soup or stew.

Newfoundland and Labrador may be boggy, rocky and cruddy for growing most things, but berries flourish here. These blueberries, partridgeberries (similar to cranberries) and bakeapples get shoveled into muffins, pies and jams. The best time of year for the harvest is mid-August. PEI rivals Idaho for being the potato capital of North America and it's said the island's tubers have a unique flavor due to the rich, red soil. The Canadian Potato Museum in O'Leary shows off all the things you can do with these hearty treats and you can usually taste samples of tasty potato-based fudge. The Annapolis Valley of Nova Scotia is known for its apples and throws a huge Apple Blossom Festival through the production areas in early June every year. Everywhere in the region you'll find roadside stalls selling strawberries July through August.

Each province also produces its own beef and poultry and you'll find these very good-quality products on menus of better restaurants that promote locally sourced ingredients. Keep an eye out for Cows ice cream, which is produced locally in PEI and is one of the region's best-known frozen treats.

Bottoms Up!

Moosehead is the region's best-known beer, brewed in Saint John, New Brunswick. In Newfoundland, Quidi Vidi microbrews flow through the provincial taps; try Eric the Red. Beer lovers will also enjoy the crisp, globally recognized beer from Alexander Keith's Brewery in Halifax, which has a burgeoning craft-brew scene, popularised by the Garrison Brewing Company, which makes a number of brews including some interesting seasonal flavors such as Sugar Moon Maple. Up-and-coming craft breweries in Nova Scotia include Cape Breton's Big Spruce Brewing, which brews an organic and aptly named 'Kitchen Party Pale Ale,' and the Authentic Seacoast Brewing company (at the Rare Bird Pub), which makes a dark, rich coffee stout from self-roasted beans.

Top Foodie Spots

Fleur de Sel,
Lunenburg,
Nova Scotia

Le Caveau,
Grand Pré,
Nova Scotia

Lot 30,
Charlottetown,
Prince Edward
Island

Chinched,
St John's,
Newfoundland

Rossmount Inn,
St Andrews
By-the-Sea,
New Brunswick

WORTH THE TRIP RESTAURANTS

Some of the best restaurants in these provinces are located in out-of-the-way villages or bucolic areas that make you combine your meal with a road trip. Locals as well as visitors don't seem to find this a hardship, though, as many of these eateries have been open for years and manage to stay full throughout summer (most shut in winter).

Our favorites include:

Bonavista Social Club (p193) Bonavista, Newfoundland

Inn at Bay Fortune (p157) Bay Fortune, Prince Edward Island

Shipwright's Cafe (p164) Margate, Prince Edward Island

Wild Caraway (p83) Advocate Harbour, Nova Scotia

Charlotte Lane (p67) Shelburne, Nova Scotia

Regional Specialties

Bakeapple, Newfoundland

Fiddleheads, New Brunswick

Oat Cakes, Cape Breton, Nova Scotia

Solomon Gundy, Southshore, Nova Scotia

Dulse, Grand Manan Island, New Brunswick

Éclairs, St Pierre & Miquelon, Newfoundland

Cod Tongues, Newfoundland

Boutique wineries are also uncorking their bottles in Nova Scotia, mostly in the Annapolis Valley, Bear River area and on the Malagash Peninsula. Domaine de Grand Pré, Blomidon Estate Winery and Jost Vineyards are the biggest, and these are the wines that you'll find in many fine restaurants in Nova Scotia and occasionally beyond. Newer wineries to sample include Benjamin Bridge, which makes a delicious, crowd-pleasing lightly sparkling white called Nova 7 (do yourself a favor and try some) and Luckett Vineyards, which makes good red, whites and fruit wines – both of these are in the Gaspereaux Valley near Wolfville. Rossignol Winery on PEI specializes in delicious and well-respected fruit wines but has begun to focus more on regular wines as well. New on the scene in PEI, Newman Estate is getting rave reviews for its medium-bodied fruity reds.

The Glenora Distillery on Cape Breton Island produces a very sip-worthy single-malt whisky and a group in Guysborough, Nova Scotia, has plans to open an even bigger distillery on their shores. Lunenburg, Nova Scotia's Ironworks Distillery, produces a Bluenose Dark Rum which is smooth as silk poured over a cube of ice. Prince Edward Distillery makes award-winning spirits from, you guessed it, potatoes, as well as a few grain-based beverages. Just around the corner, Myriad View cooks up a tonsil-searing 'Strait Lightning' that's 75% alcohol and the only legal moonshine in Canada. Newfoundland is famous for its Screech, a brand of rum that's actually made in Jamaica.

A signature Canadian drink worth trying is the Caesar, a Bloody Mary-ish cocktail made with Clamato (a tomato and clam juice–based beverage), vodka, hot sauce and Worcestershire sauce. It's a good Sunday morning hair-of-the-dog drink, imbibed on ice in a salt-rimmed glass and garnished with lime and a stalk of celery.

You can get quality coffee, including espresso and cappuccino, in cities. Barring that, the ubiquitous Tim Hortons doughnut shops brew a respectable cup.

Celebrations

Food and drink are a big part of celebrating in Atlantic Canada. Summer has seafood festivals, autumn is Thanksgiving, winter has Christmas get-togethers and spring's Easter holidays traditionally feature generous family feasts with plenty of meat dishes, salad bowls, giant desserts, beer and wine. A hearty, family-focused Sunday dinner is also a common event.

Several towns showcase their special cuisines with annual festivals:

➼ **Lobster Carnival** (p85) Pictou, Nova Scotia

➼ **Tyne Valley Oyster Festival** (p168) Tyne Valley, PEI

➼ **Digby Scallop Days** (p71) Digby, Nova Scotia

➼ **Fall Flavours** (p149) Charlottetown, PEI

Where to Eat & Drink

Even the smallest town usually has a midpriced restaurant. In places where this is not the case, your lodging host will likely serve food; for instance, many B&Bs serve meals beyond breakfast for a price and if you prearrange it. Atlantic Canada doesn't feature many fine-dining establishments outside of cities and college towns, but a few do turn up in unexpected, out-of-the-way places. A pub is often the cheapest place to get a good meal.

While there are many variations, most restaurants open for lunch (usually between 11:30am and 2:30pm) and dinner from 5:30pm (some fancy establishments only open for dinner). Midrange and family restaurants often stay open all day. In small towns and rural areas many restaurants close at 8pm but times vary and often depend on how busy the restaurant is that day.

Quick Eats

In addition to farmers markets in cities, roadside stands offer enticing seasonal produce in rural areas. Do yourself a favor and pick up a container of strawberries (best in June) or blueberries (August).

The food truck movement is catching on in Halifax. Some of the most popular are **Food Wolf** (www.thefoodwolf.com) for 'internationally inspired comfort food' and **Nomad Gourmet** (www.nomadgourmet.ca), with a fabulously painted truck serving burgers, burritos and waffle sandwiches. Outside the cities, you might come across the occasional roadside van selling fish and chips, and lots of seafood markets serve inexpensive lobster rolls, sandwiches and chowder. Poutine (French fries topped with gravy and cheese) isn't as prevalent here as in some other areas of Canada, but if you do spy a chip truck, go for it!

Vegetarians & Vegans

Vegetarians will be well catered for in the region's principal cities, such as Halifax, Fredericton and St John's, but as you move away from urban areas your options become extremely limited. Vegans can expect an even rougher ride. Strict adherents should stick to any vegetarian-only eateries they come across, since 'vegetarian' items in mainstream restaurants may well have been prepared with meat stock or lard.

> **Farmers Market Forages**
>
> ....
>
> Halifax Seaport Farmers Market, Nova Scotia
>
> ....
>
> Dieppe Market, Moncton, New Brunswick
>
> ....
>
> Boyce Farmers Market, Fredericton, New Brunswick
>
> ....
>
> Old City Market, Saint John, New Brunswick
>
> ....
>
> Charlottetown Farmers Market, Charlottetown, Prince Edward Island
>
> ....
>
> Bidgood's, Goulds, Newfoundland

TRAVEL YOUR TASTEBUDS

Head-scratching foods you may encounter in Nova Scotia and Prince Edward Island include Solomon Gundy (a pickled-herring and chopped-meat combo) and Lunenburg pudding (pork and spices cooked in the intestines of a pig). Dulse is an edible seaweed; New Brunswick's Grand Manan Island is famous for it. Fiddleheads are a fern's first shoots that are served like vegetables in the region. Figgy duff (a sweet pudding with raisins and molasses) and jig's dinner (meat and vegetables boiled together and eaten with pickles, gravy and figgy duff) are just a few of Newfoundland's colorfully named dishes.

Tip around 15% (pretax) in restaurants and bars with good table service, but don't tip the full 15% unless the service has been worth it. Also check that a gratuity hasn't been automatically added to your bill – a growing practice.

Specialty health-food shops are found almost exclusively in the larger cities or hip college towns so you'll want to stock up on supplies before going to more remote regions. Chinese eateries occasionally pop up in remote areas and may be another option. Many fine restaurants (some that have unexpected rural locations) will nearly always cater to dietary restrictions, as will many B&Bs.

Habits & Customs

Atlantic Canadians follow the tradition of eating morning breakfast, midday lunch and early-evening dinner. Expect the generally high standards of North American restaurant and bar service to apply throughout the region. Table service is common at most pubs, although you can still order at the bar as well. Don't forget to give a tip to your table server, and consider dropping some change in the bar-server's pot if you stick around for a few beers.

All of the Atlantic provinces have adopted widespread smoking bans.

Landscape & Wildlife

From unexplored wilderness to dramatic coastlines and phenomenal wildlife, the provinces of Atlantic Canada are a nature-lover's dream. It's a place where you are as likely to see thousands of seabirds resting on a passing iceberg as a moose crossing the road, and, if you're lucky, you may spot feeding blue whales or a wandering polar bear in Newfoundland or Labrador.

A Geologist's Dream

The spectacular landscapes of Atlantic Canada are both their charm and their challenge. Due to the rugged land and crumpled coastlines, the traditions of isolated villages and homesteads have been preserved to a greater extent than perhaps anywhere else in North America, but the difficulty of coaxing crops from the rocky soil or transporting goods to market keeps much of the region economically depressed to this day.

For geologists this region hides great wealth, not just in rich ore deposits but in the record of earth history preserved by the rocks. This is where two significant geologic provinces converge: Labrador forms the eastern rim of the vast Canadian Shield, the greatest exposure of ancient rocks on the earth's surface; while the other Atlantic provinces perch themselves at the northern tip of the Appalachian Mountains, which is the single most important topographic feature of eastern North America.

Sitting at this great convergence, Atlantic Canada offers a visually dramatic snapshot of more than one billion years of earth history, ranging from the red sandstone cliffs of Northumberland Strait to the famed granite headlands at Peggy's Cove, Nova Scotia. And perhaps even more fascinating for the visitor are the many signs of the massive Pleistocene ice sheet that smothered the region with ice a mile deep as recently as 20,000 years ago: the thrilling fjords of the north, the rounded mounds of Nova Scotia (known locally as drumlins), the tens of thousands of small shallow lakes.

In its simplest form, the geologic story is that Atlantic Canada formed from the fragments and pieces left over after North America and Africa collided and crushed an ocean between them 400 million years ago. In the process of swinging into each other with tremendous force, the two continents compressed and folded seafloor sediments into a giant mountain chain that has eroded over millions of years into the rolling hills we now call the Appalachian Mountains. Mixed into this mélange are the many different pieces of smaller land masses trapped between the colliding continents.

When North America and Africa went their separate ways 180 million years ago, they each left part of their coastline behind. This may be best observed in Newfoundland, for its western third is a remnant of the ancestral North American coastline, its middle third is a slice of ancient seafloor, and its eastern third once belonged to northern Africa.

At the Fundy Geological Museum, 'time travel' with interactive exhibits and visit a lab where dinosaur bones are being cleaned and assembled.

But geology never stops at the simple story, and for the traveler who's enthusiastic about the subject, this region never runs out of surprises. Even if you don't study rocks or get excited by fossils, you cannot ignore the stunning outcroppings and rock types visible at nearly every stage of your journey. There are, for example, sea stacks, drowned coastlines, glacial grooves, and erratics everywhere – what more could you ask for?

Critters of the Great North

Whether you come for a glimpse of caribou, whales or moose, Atlantic Canada's wildlife is plentiful, if elusive. Many people travel to the region to see the incredible numbers of seabirds and whales that can be spotted from coastal bluffs or on whale-watching trips, and these sightings are nearly guaranteed. Polar bears, however quintessentially Canadian they may be, are only present in the far north of this region.

The plants and animals of Atlantic Canada are even more amazing when you realize that the entire region was completely buried in ice only 20,000 years ago and was not accessible for life until about 10,000 years ago. Where all these critters came from and how they got here so quickly is anybody's guess!

Mammals

If you needed one single reason to visit Atlantic Canada, it might be the world-class encounters with whales that gather in these food-rich waters. Around 22 species of whale and porpoise can be seen on whale-watching tours, which are offered from countless coastal harbors. Leaping and diving humpback whales are most common throughout the region, but you might also catch a glimpse of the highly endangered North Atlantic right whale or even the largest leviathan of all, the blue whale.

Closer to shore or out on the ice, it's common to see seals, including the snowy white young of the harp seal in winter. Harbor and gray seals are easily observed, though in winter they seek out the edges of the pack ice.

Land animals are also a powerful draw. Fox, bear and otter are widespread throughout the region. Rabbits are everywhere. On Newfoundland there are more than 100,000 moose and there are many more on Cape Breton Island. They do stick to the woods, however, so unless you're a hiker, the highest likelihood of seeing them is on the road – a very good reminder to drive slow (hitting a moose often does more damage to the car and driver than it does the moose). As you travel north the animals become even more exotic. From Newfoundland north you will find polar bear, arctic fox, wolf, lynx, and musk ox. Labrador has the largest herd of caribou in the world, as well as wolves that follow the long lines of migrating caribou.

The white hairs on a polar bear are hollow and trap sunlight to help keep the animal warm in frigid temperatures.

FABULOUS FOSSILS

Kids will be especially intrigued by the region's fossils, many of which are on display in various parks and museums. They include fossil footprints, dinosaur bones and fossilized creatures that look like they're from outer space. In New Brunswick province, you can see remains of the first life to walk on land in North America (a giant centipede, just in case you're wondering) as well as evidence of the most primitive terrestrial plants. Nova Scotia, however, holds the most accessible fossil viewing at the Unesco Joggins Fossil Cliffs; you can also search for fossils and semiprecious stones in the low-tide flats around Parrsboro in Nova Scotia (but note you can't actually keep the fossils).

THE GRAND BANKS

Banks are a funny name for a shallow area, but in the case of the Grand Banks off New-foundland's southeast coast it's no laughing matter. Until recently this was considered the greatest site in the world for ocean fish and the animals that came to feed on them. Even today, with the fish nearly hunted out, millions of seabirds and uncounted whales come to feed in the rich waters. This area is incredibly productive because the continental shelf off the coast of Newfoundland sticks out like a thumb to intercept the south-flowing waters of the frigid Labrador Current right at the point where they mingle with the warm north-flowing waters of the Gulf Stream. The mix of warmth and nutrient-rich Arctic waters cre-ates an explosion of plankton that feeds everything from the smallest fish to the biggest whale. And because the shallow waters allow sunlight to penetrate to the ocean floor, the food chain is active at all depths.

Birds

Seabirds are the primary wildlife attraction in Atlantic Canada, and rightly so. There are few places in North America where it's easier to see outstanding numbers of seabirds such as razorbill, Atlantic puffin, common murre, and northern gannet. Huge nesting colonies on rocky islands and promontories may contain more than a million birds, but these merely hint at the numbers that once nested here before market hunters slaughtered uncounted millions of birds.

Mudflats and shorelines, especially along the Bay of Fundy, are famous for the tremendous quantities of shorebirds they attract during the May and August migration. Upwards of two million birds stop here annually. On nearby beaches, the endangered piping plover tries to hold its own against the trespass of invading sunbathers and beach walkers – please respect signs that warn you of this bird's home.

On Cape Breton Island and in Newfoundland and Labrador you're very likely to see bald eagles, Canada's largest bird of prey and the only eagle exclusive to North America. The birds can weigh up to 6.8kg (females are larger than males) and the wing span is around 2m. Besides their sheer size, you'll know them when you see them thanks to their distinctive white heads and brown bodies. Keep an eye out for their massive nests, often high in the trees along the coast, that weigh around 2 tons.

Fish

More than any other animal, fish have placed Atlantic Canada on the map, in particular the northern cod. With the collapse of the great cod fishery, other species such as halibut, mackerel, haddock, and herring have grown in economic importance. In the region's many lakes and rivers, fishers seek out trout, bass, salmon, and river herring (with the quaint name 'alewives').

Insects

Although it is easy to focus on the region's showiest animals, we cannot ignore the one that is smallest but not least in Atlantic Canada. It has been said that the diminutive black fly has single-handedly maintained the wild splendor of Labrador. This may sound like an exaggeration until you set foot onto the shore in midsummer and are blanketed in insects against which you are defenseless. Second only to the black fly are pro-lific mosquitoes. If it's any consolation, every animal from ant to moose is tormented equally by these creatures, so they're not picking on you.

NATIONAL & PROVINCIAL PARKS

Atlantic Canada has taken its park systems seriously and many important sites are protected within both national and provincial parks. Nova Scotia alone has more than 120
parks, but even Newfoundland and Labrador, which are so sparsely settled as to be parks
in their own right, have a total of 34 parks.

Not all parks are set up for camping, but they are all worthy of a visit. In a few parks
it is possible to plan extended hiking and camping trips, but all of them offer splendid
opportunities for activities ranging from picnicking to beachcombing to kayaking and
cycling. Those that are open in the winter are favored by cross-country skiers and
snowshoers.

But what can be most troubling to those unaccustomed to them are
North American leeches (also called freshwater leeches or medicinal
leeches) found in many fresh-water lakes, slow-moving streams and
marshes. These 5cm long parasites usually spend their days chilling out
under rocks or leaves in the cool, mucky bottoms, but water disturbances
(such as a splash of diving in or stepping out into the water for a swim),
is a bit akin to a dinner bell and out they swim looking for grub. While
being a meal for a leech can be very disturbing, the bites are painless and
the critters carry no diseases. If you do get bitten, you can opt either to
let the leech eat its fill and drop off, or try to release it's suction with a
fingernail or sharp flat object before gently pulling it off. Salt or insect
repellent can work to suffocate the leech.

World Heritage Sites

Gros Morne
National Park,
Newfoundland

L'Anse aux Mead-
ows National
Historic Site,
Newfoundland

Old Town
Lunenburg, Nova
Scotia

Joggins Fossil
Cliffs, Nova
Scotia

The Landscapes
of Grand Pré,
Nova Scotia

Plants

Although Atlantic Canada presents some tree diversity in its southern
reaches with a mix of birch, maple and ash, vast areas of forest are completely dominated by spruce as you head north. And at some point even
those homogenous forests give way to soggy tundra that stretches to the
Arctic. Surprisingly, the area can be rich with abundant wildflowers during the short growing season.

The yellow dandelion-like flowers of the coltsfoot may be the first ones
to come out each spring, but far more attention is given to the region's
delightful midsummer orchid displays, including showy lady's slipper,
which may carpet entire boggy areas. Blue lupines seem to bloom everywhere, and many other varieties and colors can be found.

The most common shrubs, especially in Newfoundland and Labrador,
are those in the heath family, including blueberries, cranberries and other delicious berries that grow in profusion in August. Wild roses bloom
along the coasts from late June through August.

Perhaps the most curious plant is the odd lichen called caribou moss.
Growing in such a dense spongy carpet that other plants cannot get a
toehold, this pale greenish moss may be the most dominant plant in the
northern forests. It is an important food source for caribou, hence its
name, and is often mixed with seal meat to vary the diets of sled dogs.

Environmental Issues

Early Europeans explorers were dumbfounded by the apparently inex-
haustible numbers of animals they encountered in Atlantic Canada. It
was a scene of such incredible abundance that they thought it would
never end, so they bent their will toward exploiting and profiting from
the natural wealth in every way possible. The result is only too predict-
able and sad: animals lost forever include the mythical great auk, the
Labrador duck and the sea mink. Today Atlantic Canada is facing the
horrifying prospect that the greatest fishery in the world, the uncounted

millions of cod that sustained their provincial livelihood for 400 years, may have come to an end when cod were listed as endangered in 2003. Even with fishing limitations the recovery of stocks is hindered by the proliferation of species that cod and other predator fish once fed on, such as herring and snow crab, which eat fish eggs, making it even more difficult for the fish to make a comeback. In the end, not only has the environment suffered great damage, but so have the villages and traditions that needed the fish for their survival.

ATLANTIC CANADA'S TOP NATURAL AREAS

PARK	FEATURES	ACTIVITIES	BEST TIME TO VISIT
NOVA SCOTIA			
Cape Chignecto Provincial Park	largest and newest park in province, rugged wilderness; old growth forest, deer, moose, eagles	hiking, backcountry camping	Jun-Oct
Kejimkujik National Park	pristine wilderness, network of glacial lakes; otter, loon, bald eagles	canoeing, camping, hiking	late Sep–early Oct
Cape Breton Highlands National Park	dramatic oceanside cliffs, world-famous scenic drive; whales, bald eagles, seabirds, bear, moose, wild orchids	hiking, camping, sight-seeing, whale-watching	May-Oct
NEW BRUNSWICK			
Fundy National Park	sandstone cliffs, extensive beach, dramatic tides; bear, moose, beaver, peregrine falcons	mountain biking, bird-watching, hiking	year-round
Kouchibouguac National Park	lagoons, white-sand beaches; moose, deer, bear	strolling, clam digging, cycling, skiing, kayaking, bird-watching	year-round
PRINCE EDWARD ISLAND			
Prince Edward Island National Park	red sandstone bluffs, dunes, beaches; red foxes, piping plover, sandpipers	bird-watching, beach walking, swimming, picnicking	May-Sep
NEWFOUNDLAND			
Cape St Mary's Ecological Reserve	rugged ocean cliffs; one of the most accessible seabird colonies in North America, nesting gannets, whales	bird-watching	Mar-Aug
Terra Nova National Park	craggy cliffs, many sheltered inlets, lakes, bogs; moose, beaver, bald eagles, whales	kayaking, fishing, camping	mid-May–mid-Oct
Witless Bay Ecological Reserve	offshore islands, icebergs, more than one million breeding seabirds, feeding whales	bird-watching, whale-watching	Jun-Aug

Unfortunately, resource exploitation continues unabated on several other fronts. Some $3 billion a year is generated from logging, with half of the production coming from New Brunswick. Vast ore deposits are being explored and developed all the time, with huge areas stripped of their forest and soil cover to access coal, iron, nickel and other mineral resources.

The newest threat to the environment, yet a perk for jobs and suffering local economies, is hydraulic fracturing for natural gas exploration (often called fracking). The technique involves drilling into shale or coal-bed deposits and injecting a water and chemical fracking fluid filled with ceramic beads into the holes. The beads hold open the cracks allowing natural gas to rise to the surface and be collected. The environmental risks here are many, including a huge use of valuable fresh water and the risk of fracking chemicals leaking into the water table and ocean. Fracking rigs also emit large amounts of greenhouse gases into the atmosphere. What is particularly troubling is how much exploitation occurs in seldom-visited parts of Labrador, where there is little public scrutiny or attention.

Survival Guide

Directory A–Z

Accommodations

Seasons

➧ Peak season high pricing is in summer, from mid-June to early September.

➧ It's best to book ahead during summer and during holidays and major events when rooms can be scarce.

Amenities

➧ Most properties offer in-room wi-fi. It's typically free in budget and midrange lodgings, while top-end hotels can sometimes still charge a fee, although this trend is diminishing.

➧ Almost all smaller properties (especially B&Bs) and most large chains in North America are now 100% smoke-free. A handful of smaller chain motels may have rooms set aside for smokers.

➧ Air-conditioning is not a standard amenity at most budget and midrange places. If you want it, be sure to ask about it when you book. If you want it, be sure to ask about it when you book.

Discounts

➧ In winter, prices can plummet by as much as 50%.

➧ Membership in the American Automobile Association (AAA) or an associated automobile association, American Association of Retired Persons (AARP) or other organizations also yield modest savings (usually 10%).

➧ Check hotel websites for special online rates. The usual suspects also offer discounted room prices throughout Canada.

B&Bs

➧ **Bed & Breakfast Online** (www.bbcanada.com) is the main booking agency for properties nationwide.

➧ B&B accommodations is commonplace in Atlantic Canada and can be a great way to experience true Maritime hospitality.

➧ In Canada, B&Bs (known as *gîtes* in French) are essentially converted private homes whose owners live on-site. People who like privacy may find B&Bs too intimate, as walls are rarely soundproof and it's not uncommon to mingle with your hosts and other guests.

➧ Standards vary widely, sometimes even within a single B&B. The cheapest rooms tend to be small with few amenities and a shared bathroom. Nicer ones have added features such as a balcony, a fireplace and an en-suite bathroom. Breakfast is always included in the rates (though it might be continental instead of a full cooked affair).

➧ Not all B&Bs accept kids, while others cater to them.

➧ Minimum stays (usually two nights) are common, and many B&Bs are only open seasonally.

Camping

Canada's Maritime and Atlantic provinces are filled with campgrounds – some federal or provincial, others privately owned. Private campgrounds sometimes cater only to trailers (caravans) and recreational vehicles (RVs), and may feature convenience stores, playgrounds and swimming pools. It is a good idea to phone ahead to make sure the size of sites and the services provided at a particular campground are suitable for your vehicle.

Season Varies by location, but most campsites are open from May to September. Some campgrounds remain open for maintenance year-round and may let you camp at a reduced rate in the off-season. This can

---

BOOK YOUR STAY ONLINE

For more accommodations reviews by Lonely Planet authors, check out http://lonelyplanet.com/hotels/. You'll find independent reviews, as well as recommendations on the best places to stay. Best of all, you can book online.

be great in late autumn or early spring when there's hardly a soul tramping about. Winter camping, though, is only for the hardy.

Facilities Vary widely. Backcountry sites offer little more than pit toilets and fire rings, and have no potable water. Unserviced (tent) campgrounds come with access to drinking water and a washroom with toilets and sometimes showers. The best-equipped sites feature flush toilets and hot showers and electrical and sewer hookups for RVs. The most popular national parks usually have some permanent tents (called oTENTiks), cabins and even yurts: these swanky digs (by camping standards) are exceptionally popular and sell out fast.

Fees In national and provincial parks, fees range from about $22 to $40 for tents up to $45 for full hookup sites per night; fire permits often cost a few dollars extra. Backcountry camping costs about $16 per night. Private campgrounds tend to be a bit pricier.

Availability A first-come, first-served basis is used at most government-run sites, which fill up quickly, especially in July and August. The mainstay of national parks now require bookings be made online: www.pccamping.ca.

Homestays & Holiday Rentals

How would you feel about staying on the couch of a perfect stranger? If it's not a problem, consider joining an organization that arranges homestays. The following groups charge no fees to become a member, and the stay itself is also free.

Couch Surfing (www.couchsurfing.com)

Hospitality Club (www.hospitalityclub.org)

Another option is a holiday rental where individuals rent out anything from a room in their house to private cabins or even their whole house. Locations are equally variable – you can find an apartment in Halifax to cottages deep in the woods of New Brunswick. Great bargains can be found

and this can be a fantastic option for families in particular. The following sites offer the most listings in the region:

Airbnb (www.airbnb.com)

VRBO (www.vrbo.com)

Hostels

Canada has independent hostels as well as those affiliated with Hostelling International (HI). All have dorms ($25 to $35 per person on average), which can sleep from two to 10 people, and many have private rooms (from $60) for couples and families. Rooms in HI hostels are generally gender segregated and the consumption of alcohol and smoking is prohibited; nonmembers pay a surcharge of about $4 per night.

Bathrooms are usually shared and facilities include a kitchen, lockers, internet access, laundry room and common TV room. Most hostels, especially those in big cities, are open 24 hours. If not, ask if you can make special arrangements if you're arriving late.

For additional information and online reservations:

Backpackers Hostels Canada (www.backpackers.ca) Independent hostels.

Hostelling International Canada (www.hihostels.ca) HI hostels.

Hostels.com (www.hostels.com) Independent and HI hostels.

Hotels & Motels

Most hotels are part of international chains, and the newer ones are designed for either the luxury market or business people. Rooms have cable TV and wi-fi, other facilities may include swimming pools and fitness and business centers. Rooms with two double or queen-sized beds sleep up to four people, although there is usually a small surcharge for the third and fourth person. Many places advertise that 'kids stay free,' but sometimes you have to pay extra for a crib or a rollaway (portable bed).

In Canada, like the US (both lands of the automobile), motels are ubiquitous. They dot the highways and cluster in groups on the outskirts of towns and cities. Although most motel rooms won't win any style awards, they're usually clean and comfortable and offer good value for travelers. Many regional motels remain your typical mom-and-pop operations, but plenty of North American chains have also opened up around the region.

University Accommodations

In the lecture-free summer months, some universities and colleges rent beds in their student dormitories to travelers of all ages. Most rooms are quite basic, but with rates ranging from $30 to $80 a night, often including breakfast, you know you're not getting the Ritz. Students usually qualify for small discounts.

Customs Regulations

The **Canada Border Services Agency** (www.cbsa.gc.ca) has the customs lowdown. A few regulations to note:

Alcohol You can bring in 1.5L of wine, 1.14L of liquor or 24 355mL beers duty-free.

Gifts You can bring in gifts totaling up to $60.

Money You can bring in/take out up to $10,000; larger amounts must be reported to customs.

Personal effects Camping gear, sports equipment, cameras and laptop computers can be brought in without much trouble. Declaring these to customs as you cross the border might save you some hassle when you leave, especially if you'll be crossing the US-Canadian border multiple times.

Pets You must carry a signed and dated certificate from a veterinarian to prove your dog or cat has had a rabies shot in the past 36 months.

Prescription drugs You can bring in/take out a 90-day supply for personal use (though if you're bringing it to the USA, know it's technically illegal, but usually overlooked for individuals).

Tobacco You can bring in 200 cigarettes, 50 cigars, 200g of tobacco and 200 tobacco sticks duty-free.

Discount Cards

Discounts are commonly offered for seniors, children, families and people with disabilities, though no special cards are issued (you get the savings onsite when you pay). AAA and other automobile association members also receive various travel-related discounts. Many cities have discount cards for local attractions.

➡ **International Student Identity Card** (www.isic. org) provides students with discounts on travel insurance and admission to museums and other sights. There are also cards for non-students under 26 and for full-time teachers.

➡ **Parks Canada Discovery Pass** (www.pc.gc.ca/ar-sr/lpac-ppri/ced-ndp.aspx; adult/child/family $68/34/137) provides access to nearly 100 national parks and historic sites for a year around Canada. Can pay for itself in as few as seven visits over daily entry fees; also provides quicker entry into sites.

Electricity

120V/60Hz

120V/60Hz

Food

For an introduction to the region's food scene, see p240.

Health

Before You Go
HEALTH INSURANCE

Canada offers some of the finest health care in the world. The problem is that, unless you are a Canadian citizen, it can be prohibitively expensive. It's essential to purchase travel health insurance if your regular policy doesn't cover you when you're abroad. Check www. lonelyplanet.com/bookings for supplemental insurance information.

Bring medications you may need clearly labeled in their original containers. A signed, dated letter from your physician that describes your medical conditions and medications, including generic names, is also a good idea.

VACCINATIONS

No special vaccines are required or recommended for travel to Canada. All travelers should be up to date on routine immunizations.

In Canada
AVAILABILITY & COST OF HEALTH CARE

Medical services are widely available. For emergencies, the best bet is to find the nearest hospital and go to its emergency room. If the problem isn't urgent, call a nearby hospital and ask for a referral to a local physician, which is usually cheaper than a trip to the emergency room (where costs can be $500 or so before any treatment).

Pharmacies are abundant, but prescriptions can be expensive without insurance.

EATING PRICE RANGES

The following price ranges refer to a main course.

$ less than $15

$$ $15–25

$$$ more than $25

IMMUNIZE YOURSELF

VACCINE	RECOMMENDED FOR	DOSAGE	SIDE EFFECTS
chickenpox	travelers who've never had chickenpox	2 doses 1 month apart	fever, mild case of chickenpox
influenza	all travelers during flu season (November through March)	1 dose	soreness at the injection site, fever
measles	travelers born after 1956 who've had only 1 measles vaccination	1 dose	fever, rash, joint pains, allergic reactions
tetanus-diphtheria	all travelers who haven't had booster within 10 years	1 dose lasts 10 years	soreness at injection site

However, Americans may find Canadian prescription drugs to be cheaper than drugs at home. You're allowed to take out a 90-day supply for personal use (though know it's technically illegal to bring them into the USA, but usually overlooked for individuals).

ENVIRONMENTAL HAZARDS

Cold exposure This can be a significant problem, especially in the northern regions. Keep all body surfaces covered, including the head and neck. Watch out for the 'Umbles' – stumbles, mumbles, fumbles and grumbles – which are signs of impending hypothermia.

Heat exhaustion Dehydration is the main contributor. Symptoms include feeling weak, headache, nausea and sweaty skin. Lay the victim flat with their legs raised, apply cool, wet cloths to the skin, and rehydrate.

INFECTIOUS DISEASES

Most are acquired by mosquito or tick bites, or environmental exposure. The **Public Health Agency of Canada** (www.phac-aspc.gc.ca) has details on all listed here.

Giardiasis Intestinal infection. Avoid drinking directly from lakes, ponds, streams and rivers.

Lyme disease Occurs mostly in southern Canada. Transmitted by deer ticks in late spring and summer. Perform a tick check after you've been outdoors.

West Nile virus Mosquito-transmitted in late summer and early fall. Prevent by keeping covered (wear long sleeves, long pants, hats, and shoes rather than sandals) and apply a good insect repellent, preferably one containing DEET, to exposed skin and clothing.

MEDICAL CHECKLIST

➡ acetaminophen (eg Tylenol) or aspirin

➡ anti-inflammatory drugs (eg ibuprofen)

➡ antihistamines (for hay fever and allergic reactions)

➡ antibacterial ointment (eg Neosporin) for cuts and abrasions

➡ steroid cream or cortisone (for poison ivy and other allergic rashes)

➡ bandages, gauze, gauze rolls

➡ adhesive or paper tape

➡ safety pins, tweezers

➡ thermometer

➡ DEET-containing insect repellent for the skin

➡ permethrin-containing insect spray for clothing, tents and bed nets

➡ sunblock

➡ motion-sickness medication

TAP WATER

Tap water in Canada is safe to drink.

Insurance

Make sure you have adequate travel insurance, whatever the length of your trip. At a minimum, you need coverage for medical emergencies and treatment, including hospital stays and an emergency flight home. Some policies specifically exclude 'dangerous activities' such as skiing or even hiking. Make sure to check the fine print if you plan on doing any outdoor activities. Medical treatment for non-Canadians is very expensive.

Also consider insurance for luggage theft or loss. If you already have a homeowners' or renters' policy, check what it will cover and only get supplemental insurance to protect against the rest. If you have prepaid a large portion of your vacation, trip cancellation insurance is worthwhile.

Worldwide travel insurance is available at www.lonelyplanet.com/travel-insurance. You can buy, extend and claim online anytime – even if you're already on the road.

Internet Access

It's easy to find internet access. Libraries, schools and community agencies in practically every town provide free high-speed internet terminals for public use. Usage time is usually limited to blocks of

30 minutes. Internet cafes are limited to the main tourist areas, and access generally costs from $2 per hour.

Wi-fi is almost universally available at lodgings throughout Atlantic Canada and free public wi-fi hotspots are becoming increasingly prevalent.

Legal Matters

Police

If you're arrested or charged with an offense, you have the right to keep your mouth shut and to hire any lawyer you wish (contact your embassy for a referral, if necessary). If you cannot afford one, be sure to ask to be represented by public counsel. There is a presumption of innocence.

Drugs & Alcohol

The blood-alcohol limit is 0.08% and driving cars, motorcycles, boats and snowmobiles while drunk is a criminal offense. If you are caught, you may face stiff fines, license suspension and other nasty consequences.

Consuming alcohol anywhere other than at a residence or licensed premises is also a no-no, which puts parks, beaches and the rest of the great outdoors off limits, at least officially.

Avoid illegal drugs, as penalties may entail heavy fines and possible jail time, as well as a criminal record. The only exception is the use of marijuana for medical purposes, which became legal in 2001. Meanwhile, the decriminalization/legalization of pot possession for personal use remains a subject of ongoing debate among the general public and in the parliament.

LGBTI Travelers

Canada is one of the most LGBT-friendly countries on the planet, although you might still come across uncommon pockets of prejudice in rural areas. In 2005,

Canada became the fourth country in the world to legalize same-sex marriage.

Halifax is by far this region's gayest city, with a humming nightlife scene, publications and lots of associations and support groups. It has a sizeable pride celebration, too, which attracts big crowds. While very low-key, Prince Edward Island also has a decent-sized gay population and has a small pride event in July.

The following are good resources for gay travel; they include Canadian information, though not all are exclusive to the region.

Damron (www.damron.com) Publishes several travel guides, including *Men's Travel Guide, Women's Traveller* and *Damron Accommodations;* gay-friendly tour operators are listed on the website too.

Gay Canada (www.gaycanada. com) Search by province or city for queer-friendly businesses and resources.

Lesbian & Gay Hospitality Exchange International (www. lghei.org) A network of gay and lesbian hosts who offer travelers accommodations in their homes or offer hospitality to visitors.

Out Traveler (www.outtraveler. com) Gay travel magazine.

Purple Roofs (www.purpleroofs. com) Website listing queer accommodations, travel agencies and tours worldwide.

Queer Canada (www.queercanada. ca) A general resource.

Xtra (www.xtra.ca) Source for gay and lesbian news nationwide.

Maps

Most tourist offices distribute free provincial road maps.

For extended hikes or multiday backcountry treks, it's a good idea to carry a topographic map. The best are the series of 1:50,000 scale maps published by the government's Centre for Topographic Information. These

are sold by around 900 map dealers around the country. For details, refer to: www. nrcan.gc.ca/earth-sciences/ geography/topographic-information.

Money

ATMs are widely available and credit and debit cards are accepted almost everywhere.

ATMs

Many grocery and convenience stores, airports, and bus, train and ferry stations have ATMs. Most are linked to international networks, the most common being Cirrus, Plus, Star and Maestro.

Most ATMs also spit out cash if you use a major credit card. This method tends to be more expensive because, in addition to a service fee, you'll be charged interest immediately (in other words, there's no interest-free period as there is with purchases). For exact fees, check with your bank or credit-card company.

Visitors heading to more remote regions (such as Newfoundland) won't find an abundance of ATMs, so it is wise to cash up beforehand.

Scotiabank, common throughout Canada, is part of the Global ATM Alliance. If your home bank is a member, fees may be less if you withdraw from Scotiabank ATMs.

Credit & Debit Cards

Major credit cards such as MasterCard, Visa and American Express are widely accepted in Canada, except in remote, rural communities where cash is king. You'll find it hard or impossible to rent a car, book a room or order tickets over the phone without having a piece of plastic. Note that some credit-card companies charge a transaction fee (which is around 3% of whatever you purchased); ensure you check with your provider to avoid surprises.

For lost or stolen cards, these numbers operate 24 hours:

American Express (☎800-869-3016; www.americanexpress.com)

MasterCard (☎800-622-7747; www.mastercard.com)

Visa (☎800-847-2911; www.visa.com)

Currency

Canadian coins come in 5¢ (nickel), 10¢ (dime), 25¢ (quarter), $1 (loonie) and $2 (toonie or twoonie) denominations. The gold-colored loonie features the loon, a common Canadian waterfowl, while the two-toned toonie is decorated with a polar bear.

Canada has a full series of plastic/polymer notes in circulation. The currency comes in $5 (blue), $10 (purple), $20 (green) $50 (red) and $100 (gold) denominations.

Taxes & Refunds

Canada's federal goods and services tax (GST), variously known as the 'gouge and screw' or 'grab and steal' tax, adds 5% to just about every transaction. Most provinces also charge a provincial sales tax (PST) on top of it. Taken together, they are known as the Harmonized Sales Tax (HST). At time of writing, each province had recently increased its tax rates to equate to a 15% HST.

Unless otherwise stated, taxes are not included in our listed prices.

You might be eligible for a rebate on some of the taxes. If you've booked your accommodation in conjunction with a rental car, plane ticket or other service (ie if it all appears on the same bill from a 'tour operator'), you should be eligible to get 50% of the tax refunded from your accommodation. Fill out the GST/HST Refund Application for Tour Packages form available from the Canada Revenue Agency at: www.cra-arc.gc.ca/E/pbg/gf/gst115.

Tipping

Tipping is standard practice. Rates are as follows:

Restaurant waitstaff	15-20%
Bar staff	$1 per drink
Hotel bellhop	$1-2 per bag
Hotel room cleaners	$2 per day
Taxis	10-15%

Opening Hours

The following list provides standard opening hours for high-season operating times.

Banks 10am to 5pm Monday to Friday, some open 9am to noon Saturday

Museums 10am to 5pm, may close on Monday

Restaurants 8am to 11am & 11:30am to 2:30pm Monday to Friday, 5pm to 9:30pm daily, some open 8am to 1pm weekends

Bars 5pm to 2am

Clubs 9pm to 2am Wednesday to Saturday

Shops 10am to 6pm Monday to Saturday, noon to 5pm Sunday

Supermarkets 9am to 8pm, some open 24 hours

Post

Canada's national postal service, **Canada Post/Postes Canada** (www.canadapost.ca), is neither quick nor cheap, but it is reliable. Stamps are available at post offices, drugstores, convenience stores and hotels. Many Shopper's Drug Mart branded pharmacies have Canada Post agencies in the rear of the store, though the counters do not always have the same opening hours as the pharmacies themselves.

Postcards or standard letters cost $1 within Canada, $1.20 to the USA and $2.50 to all other countries. Travelers often find they have to pay high duties on items sent to them while in Canada, so beware.

Public Holidays

Canada has 10 national public holidays a year and more at the provincial level. Banks, schools and government offices close on these days.

National Holidays

New Year's Day January 1

Good Friday March or April

PRACTICALITIES

➡ **Newspapers** The most widely available newspaper is the Toronto-based **Globe and Mail** (www.globeandmail.com). **Maclean's** (www.macleans.ca) is Canada's weekly news magazine. The Maritimes' regional principal dailies are the **Chronicle Herald** (www.chronicleherald.ca) in Halifax, the **Guardian** (www.theguardian.pe.ca) in Charlottetown, the **New Brunswick Telegraph-Journal** (www.telegraphjournal.com) in Saint John and **The Telegram** (www.thetelegram.com) in St John's.

➡ **TV** The Canadian Broadcasting Corporation (CBC) is the dominant nationwide network for both radio and TV. CTV Atlantic is the major competition.

➡ **Weights & Measures** Officially Canada uses the metric system, but imperial measurements are common for many day-to-day purposes.

➡ **Smoking** Banned in all restaurants, bars and other public venues nationwide. The majority of hotels and B&Bs are also smoke free.

UNIQUELY CANADIAN CELEBRATIONS

National Flag Day February 15; commemorates the first time the maple-leaf flag was raised above Parliament Hill in Ottawa, at the stroke of noon on February 15, 1965.

Victoria Day late May; this day was established in 1845 to observe the birthday of Queen Victoria and now celebrates the birthday of the British sovereign who's still Canada's titular head of state. Victoria Day marks the official beginning of the summer season (which ends with Labour Day on the first Monday of September). Some communities hold fireworks.

National Aboriginal Day June 21; created in 1996, it celebrates the contributions of Aboriginal peoples to Canada. Coinciding with the summer solstice, festivities are organized locally and may include traditional dancing, singing and drumming, storytelling, arts and crafts shows, canoe races and lots more.

Canada Day July 1; known as Dominion Day until 1982, Canada Day was created in 1869 to commemorate the creation of Canada two years earlier. All over the country, people celebrate with barbecues, parades, concerts and fireworks.

Thanksgiving Day mid-October; first celebrated in 1578 in what is now Newfoundland by explorer Martin Frobisher to give thanks for surviving his Atlantic crossing, Thanksgiving became an official Canadian holiday in 1872 to celebrate the recovery of the Prince of Wales from a long illness. These days, it's essentially a harvest festival involving a special family dinner of roast turkey and pumpkin, very much as it is practiced in the US.

Easter Monday March or April

Victoria Day Monday before May 25

Canada Day July 1; called Memorial Day in Newfoundland

Labour Day First Monday of September

Thanksgiving Second Monday of October

Remembrance Day November 11

Christmas Day December 25

Boxing Day December 26

Provincial Holidays

Some provinces also observe local holidays, with Newfoundland leading the pack.

St Patrick's Day Monday nearest March 17

St George's Day Monday nearest April 23

National Day Monday nearest June 24 in Newfoundland

Orangemen's Day Monday nearest July 12 in Newfoundland

Civic Holiday First Monday of August everywhere *except* Newfoundland and PEI

School Holidays

Children break for summer holidays in late June and don't return to school until early September. University students get even more time off, usually from May to early or mid-September. Most people take their big annual vacation during these months.

Telephone

Canada's phone system is almost identical to the US system.

Domestic & International Dialling

Canadian phone numbers consist of a three-digit area code followed by a seven-digit local number. In many parts of Canada, you must dial all 10 digits preceded by 1, even if you're calling across the street. In other parts of the country, when you're calling within the same area code, you can dial the seven-digit number only, but this is slowly changing. The pay phone or phone book where you are should make it clear which system is used.

For direct international calls, dial ☑011 + country code + area code + local phone number. The country code for Canada is 1 (which is the same as for the USA, although international rates still apply for all calls made between the two countries).

Toll-free numbers begin with ☑800, 877 or 866 and must be preceded by 1. Some of these numbers are good throughout Canada and the USA, others only work within Canada, and some work in just one province.

Cell Phones

Local SIM cards can be used in unlocked GSM 850/1900 compatible phones.

If you have an unlocked GSM phone, you should be able to buy a SIM card from local providers such as **Telus** (www.telus.com), **Rogers** (www.rogers.com) or **Bell** (www.bell.ca). Bell has the best data coverage.

US residents can often upgrade their domestic cell phone plan to extend to Canada. **Verizon** (www.verizonwireless.com) provides good results.

Reception can be poor in rural areas, regardless of your carrier.

Phonecards

Prepaid phonecards usually offer the best per-minute

rates for long-distance and international calling. They come in denominations of $5, $10 and $20 and are widely sold in drugstores, supermarkets and convenience stores. Beware of cards with hidden charges such as 'activation fees' or a per-call connection fee. A surcharge ranging from 30¢ to 85¢ for calls made from public pay phones is common.

Time

Canada spans six of the world's 24 time zones. The Eastern zone in Newfoundland is unusual in that it's only 30 minutes different from the adjacent zone. The time difference from coast to coast is 4½ hours.

Canada observes daylight saving time, which comes into effect on the second Sunday in March, when clocks are put forward one hour, and ends on the first Sunday in November.

In Francophone areas, times are usually indicated by the 24-hour clock.

Time difference between cities

Vancouver	3pm
New York City, Toronto & Montréal	6pm
Halifax, Fredericton & Charlottetown	7pm
Newfoundland	7:30pm
London	11pm

Tourist Information

The **Canadian Tourism Commission** (www.canada. travel) is loaded with general information, packages and links.

All provincial tourist offices maintain comprehensive websites packed with information helpful in planning your trip. Staff also field telephone inquiries and,

upon request, will mail out free maps and directories about accommodations, attractions and events. Some offices can also help with making hotel, tour or other reservations.

For detailed information about a specific area, contact the local tourist office, aka visitors center. Just about every city and town has at least a seasonal branch with helpful staff, racks of free pamphlets and books and maps for sale.

Provincial tourist offices include:

Tourism New Brunswick (☎800-561-0123; www.tourism newbrunswick.ca)

Newfoundland & Labrador Tourism (☎800-563-6353; www. newfoundlandlabrador.com)

Tourism Nova Scotia (☎800-565-0000; www.novascotia.com)

Prince Edward Island Tourism (www.tourismpei.com)

Travelers with Disabilities

Canada is making progress when it comes to easing the everyday challenges facing people with disabilities, especially the mobility-impaired.

Many public buildings, including museums, tourist offices, train stations, shopping malls and cinemas, have access ramps and/or lifts. Most public restrooms feature extra-wide stalls equipped with hand rails. Many pedestrian crossings have sloping curbs.

Newer and recently remodeled hotels, especially chain hotels, have rooms with extra-wide doors and spacious bathrooms.

Interpretive centers at national and provincial parks are usually accessible, and many parks have trails that can be navigated in wheelchairs.

Rental agencies offer hand-controlled vehicles and vans with wheelchair lifts at no additional charge, but you must reserve them in advance.

For accessible air, bus, rail and ferry transportation check **Access to Travel** (www. accesstotravel.gc.ca), the federal government's website. In general, most transportation agencies can accommodate people with disabilities if you make your needs known when booking.

For more information, download Lonely Planet's free Accessible Travel guide from http://lptravel.to/ AccessibleTravel.

Other organizations specializing in the needs of travelers with disabilities:

Access-Able Travel Source (www.access-able.com) Lists accessible lodging, transport, attractions and equipment rental by province.

Mobility International (www. miusa.org) Advises travelers with disabilities on mobility issues and runs an educational exchange program.

Society for Accessible Travel & Hospitality (www.sath.org) Travelers with disabilities share tips and blogs.

Visas

Visitor Visa

With the exception of US nationals, all visitors to Canada require either an electronic travel authorization (eTA; visa-waiver) or a formal visa.

Currently, visas are not required for citizens of 46 countries – including most EU members, Australia and New Zealand – for visits of up to six months.

To find out if you need an eTA or are required to apply for a formal visa, go to www.cic. gc.ca/english/visit/visas.asp.

Visitor visas – aka Temporary Resident Visas (TRVs) – can now be applied for online at www.cic.gc.ca/english/ information/applications/ visa.asp. Single-entry TRVs ($100) are usually valid for a maximum stay of six months from the date of your arrival in Canada.

A separate visa is required for all nationalities if you plan to study or work in Canada.

Visiting the USA

Admission requirements are subject to frequent change. **The US State Department** (www.travel.state.gov) has the latest information, or check with a US consulate in your home country.

Under the US visa-waiver program, visas are not required for citizens of 38 countries – including most EU members, Australia and New Zealand – for visits of up to 90 days (no extensions allowed), as long as you can present a machine-readable passport (e-Passport) and are approved under the **Electronic System for Travel Authorization** (www. cbp.gov/esta). Note you must register at least 72 hours before arrival and there's a US$14 fee for processing and authorization.

All visitors, regardless of their country of origin, are subject to a US$6 entry fee at land border crossings. Note that you don't need a Canadian multiple-entry TRV for repeated entries into Canada from the USA, unless you have visited a third country.

Volunteering

Volunteering provides the opportunity to interact with local folks and the land in ways you never would just passing through. Many organizations charge a fee, which varies depending on the program's length and the type of food and lodging it provides. The fees usually do not cover travel to Canada. Groups that take volunteers:

Churchill Northern Studies Centre (www.churchillscience.ca) Volunteer for six hours per day (anything from stringing wires to cleaning) and get free room and board at this center for polar bear and other wildlife research.

World-Wide Opportunities on Organic Farms (www.wwoof. ca) Work on an organic farm, usually in exchange for free room and board; check the website for locations throughout Canada.

Women Travelers

Canada is generally a safe place for women to travel, even alone and in the cities. Simply use the same common sense as you would at home.

In bars and nightclubs, solo women are likely to attract a lot of attention, but if you don't want company, most men will respect a firm 'no thank you.' If you feel threatened, protesting loudly will often make the offender slink away – or will at least spur other people to come to your defense. Note that carrying mace or pepper spray is illegal in Canada.

Physical attack is unlikely, but if you are assaulted, call the police immediately or contact a rape crisis center. A complete list is available from the **Canadian Association of Sexual Assault Centres** (☎800-726-2743; www.casac.ca).

Resources for women travelers:

Journeywoman (www.journey woman.com) A comprehensive travel resource for women, by women.

Her Own Way (www.travel.gc.ca/ travelling/publications/her-own-way) Published by the Canadian government for Canadian travelers, but contains a great deal of general advice.

Women Welcome Women Worldwide (www.womenwelcome women.org.uk) A member's network of women to meet, greet and welcome those from abroad.

Work

Permits

In almost all cases, you need a valid work permit to work

in Canada. Obtaining one may be difficult, as employment opportunities go to Canadians first. Before you can even apply, you need a specific job offer from an employer who in turn must have been granted permission from the government to give the position to a foreign national. Applications must be filed at a visa office of a Canadian embassy or consulate in your home country. Some jobs are exempt from the permit requirement. For full details, check with **Citizenship & Immigration Canada** (www.cic.gc.ca).

Employers hiring temporary service workers (such as hotels, bars, restaurants or resorts) and construction, farm or forestry workers sometimes don't ask for a permit. If you get caught, however, you can kiss Canada goodbye.

Finding Work

Students aged 18 to 30 from over a dozen countries, including the USA, UK, Australia, New Zealand, Ireland and South Africa, are eligible to apply for a spot in the **Student Work Abroad Program** (www.swap.ca). If successful, you get a six-month to one-year, nonextendable visa that allows you to work anywhere in Canada in any job you can get. Most 'SWAPpers' find work in the service industry.

Even if you're not a student, you may be able to spend up to a year in Canada on a 'working holiday program' with **International Experience Canada** (www. cic.gc.ca/english/work/iec). The Canadian government has an arrangement with several countries for people aged 18 to 30 to come over and get a job; check the website for participants. The Canadian embassy in each country runs the program, but basically there are quotas and spaces are filled on a first-come, first-served basis.

Transport

GETTING THERE & AWAY

Flights, cars and tours can be booked online at lonely planet.com/bookings.

Entering the Country

Visitors to Canada must hold a valid passport with at least six months remaining before its expiration. Visitors from visa-exempt countries (with the exception of the US) are required to purchase an electronic travel authorization (eTA, $7), similar to the USA's ESTA visa-waiver, before departing their home country. Visitors from non-visa waiver countries must apply for the appropriate visa, prior to arriving in Canada.

Once you arrive in Canada, the border officer will ask you a few questions about the purpose and length of your visit. Questioning may be more intense at land border crossings and your car may be searched. Once the immigration officer has verified your passport, eTA/visa and travel plans, you'll go through customs.

For updates (particularly regarding the rules for crossing land borders), check the websites for the **US State Department** (www.travel.state.gov) and **Citizenship & Immigration Canada** (www.cic.gc.ca).

Having a criminal record of any kind, including any drunk-driving related charges, may keep you out of Canada. If this affects you, be sure to contact the Canadian embassy or consulate in your home country.

Passport

All international visitors, with the exception of travelers from the US, require a passport to enter Canada.

Visitors from the US require a valid US passport, passport card, enhanced drivers license or NEXUS card to enter Canada at a land or sea border crossing. However, when traveling by air to/from Canada, US citizens are required to present a US passport book or NEXUS card only.

See the Western Hemisphere **Travel Initiative** (www.getyouhome.gov) for approved identification documents.

Air

Airports

While Halifax has the region's largest airport, Moncton is also busy and may offer lower fares than Halifax. For visitors heading to Newfoundland, Deer Lake is a great option if you are centering your travels on the west coast. It's now possible to fly direct to Charlottetown, Prince Edward Island, from Toronto, Ontario.

CLIMATE CHANGE & TRAVEL

Every form of transport that relies on carbon-based fuel generates CO_2, the main cause of human-induced climate change. Modern travel is dependent on aeroplanes, which might use less fuel per kilometer per person than most cars but travel much greater distances. The altitude at which aircraft emit gases (including CO_2) and particles also contributes to their climate change impact. Many websites offer 'carbon calculators' that allow people to estimate the carbon emissions generated by their journey and, for those who wish to do so, to offset the impact of the greenhouse gases emitted with contributions to portfolios of climate-friendly initiatives throughout the world. Lonely Planet offsets the carbon footprint of all staff and author travel.

Atlantic Canada's main airports:

Charlottetown, Prince Edward Island (YYG; ☑902-566-7997; www.flypei.com; 250 Maple Hills Ave)

Deer Lake, Newfoundland (YDF; ☑709-635-3601; www.deerlakeairport.com; 1 Airport Rd; 🔊)

Fredericton, New Brunswick (YFC; ☑506-460-0920; www.frederictonairport.ca)

Halifax, Nova Scotia (YHZ; ☑902-873-4422; www.hiaa.ca; 1 Bell Blvd)

Moncton, New Brunswick (YQM; ☑506-856-5444; www.gmia.ca)

St John's, Newfoundland (YYT; ☑709-758-8500; www.stjohnsairport.com; 100 World Pkwy; 🔊)

Sydney, Nova Scotia (YQY; ☑902-564-7720; www.sydney airport.ca; 280 Silver Dart Way)

Airlines

The region is not particularly well serviced, and flight and airline choices are limited. Many visitors will need to fly into Montréal, Toronto, or a US hub city such as New York, and then connect with another flight to reach their destination in Atlantic Canada. Most flights are via the national flagship carrier Air Canada; it's one of the world's safest airlines, though locals often gripe about its stiff prices. Subsidiary Air Canada Jazz operates the majority of flights to and within the Atlantic region.

Other companies that are based in Canada and are serving international destinations are the charter airline Air Transat and discount airline WestJet. There are numerous US airlines that also serve Atlantic Canada, which are worth researching.

Airlines operating to/from the region include the following:

Air Canada (AC; ☑888-247-2262; www.aircanada.com)

Air St-Pierre (PJ; ☑877-277-7765; www.airsaintpierre.com)

Air Transat (TS; ☑877-872-6728; www.airtransat.com)

American Airlines (☑800-433-7300; www.aa.com)

Condor (www.condor.com)

Delta (DL; ☑800-241-4141; www.delta.com)

Iceland Air (www.icelandair.com)

Porter Airlines (PD; ☑888-619-8622; www.flyporter.com)

Provincial Airlines (☑800-563-2800; www.palairlines.ca)

United Airlines (UA; ☑800-241-6522; www.united.com)

WestJet (WS; ☑888-937-8538; www.westjet.com)

Land

Border Crossings

There are three major border crossings between New Brunswick, Canada, and Maine, USA. They are Calais–St Stephen, Madawaska–Edmundston and Houlton–Woodstock. The website for the **Canadian Border Services Agency** (www.cbsa-asfc.gc.ca/bwt-taf/menu-eng.html) has details on estimated wait times. In general, waits rarely exceed 30 minutes, except during the peak summer season and holidays.

When returning to the USA, check the website for the **US Department for Homeland Security** (http://apps.cbp.gov/bwt/) for border wait times.

Bus

Maritime Bus (☑800-575-1807; www.maritimebus.com) plies the roads from Saint John (New Brunswick), as far as Rivière-du-Loup (Québec), up through Charlottetown (PEI) and to Nova Scotia as far as Halifax and up to Cape Breton Island to North Sydney (for ferry connections to Newfoundland). From Rivière-du-Loup, you can connect onto the **Orleans Express** (www.orleansexpress.com) to head farther afield into Québec. The changeover is pretty seamless.

At the time of writing there was no public bus to get to destinations south of Saint John or to Maine in the USA. Your best bet until someone fills this niche is with a shuttle bus company like **Eastlink** (www.eastlink shuttle.com), which offers door-to-door service from Calais (Maine) to many destinations throughout New Brunswick, PEI and Nova Scotia. From Calais in Maine you can take Greyhound buses to other destinations in the USA.

Car & Motorcycle

The USA's extensive highway network connects directly with the Canadian system at numerous key points along the border. These Canadian highways then go on to meet up with the east–west Trans-Canada Hwy, an excellent way to traverse the country.

If you're driving into Canada, you'll need the vehicle's registration papers, proof of liability insurance and your home driver's license. Cars rented in the USA usually can be driven into Canada and back, but make sure your rental agreement says so. If you're driving a car registered in someone else's name, bring a letter from the owner authorizing use of the vehicle in Canada.

Train

VIA Rail (☑888-842-7733; www.viarail.ca), Canada's national rail line, offers one service to the Atlantic region: a Montréal to Halifax train (advance purchase adult/child two to 11 years $135/68, 22 hours) that runs daily except Tuesday, and includes several stops in New Brunswick and Nova Scotia. It leaves Montréal at 7pm, and arrives in Halifax at 5:50pm the next day.

Visitors coming from the USA can hop aboard America's national rail line, **Amtrak** (www.amtrak.com), which has daily service connecting New York City and Montréal.

Sea

Ferry

Various (although dwindling) ferry routes connect Atlantic Canada to the USA and the French territory of St Pierre and Miquelon:

Nova Scotia (www.ferries.ca) Links Yarmouth and Portland, Maine.

New Brunswick (www.east coastferriesltd.com) Links Deer Island to Eastport, Maine. At time of writing, there were rumors that this service would be discontinued.

Newfoundland (www.stpierre ferry.ca) Links the Burin Peninsula to the French territory of St Pierre and Miquelon.

GETTING AROUND

Public transportation is available in cities and between larger towns, but most visitors rent a car for flexibility.

Car Good-value rentals are available in Nova Scotia and New Brunswick. There are fewer vehicles and higher prices in Prince Edward Island. In Newfoundland, this is even more the case.

Train Clean, economical and reliable VIA Rail connects Halifax to Montréal via New Brunswick.

Bus Cover more ground than trains; places not serviced by buses usually have private shuttle services for similar fares, more cramped seating and door-to-door service.

Air

Airlines in Nova Scotia, New Brunswick & Prince Edward Island

Most regional flights within the Maritimes are operated by Air Canada. Small provincial airlines fly out to the more remote portions of the region. Fares in such noncompetitive markets can be high.

Other carriers flying within Atlantic Canada:

Air St-Pierre (PJ; ☑877-277-7765; www.airsaintpierre.com)

Porter (PD; ☑888-619-8622; www.flyporter.com)

Provincial Airlines (☑800-563-2800; www.palairlines.ca)

Air Passes

Star Alliance (www.star alliance.com) members Air Canada, United Airlines and US Airways have teamed up to offer the North American Airpass, which is available to anyone not residing in the USA, Canada, Mexico, Bermuda or the Caribbean. It's sold only in conjunction with an international flight operated by any Star Alliance–member airline. You can buy as few as three coupons or as many as 10. Prices start at around C$750 for three flights.

Bicycle

The Maritime provinces, particularly Prince Edward Island, are ideal for bicycle touring.

Transportation

➡ By air: most airlines will carry bikes as checked luggage without charge on international flights, as long as they're in a box. On domestic flights they usually charge between $30 and $65. Always check details before you buy the ticket.

➡ By bus: **Maritime Bus** (☑800-575-1807; www. maritimebus.com) only charges $5 per bike and also offers boxes ($6.50) or bags ($5.65) to pack them in. Bikes only travel on the same bus as the passenger if there's enough space. To ensure that yours arrives at the same time as (or before) you do, ship it a day early.

➡ By train: **VIA Rail** (☑888-842-7733; www.viarail.ca) will transport your bicycle for $25. There are no trains with bike racks that run through this part of Canada so you'll have to dismantle and pack your bike to put on as baggage.

Rental

Outfitters renting bicycles exist in most tourist towns; many are listed throughout this guide. Rentals cost around $15 per day for touring bikes and $25 per day for mountain bikes. The price usually includes a helmet and lock. Most companies require a security deposit of $20 to $200.

Purchase

Buying a bike is easy, as is reselling it before you leave. Specialist bike shops have the best selection and advice,

---

CYCLING RULES & RESOURCES

➡ Cyclists must follow the same rules of the road as vehicles, but don't expect drivers to always respect your right of way.

➡ Since 2015, it has been mandatory for cyclists in all Maritime provinces to wear an approved helmet.

➡ The **Better World Club** (www.betterworldclub.com) offers emergency roadside assistance for cyclists. Membership costs $40 per year, plus a $12 enrollment fee, and entitles you to two free pick-ups and transport to the nearest repair shop or home, within a 50km radius of where you're picked up.

but general sporting-goods stores may have lower prices. Some bicycle stores and rental outfitters also sell used bicycles. To sniff out the best bargains, scour flea markets, garage sales and thrift shops, or check the notice boards in hostels and universities. These are also the best places to sell your bike.

Boat

The watery region hosts an extensive ferry system. Walk-ons and cyclists should be OK anytime, but call ahead for vehicle reservations or if you require a cabin berth. This is especially important during peak season (July and August).

Bay Ferries (☑888-249-7245; www.ferries.ca) Year-round service between Saint John, New Brunswick, and Digby, Nova Scotia.

Coastal Transport (☑506-662-3724; www.coastaltransport. ca) Ferry from Blacks Harbour to Grand Manan in the Fundy Isles, New Brunswick.

CTMA Ferries (☑418-986-3278, 888-986-3278; www.ctma.ca) Daily ferries to Québec's Îles de la Madeleine from Souris, Prince Edward Island.

East Coast Ferries (☑506-747-2159, 877-747-2159; www. eastcoastferries.nb.ca) Connects Deer Island to Campobello Island, both in the Fundy Isles, New Brunswick.

Labrador Marine (☑866-535-2567, 709-535-0810; www. labradormarine.com) Connects Newfoundland to Labrador.

Marine Atlantic (☑800-341-7981; www.marine-atlantic.ca) Connects Port aux Basques and Argentia in Newfoundland with North Sydney, Nova Scotia.

Northumberland Ferries (☑902-566-3838, 888-249-7245; www.ferries.ca) Connects Wood Islands (PEI) and Caribou, Nova Scotia.

Provincial Ferry Services (☑709-627-3492; www.gov.nl.ca/ ferryservices; round-trip Fogo vehicle/passenger $18/6) Operates coastal ferries throughout Newfoundland.

Bus

Maritime Bus (☑800-575-1807; www.maritimebus.com) is the main operator of services within the Maritimes and has routes around and between all four provinces.

DRL Coachlines (☑888-263-1854; www.drl-lr.com) operates bus services on the island of Newfoundland.

Discount passes are not offered.

Costs

Bus travel is cheaper than other means of transport. Advance purchases (four, seven or 14 days) save quite a bit, too.

Sample fares on Maritime:

➡ Halifax to North Sydney ($68.50, seven hours)

➡ Halifax to Charlottetown ($58.25, 5½ hours)

➡ Charlottetown to Moncton ($33.75, 3½ hours)

Sample fares available on DRL Coachlines:

➡ St John's to Corner Brook ($103, 10½ hours)

➡ St John's to Port aux Basques ($126, 13½ hours).

Reservations

Tickets can be bought online or at bus terminals for Maritime and on the bus (cash). Tickets on DRL can only be purchased on the bus, with cash: there are no phone or online sales. Show up at least 30 to 45 minutes prior to departure.

Car & Motorcycle

Automobile Associations

Auto-club membership is a handy thing to have in Canada. Try the following:

Better World Club (www. betterworldclub.com) Donates 1% of its annual revenue to environmental cleanup efforts. It offers service throughout the USA and Canada, and also has a roadside-assistance program for bicycles.

Canadian Automobile Association (www.caa.ca) Offers services, including 24-hour emergency roadside assistance, to members of international affiliates such as AAA in the USA, AA in the UK and ADAC in Germany. The club also offers trip-planning advice, free maps, travel-agency services and a range of discounts on hotels, car rentals etc.

Bring Your Own Vehicle

There's minimal hassle driving into Canada from the USA as long as you have your vehicle's registration papers, proof of liability insurance and your home driver's license.

Driver's License

Visitors can legally drive for up to three months with their home driver's license.

If you're spending considerable time in Canada, think about getting an international driving permit (IDP), which is valid for one year. Your automobile association at home can issue one for a small fee. Always carry your home license together with the IDP.

Fuel

➡ Gas is sold in liters.

➡ At the time of writing, the average for midgrade fuel was $1.05 per liter.

➡ Prices are higher in remote areas.

➡ Fuel prices in Canada are usually higher than in the USA, so fill up south of the border.

➡ Most gas stations are self-service.

➡ Finding a gas station is generally easy except in sparsely populated areas such as Labrador and Newfoundland's South Coast.

➡ Finding spare parts can be difficult far from big cities.

➡ When traveling in remote regions always bring some tools and a spare tire.

Insurance

Canadian law requires liability insurance for all vehicles, to cover you for damage caused to property and people.

The minimum requirement is $200,000 in all Maritime provinces.

Americans traveling to Canada in their own car should ask their insurance company for a nonresident interprovince motor vehicle liability insurance card (commonly known as a 'yellow card'), which is accepted as evidence of financial responsibility anywhere in Canada. Although not mandatory, it may come in handy in an accident.

Car-rental agencies offer liability insurance. Collision damage waivers (CDW) reduce or eliminate the amount you'll have to reimburse the rental company if there's damage to the car itself. Some credit cards cover CDW for a certain rental period, if you use the card to pay for the rental, and decline the policy offered by the rental company. Always check with your card issuer to see what coverage they offer in Canada.

Personal accident insurance (PAI) covers you and any passengers for medical costs incurred as a result of an accident. If your travel insurance or your health insurance policy at home does this as well (and most do, but check), then this is one expense you can do without.

Rental

CAR

To rent a car in Canada you generally need to:

➡ be at least 25 years old

➡ hold a valid driver's license (an international one may be required if you're not from an English- or French-speaking country)

➡ have a major credit card

Some companies will rent to drivers between the ages of 21 and 24 for an additional charge.

You should be able to get an economy-sized vehicle for about $25 to $65 per day. Child safety seats are compulsory (reserve them when you book) and cost about $13 per day.

Car-rental prices can double in July and August, and it's essential to book ahead in prime tourist spots such as Charlottetown or St John's, as there often just aren't enough cars to go around.

International car-rental companies usually have branches at airports and in city centers; note that ferry terminals often do not have branches. Major chains include Avis, Budget, Enterprise, Hertz and Thrifty.

On-the-spot rentals often are more expensive than prebooked packages (ie rental cars booked online or with your flight).

MOTORCYCLE

The **Motorcycle Tour Guide** (www.motorcycletourguidens. com) is a great reference for bikers visiting Nova Scotia.

Northeastern Motorcycle Tours (☑802-463-9853; www. motorcycletours.com) runs tours along the Cabot Trail from Maine, USA.

RECREATIONAL VEHICLES

Rentals cost roughly $160 to $265 per day in high season for midsize vehicles, although insurance, fees and taxes add a hefty chunk. Diesel-fueled RVs have considerably lower running costs.

Road Conditions & Hazards

Road conditions are generally good, but keep the following in mind:

➡ Fierce winters can leave potholes the size of landmine craters. Be prepared to swerve. Winter travel in general can be hazardous due to heavy snow and ice, which may cause roads and

bridges to close periodically. **Transport Canada** (www. tc.ca/road) provides links to road conditions and construction zones for each province.

➡ If you're driving in winter or in remote areas, make sure your vehicle is equipped with four-seasonal radial or snow tires, and emergency supplies in case you're stranded.

➡ Distances between services can be long in sparsely populated areas so keep your gas filled up whenever possible.

➡ Moose, deer and elk are common on rural roadways, especially at night. There's no contest between a 534kg bull moose and a Subaru, so keep your eyes peeled.

Road Rules

➡ Canadians drive on the right-hand side of the road.

➡ Seat-belt use is compulsory. Children under 18kg must be strapped in child-booster seats, except infants who must be in rear-facing safety seats.

➡ Motorcyclists must wear helmets and drive with their headlights on.

➡ Distances and speed limits are posted in kilometers. The speed limit is generally 40km/h to 50km/h in cities and 90km/h to 110km/h outside town.

➡ Slow down to 60km/h when passing emergency vehicles (such as police cars and ambulances) stopped on the roadside with their lights flashing.

➡ Turning right at red lights after coming to a full stop is permitted in all provinces.

➡ Driving while using a hand-held cell phone is illegal in Newfoundland, Nova Scotia and Prince Edward Island.

➡ Radar detectors are not allowed. If you're caught driving with a radar detector, even one that isn't being operated, you could receive a fine of $1000 and your device may be confiscated.

➡ The blood-alcohol limit for drivers is 0.08%. Driving while drunk is a criminal offense.

Hitching & Ride Sharing

Hitchhiking is never entirely safe in any country and we don't recommend it. That said, in remote and rural areas in Canada it is not uncommon to see people thumbing for a ride.

➡ If you do decide to hitch, understand that you are taking a small but potentially serious risk. Remember that it's safer to travel in pairs and let someone know where you are planning to go.

➡ Hitchhiking is illegal on some highways and in the provinces of Nova Scotia and New Brunswick, although you'll see people hitching there anyway.

Local Transport

Bicycle

Cycling is more of a recreational activity than a means of local transportation in Atlantic Canada. City bike paths are not common. Still, most public transportation allows bicycles to be brought on at certain times of day.

Bus

The only cities in the region with municipal bus services are Fredericton, Saint John, Moncton, Halifax, Sydney and St John's. The Annapolis Valley has an excellent re-

gional bus service between Wolfville and Bridgetown. Elsewhere the private car is king.

Ride Sharing

Many hostels have ride-share boards that can be a boon if you're traveling without a car.

Taxi

Taxis usually are metered, with a flag-fall fee of $3 and a per-kilometer charge around $1.75. Drivers expect a tip of between 10% and 15%. Taxis can be flagged down or ordered by phone.

Train

Train travel is limited within the region. Prince Edward Island and Newfoundland have no train services. Nova Scotia and New Brunswick are served along the **VIA Rail** (☑888-842-7733; www.viarail. ca) Montréal-to-Halifax route. For a train schedule, check the website. Most stations have left-luggage offices.

Western Labrador is also accessible by train with the Quebec Northshore & Labrador Railway. There are twice weekly services from Sept Îles, Québec, to Labrador City. There is no website so you'll have to call for current prices and information.

Classes

There are four main classes:

Economy class buys you a fairly basic, if indeed quite comfortable, reclining seat with a headrest. Blankets and pillows are provided for overnight travel.

Sleeper class is available on shorter overnight routes. You can choose from compartments

with upper or lower pullout berths, and private single, double or triple roomettes, all with a bathroom.

Touring class is available on long-distance routes and includes Sleeper Class accommodations plus meals, access to the sightseeing car and sometimes a tour guide.

Business class provides access to a business lounge with spacious seats, free non-alcoholic beverages, high-speed wi-fi and more.

Costs

Taking the train is more expensive than the bus, but most people find it a more comfortable way to travel. June to mid-October is peak season, when prices are about 40% higher. Buying tickets in advance (even just five days before) can yield significant savings.

Reservations

Tickets and train passes are available for purchase online, by phone, at VIA Rail stations and from many travel agents. Seat reservations are highly recommended, especially in summer and for sleeper cars.

Train Passes

VIA Rail offers the Canrailpass-System, good for seven trips on any train during a 21-day period. All seats are in economy class; upgrades are not permitted. You must book each leg at least three days in advance, online, or by phoning the reservations center. Passes start at $699 (low season).

Language

English and French are the official languages of Canada. You'll see both on highway signs, maps, tourist brochures, packaging etc.

New Brunswick is Canada's only officially bilingual province, although only about one third of the population speaks both French and English. French is widely spoken, particularly in the north and east of the province. Nova Scotia also has a significant French-speaking population. The strongest French Acadian ancestry on Prince Edward Island is found in Région Évangéline, where some 6000 residents still speak French as their first language.

You'll find that the French spoken in Canada is essentially the same as in France, and locals will have no problem understanding more formal French.

French pronunciation is pretty straightforward for English speakers, as the sounds can almost all be found in English. The exceptions are nasal vowels (represented in our coloured pronunciation guides by o or u followed by an almost inaudible nasal consonant sound m, n or ng), the 'funny' u (ew in our guides) and the deep-in-the-throat r. Bearing this in mind and reading the pronunciation guides in this chapter as if they were English, you shouldn't have problems being understood. Syllables in French words are, for the most part, equally stressed. English speakers tend to stress the first syllable, which is unusual in French, so try adding a light stress on the final syllable to compensate.

WANT MORE?

For in-depth language information and handy phrases, check out Lonely Planet's *French Phrasebook*. You'll find it at **shop.lonelyplanet.com**, or you can buy Lonely Planet's iPhone phrasebooks at the Apple App Store.

BASICS

Hello.	*Bonjour.*	bon·zhoor
Goodbye.	*Au revoir.*	o·rer·vwa
Excuse me.	*Excusez-moi.*	ek·skew·zay·mwa
Sorry.	*Pardon.*	par·don
Yes./No.	*Oui./Non.*	wee/non
Please.	*S'il vous plaît.*	seel voo play
Thank you.	*Merci.*	mair·see
You're welcome.	*De rien.*	der ree·en

How are you?
Comment allez-vous? ko·mon ta·lay·voo

Fine, and you?
Bien, merci. Et vous? byun mair·see ay voo

My name is ...
Je m'appelle ... zher ma·pel ...

What's your name?
Comment vous appelez-vous? ko·mon voo· za·play voo

Do you speak English?
Parlez-vous anglais? par·lay·voo ong·glay

I don't understand.
Je ne comprends pas. zher ner kom·pron pa

ACCOMMODATIONS

Do you have any rooms available?
Est-ce que vous avez des chambres libres? es·ker vo za·vay day shom·brer lee·brer

How much is it per night/person?
Quel est le prix par nuit/personne? kel ay ler pree par nwee/per·son

Is breakfast included?
Est-ce que le petit déjeuner est inclus? es·ker ler per·tee day·zher·nay ayt en·klew

a ... room	*une chambre ...*	ewn shom·brer ...
single	*à un lit*	a un lee
double	*avec un grand lit*	a·vek un gron lee

air-con	*climatiseur*	klee·ma·tee·zer
bathroom	*salle de bains*	sal der bun
campsite	*camping*	kom·peeng
dorm	*dortoir*	dor·twar
guesthouse	*pension*	pon·syon
hotel	*hôtel*	o·tel
window	*fenêtre*	fer·nay·trer
youth hostel	*auberge de jeunesse*	o·berzh der zher·nes

DIRECTIONS

Where's ...?
Où est ...?   oo ay ...

What's the address?
Quelle est l'adresse?   kel ay la·dres

Could you write the address, please?
Est-ce que vous pourriez   es·ker voo poo·ryay
écrire l'adresse,   ay·kreer la·dres
s'il vous plaît?   seel voo play

Can you show me (on the map)?
Pouvez-vous m'indiquer   poo·vay·voo mun·dee·kay
(sur la carte)?   (sewr la kart)

at the corner	*au coin*	o kwun
at the traffic lights	*aux feux*	o fer
behind	*derrière*	dair·ryair
in front of ...	*devant ...*	der·von ...
far (from ...)	*loin (de ...)*	lwun (der ...)
left	*gauche*	gosh
near (to ...)	*près (de ...)*	pray (der ...)
next to ...	*à côté de ...*	a ko·tay der...
opposite ...	*en face de ...*	on fas der ...
right	*droite*	drwat
straight ahead	*tout droit*	too drwa

EATING & DRINKING

A table for (two), please.
Une table pour (deux),   ewn ta·bler poor (der)
s'il vous plaît.   seel voo play

What would you recommend?
Qu'est-ce que vous   kes·ker voo
conseillez?   kon·say·yay

What's in that dish?
Quels sont les   kel son lay
ingrédients?   zun·gray·dyon

I'm a vegetarian.
Je suis   zher swee
végétarien/   vay·zhay·ta·ryun/
végétarienne.   vay·zhay·ta·ryen (m/f)

I don't eat ...
Je ne mange pas ...   zher ner monzh pa ...

Cheers!
Santé!   son·tay

That was delicious.
C'était délicieux!   say·tay day·lee·syer

Please bring the bill.
Apportez-moi   a·por·tay·mwa
l'addition,   la·dee·syon
s'il vous plaît.   seel voo play

Key Words

appetiser	*entrée*	on·tray
bottle	*bouteille*	boo·tay
breakfast	*déjeuner*	day·zher·nay
children's menu	*menu pour enfants*	mer·new poor on·fon
cold	*froid*	frwa
delicatessen	*traiteur*	tray·ter
dinner	*souper*	soo·pay
dish	*plat*	pla

food	*nourriture*	noo·ree·tewr
fork	*fourchette*	foor·shet
glass	*verre*	vair
grocery store	*épicerie*	ay·pees·ree
highchair	*chaise haute*	shay zot
hot	*chaud*	sho
knife	*couteau*	koo·to
local speciality	*spécialité locale*	spay·sya·lee·tay lo·kal
lunch	*dîner*	dee·nay
main course	*plat principal*	pla prun·see·pal
market	*marché*	mar·shay
menu (in English)	*carte (en anglais)*	kart (on ong·glay)
plate	*assiette*	a·syet
spoon	*cuillère*	kwee·yair
wine list	*carte des vins*	kart day vun
with	*avec*	a·vek
without	*sans*	son

Meat & Fish

beef	*bœuf*	berf
chicken	*poulet*	poo·lay
fish	*poisson*	pwa·son
lamb	*agneau*	a·nyo
pork	*porc*	por
turkey	*dinde*	dund
veal	*veau*	vo

Fruit & Vegetables

apple	*pomme*	pom
apricot	*abricot*	ab·ree·ko
asparagus	*asperge*	a·spairzh
beans	*haricots*	a·ree·ko
beetroot	*betterave*	be·trav
cabbage	*chou*	shoo
celery	*céleri*	sel·ree
cherry	*cerise*	ser·reez
corn	*maïs*	ma·ees
cucumber	*concombre*	kong·kom·brer
gherkin (pickle)	*cornichon*	kor·nee·shon
grape	*raisin*	ray·zun
leek	*poireau*	pwa·ro
lemon	*citron*	see·tron
lettuce	*laitue*	lay·tew
mushroom	*champignon*	shom·pee·nyon
peach	*pêche*	pesh
peas	*petit pois*	per·tee pwa

(red/green) pepper	*poivron (rouge/vert)*	pwa·vron (roozh/vair)
pineapple	*ananas*	a·na·nas
plum	*prune*	prewn
potato	*pomme de terre*	pom der tair
prune	*pruneau*	prew·no
pumpkin	*citrouille*	see·troo·yer
shallot	*échalote*	eh·sha·lot
spinach	*épinards*	eh·pee·nar
strawberry	*fraise*	frez
tomato	*tomate*	to·mat
turnip	*navet*	na·vay
vegetable	*légume*	lay·gewm

Other

bread	*pain*	pun
butter	*beurre*	ber
cheese	*fromage*	fro·mazh
egg	*œuf*	erf
honey	*miel*	myel
jam	*confiture*	kon·fee·tewr
lentils	*lentilles*	lon·tee·yer
oil	*huile*	weel
pasta/noodles	*pâtes*	pat
pepper	*poivre*	pwa·vrer
rice	*riz*	ree
salt	*sel*	sel
sugar	*sucre*	sew·krer
vinegar	*vinaigre*	vee·nay·grer

Drinks

beer	*bière*	bee·yair
coffee	*café*	ka·fay
(orange) juice	*jus (d'orange)*	zhew (do·ronzh)
milk	*lait*	lay
red wine	*vin rouge*	vun roozh

Signs	
Entrée	Entrance
Femmes	Women
Fermé	Closed
Hommes	Men
Interdit	Prohibited
Ouvert	Open
Renseignements	Information
Sortie	Exit
Toilettes/WC	Toilets

tea	*thé*	tay
(mineral) water	*eau (minérale)*	o (mee·nay·ral)
white wine	*vin blanc*	vun blong

EMERGENCIES

Help!
Au secours! — o skoor

I'm lost.
Je suis perdu/perdue. — zhe swee pair·dew (m/f)

Leave me alone!
Fichez-moi la paix! — fee·shay·mwa la pay

There's been an accident.
Il y a eu un accident. — eel ya ew un ak·see·don

Call a doctor.
Appelez un médecin. — a·play un mayd·sun

Call the police.
Appelez la police. — a·play la po·lees

I'm ill.
Je suis malade. — zher swee ma·lad

It hurts here.
J'ai une douleur ici. — zhay ewn doo·ler ee·see

I'm allergic to ...
Je suis allergique ... — zher swee za·lair·zheek ...

Where are the toilets?
Où sont les toilettes? — oo son lay twa·let

SHOPPING & SERVICES

I'd like to buy ...
Je voudrais acheter ... — zher voo·dray ash·tay ...

May I look at it?
Est-ce que je peux le voir? — es·ker zher per ler vwar

I'm just looking.
Je regarde. — zher rer·gard

I don't like it.
Cela ne me plaît pas. — ser·la ner mer play pa

How much is it?
C'est combien? — say kom·byun

It's too expensive.
C'est trop cher. — say tro shair

Can you lower the price?
Vous pouvez baisser le prix? — voo poo·vay bay·say ler pree

Question Words		
How?	*Comment?*	ko·mon
What?	*Quoi?*	kwa
When?	*Quand?*	kon
Where?	*Où?*	oo
Who?	*Qui?*	kee
Why?	*Pourquoi?*	poor·kwa

There's a mistake in the bill.
Il y a une erreur dans la note. — eel ya ewn ay·rer don la not

ATM	*guichet automatique de banque*	gee·shay o·to·ma·teek der bonk
credit card	*carte de crédit*	kart der kray·dee
internet cafe	*cybercafé*	see·bair·ka·fay
post office	*bureau de poste*	bew·ro der post
tourist office	*office de tourisme*	o·fees der too·rees·mer

TIME & DATES

What time is it?
Quelle heure est-il? — kel er ay til

It's (eight) o'clock.
Il est (huit) heures. — il ay (weet) er

It's half past (10).
Il est (dix) heures et demie. — il ay (deez) er ay day·mee

morning	*matin*	ma·tun
afternoon	*après-midi*	a·pray·mee·dee
evening	*soir*	swar
yesterday	*hier*	yair
today	*aujourd'hui*	o·zhoor·dwee
tomorrow	*demain*	der·mun
Monday	*lundi*	lun·dee
Tuesday	*mardi*	mar·dee
Wednesday	*mercredi*	mair·krer·dee
Thursday	*jeudi*	zher·dee
Friday	*vendredi*	von·drer·dee
Saturday	*samedi*	sam·dee
Sunday	*dimanche*	dee·monsh
January	*janvier*	zhon·vyay
February	*février*	fayv·ryay
March	*mars*	mars
April	*avril*	a·vreel
May	*mai*	may
June	*juin*	zhwun
July	*juillet*	zhwee·yay
August	*août*	oot
September	*septembre*	sep·tom·brer
October	*octobre*	ok·to·brer
November	*novembre*	no·vom·brer
December	*décembre*	day·som·brer

TRANSPORTATION

Public Transportation

boat	bateau	ba·to
bus	bus	bews
plane	avion	a·vyon
train	train	trun

I want to go to ...
Je voudrais aller à ...   zher voo·dray a·lay a ...

Does it stop at ...?
Est-ce qu'il s'arrête à ...?   es·kil sa·ret a ...

At what time does it leave/arrive?
À quelle heure est-ce   a kel er es
qu'il part/arrive?   kil par/a·reev

Can you tell me when we get to ...?
Pouvez-vous me   poo·vay·voo mer
dire quand   deer kon
nous arrivons à ...?   noo za·ree·von a ...

I want to get off here.
Je veux descendre   zher ver day·son·drer
ici.   ee·see

first	premier	prer·myay
last	dernier	dair·nyay
next	prochain	pro·shun

a ... ticket	un billet ...	un bee·yay ...
1st-class	de première classe	der prem·yair klas
2nd-class	de deuxième classe	der der·zyem las
one-way	simple	sum·pler
return	aller et retour	a·lay ay rer·toor

aisle seat	côté couloir	ko·tay kool·war
cancelled	annulé	a·new·lay
delayed	en retard	on rer·tar
platform	quai	kay
ticket office	guichet	gee·shay
timetable	horaire	o·rair
train station	gare	gar
window seat	côté fenêtre	ko·tay fe·ne·trer

Driving & Cycling

I'd like to hire a ...	Je voudrais louer ...	zher voo·dray loo·way ...
car	une voiture	ewn vwa·tewr
bicycle	un vélo	un vay·lo
motorcycle	une moto	ewn mo·to

Numbers

1	un	un
2	deux	der
3	trois	trwa
4	quatre	ka·trer
5	cinq	sungk
6	six	sees
7	sept	set
8	huit	weet
9	neuf	nerf
10	dix	dees
20	vingt	vung
30	trente	tront
40	quarante	ka·ront
50	cinquante	sung·kont
60	soixante	swa·sont
70	soixante-dix	swa·son·dees
80	quatre-vingts	ka·trer·vung
90	quatre-vingt-dix	ka·trer·vung·dees
100	cent	son
1000	mille	meel

child seat	siège-enfant	syezh·on·fon
diesel	diesel	dyay·zel
helmet	casque	kask
mechanic	mécanicien	may·ka·nee·syun
petrol/gas	essence	ay·sons
service station	station-service	sta·syon·ser·vees

Is this the road to ...?
C'est la route pour ...?   say la root poor ...

(How long) Can I park here?
(Combien de temps)   (kom·byun der tom)
Est-ce que je peux   es·ker zher per
stationner ici?   sta·syo·nay ee·see

The car/motorbike has broken down (at ...).
La voiture/moto est   la vwa·tewr/mo·to ay
tombée en panne (à ...).   tom·bay on pan (a ...)

I have a flat tyre.
Mon pneu est à plat.   mom pner ay ta pla

I've run out of petrol.
Je suis en panne   zher swee zon pan
d'essence.   day·sons

I've lost my car keys.
J'ai perdu les clés de   zhay per·dew lay klay der
ma voiture.   ma vwa·tewr

Where can I have my bicycle repaired?
Où est-ce que je peux   oo es·ker zher per
faire réparer mon vélo?   fair ray·pa·ray mon vay·lo

LANGUAGE TRANSPORTATION

Behind the Scenes

SEND US YOUR FEEDBACK

We love to hear from travelers – your comments keep us on our toes and help make our books better. Our well-traveled team reads every word on what you loved or loathed about this book. Although we cannot reply individually to your submissions, we always guarantee that your feedback goes straight to the appropriate authors, in time for the next edition. Each person who sends us information is thanked in the next edition – the most useful submissions are rewarded with a selection of digital PDF chapters.

Visit **lonelyplanet.com/contact** to submit your updates and suggestions or to ask for help. Our award-winning website also features inspirational travel stories, news and discussions.

Note: We may edit, reproduce and incorporate your comments in Lonely Planet products such as guidebooks, websites and digital products, so let us know if you don't want your comments reproduced or your name acknowledged. For a copy of our privacy policy visit lonelyplanet.com/privacy.

OUR READERS

Many thanks to the travelers who used the last edition and wrote to us with helpful hints, useful advice and interesting anecdotes: Alexander Haberl, Alfred Hall, Ameen Kanji, Anne Widya, Christine Zielhuis, Claudia Börner, David Brick, Judith Bird, Nathaniel Popkin, Peter Tomlinson, Shelley Mitchell

WRITER THANKS

Korina Miller

Thank you to Alex Howard for inviting me to join this project and to the team of travel-thirsty authors who helped make it great. Thank you to the many Albertans who shared their stories, insight and love for their province. Thanks to Kajsa Erickson for acquainting me with Calgary's wilder side during the height of Stampede; to my parents and daughters, Simone and Monique, for camping out in the Rockies with me; and to Kirk and Bing for keeping the home fires burning. And finally, thanks to my chiropractor, Dr Bob Mabee for straightening me out after driving 4500km in 10 days.

Benedict Walker

Heartfelt thanks to my ever-patient and supportive mother, Trish Walker, to the folks at LP, especially Alexander Howard for giving me this opportunity and my editors, Kristin Odijk and Saralinda Turner. In Canada, love and gratitude to Cherly, the Cowies and Mr Mikey Brown. To my mates Carl, Matt and Baker

Paul in NS and to Brittany, Kaylin and Rae-Anne in PEI: thanks all for your friendship, encouragement and local knowledge.

Kate Armstrong

Many thanks to Alexander Howard at LP plus the many locals who gave nothing but Acadian and Maritimes hospitality. Three cheers to those who advised on local tourism: Alison Aiton and Stacey Russell (Fredericton), Jillian MacKinnon (Saint John), Jillian Somers and Colette McLaughlin (Moncton) and Janice Arseneault (Edmunston). A shout out to Jay Remer for his help in St Andrews. Finally, *merci* to all the helpful Canadian enthusiasts along the way who know that their region is a special one.

Carolyn McCarthy

Many thanks go out to the good people of Newfoundland for their warm welcome and hospitality. My gratitude goes out to Carolyn Cook for her camping gear and adventure know-how, Bernadette Walsh for her total expertise, Terri Coles for her journalistic insights, Kathleen Kearns for her tips and my hosts Elissa and Mark.

ACKNOWLEDGEMENTS

Climate map data adapted from Peel MC, Finlayson BL & McMahon TA (2007) 'Updated World Map of the Köppen-Geiger Climate Classification', Hydrology and Earth System Sciences, 11, 163344.

Cover photograph: Peggy's Cove, Halifax, DOPhoto/ Shutterstock©

THIS BOOK

This 4th edition of Lonely Planet's *Nova Scotia, New Brunswick & Prince Edward Island* was researched and written by Korina Miller, Benedict Walker, Kate Armstrong and Carolyn McCarthy. The previous edition was researched and written by Celeste Brash, Caroline Sieg and Karla Zimmerman. This guidebook was produced by the following:

Destination Editor Alexander Howard

Product Editors Jenna Myers, Alison Ridgway

Senior Cartographer Corey Hutchison

Book Designer Katherine Marsh

Assisting Editors Katie Connolly, Gabby Innes, Helen Koehne, Kristin Odijk, Chris Pitts, Saralinda Turner

Cover Researcher Naomi Parker

Thanks to Joel Cotterell, Liz Heynes, Andi Jones, Claire Naylor, Karyn Noble, Martine Power, Kirsten Rawlings, Tony Wheeler

Index

Map Legend

Sights
- Beach
- Bird Sanctuary
- Buddhist
- Castle/Palace
- Christian
- Confucian
- Hindu
- Islamic
- Jain
- Jewish
- Monument
- Museum/Gallery/Historic Building
- Ruin
- Shinto
- Sikh
- Taoist
- Winery/Vineyard
- Zoo/Wildlife Sanctuary
- Other Sight

Activities, Courses & Tours
- Bodysurfing
- Diving
- Canoeing/Kayaking
- Course/Tour
- Sento Hot Baths/Onsen
- Skiing
- Snorkeling
- Surfing
- Swimming/Pool
- Walking
- Windsurfing
- Other Activity

Sleeping
- Sleeping
- Camping

Eating
- Eating

Drinking & Nightlife
- Drinking & Nightlife
- Cafe

Entertainment
- Entertainment

Shopping
- Shopping

Information
- Bank
- Embassy/Consulate
- Hospital/Medical
- Internet
- Police
- Post Office
- Telephone
- Toilet
- Tourist Information
- Other Information

Geographic
- Beach
- Gate
- Hut/Shelter
- Lighthouse
- Lookout
- Mountain/Volcano
- Oasis
- Park
- Pass
- Picnic Area
- Waterfall

Population
- Capital (National)
- Capital (State/Province)
- City/Large Town
- Town/Village

Transport
- Airport
- BART station
- Border crossing
- Boston T station
- Bus
- Cable car/Funicular
- Cycling
- Ferry
- Metro/Muni station
- Monorail
- Parking
- Petrol station
- Subway/SkyTrain station
- Taxi
- Train station/Railway
- Tram
- Underground station
- Other Transport

Note: Not all symbols displayed above appear on the maps in this book

Routes
- Tollway
- Freeway
- Primary
- Secondary
- Tertiary
- Lane
- Unsealed road
- Road under construction
- Plaza/Mall
- Steps
- Tunnel
- Pedestrian overpass
- Walking Tour
- Walking Tour detour
- Path/Walking Trail

Boundaries
- International
- State/Province
- Disputed
- Regional/Suburb
- Marine Park
- Cliff
- Wall

Hydrography
- River, Creek
- Intermittent River
- Canal
- Water
- Dry/Salt/Intermittent Lake
- Reef

Areas
- Airport/Runway
- Beach/Desert
- Cemetery (Christian)
- Cemetery (Other)
- Glacier
- Mudflat
- Park/Forest
- Sight (Building)
- Sportsground
- Swamp/Mangrove

OUR STORY

A beat-up old car, a few dollars in the pocket and a sense of adventure. In 1972 that's all Tony and Maureen Wheeler needed for the trip of a lifetime – across Europe and Asia overland to Australia. It took several months, and at the end – broke but inspired – they sat at their kitchen table writing and stapling together their first travel guide, *Across Asia on the Cheap*. Within a week they'd sold 1500 copies. Lonely Planet was born.

Today, Lonely Planet has offices in Franklin, London, Melbourne, Oakland, Dublin, Beijing and Delhi, with more than 600 staff and writers. We share Tony's belief that 'a great guidebook should do three things: inform, educate and amuse'.

OUR WRITERS

Korina Miller

Plan Chapters, Understand Chapters, Survival Guide Korina grew up on Vancouver Island and has been exploring the globe independently since she was 16, visiting or living in 36 countries and picking up a degree in Communications and Canadian Studies, an MA in Migration Studies and a diploma in Visual Arts en route. As a writer and editor, Korina has worked on nearly 60 titles for Lonely Planet and has also worked with LP.com, BBC, the *Independent*, the *Guardian*, BBC5 and CBC, as well as many independent magazines, covering travel, art and culture. She has currently set up camp back in Victoria, soaking up the mountain views and the pounding surf.

Benedict Walker

Nova Scotia, Prince Edward Island Born in Newcastle, Australia, Ben holds notions of the beach core to his idea of self, though he's traveled hundreds of thousands of kilometers from the sandy shores of home. Ben was given his first Lonely Planet guide *(Japan)* when he was 12. Two decades later, he'd write chapters for the same publication: a dream come true. A communications graduate and travel agent by trade, Ben whittled away his twenties gallivanting around the globe. He thinks the best thing about travel isn't as much about where you go as who you meet: living vicariously through the stories of kind strangers enriches one's own experience. Ben has also written and directed a play, and toured Australia managing the travel logistics for top-billing music festivals.

Kate Armstrong

New Brunswick Kate has spent much of her adult life traveling and living around the world. A full-time freelance travel journalist, she has contributed to around 40 Lonely Planet guides and trade publications and is regularly published in Australian and worldwide publications. She is the author of several books and children's educational titles.

Carolyn McCarthy

Newfoundland & Labrador Carolyn specializes in travel, culture and adventure in the Americas. She has written for *National Geographic*, *Outside*, *BBC Magazine*, *Boston Globe* and other publications. A former Fulbright fellow and Banff Mountain Grant recipient, she has documented life in the most remote corners of Latin America. Carolyn gained her expertise by researching guidebooks in diverse destinations. She has contributed to over 30 guidebooks for Lonely Planet, including *Colorado*, *USA*, *Argentina*, *Chile*, *Panama*, *Peru* and the USA National Parks guides. She is also the author of Lonely Planet's *Trekking in the Patagonian Andes*.

Published by Lonely Planet Global Limited
CRN 554153
4th edition – April 2017
ISBN 978 1 78657 334 6
© Lonely Planet 2017   Photographs © as indicated 2017
10 9 8 7 6 5 4 3 2 1
Printed in China